# Sexual Abuse Assessments

## Using and Developing Frameworks for Practice

Edited by
**Martin C. Calder**

D1341433

**Russell House Publishing**

Published in 2009 by:
Russell House Publishing Ltd
4 St George's House
Uplyme Road
Lyme Regis
Dorset DT7 3LS

Tel: 01297-443948
Fax: 01297-442722
e-mail: help@russellhouse.co.uk
www.russellhouse.co.uk

This book replaces Martin C. Calder's *The Complete Guide to Sexual Abuse Assessments*, published in 2000 by Russell House Publishing Ltd, and now out of print.

British Library Cataloguing-in-publication Data:
A catalogue record for this book is available from the British Library.

ISBN: 978-1-905541-28-7

Typeset by TW Typesetting, Plymouth, Devon

Front cover artwork by Emma Calder and Stacey Calder

Printed by the MPG Books Group in the UK

**Russell House Publishing**

Russell House Publishing aims to publish innovative and valuable materials to help managers, practitioners, trainers, educators and students.

Our full catalogue covers: social policy, working with young people, helping children and families, care of older people, social care, combating social exclusion, revitalising communities and working with offenders.

Full details can be found at www.russellhouse.co.uk and we are pleased to send out information to you by post. Our contact details are on this page.

We are always keen to receive feedback on publications and new ideas for future projects.

To my daughters Stacey and Emma

May you find as much happiness and love as you have brought into my life

Dad

# Contents

# About the Editor and Contributors

## The Editor

**Martin C. Calder** established Calder Training and Consultancy in 2005 after 20 years in frontline child protection practice. His aim has been to generate and collate the available and necessary assessment tools for frontline staff, especially in times of massive change. He also critiques central government guidance and attempts to provide remedial materials to help fill the gap left between aspiration and reality. He is contactable through his website at www.caldertrainingandconsultancy.co.uk

## The Contributors

**Sherry Ashfield** began her career in the Probation Service in 1992, holding a number of prison and community posts where she developed her interest and expertise working with women who display harmful behaviour towards children. Sherry joined the Lucy Faithfull Foundation in 1999 and works as a senior practitioner in its Female Outreach Project. This project offers assessment, intervention and consultancy services to probation and prison staff working with female sex offenders. Sherry also provides assessments for the family courts and training focused around female sexual offending for many organisations including the Probation Service, the Prison Service and NOTA.

**David Briggs** is an independent forensic clinical psychologist with a practice base in the north of England. His expertise is in the assessment and management of sexual abusers in family contexts. David consults to agencies throughout the UK and is a member of the management group of NOTA.

**Rachael M. Collie**, MA, DipClinPsyc. is a New Zealand trained clinical psychologist who has worked in the clinical forensic field for the Corrections Department and in private practice since 1996. She currently teaches clinical and forensic psychology at Victoria University of Wellington, New Zealand. She is also completing her PhD on personality processes in sexually violent offenders.

**Dr Leam A. Craig** is a Consultant Forensic Psychologist and Director of Forensic Programmes with Forensic Psychology Practice Ltd. His current practice includes direct services to forensic NHS Adult Mental Health Trusts and consultancy to Prison and Probation Services. He coordinates community-based treatment programmes for sexual offenders with learning disabilities and acts as an expert witness to civil and criminal courts in the assessment of violent and dangerous offenders. His doctoral research investigated the assessment, treatment and management of sexual offenders and he has published numerous research articles and chapters in a range of research and professional journals. He is an Honorary Lecturer in Forensic Psychology at the Centre for Forensic and Family Psychology, University of Birmingham, UK.

**Andrew Durham** has the Advanced Award in Social Work and a Ph.D. in Applied Social Studies from the University of Warwick, which researched into the impact of child sexual abuse. He is the Consultant Practitioner, managing the Sexualised Inappropriate Behaviours Service (SIBS) a countywide Children's Services provision in Warwickshire, and is a visiting lecturer at the University of Warwick. He also works as an independent consultant. He is the author of the books *Young Men Surviving Child Sexual Abuse – Research Stories and Lessons for Therapeutic Practice* (2003) and *Young Men Who Have Sexually Abused – A Case Study Guide* (2006) both published by John Wiley. He has also published a range of other papers and chapters on the subject of child sexual abuse. andrewdurham@warwickshire.gov.uk

**Hilary Eldridge** is Chief Executive of the Lucy Faithfull Foundation, a child protection charity preventing and working with child sexual abuse. She has worked with sex offenders and their families since 1975. She co-authors and monitors assessment and treatment programmes for adult male offenders, female offenders, young people and their families. Specialising in developing interventions to suit the specific needs of female sex offenders, she has published book chapters and has consulted to and provided training on this subject to a wide range of agencies. She is an Honorary Lecturer in Forensic Psychology at the University of Birmingham.

**Ian Elliott** is a Research Psychologist with the Lucy Faithfull Foundation, where he is engaged in projects relating to both female sexual offending and child pornography offences. Ian is researching a PhD at the University of Birmingham, exploring the potential application of contemporary adult sexual offence theory to child pornography offences, and is also a Course Tutor in Forensic Psychology. He has published and presented research findings at both national and international conferences.

**Dr Rachel Fyson** is currently a lecturer in Social Work in the School of Sociology and Social Policy, University of Nottingham. She has previously worked as a Research Fellow for the Ann Craft Trust (a national charity which works to prevent the abuse of people with learning disabilities) and the Norah Fry Research Centre, University of Bristol (an internationally recognised centre of excellence in learning disability research). Prior to becoming an academic she worked for many years with both children and adults with learning disabilities. Her research interests include issues around sexual abuse, learning disability, interagency working and policy implementation. She undertook the first UK study into the response of statutory education and social services to young people with learning disabilities who display sexually inappropriate or abusive behaviours. Rachel.Fyson@nottingham.ac.uk

**Theresa A. Gannon**, BSc, DPhil, C.Psychol (Forensic) is Senior Lecturer and Director of the MSc in Forensic Psychology at the University of Kent, UK. Theresa is also the developer and lead facilitator for Sexual Offender Treatment at the Trevor Gibbens Unit, Kent. Her research interests include sexual offender rehabilitation, sexual offenders' cognition, and attitudes toward offender rehabilitation and reintegration into society.

**Roger B. Hutchinson** was until recently the clinical head of the Learning Disability Service in North Derbyshire. He retired from post as a Consultant Clinical Psychologist to take up a partnership in the Forensic Psychology Practice Ltd. Whilst working in North Derbyshire he developed the Intensive Support Service which provided a framework for the treatment and management of clients with a learning disability who presented with significant forensic risk. This framework was based around a 'Supported Housing' model. The team involved with this development won a national NHS award for the 'Risk Management Team of the Year'.

**Lucy King**, MA. (Dist. In Psychology), PGDipClinPsyc, is Principal Advisor with the New Zealand Department of Corrections Community Probation and Psychological Services in New Zealand. She has 11 years of experience working as a clinical psychologist with diverse offender populations, including high risk, violent and sexual offenders. In her Principal Advisor role she is responsible for ensuring the best practice delivery of correctional assessments and rehabilitative interventions for offender populations, and has responsibility for monitoring ongoing standards of training, supervision and programme delivery. She also has a key role in facilitating research that will contribute to improved treatment integrity and outcome (i.e. reducing re-offending).

**Dr L.C. Miccio-Fonseca** has published in the area of sex offenders and victims of sexual abuse. Her clinical background is extensive including writing, consulting, clinical research, forensic psychologist, clinical supervision and expert witness in cases of sexual abuse with individuals of all ages and both genders. Dr Miccio-Fonseca is highly specialised in the area of sex disorders, the paraphilias, maintaining a practice in her field of specialisation in Southern California. Her ongoing research on sex offenders has led to the development of unique tools for assessing sexually abusive individuals. Her seven-year research project was selected for presentation by the International Congress on the Treatment of Sex Offenders (Minneapolis, Minnesota, 1993, Caracas, Venezuela 1998, Toronto, Canada, May 2000).

Dr Miccio-Fonseca's clinical research studies have been presented to the American Psychological Association (APA), the American Professional Society on the Abuse of Children (APSAC), the California Department of Social Services, The Association for the Treatment of Sexual Abusers (ATSA), the American Association of Sex Education Counselors and Therapists (AASECT), the California Coalition on Sexual Offending (CCOSO), The Society for the Scientific Study of Sex (SSSS), the California State Psychological Association (CSPA), The Committee on Juvenile Justice, The State Bar of California, the National Council of Juvenile and Family Court Judges and The National Task Force on Juvenile Sex Offending of the National Adolescent Perpetrator Network, and others.

Developing assessment tools is also an area of expertise. Dr. Miccio-Fonseca published a first of its kind versatile inventory used in exploring erotic development, *The Personal Sentence Completion Inventory (PSCI, 1994)*. The *PSCI* is used in psychological evaluations by other notable clinicians. The late Dr John Money, famous international sexologist from Johns Hospital University called the *PSCI* 'innovative and strongly recommends it without reservation'. *The Personal Sentence Completion Inventory (PSCI, 1994)* is also a tool used to devise a structured 9-10 week group discussion programme around one's own development with regard to their sexuality. It has been used widely and is reported to be a powerful tool.

More recently, Dr Miccio-Fonseca created a new unique innovative risk assessment tool, *MEGA* that was presented at the Association for the Treatment of Sexual Abusers (ATSA) September 2006 in Chicago; response to the tool has been extraordinary. *MEGA* meets the demands of best standards of practice; the tool is empirically guided by the research on youth. It is a first of its kind inventory used in assessing sexually abusive youth both males and females: *Multiplex Empirically Guided Inventory of Ecological Aggregates for Assessing Sexually Abusive Children and Adolescents (Ages 19 and Under) (MEGA)*.

*Every single* item in *MEGA* is empirically anchored and guided by the research *on minors* (with males and females), not adults; it is the only assessment tool that can make such a claim. *MEGA* is also a first of its kind inventory that is able to do follow up (with males and females) measuring change over time with the *MEGA* scales, *Risk Scale, Static Scale, Dynamical Scale, Protective Scale, Principle (severity) Scale*. *MEGA* assesses *idiosyncratic* changes in the youth as it relates to risk for sexually abusive behaviours. The Kentucky Department of Juvenile Justice has selected to use *MEGA* implementing it statewide; it is one of the validation sites for *MEGA*.

International validation sites have also been established; individuals in Israel and Taiwan have expressed an interest. The Child and Parent Resource Institute (CPRI), in London Ontario, Canada, a provincially operated regional resource center (covering a 17 county catchment area) provide specialised (tertiary) diagnostic assessment, research and short-term treatment services for children and youth, is also one of the validation sites for *MEGA* . Other sites are located in Stockton and Berkeley California. As of this writing (April 2007) the data collection for follow-up validation data is an $N = 500 +$ ; this will be one of the largest studies done in the field on measuring empirically anchored dynamic factors and risk factors directly related to minors of all ages and both genders.

**Dr Ethel Quayle** was a lecturer in the Department of Applied Psychology, University College Cork and, from 2003, director of the COPINE project.

She trained as a clinical psychologist with a special interest in sexual offending and has focused for the last twelve years on victimisation of children through Internet abuse images. Recent research has led to the development of a CBT website for offenders and the development of guidelines for working with young people who engage in problematic sexual behaviour in relation to the new technologies. She is co-author of *Child Pornography: An Internet Crime* (2003), Brunner and Routledge; *Only Pictures? Therapeutic Approaches with Internet Offenders* (2006), and *Viewing Child Pornography on the Internet. Understanding the Offence, Managing the Offender, Helping the Victims* (2005), both by Russell House Publishing, and has published in academic and professional journals. In September 2008 she moved to the University of Edinburgh School of Health in Social Science where she continues the COPINE research.

**Lucinda A. Rasmussen**, Ph.D., LCSW is a tenured associate professor of social work, has extensive clinical, teaching, and research experience in the areas of family violence and child maltreatment. She has taught social work practice classes at San Diego State University School of Social Work since 1995 and has been the School's Graduate Advisor since 2002. Dr Rasmussen completed post-doctoral clinical training at SHARPER FUTURE, San Diego as a therapist providing group treatment to adult sex offenders, and is a Licensed Clinical Social Worker in California and Utah. Her clinical experience includes 10 years as a clinical social worker at Primary Children's Medical Center in Salt Lake City, specialising in the treatment of sexually abused children and children with sexually abusive behaviour problems.

Dr Rasmussen's research focuses on child sexual abuse and family violence, particularly the assessment and treatment of youth aged 5-19 who have sexual behaviour problems or are sexually abusive. Her research includes a five-year retrospective study on juvenile sex offender recidivism, published in *Sexual Abuse: A Journal of Research and Treatment,* and a study applying Motivational Interviewing to women in a domestic violence shelter that is at press and due to be published in the *Journal of Aggression, Maltreatment, and Trauma.*

Dr Rasmussen conceptualised a comprehensive, integrative practice model for treating the effects of traumatic experiences, the Trauma Outcome Process (*TOPA* model). She has written about the *TOPA* model in four articles in the *Journal of Child Sexual Abuse*, a book that she co-authored, *Treating Children with Sexually Abusive Behavior Problems: Guidelines for Child and Parent Intervention,* and in two chapters that she contributed to books on sexually abusive youth (that were edited by Martin Calder and published in the United Kingdom). Dr Rasmussen has presented the *TOPA* model internationally in Israel at conferences sponsored by ASHALIM in

Jerusalem and the Israeli Association for Child Protection in Tel Aviv, and to social workers and psychologists working in Tijuana, Baja California, Mexico. She has presented the *TOPA* model in various cities in the United States at conferences of the: Association for the Treatment of Sexual Abusers (ATSA), Children's Hospital San Diego International Conference on Responding to Child Maltreatment, International Conference on Violence, Abuse, and Trauma (IVAT); California Coalition on Sexual Offending (CCOSO), National Adolescent Perpetrator Network (NPAN), and National Association of Social Workers (NASW) among others, and in training institutes sponsored by the Sexual Abuse Treatment Education and Prevention Services (STEPS) and the Utah Network on Juveniles Offending Sexually (NOJOS).

Dr Rasmussen is currently a research consultant in the validation research for a new innovative risk assessment tool: the *Multiplex Empirically Guided Inventory of Ecological Aggregates for Assessing Sexually Abusive Children and Adolescents (Ages 19 and Under) (MEGA)*, constructed by her colleague, L.C. Miccio-Fonseca, Ph.D., a Clinical Psychologist and Clinical Researcher. It is the first risk assessment tool to be applicable to all sexually abusive youth including adjudicated and non-adjudicated youth, females, children under 12, and developmentally delayed youth. Validation sites for *MEGA* have been established nationally and internationally with data collection currently (January 2008) at $N = 600+$.

A long-term advocate for sexually abused and other traumatised children, Dr Rasmussen actively contributes her time and expertise to the sexual abuse treatment community. Dr. Rasmussen serves as an officer on the Board of Directors of the California Coalition on Sexual Offending (CCOSO), a statewide organisation dedicated to addressing the problem of sexual abuse in our communities. lucindarasmussen@cox.net

**Lynda Regan** has worked with children and families in various settings for over 20 years. She was a social worker on a busy area team for eleven years before moving into therapeutic work at Salford Cornerstone Project in 1997. She manages a growing team of staff who are committed to supporting children and their families to move forward from sexual or domestic abuse, as well as helping to develop skills of other professionals in relation to working with children and families. Contact is held on RHP database as she is an author in her own right.

**Graeme Richardson** has worked in the field of conduct-disordered children, juvenile delinquency, serious young offenders, and mentally disordered young offenders since 1985. He first worked as a residential social worker in the largest residential facility in the UK. He then worked as a trainee psychologist specialising in residential childcare, secure care, and young offenders in this same residential facility. He qualified in Clinical Psychology in 1991 and returned to work with young people in residential care and young offenders in secure facilities. He has worked in an NHS Adolescent Forensic Mental Health Service based in Newcastle since its inception in 1993. He has applied clinical and forensic psychology in several service settings, which have included social services residential care, secure residential care, young offender prisons, an NHS outpatient clinic, and a medium secure NHS hospital. He has published in the areas of adolescent sexual offenders, adolescent interrogative suggestibility and false confessions, and risk assessment and risk management. He is an accredited Risk of Harm trainer for the Scottish Risk Management Authority, and a consultant with the Cognitive Centre Foundation UK, which provides training and support services to organisations that work with offenders. Graeme.Richardson@ntw.nhs.uk

**Susan L. Robinson**, LICSW, is a licensed clinical social worker who specialises in sexual abuse and trauma at the New England Counseling and Trauma Center in Williston, Vermont. Ms Robinson wrote the first workbook specifically designed for teenage girls who have sexually abused entitled *Growing Beyond: A Workbook for Teenage Girls* published by NEARI Press. She also wrote a treatment manual to use in conjunction with the workbook, and has authored chapters on the assessment and treatment of sexually abusive girls (*Considerations for the Assessment of Female Sexually Abusive Youth*, and *Adolescent Females with Sexual Behavior Problems: What Constitutes Best Practice*). Ms Robinson speaks nationally on the subject of female sexual abuse. She is interested in the development of a risk assessment protocol for females engaging in sexually abusive behaviours, and in developing specialised treatment programmes for this population. surobin@hotmail.com

**Ian Stringer** is a Consultant Clinical and Forensic Psychologist and Director of Forensic Psychology Practice Ltd. His practice background includes direct services to Special Hospitals, youth treatment centres, and regional secure units. He acts as a consultant to several National Health Services Adult Mental Health Trusts, and with sex offender treatment programmes for people with learning disabilities. In addition, he acts as an expert witness to civil and criminal courts in the assessment of violent and dangerous offenders. He has published numerous research articles and chapters on the assessment of sex offenders in a range of research and professional journals. He is an Honorary Research Fellow at the Centre for Forensic and Family Psychology School of Psychology, University of Birmingham.

**Tony Ward**, PhD, MA. (Hons), DipClinPsyc, is Professor of Clinical Psychology and Clinical Director at Victoria University of Wellington, New Zealand. He was previously director of the Kia Marama Programme for sexual offenders at Rolleston Prison, Christchurch, New Zealand and has also taught clinical and forensic psychology at Canterbury and Melbourne Universities. His research interests include the offence process in offenders, cognitive distortions and models of rehabilitation. He has published over 235 research articles, chapters and books and his recent books include *Theories of Sexual Offending* (Wiley, 2006) and *Rehabilitation: Beyond the Risk Paradigm* (Routledge, 2007).

# Preface

There has been – and continues to be – an immense problem with the recognition, assessment and management of sexual abuse. New research and practice wisdom have taken forward our ideas of best practice. But too much of the useful research that can help with assessments remains fragmented and inaccessible to practitioners, acting as a barrier to evidence-based assessment practice.

Moreover, in the UK, government guidance has expanded both the definitional boundaries and the expectation on workers and agencies. But there remain few if any useful materials emanating from central government on how to undertake this essential area of work with victims, perpetrators and carers.

This is a significant new book, which replaces *The Complete Guide to Sexual Abuse Assessments* (RHP, 2000 now out of print). With all material from the original book fully reworked and expanded, together with addressing elements of new government guidance, it confronts these challenges, and in so doing provides a contemporary view of the breadth of concerns.

It:

- Updates the assessment frameworks, incorporating the latest research and practice wisdom.
- Adds several new frameworks including those concerning rape, learning disability and the internet, all areas now included in government definitions of sexual abuse.

All this provides a broad canvas from which to extract up-to-date ideas across many complex situations. However, work in some of these areas is not that well developed at present, and these have not been extensively addressed in this volume. Instead, by drawing on the experience of a wide range of professionals and professional disciplines, this otherwise comprehensive edition is critically selective in providing the latest evidence-based practice and theory for busy practitioners, academics, students and researchers.

The wealth of information covered by this book may not give all the answers to what is a constantly evolving and wide-ranging problem in all societies, but what it will *certainly* give is contemporary pointers to providing the most appropriate assessments, and an opportunity to encourage reflective practice.

Much is to be found here which will be invaluable in directing all those involved in child protection, safeguarding children or community safety towards reducing sexual abuse victimisation and re-victimisation, and helping those for whom the harm has already occurred to recover from their experiences.

# Introduction

It is a great privilege to have been able to edit such a wide ranging set of chapters that have attempted to offer us a contemporary view of the breadth of concerns that unify under the sexual abuse umbrella. Although this is in effect a second edition (replacing *The Complet Guide to Sexual Assessments*) there has been considerable movement in the research and theory associated with sexual abuse since that original book was published in 2000. To ensure the reader has been provided with the latest views I have called upon a wide range of professionals across different countries and across different professional disciplines. The book is aimed at those practitioners who have to be familiar with a wide range of concerns for the safety of children and young people yet are starved of the time and the necessary resources to be able to equip themselves in their task. The sheer size of the sexual abuse problem could mean that we need a detailed book examining each of the chosen areas, although this would become unwieldy and time consuming for the reader. The aim of the book is thus to furnish the frontline practitioner as well as their managers with an overview of the key assessment areas within their domain and to help them to either undertake or better commission the required assessment.

The book is badly needed in the field for other structural and political reasons. There has been an alarming demise of sexual abuse cases entering the child protection system over recent years (see Finkelhor and Jones, 2004), despite an expansion of the areas captured under the definitional umbrella: children involved in prostitution, children and young people who sexually abuse, organised abuse, female genital mutilation and internet sexual abuse (see Calder, 2006). This raises some critical questions about whether sexual abuse has declined or we are failing to recognise and manage it effectively.

Finkelhor and Jones (2004) identified the following reasons in the United States:

- **Increasing conservatism within the child protective services (CPS).** In this view, sexual abuse cases were declining in state caseloads because CPS was adopting more conservative standards regarding 'questionable' cases (e.g., allegations arising in divorces and custody disputes) or cases with weak initial evidence.
- **Exclusion of cases that do not involve caretakers.** In this view, CPS was increasingly excluding from its jurisdiction sexual abuse cases in which the perpetrator was not a primary caregiver.
- **Changes in CPS data collection methods or definitions.** In this view, the decline was due to changes in the way CPS tabulated or counted its cases, such as

changing from a three-tiered classification system (substantiated/indicated/ unsubstantiated) to a two-tiered system (substantiated/unsubstantiated).

- **A real decline in the incidence of sexual abuse.** In this view, there was a reduction in the number of children actually being abused as a result of increased prevention efforts, more prosecution and incarceration of offenders, or other social or cultural changes.
- **Less reporting to CPS due to a sexual abuse backlash.** In this view, negative publicity about sexual abuse cases and the potential liability of professionals who report suspected abuse made the public and professionals more reluctant to report sexual abuse.
- **A diminishing reservoir of older cases.** In this view, there had been a reduction in the supply of older but previously undisclosed cases available for new disclosures but no true decline in new cases.

Some of the suggested reasons for the declining numbers in the UK have included:

- Failure to recognise?
- Failure to manage?
- More confidence in informal management? Not wanting to subject mothers to a punitive child protection process.
- Alternative systems such as MAPPA and Sex Offender Registration and family support/children in need?
- Co-existence of domestic violence and cases being managed under emotional abuse?
- Impact of prevention strategies?
- Natural reduction over time
  - ○ Not reduced sexual abuse but retrospective disclosures addressed
  - ○ Challenge is the expansion of sexual abuse in professional guidance

Whatever the underlying causes of this reduction we do need to equip staff with tools to do the job expected of them: to protect children and mothers and hold the perpetrator responsible for their behaviour. This book is just one useful part of their toolkit. Happy reading, and let us hope it can assist in reducing sexual abuse victimisation and re-victimisation and also help those where the harm has already occurred to recover from their experiences.

## Lessons from the Bichard Inquiry

There have been other high profile issues raised since publication in 2000 of the book that this one replaces. Ian Huntley was convicted at the Old Bailey on 17 December 2003 of the murder of Holly Wells and Jessica Chapman. Maxine Carr was found guilty of conspiring to pervert the course of justice. There was widespread public concern when it became clear that Ian Huntley had been known to the authorities over a period of years. In fact, he had come to the attention of Humberside Police in relation to allegations of eight separate sexual offences from 1995 to 1999. This information had not emerged during the vetting check, carried out by Cambridgeshire Constabulary at the time of Huntley's appointment to Soham Village College late in 2001. The major concerns were how this had happened and whether it was probable that similar cases had also 'slipped through the net'. On 18 December, the Home Secretary announced the launch of an independent inquiry into the manner in which the police had handled intelligence about Ian Huntley's past and about the vetting processes, which ultimately led to his employment in a local school. Sir Michael Bichard was appointed as Chairman of the Inquiry. The Secretary of State for Education and Skills, Charles Clarke, also advised that the North East Lincolnshire Area Child Protection Committee had commissioned a Serious Case Review.

One of the key failings was the inability of the police and social services to identify Huntley's behaviour pattern soon enough. That was because both viewed each case in isolation and because social services failed to share information effectively with the police. It was also because there were 'systemic and corporate' failures in the way in which Humberside Police managed their intelligence systems. The Child Protection Database (CPD) was largely worthless because the information put onto it was regarded as unreliable. The various investigations of Huntley from 1995 onwards might well have been different if the police officers involved had known about past incidents.

In late 2001, Huntley applied for the post of caretaker at Soham Village College, a school that before and after these events has shown itself to be excellent and well led. Nonetheless, on this occasion there were errors in the school's recruitment process. The five open references that Huntley provided were, by their nature, unreliable and should not have been accepted. It was not the practice of the school normally to do so. In addition, Huntley's employment history was not adequately checked and it contained gaps including, the Inquiry discovered, one undisclosed employer from whom no reference was sought.

Soham Village College retains Education Personnel Management Limited (EPM), as a personnel service provider. One of EPM's directors would have signed the Police Check Form, to confirm that the particulars Huntley provided had been verified. They did not, in practice, however, check all those particulars, including details such as previous addresses.

Many of the improvements suggested lay with central government charged with the task of considering a new system for registering those working with children and vulnerable adults and a national IT intelligence system. However there were a number of other messages that needed to be addressed locally, such as the need for clear guidance on record creation, retention, review, deletion and the sharing of information; and how to better manage the issue of underage sex which was not taken sufficiently seriously by the police or social services generally. Bichard proposed that social services should, other than in exceptional circumstances, notify the police about sexual offences committed or suspected against children; national guidance should be provided to assist social services departments in making the decision about when to notify the police or not; social services records, in particular the Integrated Children's System (ICS), should record those cases where a decision is taken not to notify the police; the decision making in these cases should be inspected by the Commission for Social Care Inspection.

Head teachers and school governors should receive training on how to ensure that interviews to appoint staff reflect the importance of safeguarding children. From a date to be agreed, no interview panel to appoint staff working in schools should be convened without at least one member being properly trained. The relevant inspection bodies should, as part of their inspection, review the existence and effectiveness of a school's selection and recruitment arrangements.

There is a need to urgently clarify the circumstances and process for requests to DFES List 99, police etc, as this is often unclear locally.

There is huge variance in recruitment of staff and in police checks. Many administrative staff who have access to sensitive information and data may never have been police checked, yet there are volunteers providing essential services to children and young people in the community who should be police checked, but are not routinely appointed in such a way.

The maintenance of information on various information sharing systems, such as ISA, ICS, etc needs clarification to avoid any confusion about how such initiatives knit together and how they work individually or corporately.

Training issues in relation to the Sexual Offences Act 2003 and especially the new offence of 'grooming' is indicated. Detailed work is required to develop new systems to control further the safe appointment of people working with children. Identified groups include head-teachers and school governors.

## Ian Huntley Serious Case Review – Key Findings and Recommendations

There were nine young women with whom Ian Huntley was known to have a relationship or sexual involvement between 1995 and 2001 and who were also known to one or more of the statutory agencies. Seven of them were under 16 at the time of their involvement with Ian Huntley. In addition to these nine cases, Ian Huntley was suspected of being implicated in four allegations of rape in April and May 1998 and May and July 1999. Only the police were involved in these cases. The inability to locate social services case files were a key feature in some of the cases – either plainly lost or destroyed in accordance with departmental policy. There is a concern that no police checks were done by social services departments when concerns emerged about girls under 16 living with Ian Huntley. Local practice would not allow this to happen quickly unless the child was on the child protection register. Ian Huntley was not cautioned even when he admitted to *USI*. Had social services identified to the police they were aware this behaviour was not an isolated one, their response may well have been more interventionist. There was also evidence of a change in Huntley's behaviour when the circumstances of individual cases were examined. Changes from exploitative relationships with young women, close to the age of sexual consent, to a violent attack on a much younger girl.

## Safeguarding Vulnerable Groups Bill February 2006

The Bill is one of the central planks of the government's response to the Bichard Inquiry. The principal changes introduced by the Bill are:

- The scrapping of existing lists of people deemed to pose an employment risk to vulnerable groups. These lists operate under different legislation and with different criteria and procedures and are: List 99 (maintained under section 142 of the Education Act 2002), the Protection of Children Act (POCA) List (maintained under the Protection of Children Act 1999) and the Protection of Vulnerable Adults (POVA) List (maintained under Part 7 of the Care Standards Act 2000).
- The replacement of these lists with two aligned barred lists – one for those who are barred from working with children (the 'children's barred list'), and one for those who are barred from working with vulnerable adults (the 'adults barred list')
- The creation of an Independent Barring Board. This Board will maintain both lists and will make decisions about whether an individual should be included in a barred list.
- The creation of two categories of activity: regulated and controlled. Regulated activity will cover close contact work in key settings such as schools and care homes and key positions of responsibility such as the children's commissioner and the director of adult social services. Controlled activity will cover ancillary work in health and further education settings such as cleaning, catering and administration.
- A barred individual will not be able to work in a regulated activity post, but may, in certain circumstances and subject to adherence to rules established in guidance, work in a controlled activity post
- There will be a series of criminal offences: For example, employers will be committing an offence and will face penalties if they employ people to work with children and vulnerable adults that they know are barred – although this may not apply to parents. Employers could also face a fine if they employ someone who has not been through the new central vetting system or fail to make a check of the system. These same penalties – fines and sentences – will also be applied to employees.

Full details of the Bill http://www.publications.parliament.uk/pa/ld200506/ldbills/079/2006079.pdf

**Martin C. Calder**
Calder Training and Consultancy www.caldertrainingandconsultancy.co.uk

# References

Bichard Report (2004). London: TSO.

Calder, M.C. (2000) The Complete Guide to Sexual Abuse Assessments. Lyme Regis: Russell House Publishing.

Calder, M.C. (2006) The Demise of Sexual Abuse and Professional Barriers to Effective Identification, Assessment and Management. Presentation to Norfolk Safeguarding Board.

Finkelhor, D. and Jones, L.M. (2004) Explanations for the Decline in Child Sexual Abuse Cases. *Juvenile Justice Bulletin*, January 2004, 1–12.

# CHAPTER 1

# Victims of Child Sexual Abuse (CSA): Frameworks for Understanding Impact

*Martin C. Calder*

## Introduction

This chapter is an attempt to provide a map through the mountain of materials that exist in this subject area and to provide workers with the compass to navigate the terrain. Although this chapter restricts itself to sexual abuse, there are a great many parallels between the experiences of being exposed to sexual abuse and domestic violence (Calder, 2003). The chapter will address different types of victims, primary and secondary victimisation, impact frameworks and resilience considerations.

## Victims of sexual abuse

It is important to acknowledge that the literature does not provide an exclusive definition of being a victim, as illustrated in Figure 1.1 below. This typology is a generic one and when applied to the particular circumstances of sexual abuse would affront most victims who are completely innocent but where the perpetrator tries to displace responsibility on to the victim and this is often mirrored unwittingly by the professional response system. This chapter will hopefully furnish the reader with the evidence to support such an assertion and in doing so encourages a sensitive supportive response.

Petrunik (2003) has pointed out that the more scared, pure or innocent the victim, the more profane or unclean the assault and the person committing it are considered to be. The obverse of this would be that the less repulsive behaviour, with victims considered to be less 'innocent' would find itself pushed down the scale of

| Type of victim | Description |
|---|---|
| The completely innocent | These victims shoulder no guilt at all. They are truly innocent and did nothing to precipitate the victimisation. |
| The victim with minor guilt | These victims share some guilt in the experience. An example is a woman who provokes a miscarriage and dies as a result. In this case, she did not intend to die but did so as a result of her own actions. |
| The victim as guilty as the offender | These victims through their own actions or deeds provoke some type of action by themselves or on behalf of someone else whereby they become victims of the committed crime. An example of this type of victim is a woman who pleads with someone else to make her crying baby be quiet. Although she may not be the person who injures the child, her actions and deed precipitated the violence. |
| The victim as more guilty than the offender | These victims actually provoke the incidents in which they become victims of crime. An example of this type of victim is a person who wants to kill himself but cannot, therefore, he pulls a gun on a law enforcement officer, forcing the officer to kill him. |
| The victim as most guilty | These victims actually provoke the violence on behalf of others and end up either wounded or assaulted by self-initiated actions. An example of this type of victim is a person who provokes a fight with another and is then killed in self-defence. |
| The simulated or imaginary victim | These victims are not really victims at all but, because of paranoia, senility, or some other mental health problem, believe that they are consistently under attack or being stalked by someone or something in the environment. An example of this type of victim is a person who is always complaining to the police that he is the victim of electrical probes by aliens from another planet. |

**Figure 1.1**  Hagan's Typology of Victims                                                    (Hagan, 1990)

potential dangerousness. This notion suggests a hierarchy of victims, with innocent children at the top and then moving through a series of victim categories who may become increasingly less deserving of care, concern or protection. This may be an unpalatable proposition. Yet consider the reactions to sexual assaults on prostitutes compared with those on 'ordinary' women. Our perceptions are closely linked with how we feel about certain activities and how at risk we believe our family and friends might be. In a sense this says something about crime coming 'close to home' in that it is a concern with becoming a victim (Nash, 2006). There is also another important consideration – public perceptions regarding sexual abuse and culpability. The serious sexual assault on women is often framed by negative views of women from males, such as notions of 'deserving it' or really 'wanting it', thus excluding the perpetrator from blame. These notions have also found their way into judicial statements and continue to reflect a male-centric and commodified view of women that absolves men of culpability and places blame on victims. In the Ealing Vicarage rapes three offenders broke into the vicarage and carried out the attacks in front of the victim's father. They received sentences of three and five years, passing longer sentences for the burglary than the rape. Mr Justice Leonard stated that his sentencing decision was in part determined by what he regarded as a 'remarkable recovery' on the part of the victim and his view that her trauma was 'not so very great'.

A child who has been abused sexually is often referred to as a 'sexually abused child' or a 'sexual abuse victim.' Referring to the child as such is necessary given that it correctly describes the experience that the child has undergone and is needed for child protection, evaluation, intervention, etc. Yet, the automatic use of such a reference also facilitates its functioning as a label with impact beyond its original intent. Given the stigmatising impact that labelling within the context of education and mental illness has been shown to have on interpersonal relationships, children who are identified as sexually abused may be similarly negatively affected by such a label (Holguin and Hansen, 2003). Given the potential for 'sexual abuse' to function as a label, the variety of individuals who come in contact with children who have been sexually abused may be subject to altering their expectations or manner of interacting with the child based solely on the label. Children who have been identified as sexually abused usually experience a system of interventions characterised by contact (eg interviews, therapy, etc.) with a number of adults. In addition to contact with teachers and parents, children who have been identified as sexually abused often come into contact with psychologists, investigators, social workers, nurses, doctors, and lawyers. Concern for the abused child in these circumstances is created by the notion that the expectation of negative consequences of CSA may possibly have iatrogenic potential, together with the fact that there is an existing, albeit preliminary, literature base suggesting that "sexual abuse" functions as a label resulting in a perceiver bias and subsequent overestimation in negative expectancies. The sexually abused child's extensive interaction with a wide array of adults may be providing a big dose of negative expectancies, which in turn may be fostering an environment with iatrogenic potential. CSA is clearly an important societal problem in need of further understanding. In addition to any direct, negative effects of CSA there may also be an additional impact from the label itself.

## Developing a contextual matrix of the experiences of sexual abuse

The potential effects of childhood sexual abuse include a wide disarray of dysfunctional outcomes for victims during their childhood and as adults. Victims of sexual abuse often experience emotional, developmental, behavioural and communication problems in childhood. They also may experience pervasive fears and feelings of helplessness and depression as well as somatic complaints. They are over-represented in special educational programmes and in the eating disorder population as infants and adults as well as among prostitutes and among people at risk of suicide, substance abuse, sexual dysfunction, multiple personality, hysterical seizures and other psychiatric and mental health problems. Another negative outcome may be the increased risk of the sexually abused becoming sexually abusive to others. It seems widely accepted that sexual abuse is a learned behaviour and as such although not all sexually abused children become adult sexual offenders, they are at increased risk of developing offending behaviours.

The experience of sexual victimisation is both the same as and different from other abusive behaviours. Although sexual abuse involves emotional betrayal and psychological distress, the relationship may also meet the vulnerable child's emotional need for attention and nurturance (Summit, 1983) thus creating psychological confusion for the victim. Sexual abuse is dependent upon exploitation of the victim by the offender, yet frequently the victim is the one who feels guilty and stigmatised.

Berliner (2002) noted that some of the negative outcomes are the direct result of the traumatic impact of the sexual or physical abuse experiences. Other effects derive from the familial context within which the abuse occurs. Unlike traumas inflicted by non-family members, child abuse threatens the fundamental assumption that parents and other relatives will protect and act in the best interest of their kin. Abuse is also associated with attachment status. Children are thought to develop secure or insecure patterns of attachment based on their early experiences with caretakers and these patterns are believed to contribute to internal working models of relationships that can extend to other relationships. Parents who are consistently responsive to children's efforts to seek closeness or comforting engender secure attachment, while parents who are inconsistent, rejecting, or a source of harm can produce insecure attachment styles in children. Insecure attachment may be manifested in anxious, angry, aloof, disorientated or manipulative behaviour with caretakers. Not surprisingly, abused children are more likely to be insecurely attached than non-abused children. Insecure attachment may precede or be the result of these experiences. Parents who are inconsistent or rejecting may be at higher risk to commit abuse or to fail to protect children from abuse experiences. Alexander (1992) has proposed a relationship between insecure attachment and sexual abuse in which children who have anxious ambivalent styles may accept abusive behaviour while avoidant children who are indiscriminate in their relationships with adults become vulnerable to exploitation by extra-familial offenders. There is some evidence that sexually abused children suffer from disruptions in attachment behaviour (Toth and Cicchetti, 1996). Disturbed relating within primary caretaker relationships may set the stage for impaired social adjustment, for example with peers that are an important ingredient of normal developmental growth.

Daigneault et al. (2004) highlighted three conclusions that could be drawn from the child sexual abuse outcome studies results. First, no single symptom or syndrome seems to characterise a majority of victims across gender and age categories. Second, approximately one third of child and adolescent survivors present no measurable symptom. Third, adolescent child sexual abuse survivors present more co-occurring diagnoses than do other adolescents.

## Short-term effects of sexual abuse

These may vary from child to child, although certain symptoms may be seen in many victims. Short-term symptoms are usually the result of the anxiety, stress, and fear caused by the abuse. They include:

- **Anxiety:** is a state of heightened emotional arousal. The abused child may be preoccupied and worried about the abuse – unable to stop thinking about it.
- **Fear:** every threat possible has been made to children to keep them quiet. The fear induced by such threats is responsible for much of the child's anxiety.
- **Nightmares and sleep problems:** are often a terrifying re-enactment of the abuse or of dreams involving monsters or other frightening events. Children may stay awake to prevent any recurrence of the abuse.
- **Acting out and general misbehaviour:** sexually abused children are often seriously distressed and their unhappiness can lead to acting out and misbehaviour at home and in school. Their academic performance may deteriorate. Older children may run away, abuse drugs or alcohol, become promiscuous, or engage in illegal conduct.
- **Withdrawal:** Some children withdraw rather than acting out, retreating into their own shells.
- **Regression:** to an earlier stage of development, such as returning to wetting the bed.
- **Poor self-concept:** occurs when they think the abuse was their fault and they feel damaged by that as well as the abuse itself.
- **Depression:** sexual abuse makes children sad. For some children, they become clinically depressed and this is a serious psychiatric problem that goes beyond transitory sadness.
- **Inappropriate sexual behaviour:** some children develop sexual developmentally

inappropriate behaviour as a result of their sexual abuse.

- **Post-traumatic stress disorder:** children with symptoms of PTSD may repetitively act out their abuse in play. They may have stomach aches and headaches. They try to avoid people and things that remind them of the abuse.

(Myers, 1997: 30–2)

Figure 1.2 provides further details around the short-term effects.

## Long-term effects of child sexual abuse

A great number of difficulties may lie ahead for children who have been sexually abused. The following information highlights just how sexual abuse can take its toll in the victims' lives. Briere (1992) has set out seven psychological disturbances found in adult and adolescent survivors:

- **Post-traumatic stress disorder:** as above.
- **Cognitive distortions:** embrace the feelings of helplessness, chronic danger, self-deprecation and pessimism about the future.
- **Dissociation:** is a defensive disruption in the normally occurring connections between feelings, thoughts, behaviour and memories, consciously or unconsciously invoked in order to reduce psychological distress.
- **Altered emotionality:** includes depression, fear and anxiety.

| Initial effect categories | Presenting symptoms |
|---|---|
| Emotional and psychological distress (similar to females) | • Fear<br>• Problems with self-concept and self-esteem<br>• Guilt and shame<br>• Marked anxiety<br>• Depression<br>• Sleep disturbance<br>• Withdrawal and isolation<br>• Anger and aggressiveness<br>• Suicidality<br>• DependencyBehaviour problemsHomophobic concerns<br>• Aggressive and controlling behaviour<br>• Infantile behaviour<br>• Paranoid/phobic behaviour<br>• Sexual language and behaviours<br>• Dreams of being chased, punished, or isolated<br>• Body image concerns<br>• Setting fires<br>• Running away<br>• Failure to develop trust and intimacy<br>• Enuresis and encopresis<br>• Prostitution<br>• Suicide attempts or ideation<br>• Hyperactivity<br>• Regressive behaviours (thumb sucking)<br>• Declining school performance and school avoidance<br>• Drug and alcohol abuse<br>• Delinquency |
| Sexual problems and concerns | • Confusion/anxiety over sexual identity<br>• Inappropriate attempts to reassert masculinity<br>• Recapitulation of the victimising experience<br>• Sexualised behaviour<br>• Difficulties with interpersonal relationships<br>• Problems with sexual performance |

**Figure 1.2**  The short-term effects of sexual abuse on males

| Subsequent effect categories | Presenting symptoms |
|---|---|
| Emotional and psychological distress | • Anger/rage<br>• Self-concept/self-esteem problems<br>• Relationship problems<br>• Suicidality<br>• Depression<br>• Self-mutilation<br>• Fantasies of retribution<br>• Focus on confrontation<br>• Shame<br>• Inability to protect themselves |
| Relationship difficulties | • Difficulties in establishing and maintaining intimate relationships<br>• Difficulties talking about feelings<br>• Promiscuity/unfaithfulness<br>• Inability to form relationships with other men<br>• Involvement in abusive relationships in adulthood |
| Sexuality and sexual problems | • Dissatisfaction with sexual interactions<br>• Avoidance of sexual interactions<br>• Poor sexual self-esteem<br>• Preoccupation with sexual thoughts<br>• Fascination with pornography<br>• Compulsive masturbation<br>• Multiple sexual partners<br>• Sexual dysfunction (difficulties with erections; impotence; ejaculation problems, etc.)<br>• Inhibited sexual desire<br>• Prostitution |
| Sexual orientation | • Masculine identity confusion<br>• Sexual identity confusion<br>• Homosexuality |
| Addictive behaviours | • Chemical dependency<br>• Alcohol use<br>• Compulsive overeating<br>• Compulsive overworking<br>• Compulsive spending<br>• Compulsive sexual behaviour<br>• Compulsive relationships |
| Cyclical victimisation | • Sexually abusive behaviours towards others |

**Figure 1.3** The long-term effects of sexual abuse on males

- **Impaired self-reference:** refers to the difficulties the victims experience relating to themselves.
- **Disturbed relatedness:** includes problems with interpersonal relationships, especially intimate and sexual.
- **Avoidance:** many adults avoid pain by engaging in behaviours that consciously or unconsciously lessen their distress. These include the use of alcohol, drugs, self-mutilation, compulsive sexual behaviour, and eating disorders.

For more detailed reviews, see Beitchman et al. (1991, 1992); Browne and Finkelhor (1986); Finkelhor (1990); and Kendall-Tackett et al. (1993), and Figure 1.3.

## Differences in impact between male and female victims

It is important to record at the start of this section that there are a great many similarities between male and female victims of child sexual abuse:

both are likely to be abused by older males or siblings, and the range of the sexual assaults are similar; both are equally reluctant to report the abuse; both are equally fearful of the disclosure and its aftermath; both exhibit acute problems from the effects of the abuse; and both need considerable support to recover from their experiences.

Bolton et al. (1989) noted that male victims are less likely to report their sexual abuse, thus creating a situation of self-victimisation for themselves. The least reported abuse is actually that by their mothers, although the focus of much writing is on the effects of abuse by other men. If and when they disclose their abuse it may be followed by them minimising the impact to distance themselves from homosexual labelling whilst preserving their macho image. This feeds the public perception of the abuse being less traumatic than that for females. Male children are often sexually abused more outside the family (Finkelhor, 1984) and in the presence of other victims. Coercion, whilst a feature of all abuse, often becomes a very real overt feature for older male victims.

Although males and females suffer from the same long-term effects, males tend to react somewhat differently from females to the abuse itself. This is because we raise boys and girls differently, have different expectations of them, and tend to view male and female victims slightly differently. Males are supposed to be dominant and aggressive, while females are traditionally viewed as submissive and passive. We can have more difficulty empathising with male victims, as we believe they should protect themselves in any situation, and any failure to do so is seen as a sign of weakness. Engel (1994) argued that this ostensibly creates a situation in which the male victim of child sexual abuse is re-victimised by his culture and his own tendency to be critical of himself. He may see himself as a coward for allowing it to happen in the first place and for not avenging the crime. Many male victims may feel they did something to encourage the advances and this can lead to them questioning their sexual orientation. Homosexuality is an added burden in today's society. Some males are unable to define themselves as sexual beings at all, because sexuality has become associated with abuse in their minds. If the perpetrator was their role model then they may conclude that 'being a man' means being abusive. They may feel less masculine than other males, and believe that no

female would want to know them now. Adult male victims can have a variety of sexual problems, including an inability to achieve or maintain an erection, premature ejaculation, fears of specific sexual acts, particularly those performed on them. Some become sexually controlling of women and become daredevils, risking their lives to prove their manhood.

Unless a boy who has been sexually abused by a man also had access to non-abusing males, they may assume that all males become perpetrators as they grow up. They may want to convince themselves that they have not been damaged by what would be considered by many to be a homosexual encounter, and he may then become deliberately sexually aggressive towards women. Fears about issues relating to homosexuality are thought to be one of the main reasons boys are reluctant to disclose sexual abuse by men, despite that there is a high degree of crossover between gender.

Briere (1992) writes that:

> *Treatment should also address sex differences in how child abuse is cognitively processed. Because boys and men are expected to be strong and aggressive, victimisation may be more of a sex role violation for them than it is for girls and women. This additional trauma can result in somewhat different cognitive responses to abuse for male and female survivors ... Many sexually abused males have sexual concerns related to early molestation. Heterosexual boys and men may believe that childhood sexual abuse by another male has caused them to be latently homosexual – a fear that, in a culture as homophobic as ours, may result in compensatory masculinity or over-involvement in heterosexual activity. Conversely, homosexual men who were sexually abused by males may be concerned that their sexual orientation somehow caused them to be abused by men, or that their abuse somehow caused them to be homosexual – conclusions that can lead to feelings of guilt, shame and self-betrayal.*

Much of the research on the effects of sexual abuse focus on the sequelae in women and not men. It is important to note the particular issues as they differentially impact on male victims. Research has shown that only one in three boys with a history of child sexual abuse disclose in comparison to two in five girls (Finklehor et al., 1990). Finkelhor (1979) postulates that our society casts men as sexually active and women as sexually passive, thus attributing more consent and less exploitation into male victims. Indeed, Pierce and Pierce (1985) in a sample of sexual abuse victims found that 12 per cent of boys compared to 3 per cent of girls were believed to have encouraged their sexual abuse.

## *An integrative matrix*

Gail Ryan and colleagues (1999) produced a very integrative matrix for understanding the range of individual experiences of sexual abuse (see Figure 1.4) as an attempt to contain and organise the vast diverse literature that had emerged in this area in the preceding twenty years or so. Just laying out all these variables in a systematic fashion impresses on us the complexity of the issue as well as the uniqueness of each victim's experience path.

With a renewed respect for the complexity of the experiences of sexual abuse, they began to hypothesise which variables in the child, the family and the prior life experience might be most relevant and influential in shaping how the child perceives and accommodates the experience of sexual abuse in the context of their view of the world (see Figure 1.5).

The final matrix (Figure 1.6) provided a map on which to plot different developmental pathways that traverse (rather than begin with) the experience of sexual abuse. The implications of such a contextual view are enormous and support a more personal and holistic approach to child victims. Although victims share common issues, the ways that they manage and interpret these issues cannot be assumed. Workers must put aside personal bias and be open to explore the meaning of sexual victimisation in the context of the client's life experience. Hindman (1989) had earlier indicated that a series of perceptual variables cannot be gleaned from the records but can be discovered by a worker's willingness to hear from clients about their unique experiences. Each client's life experience is also affected by the equally complicated matrices of the people around them (especially those of family members).

## Multiple dynamic models

Freeman and Morris (2001) defined multiple dynamic models as they are concerned with the influence of multiple factors relating to the abusive situation and not just the abusive acts. Several models fall into this category: child sexual abuse accommodation syndrome (Summit, 1983); traumagenic dynamics (Finkelhor and Browne, 1985); process of sexual abuse (Sgroi, 1982); a

triangular framework for linking offender action and victim experience (Warner, 2000) and traumagenic states (James, 1990).

## *The child sexual abuse accommodation syndrome (Summit, 1983)*

The syndrome includes five categories, two of which are preconditions to the occurrence of sexual abuse and define basic childhood vulnerability, whilst the remaining three are sequential contingencies following sexual abuse.

### Secrecy

Sexual abuse mostly occurs when the perpetrator and the child are alone and it must never be shared with anyone else. The perpetrator often attaches a danger to breaking this secrecy, such as 'do not tell your mother: she will . . . (hate you, kill you, send me away, get sick, be upset, etc.)'. This usually alerts the victim to the fact that this something is bad and dangerous. Unless the victim can find some permission and power to share the secret and unless there is the possibility of an engaging, non-punitive response to disclosure, the child is likely to spend a lifetime in what comes to be a self-imposed exile from intimacy, trust and self-validation.

### Helplessness

Children are basically helpless within authoritarian relationships. They are advised to avoid the attention of strangers, but are required to be obedient and affectionate with any adult entrusted with their care. This is ironic given that children are three times more likely to be harmed by a trusted adult than a stranger. The fact that the adult is often in a trusted and loving position only increases the imbalance of power. Children cannot consent to such a sexual relationship, and it is unfair to expect them to resist the abuse given the difference in size and strength. Children are powerless in these situations.

### Entrapment and accommodation

Once sexual abuse has started, it frequently assumes a compulsive, addictive pattern and continues over a period of time, often until the children become autonomous or until discovery. Since few cases are believed to come to the attention of family or professionals, the only

**Experience of Sexual Abuse**

Age/Developmental Stage

| Sexual humiliation or trauma | Hands off: peep, flash, obscenity | Observation: nudity, sexual abuse of other; pornography: literature, photo, video; uncomprehendable sexual stimuli | Hands on: fondling, genital stimulation, frottage | Penetration: oral, vaginal, anal; digital, penile, objectile | Genital injury |
|---|---|---|---|---|---|

| Relationship of abuser: | Stranger | Peer | Adolescent | Sibling | Known adult | Caretaker | Parent |
|---|---|---|---|---|---|---|---|

| Child's perception of relationship: | Roles/expectations | | Casual/authority/dependency | | Trust/distrust | |
|---|---|---|---|---|---|---|

| Duration: | Onetime | Repetitive | Chronic |
|---|---|---|---|

| Method of engagement | Seduction | Trickery | Bribes/lures | Coercion | Threat of loss | Threat of force | Force | Violence |
|---|---|---|---|---|---|---|---|---|

| Child's perception: | Cognitive: Understanding of offender's distortions | Physical: pain, arousal, comfort | Emotional: fear, anxiety, pleasure | Secondary gains or motive |
|---|---|---|---|---|

**Discussions**

| Expedient | Delayed | Nondisclosure |
|---|---|---|
| Effective Intervention | Ineffective Intervention | No Intervention |

Consequences of disclosure:

Victim: fear, shame, guilt, blame, placement, loss of family, not believed – abuse continues

Family: rage, confusion, intrusion, break up, loss of members, denial/minimisation

Offender: deny or admit, legal threats, personal threats, suicide, loss

**Outcomes**

Issues: Anxiety, humiliation, lack of control, helplessness, vulnerability, powerlessness, embarrassment, shame, guilt, put down, betrayed, devalued, post-traumatic stress, loss, confusion, sexual, cognitive role, boundary, relationship

Characteristics: Poor self-image, lack of trust, distorted thinking, negative expectations, rejection, failure, personalising sexual offence, depersonalising others, preoccupation, depression, fear of intimacy, sadness, deviant sexual arousal, indiscriminate external locus of control

Manifestations: setting self up, power/control behaviours, phobias, withdrawal, isolating, post traumatic stress disorder, unrealistic expectations, irresponsible behaviours, thinking errors, putting self down, somatic complaints, attention deficit, learning disability, promiscuity, aggression, self destructive behaviour, sexual acting out, sexual abuse perpetration/re-victimisation

**Figure 1.4** Experience of sexual abuse (Ryan et al., 1999. Reproduced by permission of Gail Ryan)

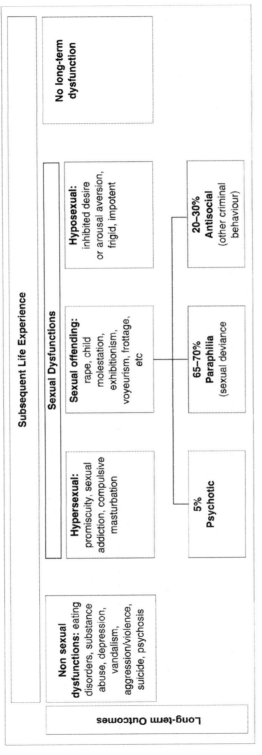

**Figure 1.4**   *Continued*

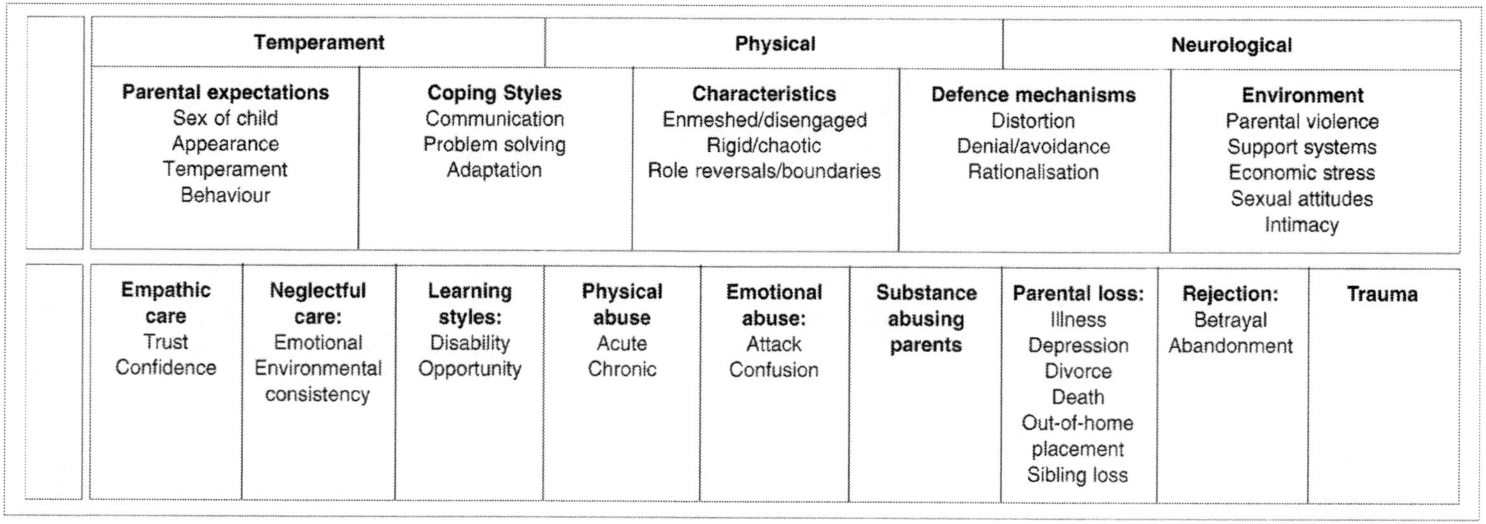

| Temperament | | | Physical | | | Neurological | |
|---|---|---|---|---|---|---|---|
| **Parental expectations** Sex of child Appearance Temperament Behaviour | **Coping Styles** Communication Problem solving Adaptation | | **Characteristics** Enmeshed/disengaged Rigid/chaotic Role reversals/boundaries | **Defence mechanisms** Distortion Denial/avoidance Rationalisation | | **Environment** Parental violence Support systems Economic stress Sexual attitudes Intimacy | |
| **Empathic care** Trust Confidence | **Neglectful care:** Emotional Environmental consistency | **Learning styles:** Disability Opportunity | **Physical abuse** Acute Chronic | **Emotional abuse:** Attack Confusion | **Substance abusing parents** | **Parental loss:** Illness Depression Divorce Death Out-of-home placement Sibling loss | **Rejection:** Betrayal Abandonment | **Trauma** |

**Figure 1.5**    Early life experience (Ryan et al., 1999. Reproduced by permission of Gail Ryan)

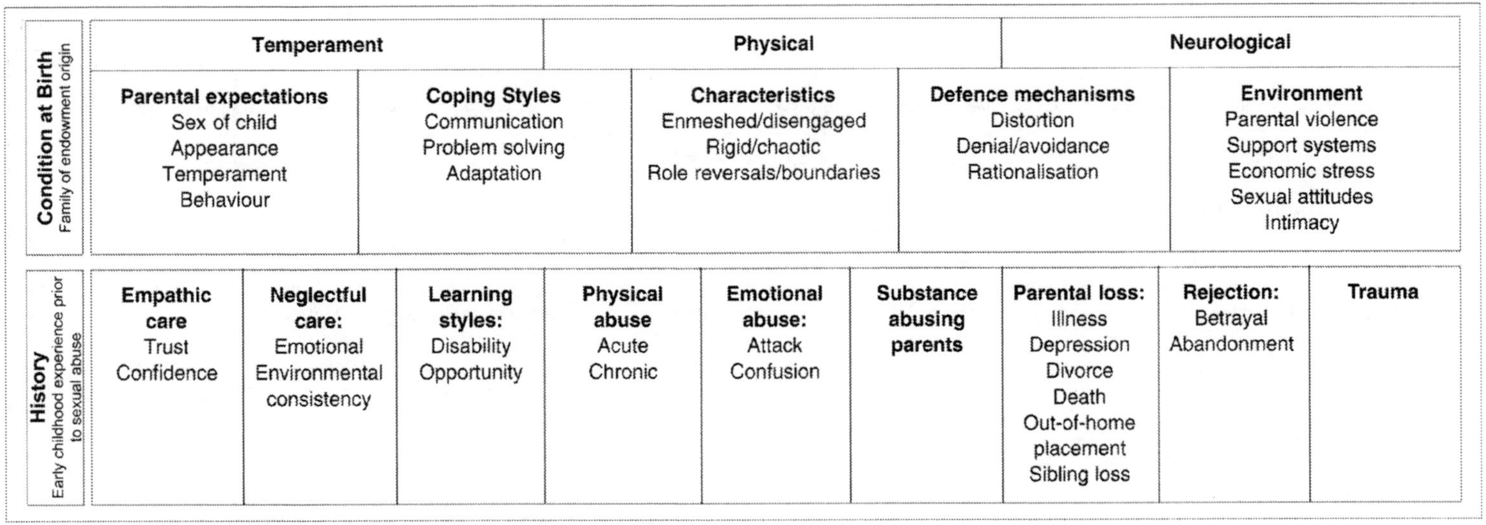

| | Temperament | | Physical | | Neurological |
|---|---|---|---|---|---|
| **Parental expectations**<br>Sex of child<br>Appearance<br>Temperament<br>Behaviour | **Coping Styles**<br>Communication<br>Problem solving<br>Adaptation | **Characteristics**<br>Enmeshed/disengaged<br>Rigid/chaotic<br>Role reversals/boundaries | **Defence mechanisms**<br>Distortion<br>Denial/avoidance<br>Rationalisation | **Environment**<br>Parental violence<br>Support systems<br>Economic stress<br>Sexual attitudes<br>Intimacy | |
| **Empathic care**<br>Trust<br>Confidence | **Neglectful care:**<br>Emotional<br>Environmental<br>consistency | **Learning styles:**<br>Disability<br>Opportunity | **Physical abuse**<br>Acute<br>Chronic | **Emotional abuse:**<br>Attack<br>Confusion | **Substance abusing parents** | **Parental loss:**<br>Illness<br>Depression<br>Divorce<br>Death<br>Out-of-home placement<br>Sibling loss | **Rejection:**<br>Betrayal<br>Abandonment | **Trauma** |

**Condition at Birth**
Family of endowment origin

**History**
Early childhood experience prior to sexual abuse

**Figure 1.6** Contextual matrix: sexual abuse in the context of whole life experience (Ryan et al., 1999. Reproduced by permission of Gail Ryan)

**Experience of Sexual Abuse**

**Sexual humiliation or trauma**

| Hands off: peep, flash, obscenity | Observation: nudity, sexual abuse of other; pornography: literature, photo, video; uncomprehendable sexual stimuli | Hands on: fondling, genital stimulation, frottage | Penetration: oral, vaginal, anal; digital, penile, objectile | Genital injury |

**Age/Developmental Stage**

**Relationship of abuser:**

| Stranger | Peer | Adolescent | Sibling | Known adult | Caretaker | Parent |

**Child's perception of relationship:**

| Roles/expectations | Casual/authority/dependency | Trust/distrust |

**Duration:**

| Onetime | Repetitive | Chronic |

**Method of engagement**

| Seduction | Trickery | Bribes/lures | Coercion | Threat of loss | Threat of force | Force | Violence |

**Child's perception:**

| Cognitive: Understanding of offender's distortions | Physical: pain, arousal, comfort | Emotional: fear, anxiety, pleasure | Secondary gains or motive |

**Discussions**

| Expedient | Delayed | Nondisclosure |
| Effective Intervention | Ineffective Intervention | No Intervention |

**Consequences of disclosure:**

| Victim: fear, shame, guilt, blame, placement, loss of family, not believed – abuse continues | Family: rage, confusion, intrusion, break up, loss of members, denial/minimisation | Offender: deny or admit, legal threats, personal threats, suicide, loss |

**Outcomes**

**Characteristics:** Poor self-image, lack of trust, distorted thinking, negative expectations, rejection, failure, personalising sexual offence, depersonalising others, preoccupation, depression, fear of intimacy, sadness, deviant sexual arousal, indiscriminate external locus of control

**Issues:** Anxiety, humiliation, lack of control, helplessness, vulnerability, powerlessness, embarrassment, shame, guilt, put down, betrayed, devalued, post-traumatic stress, loss, confusion, sexual, cognitive role, boundary, relationship

**Manifestations:** setting self up, power/control behaviours, phobias, withdrawal, isolating, post traumatic stress disorder, unrealistic expectations, irresponsible behaviours, thinking errors, putting self down, somatic complaints, attention deficit, learning disability, promiscuity, aggression, self destructive behaviour, sexual acting out, sexual abuse perpetration/re-victimisation

**Figure 1.6** *Continued*

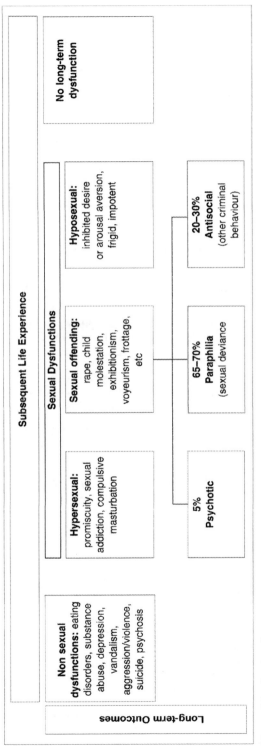

Figure 1.6   *Continued*

healthy option for the victim is to learn to accept the situation and survive. They learn to accommodate the sexual abuse, which frequently escalates and this is coupled with a realisation by the victim of the betrayal from the perpetrator. They do so by employing a number of accommodation mechanisms which might include delinquency, self-mutilation and concealing any sign of conflict or distress.

## Delayed, conflicted and unconvincing disclosure

However the sexual abuse comes to light, the child has to cope with the process of investigation (either by the family or by professionals) and the subsequent consequences of the disclosure or discovery. There are often many barriers to belief of the allegations, particularly that the abuse has been going on for some time and they never reported it. How could the child wait so long before telling their mother? The perpetrator is rarely successfully prosecuted or convicted, and some children may be removed from home. Mothers and workers need to assume a position of believing, accepting, supporting and protecting the child.

## Retraction

Whatever a child says about sexual abuse, they are likely to reverse it. They experience guilt if the family has disintegrated and the outcome is a reflection of the perpetrator's threats. They frequently bear the responsibility for the abuse and the outcome. As a result, they become aware that it is better to capitulate and restore a lie for the sake of the family. For many, a retraction of the allegations follows. The lie carries more credibility than the most explicit claims of incestuous entrapment, as it serves to restore the precarious equilibrium in the family and lets the professionals off 'the hook' of having to act. The child learns not to complain, and the adults learn not to listen. The professionals learn not to believe rebellious children who try to use their sexual power to destroy 'well-meaning parents'. Children are thought to recant either because they have been subjected to pressure from the perpetrator or family members or because their report has produced negative consequences to themselves or others. Many children report fears about telling or regret the disclosure because of the outcome (Sauzier, 1989). Even when children

do report abuse that is later confirmed, their accounts frequently are marked with inconsistencies and tentativeness (Sorenson and Snow, 1991). Recantation can occur in between one-fifth (Sorenson and Snow, 1991) to one-third of cases (Sahd, 1980). Whilst not diagnostic of abuse, recantation is a typical reaction of a child who has been abused and has disclosed the abuse. Reiser (1991) reviewed the available literature on this topic and provided the following reasons for child recantation:

### False allegations

Crewdson (1988) reported that only 2 to 4 per cent of allegations were false, with almost all the false allegations coming from older teenage girls.

### Secrecy

Child sexual abuse is characterised by secrecy. Most ongoing sexual abuse is never disclosed, at least not outside the immediate family. The family often has rigid boundaries between itself and the outside world creating an exaggerated feeling of family loyalty and traps the victim in a web of secrecy. Disclosure of the sexual abuse by the child is thus unacceptable behaviour and following the consequences, the child tries to return to the earlier and often easier secretive stance.

### Denial

Denial may be a factor in recantation. In these situations the inability to recognise consciously certain feelings or experiences may defend against the experience of disclosure, the abuse experience itself, or both.

### Lack of support and pressure to recant

Many children recant because they are not getting enough support from those responsible for their safety or they are under direct pressure to take back their admission. The experience of sexual abuse can create a great deal of fear, guilt, and confusion in children, and so recantation is an inviting option even when children are getting support for their admission. In addition to the lack of control, children operate in a time frame very different from that of adults and so a month of having their mother furious at them for disrupting the family may be experienced by the child as unbearable. Children may also be under direct pressure from family members to recant as they try to manage the loss of financial support, etc. They may actually find themselves in a situation seemingly worse than they were before the disclosure, and this can induce recantation.

### Societal attitudes

Many people believe that children are not credible witnesses. This can lead to them adopting a position which blames the victim as well as denying the abuse. In some situations, a retraction may automatically cause them to doubt the credibility of the victim.

### Child and family interacting variables

The detailed child protection procedures and legal requirements often seemingly prolong the trauma for the child victim, for many years later in some situations. Bearing this in mind, it is quite easy to see why either a child (or with parental encouragement) recants.

### Intervening events

It is not unusual for a delay in concluding court proceedings and this maintains the child and their families in crisis during this time. Worse than this, a court case can sometimes have the effect of delaying treatment services. It is not uncommon to find that as more time passes between the child's initial report of the abuse and the judicial resolution of the case, the risk of recantation increases.

### The problems with recantation

Children will not be able to process what has happened to them if they are not able to talk about it. Talking about traumatic events is widely recognised as an effective way of coming to terms with what has happened. The failure to confront the effects of the sexual abuse may increase the child's vulnerability to further victimisation, given her feelings of low self-esteem and a perception that her family and the system are unresponsive. Given the family's reaction to their initial report and their happiness with the recantation, the victim is certainly less likely than before to report again should the perpetrator re-victimise her. If no prosecution takes place, or if the abuse is not confirmed, the victims may well return to live in the abusive situation with no protection. They run the risk of being abused

again. Family members, who never believed the victim and welcomed the recantation, will not safeguard the child in the home and may see no reason to supervise perpetrator-children contact. Recantation may offer the victim with a short-term solution to some of the pressure they are experiencing, but in the long run it is likely to lead to even greater trauma because the children must now continue to lie and to live with the fact that they are lying (adapted from Marx, 1996; and Reiser, 1991).

## Traumagenic dynamics

This model was developed by Finkelhor and Browne (1985, 1986, 1988) and is probably the most influential and important framework for understanding the impact of sexual abuse. It is an eclectic, comprehensive model that suggests a variety of different dynamics to account for the variety of different types of symptoms (Finkelhor, 1988: 68). They offer us four traumagenic (trauma-causing) dynamics, defined as 'an experience that alters a child's cognitive or emotional orientation to the world and causes trauma by distorting the child's self-concept, worldview, or affective capacities'. The model allows sexual abuse to be conceptualised as a situation or a process rather than simply as an event, and this is important as different parts of the process contribute different traumagenic dynamics. The latter are not restricted to one part of the process, operating before, during, and after the sexual contact. Most of the effects that have been noted in the literature can be conveniently categorised and explained by one or two of the dynamics. Whilst the fit is not perfect, it does offer a plausible framework for the variety and diversity of impacts noted (Finkelhor and Browne, 1988: 77). They also note that different traumagenic dynamics lead to different types of trauma, and that each of the dynamics themselves is an ongoing process.

The experiences of sexual abuse can be analysed in terms of four traumagenic dynamics – traumatic sexualisation, stigmatisation, betrayal and powerlessness. Each dynamic is a clustering of injurious influences with a common theme. There are no direct correlates between effects and dynamics, although there are many affinities. The issue of gender is an important one here, given the differential impact victims experience. As always, there are differing views on impact across the sexes. Barbaree, Hudson and Seto (1993: 8) in a review of the literature found the effects to be broadly similar whether the victim is male or female although Friedrich (1988) found real differences, finding that boys tend to externalise their responses whilst girls internalise theirs. Girls who do not follow this pattern tend to have a close relationship with the abuser and have suffered a high frequency and more serious forms of sexual abuse (Print and Dey, 1992). Whatever you accept, you need to acknowledge that the knowledge base is drawn almost entirely from female victims. Mendel (1995: 77) argued that whilst it seems reasonable to hypothesise that the four traumagenic dynamics are present in male victims, it is likely that several differences exist between males and females in terms of the salience or potency of the four: it would appear that the degree of stigmatisation surrounding male sexual victimisation is far greater than that experienced by females, and the dynamic of powerlessness holds different meanings for each sex, standing at odds with the male role expectation of powerful competence and self-reliance.

Having reviewed the positive aims of the model, let us move on to consider the individual traumagenic dynamics individually and in more detail:

**1. Traumatic sexualisation:** was defined by Finkelhor and Browne (1986: 181) as 'a process in which a child's sexuality (including both sexual feelings and sexual attitudes) is shaped in a developmentally inappropriate and interpersonally dysfunctional fashion as a result of the sexual abuse'.

Finkelhor (1988: 69) offered us several distinct processes, which combine to contribute to traumatic sexualisation:

- Sexually abused children are often rewarded, by perpetrators, for sexual behaviour that is inappropriate to their level of development.
- Because of the rewards, sexually abused children learn to use sexual behaviour, appropriate or inappropriate, as a strategy for manipulating others to get their needs met.
- Because of the attention that they receive, certain parts of sexually abused children's anatomy become fetishised and given distorted importance and meaning.
- Children become confused and acquire outright misconceptions about sexual behaviour and sexual morality as a result of things that perpetrators tell them or ways that they behave.

- A child's sexuality can become traumatised when frightening and unpleasant memories become associated in the child's mind with sexual activity.

Finkelhor noted that these were among the most important of the dynamics that traumatise a child's sexual capacities. He also noted that they are among the dynamics unique to sexual abuse. We have to accept that experiences of sexual abuse will vary dramatically in terms of the amount and kind of traumatic sexualisation that they provoke (Browne and Finkelhor, 1986). The same authors went on in a later article (1988: 60) to explore the debate on what kinds of abuse are more or less traumagenic. Groth (1978) contends that sexual abuse generates the greatest trauma when:

- It continues over a long period of time.
- Occurs with a closely related person.
- Involves penetration.
- Is supported by aggression.

There are several other important considerations that should be added to this list:

- Evoking a sexual response from the child.
- It depends on the degree of the child's understanding as this develops over time even if the child is very young, the abuse takes on new meanings at each stage of their development (Finkelhor and Browne, 1986: 182).
- Non-disclosure of the abuse (Finkelhor, 1979).
- The age of the victim (Finkelhor and Browne, 1988: 61).
- The gender of the perpetrator (males being the most traumatic) (Russell, 1986).
- The age of the perpetrator – with adults being more traumatic than juveniles (Russell, 1986).
- Parental reaction – is more traumatic when negative (Finkelhor and Browne, 1986: 61).
- Removal of the victim from their home.

Sexual abuse experiences can vary dramatically in terms of the amount and kind of traumatic sexualisation they provoke. It is plausible to hypothesise that it is associated with impacts on sexual behaviour, where the effects would include sexual dysfunction, promiscuity, sexual anxiety, and low sexual self-esteem (Finkelhor and Browne, 1988: 65). Children who have been traumatically sexualised emerge from their experiences with inappropriate repertoires of sexual behaviour, and their experiences may initiate the motivation to abuse. Child sexual abuse has the capacity to arouse juveniles sexually before they have the appropriate developmental capacity to cope. Certainly sexual aggression can present as a behavioural manifestation of early traumatic sexualisation (Elliott and Butler, 1994).

**2. Betrayal:** 'refers to the dynamic in which children discover that someone on whom they are vitally dependent has caused them harm – this could be the actions of the abuser through their manipulation or lies, or by the failure to protect or believe the victim by a family member' (Finkelhor and Browne, 1986: 182).

Betrayal is present to some degree in most abuse situations, and can operate in several ways eg at the time of the abuse itself or belatedly in the realisation that they were tricked into doing something bad. Abuse by family members or trusted person has the greatest potential for betrayal, particularly when the closeness of the relationship is considered. Regardless of the relationship, the degree of harm experienced by the child will be related to how taken-in they feel by the abuse (Finkelhor, 1988: 70) as well as the family's response to the disclosure. Where the child is disbelieved, blamed or ostracised, the degree of betrayal will be perceived to be higher than those who were supported (Finkelhor and Browne, 1986: 183). The greatest sense of betrayal often comes when the mothers are unwilling or unable to believe and protect them. Even where parents do believe and support the child, they may still feel betrayed as they assumed that they were capable of warding off all harm (Finkelhor, 1988: 70). Finkelhor and Browne (1988: 65) linked this factor with effects such as depression, dependency in extreme forms, impaired ability to trust and to judge the trustworthiness of others, and anger. Some of the manifestations of these might be a vulnerability to subsequent abuse and exploitation.

**3. Powerlessness:** 'refers to the process in which the child's will, desires, and sense of efficacy are continually contravened' (Finkelhor and Browne, 1986: 183).

Finkelhor (1988: 71) argued that there were two main components to the traumagenic dynamics of powerlessness:

- A child's will and wishes are repeatedly overruled and frustrated.
- A child experiences the threat of injury or annihilation.

Many aspects of the sexual abuse experience can contribute to powerlessness, but certain of them are particularly significant and particularly common:

- A basic kind of powerlessness occurs when a child's fantasy and body space are repeatedly invaded against their will, regardless of whether this occurs through force or deceit. The latter may exacerbate the powerlessness experienced.
- The experience of violence, coercion and a threat to life forms the second core form of powerlessness, which is again exacerbated and reinforced when their attempts to halt the abuse are frustrated. It is increased when the child feels fear, and they are unable to make adults understand or believe what is happening, or when they realise how conditions of dependency have them trapped in the situation. Children are arguably powerless whether or not force is used (Finkelhor and Browne, 1986: 183).
- Ongoing vulnerability, entrapment, and the associated emotions of fear and anxiety also contribute to the dynamic (Finkelhor, 1988: 72).

Clearly, the dynamic of powerlessness distorts the child's sense of ability to control his or her own life (Finkelhor, 1988: 68). This can be offset by trying to give them some say in the way in which the abuse ends. Finkelhor and Browne (1988: 68) relate this factor to manifestations which includes nightmares, somatic complaints, depression, running away, school problems, employment problems, vulnerability to subsequent victimisation, aggressive behaviour, delinquency, and/or becoming an abuser.

**4. Stigmatisation:** 'refers to the negative connotations (eg badness, shame and guilt) that are communicated to the child surrounding experiences of molestation and that then become incorporated into the child's self-image' (Finkelhor and Browne, 1986: 184).

These negative messages are communicated in several ways:

- They can come directly from the perpetrator, who may blame the victim ('you seduced me') or denigrate ('you bitch') or shame the victim about the behaviour.
- From attitudes that the victim hears from other persons in the family or community, or from people in their environment who may impute

other negative characteristics to the victim (loose morals, spoiled goods, or 'queer' in the case of boys) as a result of the abuse.

- Perpetrators may say it indirectly through their furtiveness and pressures for secrecy.
- Stigmatisation may grow out of the child's prior knowledge or sense that the activity is considered deviant and taboo.
- It is reinforced if, after disclosure, people react with shock or hysteria or blame the child for what has transpired (Finkelhor and Browne, 1988: 64–5).
- If the perpetrator uses tricks and bribes which the child feels implicates them in the abuse and sets them out as socially unacceptable, eg drink, drugs, truancy.

The dynamic of stigmatisation clearly distorts the child's sense of his or her own value of worth (Finkelhor, 1988: 68). It occurs in various degrees in different abuse situations. We therefore need to consider this as a possibility in each presented case. An example would be that some are told that it is their fault, whilst others are not (Finkelhor and Browne, 1988: 64–5). Others may be too young to have much awareness of social attitudes and thus suffer little stigmatisation as a result. Others may have to manage powerful religious and cultural taboos on top of the usual stigma. Retaining the abuse as a secret may increase the sense of stigma since it reinforces the sense of being different. In contrast, children who find out that such experiences occur to many other children may have some of their stigma assuaged (Finkelhor and Browne, 1988: 64). These authors relate this dynamic to such long-term effects such as guilt, poor self-esteem, a sense of being different and isolated, and secondary problems such as drug and alcohol abuse, criminal involvement, suicidal ideation, and attempts (p65). Any accommodation of the perpetrator's own distorted rationalisation can lead to the victim's personal stigmatisation (Ryan, 1991).

### The process of sexual abuse model (Sgroi, 1982)

The sexual abuse of children follows a predictable pattern of stages or phases (Sgroi, 1982) and mothers will have an increased ability to understand the impact of sexual abuse when they understand the process through which sexual abuse usually progresses. It will also help them to understand why it is often so difficult for the child to tell.

### Engagement or entrapment stage

The perpetrator initiates the contact with the child by offering bribes or rewards or by offering special attention and affection. This is referred to as 'grooming' the victim. Sexual abuse usually is well planned by the perpetrator who uses his close and trusted relationship with the child and family to access the child.

### Sexual interaction stage

Once the child responds to this special attention, the adult begins some form of sexual activity. The sexual interaction is usually progressive and may include one or more of the following: showing pornographic pictures, using sexually graphic language, undressing, touching, masturbation, kissing, vaginal or anal penetration, fellatio, etc.

### Secrecy stage

Once the sexual activity has begun, the adult imposes secrecy by threatening that no-one will believe them if they tell; the pets will be hurt if they tell; the family will be split up if they tell; something bad will happen to the abuser if they tell; or that the child may be removed from the family. It is for these reasons that some children never tell of their abuse, and if they do, it is many years later. For example, Etherington (1995) found that the average duration for male victims to disclose was 20 years.

### Disclosure stage

Disclosure occurs when secrets are told or discovered and this creates the crisis discussed in detail earlier in this chapter.

### Suppression stage

This is a critical stage for the child who has disclosed. If family members react by blaming or dismissing the allegations, the disclosure may be withdrawn. Without adequate supports, the child may believe the threats from the abuser.
Recanting is most common in situations of incest and other family members do not support them. Recantation can occur also when the child realises the consequences of their disclosure.

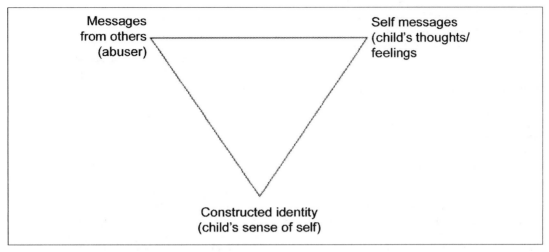

**Figure 1.7**   The triangle of effects (Warner, 2000)

## A triangular framework linking offender action and victim experience (Warner, 2000)

In order to sexually abuse children, abusers must trick the children into complying with their demands and keeping silent about the abuse. Abusers set up particular versions of identity and experience that construct abusers as blameless, position children as guilty, and also dissuade others from asking questions and recognising harm. The negative messages which surround the abuse and which are reinforced by the abuser and directed towards the child, may then become internalised by the child. And because it is the mind-tricks that harm children, such feelings may perpetuate long after the original abuse has ceased.

The messages the abuser gives the child through actions and words affect the child's sense of self. The more important the abuser is to the child, the more powerful are the actions/words. Over time the messages received become so fixed that people no longer have a sense that they were ever told them.

### Phase 1: Targeting

#### Making the child feel good

The abuser must first establish a positive relationship with the child and those people who could act to protect that child. They may already be there, ie teacher, parent, religious leader, or they target women who have children.

### Making the child feel confused

The abuser gradually alters his behaviour with the child. Hugs and physical games gradually have a sexual element introduced. The child may not trust his own feelings of disquiet. The abuser maintains a consistent relationship with everyone else. The child feels the problem is with himself. His confusion is increased because his perception of the abuser is at odds with everyone else. Also parts of the relationship are still good – adding to the confusion. The child may feel guilty if he instigated the hugs or games. The child's confusion can result in lowering of trust in all his relationships and therefore his ability to tell others. Ultimately he will feel unable to trust his own judgements and his self esteem will gradually erode.

### Making the child feel sad or angry

The child feels betrayed. The abuser both failed to protect and actively caused harm. Betrayal is most keenly felt when children are abused by someone close to them or someone they respect. The child feels the loss of the relationship with the abuser and also with other people. The child has a huge secret that separates them from others. This can be intense if the child believes others know about it, but don't protect. This can lead to powerful feelings of sadness and despair. Anger in the child may be directed at himself or other targets less frightening than the abuser. Feelings of anger and sadness can become integrated into the child's sense of self as a generalised feeling of alienation. The child may find it difficult to feel good about anything and feels separate and alone.

### Making the child feel responsible

The child may come to believe that the change in the relationship is about the 'bad' character of the child and that the child seduced the adult. The child feels that they, not the abuser, is responsible. The child may believe that their availability makes them 'easy' rather than the situation they are in has increased their vulnerability. The repetition of abuse reinforces the powerlessness of the child. The child's positive self-concepts are gradually eroded. The child feels responsible and powerless. The child may see himself as both seducer and eternal victim.

## Phase 2: Grooming for compliance

### Make the child feel normal

The abuser tries to convince the child that what they are doing is not abuse. This denies the reality of betrayal and reduces the abusers own inhibitions against abusing. They persuade themselves that the child wanted sexual contact and that this is the usual way to express love and affection. If the child loves trusts respects that person, the child will be more ready to believe this too. Feeling 'normal' may be a great relief to the child and the child may have a stake in maintaining a sense of normality.

If the child has limited access to other relationships in which different messages can be found, they will be more likely to accept the reality constructed through the abusive relationship. In order to maintain any positive sense of self, the child must believe that the sexual relationship they have with the abuser is, indeed, normal.

### Making the child feel isolated

Secrecy and isolation create the perfect conditions for concealing abuse. Apparently 'normal' 'respectable' families from the dominant class: white, heterosexual, two parent family, with money, may be less likely to be challenged by the public. No one hears what goes on in a large detached house. Secrecy and isolation also create the perfect emotional conditions for concealing

abuse. Abusers therefore isolate children so that their only, or major, source of information about themselves comes through the experience of the abuse and the messages of the abuser. The abuser may not only isolate children within families but from their friends and the wider community. Children may be refused permission to visit friends or to go to after school activities.

### Making the child feel alienated

The abuser may increase the child's sense of isolation by attempting to alienate the child from all other relationships. They may tell the child their mother knows but doesn't care. They may set up divisions between siblings ie spoiling the abused child. The child's behaviour may deteriorate and the abuser may use this to discredit the child. They may label them a trouble maker. People may come to believe that the child can't be trusted. The child's negative version of self is reinforced. The abuser may tell the child that their community would reject them if they tell or that they wouldn't be believed because they are disabled, black, or working class. Such alienation continues long after the abuse has ceased.

## Phase 3: Grooming for offending

### Making the child feel guilty

Guilty feelings are especially engendered where the child has been made to be an active participant in the abuse. This includes activities the child has been made to perform on the abuser or other children or when the child has been sexually aroused. The abuser may tell the child that they really wanted to have sex because they obviously enjoyed it. Despite the child's abhorrence of 'doing sex' with their abuser, their own body betrays them by responding to their demands. As such they can no longer trust themselves. Feelings of self betrayal and disgust may increase their sense of guilt. Their guilt may be exacerbated because of feelings that they should have stopped it earlier. Children accept their failure to speak out as indicating guilt rather than their naivety.

### Making the child feel bad

If the abuser justifies his actions by using widely held stereotypes of male sexuality that depict men as being ruled by their genitals, this has profound implications for the children they abuse. A girl may feel entirely responsible for the abuse, because only she can stop it – men can't do this themselves. She may fear telling because she feels people will condemn her. A boy is in the role of victim (against his gender role) but he may also be made to abuse others (within his gender role). He is therefore twice guilty: for acting 'like a girl' and being abused; and acting 'like a man' and abusing others. Some boys who are abused by men may fear, if they disclose, being pathologised for being homosexual.

## Phase 4: Grooming to stop disclosure

### Making the child feel powerful

The child may believe that because they actively sought out the abuser's hugs and games, this makes them responsible for the subsequent sexual abuse. The abuser may act as if their relationship is based on the choices the child makes, rather than their demands. They may interpret the child's inability to say 'no' as active agreement for the sexual relationship to continue. They may interpret their body's responses as an active desire for them. The abuser may feel the child is responsible for invoking their arousal and they therefore cannot be held responsible. The child's inability to stop the abuse re-invokes their primary feelings of helplessness. They may come to believe that they have power over the abuser. Accepting responsibility means that they can internalise a version of self that is powerful, however bad they feel about themselves. Precisely because experiences of sexual abuse can make children feel so helpless, they may accept their identity as powerful; because, the moment they feel strong, they deny their sense of self as fundamentally weak.

### Making the child feel ashamed

If children are made to feel a sense of shame, it is less likely they will speak out. Secrecy invokes feelings of shame. Children often have a feeling of loyalty towards abusers and protect them from the outside world who would not understand. As the child learns that what is happening is regarded as dirty or wrong, this will have a deleterious effect on their self-image. The sense of shame will be reinforced by ordinary conversations in school. Girls will recognise themselves as 'slags' and boys as 'queer'. The prejudices of the wider society reinforce the

messages received through the abuse. Secrecy is the only thing that can keep their shame hidden.

### Making the child feel like a freak

The child's sense of being different may become another negative component of their identity. This adds to feelings of isolation and alienation. The child who believes they are a freak may withdraw from relationships for fear of contaminating others or in the belief that others will reject them. The more bad and dirty they believe themselves to be the more they feel they deserve the abuse and are less likely to tell. The abuser may emphasise their difference from others both to the child and other carers. They may become known as a 'bad' child who is always in trouble. Behaviours such as self-harm or hearing voices further confirm their strangeness. A child's accounts of abuse may be dismissed as symptoms of a mental disorder or because they lie so often.

### Making the child feel worthless

In the act of abuse children's rights over their bodies are denied making them feel worthless. Children with disabilities often have less 'rights' to having a private body. It is more difficult for them to develop a sense of what is abuse and what is not. If attempts to tell have gone unheard they will feel more worthless. They feel people don't care about them. Communication problems due to lack of vocabulary, age or disability can prevent them from disclosing. Abusers may use coded language to conceal abuse – using everyday words for sexual words, so that if a child tries to explain they are misunderstood.

### Making the child feel powerless

Children learn that they have no choice or control over what happens to them. They live with the constant threat of it happening again. A profound sense of helplessness can be internalised. The child tries to find reasons why it is happening and can believe that they have done something wrong and if only they could be 'good' it would stop. They come to learn that whatever they do has no effect, which further confirms their helplessness. Feelings of helplessness and badness add to the child's sadness which further depresses the child's ability to tell. Being vulnerable also engenders feelings of fear and anxiety. Fear of being re-abused may be present for the child at all times. The child internalises their role as a victim.

## Making the child feel scared or anxious

Both indirect and direct threats are the final mechanisms of control which silence children by engendering feelings of anxiety and fear. Threats can include the removal of positives, such as love, as well as the addition of negatives such as pain. Threats can also be levelled at people and things the child loves, such as carers, siblings, animals and toys. 'If you don't let me do this to you, I will do it to your sister or brother.' Children sometimes do not tell because of a fear of making others angry, for example, if they were truanting from school, drunk or somewhere they shouldn't be. Children may not understand that sexual assault is a greater crime than being drunk or playing truant. They may fear speaking out will cause the break up of the family or cause trouble for the family. The single most important factor that can ameliorate the effects of sexual abuse is that the child or adult is believed. If the person is not believed then that person's sense of betrayal, worthlessness and isolation is increased. Once the process of disclosing has begun, children may once again feel that they have very little control over what happens to them. The phased model can be represented in tabular format that links the abuser modus operandi through comments with how such messages are received by the child.

## *Traumagenic states (James, 1990)*

James (1990) argued that trauma is the psychological impact of the abuse on the young person. The nine traumagenic states that she articulated (and which represent an expansion of Finkelhor and Browne's work) provide us with a useful framework for evaluating the impact of trauma. This is important when we know that a child's experience of the event can differ significantly from what the worker might anticipate.

## Self-blame

It is important that the child truly believes that the sexual abuse is not their fault, as children frequently blame themselves for almost everything that happens to them. This self-blame belief is embedded in the child's cognitive understanding and in his affective, sensory, and muscle memory.

## Powerlessness

Many children hold on to the powerlessness they experienced when abused and that feeling expands to become their self-image. Children do tend to be powerless by definition, eg have to go to school, are financially dependent, etc. Some victims attempt to be powerful in self-destructive ways eg truancy, drinking. Workers need to show children areas of their lives where they can be powerful and give them strategies to be powerful in appropriate ways.

## Loss and betrayal

The losses sustained by abused children are enormous, and may include the attention they used to receive, loss of a parent, home, friends, school, identity, and everything familiar. Betrayal and the child's subsequent loss of trust disturb the very foundation of their development. For example, betrayal by a loved caregiver is translated into 'I am no good. I don't deserve better treatment. The world is threatening'. A child who cannot trust their primary caregiver is unlikely to feel able to trust anyone.

## Fragmentation of bodily experience

People who have been sexually abused appear to have encoded the event through sensory and muscular memory as well as affective memory. With specific stimuli such as an odour, or a certain touch to the body, they relive the event again and experience the original trauma with its attendant feelings. A child may be able to achieve some cognitive understanding that what happened was not their fault, and she may be able to freely express her myriad feelings related to the event. However, mastery of the trauma is not complete unless it includes bodywork that allows the child to reclaim ownership of her body and to feel a sense of respect and mastery on a basic physical level.

## Stigmatisation

Abused children experience a deep sense of shame and feel alienated from others because of their experiences, regardless of the nature of the abuse. Many of these children believe that anyone can look at their faces and know what has happened to them; they frequently avoid eye contact, and stay hidden in a variety of ways. Other stigmatised children try to compensate for their perceived status of not being good enough with a driven need to achieve. Usually, however, no amount of achievement compensates for the child's feelings of shame and diminished self-worth, because the awards do not accrue to the child's hidden, damaged self.

## Eroticisation

Children who have learned that they are of special value as sexual objects who have experienced control over an adult's sexual behaviours, who have been taught to behave in ways that are provocative to those who sexually exploit children, and who have experienced intense excitement in the process of being sexually abused often become eroticised. The entire persona of the eroticised child is wrapped around their view of themselves as being valued only for their sexuality. In adulthood, these people may place themselves in high-risk situations, re-enacting the intensity of their early, forbidden experiences.

## Destructiveness

Destructive children quietly or outrageously engage in a wide range of behaviours that result in others disliking and punishing them. The loss of impulse control in some leads to frightening displays of their own rage.

## Dissociative/multiple personality disorder

Traumatising child abuse has been identified as a predisposing factor in 95 per cent of a thousand documented cases of multiple personality disorder. Dissociative disorders can provide an efficient way for a child to cope with their difficulties.

## Attachment disorder

Attachment disorders in children can result from repeated traumatising events, which keep a secure attachment from forming, or from a single event that threatens a child's attachment relationship. They may exhibit indiscriminate clinging to an adult to denying that anything is amiss; they can be demanding or overtly compliant; or they may give their carers nothing back emotionally.

Croll (1991) noted that sexual abuse can impact on children in other ways:

- **Role reversal:** occurs when they are expected to care for or meet the needs of adults.
- **Silence and deception:** results from the strain of carrying the burden of the secret.
- **Regression:** sexual abuse may arrest the child's emotional development at the developmental stage the young person was in when the abuse began and therefore behaviours may be exhibited that are younger than their chronological years (immature play, speech, social skills, etc.).
- **Memory loss:** is common as this enables the child to bury them until they become strong enough or supported enough to recall them.

## Ten impact areas (Porter et al., 1982)

The following framework highlighting the ten impact areas has been very influential in the field of practice. The authors note that the first five impact areas are likely to affect all children who have been sexually abused, regardless of the identity of the perpetrator. The last five issues are much more likely from intra-familial sexual abuse victims, although they cannot be excluded from other groups.

## 'Damaged goods' syndrome

In most cases, a child victim of sexual abuse feels damaged by their experiences. The 'damaged goods' syndrome is an amalgam of reactions:

- Physical injury or fear of physical damage.
- Societal responses, particularly those of the immediate family who may reinforce the victim's feelings of damage.

## Guilt

Some sexually abused children do not feel guilty about their behaviour prior to the disclosure of the secret of the sexual activity. However, intense guilt feelings following disclosure of sexual abuse are practically a universal victim response. Children who have been sexually abused usually experience guilt on three levels:

- Responsibility for the sexual behaviour.
- Responsibility for the disclosure.
- Responsibility for the disruption to all the family members.

## Fear

All child victims of sexual abuse can be expected to be fearful of the consequences of the sexual activity as well as the disclosure. Child victims may also fear subsequent episodes of sexual abuse both before and after the disclosure as well as reprisals from the abuser after disclosure. These fears may be expressed on a conscious level or they may be manifested by sleep disturbance, especially in the form of nightmares.

## Depression

Nearly all victims will exhibit some symptoms of depression after the disclosure of sexual abuse. Children who are victims of ongoing sexual abuse may appear depressed prior to disclosure as well. There may be overt signs of depression with the child appearing sad, subdued, or withdrawn. Or it may be masked and expressed as complaints of fatigue or physical illness. Some children may act out their despair with self-mutilation or suicide attempts.

## Low self-esteem and poor social skills

Fear of physical injury, societal response to the sexually abused child, experiencing guilt and shame for participating in the sexual behaviour, for disclosure and the subsequent disruption – all these feelings tend to undermine the victim's self-esteem. Low self-esteem combined with a feeling of being somehow spoiled or damaged in turn tend to undermine the child's self-confidence. Many victims of intra-familial child sexual abuse have been pressured by their parents to limit outside relationships and to depend only upon interaction with other family members to meet their social needs thus causing them to possess few social skills. This is aggravated further if they have attempted, and failed, to make friends of the same age. Victims often feel helpless and are rarely assertive on their own behalf. They also often describe themselves in derogatory terms. Some find themselves so unappealing that they will initiate a series of sexual relationships to prove they are 'desirable'.

## Repressed anger and hostility

Although they may appear outwardly passive and compliant, most sexual abuse victims are inwardly seething with anger and hostility. They are angry with the perpetrators for abusing them; they are angry with non-abusing parents for their failure to protect; they may be angry at neighbours, extended family and friends, possibly for their responses to the disclosure. In most cases, the anger is repressed rather than expressed or acted out. It may be characterised by depression or withdrawal, and occasionally in psychotic symptomatology.

## Inability to trust

A child who has been sexually victimised by a known and trusted person can be expected to have difficulty in developing trusting relationships thereafter. The degree of impairment will depend on a variety of factors, which might include:

- The identity of the perpetrator.
- The relationship between the victim and the perpetrator.
- The age of the young person when the abuse began and the length of time over which it occurred.
- The extent of the abuse.
- The type of sexual activity involved in the abuse.
- The degree of pleasure or discomfort experienced as a result of the abuse.
- The degree of force used to coerce the child.
- How others responded to the child's disclosure.
- The support persons available to the child post-disclosure.
- The point at which the abuse was disclosed.
- The personality structure and coping style of the victim.

(adapted from Tower, 1989)

The significance of these will vary from child to child. Frequently, the child's inability to trust is a direct consequence of broken promises from the perpetrator and others. No two children are alike and thus every child's reaction to their experiences of abuse will be unique. One child may fall apart whilst another will not.

## Blurred role boundaries and role confusion

Child sexual abuse is disorientating because the victims frequently experience role confusion due to the inevitable blurring of role boundaries between the perpetrator and the child. For an adult who occupies a power position to turn to a relatively powerless child for a sexual relationship implies a profound disregard for the usual societal role boundaries. Although the sexual activity is primarily in the service of non-sexual needs, the premature and inappropriate sexual experience with an adult generates a great deal of role confusion for the child victim. If the adult is a parent then the role confusion is magnified.

## Pseudo-maturity and failure to complete developmental tasks

Child sexual abuse is disruptive because the extensive stimulation and preoccupation with the sexual relationship tends to interfere with the accomplishment of age-appropriate developmental tasks of childhood and adolescence. In addition, role confusion often leads to the child's premature assumption of an adult role in the family. As sexually abused children assume more adult responsibilities, the gap widens even further between them and their peers. If this is identified by peers then this isolation becomes permanent.

## Trauma

Traumatic incidents represent incidents of major change. Parkes (1996) describes that we carry within our own minds our own unique and complex model of the world. This assumptive world contains images from our own experience, our values and the elements by which we assess our environment and people whom we meet. Our assumptive world also provides us with the basis on which we attribute emotions such as fear, security and significant factors within our unique life plans. Traumatic events alter our assumptive world in three key ways by shattering three basic assumptions:

- A belief in personal invulnerability.
- The perception of the world as meaningful and comprehensible.

- The view of ourselves in a positive light.
(Janoff-Bulman, 1992)

The ordered world can become chaotic and unpredictable. Individuals often discover that they may not have reacted as positively as they had envisaged they would when confronted with a traumatic incident. For some parents or carers they may feel guilty that they did not do enough to help someone.

Carlson and Dalenberg (2000) developed a useful conceptual framework for understanding the impact of traumatic experiences. Defining traumatic events as only those involving injury or death erroneously excludes some events that are potentially traumatic. The requirement that a person must fear injury or death to be traumatised assumes that imminent injury or death are the only experiences that would cause emotional pain or arousal severe enough to precipitate PTSD. This is an assumption that has not been supported empirically or by any theoretical formulation that explains why events that do not involve injury or death are necessarily excluded from the definition of trauma. In fact, evidence that events that do not involve injury or death can be traumatic stressors is beginning to emerge.

Defining traumatic events as only those involving fear, helplessness, or horror has the advantage of taking into account the interaction between the event and the individual that is critical to include in theories of trauma. But this criterion seems too restrictive, as it does not define an event as traumatic if a person dissociates at the time of trauma and does not report feeling fearful, helpless, or horrified (Briere, 1996). Clinical reports of dissociative experiences at the time of trauma (such as derealisation, depersonalisation, and gaps in awareness) have been labelled peri-traumatic dissociation. The term *peri-traumatic* is used to denote 'around the time of the trauma.' Derealisation includes experiences of distortions in perceptions of the environment or objects, whereas depersonalisation includes distortions in perceptions of oneself or parts of oneself. Gaps in awareness would be experienced as a lack of recall of important aspects of the traumatic event.

There are three defining features of traumatic events: a lack of control over what is happening; the perception that the event is a highly negative experience; and the suddenness of the experience. All three elements are necessary for traumatisation to occur, though an event may not be traumatic even if all three are present.

In the face of sudden danger, humans and other animals exhibit an innate 'fight or flight' response that aids them in coping with or fleeing from danger. The fight or flight response is characterised by high levels of physiological and affective arousal that are typically experienced as fear or anger. The phenomenon of high arousal in the face of danger seems to be an unlearned, preparatory response of the body and the mind to danger. In other words, when you experience loss of control over your safety, your body and mind automatically go on red alert in an attempt to regain control. The red alert status might involve being hyperalert or hypervigilant to one's surroundings and having an increase in physiological arousal to allow for flight or defence. Aggressive behaviours are also a natural response to danger. Such behaviours can be understood as an attempt to gain control over an unpredictable environment. This response to danger would seem to be an unlearned survival instinct. In addition, a 'freezing' response in response to imminent danger has also been observed in animals. Such a response might be a way to increase the chances for survival when fleeing or fighting are not viable options. In contrast to the high arousal of the fight or flight response, a freeze response would be characterised by a parasympathetic physiological response and a numbing of emotions.

During fight or flight or freezing responses at the time of trauma, cognitive distortions frequently occur that also seem to facilitate coping. Dissociative experiences such as depersonalisation and derealisation may help the individual continue to function by narrowing or distorting their experience of themselves or the world around them.

A complete conceptual framework for the impact of traumatic experiences must explain why peri-traumatic responses to traumatic events persist once the event is over and why new symptoms arise. If you are in a dangerous or frightening situation and feel fearful, helpless, horrified, or dissociated, why might you still have these or other symptoms weeks, months, or even years after you are out of danger? Several behavioural and cognitive theories can be applied to traumatic experiences to explain persistence of trauma responses.

Though there is tremendous individual variation in how people respond to sudden, uncontrollable, and negative events, there are two basic categories of responses that are common following a wide range of traumatic events: re-experiencing and avoidance symptoms. Re-experiencing symptoms occur when a person is cued by a conditioned stimulus that has been associated with the trauma. Avoidance symptoms occur because they afford relief from the anxiety associated with trauma-related stimuli. The distinction between re-experiencing and avoidance symptoms can get blurred sometimes because what appears to be avoidance may be re-experiencing of disconnections felt at the time of trauma. Both sets of responses can be manifested cognitively, affectively, behaviourally, and physiologically (see Figure 1.8 below).

Five factors are proposed that influence the response to trauma including biological factors; developmental level at the time of trauma; severity of the stressor; social context; and prior and subsequent life events (see Figure 1.9 overleaf).

In addition to the core or primary trauma symptoms of re-experiencing and avoidance, there are at least eight major types of response to trauma that are either secondary to or closely

| Mode | Re-experiencing | Avoidance |
|------|-----------------|-----------|
| Cognitive | Intrusive thoughts, intrusive images | Amnesia for trauma, derealisation/depersonalisation |
| Affective | Anxiety, anger | Emotional numbing, isolation of affect |
| Behavioural | Increased activity, aggression | Avoidance of trauma-related situations |
| Physiological | Physiological reactivity to trauma reminders | Sensory numbing |
| Multiple modes | Flashbacks, nightmares | Simultaneous avoidance in multiple modes |

**Figure 1.8**  Manifestations of re-experiencing and avoidance across modes of experience (Carlson and Dalenburg, 2000)

| Biological factors | Developmental level at the time of the trauma | Severity of the stressor | Social context | Prior and subsequent life events |
|---|---|---|---|---|
| Three major biological factors can influence responses to trauma. These are a genetic predisposition to vulnerability or resilience to trauma, a non-genetic biological predisposition, and biological alterations in function that occur in response to prior traumatic experiences. Personality researchers have only recently begun to explore the possibility that innate, biological tendencies in brain function are associated with temperament and affective responses to stressful, negative events. | Responses to trauma will be greatly influenced by the level of emotional, social, and cognitive development of the individual at the time of trauma. This is especially true during childhood, when development is not yet complete. In general, children at earlier stages of development will have more severe responses to traumatic stressors, but at times, lower levels of development may protect a child from experiencing a negative valence and uncontrollability. There may also be an interaction between the trauma and the attachment when trauma occurs before or during attachment formation. This can be particularly problematic when the trauma takes the form of abuse inflicted by an attachment figure. Higher levels of cognitive and social skills might enable a child to exert more control over his or her environment following a trauma, thus reducing his or her anxiety and possibly avoiding further stress or traumatic experiences. In | Objective characteristics of an event such as its intensity, nature, and duration all contribute to its severity because they shape the individual's perceptions of the controllability and negative valence of the event. Conversely, an individual's subjective impressions and perceptions can greatly affect the perceived intensity and nature of a traumatic experience by influencing the valence and perceived controllability of an experience. Traumas that are more intense are more likely to provoke overwhelming fear and helplessness because of their more negative valence. The nature of a traumatic experience can also greatly affect an individual's response. Given a constant level of intensity, traumatic experiences of greater duration tend to cause more severe responses because there is a longer period when the person feels unable to control the aversive event. This greater feeling of uncontrollability will result in a higher level of anxiety and | An individual's social context exerts an influence on his or her responses to trauma both before and after the event. Before the event, the community and family environment shape the individual's general expectancies about controllability and negative valence. Through this process, an individual's social context can strengthen or weaken his or her ability to cope with a traumatic stressor. Pre-traumatic community environment variables that are likely to impact on post-traumatic responses include poverty, level of violence, and concern for individual community members. Pre-traumatic family environment variables that are likely to impact on post-traumatic responses include neglect, psychological maltreatment, substance abuse, caretaker mental disorders or suicidality, disciplinary methods, poverty, and domestic violence. Post-traumatic community and family social support are also important parts of social context that would influence | One viewpoint is that experiencing stressful events may 'inoculate' a person so that they are more resistant to subsequent stressful events. Some have proposed that infrequent, relatively low-level stressors might produce a toughening effect that desensitises the individual to the effects of later stressors On the other hand, prior stressful events may impair a person's ability to cope with trauma. |

Figure 1.9  Factors that influence the response to trauma (developed from Carlson and Dalenberg, 2000)

| Biological factors | Developmental level at the time of the trauma | Severity of the stressor | Social context | Prior and subsequent life events |
|---|---|---|---|---|
|  | addition, a child with more advanced social and cognitive skills might be more able to obtain social support after a trauma and benefit from its effects. | more intense later symptoms. Traumas of very long duration, such as being a prisoner of war, are likely to have the added effect of producing despair and depression because of the ongoing inability to control aversive events. In turn, despair and depression generated by traumas of longer duration will inhibit recovery following trauma. | responses to trauma. Post-traumatic social support can help restore a person's feelings of controllability and can help reduce the negative valence of an experience. Post-traumatic family social support might include taking care of the trauma victim following the event, being available and willing to hear about the traumatic event, and demonstrations of support through cards, letters, or calls. |  |

**Figure 1.9** *Continued*

associated with traumatic experiences. Secondary responses are not directly caused by the traumatic experience, but occur later as a result of problems with re-experiencing and avoidance. They can be considered the 'second wave' of symptoms following trauma. Associated responses are those that result from exposure to concomitant elements of the traumatic environment. These responses are also not directly related to being overwhelmed with fear – they are caused or shaped by the social environment or other circumstances accompanying or following the trauma.

### Post-Traumatic Stress Disorder (PTSD)

This model was originally designed to explain certain psychiatric reactions of combat veterans in World War One. These veterans were observed to repeat over and over again traumatic situations, which they had experienced. Their hope was to gain mastery of the trauma by recreating it in an environment in which they could control and reshape it.

Mendel (1995: 77–8) offered us a working definition of PTSD, which is:

> . . . the development of characteristic symptoms following a psychologically distressing event that is outside the range of usual human experience . . . The stressor producing this syndrome would be markedly distressing to almost anyone, and is usually experienced with intense fear, terror and helplessness. The characteristic symptoms involve re-experiencing the traumatic event, avoidance of stimuli associated with the event or numbing of general responsiveness, and increased arousal.

This framework was extended to sexual abuse victims when similarities between victims of war were noted. Finkelhor (1988: 63) outlined several significant effects of putting sexual abuse into the PTSD framework:

- It provides a clear label and description of a phenomenon that many victims of child sexual abuse are suffering from.
- It has suggested that the effects of sexual abuse need to be looked at in a structured way.
- It frames sexual abuse in a wider context and erects bridges to other types of trauma.
- It has brought a new interest in sexual abuse.
- It has increased the salience of the problem by adding to it the list of well-recognised psychological stressors.

- Considering sexual abuse as a form of PTSD may act to reduce some of the lingering stigma that clings to victims.

Finkelhor (1998: 62–3) reported the following components to PTSD:

- The existence of a recognisable stressor that would evoke significant symptoms of distress in almost anyone.
- The re-experiencing of the trauma either through recurrent intrusive recollections, dreams, or sudden feelings.
- A numbing of responsiveness or reduced involvement in the external world indicated by diminished interest in activities, feelings of estrangement from others, and constricted affect.
- In addition, at least two of the following set of symptoms also need to be present:
  - o hyper-alertness
  - o sleep problems
  - o survival guilt
  - o problems with memory or concentration
  - o avoidance of activities or the intensification of symptoms when exposed to stimuli related to the traumatic event.

There are problems with regarding this as the only dynamic factor in the transmission of sexual abuse through the generations. It also has limited ability in explaining the unique and particular characteristics of sexual abuse. The fact that the traumatic experiences of abuse survivors occur during childhood, the sexual nature of the trauma, the tendency of sexual abuse to comprise an ongoing relationship rather than a single event, and the involvement of trusted caregivers and family members in most instances of the trauma make childhood sexual abuse quite distinct from military battles and natural disasters (Mendel, 1995: 78).

Finkelhor (1988: 64) provided us with a detailed critique of the application of PTSD to child sexual abuse. He explored some serious limitations of locating sexual abuse in this framework: it does not adequately account for all the symptoms, and thus only accurately applies to certain victims, and it does not truly present a theory that explains how the dynamics of sexual abuse lead to the symptoms noted. He concluded that understanding the problem of sexual abuse will not benefit from being subsumed within a diluted and a theoretical notion of PTSD. He

preferred to delineate a separate syndrome because of the unique characteristics of responses to sexual abuse (p68).

The concept of PTSD has produced a variety of theoretical models that may be used to explain its impact on traumatised individuals. These models are derived from biological, physiological, cognitive behavioural and psychodynamic frameworks. This variety is conducive to examination of the many facets of PTSD. Insights from one theoretical model appear to complement rather than contradict insights derived from another theoretical source.

## Psychobiological model

Biological aspects can offer us some useful insights into such symptom clusters as intrusive phenomena, arousal and avoidance. Conditional automatic responses have included increased blood pressure, muscle tension and skin resistance, as well as flashbacks. In most cases the impact of a traumatic event is temporary and the hyper-alerted systems return to baseline functioning levels. However, when the impact persists, feelings of loss of control and helplessness can be experienced. Sleep disturbances are also widely reported by those experiencing PTSD. Those who experience sleep deprivation appear to present in two categories. Each of these forms cause distress for the sufferer and can affect the sleep of a spouse or partner. Those who anticipate a disturbed night with intrusive and distressing dreams try to delay going to sleep by indulgence in alcohol or sleep medication. Many explain these acts as a means of attempting to block out the distressing dreams. Those with associated depressive symptoms of this syndrome often become very anxious and distressed if a pattern of early awakening is established. These aspects can result in exhaustion and be very serious to a person's general well-being when they are trying to maintain a normal work life and relationships.

## Responding to psychosocial reactions

These psychobiological aspects of post-trauma reaction are of paramount importance. The sustained inappropriate hyperstimulation of the hormonal system may have major implications for those who are called on to respond to be involved in multiple traumatic events. Opioid release produces analgesia and can contribute to psychosocial withdrawal. This may well be the explanation needed for families and friends, who report that the person remains 'aloof' from their attempts to love, support and encourage. This can create friction within the support network when they find their efforts being rejected.

While these reactions contribute to initial survival in a threatening environment, in the longer term they may give rise to more persistent neurobiological responses which become maladaptive. Such maladaptive neurobiological responses may affect future reactions to similar stimuli. They may also affect a person's ability to process and learn from the experience.

## Psychoanalytical models

Trauma as an incident '. . . which involved the breaching of a protective shield or stimulus barrier, which normally functions to prevent the overwhelming of the mind (ego) from internal and external stimuli, by means of managing or binding the excitation'.

Freud argued that 'a flood of unmanageable impulses' would cause 'disturbances on a large scale' and set 'in motion every defensive measure'. Freud drew attention to the fact that 'repetition compulsion' formed the basis for re-experiencing disturbing and catastrophic events and could be an attempt to master such memories. The person's fixation with the trauma is alternated with attempts to avoid any remembrance of the event.

In 1926, Freud elaborated his theory by linking these reactions to the helplessness of the ego, which he felt was the core of the traumatic experience. He further suggested that anxiety could be used as a signal of the possibility of the reoccurrence of the trauma experience. This formed a link with the phenomenon of increased arousal in PTSD.

The complexity of PTSD is reflected in the way that psychoanalytic psychotherapists appear to be adapting their theoretical approaches to aspects of trauma rather than suggesting one overall approach to the total disorder. Fear of annihilation is described as a key feature of trauma in terms of a psychoanalytic model by Hopper (1991).

Psychoanalytical models have much to contribute to our understanding of how

individuals react to situations of chaos and re-establish their own unique sense of order. It is interesting to trace their evolution from Freud through to present-day theorists.

### The four psychologies: a comprehensive model (Weitzman, 2005)

Pine (1990), purports that the major developmental theories of personality can be categorised into essentially four relatively autonomous, yet interrelated perspectives or *domains* of personality functioning, each having its own central role of *motivational status* in human functioning. He describes these as the domains of ego, object, self and drive. Although he uses the idea of interdependence and multiple function to describe the interaction among domains, he also says that these domains of personality function essentially as *parallel partners* and that each has a specific set of associated psychological *issues*. Thus, for example, the domain of self is associated with such issues as self-agency, self-esteem, self-regulation, body-self-integrity, self-representation and other *issues* of the self-psychology model. Likewise, the domain of ego is associated with ego adaptations, learning, cognition, ego defences and defects. The domain of drive is associated with more biologically based issues such as sensation and impulse, sexuality and aggression, and includes the central concepts of conflict and anxiety. Finally, the domain of object is associated with attachment-seeking, internalisation and differentiation of objects, relationship and mental representations as they are relived in the current life of the individual.

### Self domain

When all goes well, the young child in the domain of self is buoyant. The healthy child has ample self-affection and a natural curiosity about the world around him, an outgrowth of positive caretaking, attunement, and the robust expression of primary narcissism and the grandiosity of the earliest stages of self-development, including a sense of well-being in his body, its sensations and functions. This inflation is gradually transformed by experience into a less grandiose, more realistic appreciation for oneself, others and the social environment as the child integrates disappointments and frustrations and learns, about their own limitations.

The issues at stake in the domain of self are about how a child feels about himself and the external world. It is primarily an affective domain whose principles are self-esteem, self-regulation, self-image, self-agency, body-self, self-cohesion, and self-object relationships. In the good-enough family, the child comes to esteem himself, take pleasure in his own needs, opinions and feelings. The child learns to modulate emotional reactions to stress and manage feeling-states. He trusts his body and lives in his body where he experiences continuity between his needs, feelings and thoughts.

Buoyancy in a child can wither away if trauma is inflicted during the formative stages of self-development. The self-domain, like the other domains, is a work in progress. Any phenomena in a formative process can go awry if too little (severe neglect) or too much stimulation (severe abuse) is introduced. Severe over stimulation in the form of trauma can seriously impact a child's self-development. Sufficiently prolonged and hostile experiences can lead to self-doubt, insecurity, shame and worthlessness and self-defeat (Diehl and Prout, 2002). Curiosity and joy can be dimmed by overwhelmingly inhospitable circumstances. Survival-threatening experiences can corrupt the child's sense of being an agent of his own actions, moving the locus of control outside his own body. Helplessness, passivity, lack of initiative and self-doubt can become significant clinical problems for the child.

## Ego domain

The domain of ego is principally about the child's capacity for control of his own impulses and needs, and adaptation to the demands of the world around him. The issues of the ego domain are about building ego structures, superego development, ego defects and defences. It is about how the child learns, problem-solves, uses language and symbolic communication, develops cognitively, thinks, judges and copes. In the good-enough environment, the child's ego capacities are gradually built-up through constructive experiences, encouragement by caretakers to experiment, to try new things, to involve himself in activities and to master his body through play and action. He learns to value words and language when his communications are met with mutual vocalisation. The unfolding

of healthy cognitive schemata is aided by the logical and consistent pattern of responses by others to his needs.

Trauma to the developing ego can interfere with any one of these crucial functions. In threatening environments, the child's innate desire to learn and explore can be stilled by fear. Many abused children avoid novel learning experiences out of fear of failure and shame.

Children in abusive homes are not generally encouraged to use meaningful problem-solving strategies and communication skills as routine ways to resolve conflict. Abusive homes tend to lack structure, routine and consistency and do not foster mastery or internal controls in the child, nor inhibit impulsivity or reward logic, though there are certainly abusive homes with repressive environments where fearful children are rigidly obedient and develop false-selves to cope with their adversaries. They are frequently homes dominated by considerable anarchy. Rules and reason are not part of the child's daily experience. Hence, these environments engender cognitive impairments, verbal deficits, and impulsivity that reflect the illogic and unpredictability of the environment (Banyard, Williams, and Siegel, 2003; Dilillo and Damashek, 2003).

In order to survive chronic onslaughts of aggression, rejection and other maltreatment, the child's ego defences have to work overtime. Denial, projection, displacement, identification with the aggressor and other defences can make exaggerated claims on the ego in order to protect it from danger or disintegration. Dissociation and out of body experiences permit the sexually abused child to leave the scene of the crime.

## Object domain

The object domain is about attachment and relationship. The central issues are about forming secure and warm relationships with others through the empathic bond of early parent child interactions. When all goes well, the child in this domain is able to internalise positive, whole and integrated mental representations of himself and others that form the template for all future relationships. Securely attached children who live in responsive, nurturing homes develop representations of reliability, consistency and warmth. The child develops both object constancy and wholeness, and capacity for ambivalence towards others and integration of good and bad parts into a balanced whole.

Healthy object-related children develop powerful identification with parent-objects, adopting core values, beliefs and styles of coping. These children learn autonomy through supportive interactions by the parent who takes pleasure in their growing independence. Their ability to tolerate ambivalence toward others – the integration of good and bad part-objects, allows them to develop and maintain enduring relationships.

Trauma in the object domain is principally about attachment disorder and arrest in relationships, intimacy and basic trust. Dependent needs that are frustrated too often, much less denied or thwarted by a disturbed parent eventually leads to dependency conflicts, or worse, psychopathic detachment.

## Drive domain

The chief issues of the drive domain are about biologically based impulses toward sexuality and aggression. These biologically driven impulses form the basis of healthy sexuality, intimacy and assertiveness when modulated by the caretaking system of the family. In propitious circumstances, these urges are modified by resolution of the various psychosexual stages, culminating in the harnessing of impulses through successful resolution of the Oedipal stage. The outcome of this process is a child who can relate well to others, use his superego to modulate impulses, seek intimacy in an appropriate fashion, and use aggressive impulses to accomplish work and be industrious; that is, channel and sublimate such impulses into constructive ways of being.

Unpropitious circumstances and trauma in the drive domain lead to difficulties with impulse control, over-activity, excitability, distractibility and over stimulated sexual and aggressive urges. Over stimulation of sexual and aggressive impulses can lead to sexual acting out, over-determined drives toward sexual gratification as substitutes for real love, and preoccupations with power and control through defensive, aggressive domination. Older children who have had some superego development can become over controlled and repressed as a defensive reaction to over stimulation. In others, sexual and aggressive impulses can become fused as a response to sexual exploitation, resulting in delinquent sexual acting out – as is evident of many sexual offenders. Children with drive domain disorders have problems with

self-control and primitive, poorly modulated affect and impulsivity.

### Cognitive behavioural models

Bowlby (1979) has written of the need for an individual who has been subjected to an extraordinary experience to deal with it by mastering the extraordinary information received from the event. Such mastery is essential if the person is to gain congruence between the new information and the person's existing mind models. This would mean that the traumatic experience becomes integrated into normal cognitive schemata in such a way that it no longer represents a threat to the person's view of their total world. PTSD would therefore be classed as a flawed integration of traumatic information into the individual's cognitive schemata.

Horowitz (1990) postulates that PTSD results from incomplete cognitive processing. The negative and overwhelming nature of such information creates problems for the individual as they seek to integrate this traumatic information into their existing schemata to regain a harmony in their lives. Such recall may be resisted by the individual in the form of denial.

Horowitz's model of PTSD is a two-phase model, with alternating intrusion-repetition and denial-numbing. He suggests that the avoidant intrusion cluster symptoms of PTSD – denial of the event, avoidance and numbness – result when the inner inhibitory control mechanisms predominate over the repetition of information into the conscious mind as characterised in the intrusion symptom cluster. At other times, the intrusion symptoms can dominate over the avoidance state.

### Behavioural models of PTSD

Mowrer's theory (1947) proposes that two types of learning – classical and instrumental – are present in acquired fear and avoidance which present after trauma. Neutral stimuli, such as smells, sounds, shapes or words, when associated with painful traumatic events, can evoke painful responses. Such responses can then be described as conditioned responses to the trauma when they produce or recreate painful responses such as fear and anxiety. This model reminds us that ordinary everyday stimuli can be turned into traumatic stressors by the association with the traumatic event.

Mowrer's theory also included instrumental conditioning as an explanation of the development of such behaviours as escape and avoidance. These behaviours can be utilised as a means of reducing exposure to an aversive conditioned stimulus.

Mowrer's work gives us insights into how responders, who are repeatedly exposed to stimuli associated with trauma, can use escape/avoidance behaviours in an effort to minimise the impact of the painful response which the stimuli may elicit even in non-traumatic environments. Animal experiments indicate that the longer the duration and the greater the intensity of the original trauma, the more these conditioned responses may be evidenced. A lack of understanding on how painful reactions can be triggered must surely add to the negative reactions experienced. This work would suggest that in any form of pre-crisis training there would be a need to address this possible reaction with responders in an effort to minimise the impact of such reactions in the post-trauma stage.

### Cognitive models of PTSD

The theory of learned helplessness has been proposed as an explanation of the numbing effect and passivity sometimes seen in PTSD. This learned helplessness is similar to feelings associated with victimisation.

The process by which individuals attach meaning to a traumatic event – cognitive appraisal – has been explored by several researchers. If the traumatic event happened in situations which were deemed to be safe, the reactions experienced were different in severity and intensity. A rape victim who felt she was in a safe environment suffered more reaction to the rape than a victim who appraised that she was in an at-risk situation prior to the rape.

Cognitive models afford us explanations of some of the symptoms that contribute to behavioural changes. They also alert us to some of the factors that it may be possible to influence by pre-crisis training.

### Information processing model

One of the most significant models for understanding PTSD is the information processing model proposed by Horowitz (1986). 'Information overload' can occur when too much information is received at the time of crisis, use the term 'completion tendency' to describe the situation where important information is processed until reality and cognitive models match. Incomplete information processing is experienced when new information has only been partially processed and the information remains an 'active form of memory'.

Horowitz postulates that traumatic incidents involve the intake of massive amounts of new information that is outside our usual realm of experience. As a direct result, most of the information cannot be matched to a person's existing cognitive schemata. The result is information overload in which new experience, ideas, effects and images cannot be integrated with self. As a result of extreme traumatisation, a person cannot process the information and it may be shunted out of awareness. Numbing and denial may be employed as defensive mechanisms to avoid this processing. As a result, the information will remain in an unprocessed active or raw form. This painful information will re-enter the mind at times as intrusive images or sensations due to 'completion tendency'. Horowitz (1976) views such intrusions as part of the information processing which must take place (see Figure 1.10)

Completion of information processing continues until the new information becomes part of 'long-term models and inner schemata'. Green et al. (1985: 6) believe that: 'At completion, the experience is integrated so it is the individual's view of the world and of him or herself, and no longer needs to be walled off from the rest of his or her personality. At this point, the trauma is no longer stored in an active state. Horowitz's model of information processing is an extension of psychoanalytic concepts of trauma. Traumatic incidents continue to destabilise our psychic equilibrium until the information is fully processed.

### Psychosocial model

It identifies factors which may aid our research for a greater understanding of why some people exposed to traumatic incidents develop PTSD and others do not. This is a very important issue which needs to be addressed in any analysis which will lead to a preventative model of intervention.

Green's diagram (Figure 1.11) indicates how pre-existing individual characteristics and the

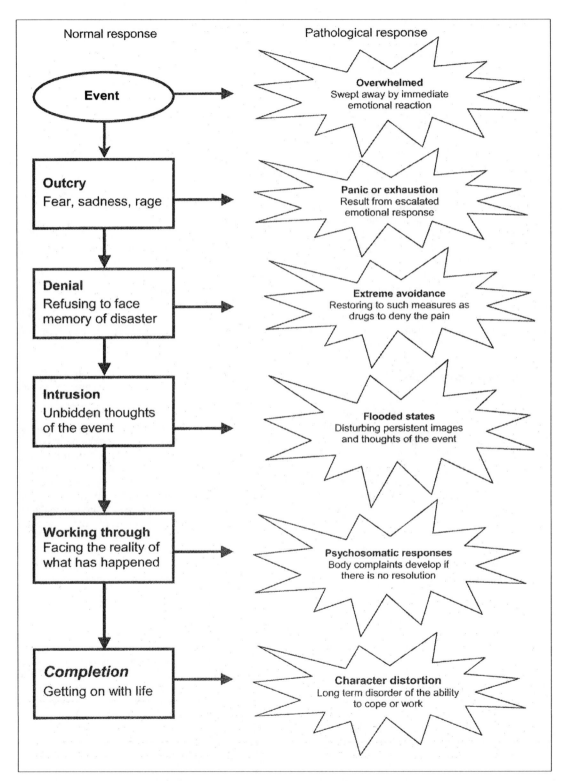

**Figure 1.10**  Normal and pathological phases of post-stress response (Horowitz, 1976)

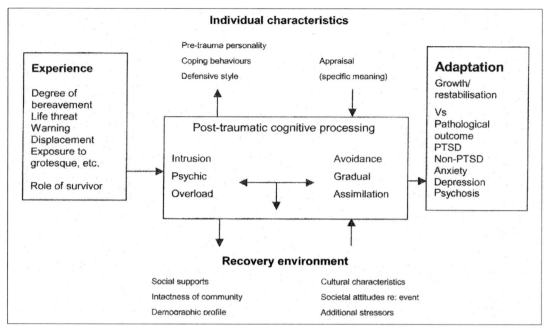

**Figure 1.11**   Psychological framework for understanding PTSD (Green et al., 1985)

recovery environment interact in a dynamic way with the post-traumatic cognitive processing. Green et al. (1985) argue that the influence of the recovery environment is often neglected in the theoretical formulation of PTSD. They believe that the qualities of the environment have a direct correlation with the outcome achieved.

## Secondary traumatic stress model

'There is a cost to caring. Professionals who listen to clients' stories of fear, pain and suffering may feel similar fear, pain and suffering because they care' (Figley, 1986: 1). The links between the reactions of primary victims and those of responders are discussed by Raphael (1986: 235) where she describes responders as 'hidden victims' (see Figure 1.12). 'The stressful effects on responders stem from the encounter with death, from sharing the anguish of the victims and their families and from role stresses.'

## Loss arising from sexual abuse

Experiences of loss may include loss related to self, interpersonal trust and innocence as relevant to sexual abuse survivor's psychological and

emotional lives. Bourdon and Cook (1993) identified five categories where survivors of sexual abuse may experience loss: developmental, relational, sexuality, self-esteem and other. The most difficult losses were identified as loss of trust, self-love and self-identity. Murthi and Espelage (2005) added further considerations to the loss framework concept by identifying a three-dimensional loss structure involving loss of optimism (eg loss in ability to dream about the future) loss of self (eg feeling lost and helpless) and loss of childhood (eg grew up too fast). They also established that child sexual abuse (before the age of 12) was related to higher levels of distress as compared to child sexual abuse (after the age of 12) across two loss dimensions: losses in relation to self and childhood.

## Grief reactions in sexually abused children

It is important that we have some understanding about the process of grieving that the sexually abused child may go through. Hopkins and Thompson (1984) explored issues of loss and mourning in victims of rape and sexual assault.

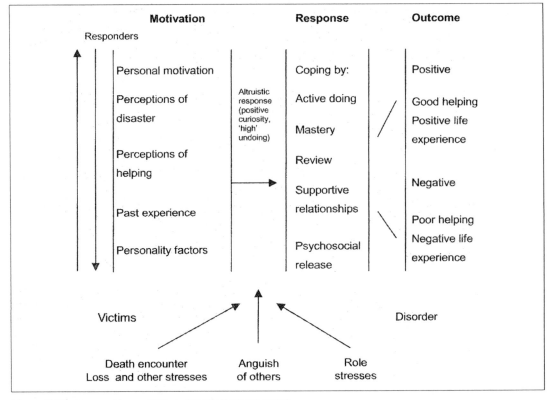

**Figure 1.12**   Responders as hidden victims (Raphael, 1986)

They noted that there are two components to an individual's response to loss: the need to mourn and a change in self-image: of self and others. Their most serious wounds may not be visible and this can foreclose empathy. The need to mourn is well established. Recovery from loss includes working through the various psychological stages which loss engenders as well as coping with a variety of behavioural manifestations. Total acceptance of the loss is the final stage of a successful mourning. There are often three general areas of loss: trust, freedom and ego identity. Trust is one of the more easily recognised losses. Freedom implies the exercising of choices, yet victims of sexual abuse lose important options and choices, thus curtailing their freedom. For example, they may question what clothes to wear, what make-up to use, and whether to accept a lift home with a male. They forego these choices in an effort to gain security, but the price of such security is the loss of freedom, of autonomy and independence. The fruits of ego identity – continuity, security,

credibility, confidence, certainty, control, sense of place and order, spontaneity and predictability – are lost also.

They then set out the following clearly identifiable stages of grief and reactions to sexual abuse as experienced by the child/ren:

### Shock

When the mind and the body cannot cope with severe trauma and loss, shock – the anaesthetising or numbing of feelings – is often the first reaction. One cannot take in what has occurred and shock reaction provides both time and padding. The intensity and duration of this numbness depend upon the individual and external circumstances. It is a natural and helpful defence mechanism.

### Denial

Although similar to shock in manifestation, denial is a more intellectual response to unacceptable pain or reality. The mind may eventually acknowledge the trauma, but there is no true emotional acceptance. Denial provides another explanation for the noted delay of victims in asking for relief from recurring bad dreams, irrational fears, obsessive behaviour, ruminations and psychosomatic symptoms.

## Anger

Anger, even rage, is a normal and healthy (although often uncomfortable) reaction to loss. 'Why me?' 'It isn't fair' 'How dare he'.

## Guilt

In a society committed to the belief that every effect has a cause, guilt, which may be expressed as sadness, self-doubt, painful self-criticism or shame, is a rather inevitable response to loss.

## Anxiety

The actual circumstances of the sexual abuse (fear for life, helplessness, total lack of control) as well as the immediate post-attack situation (worry about being believed, need to prove innocence, fear of ridicule and recriminations) are all powerful sources of anxiety and reflect the loss of control and autonomy victims experience. The anxiety that is reported by victims often takes the form of an unrelieved sense of foreboding or irrational fears, continuing long after the actual threatening situations. For example, changes in physical health, panic, phobic behaviour, obsessive ruminations and psychosomatic illness.

## Depression

Anger, sadness and even guilt, if not carried to extremes, are considered a part of normal good grief. However, these feelings may lead to depression, a potentially more destructive stage in the mourning process. Depression is a reaction to loss (past or present, real or imagined) based on feelings of worthlessness, unexpressed hostility, fear and anger turned against self. It results in feelings of loneliness, despair, apathy, isolation, and in regressive, helpless or self-destructive behaviour. Depression may only be a temporary response to a loss situation. The manifestations of depression seem to come out of nowhere, long after the crisis. Victims may report unusual fatigue, insomnia, and exhibit apathy if not anomie.

## Reasons for survivors to grieve

Just as it is important for us to understand the process of grieving, it is also essential that we are given some understanding about the reasons why this is important and some potential problems if the process is blocked.

When a survivor fails to grieve her losses, she perpetuates the traumatic reaction. However, many survivors are afraid of this task. A survivor may fear that once she begins grieving, she will not be able to stop. She may resist mourning out of pride or feel that if she mourns, the perpetrator has somehow won (Herman, 1992). However, Herman (1992: 190) noted, 'Mourning is the only way to give due honour to loss; there is no adequate compensation'.

There are several reasons for survivors of child sexual abuse to grieve. Some of the things survivors grieve for are being abandoned, a loss of feelings, their pasts and presents, the damage they must now heal, the time and money it takes to heal, relationships that have been ruined, and the pleasures and opportunities they missed out on while they were trying to deal with the abuse (Bass and Davis, 1992). Survivors may mourn because they have lost their moral integrity or because they cannot undo what has been done to them (Herman, 1992).

A survivor may grieve for their shattered image of the world as a safe place where children are loved and cared for and where people respect one another. Or they may grieve for the innocence they lost during the abuse (Bass and Davis, 1992) or for the childhood that was taken away from them (Herman, 1992). They may grieve for the part of them that did not survive the abuse (Bass and Davis, 1992).

If a survivor was abused by family members, they may grieve for the fact that they do not have an extended family for their children (Bass and Davis, 1992). They may grieve for their loss of belief in good parenting and trust (Herman, 1992). Some survivors also need to grieve for inheritances they will not receive or for lost family roots (Bass and Davis, 1992).

Although survivors may feel they are foolish to cry over events that happened years ago, they need to express their feelings, to grieve their losses. If they do not do this, they will be limiting themselves and their capacity to love others (Bass and Davis, 1992).

Survivors need to take their grief seriously. Bass and Davis (1992) suggested that survivors should take a period of time to grieve and mourn, just as they would if someone close to them had died. They will not fully be able to grieve unless they allow themselves the time, space, and security to do so.

If a survivor does not grieve, they limit their 'capacity for joy, for spontaneity, for life' (Bass and Davis, 1992: 119). When they were a child, they needed to suppress the feelings of fear and anger they felt during the abuse. Now these feelings must be dealt with so they can move forward with their life (Bass and Davis, 1992).

With the support of friends, survivors need to scrutinise the abuse – secure in the fact that they now are adults. This time, however, they must allow themselves to grieve. They need to express the feelings they were not permitted to express at the time of the abuse. They need to know they were heard. They also need to be comforted and to learn to comfort themselves. Bass and Davis (1992) contend that survivors will be able to move beyond their grief once they have learned to comfort themselves. Herman (1992) noted that survivors often are amazed at how little concern they feel for the perpetrators' fates once they have mourned the abuse.

### The tasks of mourning

Worden (1991) contended that certain tasks must be accomplished in order to complete the process of mourning. If these tasks are not completed, further growth and development are impaired. The first of the tasks is for the griever to *accept the reality of the loss* (Worden, 1991). Survivors must overcome their denial about the abuse. They need to realise that the abuse happened, that it was not their fault, and that they could not have prevented it. They also must stop denying that the abuse had an effect on them. Worden (1991: 12) commented, '*Belief and disbelief are intermittent while grappling with this task*'.

The second task of mourning is for the griever to *work through to the pain of grief*. Worden (1991: 13) suggested the German word *Schmerz* as useful for talking about pain. Here is what he had to say about it: 'Its broader definition includes the literal physical pain that many people experience and the emotional and behavioural pain associated with loss. It is necessary to acknowledge and work through this pain or it will manifest itself through some symptoms or other form of aberrant behaviour'. Society may feel uncomfortable with the survivor's pain and

pressure them to get over the abuse and put it behind them. This may cause the survivor to deny that they need to grieve. Survivors may try to bypass the second task by cutting off their feelings or denying their pain. Others use alcohol or drugs to keep from feeling the pain.

The third task of mourning is to *adjust to the current environment* (Worden, 1991). For the survivor, this could be a world in which the perpetrator no longer plays a key role. The survivor must adjust to their new role; they need to adjust to their sense of self and to their sense of the world.

The fourth task of mourning is to *put the trauma behind and move on with life*. For many people, this is the most difficult task to accomplish. They get stuck at this point in their grieving and later realise that their life in some way stopped at the point the loss occurred (Worden, 1991). This task is hindered if a survivor tries to hold onto the past. They may feel they never want to trust another person again because the loss from their abuse was too painful.

### The processes of mourning

While acknowledging that Worden's tasks of mourning are useful, Rando (1993) believed that mourning is better discussed in terms of four processes. One does not know until the end of the task if it has been completed successfully. At that time, the mourner has to readdress the task if the specific desired outcome has not been accomplished. When mourning is viewed as a process, it allows for more immediate feedback and for those around the mourner to focus on what she is currently experiencing (Rando, 1993).

There are two sub-processes to the first phase. The first is for the mourner to *acknowledge the death* (Rando, 1993). Rando was speaking specifically about mourning death; abuse survivors instead must acknowledge the sexual abuse or any of the losses they experienced because of it. If the survivor has not acknowledged the fact that they were sexually abused in childhood, they have no need to grieve. By not admitting how much the abuse has affected them, they fool themselves into thinking they do not need to heal and readapt their life.

The second sub-process in this first phase is for the mourner to *understand the death* (Rando, 1993) (Again, survivors should substitute 'the abuse' for 'death'.) The survivor needs not only to acknowledge the abuse but to understand some of the reasons for it – what contributed to the abuse and the circumstances surrounding it. The survivor should not use these reasons to justify their abuse. They just needs to understand them.

The second process of mourning, according to Rando (1993) is for the mourner to *react to the separation*. Once they have accepted that they were abused, the survivor must focus on how this changes their relationship with the perpetrator. Healthy mourning will be promoted if the survivor allows themselves to express all the emotions and reactions they are feeling. There are three sub-processes to this phase. The first is to *experience the pain* (Rando, 1993). The survivor must experience the pain and their feelings about the abuse. They also must experience the pain of losing their mother or the pain of trying to understand how a parent could abuse a child.

The second sub-process of this phase is to *feel, identify, accept and give some form of expression to all psychological reactions to the loss* (Rando, 1993). The survivor should identify, label, and differentiate these emotional responses (so that painful emotions can become more bearable) in order to gain control over them. The survivor must find spoken or unspoken expressions that are appropriate and personally comfortable for them (Rando, 1993). The last sub-process in this second phase is to *identify and mourn secondary losses* (Rando, 1993).

The third process of mourning is to *recollect and re-experience the deceased and the relationship* (Rando, 1993). (Again, the 'deceased' should be replaced with the 'perpetrator' here.) The survivor will have to decide what type of relationship they want to have with the perpetrator. In this process, the survivor may need to identify any unfinished business they have with the perpetrator and find a way to achieve some sort of closure. A confrontation may help the survivor to achieve some closure; however, as mentioned before, whether or not to confront should be their choice, not one forced on them. There are two sub-processes to the third process. The first is to *review and remember realistically* (Rando, 1993). The survivor needs to remember all the positive and negative aspects of their relationship with the perpetrator:

*The mourner must repeatedly review the entire relationship, the expectations and needs that initially formed it, its ups and downs, its course and development, its crises and joys – all elements of it throughout the years. As these events and features of the relationship unfold, the mourner can examine associated feelings and thoughts: negative*

*ones, such as anxiety, ambivalence, and guilt, as well as more positive ones, such as satisfaction, happiness, and meaning.*

(Rando, 1993: 49)

The second sub-process is to *revive and re-experience the feelings* (Rando, 1993). The survivor must undo the ties that bind them to the perpetrator and memories of the abuse. This does not mean that they are expected to forget about the abuse and what was done to them; rather, they should understand that they can't change the past and that they could not have prevented the abuse.

The fourth process of mourning is to *relinquish the old attachments to the deceased [or perpetrator] and the old assumptive world* (Rando, 1993). The 'assumptive world' is an organised schema in which, based on their previous experiences, a person assumes certain things to be true about the world and themselves. 'The assumptive world is viewed as being fuelled by the individual's experiences, memories, and needs, and confirmed through experiences, behaviour and interaction patterns, and role relationships' (Rando, 1993: 50). If the survivor repressed the abuse and remembered it years later, the fact that they were abused may not fit in with *their global assumptions* (ie those pertaining to the world; Rando, 1993). If the survivor's mother was the perpetrator, this may interfere with their *specific assumptions* about their mother (ie she was caring, loving, and protecting).

According to Rando (1993) the fifth process of mourning is to *readjust to move adaptively into the new world without forgetting the old*. After releasing the attachment to the old assumptive world and to the perpetrator, the survivor is able to establish new connections that are appropriate with the changes that have taken place. The word 'move' denotes action and suggests that the survivor will be able to progress to a place where they can function. The word 'adaptively' suggests that the survivor will be able to adjust and adapt to the change. There are four subprocesses to this phase of mourning. The first is to *revise the assumptive world* (Rando, 1993: 52–3). The survivor needs to modify their assumptive world, which was violated with the knowledge of their abuse. The extent to which they need to do this depends on six things:

- The perpetrator's importance and centrality to the survivor's life.

- The types and number of roles the perpetrator played in the survivor's life.
- The meaning the perpetrator gave to the survivor.
- The pattern of interaction the survivor had established with the perpetrator.
- The type of abuse perpetrated and the degree to which it violated 'other needs, feelings, thoughts, behaviour and interaction patterns, hopes wishes, fantasies, dreams, assumptions, expectations, and beliefs'.
- The number, type, and quality of secondary losses.

The more numerous or important to the survivor the violations were, the more they will need to reconstruct their assumptive world. The second sub-process to the fifth phase of mourning is to *develop a new relationship with the deceased [perpetrator]* (Rando, 1993). The survivor must decide what kind of relationship they want to have with the perpetrator or if they want to have one at all.

The third sub-process is to *adopt new ways of being in the world* (Rando, 1993). In order for the survivor to be healthy in their mourning process, they cannot pretend that the abuse did not occur or has not affected them in some way. They may have to take on new roles, learn new skills, change some behaviours and establish new relationships.

The fourth sub-process is to *form a new identity.* 'With a new assumptive world, a new relationship with the deceased (perpetrator) and the acquisition of new skills, behaviours, roles, and relationships, the mourner is no longer the same person they used to be' (Rando, 1993, p59). They need to change their image of themselves to reflect this new reality. The part of them that was victim should no longer define their sense of self and identity. They may feel they are losing a part of themselves and need to mourn that. However, in the case of sexual abuse, the part they lose is the *victim self*, which is replaced by a more positive sense of self as a *survivor*.

The sixth and final process in Rando's (1993) *'six processes of mourning'* is for the survivor to *reinvest*. The energy once invested in the relationship with the perpetrator and in dealing with the issues of the abuse must be reinvested into something more healthy, something that benefits the survivor by giving them a sense of satisfaction. For example, they can do volunteer work with sexually abused children; they can establish a healthy relationship with someone who will not abuse them in any way, letting them know they are worthy of love; or they can return to school and get or finish a degree.

### Common behaviours associated with grief

According to Worden (1991) many people who experience acute grief reactions exhibit some of the same behaviours. He broke the behaviours into four categories: feelings, physical sensations, cognitions and behaviours.

### Feelings

Some feelings commonly associated with the process of grieving are sadness, anger, guilt and self-reproach, anxiety, loneliness, fatigue, helplessness, shock, yearning, emancipation, relief, and numbness (Worden, 1991). These are all normal reactions and should not be considered pathological. However, if they last for extended periods of time, the grief may be considered complicated (Worden, 1991).

### Physical sensations

Worden (1991) noted that the physical sensations surrounding grief are often overlooked, even though they are important during grieving. The physical sensations Worden listed include hollowness in the stomach, tightness in the chest or throat, over-sensitivity to noise, a sense of depersonalisation, breathlessness or feeling short of breath, muscle weakness, lack of energy, and dry mouth (adapted from p25).

### Cognitions

Worden (1991) listed five cognitions that commonly accompany the grieving process: disbelief, confusion, preoccupation, sense of presence, and hallucinations.

### Behaviours

Worden (1991) listed several behaviours often reported by those who are grieving. Following is a list of behaviours common among survivors grieving issues of abuse: sleep disturbance, appetite disturbance, absent-minded behaviour, social withdrawal, sighing, restless over-activity, and crying. Survivors may experience any or all of these behaviours.

# The victim's response cycle (Simon-Roper, 1996)

Simon-Roper provided us with a useful model for understanding the unique relationship between the child victim and their perpetrator in cases of incest. It is in the context of this relationship that the development of thoughts, feelings and behaviours that form the victim's response cycle are encouraged. In this model, the cycle begins with the child's negative self-view that can develop from a number of sources such as being in an abusive relationship for some time. They may have received mixed messages about what is expected of children (role confusion) and these contribute to the disruption in the child's mastery of developmental tasks, which can create a painful, conflicted view of self which they attempt to compartmentalise in order to function. This can lead to poor self-image and lack of confidence. The child may also be confused about interpersonal relationships as the perpetrator may discourage them from social activities which affects their ability to make friends outside of the home and prevents the opportunity to learn social skills. Any attempts to relate to others may be rejected and the child then withdraws in order to protect themselves. This has the potential to isolate them and they may use a variety of 'coping' skills, such as self-mutilation or substances ('acting out behaviours) or developing dissociative qualities. As the relationship with the perpetrator continues, the child becomes aware as to when the behaviour becomes pre-abusive, such as being bought special toys. They then learn how to respond in a way that will assure the most predictable abuse experience, thus offering them a small degree of control. After the abuse has occurred, children often report a sense of responsibility for maintaining the abuse (especially due to the anticipatory behaviours) which induces a sense of shame which is intensified by a fear of rejection and the negative self-image that the abuse has created. Children continue to respond with new coping strategies (such as caretaking or pseudo-mature behaviours) to deal with these feelings, and they may elicit positive responses from others, including the abuser, who see them as justification for their abusive behaviour and not attempts by the child to soothe themselves. This increased emotional comfort increases the likelihood of re-abuse occurring, thus reinforcing the victim's responses as they have been beneficial in their ability to survive.

# The process of victimisation: the victim's perspective (Berliner and Conte, 1990)

As each victim's experience of the abuse will differ and their response to it will be determined by their own personal resources and perspective on life, a wide range of effects can be observed (Davenport et al., 1994).

Berliner and Conte elicited the views of 23 children between the ages of 10 and 18 who had been sexually abused to explore the process of victimisation as they perceived it. They found no single pattern of sexual abuse victimisation and a startling variety of types of relationships.

## *Attitude towards the perpetrator*

The children described ambivalent feelings for the perpetrator. The majority described the relationship as positive: others described it as neutral or negative. They reported a range of emotions: over half said that they loved him, liked him, needed or depended on him. Almost half also endorsed the statement 'I hated him'. Some had known the offender their whole lives, whilst for others the length of time they knew him before the abuse started ranged from 5 to 10 years to 6 months or less. There were positive comments on the quality of the relationship ('We were really good friends, best friends'); neutral comments ('He was just around'); and negative comments ('He was a rough guy').

## *Pre-abuse indicators*

Many of the children described the perpetrator as doing or saying things before the abuse which caused them to feel the perpetrator was thinking of them in a sexual way, thus representing 'warning signs' that the abuse was about to take place (often recognised as such retrospectively). These included treating them differently from other children, often in an age-inappropriate way; telling them not to tell their mother about the things that happened; or telling them private things about their mother, etc.

The perpetrator rarely respected privacy, engaged in a lot of physical contact, and would touch them in their sexual parts or expose themselves-ostensibly accidentally. The majority of the children did not know that they were being sexually abused initially.

## Perpetrator statements

The children confirmed that in most cases perpetrators made statements about the sexual activity to justify it. For example, 'I'll only do it one more time'; 'I am teaching you about sex'; 'I am lonely'; 'I need love and affection, too', etc. They would use these to try to persuade the child that it was acceptable or to minimise the seriousness.

## Coercion

Almost all of the children reported some type of coercion either to gain co-operation or to prevent reporting. A majority said there were threats, relating either to physical harm to the child, abandonment or rejection, or consequences to the perpetrator. In many cases the coercion was indirect and accomplished by some form of bribery or by exploiting the child's needs or vulnerability. Most children were told to keep the abuse secret.

## Child vulnerability

In many cases the sexual abuse relationship filled a significant deficit in the child's life, or disclosure posed a serious threat to the child's or parents' situation.

## Current beliefs

They expressed regret at not telling, because 'emotionally it screwed me up. I hate men. I hate my mother . . .'

# The 'Stockholm syndrome' (Doyle, 1997)

The phrase 'Stockholm syndrome' derives from events during and after a bank robbery in the Swedish capital in 1973, when bank employees held hostage showed loyalty and affection to the robbers and used their own bodies to protect them from police fire when the robbers surrendered. It can be used to describe the way in which individuals can form an attachment to their persecutor, with them trying to protect their perpetrator. They show gratitude and loyalty towards them, turning hostility away from their oppressor and onto potential rescuers. Some eventually adopt the perpetrator's values and beliefs and emulate the abusive behaviour. This

process can be applied to sexually abused children.

## Compliance and denial

The inability to escape leads to frozen fright, which is not just a suspension of emotional response and activity, but a total focusing of energy and attention on the source of threat. In this state, the victim will become quiet and compliant. This is often safer than trying to resist when the odds are overwhelming and the perpetrator is determined to exert power. Another early response to threat is denial – often of the reality or the severity of the situation. This is a useful temporary state, which helps people from being overwhelmed, but it becomes counterproductive if entrenched. They may dismiss the severity, pain and distress of their abuse, and this can lead to a view that there is no harm in treating others in the same way.

## Coping with fear and anger

Frozen fright, shock, numbness and denial are all passive emotions. This state of passivity does not always continue. These responses can be replaced by more active and possibly more painful emotions, namely fear and anger. The uncomfortable feeling of powerlessness is all the greater if the victim fears the perpetrator. In order for the level of fear to be tolerated, it is usually repressed. It can lead to anger against society or the helping professionals rather than their perpetrator, leading to a rejection of all adults and authority figures. It can also be projected against vulnerable others, especially other children who remind them of their own frailty and powerlessness.

## Hope and gratitude

In order to preserve hope, victims will convince themselves that the perpetrator is basically good and suppress a reminder of their malevolence. This can lead to them believing that not only is the perpetrator good but the behaviour and beliefs are equally good.

## Deserving, deprecation and depression

Many victims come to a logical conclusion that, if their tormentor is good and yet they are suffering, it must be because they are bad or have in some way deserved the abuse. They can turn their anger and self-deprecation inwards and become depressed.

### Accepting and adapting

The final stage for many victims is one of acceptance, and this has attached dangers. The child may not complain about the abuse and they may be poorly motivated to seek help to escape from the situation. They may also accept the beliefs, values and behaviour of their perpetrator, and do not see that their behaviour is in any way wrong.

## The impact of child sexual abuse in a developmental perspective

Finkelhor (1995) has argued that to understand the impact and nature of this abuse as well as the operation of protective factors, a developmental perspective must be adopted. Childhood is a period of enormous change in size, strength, cognitive capacities, gender differentiation, relationships, and social environments – all of which affect the potential for victimisation. Moreover, the impact of these changes, which interact with one another, is not simple. He split the developmental victimology of childhood into two domains: risk (the types of victimisation that children suffer depend on their age and level of development) and impact (how children respond to abuse depends on stage-specific capacities and vulnerabilities).

### Risk

The risk for sexual abuse appears to increase markedly between the ages of six and ten (Finkelhor and Baron, 1986). The child's age also affects the likelihood of disclosure or reporting. It appears to be much more difficult for children under six to disclose sexual abuse than for those over twelve. Over the course of their development, children both acquire and lose characteristics that make them more or less vulnerable as targets for various types of abuse. For example, sexual maturation may make the child more vulnerable to sexual crime, although there are abusers who only target young children. Children also change in their ability to protect themselves as they get older, although they may also be more likely to take risks (to drink or take drugs) that compromise such protective abilities. The environments in which children live, travel and work change over the course of their

development, dramatically affecting their risk of victimisation. The risk of victimisation is often higher in environments with more motivated perpetrators and lower in those with more capable guardians. Sexual abuse challenges this as it often occurs in the home and so the motivated perpetrators are often parents, relatives or siblings. Children do not generally choose their family so younger, dependent children cannot opt to leave such a setting when it becomes dangerous. This may account for why younger children suffer most abuse in the care of their dependants. Developmental factors affect boys' and girls' risk for victimisation in different ways. The patterns of victimisation are often less gender-specific for younger children (as they have similar activities and physical characteristics) and more so for older children (when physical and social characteristics diverge).

### Impact

Finkelhor notes that it is equally as useful to adopt a developmental perspective to impact, although this is constrained by the fragmentation of research information. Much of the extensive sexual abuse information has not adopted a developmental analysis and where developmental issues have been explored it has been in regard to how post-traumatic stress disorder differs when applied to younger children. Some authors contend that unlike adults and adolescents, younger children do not so clearly exhibit psychic numbing or experience sudden visual flashbacks. Those who have studied abuse impact with children have felt a much stronger need for models of impact that go beyond PTSD, and include the impairment of attachment or self-esteem, adoption of highly sexualised behaviour, or highly aggressive modes of interpersonal relating, failure to acquire competence in peer relations or the use of drugs, dissociation, self-injury, or other dysfunctional ways of dealing with anxiety (Briere, 1992). Based on the research on the severity of victimisation impact, developmental effects are more likely to occur under a number of conditions: the victimisation is repetitive and ongoing; it dramatically changes the nature of the child's relationship with his or her primary support system; it adds to other serious stressors; and because of its timing, the victimisation interrupts a crucial developmental transition.

It is clear therefore that childhood sexual abuse is a major risk factor for a variety of problems, both in the short-term and in terms of later adult functioning. The harm is attributable to the fact that the sexual abuse is always non-consensual, frequently developmentally inappropriate, and invariably alters the nature of the relationship within which it occurs. It can be painful, frightening, and confusing and can lead to responses in childhood that interfere with normal developmental processes and increase the risk for subsequent maladjustment in adult life.

## Resilience: the child's strength

### Resilience

Resilience is a complex construct that has been sued to describe a process or phenomena of positive adaptation in the face of significant adversity. Resilience cannot be directly measured: rather, it is inferred from this process of examining positive adaptation in conjunction with adversity. There is a lack of agreement as to the level of competence needed to reflect positive adaptation, and whether it is required in more than one domain, given the multi-dimensional influences that children experience (Luthar and Zelaro, 2003). Masten et al. (1990) delineated three types of resilient phenomena: being at high-risk and doing better on outcomes than expected; adapting well under stressful circumstances; and recovering from trauma. Although resilience was initially viewed as primarily the result of personal characteristics of the resilient child, over time a conceptual framework for resilience has emerged that emphasises three interactive factors that are seen as contributing to the development of resilience: characteristics of the child, their family and their social environment (Luthar et al., 2000).

Research on resilience focuses on the underlying factors and mechanisms that modify the negative effects of maltreatment and abuse to foster adaptive outcomes. The first wave of research focused on the short and long-term effects of sexual abuse and the second wave moved on to identify potential background variables and potential factors that mediate or moderate direct association between child sexual abuse and negative psychological outcomes. These variables have included perceived social support, family environment, coping strategies

and child sexual abuse-related variables such as age of onset, relationship to perpetrator, coerced abuse, and duration of abuse. However, characteristics of child sexual abuse such as severity sometimes fail to explain variability in outcome and sometimes show contradictory results (Ruggiero et al., 2000). Other factors are related to less severe symptomatology and seem to act as protective factors following child sexual abuse, such as parental/maternal support and participation in treatment. However, studies of disclosure (or talking about past abuses) which has been considered a necessary process toward recovery have yielded contradictory results. These indicate that disclosure can be either positively or negatively related to symptomatology depending on the response from the environment, the time elapsed since the disclosure and the voluntary nature of the disclosure (Dufour et al., 2000).

Many adult survivors identify themselves as high-functioning and appear well adjusted in their current lives. The majority of the research on resilience has examined developmental outcome in a single domain of functioning (predominantly intrapersonal functioning). However the processes underlying resilience may build over time and across domains (ie psychological well-being, physical health, romantic relationships, work competence, and parental competence and thus there is likely to be significant variability in functioning across domains of adjustment. A person may function well in one domain at the expense of functioning well in other salient domains.

O'Dougherty Wright et al. (2005) redressed the scant attention that has been given to positive adaptation following child sexual abuse and in so doing assessed resilience across intrapersonal, interpersonal and intra-familial domains. They found that a substantial number of survivors do demonstrate resilience across several domains of functioning, albeit with considerable variability across domains. When multiple adaptational domains are assessed, individuals often show significant discrepancies in how adequately they function across domains, and many individuals are successful in one domain but not in another. Of concern in their sample was the continued vulnerability of many of the mothers, with 18 per cent experiencing difficulty in every domain and 54 per cent had difficulty in two or more domains. The wide-ranging nature of the difficulties experienced highlights the need to move from a focus on the absence of psychological symptoms to a more comprehensive assessment of overall wellbeing, effective role functioning and general quality of life. They confirmed significant correlations between domains of resilience with the strong correlations between depressive symptoms and physical health and between depression and the interpersonal and intra-familial domains (marital satisfaction and perceived competence as a parent).

Children have often been perceived by adults as being in the possession of some intrinsic resilience that protects them from acutely stressful events. It is true that children have been shown to cope with traumatic events by the use of a wide range of strategies – some of which will be adaptive, while others will be less so. Coping attempts will clearly be shaped by the ongoing environment as well as particular characteristics of the child. There has been an increasing interest in processing of cognitive appraisal (how children assess the abuse impact on their ability to cope), coping strategies (what children engage in to deal with the abuse and its effects) and attributional processes (what they attribute their abuse to) and their relationship to outcome.

Research on resilience has occurred in two separate but somewhat related domains: family stress and developmental psychopathology. Both focus on positive outcomes under conditions of adversity and each is concerned with family relationships. In the family stress literature, the processes of interest are individuals' appraisals of contemporary events, how they marshal resources, and how they cope. In developmental psychopathology, the focus is on child adaptation, with parent-child relationships as a major resource variable and the major resource for successful outcomes. The general definition of resilience within developmental psychopathology involves the interactions of risks and assets that result in good outcomes. Assets and risks reside within individuals, families, neighbourhoods, and social policies and programmes. Individuals may have many assets that could potentially help them to deal successfully with risks, but if they do not use them, they do not function as assets at all. On the other hand, persons with a few assets may use them in the constructive management of adversities. Gilgun (1999) thus argues that human agency and interpretation are pivotal in resilience processes.

Individuals can be termed resilient only when they have been subjected to risk conditions (Gilgun, 1999). Risks are a component of resilience. They are probabilistic, statistical concepts. Risks predict that a portion of an at-risk group will experience adverse outcomes, but cannot predict which individuals within high-risk groups will have the associated outcome. Being a member of an at-risk group can predict only a vulnerability to the outcome. Vulnerability is thus a concept that can be applied to individuals, when they are members of at-risk groups.

Initially, the term resilient referred to so-called 'stress resistant' or 'invulnerable' children. These children were characterised as unusually competent and capable. They not only survived, they thrived under adverse circumstances. More recently, the attributes of resiliency have changed to explore the processes over time that protect one from risk. As such, resiliency is a process whereby risk was successfully engaged (Anderson, 1997). Wolin and Wolin (1993) broadened the definition of resilience further to include the individual attributes that develop as a result of finding ways to survive childhood adversity. They recognise the capacity of self-repair for anyone who must endure hardship. They emphasise that resilience is not limited to people who escape risk with few problems. People who have survived traumatic childhoods are considered resilient because they have enduring strengths that developed as a means of protecting themselves from their troubled families. Their survival is based on their survival abilities often without any assistance from their families.

Resilience has been variously defined. It has been described as the capacity for successful adaptation, positive functioning, or competence (Garmezy, 1993) despite high-risk status, chronic stress, or following prolonged or severe trauma. Garmezy (1991: 459) defined resiliency as 'the capacity for recovery and maintained adaptive behaviour that may follow initial retreat or incapacity upon initiating a stressful event'. Resilience is often operationalised as the positive end of the distribution of developmental outcomes in a sample of high-risk individuals (Rutter, 1979; 1990). Rutter (1983: 2) defined resilience as 'people who 'do well' in some sense in spite of having experienced a form of stress which in the population as a whole is known to carry a substantial risk of an adverse outcome'; and 'the positive pole of individual differences in people's response to stress and adversity' (Rutter, 1987: 316). Masten et al. (1990: 426) described it as an 'outcome of successful adaptation despite challenges or threatening circumstances . . . Good outcome despite high risk status, sustained competence under threat and recovery from trauma'.

More recently, it has been defined as 'the development of competence despite severe or pervasive adversity' (Egeland et al., 1993). It is conceived by these authors not as a childhood given, but as a capacity that develops over time in the context of person-environment interactions. From this perspective, developmental outcomes are determined by the interaction of genetic, biological, psychological, and sociological factors in the context of environmental support. According to this view, any constitutional or environmental factors may serve as vulnerability, protective, or risk variables, directly or indirectly influencing behaviour. They thus view resilience 'as developing over time through an interaction of constitutional and experiential factors in the context of a supportive environment. Adaptation is viewed in terms of successful resolution of the individual tasks most salient for given developmental periods' (p525). Rutter (1999: 119–20) defined resilience as 'the phenomenon of overcoming stress or adversity. That is, put in more operational terms, there has been a relatively good outcome for someone despite their experience of situations that have been shown to carry a major risk for the development of psychopathology'. Overall, the definitions on resilience seem to contain reference to two kinds of adaptive responses:

- The maintenance of normal development despite the presence of threats or risks (internal and external).
- Recovery from trauma.

(Staudinger et al., 1993)

Resilience can be viewed as both a set of behaviours and internalised capacities. Behaviourally, resilience means recovering from, coping with, or overcoming adversity. As internal processes, resilience refers to the capacity to maintain feelings of personal integration and a sense of competence when confronted by particular adversity (Gilgun, 1999).

In some respects, the concept of the resilient child has changed. One no longer thinks of a child as invulnerable or totally resilient. Even the child who shows remarkable degrees of success in dealing with stress has setbacks and successes at different times and in different domains (Radke-Yarrow and Brown, 1993).

Resilience is a broadly based concept of some complexity. This means that there must be a careful analysis which focuses not just on the individual or the family but on the relevant stresses and adversities in their social context (Rutter, 1999: 159). The importance of taking a broadly based approach to the assessments of children is highlighted by current ideas on protective factors. The evidence suggests strongly that children vary considerably in their responses to positive and negative experiences. Multiple protective and adverse factors may be involved at the same time. Rutter therefore suggests in summary that:

*Children may vary in their vulnerability to psycho-social stress and adversity as a result of both genetic and environmental influences; that family-wide experiences tend to impinge on individual children in quite different ways; that the reduction of negative, and increase of positive, chain reactions influences the extent to which the effects of adversity persist over time; that new experiences which open up opportunities, can provide beneficial 'turning-point' effects; that although positive experiences in themselves do not exert much of a protective effect, they can be helpful if they serve to neutralise some risk factors; and that the cognitive and affective processing of experiences is likely to influence whether or not resilience develops.*
(p119)

### Seven themes of resilience (Wolin and Wolin, 1993)

Wolin and Wolin set out seven themes of resilience, which represent clusters of strengths that interact with one another to help people survive adverse experiences. The development and maturation of each resiliency occurs in three stages – childhood, adolescence and adulthood (of which the first two stages as they affect our catchment groups will be explored in detail later). Although not every child exposed to sexual abuse has each of the areas of resilience, mothers and workers should be able to identify each child's configuration of them. Anderson (1997) argues that the seven themes of resilience provide a conceptual framework for those who are interested in uncovering strengths in sexually abused children while validating and discussing their trauma.

### Insight

Insight allows the child to question the distorted reflections of a troubled family. During the first stage of insight, children may sense the flaws in their families. Families may give them messages blaming them for the sexual abuse or may deny its occurrence. Insight continues to develop throughout adolescence, as they begin to identify the underlying problems in the family. Through changes emotionally, intellectually and in social interactions with others, they are able to grow from sensing what is wrong in their family to giving a name to the problem. For example, children who are incest victims may figure that the sexual activity is not an 'expression of affection'.

### Independence

This refers to the child's ability to distance him or herself emotionally or physically from a troubled family. Such distancing is difficult to sustain in sexually abusing families because the tendency in such families is to pull together in order to maintain the family secret. During childhood, independence and distancing are achieved by finding a protective stance – psychologically through fantasising or dissociating, or behaviourally maintaining a low profile in the family. They understand that they are not going to get the appropriate recognition from their parents so they immerse themselves in satisfying activities with others in order to gain affirmation.

### Initiative

Initiative occurs through taking risks to make one's life controllable despite the sexual abuse. During childhood exerting initiative takes the form of experimenting and learning that parts of a sexually abusing family environment are controllable and realising what is not. They may figure out ways to try to protect themselves from the sexual abuse, either by sleeping with a sibling or wearing extra clothes in bed. They may not always be successful in their attempts. In adolescence, initiative is shown through children's ability to take hold of their lives in the midst of family problems. They maintain hope that the sexual abuse will end and that they can find ways to persevere until the time comes. Focusing on the future helps them to separate from their current trauma and allows them to begin planning for life after sexual abuse.

### Relationships

In childhood, the search for people with whom to connect is often within the family in periods of

calm and then trying to distance themselves during periods of chaos. These attempts are often futile, which leads to them seeking relationships outside the immediate family, and may include dolls and pets. During adolescence, children actively seek relationships to fill the void in their own families, and they have some control over who they chose. They often pick out role models, such as parents of friends, or a teacher.

### Morality

Morality is an expression of an informed conscience and is demonstrated through empathy, compassion, and caring towards others. Throughout childhood, children feel they have got a poor deal with their family but may channel their disappointment into trying to make a difference for others. They may express their morality through judgements of what is right or wrong in their family. During adolescence, their morality may be channelled into fighting for justice at home by protecting younger family members and standing up to their perpetrator. They may demonstrate compassion towards others even though they have received little compassion themselves.

### Creativity and humour

Expressions of creativity and humour channel pain and discomfort in imaginative ways. A young child may manage adverse circumstances through play and this also helps them to heal. In adolescence they use their imagination as an important tool for managing difficult situations. The play becomes refined into creative works or a highly developed sense of humour, and these creative abilities help them process their pain and grief (Dinsmore, 1991). It may be channelled through writing, drawing, music, etc. A well-developed sense of humour not only helps them disconnect from emotional pain but helps them connect with others.

## Protective factors

*A protective factor is one that moderates against the effects of a stressful or risk situation so that the individual is able to adapt more successfully than they would have had the protective factor not been present.*

(Masten et al., 1990)

Davies (1999: 46) has argued that:

*... protective factors, either in the child or environment, mitigate risk by reducing stress, providing opportunities for growth, or strengthening coping capacities. Recent research on resilience has increasingly recognised the ongoing transactional process of development and protective factors ... It may be more appropriate to refer to protective factors as protective processes, since to be truly effective in promoting resilience they must be present across many years of the child's development.*

Masten and Coatsworth (1998: 216) noted that 'successful children [who do well despite adversity] remind us that children grow up in multiple contexts – in families, schools, peer groups ... and each context is a potential source of protective as well as risk factors'. These children demonstrate that children are protected not only by the self-righting nature of development, but also by the actions of adults, by their own actions, by the nurturing of their assets, by opportunities to succeed and the experience of success. This highlights the many protective forces that may be at work or waiting to be tapped, even in the most unpromising circumstances.

Gilgun (1999) has argued that when individuals use assets to deal constructively with risks, the assets are termed protective factors. They are therefore elements in resilience processes that counter the influence of risk. She argues that there is such a concept as cumulative protective processes, which are likely to equip individuals to cope well when confronted with risk situations.

Rutter (1990) asserted that it is conceptually important that the protective factor only has its effect in combination with the risk variable such that it either has no effect on individuals at low risk or has some effect on low risk individuals but a much greater effect on individuals in high-risk situations. Conrad and Hammen (1993) have questioned whether protective factors are conceptually useful or they are simply the opposite of risk factors. Rutter (1987, 1999) has stressed the importance of clarifying what the processes or mechanisms are that lead to the protective effect because a given variable may be a risk factor in one situation and a protective factor in another, depending on the underlying processes. It is probably useful to conceive the protective effect as a process, as there are no static variables within an individual person. Garmezy (1985) stated that there are three main types of factors that are protective against risk: personal

attributes of the child, family factors, and external social supports.

Rutter (1987) reminded us that if we want to help vulnerable youngsters, we need to focus especially on the protective processes that bring about changes in life trajectories from risk to adaptation. He included among them:

- Those that reduce the risk impact.
- Those that reduce the likelihood of negative chain reactions.
- Those that promote self-esteem and self-efficacy.
- Those that open up opportunities.

There has been a process of differentiating protective from resource factors. Conrad and Hammen (1993: 594) defined a resource factor as 'a variable that contributes to good outcomes for a person regardless of risk status'. They differentiated between factors that serve as resources (equally affecting those at high or low risk) and those that are protective (having greater positive impact on those at high risk). In their study, they found that the child, family and external attributes served mainly as resource factors. Thus, for most of the risk conditions, positive self-concept, academic success, social competence, positive perceptions of the mother, maternal social competence, having a healthy father at home, and friendships assisted children in attaining lower diagnostic ratings. Resource factors are beneficial to high-risk children, but their action is not unique to high risk.

Previous research suggests that some factors can mediate these negative outcomes. For example, the emotional support of non-offending parents towards sexually abused children has been suggested as one such factor.

Feiring et al. (1998) explored the factors mitigating the negative effects of sexual abuse on children and adolescents. A focus on such protective factors offers insight into the assessment and treatment process and does highlight the capacity for individual and/or environmental resources to operate as protective factors against the development of subsequent behaviour problems (Spaccarelli, 1994). Some evidence suggests that adolescents, compared to children, are seen as more responsible for their victimisation and, therefore, may receive less support from caregivers. This was supported by Feiring et al.'s research, although they did find that adolescents reported receiving more support from friends than did children. The social support provided by relationships with parents, siblings, extended kin, non-kin adults, and friends is known to influence psychological health and adjustment in children and adolescents, yet there is no detailed research on its buffering effects. Research does show that support from a non-offending mother is related to a better prognosis and less psychological distress (Everson et al., 1991) particularly fewer symptoms of depression and anxiety, as well as higher levels of social competence. Parental support can also serve to help victims feel less exposed to social condemnation and less isolated and stigmatised, making them less likely to develop symptoms.

Feiring et al. found that children are more likely than adolescents to report the receipt of support, and are more satisfied with the support received from adults; in particular parents and relatives. Adolescents are more likely than children to report the receipt of, and satisfaction with, support from friends. The developmental tasks of adolescents may place them at increased risk for not seeking or receiving the type of emotional support from parents that promotes better adjustment. Early adolescence is a time when few adolescents spend much time with their parents and emotionally distance themselves from established sources of support. Even when sexual abuse is disclosed, there is a conflict between support and the need for autonomy with this age group. Age is important when responsibility is broached: as many parents see children as less responsible than adolescents. The research did reaffirm the centrality of parental support in regard to post-discovery distress, with it being a salient factor in helping both children and adolescents recover from sexual abuse. In particular, those individuals who reported high satisfaction with the support received from parents indicates that parental support may buffer victims from developing psychological distress related to self-blame and low self-esteem. They found that support from relatives was related to increased sexual anxiety and eroticism, whilst support from friends was related to more hyper-arousal, perceptions of negative events by others, and eroticism. The examination of those individuals who received high support from friends is related to heightened levels of psychological distress, high levels of shame and self-blame, both of which are important processes for understanding how

victims feel and think about the sexual abuse and can help explain which children and adolescents will experience more behavioural problems over time. Overall, the findings suggest that support does not always facilitate healthier functioning post-abuse discovery. Rather, different sources of support may be differentially appropriate for the needs of the victim.

Another protective factor related to child's successful coping is high self-esteem (Garmezy, 1985) which in turn is enhanced by positive and secure love attachments (Santry and McCarthy, 1999).

The child's responses to the abuse are mediated by coping mechanisms that personal experience and family members have helped to shape. The child's typical response is to accommodate the abuse situation, and this response in part depends on the responses of family members and intervening agencies. For some children, the stress and potential damage to personality development caused by the abuse is made greater by the intervening agencies, whereas for others it is essential to resolving their feelings about the abuse and freeing themselves from feelings of guilt.

More information is needed about what happens if and when child sexual abuse comes to the attention of mothers and other adults, in order to better understand what aspects of the aftermath of the experience may lessen lasting effects and facilitate reclamation of the lives of children and the mothers.

Wyatt and Mickey (1988) studied the support of the mother and others as it mediated the lasting effects of sexual abuse. They found that 55 per cent of the abused women who received positive family support had no negative lasting effect on their attitudes to men, 21 per cent had minimal effects, 12 per cent had modest effects and 12 per cent had severe effects.

Children actively process incoming information about external events, matching this against their existing internal perceptions of how the world works. If the child finds themselves with too great a mismatch when contemplating a new event, they have a choice of changing his or her world view to incorporate the new information or simply ignoring it and persisting in their original schema. This suggests that healthy children are much more flexible than adults. A similar process operates when a child has to deal with a trauma or stressor. A developmental model posits that children actively seek to adapt to a new situation and to develop various coping mechanisms so that the thrust of development can continue. Sexual abuse is clearly a stressor and children take an active role in creating coping mechanisms for themselves. Friedrich (1988) sees the range of children's responses as reflecting individual ways of coping in which the child will either externalise or internalise the traumatic event with various psychological and social consequences. Driver (1988) postulates several basic ways for a child to resolve the 'moral double bind' of abuse. These are blocking, non-integration, or identification with the aggressor. She is of the opinion that the first three are determined by messages the child receives from the outside world and the way in which they are responded to and communicated with during intervention.

Oates et al. (1994) found that family functioning was the most significant factor influencing the adjustment of sexually abused children, 18 months after their initial referral to child protection.

Egeland et al. (1993) looked at emotional responsivity as a protective mechanism. Their findings emphasised the important protective function of parenting, or the quality of parent-child relationships, particularly early relationships. The findings suggest that effects of severe risk conditions are mediated in part by the care the child receives from their parents or caretakers. A secure attachment relationship in infancy serves a crucial protective function. Crucial for the development of such a relationship is the experience of sensitive and emotionally responsive caregiving, which can also help break an intergenerational cycle of abuse. Responsive caregiving is central in assisting the child regulate emotional response and developing confidence in the supportive presence of others. Through repeated interaction with a sensitive caregiver, the child comes to view themselves as lovable and worthwhile and to experience mastery in the environment. The child develops confidence in themselves and their ability to elicit positive responses from others through the developmental transaction of internal and external experience rather than as the result of inherent traits. In turn, these caregiving qualities may serve as protective functions in specific risk situations and have positive influence on later adaptation.

Buchanan (1999) has talked about the importance of mobilising clusters of protective factors for children even in the most unpromising situations. This constitutes an important consideration in assessment and intervention.

Davies (1999) has helpfully considered risk and protective factors from the standpoint of the child, the parent, and the community/ environment and this is consistent with the new assessment framework (DOH, 2000). Whilst he produces very detailed discussion in his book, the following Figure 1.13 points workers in the right direction.

Boushel (1993) has explored the notion of a protective framework for children in some detail. This comprises factors at the structural, cultural, personal and inter-personal levels and is again compatible with the new assessment framework. The four factors are the value attached to children, the status of women as carers, the social interconnectedness of children and carers, and the extent and quality of the protective safety nets available. The aim of her framework is to identify the main factors which need to be taken into account in a culturally sensitive and anti-oppressive assessment of the protective environment of children.

Boushel defines 'the child's protective environment' as 'a way of signifying the range of structural, cultural, personal and inter-personal factors which combine to make the child's world a more or less safe and fulfilling place' (p174).

If we are to understand the protective strategies open to parents and children we need to take account of the choices and limitations they face. Historically, the focus of structural inequality was on class, but this has now expanded to embrace the abuse of power to include discrimination based on race, gender, disability and the abuse of professional power. Such developments have also led to a better understanding of the practical and emotional difficulties faced by mothers who wish to protect their children from sexual abuse within the family and of how they and other non-abusing carers may be supported. They illustrate the need when assessing a child's protective environment to consider the extent to which each parent is afforded access to supportive financial, legal and other resources by the state, by their community and by their families. For example, discrimination in housing, employment and education subjects ethnic minority people to severe economic and social hardship. Racism makes it dangerous for people in some areas to visit family and friends and for children to go to school. Social services may deal insensitively with requests for help or

| Risk factors | Protective factors |
|---|---|
| *Child risk factors* | *Child protective factors* |
| • Prematurity, birth anomolies | • Good health |
| • Exposure to toxins in utero | • Personality factors: easy temperament; positive |
| • Chronic or serious illness | disposition; active coping style; positive self-esteem; |
| • Temperament: difficult or slow to warm up | good social skills; internal locus of control; balance |
| • Mental retardation/low intelligence | between help-seeking and autonomy |
| • Childhood trauma | • Above-average intelligence |
| • Antisocial peer group | • History of adequate development |
| | • Hobbies and interests |
| | • Good peer relationships |
| *Parent/family risk factors* | *Parent/family protective factors* |
| • Insecure attachment | • Secure attachment; positive and warm parent-child |
| • Parent: insecure adult attachment pattern | relationship |
| • Single parenthood (with lack of support) | • Parent: secure adult attachment pattern |
| • Harsh parenting, maltreatment | • Parents support child in times of stress |
| • Family disorganisation; low parental monitoring | • Household rules and structure; parental monitoring |
| • Social isolation, lack of support | of child |
| • Domestic violence | • Support/involvement of extended family, including |
| • High parental conflict | help with caregiving |
| • Separation/divorce, especially high-conflict divorce | • Stable relationships between parents |
| • Parental psychopathology | • Parents model competence and coping skills |
| • Parental substance abuse | • Family expectations of pro-social behaviour |
| • Parental illness | • High parental education |
| • Death of a parent or sibling | |
| • Foster care placement | |
| *Social/environmental risk factors* | *Social/environmental protective factors* |
| • Poverty | • Middle-class or above socio-economic status |
| • Lack of access to medical care, health insurance, | • Access to health care and social services |
| and social services | • Consistent parental employment |
| • Parental unemployment | • Adequate housing |
| • Homelessness | • Family religious faith and participation |
| • Inadequate child care | • Good schools |
| • Exposure to racism, discrimination | • Supportive adults outside family who serve as role |
| • Poor schools | models/mentors to child. |
| • Frequent change of residence and schools | |
| • Exposure to environmental toxins | |
| • Dangerous neighbourhood | |
| • Community violence | |

**Figure 1.13**   Risk and protective factor framework (Davies, 1999)

inappropriately remove or fail adequately to protect children from minority ethnic groups. Such responses diminish the likelihood of black children and women disclosing abuse to official agencies and thus reduces their access to the resources these protective services control.

Korbin (1981, 1991) has identified four factors that most acutely influence children's safety from abuse:

1. The value attached to children: In cultures where children are highly valued for their economic utility, for perpetuating family lines

and the cultural heritage, and as sources of emotional pleasure and satisfaction, maltreatment is less likely to occur.

2. Attitudes to certain categories of children: given that some may be undervalued in communities, leaving them potentially vulnerable. These include children with disabilities, unhealthy or unwanted children,

children born under difficult or stigmatising circumstances, or where there are diminished social supports.

3. The embeddedness of child rearing in social networks: Shared child-rearing provides assistance with child care tasks and responsibilities, allows for the redistribution of caring, and encourages greater consensus and closer monitoring of acceptable child rearing practices. Social interconnectedness with peers is also very important as it can provide support and contribute to the development of a confident personal identity or provide models of coping with adult behaviour.

4. Rapid social or economic change: particularly in certain areas, such as immigration and urbanisation as they may lead to increased vulnerability as children's roles and parental authority adjust to the new context.

## Mediating factors

Merrill et al. (2001) describe 'third generation' studies in the field of child maltreatment that go beyond documenting prevalence and direct links between abuse and negative outcomes to a more complex analysis of intervening mediating and moderating processes. One part of this developing area of research focuses on notions of resilience and recovery to understand variability within groups of survivors. Masten et al. (1990) described three types of resilience, including individuals who exhibit exemplary outcomes after adversity, those who while not exceptional in their functioning show positive development in the context of adversity, and finally those who may initially show negative consequences of trauma but over time recover adaptive functioning. Palmer (1997, 1999) challenged models of resilience that reflect a more linear pattern of increasing growth across time. Harvey described a model of resilience composed of several stages or types of resilience and using qualitative data showed how individuals may move back and forth between these levels over time. Her work fits with that of Barringer (1992: 15) who described survivors' healing process from child sexual abuse not as linear but 'as spiral, as a repeated traversing of the issues, layer by layer, piece by piece, sorting and resorting, until the toxicity of the abusive experiences has been released.' Luthar et al. (2000) provided a definition to span such complexity. They stated,

'resilience refers to a dynamic process encompassing positive adaptation within the context of significant adversity (Luthar et al., 2000).' They further note 'that positive adaptation despite exposure to adversity involves a developmental progression, such that new vulnerabilities and/or strengths often emerge with changing life circumstances.' An important implication of this is that all elements of resilience are not necessarily captured in childhood but should be examined across the lifespan (Luthar et al., 2000; Palmer, 1997).

Banyard and Williams (2007) used longitudinal data from a sample of female survivors of child sexual abuse to examine in an exploratory manner aspects of resilience and well-being across the early adult portion of the lifespan. Quantitative findings showed that resilience was often stable and was protective, associated with reduced risk for such things as re-exposure to trauma. Earlier resilience was also associated with more active and positive later coping and greater life and role satisfaction. Yet change was also possible, with decreased resilience associated with trauma re-exposure and many women in qualitative interviews discussing positive 'turning points' in their adult lives that lead to positive growth and change. The findings of the study are consistent with previous work that emphasises resilience as a dynamic process (eg Luthar et al., 2000) while extending such conclusions to survivors of adversity in early adulthood. Quantitative findings showed how resilient functioning when examined across multiple spheres in early adulthood can be both stable and dynamic over time. Survivor's own narratives support notions of resilience and recovery as an ongoing process that is not necessarily linear (eg Barringer, 1992). This process includes experiences of 'turning points' or 'second chances'.

Stein et al. (2000) use the case study method to make the case that in childhood significant shifts and changes in functioning can be observed. The current study extends these findings and suggests ways in which life course changes may occur even in samples of chronically stressed adults. The quantitative findings, while exploratory, do suggest that resilient functioning at one point in time does seem related to decreased risk of re-traumatisation and mental health problems later in the lifecourse. Indeed, in their study re-traumatisation is a risk factor for negative changes in competence and resilience. This finding fits with the growing attention in the trauma and maltreatment fields to understanding re-traumatisation in more detail (eg Banyard et al., 2001) though most of these studies to date focus on the relationship between re-trauma and negative consequences rather than assessing its impact on indices of competent functioning.

Historically the focus on mediating factors has been on abuse characteristics, such as the identity of the perpetrator, multiple abusers, the type of sexual acts, the frequency and duration of abuse, the recency of the abuse, and the use of force (Browne and Finkelhor, 1986). Research findings show that abused children suffer more symptomatology when the abuse is perpetrated by a father or step-father and when the abuse involves physical force and/or more invasive contact, such as penile penetration (Conte and Schuerman, 1987). Age and sex appear to be related more to the type of distress seen in children. Boys appear to have more externalising problems than girls (Friedrich et al., 1988). Children also manifest different kinds of problems at different developmental stages. Cognitive appraisal and coping may be among the most important factors for the development of problems in sexually abused children (Spaccarelli, 1994). Higher levels of cognitive functioning are correlated with greater distress (Shapiro et al., 1992) perhaps due to their ability to appreciate the implications of having been abused. Although relationship to the perpetrator, use of physical force, and type of contact are immutable characteristics not amenable to psychological interventions, recent research suggests that the level of support children receive from the non-abusing parent is a potentially modifiable variable that may be more powerful in mediating children's post-abuse adjustments. Children who receive more support from non-abusing parents appear to suffer less post-abuse symptomatology (Conte and Schuerman, 1987).

Parental support and parental responses to sexually abused children's disclosures and needs. For example, Lazarus and Folkman (1984) developed a model of stress response, in which the individual's appraisal (daughter's perception) of the taxing and endangering person-environment transaction (sexual abuse) was mediated by the daughter's perception of her mother's support, which ultimately influenced the daughter's behavioural response to the stress of sexual abuse. Those girls who perceived

themselves to be supported by their mothers were able to respond more adaptively to the stress of sexual abuse. Their appraisals of the event, via their mother's supportive activities (or lack of support) appear to have meaningfully influenced the girls' response to the stress of sexual abuse. Over the long-term there is evidence to suggest that supportive disclosure may interrupt the cycle of intergenerational abuse (Haller and Alter-Reid, 1985). Unfortunately, there is considerable evidence that non-abusing parents suffer significant levels of distress themselves following a child's disclosure of abuse (Kelley, 1990). This distress may in turn impair their ability to be as supportive as possible to their children. There is also evidence that the closer the relationship of the offender to the mother, the more likely that support will be compromised.

The quality of peer and family relationships (Lynskey and Fergusson, 1997). Alexander (1992) noted that family dysfunction not only increases the likelihood of intra-familial abuse but also may exacerbate the effects of the abuse once it has occurred. Abused children are more distressed if their families have characteristics of negative family functioning, more conflict, and less cohesion (Friedrich et al., 1987). Families of abused children often have multiple additional problems, including parental divorce, violence, psychiatric problems, and substance abuse (Elliott and Briere, 1994). Feiring et al. (1998) show that different sources of support (eg a relative, parent, or friend) can have a differential impact on feelings of competence and self-esteem. For example, they found that support from parents may be related to a general sense that one will be treated well by others. In general, less support from relatives and friends is related to better adjustment. Lower sexual anxiety is significantly related to being adolescent, being a boy, no use of force, and less support from relatives.

Parental and/or family factors in the outcome of treatment with sexually abused children, for example, Friedrich et al. (1992) found that initial levels of maternal support, and depression, family conflict and severity of abuse influenced therapy outcome with sexually abused boys. Cohen and Mannarino (1996) found a significant relationship between parental emotional distress related to the abuse and treatment outcome in sexually abused preschoolers independent of the type of treatment received. Tufts (1984) found that children whose mothers reacted in a punitive way toward them when the sexual abuse was disclosed exhibited more behavioural disturbances. Conte and Schuerman (1987) found that the victim's support system accounted for 20 per cent of the variance in the impact of sexual abuse. They also found that victims whose families had greater psychological dysfunction or significant problems fared worse than victims in emotionally supportive and relatively healthy families. Burgess et al. (1987) found that family disruption and instability contributed to the impact of child sexual abuse.

The effects of the intervention system: the various activities subsumed under the heading of professional intervention may affect the level of psychological distress. For example, multiple interviews by different personnel often increase symptoms, as does the need to give evidence in court. Placement or separation *per se* is not always distressing (Berliner and Conte, 1995).

Deblinger et al. (1999) noted that there is clear research and clinical consensus that sexually abused children who are neither believed or supported by their parents, have a poorer prognosis. Their research went further by examining the potential influence of specific maternal factors in a group of non-offending mothers whose belief and support of their sexually abused children was demonstrated by their desire to obtain treatment services. They found that certain aspects of maternal adjustment and parenting methods contributed significantly to children's post-abuse adjustment.

A mother's self-reported severity of depression was positively related to both PTSD symptoms and parent-reported internalising behaviours. Children's perceptions of particular dimensions of their mothers' parenting styles likewise were associated with their symptomatology. Specifically, the severity of the child's self-reported depression was related to their perception of their mother's parenting style as rejecting rather than accepting. Thus, children who described their mothers as accepting reported less depression. Children who experience hostility and rejection from their mothers – rather than the warmth, caring, and affection inherent in a more accepting parenting style – are more likely to view themselves negatively, a self-view more inclined to predispose to depression.

Children's perceptions of their mothers using parenting methods that were guilt and anxiety provoking were associated with more PTSD symptoms and parent-reported externalising behaviour. The extent to which mothers' parenting methods were perceived by their children as intrusive and psychologically controlling – as opposed to more individuating – was found to contribute unique variance to the extent of PTSD symptoms exhibited by their children. Because many PTSD symptoms are anxiety-based, it seems reasonable that parenting methods that instill guilt and anxiety rather than autonomy in children may have contributed to the children's increased symptoms of PTSD.

## Dissociation

Putnam and Trickett (1993) noted that dissociation is a complex psycho-physiological process manifest by a disruption in the normally integrative processes of memory, identity, and consciousness. Dissociation is conceptualised as occurring along a continuum ranging from the normal, minor dissociations of everyday life such as momentarily spacing out or daydreaming to pathological manifestations such as the profound disruptions in self and memory that occur in multiple personality disorder. It serves a number of highly protective functions in the face of intolerable pain, fear or horror. At the present time, our understanding of pathological dissociation in traumatised children and adolescents is based on clinical experience rather than on systematic study. Spontaneous trance-like states, in which the child is inattentive and unresponsive, are probably the single most common dissociative symptom in children. These blank spells impact significantly on schoolwork and other arenas of cognitive performance. The child often has no awareness of this behaviour but may be aware of missing information that their peers know. Dissociation is a natural capacity that waxes and wanes over the course of normal development, and that may be utilised by traumatised children to escape from overwhelming experiences. Frequent or prolonged use of dissociative defences is believed to seriously impair the consolidation of identity and continuity of memory in trauma victims.

## Sexual revictimisation

Research on sexual assault has revealed that as many as 27 per cent of women report a history of child sexual abuse (Finkelhor, Hotaling, Lewis, and Smith, 1990) whereas approximately 20 per cent of women report histories of adult sexual assault (Koss, 1993). Rather than being independent traumatic events, a number of studies have found that women with a history of child sexual abuse are at increased risk for adult victimisation compared to women who do not report histories of child sexual abuse.

Researchers have found that CSA survivors are at least twice as likely to be revictimised as women with no reported CSA (see Messman-Moore and Long, 2003, for a review). A number of mechanisms have been suggested to explain revictimisation.

A significant and growing body of research demonstrates the problem of repeated sexual victimisation. Building on Messman and Long's (1996) review, many recent and extensive empirical reviews of revictimisation research conclude that strong evidence of the sexual revictimisation phenomenon exists (Arata, 2002; Breitenbecher, 2001; Classen, Palesh, and Aggarwal, 2005; Messman-Moore and Long, 2002; Rich et al., 2004). One review determined that women who experienced childhood sexual abuse were two to three times more likely to experience revictimisation during their adolescence or adulthood than women without this history (Arata, 2002). In their meta-analysis from 19 studies examining revictimisation, Roodman and Clum (2001) found a moderate effect of prior victimisation for revictimisation. Furthermore, a recent population investigation of revictimisation (Desai et al., 2002) showed strong relationships between different experiences of sexual violence across the lifespan.

Classen et al. (2005) conducted a review of the empirical literature and their key findings included:

- Sexual revictimisation is a common occurrence.
- Child sexual abuse is a significant risk factor for revictimisation. In addition, severity of previous sexual victimisation differentiates between individuals who are victimised and revictimised.
- According to some research, sexual assault during adolescence places a woman at a greater risk of victimisation as an adult compared to the risk associated with childhood sexual abuse.
- Recent victimisation places one at a higher risk of revictimisation
- The likelihood of sexual revictimisation seems to increase with cumulative trauma. Survivors

of physical abuse and child sexual abuse have been found to be at a higher risk when compared to survivors of child sexual abuse who were not physically abused.

- Preliminary findings suggest that some demographic factors, such as being an ethnic minority or having a dysfunctional family background, increase the risk of revictimisation.
- Sexual revictimisation is correlated with increased distress. Revictimisation has been associated with having a psychiatric disorder, problems with addiction, and difficulties in interpersonal, behavioural, and cognitive functioning. There is a relationship between revictimisation and greater feelings of shame, blame, powerlessness, and some coping strategies.
- Sexual assault prevention programmes seem to be effective in changing attitudes but are less effective in reducing revictimisation. Programmes that are most promising appear to have longer and more involved interventions.
- Pilot studies on therapeutic interventions for individuals who are revictimised have shown some success in symptom reduction. One pilot study showed promise for a group intervention reducing revictimisation.

Arata (2000) developed a model for predicting sexual revictimisation. There are few current theories of victimisation that directly address sexual revictimisation, however, the dynamics suggested in current theories can be logically linked to revictimisation. By examining theories regarding effects of child sexual abuse and risk factors for rape, overlapping variables are found that suggest a model for revictimisation.

Koss and Dinero (1989) proposed the 'vulnerability hypothesis' as an explanation for increased risk for rape among some women. They found that women with a history of child sexual abuse, liberal sexual attitudes, and above average levels of sexual activity had the highest risk for rape. They also found that these risk factors were most predictive of rape when associated with above average alcohol use. These findings were consistent with a vulnerability hypothesis for understanding revictimisation.

In a theoretical examination of revictimisation, Chu (1992) proposed that dissociative and post-traumatic symptoms are a factor in the tendency for some child sexual abuse victims to be revictimised. In particular, in a dissociative state or in the numbing phase of PTSD, an individual would be more vulnerable to victimisation due to his or her detachment and constricted affect that might inhibit his or her awareness of potential danger. Furthermore, a history of child sexual abuse with concomitant PTSD may lead a victim to experience overwhelming shock or helplessness that may limit his or her perceptions of choices in potentially dangerous situations.

Arata (2000) attempted to combine theoretical models from both fields in an effort to identify mediating variables to revictimisation by examining both effects of child sexual abuse and risk variables for adult assault and their relationships. Theoretical models on the effects of child sexual abuse (Chu, 1992; Finkelhor and Browne, 1985) are combined with a model for predicting adult victimisation (Koss and Dinero, 1989). Koss and Dinero described the vulnerability hypothesis as the effort to identify variables that place specific women at an increased risk for sexual victimisation compared to other women. Finkelhor and Browne described traumatic sexualisation as the 'process in which a child's sexuality . . . is shaped in a developmentally inappropriate and interpersonally dysfunctional fashion as a result of sexual abuse' (p 531).

The proposed theoretical model suggests that vulnerability to revictimisation is an additive process in which traumatic sexualisation and powerlessness result from circumstances surrounding child sexual abuse. Characteristics of the child sexual abuse are hypothesised to predict self-blame and post-traumatic symptoms that then increase consensual sexual behaviour, leading to increased risk for revictimisation.

A model was developed that suggested that risk of revictimisation is related to characteristics of the child sexual abuse, post-child-abuse events, and high-risk behaviour. The final model developed suggested that child sexual abuse and adult and adolescent revictimisation are not directly related but rather are due to the effect of mediating variables. This model is beneficial in helping to understand areas in which to intervene to reduce risk of revictimisation among child sexual abuse survivors.

Grauerholz (2000) examined sexual revictimisation using an ecological framework to advance the understanding of how personal, interpersonal, and sociocultural factors contribute to child sexual abuse victims' increased risk of being sexually victimised later in life. This ecological model explores how sexual revictimisation is multiply determined by factors related to the victim's personal history (eg traumatic sexualisation), the relationship in which revictimisation occurs (eg decreased ability to resist unwanted sexual advances), the community (eg lack of family support) and the larger culture (eg blaming the victim attitudes). Figure 1.14 sets out a summary of factors hypothesised to be related to sexual revictimisation at the various levels.

Filipas and Ullman (2006) examined the psychological sequelae of child sexual abuse (CSA) and the factors that contributed to revictimisation in the form of adult sexual assault (ASA) using a survey of 577 female college students. CSA characteristics, maladaptive coping in response to CSA, degree of self-blame at the time of the abuse and currently, and post-traumatic stress disorder (PTSD) symptoms were examined as predictors of revictimisation. Results indicated that individuals who reported both CSA and ASA had more PTSD symptoms, were more likely to use drugs or alcohol to cope, act out sexually, withdraw from people, and seek therapy services. In addition, the revictimised group reported more self-blame at the time of the abuse and currently. The only factor that predicted revictimisation in this study was the number of maladaptive coping strategies used.

Characterological self-blame (ie blaming something stable within oneself) has been associated with poor outcomes, whereas behavioural self-blame (ie blaming one's actions) has been associated with positive outcomes in certain circumstances because one may be able to change future behaviour (Janoff-Bulman, 1979).

Arata (2000) studied undergraduates and found that the association of CSA with revictimisation was directly mediated by self-blame and PTSD. Victimised women may believe that they have brought the abuse on themselves and that they do not deserve to be loved unconditionally. Vicary, Klingaman, and Harkness (1995) stress the importance of studying blame attributions in sexual assault as many teenage girls continue to blame themselves, which can lead to damaging long-term psychological and physical health consequences. Furthermore, certain kinds of abusive men may target women whom they perceive as vulnerable. Maladaptive coping strategies have also been found to be associated with revictimisation.

**Ontogenic development**
The initial victimisation experience (possible effects include traumatic sexualisation, alcohol and drug abuse, dissociative disorders, low self-esteem, powerlessness, stigmatisation, learned expectancy for victimisation, social isolation running away from home, deviance, and early/premarital pregnancy)
Early family experiences (possible correlates include family breakdown, disorganisation and dysfunction, marital dysfunction, unsupportive parents, and partriarchal structure)

**Microsystem**
Exposure risk (factors increasing this risk include traumatic sexualisation, dissociative disorder, alchol abuse, involvement with deviant activities, stigmatisation, and low self-esteem)
Increased risk of perpetrator acting aggressively due to:
    Perception of victim as easy target (factors increasing this risk include stigmatisation, powerlessness, low self-esteem, lack of social/family support, and knowledge of past abuse)
    Feeling justified in behaving aggressively (factors increasing this perception include traumatic sexualisation, knowledge of past victimisation, and viewing female resistance as insincere)
    Victim's decreased ability to respond assertively and effectively to unwanted sexual advances (factors decreasing victim's ability include alcohol abuse, learned expectancy, stigmatisation, and powerlessness)

**Exosystem**
Lack of resources (related factors include low socoieconomic status, unsafe living conditions, early childbearing, single motherhood, and divorce)
Lack of alternatives (due to weak family ties or support and social isolation)

**Macrosystem**
Cultural tendency to blame victims
Good girl/bad girl construction of femininity

**Figure 1.14**   Summary of factors hypothesised to be related to sexual revictimisation (Grauerholz, 2000)

Gidycz, Hanson, and Layman (1995) indicated the need to study coping skills in understanding revictimisation experiences because maladaptive coping (eg alcohol use, having multiple sex partners) may contribute to sexual revictimisation. In a longitudinal study of college women, Himelein (1995) found that sexual victimisation in dating experiences before college was a significant predictor of revictimisation. Koss and Dinero (1989) found that, aside from CSA and sexual attitudes, alcohol use and sexual activity-indicators of maladaptive coping responses-were predictors of future victimisation.

In a national longitudinal study of 3,006 women, Kilpatrick, Acierno, Resnick, Saunders, and Best (1997) found that the biggest risks for physical or sexual revictimisation were minority status, drug use, and prior victimisation. The researchers concluded that a reciprocal relationship exists between substance use and victimisation such that criminal victimisation leads to substance use, creating risk for further victimisation, which may exacerbate substance use. Researchers have also found a link between avoidance forms of coping (eg withdrawing from others, trying to forget about the abuse) maladaptive coping (eg alcohol abuse) and PTSD

symptoms (Sinclair and Gold, 1997) which can potentially lead to revictimisation.

It is possible that avoidance coping is used to manage the intrusive symptoms associated with PTSD, leading to the negative PTSD symptoms (ie avoidance and numbing) which can result in revictimisation.

Many researchers have found a link between PTSD symptoms and revictimisation (Arata, 2000; Boney-McCoy and Finkelhor, 1995; Rowan and Foy, 1993). Furthermore, CSA victims who reported dissociating during the abuse were found to have more PTSD symptoms than women who did not report dissociating (Johnson, Pike, and Chard, 2001).

CSA severity has also been identified as a possible contributor to revictimisation, with penetration, frequent abuse, and use of force more common in revictimised women and those with more PTSD symptoms (Koverola et al., 1996). In their review of CSA sequelae, Beitchman et al. (1992) found that CSA severity and duration have been associated with more negative outcomes, including revictimisation. Moeller, Bachmann, and Moeller (1993) reported that the more types of abuse experienced in childhood (eg physical, emotional, sexual) the greater the likelihood of adult revictimisation.

Contrary to the hypothesis that CSA severity, self-blame, PTSD symptoms, and coping strategies would all predict revictimisation, the only variable found as a reliable predictor of revictimisation in this study was the use of maladaptive coping strategies. Individuals who engaged in maladaptive coping responses were almost twice as likely to be revictimised as individuals who did not use these responses. It is difficult to tease apart which specific coping responses (ie drug and alcohol use, withdrawing from people, acting out sexually or aggressively) most contributed to revictimisation. Arata (2000) found alcohol use to be a predictor of revictimisation, whereas Gidycz et al. (1995) found that the number of sex partners predicted revictimisation. It may be the case that maladaptive coping in relation to CSA may increase risk for revictimisation (eg via risky behaviours) which then increases the risk of PTSD development. Further research is needed to disentangle the specific contributors of revictimisation, which may differ in different situations or contexts (Messman-Moore and Long, 2003).

Women who have experienced revictimisation, when compared with women with a history of childhood sexual abuse but no additional sexual victimisation, described themselves as being overly nurturing, overly responsible, and having difficulty being assertive in interpersonal relationships (Classen et al., 2001). In a community sample of African American and White women, Wyatt et al. (1992) found that participants who reported childhood and adult sexual victimisation were the most likely to report high rates of unintended pregnancies. In addition, women with two or more incidents of abuse in childhood and adulthood reported frequent involvement in masturbation, cunnilingus, fellatio, vaginal and anal sex, group sex, and partner swapping. In an analysis of later data collected from the same sample, Banyard, Williams, and Siegel (2001) found that women victimised as adults and children experienced more mental health problems, including sexual dysfunction and sexual concerns, than victims of only child sexual abuse. They found no differences between those only victimised as adults and those victimised as adults and children. These results, however, could reflect the small sample of 12 women with adult-only victimisation.

The literature suggests a relationship between childhood sexual victimisation and participation in risky sexual activities, such as multiple sexual partners, not using birth control, engaging in unprotected sex, and sexual non-assertiveness. Similar psychological issues and risky behaviours have been found in women who have been sexually assaulted in adulthood. Specifically, adult victimisation has been associated with unintended pregnancies, negative attitudes about sex, decreased comfort with sexuality, sexual dysfunction, and feelings of vulnerability.

Miner et al. (2006) reported on the associations of sexual revictimisation (experiencing sexual abuse in childhood and adulthood) in a sample of 230 African American women who are low-income. Data indicate that women who experience sexual revictimisation are more at risk for emotional stress and psychological pathology than women with no history of abuse. In addition, women who are revictimised appear to be at greater risk for emotional problems than women sexually abused only as a child or sexually assaulted only as adults. Revictimisation also appears to be associated with an increased probability of engaging in prostitution, even higher than women with childhood- or adult only victimisation, who showed increased probability when compared to women never abused. Finally, women who are revictimised showed increased HIV risk, in that they were four times less likely than other women to consistently use condoms, but no more likely to be in monogamous relationships or less likely to have multiple partners.

Research posits that negative sequelae of victimisation may operate in two ways to place women at risk of revictimisation (Messman-Moore and Long, 2002). First, trauma consequences may increase a survivor's contact with potential perpetrators. For example, women may turn to substances to manage PTSD symptoms following rape and, in turn, substance abuse and substance dependency may lead these women into situations where they are exposed to male perpetrators (Logan et al., 2002). Second, perpetrators may be able to identify and act upon the victim-survivors' vulnerabilities (Messman-Moore and Long, 2002; Noll, 2005). For example, one robust correlate of subsequent victimisation is revictimised women's reduced capacities for threat detection (Breitenbecher, 2001). It is possible that perpetrators may be able to assess such vulnerabilities and thus tend to target these women. Researchers have also asserted that post-assault negative sequelae likely co-occur and operate collectively to increase women's vulnerability to revictimisation (Messman-Moore and Long, 2002).

### Poly-victimisation

Finkelhor et al. (2007) coined this term to refer to multiple victimisation in explaining trauma symptomatology. They found that children experiencing four or more different types of victimisation in a single year comprised 22 per cent of their sample. Poly-victimisation was highly predictive of trauma symptoms, and when taken into account, greatly reduced or eliminated the association between individual victimisations (eg sexual abuse) and symptomatology. Poly-victims were also more symptomatic than children with only repeated episodes of the same kind of victimisation.

### Post-traumatic growth

It is important that we acknowledge that childhood abuse does not necessarily lead to a damaged life and that for some can lead to positive change and growth.

Post-traumatic growth is an emerging area of research concerned with the positive psychological changes that can follow the experience of traumatic events. According to O'Leary and Ickovics (1995) there are three possible outcomes: survival, recovery or thriving. Those who recover return to their previous level of functioning. Those who thrive, however, move beyond the original level of psychosocial functioning, flourish, and grow as a result of their experience. Post-traumatic growth experiences are therefore not just about learning to live with the effects of trauma, or about bouncing back from trauma, but are likened instead to a springboard to further individual development, thriving and personal growth (Tedeschi et al., 1998). Evidence shows that 40–70 per cent of people who experience a traumatic event later report some form of benefit from their experience (Calhoun and Tedeschi, 1999). Three main areas of growth have been identified: changes in perception of self, changes in relationships with others, and changes in philosophy of life. What remains uncertain is why some individuals grow in the aftermath of trauma whilst others do not. However we need to be cautious as the fact that childhood abuse does not necessarily lead to a damaged life and can lead to positive change is

not true for everyone. We need to guard against inadvertently implying that the person in some way has failed in not making more of their experiences or in implying that there should be something inherently positive about traumatic experiences.

Post traumatic growth experiences have been reported following sexual abuse (McMillen et al., 1995). Woodward and Joseph (2003) examined positive change processes and post-traumatic growth in people who have experienced childhood abuse. They identified three domains: inner drives, vehicles of change and psychological changes. These domains represent a distinction between those factors internal to the person, psychological processes triggered by person-environment interactions; and descriptions of psychological changes.

### Inner drive toward growth

Several of the respondents noted how they had a belief, or faith in themselves, that somehow they would survive their experience. Some referred to some form of 'inner drive', 'will to live', 'passion for living', 'fighting spirit' or 'determination' which they felt was instrumental in enabling them to survive, live, seek meaning in their experiences, and ultimately heal.

### Vehicles of change

This domain is concerned with experiences of awakening, validating, nurturing, liberating and mastering nature identified by respondents as being important in terms of bringing about or influencing areas of positive change and personal growth. Also included were experiences which bring about a sense of belonging or connection to others, including those of a religious or spiritual nature. In reflecting upon their experiences, over half of the respondents mentioned having come to a point in their lives when they realised that they had to make a decision over whether or not to take responsibility or control over the direction of their own lives. They also described how change had occurred through experiencing genuine acceptance from others, where they felt that they could be themselves. They also reported being able to give self-nurturance and care in terms of recognising, seeking, and meeting their own needs (including safety needs) as well as being more receptive to receiving nurture and care from others. Many reported about receiving love and care from significant others. Another important vehicle of change was having a sense of liberation and freedom. Feeling a sense of freedom can come from several different sources, including perceiving a sense of control; telling a secret; forgiveness; and gaining insight and awareness. Feeling free can also be exhibited in terms of behaviours, eg from walking hunched over to putting one's shoulders back and lifting one's head high. Some spoke of the liberating experience experienced through gaining a sense of accomplishment and achievement. The idea here is that life experiences of almost any kind can come to be perceived as a vehicle of change – and this may stem from a variety of events which include the death of a significant other, going to counselling, reading something, buying a house, kind words from a teacher or the love of children. Any life experience at all can serve as a vehicle for change. What appears to be important is not the event itself, but rather what the person brings to their experiences, and how they appraise events. It also highlights the importance of identifying extra-therapeutic factors in facilitating and sustaining change.

## Psychological changes

This domain relates to increased insight and understanding, recognition of changes, and the processing of experiences brought about by vehicles of change. Salient themes relate about being in touch with self, gaining new perspectives on life and developing an increased sense of the importance of relationships. Changes in self perception relates to increased self-awareness and includes being able to feel, express and process feelings, the recognition of inner strengths as well as recognition of further changes needed in their lives.

## Conclusion

This chapter has attempted to draw on the available literature to inform professional understanding and decision-making. It will hopefully act as a useful starting point against which to judge many of the sexual abuses that will be addressed in the text. Given the volume of materials that exist the reader will inevitably be signposted to the following references to pursue the detail that could not be covered in a chapter of this nature.

## References

Alexander, P.C. (1992) Application of Attachment Theory to the Study of Sexual Abuse. *Journal of Consulting and Clinical Psychology*, 60: 185–95.

Anderson, K.M. (1997) Uncovering Survival Abilities in Children who have been Sexually Abused. *Families in Society*, November–December, 592–9.

Arata, C.M. (2000) From Child Victim to Adult Victim: A Model for Predicting Sexual Revictimisation. *Child Maltreatment*, 5: 1, 28.

Arata, C.M. (1999) Cope With Rape: The Roles of Prior Sexual Abuse and Attributions of Blame. *Journal of Interpersonal Violence*, 14: 1, 62–78.

Arata, C.M. (2002) Child Sexual Abuse and Sexual Revictimisation. *Clinical Psychology: Science and Practice*, 9: 2, 135–64.

Bagley, C. and Ramsay, R. (1985) Sexual Abuse in Childhood: Psychosocial Outcomes and Implications for Social Work Practice. *Journal of Social Work and Human Sexuality*, 4: 33–47.

Banyard, V.L. and Williams, L.M. (2007) Women's Voice on Recovery: A Multi-Method Study of the Complexity of Recovery from Child Sexual Abuse. *Child Abuse and Neglect*, 31: 275–90.

Banyard, V.L., Williams, L.M. and Siegel, J.A. (2001) The Long-Term Mental Health Consequences of Child Sexual Abuse: An Exploratory Study of the Impact of Multiple Traumas in a Sample of Women. *Journal of Traumatic Stress*, 14, 697–715.

Barbaree, H., Hudson, S.M. and Seto, M.C. (1993) Sexual Assault in Society: The Role of the Juvenile Offender. In Barbaree, H.E. et al. (Eds.) op cit, 1–24.

Barringer, C.E. (1992) The Survivor's Voice: Breaking the Incest Taboo. *National Women's Studies Association Journal*, 4: 1, 4–22.

Bass, E. and Davis, L. (1992) *The Courage to Heal: A Guide for Women Survivors of Child Sexual Abuse*. New York: Harper Collins.

Beitchman, J.H. et al. (1991) A Review of the Short-Term Effects of Child Sexual Abuse. *Child Abuse and Neglect*, 15, 537–56.

Beitchman, J.H. et al. (1992) A Review of the Long-Term Effects of Child Sexual Abuse. *Child Abuse and Neglect*, 16, 101–18.

Berliner, L. (2002) The Traumatic Impact of Abuse Experiences: Treatment Issues. In Browne, K.D. et al. (Eds.) *Early Prediction and Prevention of Child Abuse: A Handbook*. Chichester: John Wiley.

Berliner, L. and Conte, J. (1990) The Process of Victimisation: The Victim's Perspective. *Child Abuse and Neglect*, 14: 29–40.

Berliner, L. and Conte, J. (1995) The Effects of Disclosure and Intervention on Sexually Abused Children. *Child Abuse and Neglect*, 19: 3, 371384.

Bolton, F.G., Morris, L.A. and Maceachron, A.E. (1989) *Males at Risk: The Other Side of Child Sexual Abuse.* Newbury Park, CA: Sage.

Boney-McCoy, S. and Finkelhor, D. (1995) Prior Victimisation: A Risk Factor for Child Sexual Abuse and for PTSD-Related Symptomatology among Sexually Abused Youth. *Child Abuse and Neglect*, 19: 12, 1401–21.

Bourdon, L.S. and Cook, A.S. (1993) Losses Associated with Sexual Abuse. *Journal of Child Sexual Abuse.* 2: 69–82.

Boushel, M. (1994) The Protective Environment of Children: Towards a Framework for Anti-oppressive, Cross-cultural and Cross-national Understanding. *British Journal of Social Work*, 24: 173–90.

Bowlby, J. (1979) *The Making and Breaking of Affectionate Bonds.* London: Tavistock.

Breer, W. (1987) *The Adolescent Molester.* Springfield, IL: Charles C Thomas.

Breitenbecher, K.H. (2001) Sexual Revictimisation among Women: A Review of the Literature Focusing on Empirical Investigations. *Aggression and Violent Behavior*, 6, 415–32.

Briere, J. (1992) *Child Abuse Trauma: Theory and Treatment of the Lasting Effects.* Newbury Park, CA: Sage.

Briere, J. and Runtz, M. (1991) Childhood Sexual Abuse: Long-Term Sequelae and Implications for Psychological Assessment. *Journal of Interpersonal Violence*, 8: 312–30.

Briere, J. (1996) Psychological Assessment of Child Abuse Effects in Adults. In Wilson, J.P. and Keane, T.M. (Eds.) *Assessing Psychological Trauma and PTSD: A Handbook for Practitioners* (pp. 43–68). NY: Guilford.

Browne, A. and Finkelhor, D. (1986) Impact of Sexual Abuse: A Review of the Research. *Psychological Bulletin*, 99: 66–77.

Buchanan, A. (1999) *What Works for Troubled Children. Family Support for Children with Emotional and Behavioural Problems.* London: Barnardo's.

Burgess, A.W., Holmstrom, L.l. and McCausland, M.P. (1977) Child Sexual Assault by a Family Member: Decisions Following Disclosure. *Victimology*, 11: 2, 236–50.

Burgess, A.W., Holmstrom, L.P. and McCausland, M.P. (1978) Divided Loyalty in Incest Cases. In Burgess, A.W., Groth, A.N., Holmstrom, L.L. and Sgroi, S.M. (Eds.) (1978) *Sexual Assault of Children and Adolescents* (pp. 115–26). Lexington, Mass: Lexington Books.

Calder, M.C. (2003) Child Sexual Abuse and Domestic Violence: Parallel Considerations to Inform Professional Responses. *Seen and Heard*, 12: 3, 14–24.

Calhoun, L.G. and Tedeschi, R.G. (1999) *Facilitating Post-Traumatic Growth: A Clinician's Guide.* London: Erlbaum.

Carlson, E.B. and Dalenberg, C.J. (2000) A Conceptual Framework for the Impact of Traumatic Experiences. *Trauma, Violence and Abuse*, 1: 4–28.

Chu, J. A. (1992) The Revictimisation of Adult Women with Histories of Childhood Abuse. *Journal of Psychotherapy Practice and Research*, 1, 259–69.

Classen, C.C., Palesh, O.G. and Aggarwal, R. (2005) Sexual Re-Victimisation: A Review of the Empirical Literature. *Trauma, Violence and Abuse*, 6: 2, 103–29.

Classen, C. et al. (2001) Interpersonal Problems and Their Relationship to Sexual Revictimisation among Women Sexually Abused in Childhood. *Journal of Interpersonal Violence*, 16, 495–509.

Cohen, J.A. and Mannarino, A. (1996) Factors that Mediate Treatment Outcome of Sexually Abused Pre-School Children. *Journal of The American Academy of Adolescent Psychiatry*, 34: 1, 1402–10.

Conrad, M. and Hammen, C. (1993) Protective and Resource Factors in High and Low-Risk Children. *Development and Psychopathology*, 5: 593–607.

Conte, J. and Schuerman, J. (1987) Factors Associated with an Increased Impact of Child Sexual Abuse. *Child Abuse and Neglect*, 11: 201–11.

Conte, J. and Schuerman, J. (1987b) The Effects of Sexual Abuse on Children: A Multidimensional View. *Journal of Interpersonal Violence*, 2: 380–90.

Courtois, C.A. (1988) *Healing the Incest Wound: Adult Survivors in Therapy.* NY: WW Norton.

Crewdson, J. (1988) *By Silence Betrayed: Sexual Abuse of Children in America.* Boston, MA: Little, Brown.

Croll, L. (1991) *Caring For Children and Young People who have been Sexually Abused.* Basildon: Breakthrough For Youth.

Daigneault, I., Tourigny, M. and Cyr, M. (2004) Description of Trauma and Resilience in Sexually Abused Adolescents: An Integrated Assessment. *Journal of Trauma Practice*, 3: 2, 23–47.

Davenport, C., Browne, K. and Palmer, R. (1994) Opinions on the Traumatising Effects of Child Sexual Abuse: Evidence for Consensus. *Child Abuse and Neglect*, 18: 9, 725–38.

Davies, D. (1999) *Child Development: A Practitioner's Guide*. NY: Guilford Press.

Deblinger, E. et al. (1989) Post-Traumatic Stress in Sexually Abused, Physically Abused and Non-Abused Children. *Child Abuse and Neglect*, 13: 403–8.

Deblinger, E., Steer, R. and Lippmann, J. (1999) Maternal Factors Associated with Sexually Abused Children's Psychosocial Adjustment. *Child Maltreatment*, 4: 1, 13–20.

Desai, S. et al. (2002) Childhood Victimisation and Subsequent Adult Revictimisation Assessed in a Nationally Representative Sample of Women and Men. *Violence and Victims*, 17: 6, 639–53.

Diehl, A.S. and Prout, M.F. (2002) The Effects of Post-traumatic Stress Disorder and Child Sexual Abuse on Self-efficacy Development. *American Journal of Orthopsychiatry*, 72: 2, 262–65.

DiLillo, D. and Damashek, A. (2003). Parenting Characteristics of Women Reporting a History of Childhood Sexual Abuse. *Child Maltreatment*, 8: 319–33.

Dinsmore, C. (1991) *From Surviving to Thriving: Incest, Feminism and Recovery*. Albany, NY: State University of New York Press.

Downs, W.R. (1993) Developmental Considerations for the Effects of Childhood Sexual Abuse. *Journal of Interpersonal Violence*, 8: 331–45.

Doyle, C. (1997) Terror and The Stockholm Syndrome: The Relevance for Abused Children. In Bates, J., Pugh, R. and Thompson, N. (Eds.) *Protecting Children: Challenges and Change*. Aldershot: Arena.

Driver, E. (1988) *Through the Looking Glass: Child Sexual Abuse after Cleveland: Alternative Strategies*. London: Family Rights Group.

Dufour, M.H., Nadeau, L. and Bertrand, K. (2000) Factors in the Resilience of Victims of Sexual Abuse: An Update. *Child Abuse and Neglect*, 24: 781–97.

Egeland, B., Carlson, E. and Sroufe, A. (1993) Resilience as Process. *Development and Psychopathology*, 5: 517–28.

Elliott, C.E. and Butler, L. (1994) The Stop and Think Group: Changing Sexually Aggressive Behaviour in Young Children. *Journal of Sexual Aggression*, 1: 1, 15–28.

Elliott, D.M. and Briere, J. (1994) Forensic Sexual Abuse Evaluations of Older Children: Disclosures and Symptomatology. *Behavioural Sciences and The Law*, 12: 261–77.

Engel, B. (1994) *Families in Recovery: Working Together to Heal the Damage of Child Sexual Abuse Cases*. Los Angeles, CA: Lowell House.

Enos, W.F., Conrath, T.B. and Byer, J.C. (1986) Forensic Evaluation of the Sexually Abused Child. *Paediatrics*, 78: 385–98.

Etherington, K. (1995) *Adult Male Survivors of Childhood Sexual Abuse*. London: Pitman Publishing.

Everson, M., Hunter, W., Runyon, D., Edelsohn, G. and Coulter, M. (1989) Maternal Support following Disclosure of Incest. *American Journal of Orthopsychiatry*, 59, 197–207.

Feiring, F., Taska, L.S. and Lewis, M. (1998) Social Support and Children's and Adolescent's Adaptation to Sexual Abuse. *Journal of Interpersonal Violence*, 13: 2, 240–60.

Figley, C.R. (1986) *Trauma and Its Wake: Volume 2: Traumatic Stress Theory, Research and Intervention*. NY: Brunner/Mazel.

Filipas, H.H. and Ullman, S.E. (2006) Child Sexual Abuse, Coping Responses, Self-Blame, Posttraumatic Stress Disorder and Adult Sexual Revictimisation. *Journal of Interpersonal Violence*, 21: 5, 652–72

Finkelhor, D. (1979) *Sexually Victimised Children*. NY: The Free Press.

Finkelhor, D. (1984) *Child Sexual Abuse: New Theory and Research*. NY: The Free Press.

Finkelhor, D. (1988) The Trauma of Child Sexual Abuse: Two Models. In Wyatt, G.E. and Powell, G.J. (Eds.) *Lasting Effects of Child Sexual Abuse*. Thousand Oaks, CA: Sage.

Finkelhor, D. (1990) Early and Long-Term Effects of Child Sexual Abuse: An Update. *Professional Psychology: Research and Practice*, 21: 325–30.

Finkelhor, D. (1995) The Victimisation of Children: A Developmental Perspective. *American Journal of Orthopsychiatry*, 65: 2, 177–93.

Finkelhor, D. (1998) The Responses of Pre-adolescents and Adolescents in a National Victimization Survey. *Journal of Interpersonal Violence*, 13: 3, 362–82.

Finkelhor, D. and Baron, L. (1986) Risk Factors for Child Sexual Abuse. *Journal of Interpersonal Violence*, 1: 43–71.

Finkelhor, D. and Browne, A. (1985) The Traumatic Impact of Child Sexual Abuse: A Conceptualisation. *American Journal of Orthopsychiatry*, 55: 4, 530–41.

Finkelhor, D. and Browne, A. (1986) Initial and Long-Term Effects: A Conceptual Framework. In Finkelhor, D. et al. (Eds.) *A Sourcebook on Child Sexual Abuse*. Beverly Hills: Sage.

Finkelhor, D. and Browne, A. (1988) The Impact of Child Sexual Abuse: A Review of the Research. *Psychological Bulletin*, 99: 1, 66–77.

Finkelhor, D. et al. (1990) Sexual Abuse in a National Survey of Adult Men and Women: Prevalence, Characteristics and Risk Factors. *Child Abuse and Neglect*, 14: 19–28.

Finkelhor, D., Ormrod, R.K. and Turner, H.A. (2007) Poly-Victimisation: A Neglected Component in Child Victimisation. *Child Abuse and Neglect*, 31: 7–26

Freeman, K.A. and Morris, T.L. (2001) A Review of Conceptual Models Explaining the Effects of Child Sexual Abuse. *Aggression and Violent Behaviour*, 6: 357–73.

Friedrich, W.N., Jaworski, T.M., Huxsahl, J.E. and Bengston, B.S. (1987) Dissociative and Sexual Behaviours in Children and Adolescents with Sexual Abuse and Psychiatric Histories. *Journal of Interpersonal Violence*, 12: 2, 155–71.

Friedrich, W.N. (1988) Behaviour Problems in Sexually Abused Children: An Adaptational Approach. In Wyatt, G.E. and Powell, G.J. (Eds.) *Lasting Effects of Child Sexual Abuse*. Newbury Park, CA: Sage.

Friedrich, W.N. et al. (1992) Psychotherapy Outcome in Sexually Abused Young Children: An Agency Study. *Journal of Interpersonal Violence*, 7: 3, 396–409.

Fromuth, M.E. (1986) The Relationship of Childhood Sexual Abuse with Later Psychological and Sexual Adjustment in a Sample of College Women. *Child Abuse and Neglect*, 10: 5–15.

Garmezy, N. (1985) Stress-resistant Children: The Search for Protective Factors. In Stevenson, J.E. (Ed.) *Recent Research in Developmental Psychopathology* (pp. 213–33). Oxford: Pergamon Press.

Garmezy, N. (1991) Resilience in Children's Adaptation to Negative Life Events and Stressed Environments. *Pediatric Annals*, 20: 459–66.

Garmezy, N. (1993) Vulnerability and Resilience. In Funder, D.C. et al. (Eds.) *Studying Lives Through Time: Approaches to Personality and Development*. Washington, DC: American Psychological Association.

Gibson, M. (2006) *Order From Chaos: Responding to Traumatic Events*. 3rd edn Bristol: The Policy Press.

Gidycz, C.A., Hanson, K. and Layman, M.J. (1995) A Prospective Analysis of the Relationships among Sexual Assault Experiences: An Extension of Previous Findings. *Psychology of Women Quarterly*, 19, 5–29.

Gilgun, J.F. (1999) Mapping Resilience as Process among Adults with Childhood Adversities. In McCubbin, H.I. et al. (Eds.) *The Dynamics of Resilient Families*. Thousand Oaks, CA: Sage.

Grauerholz, L. (2000) An Ecological Approach to Understanding Sexual Revictimisation: Linking Personal, Interpersonal and Sociocultural Factors and Processes. *Child Maltreatment*, 5: 1, 5–17.

Green, B.L., Wilson, J.P. and Lindy, J.D. (1985) Conceptualising Post Traumatic Stress Disorder: A Psychosocial Framework. In Figley, C.R. (Ed.) *Trauma and Its Wake*. NY: Brunner/Mazel.

Groth, A.N. (1978) *Men Who Rape: The Psychology of the Offender*. NY: Plenum.

Hagan, J. (1990) The Structuration of Gender and Deviance: A Power-Control Theory of Vulnerability to Crime and the Search for Deviant Role Exits. *Canadian Review of Sociology and Anthropology*, 27: 2 137–56.

Haller, O.L. and Alter-Reid, K. (1986) Incest: Comparison of Two Treatment Samples. *American Journal of Psychotherapy*, 40: 4, 554–63.

Herman, J. (1981) *Father-Daughter Incest*. Cambridge, MA: Harvard University Press.

Herman, J. (1992) *Trauma and Recovery: The Aftermath of Violence – From Domestic Violence to Political Terror*. NY: Basic Books.

Himelein, M.J. (1995) Risk Factors for Sexual Victimisation in Dating: A Longitudinal Study of College Women. *Psychology of Women Quarterly*, 19, 31–48.

Hindman, J. (1989) *Just Before Dawn: From the Shadows of Tradition to New Reflections in Trauma Assessment and Treatment of Sexual Victimisation*. Ontario, OR: Alexandria Associates

Holguin, G. and Hansen, D.J. (2003) The Sexually Abused Child: Potential Mechanisms of Adverse Influences of such a Label. *Aggression and Violent Behavior*, 8: 645–70.

Hopkins, J. and Thompson, E. (1984) Loss and Mourning in Victims of Rape and Sexual Assault. In Hopkins, J. (Ed.) *Perspectives on Rape and Sexual Assault*. London: Harper and Row.

Hopper, E. (1991) Encapsulation as a Defence against the Fear of Annihilation. *International Journal of Psychoanalysis*, 72: 602–24.

Horowitz, M.J. (1986) *Stress Response Syndromes.* (2nd ed.) New York: Jason Aronson.

Horowitz, M.J. (1990) Post Traumatic Stress Disorder: Psychotherapy. In Bellack, A.S. and Hersen, M. (Eds.) *A Handbook of Comparative Treatments for Adult Disorder.* Chichester: John Wiley.

James, B. (1990) *Treating Traumatised Children: New Insights and Creative Interventions.* Lexington, Mass: Lexington Books.

Janoff-Bulman, R. (1979) Assumptive Worlds and the Stress of Traumatic Events. *Social Cognition*, 7: 113–136.

Janoff-Bulman, R. (1992) *Shattered Assumptions: Towards a New Psychology of Trauma.* NY: Free Press.

Johnson, D.M., Pike, J.L. and Chard, K.M. (2001) Factors Predicting PTSD, Depression and Dissociative Severity in Female Treatment-Seeking Childhood Sexual Abuse Survivors. *Child Abuse and Neglect*, 25, 179–98.

Jones, D.P. and Ramchandani, P. (1999) *Child Sexual Abuse: Informing Practice from Research.* Oxford: Radcliffe Medical Press.

Kelley, S.J. (1990) Parental Stress Response to Sexual Abuse and Ritualistic Abuse of Children in Day Care Centres. *Nursing Research*, 39: 25–9.

Kelly, R.J. and Gonzalez, L.S. (1990) *Psychological Symptoms Reported by Sexually Abused Men.* Paper presented to the 3rd National Conference on The Male Survivor. Tucson, Arizona, Nov.

Kendall-Tackett, K.A., Williams, L.M. and Finkelhor, D. (1993) Impact of Sexual Abuse on Children: A Review and Synthesis of Recent Empirical Studies. *Psychological Bulletin*, 113: 1, 164–80.

Kilpatrick, D.G. et al. (1997) A 2-Year Longitudinal Analysis of the Relationships between Violent Assault and Substance Use in Women. *Journal of Consulting and Clinical Psychology*, 65: 5, 834–47.

Korbin, J.E. (1991) Cross-Cultural Perspectives and Research Directions in the 21st Century. *Child Abuse and Neglect*, 15: 67–77.

Korbin, J.E. (Ed.) (1981) *Child Abuse and Neglect: Cross-Cultural Perspectives.* California: University of California Press.

Koss, M.P. and Dinero, T.E. (1989) Discriminant Analysis of Risk Factors for Sexual Victimisation among a Sample of College Women. *Journal of Consulting and Clinical Psychology*, 57, 242–50.

Koverola, C. et al. (1996) Family Functioning as Predictors of Distress in Revictimised Sexual Abuse Survivors. *Journal of Interpersonal Violence*, 11: 2, 263–80.

Lazarus, R.S. and Folkman, S. (1984) *Stress, Appraisal and Coping.* NY: Springer.

Logan, T.K. et al. (2002) Victimisation and Substance Abuse among Women: Contributing Factors, Interventions and Implications. *Review of General Psychology*, 6: 4, 325–97.

Luthar, S. and Zelaro, L. (2003) Research on Resilience: An Integrative Review. In Luthar, S.S. (Ed.) *Resilience and Vulnerability: Adaptation in the Context of Childhood Adversities.* NY: Cambridge University Press.

Luthar, S., Cicchetti, D. and Becker, B. (2000) The Construct of Resilience: A Critical Evaluation and Guidelines for Future Work. *Child Development*, 71: 3, 543–62.

Lynskey, M,T. and Fergusson, D.M. (1997) Factors Protecting against the Development of Adjustment Difficulties in Young Adults Exposed to Childhood Sexual Abuse. *Child Abuse and Neglect*, 21: 1, 1177–90.

Macy, R.J. (2007) A Coping Theory Framework toward Preventing Sexual Revictimisation. *Aggression and Violent Behaviour*, 12: 177–92.

Marx, S.P. (1996) Victim Recantation in Child Sexual Abuse Cases: The Prosecutor's Role in Prevention. *Child Welfare*, 75: 3, 219–33.

Masten, A.S. and Coatsworth, D. (1998) The Development of Competence in Favourable and Unfavourable Environments: Lessons from Research on Successful Children. *American Psychologist*, 53: 2, 205–20.

Masten, A.S., Best, K.M. and Garmezy, N. (1990) Resilience and Development: Contributions from the Study of Children who Overcome Adversity. *Development and Psychopathology*, 2: 425–44.

Mcleer, S.V. et al. (1988) Post-Traumatic Stress Disorder in Sexually Abused Children. *Journal of The American Academy of Child and Adolescent Psychiatry*, 27: 650–4.

McMillen, C., Zuravin, S. and Rideout, G. (1995) Perceived Benefits from Child Sexual Abuse. *Journal of Consulting and Clinical Psychology*, 63: 1037–43.

Mendel, M.P. (1995) *The Male Survivor: The Impact of Sexual Abuse.* Thousand Oaks, CA: Sage.

Merrill, L. et al. (2001) Predicting the Impact of Child Sexual Abuse on Women: The Role of Abuse Severity, Parental Support and Coping Strategies. *Journal of Consulting and Clinical Psychology*, ??

Messman, T.L. and Long, P.J. (1996) Child Sexual Abuse and Its Relationship to Revictimisation in Adult Women: A Review. *Clinical Psychology Review*, 16: 5, 397–420.

Messman-Moore, T.L. and Long, P.J. (2003) The Role of Childhood Sexual Abuse Sequelae in Sexual Revictimization: An Empirical Review and Theoretical Reformulation. *Clinical Psychology Review*, 23: 4, 537–71.

Miner, M., Klotz Flitter, J.M. and Robinson, B.E. (2006) Association of Sexual Revictimisation with Sexuality and Psychological Function. *Journal of Interpersonal Violence*, 21: 4, 503–24.

Moeller, T.P., Bachmann, G.A. and Moeller, J.R. (1993) The Combined Effects of Physical, Sexual and Emotional Abuse During Childhood: Long-Term Health Consequences for Women. *Child Abuse and Neglect*, 17, 623–40.

Mowrer, O.H. (1947) On the Dual Nature of Learning: A Reinterpretation of Conditioning and Problem Solving. *Howard Educational Review*, 17: 102–48.

Murthi, M. and Espelage, D.L. (2005) Childhood Sexual Abuse, Social Support and Psychological Outcomes: A Loss Framework. *Child Abuse and Neglect*, 29: 1215–31.

Myers, J.E. (1997) *A Mothers Nightmare – Incest. A Practical Guide for Parents and Professionals.* Thousand Oaks, CA: Sage.

Nash, M. (2006) *Public Protection and the Criminal Justice Process.* Oxford: Oxford University Press.

Nelson-Gardell, D. (2001) The Voices of Victims: Surviving Child Sexual Abuse. *Child and Adolescent Social Work Journal*, 18: 6, 401–16.

Noll, J. (2005) Does Childhood Sexual Abuse Set in Motion a Cycle of Violence against Women? *Journal of Interpersonal Violence*, 20: 4, 455–62.

O'Dougherty Wright, M., Fopma-Loy, J. and Fischer, S. (2005) Multidimensional Assessment of Resilience in Mothers who are Child Sexual Abuse Survivors. *Child Abuse and Neglect*, 29: 1173–93.

O'Leary, V,E. and Ickovics, J.R. (1995) Resilience and Thriving in Response to Challenge. Women's Health: Research on Gender. *Behaviour and Policy*, 1: 121–5.

Oates, R.K. et al. (1994) Stability and Change in Outcomes for Sexually Abused Children. *Journal of The American Academy of Child and Adolescent Psychiatry*, 33: 7, 945–53.

Palmer, N. (1997) Resilience in Adult Children of Alcoholics: A Non-Pathological Approach to Social Work Practice. *Health and Social Work*, 22: 201–9.

Palmer, N. (1999) Fostering Resiliency in Children: Lessons Learned in Transcending Adversity. *Social Thought*, 19: 69.

Parkes, C.M. (1996) *Bereavement: Studies of Grief in Adult Life.* London: Tavistock/Routledge.

Petrunik, M. (2003) The Hare and the Tortoise: Dangerousness and Sex Offender Policy in the US and Canada. *Canadian Journal of Criminology and Criminal Justice*, 45, 1.

Pierce, R. and Pierce, L. (1985) The Sexually Abused Child: A Comparison of Male and Female Victims. *Child Abuse and Neglect*, 9: 191–9.

Pine, F. (1990) *Drive, Ego, Object and Self: A Synthesis for Clinical Work.* NY: Basic Books.

Porter, F.S. (1982) A Conceptual Framework for Child Sexual Abuse. In Sgroi, S.M. (Ed.) *Handbook of Clinical Intervention in Child Sexual Abuse.* Lexington, MA: Lexington Books.

Print, B. and Dey, C. (1992) Empowering Mothers of Sexually Abused Children: A Positive Framework. In Bannister, A. (Ed.) *From Hearing to Healing: Working with the Aftermath of Child Sexual Abuse.* London: Longman.

Putnam, F.W. and Trickett, P.K. (1993) Child Sexual Abuse: A Model of Chronic Trauma. *Psychiatry*, 56: 82–95.

Radke-Yarrow, M. and Brown, E. (1993) Resilience and Vulnerability in Children of Multiple-Risk Families. *Development and Psychopathology*, 5: 581–92.

Rando, T.A. (1993) *Treatment of Complicated Mourning.* Champaign, IL: Research Press.

Raphael, B. (1986) *When Disaster Strikes: Handbook for Caring Professions.* London: Hutchinson.

Reiser, M. (1991) Recantation in Child Sexual Abuse Cases. *Child Welfare*, 70: 611–21.

Rich, C.L. et al. (2004) Child Sexual Abuse and Adult Sexual Revictimisation. In Koenig, L.J. et al. (Eds.) *From Child Sexual Abuse to Adult Sexual Risk Trauma, Revictimisation and Intervention.* Washington DC: APA.

Roodman, A.A. and Clum, G.A. (2001) Revictimisation Rates and Method Variance: A Meta-Analysis. *Clinical Psychology Review*, 21: 2, 183–204.

Rowan, A.B. and Foy, D.W. (1993) Post-Traumatic Stress Disorder in Child Sexual Abuse Survivors: A Literature Review. *Journal of Traumatic Stress*, 6: 1, 3–20.

Ruggiero, K.J., Mcleers, V. and Dixon, F.J. (2000) Sexual Abuse Characteristics Associated with Survivor Psychopathology. *Child Abuse and Neglect*, 24: 951–64.

Russell, D.E. (1986) *The Secret Trauma: Incest in the Lives of Girls and Women*. NY: Basic Books.

Rutter, M. (1979) Protective Factors in Children's Responses to Stress and Disadvantage. In Kent, M.W. and Rolf, J.E. (Eds.) *Primary Prevention of Psychopathology: Volume 3. Social Competence in Children*. Hanover, NH: University Press in New England.

Rutter, M. (1983) Stress, Coping and Development: Some Issues and Some Questions. In Garmezy, N. and Rutter, M. (Eds.) *Stress, Coping and Development*. NY: Mcgraw-Hill.

Rutter, M. (1985) Resilience in the Face of Adversity. *British Journal of Psychiatry*, 147: 598–611.

Rutter, M. (1987) Psychosocial Resilience and Protective Mechanisms. *American Journal of Orthopsychiatry*, 57: 316–31.

Rutter, M. (1990) Psychosocial Resilience and Protective Mechanisms. In Rolf, A. et al. (Eds.) *Risk and Protective Factors in the Development of Psychopathology*. NY: Cambridge University Press.

Rutter, M. (1996) Stress Research: Accomplishments and Tasks Ahead. In Haggerty, R.J. at al. (Eds.) *Stress, Risk and Resilience in Children and Adolescents*. Cambridge: Cambridge University Press.

Rutter, M. (1999) Resilience Concepts and Findings: Implications for Family Therapy. *Journal of Family Therapy*, 21: 119–160.

Ryan, G. et al. (1999) *Web of Meaning: A Developmental-Contextual Approach in Sexual Abuse Treatment*. Brandon, VT: Safer Society Press.

Ryan, G.D. (1991) Juvenile Sex Offenders: Defining the Population. In Ryan, G.D. and Lane, S.L. (Eds.) *Juvenile Sex Offenders: Causes, Consequences and Corrections*. Lexington, Mass: Lexington Books, 3–8.

Ryan, G.D. (1994) Presentation to the 10th National Training Conference of The National Adolescent Perpetrator Network. Denver, Colorado, February 1994.

Sahd, D. (1980) Psychological Assessment of Sexually Abusing Families and Treatment Implications. In Holder, W. (Ed.) *Sexual Abuse of Children: Implications for Treatment*. Englewood, CO: American Humane Association.

Santry, S. and Mccarthy, G. (1999) Attachment and Intimacy in Young People who Sexually Abuse. In Calder, M.C. (Ed.) *Working with Young People who Sexually Abuse: New Pieces of the Jigsaw Puzzle*. Lyme Regis: Russell House Publishing.

Sauzier, M. (1989) Disclosure of Sexual Abuse. *Psychiatric Clinics of North America*, 12: 445–71.

Sgroi, S.M. (Ed) (1982) *Handbook of Clinical Intervention in Child Sexual Abuse*. Lexington, MA: Lexington Books.

Sgroi, S.M., Blick, L.C. and Porter, F.S. (1982) A Conceptual Framework for Child Sexual Abuse. In Sgroi, S.M. (Ed.) *Handbook of Clinical Intervention in Child Sexual Abuse*. Lexington, MA: Lexington Books.

Shapiro, F. (1992) Eye Movement Desensitization and Reprocessing (EMDR). *Journal of Traumatic Stress*, 6: 417–21.

Simon-Roper, L. (1996) Victim's Response Cycle: A Model for Understanding the Incestuous Victim-Offender Relationship. *Journal of Child Sexual Abuse*, 5: 2, 59–79.

Sinclair, B.B. and Gold, S.R. (1997) The Psychological Impact of Withholding Disclosure of Child Sexual Abuse. *Violence and Victims*, 12, 125–33.

Sorensen, T. and Snow, B. (1991) How Children Tell: The Process of Disclosure in Child Sexual Abuse. *Child Welfare*, 70: 3–15.

Spaccarelli, S. (1994) Stress, Appraisal and Coping in Child Sexual Abuse: A Theoretical and Empirical Review. *Psychological Bulletin*, 116: 340–62.

Staudinger, U.M., Marsiske, M. and Baltes, P.B. (1993) Resilience and Levels of Reserve Capacity in Later Adulthood. *Development and Psychopathology*, 5: 541–66.

Stein, H. et al. (2000) Lives Through Time: An Ideographic Approach to the Study of Resilience. *Bulletin of The Menninger Clinic*, 64: 281–305.

Summit, R.C. (1983) The Child Sexual Abuse Accommodation Syndrome. *Child Abuse and Neglect*, 7: 177–93.

Tedeschi, R., Park, C.L. and Calhoun, L.G. (1998) Post-Traumatic Growth: Conceptual Issues. In Tedeschi, R., Park, C.L. and Calhoun, L.G. (Eds.) *Post-Traumatic Growth: Positive Changes in the Aftermath of Crisis*. London: Erlbaum.

Terr, L. (1990) *Too Scared to Cry: Psychic Trauma in Childhood*. NY: Harper and Row.

Testa, M. et al. (1992) The Moderating Impact of Social Support following Childhood Sexual Abuse. *Violence and Victims*, 7: 2, 173–86.

Toth, S.L. and Cichetti, D. (1996) Patterns of Relatedness, Depressive Symptomatology and

Perceived Competence in Maltreated Children. *Journal of Consulting and Clinical Psychology*, 64: 32–41.

Tower, C.C. (1989) *Understanding Child Abuse and Neglect*. Boston: Allyn and Bacon.

Tufts New England Medical Centre, Division of Child Psychiatry (1984) *Sexually Exploited Children*. Unpublished Manuscript.

Vicary, J.R., Klingaman, L.R. and Harkness, W.L. (1995) Risk Factors Associated with Date Rape and Sexual Assault of Adolescent Girls. *Journal of Adolescence*, 18, 289–306.

Wachtel. A. and Scott. B. (1995) The Impact of Sexual Abuse in Developmental Perspective. In Bagley, C.R. and Thomlinson, R.J. (Eds.) *Child Sexual Abuse: Critical Perspectives on Prevention, Intervention and Treatment*. Toronto: Wall and Emerson.

Warner, S. (2000) *Understanding Child Sexual Abuse: Making the Tactics Visible*. Gloucester: Handsell Publishing.

Weitzman, J. (2005) Maltreatment and Trauma: Toward a Comprehensive Model of Abused Children from Developmental Psychology. *Child and Adolescent Social Work Journal*, 22: 3, 321–41.

Wolfe, D.A., Sas, L. and Wukerle, C. (1994) Factors Associated with the Development of Post-Traumatic Stress Disorder among Child Victims of Sexual Abuse. *Child Abuse and Neglect*, 18: 37–50.

Wolin, S. and Wolin, S. (1993) *The Resilient Self*. NY: Villard.

Woodward, C. and Joseph, S. (2003) Positive Change Processes and Post-Traumatic Growth in People who have Experienced Childhood Abuse: Understanding Vehicles of Change. *Psychology and Psychotherapy*, 76: 267–83.

Worden, J.W. (1991) *Grief Counselling and Grief Therapy: A Handbook for the Mental Health Practitioner*. NY: Springer.

Wyatt, G.E. and Mickey, M.R. (1987) Ameliorating the Effects of Child Sexual Abuse. *Journal of Interpersonal Violence*, 2: 403–14.

Wyatt, G.E., Guthrie, D. and Notgrass, C.M. (1992) Differential Effects of Women's Child Sexual Abuse and Subsequent Sexual Revictimisation. *Journal of Consulting and Clinical Psychology*, 60, 167–73.

# CHAPTER 2

# Assessing Children and Young People's Sexual Behaviour in a Changing Social Context

*Andrew Durham*

From an increasingly early age children and young people are bombarded with sexual information from a variety of sources – television; internet; mobile phones; sex education lessons; campaigns about 'safe sex' and sexually transmitted diseases; parental advice; abuse prevention programmes; music and fashion industry; the sex industry and not least from their peers, though not always truthful and perhaps often exaggerated. Children and young people often report that they have learnt about sex mainly from their peers. This is in many ways an indictment of the current state of sex and relationships education available for young people, although many young people are more comfortable in gaining knowledge from their peers rather than from adults. This chapter sets out a framework to help us better understand the social context of this learning, and some of the precise influences on children and young people's harmful or inappropriate sexual behaviours. With a strong emphasis on gender, power and sexuality, the framework highlights the impact of social oppression and stereotyping on young people's beliefs about their sexual identities, and about how they should behave. Following this, the chapter provides definitions of 'child sexual abuse' and 'inappropriate or harmful sexual behaviour' and sets out a further framework to assess particular sexual behaviours in accordance with a child or young person's age, development and understanding. Finally, the chapter will present some brief details of guidance for completing an initial assessment of a child or young person who has committed harmful or inappropriate sexual behaviour.

## A practice framework for understanding the social context of children and young people's harmful or inappropriate sexual behaviours

This framework draws together the multiple social influences on children and young people's behaviours. It seeks to allow diverse interpersonal language and individual experiences to be considered in a context of social oppression (Durham, 1999). The framework utilises Cooper's (1995) concept of 'organising principles', to allow for multiple dimensions of inequality and social oppression: 'Rather than basing analysis on axes of oppression, gender, class and race can be conceived as 'organizing frameworks' or less systematically 'principles' that over-determine each other in their operation and effects' (Cooper, 1995: 11). Racism, for example, is seen to interact with (determining and being determined by) other structures of social oppression, such as age, gender or sexuality. No single aspect of social oppression is seen as an absolute determinant of social power. It therefore becomes easier to account for the complexities of interpersonal relationships, for example, between a white woman and a black man, or between a white child and a black woman. The white woman may have less power by virtue of being a woman, but may have more power through being white. Similarly, a white child may have more social power than a black adult or, in certain circumstances, than a gay man. The location and social context of these power relationships can also be highly significant in determining their outcome.

The framework emphasises the significance of language, the use of particular types of language can invoke and carry forward social oppression and thereby significantly influence interpersonal power relationships. Individual words and phrases have the potential to invoke wider social understandings. In this sense, language potentially becomes a tool of oppression. Simple statements or even words could embody significant meanings, which directly relate to widespread and socially embedded oppression. For example, the use of the word 'queer' in the context of adolescent peer group relations may have a particularly powerful impact, making some people significantly more powerful and others significantly less powerful (Nayak and Kehily 1997; Durham 1999, 2003). Throughout society, sexuality and sexual desire is policed oppressively (Steinberg, Epstein and Johnson, 1997) whereby people, particularly young people, receive very powerful messages that emphasise the compulsory nature of heterosexuality, often pressurising them to demonstrate their heterosexual competencies. This is particularly pertinent for adolescent boys, where homophobia, characterised by homophobic name-calling and other bullying, becomes a significant feature of day-to-day peer group interaction (Nayak and Kehily, 1997; Durham, 1999, 2003).

The framework allows power relationships to be studied at varying inter-related levels of social interaction, in the context of widespread oppressive social and political influences. At the centre of the framework, the individual is an agent of choice and action, with wishes, beliefs and desires. Individual experiences are subject to and created by interactions with others. Each level of interaction constitutes a site of learning and influence. Each individual is a member of each level and so not only receives its influence, but also contributes to its influence on others. For example, at a peer group level or at the level of the wider political and social context, where processes of hegemony and consensus involve each individual in receiving beliefs, carrying them forward within themselves, passing them on to others and so forth. The extent of the influence will vary according to many factors, some of which may relate to class, race, gender, sexuality, age or ability. The influence of each level is interdependent, and will vary according to the individual's circumstances, age, understanding and development.

The most immediate level of interaction is family and kinship. In most circumstances, for a young child this will be the site of initial interaction, relationships and learning, and will continue to have a varying influence over time. The next level of interaction is the social network of extra-familial relationships and interactions. Within this network is located the peer group and access to other close and intimate relationships, experienced through schools and possibly pre-school networks, social and leisure contacts and work or college. The three levels – individual, family and peer group – are located in the wider social and political context, which again influences and interacts with each level, and also contributes to the determination of

interactions between the different levels. The framework delineates the apparatus of oppression and social disadvantage, as a context in which to understand diverse individual experiences. It allows analysis of interpersonal power relationships, highlighting the significance of language in mediating and carrying forward oppression, alongside recognition of the importance of power and sexuality. The framework is useful for a wide range of therapeutic practice, and in particular the field of sexual abuse where issues of power, gender and sexuality are pertinent. The framework is represented in Figure 2.1 below.

In therapeutic work with young people with sexual behaviour difficulties, we can use the framework to examine the wider social and cultural influences on their decisions to behave in a particular way. By looking at the wider social messages a young person receives about how he or she should feel and behave, we can find clues about how a diverse range of factors may have intersected and accumulated to precipitate the circumstances, thoughts, feelings and beliefs behind an abusive or inappropriate act. With the framework, we can explore the power relationship between a person initiating inappropriate or harmful sexual behaviour and the victim. The 'organising principle' of gender is a particularly significant aspect of the framework, considering that over ninety per cent of child sexual abuse is committed by men or boys (Morrison, Erooga and Beckett, 1994; Home Office, 1997). The framework allows us to explore with a boy, his received beliefs about his 'masculinity' – for example how he may have been encouraged to avoid or deny his weaknesses and vulnerabilities by not crying, or by avoiding intimacy, or simply not being encouraged to develop intimacy skills – and how they have influenced his thoughts and feelings about being a boy or a man and how this has all been processed and translated into action and behaviour (Carrigan, Connell and Lee 1987; Connell, 1987; Nayak and Kehily 1997; Durham 1999, 2003). It also allows us to consider closely, in a wide variety of ways, the meanings, textures, and dynamics of many of the interpersonal power relationships in his day to day life.

Through this framework, we can examine how young people may have internalised many oppressive stereotypes, beliefs and misunderstandings, through which they may have in some ways become able to justify their

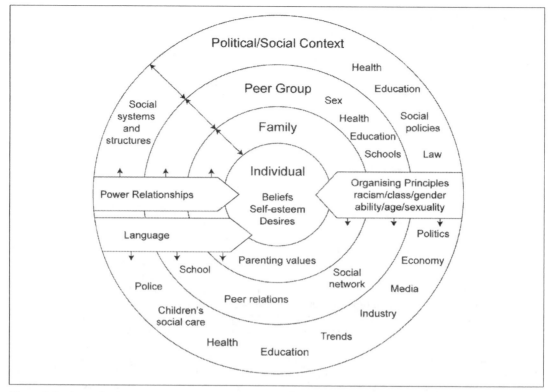

**Figure 2.1**   A practice framework for understanding the social context of children and young people's sexual behaviours (Durham, 1999)

actions to themselves, or may have generated powerful motivations for committing the abuse. For example a boy living, for whatever reason, in fear of his self-perceived heterosexual 'inadequacies' may engage in behaviours geared towards an affirmation of his heterosexual identity. He may have beliefs about his own inadequacies or incompetence through being oppressed as a young and powerless 'child' (Archard, 1993) within a chaotic family, or a family characterised by sexual aggression and domestic violence. He may have felt more powerful, or more like a 'real man' or 'one of the boys' through committing sexual acts with a weaker, younger or less powerful person. The framework can be used to explore the dynamic power differential between the young person and the person he abused. This may lead to greater insight, with the young person being helped to see where he is located within the multiple influences and discourses which may have shaped his thinking, leading him into a situation where he made the decision to sexually abuse or

behave in a sexually inappropriate way (Durham, 2006). The framework effectively gives the young person a map through which to interpret and negotiate the past, present and future landscape of his sexuality. It can assist him in negotiating positively about the future influences on his behaviour. These applications of the framework are drawn together in Figure 2.2 below.

It is important to note that whilst most young people who sexually abuse are men or boys, there are women and girls who also sexually abuse, or who have inappropriate sexual behaviours. The practice framework has an equally important application to therapeutic work with girls. In a similar way to that in which boys receive oppressive messages and beliefs about their 'masculinity', girls receive oppressive messages and beliefs about their 'femininity', that emphasise weakness, passivity, dependence and subordination to 'masculinity'. Girls receive mixed and confusing messages about their identities and their sexual behaviours, and are often pressured into subordination. Again, as

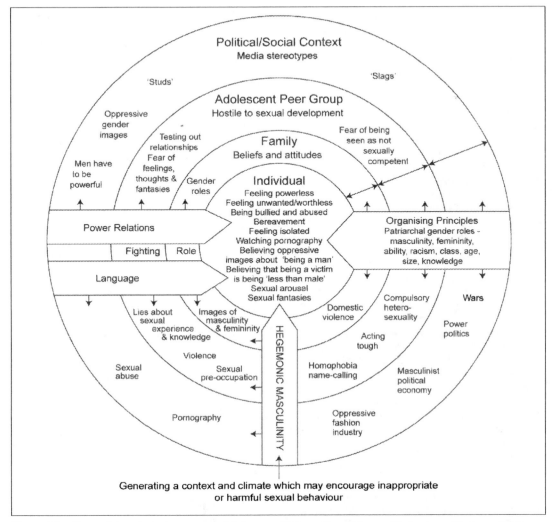

**Figure 2.2**   The social context of young people's inappropriate and harmful sexual behaviours (Durham, 2006)

with boys, the framework allows us to understand and explore with a girl, her received beliefs about her 'femininity', the influences on her thoughts and beliefs and how they are translated into day-to-day interactions. With each young person, a blank diagram of the framework can be used to help them identify and construct from their own particular circumstances the influences on their beliefs, understandings and behaviours, and the pressures to conform to a particular type of sexual identity. The practice framework also allows the practitioner to address their power relationship with the child or young person and emphasises the importance of a strongly transparent approach to therapeutic work, which explains the process from the outset and maintains a high level of respect, whilst acknowledging that some behaviours are problematic. The framework provides a theoretical underpinning for the practitioner, and provides helpful ideas for working directly with children and young people.

### Assessing sexual behaviour: typical or untypical

When working with young people's harmful or inappropriate sexual behaviours, it is important to be very clear about what these behaviours are, and which behaviours are to be considered appropriate and not harmful. It is also important to recognise that there is wide variance of opinion, standards and values within the community and across cultures and religions, about which behaviours are considered to be acceptable. Acceptability of sexual behaviours also has a historical dimension. It has long been recognised in the literature that the social context of children and young people's overall development, including not least their sexual development, is constantly changing, and is becoming increasingly more sexualised (Gill and Johnson, 1993). Recently there have been significant changes in the UK law that governs sexual behaviour. Following a reduction in the age of consent for gay male sexual activity, recent changes in UK law, *The Sexual Offences Act 2003*, have removed homophobic aspects of previous laws, again reflecting a change of values and standards. The changing social context and the wide variation of personal standards and values make it difficult to establish a baseline of acceptable or appropriate sexual behaviours.

In recent years, the changing context of young people's sexual behaviours has been escalated by developments in information technology, most notably computer technology, digital photography, mobile phones and the internet. These developments have widened significantly the social availability of explicit sexual material, including an area of particular concern, the increased production of images of child sexual abuse (Carr, 2003). Notwithstanding the direct harm this will have caused to the children involved, these images, indirectly, will go on to create further harm and will potentially have an impact on some people's perception of acceptable sexual behaviours, allowing them to attempt to justify sexual abusing to themselves and to others. The images are also likely to be used to skew children's perception of sexual acceptability as part of the process of being sexually abused. Generally the increased availability *per se*, of pornography through the internet and mobile phones will increase the probability of children and young people viewing explicit and exploitative sexual material. These factors underscore the importance of providing comprehensive sex and relationships education for children and young people from an early age. There is also evidence that it is beneficial for children and young people to be encouraged to

talk to each other in a more formalised manner, through the use of structured peer support, particularly where there has been sexual abuse (Alaggia and Michalski, 1999). Without this support, children and young people are left to cope with the many confusing and prejudiced messages propagated by the media, popular culture and the fashion industry. In considering young people's sexual behaviours, it is important to be clear about what we mean by child sexual abuse, and harmful or inappropriate sexual behaviours.

## Defining child sexual abuse and inappropriate or harmful sexual behaviour

The vast range of unique individual experiences of child sexual abuse makes it hard to achieve an encompassing definition. Some prevalence studies have recognised this by asking respondents about ranges of sexual experiences and have then applied differing definitions that show hugely variable outcomes (Kelly, Reagan and Burton 1991; Cawson et al., 2000). Influenced by these approaches and the work of Finkelhor et al. (1986) and Morrison and Print (1995), which draws a distinction between contact and non-contact behaviours, wide and lengthy definitions of both 'child sexual abuse' and 'inappropriate or harmful sexual behaviours' are proposed. These definitions present a range of options and defined behaviours (Durham 2003, 2006):

### Child sexual abuse

1. Forced or coerced sexual behaviour that is imposed on a child (person under 18 years old).
2. Sexual behaviour between a child and a much older person (five years or more age discrepancy) or a person in a caretaking role, or a sibling.
3. Sexual behaviour where the recipient is defined as being unable to give informed consent by virtue of age, understanding or ability.

### Inappropriate or harmful sexual behaviour

1. Initiated sexual behaviour which is inappropriate for a child's age and development.

2. Initiated sexual behaviour which is inappropriate in its context. For example, behaviour that is considered acceptable in privacy occurring in non-private circumstances.
3. An initiated sexual act committed:
- Against a person's will.
- Without informed consent.
- In an aggressive, exploitative or threatening manner.

### *Contact and non-contact behaviours*

- **Contact behaviours** may involve: touching, rubbing, disrobing, sucking, or penetrating. It may include rape. Penetration may be oral, anal or vaginal and digital, penile or objectile.
- **Non-contact behaviours** may involve: exhibitionism; peeping or voyeurism; fetishism (such as stealing underwear or masturbating into another's clothes); involving children in looking at, or in the production of, pornography; and obscene communication (such as obscene phone calls, and verbal and written sexual harassment or defamation).

### *Assessing children and young people's sexual behaviours*

Johnson and Feldmeth (1993) identified a continuum of four clinically derived definable clusters of sexual behaviour for pre-adolescents:

1. Natural and healthy sex play.
2. Sexually reactive.
3. Extensive mutual sexual behaviours.
4. Children who molest.

The behaviours in group one are considered to be developmentally appropriate. The remaining three groups raise varying levels of concern, in group four there are clear concerns about the victimisation of others. The behaviours corresponding to each group in Johnson and Feldmeth's model are detailed as follows:

### Group 1 – Natural and healthy sex play

- Exploratory in nature and characterised by spontaneity and light-heartedness.
- Intermittent and balanced with curiosity.
- Similar in age, size and development level.
- Embarrassed but not with strong feelings of anger, fear or anxiety.

### Group 2 – Sexually-reactive

- Often done in view of adults and may be frequent.
- Can generally be distracted, but erupt again when scared or anxious.
- Many of the behaviours are autoerotic or directed toward adults.
- No coercion.
- Not really directed outward toward others.
- A partial form of re-enactment of sexual abuse.
- Shame, guilt, anxiety and fear but not intense anger.

### Group 3 – Extensive mutual sexual behaviours

- Extensive, often habitual and may include the full spectrum of adult sexual behaviours.
- Persuasion, willing partners, not coercion.
- Often distrustful, chronically hurt and abandoned by adults.
- These children relate best to other children.
- Little desire to stop.
- Not an aggressive or retaliatory function.

### Group 4 – Children who molest

- Frequent and pervasive.
- A growing pattern of sexual behaviour problems is evident in their histories. Intense sexual confusion.
- Sexuality and aggression are closely linked.
- Bribery, trickery, manipulation or emotional or physical coercion.
- Not often physical force, as victims are chosen for their vulnerability.
- Impulsive, compulsive, and aggressive.
- Problems in all areas of their lives.

It is important to remember that children can move across these different groups, or have aspects of different groups at the same time. Being able to locate a child in one of these groups will have implications for the nature and level of intervention needed, and the risks presented to others. It is particularly important to make a distinction between children in group two and group four. Johnson and Feldmeth's categorisation is a helpful guide that emphasises the importance of assessing each child or young person, going some way to highlight the heterogeneity of children and young people's inappropriate or harmful sexual behaviours. It is important to keep sight of the uniqueness of the individual circumstances of each child, and to have a framework through which to assess a wide range of circumstances.

Hall, Matthews and Pearce (2002) analysing the sexual behaviours of a sample of children who have been sexually abused, have identified five empirically based typologies:

1. Developmentally expected sexual behaviour.
2. Unplanned interpersonal sexual behaviour (developmentally problematic).
3. Self-focused sexual behaviour (developmentally problematic).
4. Planned interpersonal sexual behaviour (developmentally problematic).
5. Planned, coercive interpersonal sexual behaviour (developmentally problematic).

These typologies involve the child's response to being sexually victimised, and have included family and parental factors in accounting for the behaviours.

### 1. Developmentally expected sexual behaviour

- No problematic sexual behaviours.
- Not actively involved or sexually aroused in their own sexual victimisation.
- Single perpetrator, usually abused individually without sibling or peer involvement.
- Non-sadistic abuse.
- Have experienced generally positive parenting.

### 2. Unplanned interpersonal sexual behaviour (developmentally problematic)

- Spontaneous and sporadic developmentally problematic interpersonal sexual behaviours.
- Actively involved in own sexual victimisation, but no arousal.
- Single perpetrator, usually abused individually without sibling or peer involvement.
- Non-sadistic abuse.
- Positive parenting – good supervision, healthy family sexual attitudes.

### 3. Self-focused sexual behaviour (developmentally problematic)

- Frequent and extensive masturbation and sexual preoccupation.
- Sexual arousal experienced during sexual victimisation.
- Single perpetrator (mainly) usually abused individually without sibling or peer involvement.

- Non-sadistic abuse.
- Blame themselves for own sexual abuse.
- Some parenting problems – some parent-child role reversal, some family violence.
- Some problematic family attitudes regarding sex, but not sexual interaction.
- Parental difficulties in setting limits on the child's sexual behaviours.

### 4. Planned interpersonal sexual behaviour (developmentally problematic)

- Interpersonal sexual behaviours – extensive adult-type sexual acts.
- Planned but not coercive sexual behaviours.
- High levels of masturbation and sexual pre-occupation.
- Active participation and sexual arousal in their own sexual victimisation.
- Experienced sadistic abuse, causing discomfort.
- Often with multiple perpetrators, multiple victim contexts.
- Poor parental boundaries; role reversal; family dysfunction; poor parental skill.
- Inadequate parental supervision– therefore potential access to other children.
- Problematic family sexual attitudes, sometimes patterns of sexualised interaction.

### 5. Planned, coercive interpersonal sexual behaviour (developmentally problematic)

- Extensive and persistent adult-type sexual behaviours – planned and coercive.
- High levels of problematic masturbation, sexual pre-occupation and sexual gestures.
- Frequent child-on-child sexual behaviours; siblings taught to act as perpetrators.
- Own sexual victimisation involved sadism, arousal and a high level of participation.
- Multiple perpetrators, abused in multiple victim contexts.
- Children experience pairing of sex and violence from an early age.
- Poor parental supervision; easy access to other children inside and outside family.
- Problematic family sexual attitudes; family dysfunction; family violence; criminality.
- Sexualised family interaction; role reversal; parental maltreatment histories.

### *A six step cumulative framework for assessing sexual behaviour*

The following accumulating criteria can be used to try and determine whether a young person's sexual behaviour is appropriate, inappropriate or harmful (derived from Pithers, Gray, Cunningham and Lane, 1993; and Johnson, 1999). A progression through each level reflects an increasing degree of concern and a stronger indication that the young person has a problem:

1. Sexual activity compared to the child's level of development.
2. Relative power between the children involved.
3. Child or young person's use of intimidation, force, trickery, or bribes.
4. Secrecy.
5. Compulsive or obsessive behaviours.
6. Progressive behaviours.

### 1. Sexual activity compared to the child's level of development

This initial step, in determining whether a sexual behaviour is a problem or not, involves comparing a child's developmental level with the type of sexual behaviour taking place. It is important to establish how the child has obtained the information about the sexual behaviours involved – has the child watched pornography, or has he or she been sexually abused? How does the behaviour balance with other aspects of the child's life and general interests? It is important to explore how the child's behaviour compares with what would be expected of other children of the same age and development.

### 2. Relative power between the children involved

A sexual behaviour is likely to be a problem if one child participating in it has more power than another. Power differentials may exist by virtue of a child's age, gender, class, race, ability – intellectual and physical, or status amongst peers. Sometimes one child may simply be in the habit of having a leadership role in a play relationship. This role may have been exploited to create opportunities to coerce another child into sexual behaviours. A child may use popularity in a similar way, or may gravitate towards much younger and developmentally less mature children.

### 3. Child or young person's use of intimidation, force, trickery, or bribes

Developmentally appropriate sexual behaviours involve curiosity and game playing, not intimidation, force, trickery, or bribes. It is

important to assess whether informed consent has been given. To give informed consent, a child or young person has to be old enough to understand what they are consenting to, and have enough knowledge and information, and be able to say yes or no without feeling under any pressure. When exploring these circumstances, it is important to remember that the discovery by adults of children's sexual behaviours will often cause anxiety in itself. It is important to establish beyond this, whether or not there is discomfort or unhappiness, and a wish to complain.

### 4. Secrecy

It is important to make a distinction between privacy, embarrassment and secrecy. Privacy is the right to protection from intrusion, while secrecy implies the avoidance of the consequences of an action that a child knows or senses is wrong or harmful. If children's sexual behaviours are discovered, they may deny them by either embarrassment or anxiety, but deliberate attempts to hide or conceal them may be a cause for concern, particularly if this is done disproportionately by one of the children involved.

### 5. Compulsive or obsessive behaviours

A compulsive behaviour involves an apparent inability to control that behaviour, while an obsessional behaviour is an apparent continual preoccupation with that behaviour. As far as a child's sexual behaviour is concerned, both or either of these may indicate that there is a problem, particularly if they have continued in spite of consistent and clear requests to stop. These behaviours would be of increasing concern if they were associated with anxiety, guilt or shame, or are causing overt discomfort to others.

### 6. Progressive behaviours

It is important to establish whether or not there is a progressive element to the behaviours: the extent to which there has been an increasing intensity or frequency of behaviour; or whether behaviours have been intensified and developed alongside fantasies. Concern is raised when the behaviours are more intrusive, are used to hurt others, or are associated in some way with anger and violence. It is also important to explore whether or not a child or young person is using distorted thinking in order to justify his or her sexual behaviours.

### *Stages of typical sexual development*

In considering these behaviours, it is important to consider what would be expected as normal or typical sexual behaviour for children and young people of different ages (Durham, 2006):

### Ages 0–5 years

At this age children are curious about most things, including their bodies. They may often be happier without any clothes on. At this age and throughout their development children may find comfort in holding or fondling their genitals. It can act as a self-comforting as well as an exciting behaviour. At these ages children will also be curious about other peoples' bodies. This may result in children trying to look at or touch other children's (of a similar age) genitals. This exploratory looking and touching will not be coercive.

### Ages 6–10 years

School age children continue to be curious about their bodies. At this age their sexual and gender curiosity may be expressed in the games they play. Games such as 'Doctors and Nurses,' 'Mummies and Daddies' may be fairly common. Boys may compare the size of their penises. Children will begin to show an interest in sexual words and rude jokes, though little interest in the opposite sex may be evident. Children may continue to be interested in their own and other peoples' bodies, especially if they begin to develop their own secondary sexual characteristics, some children may commence masturbation.

### Ages 11–12 years – pre-adolescence

As children's sexual awareness begins to develop, they may become anxious to establish relationships with their peers. They may begin to derive increasing pleasure and enjoyment from masturbation. By this age most children will have experienced some formal sex education, and may become increasingly curious about sexual knowledge. Some young people may engage in sexual activity, such as kissing and fondling with their peers. They may imitate sexual activity that they have seen or heard about. Most of these behaviours will be with members of the opposite sex, though some people may engage in sexual activities with peers of the same sex.

### Ages 13–18 – adolescence

During adolescence many young people will have gone through puberty and are likely to have increasing levels of sexual knowledge, interest and feelings, these being related to the extent of their physical development.

At this stage young people may express their developing sexuality through sexual innuendo, flirtations and courtship behaviours. They may have had sexual experiences within a peer relationship. Typical experiences can include consenting non-coital sexual behaviour (eg kissing, fondling, mutual consenting masturbation). Adolescence can also be a time when powerful emotions are experienced and expressed. These emotions may coincide with sexual experiences or be separate from them.

Although the age of consent is 16, some young people may have engaged in sexual intercourse before reaching these ages. Other young people may not have engaged in sexual activity with their peers and may have little interest in doing so. Some young people may engage in explicit sexual discussion amongst peers using sexual swear words and telling obscene jokes. They may show interest in erotic material and use it in masturbation. Some young people may become competitive and proud about their sexual activity, which may in turn create pressures and anxieties for others. It is not uncommon for young people to feel they have to lie about their involvement in sexual activity in response to this competitive peer scenario, which is often reinforced by media images.

Adolescence is a stage when young people may become conscious about developing their own identity in many respects, as a result image and fashion may become an increasing priority. This becomes closely related to the continuing development of a sexual identity. At this stage, peer influences may have a heightened significance. For some young people there may be discrepancies between sexual orientation, sexual experiences and their sexual identity.

Adolescence is also a stage when some young people become more distant from their parents or carers. Sometimes this can be paradoxical as they can be seen to be struggling with areas of their lives where adult guidance might be beneficial. This may be particularly true in relation to the development of sexual identity, and sexual behaviour. Additionally this is an area which many parents and carers find difficult or uncomfortable, particularly if this is an area which has not received open discussion at earlier stages. In these circumstances, young people may find it easier to talk to other adults or their peers.

## Guidance for completing an initial assessment of a child or young person who has committed harmful or inappropriate sexual behaviour

It is important to remember that even though a child or young person may have committed an extremely harmful act towards another child, he is still a child or young person himself. It is also important to remember that the child or young person is likely to have suffered some form of abuse, loss or disruption in his own life, which may include sexual abuse. It is therefore imperative to adhere to the principles of anti-oppressive child or young person-centred practice from the outset. In attending a therapeutic session about having committed a sexually abusive act, or behaving in a sexually inappropriate manner, a child or young person may be anxious, embarrassed or possibly afraid of the process. The practitioner's awareness of this is best stated and addressed as soon as possible. Equally, a child or young person may deny all knowledge of his alleged behaviours, or may be attending under duress, perhaps as part of a legal disposal or criminal conviction, or at the insistence of his parents. In gaining a child or young person's trust, a transparent approach is essential. The child or young person needs to know quite quickly how the practitioner is going to approach working with him, and what the ground rules are. He needs to be told that the intervention is about him and that an attempt will be made to explore fully the circumstances that have led to his reported difficulties and behaviours. The child or young person also needs to know that he will be supported through the difficult stages of the work and that the approach is not about punishment, but is about empowering the child or young person in a manner which allows him to consider his mistakes and make important steps towards an improved way of managing his life, without hurting others.

In using this guidance, it is important to keep to an approach that recognises the uniqueness of the child or young person's life, circumstances, history and personality, as being the essential context of the assessment. It should not be expected to find single causes for young people's harmful or inappropriate sexual behaviours. Causes often amount to an intersection of many events and circumstances in a child or young person's life, creating a unique pathway to the behaviours in question. The assessment is about uncovering that pathway by exposing the connections between the different experiences, and explaining how they acted together to precipitate the sexual behaviours. If the child or young person has been sexually abused, it will be necessary to address the impact of this as part of the work, being careful to emphasise that most people who have been sexually abused do not commit harmful sexual behaviours. These guidelines have been derived from Gray and Pithers (1993), Araji (1997), Gilgun (1999), Calder (2001) and Hackett (2004) and from my own practice experience, they are detailed under the following seven categories and summary:

1. The alleged harmful or inappropriate sexual behaviour
2. Sexual history
3. Developmental history
4. Social history
5. Health
6. Educational history
7. Personality, emotional regulation and self-esteem
8. Summaries, risk assessment and therapeutic proposals
(see Durham (2006) for the full questionnaire schedules for each section)

### 1. The alleged harmful or inappropriate sexual behaviour
In coming to this work, the child or young person will be well aware that information is known about his inappropriate or harmful sexual behaviours, and is likely to be anxious about being asked to discuss them. Given that this is his likely anticipation and continued anxiety, it is best to alleviate some of this tension by discussing the alleged behaviours as soon as possible – the extent to which this will be possible will vary between individual cases. It is helpful to communicate that you are aware of what has happened, and that the work is about finding solutions and making improvements in the young person's life. The questions in this area should seek to establish the young person's precise explanation and description of the

behaviours committed, their circumstances and context, and the accompanying thoughts and feelings before, during and after the behaviours, and details of any accompanying masturbatory fantasies. It is important to establish how the young person now feels about these behaviours, and the extent to which they see themselves as being responsible, and their understanding of their impact on the victim and on other members of the family, and their willingness to work towards changing their behaviours. The answers to these questions will provide important information about the on-going level of risk, and the young person's need for supervision, protection, re-assurance and so on.

## 2. Sexual history
Assessing a young person's sexual history will provide important clues as to how or why they have engaged in inappropriate or harmful sexual behaviour. Assessing sexual history will enable the practitioner to identify the extent of the young person's sexual development and understanding, alongside information concerning their sexual experiences, habits and patterns of arousal. It will provide information about the young person's sexual attitudes, the attitudes of their family, and their sexual orientation, sexual preferences etc. It will provide an opportunity for discussion about experiences of unwanted sexual contact, or exposure to sexual behaviour between others, or exposure to pornography. It will provide an initial opportunity for the practitioner to establish a dialogue about sexual matters with the young person. In doing so, it is important from the outset to establish a common understanding of the language to be used, acknowledging that people often find it uncomfortable or embarrassing to talk about sexual matters, explaining why this is currently necessary because of the young person's inappropriate or harmful sexual behaviours.

## 3. Developmental history
It is very important to have a good understanding of the young person's emotional and physical development, as a context for building an understanding of his pathway into committing harmful or inappropriate sexual behaviours. Depending on the nature and circumstances of the child or young person, and the behaviours in question, it may be necessary to have specialist medical assessments, for example if there are suspected mental health issues; learning

difficulties; speech and language difficulties; physical health issues and so on. It is important for these issues to be checked out with other key professionals during the early planning meetings that should have taken place as an initial response to the young person's behaviours. In a more generalised sense, the questions in this area will build upon the existing knowledge of the young person's emotional, physical and psychological development.

## 4. Social history
As with developmental history, there may be existing knowledge about the young person's social history. Exploring social history will give important information about how the young person currently functions in terms of friendships, social relationships, interests, leisure pursuits, attitudes and so on, and will provide clues about how they need to be helped in meeting their future needs appropriately.

## 5. Health
There may be some health issues that are directly relevant to the nature of the young person's inappropriate or harmful sexual behaviours. The presence of on-going health difficulties will in most cases be likely to have an impact on the young person's day to day feelings about themselves, their life and their social relationships.

## 6. Educational history
In terms of the young person's abilities and understanding, questions about their education will provide important information about the level and pace at which the therapeutic work should be conducted. The young person's level of educational achievement will also have a significant impact on their current and future life.

## 7. Personality, emotional regulation and self-esteem
The young person's attitudes and personality will have a significant bearing on how they are likely to receive the work, and how they are likely to view the prospect of making positive improvements for the future – making positive personal and social relationships; attitude towards others and towards the victim etc.

## 8. Summaries, risk assessment and therapeutic proposals
These questions draw together the overall conclusions of the initial assessment and set

the future therapeutic agenda for the young person.

- What are the key or essential findings of each section of the report?
- What bearings do these findings have on the reported inappropriate or harmful sexual behaviour; how do they interact to precipitate elements of risk?
- What is the nature and extent of future sexual risk presented by the young person?
- What immediate measures need to be taken to manage, contain and reduce the risks presented by the young person?
- In response to these findings, what are the key proposals for future therapeutic work?

The length of time taken to complete the assessment will often vary in accordance with the extent and nature of problems and difficulties uncovered, and with the child or young person's response in terms of openness and cooperation. Whist this assessment schedule is structured and prescriptive, it is important to keep to an approach that recognises the uniqueness of the child or young person's life, circumstances, history and personality, as being the essential context of the assessment.

## Conclusions

As a precursor to assessment, this chapter has set out an analytical framework to help us better understand the social context of children and young people's sexual behaviours. The framework had a particular emphasis on gender, power and sexuality, and how these factors interact to generate circumstances that cause some children and young people to commit harmful sexual behaviours. The rapidly changing social context of children and young people's sexual behaviours was highlighted, drawing attention to the consequent difficulty in establishing a common baseline of appropriate and acceptable sexual behaviour. It was recognised that through changes in technology children and young people are potentially gaining more access to explicit sexual material, and that quite often some of this is exploitative and harmful. The chapter has explored empirical typologies of children's sexual behaviours and has presented a six step cumulative framework for assessing sexual behaviour, alongside

information about typical or 'normal' age-related sexual behaviour. Finally the chapter presented some guidance for an initial assessment of a child or young person who has committed harmful or inappropriate sexual behaviour, reminding practitioners of the importance of a truly child or young person-centred approach. The guidance and the practice framework has highlighted the importance power relationships, and the necessity of recognising the uniqueness of each child or young person's life, circumstances, history and personality, as being the essential context of the assessment. It was emphasised that the causes of harmful or inappropriate sexual behaviours often amount to an intersection of many factors, events and circumstances in a child or young person's life, creating a unique pathway to the behaviours in question.

## References

Alaggia, R. and Michalski, J.H. (1999) The Use of Peer Support for Parents and Youth Living with the Trauma of Child Sexual Abuse: An Innovative Approach. *Journal of Child Sexual Abuse*, 8: 2, 57–73.

Araji, S.K. (1997) *Sexually Aggressive Children: Coming to Understand Them*. Thousand Oaks, CA: Sage.

Archard, D. (1993) *Children: Rights and Childhood*. London: Routledge.

Calder, M., Hanks, H., Epps, K.J., Print, B., Morrison, T. and Henniker, J. (2001) *Juveniles and Children Who Sexually Abuse: Frameworks for Assessment. Second Edition*. Lyme Regis: Russell House Publishing.

Carr, J. (2003) *Child Abuse, Child Pornography and The Internet*. London: NCH.

Carrigan, T., Connell, B. and Lee, J. (1987) Hard and Heavy: Toward a New Sociology of Masculinity. In Kaufman, M. (Ed.) (1987) *Beyond Patriarchy*. Don Mills, ON: Oxford University Press.

Cawson, P. et al. (2000) *Child Maltreatment in the United Kingdom: A Study of Child Abuse and Neglect*. London: NSPCC.

Connell, R.W. (1987) Theorising Gender. *Sociology*, 19: 2, 260–72.

Cooper, D. (1995) *Power in Struggle*. Buckingham: OUP.

Durham, A.W. (1999) *Young Men Living Through and With Child Sexual Abuse: A Practitioner Research Study*. PhD Thesis, University of Warwick.

Durham, A.W. (2003) *Young Men Surviving Child Sexual Abuse: Research Stories and Lessons for Therapeutic Practice.* Chichester: Wiley.

Durham, A.W. (2004) Children and Young People with Sexual Behaviour Difficulties: A Practice Framework for Holistic Interventions. In White, V. and Harris, J. (2004) *Developing Good Practice in Children's Services.* London: Jessica Kingsley.

Durham, A.W. (2006) *Young Men who have Sexually Abused: A Case Study Guide.* Chichester: Wiley.

Finkelhor, D. et al. (1986) *A Sourcebook on Child Sexual Abuse.* Newbury Park, CA: Sage.

Gil, E. and Johnson, T.C. (1993) *Sexualised Children: Assessment and Treatment of Sexualised Children and Children Who Molest.* Rockville, MD: Launch Press.

Gilgun, J.F. (1999) CASPARS Clinical Assessment Instruments that Measure Strengths and Risks in Children and Families. In Calder, M.C. (Ed.) *Working With Young People Who Sexually Abuse: New Pieces of the Jigsaw Puzzle.* Lyme Regis: Russell House Publishing.

Gray, A.S. and Pithers, W.D. (1993) Relapse Prevention with Sexually Aggressive Adolescents and Children: Expanding Treatment and Supervision. In Barbaree, H.E., Marshall, W.L. and Hudson, S.M. (Eds.) *The Juvenile Sex Offender.* New York, Guildford.

Hackett, S. (2004) *What Works For Children and Young People With Harmful Sexual Behaviours.* Ilford: Barnardo's.

Hall, D.K., Matthews, F. and Pearce, J. (2002) Sexual Behaviour Problems in Sexually Abused Children: A Preliminary Typology. *Child Abuse and Neglect,* 26: 289–312.

Home Office (1997) *Criminal Statistics for England and Wales 1996.* London: HMSO.

Johnson, T.C. (1999) *Understanding Your Child's Sexual Behaviour: What's Natural and Healthy.* Oakland, CA: New Harbinger.

Johnson, T.C. and Feldmeth, J.R. (1993) Sexual Behaviours: A Continuum. In Gil, E. and Johnson, T.C. *Sexualised Children Assessment and Treatment of Sexualised Children and Children who Molest.* Rockville, MD: Launch Press.

Kelly, L., Regan, L. and Burton, S. (1991) *An Exploratory Study of the Prevalence of Sexual Abuse in a Sample of 16–21 year-olds.* London: Child Abuse Studies Unit, Polytechnic of North London.

Morrison, T. and Print, B. (1995) *Adolescent Sexual Abusers.* Hull: NOTA.

Morrison, T., Erooga, M. and Beckett, C. (Eds.) (1994) *Sexual Offending against Children.* London: Routledge.

Nayak, A. and Kehily, M.J. (1997) Maculinities and Schooling: Why are Young Men so Homophobic? In Steinberg, L., Epstein, D. and Johnson, R. (1997) *Border Patrols:* Policing the Boundaries of Heterosexuality: Policing Sexual Boundaries. London: Cassell.

Pithers, W.D. et al. (1993) *From Trauma to Understanding: A Guide for Parents of Children with Sexual Behaviour Problems.* Brandon VT: Safer Society Press.

Steinberg, L., Epstein, D. and Johnson, R. (1997) *Border Patrols.* London: Cassell.

# CHAPTER 3

# Assessing Children and Youths with Sexual Behaviour Problems

*L.C. Miccio-Fonseca and Lucinda A. Rasmussen*

The assessment interview with a sexually abusive youth facing allegations of a sexual offence is unique and challenging for the professional. The concept that children and adolescents are sexual beings is not widely accepted, particularly for the younger youth – or for the developmentally delayed (whether male or female). Although sexual behaviour by adolescents is increasingly recognised as normative, many adults are blind to, or refuse to see the signs that their preadolescent or teenage children are engaging in sexual behaviours, ignoring the evidence until it is irrefutable (eg teen pregnancy). The prevalent denial within American society that children and adolescents have normative sexual behaviours not only harms those youth whose sexual behaviours are developmentally appropriate, it contributes to a hostile environment where any sexual behaviour outside the norm is viewed as an extreme aberration. Too often youth who are engaging in unlawful sexual behaviours are viewed as sexually deviant and akin to adults. Spurred on by recent legislation, people in their communities may demand that they receive the same punitive consequences as adult sex offenders (eg mandatory registration, residency restrictions, polygraph testing, etc.). When sexually abusive youth are viewed and treated as if they were adults, important developmental differences are not recognised or considered. For example, recent neuropsychological research has found that the brains of young people are still developing until their early 20s (Cauffman and Steinbery, 2000) meaning their sexually abusive behaviours are more likely to be more motivated by impulsivity and curiosity than by the planned intent to do harm shown by many adult sex offenders (Johnson and Doonan, 2006).

Crime data show that far from being an aberration, youth under the age of 18 commit a substantial proportion of sex offences, with some reports showing that in 16 per cent of rapes and at least 20 per cent of child molestations, the offender was an adolescent or preadolescent child

(Office of Juvenile Justice and Delinquency Prevention [OJJDP], 2006). Sexually abusive individuals (whether males or females – adults, adolescents or children – or individuals who are developmentally delayed) are heterogeneous; they vary considerably in their sex offences, histories, risk levels, and the degree of danger they present to the community (Chaffin, Letourneau and Silovsky, 2002). Like adult sex offenders, sexual offences committed by sexually abusive youth span a range of risk, from low, moderate, high, to very high to extremes of being lethal (Rasmussen and Miccio-Fonseca, 2007a, 2007b).

Risk levels need to be taken into account at all steps of the intervention process (ie assessment, treatment, supervision and monitoring) and the interventions individualised according to the particular needs of a youth. Failing to do so may result in treating lower risk sexually abusive youth too harshly and allocating to them scant resources that would be better directed toward effectively assessing, treating, supervising and monitoring those youthful offenders who are dangerous and at high risk to continue their problematic behaviour (Epperson, 2006). In order to accurately assess risk, professionals must use tools that:

- Comprehensively consider all relevant factors contributing to the youth's sexually abusive behaviour.
- Take into account age, gender and developmental capacities.
- Have well established reliability and validity and are specific to the population being assessed.

In this chapter, we present a new, innovative tool (ie *MEGA*) applicable to *all* sexually abusive youth under the age of 19 (male or female, adolescent or child, and youth who are developmentally delayed). We describe how this tool is used within a comprehensive, ecologically based interviewing protocol to:

- Assess the level of risk of a youth for sexually abusive behaviour.
- Identify areas that can be targeted in the treatment.
- Monitor the youth over time to determine change and improvement.

The strengths of this tool include its ability to synthesise data obtained from intake interviews and other sources, thereby increasing the accuracy of an assessment. The tool is also able to provide a baseline of risk level that can be compared every 6 months to assess and note progress.

The term 'sexually abusive youth' is used in this chapter when referring to those youth who have engaged in sexually abusive behaviour and/or have committed sex crimes, however were not adjudicated. As with adults, the legal term 'sex offender' is appropriate to use when a youth has been adjudicated for having committed a sex crime. Reasons that preclude sexually abusive youth from being adjudicated can include:

- Their sex offence was not detected or reported to the authorities.
- There was a report, but data were insufficient to render further judicial action.
- They were preadolescent children who were too young to be adjudicated according to the laws of their particular state.

## Assessing risk – risk assessment tools

Existing resources for assessing the risk of sexually abusive youth are limited to adjudicated males and are not geared for assessing females, children under 12, or the developmentally delayed. The existing risk assessment tools include: _Juvenile Sex Offender Assessment Protocol_ (_J-SOAP-II_, Prentky et al., 2000; Prentky and Righthand, 2003, 2004; Righthand et al., 2005); _Estimate of Risk of Adolescent Sexual Offence Recidivism_ (_ERASOR, Version 2.0_, Worling and Curwen, 2001; Worling, 2004); and the _Juvenile Sexual Offender Recidivism Risk Assessment Tool-II_ (_J-SORRAT-II_, Epperson et al., 2006). Two of these tools (_J-SOAP-II_ and _ERASOR, Version 2.0_) follow the traditional (but questionable) paradigm of supporting many of their items with empirical data obtained from samples of adult sex offenders. Adult research typically does not

consider developmental issues, milestones and concerns, or reflect the distinct developmental differences between adults and youth (Chaffin and Bonner, 1998; Miccio-Fonseca and Rasmussen, 2006b; Rasmussen and Miccio-Fonseca, 2007a, 2007b). Findings obtained from the _J-SOAP-II_ and _ERASOR, Version 2.0_ can be disputed because their items are based on this adult research and therefore can have no substantial validity or reliability when applied to sexually abusive youth. Although based on the research on sexually abusive youth, the third risk assessment tool, the _J-SORRAT-II_, primarily assesses static (ie non-changeable) areas in the youth's functioning. A risk assessment tool cannot evaluate whether the risk of a given youth is increasing or decreasing over time unless it has items that assess areas in the youth's life that are subject to change as he or she matures and develops the necessary self-management skills to prevent reoffence.

## The _MEGA_ risk assessment tool

The _Multiplex Empirically Guided Inventory of Ecological Aggregates for Assessing Sexually Abusive Adolescents and Children (Ages 19 and Under)_ or _MEGA_ (Miccio-Fonseca, 2006c) is a new, comprehensive risk assessment tool designed to be implemented as part of a structured assessment protocol for sexually abusive youth. _MEGA_ (and its parent tool, the ecologically framed _FISORF-1998_ [Miccio-Fonseca, 1998]) reflect a paradigm shift away from the traditional practice of using research obtained from adults to inform clinical practice with youth. Every item in _MEGA_ is supported and anchored on an extensive literature review of the most recent scientific research in the field of sexually abusive youth ages 19 and younger (both genders) (Miccio-Fonseca, 1999 – [Revised 2002–2005]; Miccio-Fonseca and Rasmussen, 2006a). Some items are associated with areas that had scant empirical data; these items were anchored to research on other variables that were closely related. Both _MEGA_ and the _FISORF-1998_ were also based on results of a 7-year research project on a sample ($N = 656$) of sexually abusive individuals and their families (Miccio-Fonseca, 1996, 2000, 2001). The sexually abusive individuals in the sample ($n = 350$) were relatively young – 72 per cent were under age 19 and 53 per cent were age 16 and under; the youngest was eight years old.

*MEGA* is composed of 7 aggregates (ie *Neuropsychological, Family Lovemap, Antisocial, Sexual Incident, Coercion, Stratagem,* and *Relationship* [*Predatory Elements*]). These 7 ecologically based Aggregates are embedded and interwoven in 4 scales for a total of 75 items. The empirically guided items in *MEGA 7 Aggregates* are geared to assessing risk and protective factors related to the functioning of the youth and his or her family. Some Aggregates assess domains that other tools (i.e. *J-SOAP-II; ERASOR, Version 2.0; J-SORRAT-II*) do not consider (eg neuropsychological factors, protective factors, levels of coercion [eg non-violent threats versus threats of bodily harm or use of weapons]). Final analysis of the *MEGA* validation sample ($N=1,184$) found moderately high internal consistency for the Aggregates (ie .409 to .749) and exceptional internal consistency for the scales (ie .816 to .848), sustaining the conceptual design of *MEGA* and evidencing that it is an empirically robust tool (Miccio-Fonseca, 2008). (See Table 1 for a brief description of the 7 Aggregates and some of *MEGA*'s elements.)

The 4 *MEGA* scales are based on methodically researched variables (related to the youth's risk for sexually abusive behaviours and/or coarse sexual improprieties) shown in the empirical research to affect the individual's functioning; these variables are known to contribute to, assist, enhance, and/or impair, or make vulnerable the individual's overall functioning and/or predisposition. Each scale assesses a different dimension for the youth relating to the empirically guided risk factors (static and dynamic) in the 7 ecological Aggregates. Together, the 7 Aggregates and 4 scales identify on first case review those areas related to the youth's risk for sexually abusive behaviour that need to be considered and targeted when making decisions related to treatment, supervision, placement, and evaluation of the youth over time. They provide an intricate network that assesses the youth's risk of sexually abusive behaviour at the initial evaluation, establishes an individualised profile, and then maps how the youth's profile and risk level change over time. Both clinicians and non-clinical professionals (eg case managers, child protective services workers, probation officers, school social workers and/or counsellors) can use *MEGA* so long as they have two or more years of experience in assessing and working with sexually abusive youth.

Encompassing all 7 ecological Aggregates, the *Risk Scale* considers risk levels related to the *overall* level of risk for sexually abusive behaviours and/or coarse sexual improprieties. It is designed to identify those youth who have a propensity for, a history of, a tendency to, engage in antisocial and even criminal behaviours. The *Risk Scale* assists in identifying the most serious and problematic youth, including those who are possibly sexually violent or possibly predatory (ie they abuse people whom they do not know or have known less than 24 hours). In very infrequent, unusual cases, the behaviours evidenced by these youth are profoundly serious and may reach levels of dangerousness or even lethality (eg threatening bodily harm, luring, using weapons). Items in the *Risk Scale* can identify and assess these youth and differentiate them from other sexually abusive youth who present a lower level of risk. The *Risk Scale* provides information that can help professionals assess critical factors that must be addressed immediately, as related to treatment planning, interventions, monitoring, and supervision.

The *Risk Scale* is composed of both *static* (historical) and *dynamic* (changeable) risk factors related to the youth's functioning within the 6 months prior to the *MEGA* assessment; it provides a baseline from which to measure the youth's progress. *Static factors* are historical; they reflect typically unchanging situations and/or behaviours that may be constitutional (eg lower level of intellectual functioning), chronic (eg a bipolar or depressive disorder that perhaps has a genetic component), environmental (eg separation from parents at an early age, history of child maltreatment or other trauma), and/or antisocial behavioural (eg history of arrests or other law enforcement involvement). Static factors may reflect areas where there was no intervention, or where interventions were attempted but were not successful. The *Risk Scale* can help identify extended services that are needed to further address these historical difficulties (ie follow-up on educational services (eg individualised plan for special education).

The *dynamic factors* in the *Risk Scale* include methodically researched variables shown in the empirical research to be related to antisocial propensities, proclivities, and behavioural patterns. These dynamic elements are flexible and malleable, observable and measurable. They yield information about specified targeted areas and can be followed for indices of change over time (every 6 months until the youth is 19 years, 11 months, and 29 days). Dynamic factors in the *Risk Scale* can be serious, urgent, critical and abrupt (eg involving a crisis occurring within the past 24 hours), or they can be acute but present for more than 24 hours, as in a sudden onset of behaviour (eg binge drinking, a sudden slew of antisocial activity or rash of sexually abusive behaviours and/or sexual offenses). They can also be more chronic (eg being unemployed, having an illness, or frequent moves and/or changes in types of residence [residential, foster care]).

The dynamic factors in the *Risk Scale* also assess the youth's propensity for disruptive, rebellious, or antisocial behaviour. This includes the youth's pattern of self-direction and self-regulation, as related to rule bound behaviours, as well as the quality and stability of the youth's relationships (eg peers, school) and/or proclivity towards participation in antisocial activity. The dynamic items in the *Risk Scale* focus on these elements that have occurred within the 6 months prior to the *MEGA* assessment and provide a baseline from which to measure the youth's progress.

The *Protective Risk Scale* consists of static and dynamic items and identifies those variables found in the scientific research literature to be related to risk for sexually abusive behaviours, but have been found to alleviate risk. The more protective variables present in the youth's life, the more likely that the risk level is mitigated, or reduced to some degree; in a word these variables contribute to *lowering the risk level*.

The *Protective Risk* items in *MEGA* hone in on how the youth has been doing overall in his and/or her overall daily functioning in various environments and situations. The dynamic factors items in the *Protective Risk Scale* directly relate to self-regulation, self-governance, and self-navigation; *Protective Risk Scale* assesses functioning that is more prosocial, as indicated by how the youth responds, adapts to, and meets the daily challenges at home, school and in the community. Such factors as attending and participating in school, engaging in assignments, and managing his or her behaviour consistently across situations and in various environments, indicate something about the youth's ability to be responsible.

The *Estrangement Scale* also consists of static and dynamic factors; however, these items are related specifically to family history and dynamics in the youth's relationships. As with the other *MEGA Scales, Estrangement Scale*

identifies those variables found in the scientific research literature to be associated with risk for sexually abusive behaviours and/or coarse sexual improprieties. *Estrangement* variables that assess static factors include historical events and/or themes reported by the youth and/his or her parents or caregivers (eg separation or loss of a parent [either by divorce or death], exposure to domestic violence, and/or the youth having been a victim of child maltreatment [ie physical, sexual, or emotional abuse and/or neglect]). Dynamic variables assessed by this scale are observable and measurable; they relate to the self-regulation of the youth and how it is evidenced in his or her relationships (eg impulsivity, degree of cooperativeness with others).

The family history of the child is in fact a Family Lovemap history, a reflected paradigm of the family's culture with regard to love, caring and loving others. Family Lovemap history reflects how individuals in the family relate to each other as well as with others (eg extended family, friends, neighbors, co-workers, classmates, authority figures, etc.). The Family Lovemap also reveals the gender-identity-roles of the characters that make up the family. Family Lovemap history reveals romantic patterns of intimate bonding and reveals the patterns of family planning (conception, infertility, and/or adoption). It also reveals patterns of separations and/or divorce, and the dynamics of remarriages. Historical patterns are modeled and reinforced over time as norms guiding relationships, both in and outside of the family. These norms impact how sexually abusive youth learn to relate to others and affect their ability to have close, intimate relationships at different levels (emotional as well as social). The modelling received in the family of origin also affects how these youth self-regulate and negotiate intense feelings in the contexts of intimacy, social relationships with peers or others in the community, interactions with teachers or other authority figures; and the like.

Youth who come from families where the Family Lovemap fosters qualities of loving and caring for one another, respect for others, honesty and responsibility, and trust in each other are likely to have significant protective factors mitigating risk for sexually abusive behaviour and/or coarse sexual improprieties. On the other hand, disruption in the youth's Family Lovemap can occur through loss of a parent or parents due to the parents' separation, divorce, death, incarceration, or behaviours of the parent(s) that physically and/or emotionally neglect or abandon the child (eg substance abuse). This may lead to a number of changes in caregivers and residences (including kinship, foster, and/or adoptive placements), all of which may provide conflicting adult role models of bonding and intimate relationships that may be confusing to the youth.

Abuse in the family (physical, sexual, emotional) vandalises the Family Lovemap, creates havoc in family members' interactions, and subsequently impairs or obstructs children's emotional development. When exposure to a chaotic and/or aversive environment characterised by tension, discord, and violence has been chronic, it can be extremely difficult for a youth to later overcome the long-term effects and make real changes in how he or she relates to others and engages in close or intimate relationships. Estrangement is often a consequence of poor role modelling, a vandalised Family Lovemap, and lack of opportunities to learn skills in authentically and responsibly interacting with others. Self-regulation and relationship difficulties may then be apparent and make an estranged youth from a family with a vandalised Family Lovemap at risk for sexually abusive behaviour and/or coarse sexual improprieties.

The validation data reported on the *MEGA Estrangement Scale* demonstrated that in all age groups and for both genders the youth in this sample had high scores, suggesting that problems with family, self-regulation, and self-navigation emerged very early in their development. Gender distribution in the means of the *Estrangement Scale* showed that overall, both male and female youth had significant family and self-regulation difficulties across all age groups; that is the scores of all age groups were notably elevated (Miccio-Fonseca, 2008). These data support the findings in the literature that sexually abusive youth come from multiproblem families (ie families with criminal backgrounds including sexual misconduct, history of child maltreatment, and family history of sexual abuse) (Mathews et al., 1997; Miccio-Fonseca, 1996; 2000).

*Persistent Sexual Deviancy Scale* consists of static items and identifies variables related to sexuality that have been found in the scientific research literature to be associated with risk for sexually abusive behaviours. Items included in the scale are age of onset of deviant sexual proclivities, frequency of sexually abusive behaviours, and whether the youth's sexual deviancy has progressed into more sophisticated and integrated sexual behaviours. The scale also gives information about the persistence of sexual improprieties and the presence of age disparity in sexual encounters.

The completed *MEGA* assessment provides a *MEGA Individualised Profile (MIP)* consisting of the youth's scores on each of the 4 Scales. The *MIP* established on the first administration of *MEGA* provides an individualised personal baseline that delineates those areas in each of *MEGA*'s 7 Aggregates that are in immediate need of attention as related to sexually abusive behaviour of the youth (Miccio-Fonseca, 2006c). The baseline data are used to inform decisions related to: treatment planning, interventions, supervision, and placement. Subsequent administrations (every 6 months) delineate changes in the youth's *MIP* (particularly in the *Risk* and *Protective Risk Scales*. MEGA can be administered every 6 months until the youth is 19 years, 11 months and 29 days. MEGA is in the process of being cross validated and is available only to approved cross validated research sites. For additional information about *MEGA*, please refer to recent publications (Rasmussen, & Miccio-Fonseca, 2007a, 2007b). *We caution clinicians that they must have the complete version of MEGA (including the instructional set found in the MEGA Manual and Rating Booklet [Miccio-Fonseca, 2006c]) before proceeding to use it in assessing risk of sexually abusive behaviour in a youth. Using MEGA to assess a youth without complying with the parameters specified in MEGA's instructional Manual and Rating Booklet would likely result in an inadequate and inaccurate assessment of the youth's functioning and level of risk.*

## Interviewing and assessing sexually abusive youth

An assessment of a sexually abusive youth needs to consider all the ecological systems that impact the youth at different levels, including the youth's:

● Biological functioning.
● Neuropsychological functioning and behaviours.
● Family dynamics.
● Environmental context (social supports in the community and culture).

The assessment conclusions and recommendations must also be ecologically valid, that is, the assessment must be able to be updated over time as the youth makes changes and demonstrates either improvement or regression. Making *MEGA* an integral part of an assessment helps the professional obtain a comprehensive and multidimensional picture of the youth's functioning. Its items serve as a structuring device for a qualitative face-to-face, empirically guided structured clinical interview. They guide the interviewer in exploring the youth's history as related to risk for sexually abusive behaviour. Exploring those protective factors found to be related to *reducing risk* is also essential; after all, many sexually abusive youth who are placed out-of-home want to be living back in their communities with their families, and it is often in their best interests to return them to their own homes. The elements in *MEGA*'s 4 scales help identify and develop the ecological systems and resources (ie school, church, other cultural supports, extended family) needed to support sexually abusive youth in their community and sustain their remission from sex crimes. Identifying and harnessing protective factors on behalf of sexually abusive youth can create a network of social supports or 'prevention team' (Gray and Pithers, 1993) that can help them improve their self-governance, gain a sense of mastery and competence, and acquire the skills to self-manage their behaviour (Katz, 1997; Rasmussen, 2004). Sexually abusive youth can best be integrated back into the community through a collaborative management approach that includes a regular (every 6 months) comprehensive assessment (ie *MEGA*), provides careful and comprehensive supervision, and adjusts interventions as needed, thus ensuring community safety.

### Ethical considerations

All professionals who deal with situations involving cases of sexual abuse should follow the legal and ethical guidelines specified by statute, their professional licensing body or the code of ethics for their particular profession. For licensed mental health professionals, these guidelines include safeguarding confidentiality, respecting people's rights and dignity, and providing informed consent to clients regarding planned treatment. (See codes of ethics of the American Psychological Association [APA, 2002] and the

National Association of Social Workers [NASW, 1999]. Likewise, professionals who are not licensed as a mental health practitioner (eg probation officers, caseworkers, teachers) and who work in sexual abuse treatment must follow the codes of conduct specified by their profession.

Discussion of the release of confidential information provides an opportunity for the professional to communicate to the youth and their parents or guardians the limitations of confidentiality. The professional should clearly state in the beginning of the interview that information disclosed in the assessment and in treatment is confidential, with certain exceptions. This includes discussing the intervention protocol that would take place should the youth become suicidal. In cases where a court has mandated the assessment, the interviewer needs to indicate that the completed assessment and ongoing treatment progress reports will be forwarded to the court and any other professionals who have a legal right to receive them (ie those providing ongoing supervision to the youth, such as probation officers or child welfare caseworkers). The interviewer should also discuss what types of information will be reported to the probation officer or caseworker on an ongoing basis. Mandated reporting requirements need to be clearly explained. The youth and the parents or guardians must understand that new disclosures of other known incidents of child abuse or of unreported sex offences by the youth will not be kept confidential but will be reported immediately to the appropriate authorities (ie child protective services or law enforcement). If new sex offences are disclosed during the assessment process or after treatment has begun, the same set of events will be set in motion as in the youth's initial sex offence (ie new investigations, interviews, arrests, additional charges, adjudications, possible custody time, etc).

Unfortunately, despite the laws and professional codes of ethics that safeguard clients, professionals' emotional responses may override ethical considerations. Cases of sexual abuse, especially those involving young children, tap into a full range of emotions and violate our value structures. When personal values and human reactions come into play, they may colour the professional's perceptions and affect their responses to the individual being interviewed. Often, sexually abusive individuals who get 'into the system' complain about being treated disrespectfully and unfairly by investigating professionals. They report violations of their civil rights, claiming that they were 'lied to' or 'tricked.' Other professionals who subsequently see these clients commonly dismiss their complaints; rarely is there an investigation for ethical violations. Complaints by sexually abusive youth (as well as their parents or guardians) are often discounted as reflective of general patterns of denial, minimisation and blame. Nevertheless, not all complaints can be ignored and attributed to denial. Professionals can in fact be very harsh when investigating, treating, or supervising sexually abusive youth or adults. They may think little of the ethical violations they perpetuate when they are disingenuous, disrespectful or overly confrontational with their clients.

An interviewer's personal values, especially those related to sexuality, can interfere with the interviewing process and prevent salient data from being obtained. The professional who deals with sex crimes must be comfortable with the topic of human sexuality and remember that each interview with a sexually abusive individual will be unique. If the interviewer is uncomfortable with discussing sexuality, then they may misjudge something that the youth says that may or may not be sexual. The interviewer might also miss identifying important variables related to the 'erotic script' associated with a sex offence (Miccio-Fonseca and Rasmussen, 2007). Interviews with sexually abusive youth and their family members are often delicate and emotionally laden. Stories from the victims can be grotesque; making it difficult for the professional to remain objective. The interviewer's discomfort with sexuality will come through; the youth being interviewed sense that the interviewer is judgmental, akin to other adults in their life. A professional's discomfort with sexuality cannot help but taint the interview, contaminating conclusions and recommendations. Although professionals' failure to manage their own personal values and judgments is quite likely to compromise the validity of an assessment, this issue has seldom been studied in the research literature or discussed in professional conferences.

Informed consent is another legal and ethical requirement that is sometimes overlooked or ignored in sex offender treatment. The rights that a client normally has to consent for treatment are curtailed for sexually abusive individuals, both adults and youth. The court mandates that the youth and his or her family *will* participate in treatment, often through the threat that the youth will be placed in custody, should they refuse. In some treatment programs, commencing treatment may be conditional on the youth and his or her parents or guardians signing release of information forms that allow the therapists to access records from systems previously involved with the youth and his or her family (ie health care, mental health agencies or treatment programs, schools). Although such records are essential for a comprehensive assessment, the manner by which they are obtained can sometimes be suspect. Sometimes professionals indicate to their clients that the referring agency (eg juvenile probation) will be contacted if the youth or their parents or guardians refuse to sign the requested releases of information. When professionals exert this type of undue pressure for clients to waive their confidentiality, the clients' signed consent for releasing information is really perfunctory.

### Preparing for the interview

Sexually abusive youth generally enter treatment via judicial intervention and oftentimes as soon as their adjudication is concluded. They were identified as committing a sex offence (through the disclosure of a victim or others' observations), investigated and arrested by police, and adjudicated. If at all possible, the interviewer should gather and review all available information from investigative agencies (eg child protective services, law enforcement, and juvenile probation) prior to interviewing a sexually abusive youth. All notations and data should be gathered in a competent and ethical manner. Important information usually accumulated in these cases by these agencies includes:

- Police reports.
- Disposition of child protective services reports.
- Pre-sentence reports completed by juvenile probation.
- Disposition and orders by the juvenile court.

Sometimes the information will also include the findings of the examining physician or social workers at the hospital where an evidentiary examination took place. Other records that are important to obtain regarding the youth include:

- Health records from physicians or psychiatrists.

- Mental health records from previous therapists or treatment programs.
- Educational records from teachers, school counsellors, and school officials (including findings of educational testing).
- Records from employers or those who have supervised the youth in volunteer work.

These records, as well as records from agencies or programs where the youth and his or her family have previously received treatment can only be obtained through a release of information form signed by the youth and their parents and guardians.

### Developmental considerations

The age and developmental stage of a youth *always* need to be considered in an assessment. Failing to tailor questions according to the developmental capacities of the youngster can adversely affect the assessment and is likely to invalidate the findings. Questionable results can impact interventions later employed with the youth in both treatment and supervision. The interviewer must be aware of several factors when assessing adolescents and children that are not even considered when assessing an adult. This is especially the case when interviewing very young children (under age 8). Children's brains are still developing; they do not yet have the cognitive structures necessary for abstract thinking and concepts and have limited verbal skills when compared to adolescents. Young children are generally poor historians and may have difficulty reporting sequential historical events (eg dates, times, specific events). The interviewer should anchor questions related to sexually abusive behaviour within time frames, events that are important to the child (eg holidays, birthdays, first day of school, the time of year when the child moved to a new neighbourhood or enjoyed a particular activity, such as swimming during the summer, or playing in the snow in the winter).

The assessment of a child or adolescent who has been sexually abusive often takes place after they have been interviewed by social workers from child protective services or the police. The interviewer should keep in mind that these previous interviews may adversely affect the child's interactions with other adults conducting similar interviews. Children's reports of sexual abuse or sexually abusive behaviour are easily contaminated when they are interviewed multiple times by multiple interviewers (with varied professional experience) and with multiple methods of interviewing. Great care must be taken when interviewing young children, for they can be easily led by the interviewer and are easily confused.

The assessing professional may see disparity between the youth's chronological and developmental age, indicating that a different approach to the interview is needed. Questions may need to be simplified or different terminology used (especially when interviewing young children or youth who are developmentally delayed). It is important to carefully observe the youth and ensure that he or she understands the questions asked or the terms used. Youth who seem hostile or resistant may not necessarily be oppositional; they may be having trouble understanding the interviewer and what is expected in the interview. When the interviewer is alert to fine developmental distinctions and observant of the youth's responses in the interview, the findings of the assessment and hypotheses that attempt to explain the youth's sexually abusive behaviour are likely to be more accurate. Tailoring the interviewing according to the developmental capacities of the youth is likely to enhance rapport, which in turn is likely to maximise the information obtained.

Assessments of sexually abusive youth often ignore or are insensitive to the special issues and concerns of the population of youth who have:

- Developmental disabilities.
- Low intellectual functioning.
- Physical disabilities (eg impairments in vision, hearing or speech).

Developmentally delayed sexually abusive youth have been identified by a mental health or social service system as having impaired cognitive functioning and delays in achieving expected developmental milestones. They meet diagnostic criteria for mental retardation, that is, their limitations in cognitive functioning are significant, as are their 'conceptual, social, and practical adaptive skills' (American Association of Mental Retardation, 2006). These youth generally have a documented history of receiving services and accommodations (eg financial aid, special education or other academic services, vocational training). Low functioning youth typically function at a higher level than developmental delayed youth. When compared to youth of normal intelligence who are on track developmentally, low functioning youth have limited cognitive functioning or impaired social skills. Less likely than developmental delayed youth to be identified by mental health or social service professionals as having developmental problems, low functioning youth often do not receive needed special services or accommodations.

Acknowledging the disparity of developmental versus actual age assists the interviewer in estimating the youth's capacity to understand the seriousness of the allegations of sexually abusive behaviour and the potential consequences. The interviewer will see nuances of behaviour, verbiage and gestures that assist in assessing chronological versus developmental age. Does the youth appear to be his or her stated age, or look younger or older? Youthful sex offenders are often emotionally younger than their chronological age would indicate; this may sometimes be seen in regressive behaviours (eg reports of acting 'silly,' engaging in horseplay characteristic of younger children, insisting on playing games designed for very young children, eg Candyland, etc.). When children or adolescents appear older, we tend to expect more; we often expect them to have a cognitive understanding of their sex offence and the impact of their behaviour on others. A 15 year-old male adolescent who looks about 18, will often provide responses that reflect his developmental emotional age. It is important that interviewers are not misled by the youth's apparent age, but objectively assess verbal responses and behaviour to ascertain their developmental and emotional age. Observed developmental delays must be carefully documented in the assessment findings and in the interviewer's recommendations in order to ensure that these youth receive the sustained assistance and services needed to function at an optimal level.

*MEGA* has been designed with items that assess the particular needs of young children, developmentally delayed or low functioning youth, and youth who have limitations in physical capacities). The *Neuropsychological* and *Family Lovemap Aggregates* of *MEGA* are particularly informative for assessing developmental capacities and identifying factors in early development that may increase risk for sexually abusive behaviour. Using these

Aggregates when completing an assessment is likely to facilitate a more accurate and comprehensive assessment. Other Aggregates in *MEGA* (ie *Antisocial, Sexual Incident, Coercion, Stratagem,* and *Relationship* [*Predatory Elements*]) also apply to children under 12; however, clinicians and non-clinical professionals *must be very careful in applying the various items*. 'Very few children have predatory or antisocial elements in their sexually abusive behaviour, make threats of bodily harm, use physical force, or use a weapon' (Miccio-Fonseca and Rasmussen, 2007; Rasmussen and Miccio-Fonseca, 2007a, 2007b). Nevertheless, *MEGA* can be beneficial when assessing the small percentage of sexually abusive children under 12 who display antisocial behaviour, show extreme coercion, or are predatory in abusing strangers or casual acquaintances.

### Behavioural observations

All aspects of the youth being assessed are important to note, beginning with observations of his or her initial overall presentation. Is the youth appropriately dressed for the weather? The youth's attire can imply a variety of things. Inappropriate dress could indicate neglect and poor parenting; or that the youngster's sensing system is impaired and disconnected with the immediate environment (eg dressing in tank tops and shorts when it's about 50 degrees or colder outside). Coming to the interview in an unkempt and dishevelled state might also indicate neglect, or it might be a sign that the youth is not taking care of personal hygiene due to being severely depressed. The interviewer should pay attention to subtle nuances of all aspects of the youth's overall appearance, including such apparent trivialities as hair do's, hair colour, style of clothing, logos on clothing (eg music, art, lyrics, designs) tattoos, or types of body piercing. Things that are obvious to an observer may give an indication of the youth's self-concept and how they wish to present to the world.

During the interview, the interviewer should pay close attention to all aspects of the youth's communication style: body language; speech patterns (eg tone, rate, quantity); automatic phrases; facial expressions; verbal and utterances (eg sucking sounds); physical changes (eg fidgeting throughout the interview) and other verbalisations or behaviours. Observing how the youth makes eye contact often reveals something about their level of social skills, although it may also be indicative of cultural factors. Likewise, verbal skills reveal whether the youth has the capacity to relate well socially, as well as suggest their level of intellectual functioning and education. Clear and articulate responses are generally a measure of above average intelligence. Limited verbal skills may indicate developmental delays, problems in auditory or cognitive processing, or in some cases, socially withdrawn behaviour characteristic of depression, or that the youth has not had a consistent education history. People with good verbal skills are certainly easier to interview, but they may also be more adept at distracting the interviewer. American adolescents have a tendency to use such innocuous phrases as 'all that stuff', or 'you know', 'awesome,' 'I go' or 'he goes,' or 'an' everything'. The interviewer should not presume to know what sexually abusive youth are trying to convey without checking to see what the phrases actually mean to them.

### Aligning with the youth

The skilled interviewer must know how to align with the individual being interviewed. Discussing intimate sexual activities with an unknown adult is understandably uncomfortable and threatening; it is expected that the youth will be very reluctant to engage with the interviewer. The first few minutes set the tone for the entire interview. The interviewer can do little things to help put the youth at ease (eg talking briefly about the youth's trip to the interviewer's office; asking about what the youth did during that day before coming to the appointment). Multiple interviews (eg by police, social workers from child protective services, other therapists) result in what is known as 'a practice effect', and this in turn can jeopardise the validity of the interview. The 'practice effect' teaches the youth what to expect; they inadvertently become more prepared, can anticipate the questions that might be asked, and have learned how to respond. The kind of information that a youth decides to disclose in a new interview may have less to do with 'being in denial' and more a self-protective response generated by previous critical and judgmental reactions of other interviewers.

### Environmental variables that make a difference for interviewing

Manipulating certain relatively simple environmental variables can make a great

difference when conducting an interview. The interview should be conducted in a private space, with only the interviewer and the youth present. Interruptions during the interview should be avoided in order to allow the free flow of the youth's disclosure of embarrassing sexual experiences. This may be the first time that the youth has been asked to discuss his or her sexual proclivities. Experiencing embarrassment and shame is often part of the youth telling about his or her sexually abusive behaviour or traumatising experiences. Privacy makes disclosures easier for the youth to handle. The interviewer can maximise the potential for full disclosure by being attentive to the youth's needs. Simply stating how long the interview will last can diffuse anxiety. This provides a predictable time frame and helps the youth have some idea of what to expect. The youth's response when told about the length of the interview can help the interviewer gauge how the youth is dealing with being interviewed. Taking into account physical needs (eg not starting an interview just prior to a meal [particularly if interviewing a young child]; asking if the youth needs to go to the restroom) is also important. Interruptions make it difficult to sustain the pace and flow of information.

Uninterrupted time facilitates the youth's disclosure and allows the interviewer to pace and direct the focus of the interview. Although there is a structure in the interviewing process, the interviewer needs to be ready to adjust if the youth takes a different route. The interviewer's flexibility will allow the youth to disclose sufficient information and detail, possibly revealing other sex offences, unreported victims, or the youth's own traumatic experiences, including past abuse (eg sexual, physical, emotional or exposure to domestic violence). Skilful interviewing can guide the youth in disclosing and obtain critical information related to the youth's history and current risk for sexually abusive behaviour.

Careful interviewing is necessary when assessing the youth's level of responsibility for alleged sexually abusive behaviour. The interviewer must be alert to those questions and areas of inquiry that elicit the most emphatic or fully developed responses and those that seem to produce responses that are vague or desultory. Persons alleged to have committed sexually abusive acts or sex crimes are typically guarded, defensive and disinclined to open up; this is particularly true if the person is innocent and no effort has been made by investigators or interviewers to keep this possibility in mind. It is imperative that interviewers are objective and 'play fair and square' and do not automatically assume that youth are guilty of the sex offences they are alleged to have committed, or that their statements disputing the allegations represent a conscious effort at denial. The interviewer must remain open to what the youth is saying and not immediate discount the youth's self-report as unreliable and self-serving. Professionals who are sceptical of the youth's self report (and communicate this doubt, either verbally or nonverbally) are not likely to elicit much disclosure. In order to fully disclose their sexually abusive behaviour and traumatic experiences, youngsters must feel that they are believed, or that interviewers will at least consider that what they are saying may be true. If the interviewer comes across as judgmental, the youth is likely to shut down and the opportunity to elicit disclosure will be missed.

A judgmental stance also interferes with objectivity. Failing to be objective in interviews can result in regrettable mistakes with profoundly devastating results for youth and their families and possibly the professional (in terms of malpractice suits and loss of license). Interviewers need to be acutely aware that there are many cases of innocent people being arrested, tried and convicted of a sex crime only to be released from incarceration years later when their conviction is overturned due to new information disputing eyewitness accounts or providing DNA evidence that supports their innocence. Being adjudicated (and perhaps placed in custody) for a sex offence is likely to have a far-reaching impact for sexually abusive youth and their families. Their educational and career goals may no longer be attainable. They will carry the stigma of being labelled a sex offender. Recent federal legislation (ie Adam Walsh Act) also means that many sexually abusive youth will be subject to restrictive laws (eg registration and residency requirements). Their names will be published on the internet for their peers, friends, extended family members, and neighbours to see. These are foreseeable consequences for youth who are sexually abusive, but they are unacceptable penalties for those youth who are innocent and have been erroneously assessed in an evaluation to be 'in denial'.

Observing how an alleged sexually abusive youth handles being confronted with the allegations is a good indication of the general development of the interview. The stance of the youth, as exemplified by levels of cooperation, compliance and motivation, may change throughout the interview. If the alleged sexually abusive youth is in denial and is uncooperative, the interview will seem long and endless for all parties involved. On the other hand, when a youth is motivated, cooperates with the interviewer and takes responsibility for their offences, the interview flows well and both the youth and the interviewer feel a sense of accomplishment at its completion.

It is important to keep in mind that the youth will also be observing the interviewer's body language and other behavioural responses and responding accordingly. The interviewer's reactions can significantly influence the responses of the youth. Stories of child sexual abuse are sometimes grotesque and can be depressing and shocking, making it very difficult to listen to without having some kind of emotional response. The interviewer must always monitor his or her internal reactions and external expressions so that sexually abusive youth are not thwarted in their disclosures of abuse-related content.

The interviewer should document all observations in the above areas while the interview is in progress. Methods of recording may include: notations with pen and paper, audio recording, video recording, or computer input recording; all done with appropriate consent from the youth and their parents or guardians.

## Stories of incidents of sexual abuse sound different: they should be, they are told by humans

The interviewer must be aware that individuals' stories of incidents of sexual abuse in any particular case will often consist of varied accounts of the same incident. Stories of sexual abuse vary according to individuals' perceptions of their experiences. Sometimes it will appear as though the reported victim and the alleged sexually abusive youth are talking about something else entirely. Sometimes the sexually abusive individual's verbal skills are superior to those of the victims. The victims, especially young children, may be largely inarticulate, providing inadequate and unclear explanations and descriptions. Being frightened, ashamed and embarrassed, they are likely to omit events and miscalculate dates and places. This can affect the clarity and accuracy of the police report documenting the victims' statements.

The interviewer should watch for and take note of how the youth's account of the abusive incident differs from the account given by the victim. In some cases, neither the victim nor the sexually abusive youth remember details of the incident. Often time gaps and contradictions about events are found in the record. Memories of abusive incidents (of either the victim or the offender) are contaminated by the events that take place following disclosure of the abuse (eg investigations by child protective services and law enforcement, placement in foster care, arrest and detention). The investigative process is often disorienting. Like victims in shock, sexually abused children and/or sexually abusive youth may not always remember what they stated earlier during their first interview with child protective services or the police. This does not mean that they lack credibility. Memory and other psychological processes can be significantly impacted by the trauma of being investigated, arrested and adjudicated.

Using the victim's or sexually abusive youth's own language (actual terms, slogans, slang and/or expressions) is *most important*. Important disclosures often take place when the interviewer is able to skilfully frame questions in ways that trigger the youth's memories associated with trauma or an abusive incident. The interviewer can help the youth recall and describe specific details of the abusive incident by asking questions about the 'field' or background of the event. These questions can be useful in triggering the youth's memories. For example the interviewer might ask such things as: Was it noisy? Was there music? What was the weather like? What was the time of day? What were you doing before (or after) the event? Helping the youth to recall the incident slowly, step by step, can trigger memories (Perry and Orchard, 1992).

Using a simple time guide during the interview is also helpful when assessing a youth's experiences related to sexual abuse. For example, when asking about a particular event, the interviewer might inquire about the season of the year, where the family was living, the school the child attended, the child's grade in school and/or his or her teacher at the time. Such questions typically elicit a range of responses and help put things into a historical context for both the youth and the professional obtaining the information.

Using major holidays or other significant family events as a time guide can also be helpful. The interviewer might inquire if an incident of sexual abuse took place around a family member's birthday, close to a holiday (eg July 4th, Thanksgiving, Christmas, Hanukkah, New Year's Day) during a time when school was out (eg spring break, summer vacation) or when the family took a trip out of town (eg vacations, weddings, funerals, etc.). Recalling family stressors (eg a family member's hospitalisation or illness, a parent's unemployment) might also trigger the youth's memory of the abuse and elicit disclosures. Memories of abuse might also be associated with significant events in the community and/or nation that took place during the time frame of the abuse (eg 9/11, the beginning of the war in Iraq, Election Day, Hurricane Katrina, Southern California wildfires).

When sexual abuse is severe and chronic over an extended period of time memory recall for either a victim or an offender is more severely impacted. It may be more hazy, inconsistent, distorted, or unavailable. They may not recall when the events in question started and just when they ended. It is not uncommon to find interviewers who become frustrated because the victim and/or the sexually abusive youth are 'not reporting consistently.' It may be simply that the youth, particularly if a young child, is not able to cite exact dates, frequencies, or locations where the sexual trauma took place. Both the initiation of trauma, and the receiving of trauma, affects memory. It is important to carefully document what the youth reports to have seen, heard, smelled, tasted and touched. It will, in the long run, help the youth (either a victim or an abuser) piece together a number of experiences that can later be put into a more clear and logical time frame.

Defences of denial, minimisation and blame are commonly found in families where there has been a sexual molestation. Many sexually abusive youth have learned to blame others or use denial and minimisation by watching their parents or other family members use such defences. Denial can function on a long-term basis and over an extended period of time. Some sexually abusive youth will continue to deny their offences in spite of the most blatant evidence. If the interviewer persists in confronting the youth's denial in a demanding and demeaning manner, it will only create distance, further entrench the denial, and may produce an impasse. The feeling of 'being stuck' and or of 'not getting anywhere' will be apparent. If this happens, the interviewer has lost ground and needs to find a way to recover. It generally is unwise to interrupt an interview; however, when arriving at such impasses, it may be wise to stop the interview and allow the youth to take a short break. Taking a break can reduce the youth's defensiveness and resistance, while allowing the interviewer to re-focus and then resume the interview with a different tone. Recognising and acknowledging that an impasse in the interview has occurred can dissipate the frustration of both the interviewer and the youth and allow the task to continue on a different footing. Introducing other areas of explorations can lead to new and valuable information. By acknowledging the need for a slower pace and more patience in listening to the youth, the interviewer will overcome the impasses that do occur.

Risk level remains high when a youth consistently denies or claims that he or she cannot recall the abusive incident or the steps that led to it. Without this important information, a prevention plan cannot be structured. The risk level is increased since variables to reduce risk (ie the steps the youth took to engage in sexually abusive behaviours) cannot be identified, because they cannot be recalled. The youth is at high risk and any prevention plan is seriously faulty.

### The importance of defining the terms

A definition of terms begins with the person being interviewed. As with beginning the interview and aligning with the youth, the assessment of sexually abusive behaviour is predicated on the interviewer clearly understanding the meaning of the terms and expressions used by the youth. Interviewers must realise that youth differ significantly from adults in the language they use and the terms they employ. What is common language to the interviewer may not necessarily be common to the youth and vice versa. It is important to avoid making assumptions. Listening and doing one's best to understand the terms that a youth uses and defines increases the accuracy of information gathering, generates fewer errors, and creates a better management of the case. The youth's level of understanding of the terms he or she is using must be established. Terms can be confusing, especially since slang is commonly used to describe specific sexual behaviour. For example, what exactly do youngsters mean when they say:

'He was doing it to me'? Many times interviewers fail to ask sexually abusive youth to clearly explain or define terms and expressions they use in the interview. The interviewer operates in a vacuum, relying on their own assumptions as to what the youth means without checking it out or asking for clarification and/or additional description.

Certain considerations must be made with regard to the person being interviewed, particularly when he or she is a youth. What are the youth's cognitive abilities? How much does the youth *really* understand? Can the interviewer determine that level at which 'real' communication is taking place? Does the interviewer use words, phrases, and sentences that can be easily understood by the youth? Are operational terms defined so the youth can in fact be aware of what is being asked? Does the youth have the cognitive skills needed to understand the meaning of abstract terms? Patience is critical to a successful interview. The interviewer must take the time to check out whether or not the youth understands the questions. When youth do not understand what is being asked, they may feign understanding. Youth are often conditioned in their families to want to please adults. Some youth may think they will incur an adult's displeasure if they ask for terms to be clarified. On the other hand, other youth will become hostile, resistant and oppositional when they do not understand what is being asked. As many as 75 per cent of sexually abusive youth have learning disabilities (Courtney, Misch, and Burker, 2003); it is important that the interviewer take this into account and ensure that every effort is made to present information in a way that the youth can easily understand.

Language skills vary, especially when dealing with cross-cultural influences. When interviewing bilingual youth, it is critical to evaluate the youth's degree of fluency in the language spoken by the interviewer. If the interviewer is not fluent in the primary language spoken by the youth, he or she will need to assess whether or not an interpreter needs to be present during the interview. This of course presents significant ethical concerns, as the interviewer will need to apprise the interpreter of the legal and ethical rights of the youth and obtain the interpreter's commitment to keep what is discussed in the interview confidential. The act of bringing in an interpreter introduces a potential confounding variable that must be closely monitored. It compromises the interview on a variety of levels (ie less privacy, less confidential, greater discomfort in discussing intimacy with yet another party, overall impact on the youth's level of motivation and cooperation).

Aside from language and bilingual issues, the interviewer must also take into account the learning style of the youth (Longo, 2004). Many youth, particularly those who have a learning disability or are developmentally delayed, will understand and express themselves much better if:

• Information is presented to them visually.
• They are allowed to use nonverbal means of communication during the interview.

If the youth being interviewed is a young child or is an adolescent who seems to be visually oriented, the interviewer might allow them to use drawings when responding to questions or initiating communication. Puppets, dolls, books and stories are frequently used in interviewing children. Full anatomical dolls are useful tools, regardless of the age of the child or adolescent, and can be an effective means of gathering specific information about the sexual behaviours in question. They are especially helpful when interviewing young children (Bentovim et al., 1999). These nonverbal methods of communication (ie art, books, stories, puppets and dolls) are also helpful in alleviating the anxiety of the youth and facilitating a more open disclosure of the details of their sexually abusive behaviour or their own victimisation (Rasmussen, 2001; Rasmussen and Cunningham, 1995).

A method for ascertaining whether sexually abusive youth are clearly understanding the interviewer's questions is to ask them to say in their own words what they think is going on or describe the topic currently under discussion. If a youth 'parrots' words, that is, uses the exact same words that the interviewer has said, it is likely that they are merely 'replaying' information. The interviewer needs to 'check in,' assuring that the youth is on the same wavelength. If the interviewer 'fills in the gaps' with their own interpretation of what occurred, using language that is different from that of the youth or the victim, distortions are inevitable and the resulting report of the assessment will be inaccurate and invalid.

### Taking an ecological history

A critical component of an assessment of a sexually abusive youth is obtaining a comprehensive history. The systems influencing the youth are classified into four broad ecological domains:

• Psyche/soma (ie physiological, cognitive and emotional functioning).
• Family Lovemap (see discussion related to family dynamics later in this chapter).
• Social fabric (ie the youth's immediate social network).
• Mezzo and macro community and culture (ie the environmental context).
   (Rasmussen and Miccio-Fonseca, 2007a: 184)

A comprehensive assessment must address all these components.

The professional's role will determine the focus and purpose of the interview and the type of information obtained. Child protective services workers focus their interviewing on protection issues for the vulnerable children involved. For law enforcement, the focus of the investigative phase of the case is on the present crime and possible past offences. In mental health services, the reverse is true, the focus being on individual and family history, physical and medical history, developmental history (which includes erotic development) peer relationships, academic aspects, and employment.

An effective way to gather historical information is by breaking up the information into categories. *MEGA* is helpful in this regard, as the 7 Aggregates (ie *Neuropsychological, Family Lovemap, Antisocial, Sexual Incident, Coercion, Stratagem,* and *Relationship* [*Predatory Elements*]) assist in structuring the history in different categories. As the history is taken, a picture slowly but surely emerges and fits a pattern of a set of familiar variables that materialise and represent the pathology of the youth's sexually abusive behaviour. The more information assembled, the better and the more comprehensive the assessment.

Developmental indicators of pathology can be found in the process of history taking. For example, sexually abusive youth often have a history of other antisocial activities (eg stealing, fighting, non-sexual offences, fire setting) that may have been observed in school (ie documented by school suspensions or expulsions) or resulted in prior involvement of law enforcement for nonsexual offences. Indeed research indicates that prior nonsexual offences are a significant risk factor for recidivism (Kahn and Chambers, 1991; Rasmussen, 1999a; Schram, Milloy, and Rowe, 1991; Worling and Curwen, 2000). Certainly a history of high risk behaviours (eg fire setting, aggression toward peers or adults) is significant if the youth is to be placed in a foster home or residential facility. The level of risk must be carefully evaluated through exploring such information as the youth's age when the antisocial activity began, together with circumstances and consequences, both formal (ie school suspensions and expulsions; arrest, detention, and adjudication, referral to child protective services, out-of-home placement) and informal (ie consequences imposed by parents, foster parents or guardians).

Some sexually abusive adolescents have a history of abusing pets. Parents or guardians report that they lacked empathy or sensitivity for animals. As young children, these youth may have been either sexual or unusually cruel with pets or other animals (eg pulling the pet's tail, twisting limbs, hitting or kicking the animal, grabbing the animal's genitals and squeezing them). In extremely rare cases, a youth (child or adolescent) may torture, maim or kill an animal or force it to participate in a sexual act (ie bestiality). Interviewers need to assess for animal abuse, as its presence is indicative that the youth is high risk.

### Sexual history

Taking a history of the youth's actual sexual behaviours in question is not an easy task. The reasons for taking a sexual molestation history can be for investigative purposes or for assessment or treatment. Initial disclosures of some important areas are usually limited.

History of the youth's own sexual trauma is crucial information and may give instructive clues about the factors that contributed to the youth's sexually abusive behaviour, as well as assist in identifying the areas that need to be further assessed and addressed in the treatment. Sexually abusive youth often report being sexually abused or sexually traumatised when younger, usually by a known family member or friend. Approximately 60 per cent of boys and 80 per cent of girls who are sexually victimised are abused by someone known to the child or the child's family (Lieb, Quinsey, and Berliner, 1998). A comprehensive assessment needs to include specific details about the youth's sexually abusive behaviour, as well as their sexual victimisation or

other traumatic experiences (eg physical abuse, emotional abuse, neglect, abandonment, exposure to domestic violence, exposure to community violence).

The professional is responsible for being comfortable with sexual topics and keeping his or her own values related to sexuality in check. Importantly the professional should also be responsible for being informed about the current studies in human sexuality as they relate to societal norms of sexual human development and behaviors. The interviewer needs to use the youth's own words when asking questions about the youth's sexual history. Matching the youth's language can facilitate developing therapeutic rapport and eliciting disclosure. Youth and adults are seldom at ease discussing sexuality. A comfortable tone must be established before approaching this aspect of the individual's private life.

An area that is rarely explored, discussed in professional journals or conferences, or reported in assessments is the individual's erotic development. Perhaps the most neglected aspect of child development is the erotic aspect, namely the history of the child's sexuality (Miccio-Fonseca, 1994/1997; Money, 1986, 1988; Williams and Money, 1980). Most parents are unaware of the sexual aspects of a child's private world. When youth are interviewed alone, without any family member present, they can be quite candid and open about their sexuality. On the other hand, some youth may be quite reticent, never admitting any incidents of sexual behaviours (normative or abusive). An interviewer can establish a comfortable atmosphere that facilitates disclosure of sexual material by asking such questions as:

- Tell me something you've not told anyone else.
- Tell me two things about yourself that you are afraid that your parents or friends would find out.
- Tell me a well kept secret you kept from your parents and friends when you were younger.

The interviewer may find that youth who have been sexually traumatised have been exposed to an aspect of sexuality that is out of 'normal experience.' Children who are victims of sexual assault, incest or sexual molestation are generally exposed to aspects of sexuality, sexual behaviours or sexual materials prior to their sexual readiness age; that is, before they are developmentally prepared to integrate the experience. These children are 'eroticised'; they have been prematurely exposed to sexual material, either in the form of media (ie magazines, TV, video, movies) or actual sexual behaviours, either observed, or participatory beyond their sexual readiness age (Miccio-Fonseca, 1994/1997; Miccio-Fonseca and Rasmussen, 2006b; Rasmussen and Miccio-Fonseca, 2007a, 2007b). They may have difficulty incorporating their experience with sexuality with other aspects of their life. Eroticised children who grow up in abusive or neglectful homes, or are removed from their home and placed in foster or residential care, often do not receive the help they need. Eroticisation should be taken into account when making recommendations about treatment planning and ongoing supervision of the youth.

Identifying the onset of the sexual abuse or sexual molestation (whether the youth's sexually abusive behaviour or own victimisation) is important, in order to assess not only its duration, but also the developmental state of the youth at the time. Frequency of the molestation often indicates the erotic patterns of the sexually abusive youth. Pattern of sexual behaviours, duration, and frequency are variables used to determine the youth's risk level for sexually abusive behaviours in the community.

Specific sexual behaviours charged to the youth must be clearly described; for example: fondling of the breasts or the genitals, oral copulation on the giving or receiving end; whether physical force or weapons was used or implied; whether the sexual contact included anal sex, penile or digital penetration, or insertion of foreign objects. Was there sexual intercourse (penile vaginal penetration)? Was it full penetration or partial? If the offence consisted of digital penetration, was it full or partial penetration? Also, in very rare cases, the youth may have engaged in unusual behaviours, such as urinating on others or forcing another person to receive an enema. The interviewer needs to ascertain these various aspects of the sexually abusive behaviour.

## Impairment in erotic and physical development

Individuals who are over 18 and have sex disorders many times do not really know what constitutes appropriate and inappropriate sexual behaviours. It is difficult for professionals to identify what 'appropriate' and 'inappropriate' sexual interactions are for youth raised in unconventional households. These youths' perceptions of what is 'normal' and their tolerance level for abnormal experiences varies greatly from those of their counterparts raised in conventional households. For these youth, erotic development seems to follow unusual developmental lines, which puts them at risk for severe problems in courtship and romantic bonding. Such things as crushes and other romantic connections, love dreams, erotic dreams (sexual dreams) and nocturnal emissions ('wet dreams') are generally experienced either early in their development (before their sexual readiness age) or not at all. Erotic self-stimulation (masturbation) also commences early or not at all.

## Physical development and physical medical history

An assessment of a youth must consider not only psychological and emotional developmental aspects, but also physical development and characteristics. A physical description of the youth assists in assessing the other aspects of their functioning. This description of the current physical appearance also includes all the demographics: age, race, gender, educational level (which are documented on the informational page in *MEGA*). Although it is often an important indicator of impaired development, physical appearance is seldom mentioned in histories of children. Regrettably, there is typically little comment in assessment reports on the health of the child. The impact of a lack of emotional bonding on a child can be observed in the child's failure to pass through developmental milestones successfully and is evident in the child's physical development. Children who are victims of abuse and sexually abusive youth often have health histories characterised by frequent illnesses or other health concerns. They are frequently under or over weight, subject to frequent colds, ear aches or infections, and other kinds of chronic somatic discomfort such as stomach aches, irregularity and headaches. It is important for the interviewer to assess for these symptoms in the child or adolescent and note them if they are present.

Sexually abusive male adolescents often appear to be either under-developed, or over-developed in stature, physical size, and muscle mass. Over-development contributes to their looking older than their stated age. More often, the youth is an awkward young-looking male who has yet, in many cases, to develop secondary sexual characteristics. The muscle mass of an under-developed adolescent is still boy-like; body hair is still fine and sparse, not yet coarse. The youth's facial hair is also fine and rarely developed. The sexually abusive female adolescent also usually appears to be either under-developed, or over-developed in stature, physical size, breast development, and perhaps has an early onset of menses. When over-developed, these physical characteristics contribute to the sexually abusive female adolescent looking older than her stated age.

Other related physical aspects to be included in the assessment are:

- Any impending medical condition (if the condition requires immediate medical consultation, this should be done).
- Any physical disabilities with details of the cause, occurrence, treatment and/or therapy.

The interviewer should assess whether the alleged sexually abusive youth experienced a significant physical injury during the assault or offence. If so, what kind of injury? Was there an evidentiary and/or medical examination? This is very important, particularly in case of a head injury. Head injuries are of special significance, as they may contribute to impairment in memory. There is also some research indicating that head injury can predispose an individual to be physically abusive (Rosenbaum, Geffner, and Benjamin, 1997).

Physical history must also include the area of the general health of the parents, which gives information about the youth's inherited characteristics. It is important to identify whether the youth is at risk for diseases (eg diabetes, cancer) or neuropsychological conditions (eg depression, bipolar disorder, schizophrenia, attention deficit disorder) that may have a genetic component. The parents' physical health history also gives a picture of the developmental background that the sexually abusive youth may have had.

Problems in the physical development of sexually abusive youth may contribute to associated problems in emotional functioning. These youth are often immature, impulsive, and have difficulty delaying gratification. Their sensing system, be it the eyes, the ears, the nose,

and touch may be impaired. For example, they may have difficulty in sensing temperature (ie coldness, heat) and may not be aware of the actual heat of an item that they are handling or picking up (ie hot pot, bowl). The health histories of both female and male sexually abusive adolescents frequently show signs of possible organic, neurological problems. These youth are commonly reported to have problems related to their sense of sight (eg blurred vision, sensitivity to light, seeing shadows). They also appear to be more likely to need glasses and often have a history of wearing glasses from a young age. Another common symptom among sexually abusive youth is having a hearing problem. Often these youth have a history of early childhood ear infections, many times accompanied by high fevers. A history of ear difficulties may have been severe enough to require surgery to place tubes in the child's ears (usually before the age of seven). Many children have tubes placed in their ears, however, and we do not know if there are data to show that this is any more likely for sexually abusive youth. Often language development of sexually abusive youth has been slow and difficult, especially if there are hearing problems. Although this is not addressed as a risk factor for sexually abusive behaviour in the empirical research, the first author notes that her clinical experience has shown that speech impediment is the most commonly reported language problem of sexually abusive youth, especially with enunciation and pronunciation. Stuttering, although not as common, is also found in histories of some sexually abusive youth and may be evident in the interview. A history of both short and long term speech therapy is often found in the elementary school records of these youth.

Sexually abusive youth are at risk for a number of other symptoms, including: history of thumb sucking, nail biting, enuresis, and defecating in underwear (encopresis or smearing faeces). The first author has found in her 25 years of clinical experience that a history of encopresis is often a good indicator that the youth may have been a victim of anal penetration. Immune system deficiency problems can also be seen in the health histories of many sexually abusive youth, making them more susceptible to frequent colds, flu, irritable bowel syndrome or other stomach complaints, or respiratory problems (eg asthma).

Acquiring information in separate interviews from the parent and the sexually abusive youth

**Table 3.1**   The 7 aggregates of *MEGA*

| | |
|---|---|
| *Neuro-psychological aggregate* | Assesses elements related to neuropsychological functioning including lower level of intellectual functioning, history of epilepsy, attention problems/deficits, special education. |
| *Family lovemap aggregate* | Assesses several aspects of the youth's family background including: *Family Lovemap* (Miccio-Fonseca, 2005, 2006a, 2007) (ie family's sexual history and family's familial psycho-sexio-social history); family history of experiencing various types of abuse; youth's individual history of experiencing various types of abuse. |
| *Antisocial aggregate* | Assesses the youth's history of law enforcement involvement (nonsexual offences) and other antisocial behaviour (eg behaviour problems at school, animal abuse) that may bring youth to the attention of authority figures (eg parents, preschool or day care workers, teachers, residential staff). |
| *Sexual incident aggregate* | Assesses the number of incidents of non-consensual, sexual behaviour, and whether the youth's behaviours show progression across time and situations, or into more sophisticated sexual behaviours involving penetration. |
| *Coercion aggregate* | Assesses the degree of coercion that the youth uses in influencing another person or persons to comply with a sexual behaviour including: intimidation or use of force; use of general threats and threats of bodily harm or threats of lethal consequences, and whether the youth has utilised a weapon or weapons for the purposes of procuring compliance in sexual behaviour from another person or persons, and the type of weapon used (eg rocks, guns, knives, tyre lever, baseball bat, poles and sticks, air gun, hammer, chains, and explosives). |
| *Stratagem aggregate* | Assesses behaviours of the youth that may suggest intent or motivation for engaging in the sexual behaviour including: use of deceit, trickery, and lying; evidence of planning. |
| *Relationship aggregate (predatory elements)* | Assesses the relationship that the youth has with the person or persons involved in the sexual behaviour, whether there is an age difference or difference in mental capacity, or difference in physical capacity, and whether the relationship is 'predatory' (ie a relationship with a stranger or casual acquaintance that the youth engages in for the primary purpose of carrying out abusive dynamics of manipulation and coercion). |

about his or her health history usually reveals conflicting information. That is, a parent may report no history of their child defecating in underwear, and yet the youth reports that they stopped defecating. Such discrepancies in information are not only important data for assessment, but they also are an indicator of the quality of parent/child relationship.

Sometimes an evidentiary exam reveals indications that a youth has a sexually transmitted disease. A culture should be taken and a recommendation for a follow up be made. Many times the results are only available days or even weeks after the culture is taken. The youth (and sometimes the parents and/or guardians) may not understand the importance of a medical follow up for evaluation and possible treatment, particularly if they have developmental delays or is a child under 12. This must be noted, and the professional should make a follow up call to the youth and their parent or guardian. Obviously, sexually transmitted diseases left untreated have devastating effects.

### Family history and composition (family lovemap and antisocial aggregates)

The importance of assessing the history of the family and its dynamics cannot be overemphasised. Taking a family history is like standing back, looking at a photograph or tapestry, and scanning the people that surround the individual. The assessing professional must carefully study the fabric of the youth's family. Within this fabric are the people in the immediate family and those who make up the extended family. The family norm today in American society is no longer the nuclear family with two natal parents that have had no previous marriages or produced other offspring. The great majority of children in today's American families have a network of family relationships that include:

- Natal parents, full blooded siblings, and natal extended family (ie grandparents, aunts and uncles, cousins, etc.).
- Step-parents, step-siblings, and their extended families.

- Half siblings and their half sibling's other parent and extended family.

Children may be aware of these different related and non-related individuals and have close relationships with many, but usually not all of them. The various configurations of relationships are difficult to keep track of. There are the grandparents of the step-siblings and all their uncles and aunts who may also have had multiple marriages and offspring. Then there are their half-siblings' parents and aunts and uncles, who also have had multiple marriages and offspring producing a multitude of cousins. And these cousins also have half-siblings and step-siblings with their extended family. The identity of a family takes on mutations and complexity; it is not surprising that interpersonal boundaries, family lines and what constitutes an 'appropriate' relationship become obscure.

Within the intricate fabric of multiple relationships in the family of a sexually abusive youth, there is typically a generational history of sexual abuse, sexual assault, and other types of abuse or child maltreatment (eg physical abuse, exposure to domestic violence, neglect, abandonment, emotional abuse). Abuse vandalises the *Family Lovemap* (ie the romantic and erotic bonding in the family – see definition in Table 3.1) (Miccio-Fonseca, 2005, 2006a, 2007). The empirical research supports that sexually abusive youth typically have experienced stressful and often chaotic family environments, including disruptions in attachment (Friedrich, 2002; Pithers, Gray, Busconi, and Houchens, 1998a, 1998b; Rasmussen, 2001; Rich, 2006); impairment in romantic and erotic bonding (Miccio-Fonseca, 2005, 2006a, 2007); exposure to domestic violence (Bonner, Walker, and Berliner, 1999); and blurred family boundaries (both enmeshed and disengaged) (Burton et al., 1998; Gil and Johnson, 1993; Hall, Mathews, and Pearce, 1998, 2002; Johnson, 2000; Rasmussen, 1999b). The *Family Lovemap Aggregate* of *MEGA* assesses for these various types of child maltreatment and evaluates the impact of a stressful family environment in increasing risk for sexually abusive behaviour.

In many families of sexually abusive youth, the roots of abusive patterns and violence can be traced back from generation to generation (ie from the youth, to parents, grandparents, great-grandparents, great-great grandparents, etc.) with multiple victims and sexually abusive individuals scattered throughout the family's history. This history of sexual abuse or sexual assault is not only in the natal family history, but also interestingly in step-family relationships as well. Assessing family history and dynamics is critical to identifying unreported abuse, unknown victims and abusers in a family.

When assessing the current generation of the youth's family, the interviewer may find that the youth and other children in his or her family (eg siblings, nieces, nephews, and cousins) did attempt to disclose their abuse to others (eg family member, friend or neighbour, teacher). In some cases, the person whom the child or adolescent trusted followed through and reported the abuse to authorities; in fact, there may have been a number of calls that were made to either police or child protective services. Child protective services documentation may show that multiple complaints were cited, or even that the abusive individuals were prosecuted for child molestation. Nevertheless, in all too many cases, responses of adults to the child's initial disclosures are inadequate. Sometimes the abused child must disclose again and again to different adults before a report to authorities is made. In other cases, the response of the 'system' is inadequate; the referral is determined to be 'unsubstantiated' and no intervention (ie supervision by child protective services or probation, or therapy by a licensed mental health professional) takes place.

A comprehensive assessment of the family history of a sexually abusive youth may uncover other victims who have been, or are currently being abused. The assessment is critical to identifying the victims and ensuring that they receive treatment. In many cases, providing treatment to the sexually abusive youth also includes finding treatment resources for not only currently identified victims, but also for other abused and abusive family members. On the surface, basic questions such as asking for information about the youth's natal parents appear to be easy, but the interviewer quickly discovers the complexity and permutations of relationships within the family and the implications that assessment data has in revealing undisclosed and/or unreported incidents and victims of sexual abuse (or other abuse).

### Marital history of parents

The marital and intimate partnership history of each parent provides important information about the previous relationships in the family. If there were children from previous marriages or intimate partner relationships, inquiry about how each partner bonded and parented these children can give a picture of the stability of his or her romantic relationships and skills as a parent. Also, tracing the separations and divorces of the youth's parents and in the family history provides information about the primary attachments, working models of relationships and developmental losses suffered by one or both partners and by the family as a whole (Bowlby, 1988; Davies, 1999).

The number of children the mother had, or the father has fathered, adds to the picture (or tapestry) of the family. Information regarding the parent/child relationship and frequency of contact when children are not living with their natal parent can be instructive to the interviewer. How parents maintain contact with their children from prior relationships is an indicator of how they are fulfilling their role as parents, as well as the degree of detachment or enmeshment among family members.

## Unconventional households (family lovemap and antisocial aggregates)

Many sexually abusive youth come from unconventional households where relationships are tenuous and transitory. Romantic relationships amongst the adults in the family are usually very abusive (physically, emotionally and sexually). Many times these relationships are not of long duration; they are not usually sustaining or consistent. The transient nature of family relationships (with a parent having a number of different partners and the children experiencing several moves and changes in schools) often contributes to sexually abusive youth being poor historians with regard to their own family history.

The professional who interviews a number of families finds commonalities related to abusive patterns and tenuous relationships, but also an incredible heterogeneity in family histories. Family history taking also reveals a picture of family ties, strengths, and family alignments. Whenever possible, the interviewer should attempt to interview the sexually abusive youth's parents, siblings, and extended family members who are significantly involved with the youth. The process of taking the history of a family informs the interviewer how the youth relates to

his or her parents, siblings, and extended family and how the family functions as a whole. Families of sexually abusive youth are often characterised by lack of deep emotional bonding. A problematic parent-child relationship has been found in the research to be a risk factor for sexually abusive behaviour (Worling and Curwen, 2000, 2001).

Asking the youth simple questions (eg ages of siblings, the full name of natal parents, or how long parents have been married) gives a glimpse of how much the youth knows about their own family history. Asking children and adolescents how their parents met, or if their parents are divorced, why did they divorce, can be quite revealing in terms of how much the youngsters know about their parents. Inquiry as to the number of marriages or significant other relationships, can give a hint of 'traffic' in the home in terms other individuals coming into the family system and living within the home. The number of divorces, reasons for divorces and separations, reports of significant losses such as illnesses and deaths, are important data that reveal the youth's knowledge about their family, as well as gauge the level of communication within the family. The composition of the family, coupled with historical information, is an indication of the ambience of the family environment.

Gathering historical information often reveals a family history of occasional judicial involvement. Exploring which family members have been involved with the law in terms of offences, arrests, prison sentences, probation supervision and the like, can uncover patterns of abuse over an extended period of time. Research supports that families in which sexual abuse takes place have members with antisocial patterns of behaviour and criminal involvement. For example, Miccio-Fonseca's (1996) study of 656 adult and adolescent sex offenders and their families, found 63 per cent (29 per cent females and 34 per cent males) reported having a family member who tried to physically hurt or kill someone.

## Academic history (Neuropsychological, Family Lovemap and Antisocial Aggregates)

Academic history is a crucial area to assess, especially for youthful offenders who become either dependents or wards of the Juvenile Court.

Having comprehensive educational data is essential, whether the assessing professional is a clinical psychologist providing an evaluation to the court, a clinical social worker providing therapy or a probation officer or social worker seeking placement for the youngster. These data are needed whether the youth remains in their home and community or is placed in out-of-home care (eg foster care, group home, residential facility, secure custody).

The items of the *Neuropsychological Aggregate* of *MEGA* help delineate important academic information to obtain in an assessment. These items provide assessment data related to attention problems/deficits, intellectual functioning and other neuropsychological concerns. This is critically important since research has shown that nearly half of sexually abusive youth have attention problems/deficits (Araji, 1997; Bonner et al., 1999; Pithers et al., 1998b). Assessing academic functioning also involves reviewing the results of educational testing and seeing if the youth has been diagnosed with learning disabilities, and if so, whether the youth was enrolled in an individual educational program (IEP). It is important to determine whether the IEP is current, if the youth is making progress on stated goals and objectives, and whether the current IEP adequately addresses the youth's educational needs. When past and current educational records are made available, educational needs can more readily be identified and the success of the youth's overall placement is enhanced. Knowing that a youth is placed in special education is also important in monitoring the youth, as research indicates that youth who have received special education are more at risk to re-offend sexually (Epperson et al., 2006).

There is a wide variation in the academic performance of sexually abusive youth from below average, average, high average, or even superior level, so any conclusions related to academic functioning and risk for sexually abusive behaviour are equivocal. Often, sexually abusive youth may have a long history of problems with academics and scholastic behaviour. Sometimes scholastic problems arise approximately at the time that the youth's own sexual abuse or first incidents of sexually abusive behaviour first took place. Teachers and other school personnel can often give actual dates of behavioural changes and of academic difficulties of the sexually abusive youth, which can then be compared against significant events in the youth's life to identify relevant stressors that affected academic performance.

The *Neuropsychological* and *Antisocial* aggregates of *MEGA* provide guidelines for knowing what academic information is important to collect, as well as framing questions to ask the youth's teachers and counsellors. Talking to school personnel is always informative. The teachers, school counsellors, and vice-principals can give information regarding the youth in question, providing such data as: history of parental involvement in the youth's academics or IEP; current behavioural problems; and history of truancy, school suspensions, and expulsions. These are all important factors to consider if the youngster is to be placed in a residential setting or foster home. If there is a long history of school absences, it is important to explore how the youth spent their time, with whom and so forth. This exploration may lead to other disclosures of antisocial behaviours (eg stealing, breaking and entering, drug involvement or other delinquent behaviour or nonsexual criminal involvement), which research has shown to be associated with risk for sexually abusive behaviour (Miccio-Fonseca, 1999: Revised 2002–2005; Prentky and Righthand, 2003). In fact, research on recidivism has shown that sexually abusive youth are significantly more at risk to re-offend with a nonsexual offence than with a sexual offence (Miner, 2002; Rasmussen, 1999a).

*MEGA*'s *Neuropsychological* aggregate is especially helpful in gathering data related to the youth's health and mental health concerns that may manifest in the school setting. Attention problems and problems in self-regulation are frequent mental health issues found in sexually abusive youth (Miccio-Fonseca, 2001; Pithers et al., 1998b). Attention problems are often associated with problems in academic and behavioural functioning (which are assessed by *MEGA*'s *Antisocial Aggregate*). Problems in self-regulation of emotions and impulses relate not only to the youth's behaviour, but also their emotional functioning and mental health. The school nurse is also a resource for obtaining general impressions of health, somatic problems and use of medication. The nurse may be aware that the youth is depressed or has difficulty regulating anger. At times the nurse's office can become a 'hang out' place for youth to go. The school nurse has an opportunity to notice the youth's peer relationships and comments that the youth's peers make about him or her, which provides valuable information about the youth's social functioning and social skills. The nurse can also comment on parental or family encounters and interactions that school personnel have with the youth. Gathering information about the sexually abusive youth from school officials can be invaluable, since the child on occasion will complain to a school official about conditions of home life.

Older adolescent sexually abusive youth (age 16–19) often have limited educational options. Their academic and/or school behavioural problems may have resulted in them being transferred to an 'alternative high school' or referred to some type of vocational training. When this is the case, it is helpful to obtain information about the youth's performance in vocational training, as well as explore options for continued vocational training or employment. Vocational options can be critical to facilitating a successful re-entry for sexually abusive youth who have been placed outside their community.

### Employment history (Neuropsychological, Family Lovemap and Antisocial Aggregates)

Employment history should be explored for both young adult and older adolescent youth, for it provides behavioural information. Employment provides sexually abusive youth with resources for themselves and their family. How the youth manages these resources can be telling. Squandering money to support his or her own wants as opposed to allocating it to meet basic needs (eg food, housing, clothing, etc.) can mirror the lack of personal responsibility that the youth shows in other areas of his or her life.

The employment record provides information on stability of employment, level of responsibilities, and relationships with co-workers and supervisors. Length of employment, reasons for leaving, types of jobs, promotions, all give a picture of the youth's 'social' identity. Some sexually abusive youth are able to perform well at their employment. Their evaluations are excellent, and they show conscientious, responsible and highly motivated work habits. Other youth show a pattern of irresponsibility in their first jobs (eg poor attendance, lack of motivation, failure to perform job tasks). As with academic history, the association of problems with employment and

risk for sexually abusive behaviour is not established. Nevertheless, it can be hypothesised that youth who have academic and behavioural problems in school might also be likely to have periods of unemployment already apparent (even before they enter the adult world of work).

Although it is a rich and untapped bank of knowledge, the employment record of sexually abusive individuals is mostly overlooked as a source of information related to their sexually offending behaviour. A youth's employment history may reveal information that is suspect, particularly for those youth whose offences involve molesting children. For example, an employer may have terminated the youth due to evidence of inappropriate sexual behaviours with children. Although it is inappropriate to diagnose young sexually abusive youth with paedophilia (see the Diagnostic and Statistical Manual of Mental Disorders – TR, 2000: 572) some older adolescents do show deviant sexual arousal to young children (Worling and Curwen, 2001). An interviewer needs to carefully assess the job history of these youth, as well as any volunteer work that they have done in community organisations. Youth who have offended against and have deviant sexual interest in children may manage to get jobs with direct access to children (ie coach, gym counsellor, teacher aide, peer counsellor at a school, library, teen centre or boys and girls club). They may take jobs in fast food restaurants, movie theatres, parks or other places where children gather. They may readily volunteer to baby-sit, coach team sports, serve as camp counsellors or be scout leaders. Family members or friends who are unaware of the youth's sexual proclivities may hire them to baby-sit young children (eg siblings, cousins, nieces, nephews, family friends). Assessing employment history and volunteer experience can reveal the youth's manipulative tactics, as well as highlight and provide valuable information related to his or her behavioural patterns of accessing victims and offending.

### Risk to the community

The primary consideration of initial assessment is identifying the youth's risk for sexually abusive behaviours. What is the level of risk for recurrence? A comprehensive assessment needs to be done to answer this question. *MEGA* provides a viable method for structuring an assessment and gathering data on a multitude of variables that need to be considered when estimating the level of risk that a youth represents or poses. It improves the accuracy of the assessment since its items are empirically guided; that is, they are based on variables that have been found in the research on sexually abusive youth to be empirically associated with risk for sexually abusive behaviour. The background of the sexually abusive youth, the nature and circumstances of the offence, and the immediate resources for intervention with the youth must all be considered when attempting to determine the risk level of a youth. Youth who offend for the first time are less of a risk than those who have a chronic history of offences (Epperson et al., 2006; Prentky and Righthand, 2003, 2004; Worling and Curwen, 2001). A systematic review looking at 12 studies of recidivism in sexually abusive youth found that a prior offence history, whether nonsexual offending, sexual offending or both, to be the most documented and significantly correlated factor in predicting recidivism (Gerhold, Brown, and Beckett 2007). Some research has shown that having multiple female victims was significantly associated with risk for sexual recidivism (Rasmussen, 1999a).

Chronic sexually abusive youth have engrained behaviour patterns that are self-gratifying and more difficult to change. Nonetheless, the fact that they are still youth means that they are still developing and are therefore more amenable to change than adult sex offenders. Given the neuropsychological research showing that the brain continues to develop until youth are in their mid 20s (Cauffman and Steinbery, 2000) sexually abusive youth can be expected to gain better self-regulation of emotions and impulses as they mature. This likely reduces their risk for recidivism for a sexual offence. The chronicle of the youth's offences and personal and family history must be assessed in order to formulate an individualised treatment program and select interventions that will be most beneficial.

*MEGA* assessment provides a comprehensive and objective method for assessing the youth's risk level and guiding placement decisions. Treatment options for sexually abusive youth consist of remaining in the community and being treated on an outpatient or day treatment basis, or being placed in a treatment facility. Treatment resources for sexually abusive youth are scarce, whether they consist of outpatient therapy, day treatment, or residential care. Sexually abusive youth who are assessed as

being lower risk and able to remain in the community may continue to live in their own home, stay with extended family or friends, or reside in a foster home. Wherever the placement is, caution should be taken that no children will be accessible to the sexually abusive youth. Vigilant supervision needs to be provided, and those individuals doing the supervision (ie parents, foster parents, extended family members, family friends) need to be advised and instructed on just what 'supervising' means. All too often this concept of supervision is used quite loosely, without professionals giving the supervising parties any real guidelines as to how to supervise, what to look for, and what interventions to make in case of problems. The supervisors many times 'supervise' according to their own concepts of 'supervision,' which may leave potential victims unprotected and youthful offenders free to offend again.

If the risk level of the youth is determined to be too high for them to safely reside in the community, a more intensive treatment setting must be found. Options include inpatient hospitalisation, a residential treatment program, or a correctional facility. Regardless of whether a youth's placement is outpatient, inpatient or residential, the Containment model, increasingly considered the gold standard of treatment for adult sex offenders, is generally applied. The Containment model is a collaborative and multidimensional model of intervention consisting of four components: treatment, supervision, polygraph testing, and victim advocacy/education (San Diego County Sex Offender Management Council, 2003). Inpatient, day treatment, and residential facilities employ the treatment component on a higher frequency rate and generally incorporate the educational component. Although we (the authors) agree with most components of the adult Containment model, we believe that polygraph testing should be used extremely judiciously unless of course there are well established standards of validity and reliability for individuals under the age of 18. We object to the use of polygraph testing with youth, however, because the standards for youth are not well established and there is no documented evidence that polygraph testing is valid and reliable for youth under the age of 18. It is a little known fact that polygraph examiners do not receive specialised training on child development and/or how to adjust polygraph testing to the developmental stage and age of the youth (American Polygraph Association, 2004a, 2004b). We believe that polygraph testing of younger youth raises significant ethical concerns. A better alternative for eliciting disclosure is for the interviewer to complete a comprehensive assessment as outlined in this article and as guided by the *MEGA* risk assessment tool.

Whether a sexually abusive youth remains in the community or is placed out of the community in a treatment facility, *MEGA* can be a valuable tool to help guide treatment planning and monitor the youth's progress over time. Its *Risk Scale* is geared toward identifying the changes that the youth makes in those risk factors that are dynamic and changeable. Also, *MEGA*'s *Protective Risk Scale* helps identify new resources that become available to the youth, either through the youth's home and community, or as a natural result of the interventions given to the youth.

Effectively and ethically assessing a sexually abusive youth means probing into the private world of their sexuality with a minimum of threat to that person, even though it may explore the most intimate aspects of erotic development and elicit the most carefully guarded personal information. For example, it is not uncommon for an interviewer to discover a respondent's sexual turn-ons, however unconventional they might be. The interview provides an environment where a sexually abusive youth may reveal private and hitherto undisclosed information including: sexual fantasies, past or current experiences of being sexually or otherwise abused or harassed, and detailed descriptions of his or her sexually abusive or sexually violent behaviour. The interviewer who ventures into this private territory must be guided by an objective map that outlines the lay of the land and identifies the factors placing the youth at risk to be sexually abusive and to engage in recurring sexual offences. The new risk assessment tool *MEGA* provides that map and is a valuable asset when assessing any sexually abusive youth under the age of 19, whether male or female, adolescent or child, or developmentally delayed.

# References

American Association on Mental Retardation (2006) *Policies: Definition of Mental Retardation*. Retrieved March 19, 2006 From: Http://Www.Aamr.Org/Policies/Faq_Mental_Retardation.Shtml

American Polygraph Association (2004a) Division III, *Standards of Practice*. Chattanooga, TN: APA.

American Polygraph Association (2004b) Division V, *By Laws Standards of Practice*. Chattanooga, TN: APA.

American Psychiatric Association (2000). *Diagnostic and statistical manual of mental disorders* (4th ed., text revision). Washington, DC: American Psychiatric Association.

American Psychological Association (2002) *Ethical Principles of Psychologists and Code of Conduct*. Washington, DC: Retrieved November 6, 2007 From: Http://Www.Apa.Org/Ethics/Code2002.Html

Araji, S.K. (1997) *Sexually Aggressive Children: Coming to Understand Them*. Thousand Oaks, CA: Sage.

Bentovim, A. et al. (1999) Facilitating Interviews with Children who have been Sexually Abused. *Child Abuse Review*, 4: 4, 246–62.

Bonner, B.L., Walker, C.E. and Berliner, L. (1999) *Children with Sexual Behaviour Problems: Assessment and Treatment*. Washington, DC: Department of Human Services.

Bowlby, J. (1988) *A Secure Base: Clinical Applications of Attachment Theory*. London: Routledge.

Burton, J. et al. (1998) *Treating Children with Sexually Abusive Behaviour Problems: Guidelines for Child and Parent Intervention*. New York: Haworth Press.

Calder, M., Hanks, H., Epps, K.J., Print, B., Harrison, T. and Hennicker, J. (2001) *Juveniles and Children Who Sexually Abuse: Frameworks for Assessment*. 2nd edn. Lyme Regis: Russell House Publishing.

Cauffman, E. and Steinberg, L. (2000) (Im)Maturity of Judgment in Adolescence: Why Adolescents may be less Culpable than Adults. *Behaviour, Science and Law*, 18: 6, 741–60.

Chaffin, M. and Bonner, B. (1998) 'Don't Shoot, We're Your Children': Have We Gone too far in our Response to Adolescent Sexual Abusers and Children with Sexual Behaviour Problems? *Child Maltreatment*, 3: 4, 314–6.

Chaffin, M., Letourneau, E. and Silovsky, J. (2002) Adults, Adolescents and Children who Sexually Abuse Children. In Meyers, J.E. et al. (Eds.) *The APSAC Handbook on Child Maltreatment*. 2nd edn. Thousand Oaks, CA: Sage.

Courtney, S., Misch, G. and Burke, C. (2003) *San Diego County Sexually Abusive Youth Profile*. San Diego, CA: San Diego Association of Governments Retrieved September 8, 2005

From: Http://Www.Sandag.Org/Uploads/ Publicationid/Publicationid_1036_2836.Pdf-Micro

Davies, D. (1999) *Child Development: A Practitioner's Guide*. New York: Guilford.

Epperson, D. (2006) *Resolving Public Policy Conflicts through the Presentation of Accurate Risk Assessment as a Prevention Strategy: Development of the J-SORRAT-II as an Illustration*. Address at Ninth Annual Training Conference of The California Coalition on Sexual Offending. San Mateo, CA.

Epperson, D.L. et al. (2006) Actuarial Risk Assessment with Juveniles who Offend Sexually: Development of the Juvenile Sexual Offence Recidivism Risk Assessment Tool-II (JSORRAT-II). In Prescott, D. (Ed.) *Risk Assessment of Youth who have Sexually Abused: Theory, Controversy and Emerging Strategies*. Oklahoma City, OK: Woods 'n' Barnes.

Friedrich, W.N. (2002) *Psychological Assessment of Sexually Abused Children and their Families*. Thousand Oaks, CA: Sage.

Gerhold, C., Brown, K. and Beckett, R. (2007) Predicting Recidivism in Adolescent Sexual Offenders. *Aggression and Violent Behaviour* 12, 427–38.

Gil, E. and Johnson, T.C. (1993) *Sexualised Children: Assessment and Treatment of Sexualised Children who Molest*. Walnut Creek, CA: Launch Press.

Gilgun, J.F. (1999) CASPARS Clinical Assessment Instruments that Measure Strengths and Risks in Children and Families. In Calder, M.C. (Ed.). *Working with Young People Who Sexually Abuse: New Pieces of the Jigsaw Puzzle*. Lyme Regis: Russell House Publishing.

Gray, A.S. and Pithers, W. D. (1993) Relapse Prevention with Sexually Aggressive Adolescents and Children: Expanding Treatment and Supervision. In Barbaree, H.E., Marshall, W.L. and Hudson, S.M. (Eds.) *The Juvenile Sexual Offender*. New York: Guilford Press.

Hackett, S. (2004) *What Works for Children and Young People with Harmful Sexual Behaviours*. Ilford: Barnardo's.

Hall, D.K., Mathews, F. and Pearce, J. (1998) Factors Associated with Sexual Behaviour Problems in Young Sexually Abused Children. *Child Abuse and Neglect*, 22: 1, 1045–63.

Hall, D.K., Mathews, F. and Pearce, J. (2002) Sexual Behaviour Problems in Sexually Abused Children: A Preliminary Typology. *Child Abuse and Neglect*, 26, 289–312.

Johnson, T.C. (2000) Sexualised Children and Children who Molest. *Siecus Report*, 29: 1, 35–9.

Johnson, T.C. and Doonan, R. (2006) Children Twelve and Under with Sexual Behaviour Problems: What We Know in 2005 that we Did Not Know in 1985. In Longo, R.E. and Prescott, D.S. (Eds.) *Current Perspectives in Working with Sexually Aggressive Youth and Youth with Sexual Behaviour Problems*. Holyoke, MA: NEARI Press.

Kahn, T.J. and Chambers, H.J. (1991) Assessing Re-offence Risk with Juvenile Sexual Offenders. *Child Welfare*, 70: 3, 333–45.

Katz, M. (1997) *On Playing a Poor Hand Well: Insights from the Lives of Those who have Overcome Childhood Risks and Adversities*. New York: WW Norton.

Lieb, R., Quinsey, V. and Berliner, L. (1998) Sexual Predators and Social Policy. In Tonry, M. (Ed.) *Crime and Justice*. Chicago, IL: University of Chicago.

Longo, R.E. (2004) An Integrated Experiential Approach to Treating Young People who Sexually Abuse. *Journal of Child Sexual Abuse*, 13: 3, 193–213.

Miccio-Fonseca, L.C. (1994/1997) *Personal Sentence Completion Inventory, an Inventory that Explores Erotic Development and Sexual Functioning. A Supplemental Tool for the Clinician in Assessments and Evaluations*. San Diego, CA: Clinic for the Sexualities; Brandon, VT: Safer Society Press.

Miccio-Fonseca, L.C. (1996) Research Report: on Sex Offenders, Victims and Their Families. *Special Edition, Journal of Offender Rehabilitation*, 23: 3, 71–83.

Miccio-Fonseca, L.C. (1998) *Fonseca Inventory of Sex Offenders' Risk Factors*. San Diego, CA: Author.

Miccio-Fonseca, L.C. (1999 – Revised 2002, 2003, 2004, 2005) *Fonseca Inventory of Sex Offenders' Risk Factors (FISORF) – Professional Manual*. San Diego, CA: Author.

Miccio-Fonseca, L.C. (2000) Adult and Adolescent Female Sex Offenders: Experiences Compared to other Females and Male Sex Offenders. *Journal of Psychology and Human Sexuality*, 11, 75–88.

Miccio-Fonseca, L.C. (2001) Somatic and Mental Symptoms of Male Sex Offenders, a Comparison among Offenders, Victims and Their Families. *Journal of Psychology and Human Sexuality*, 13, 103–14.

Miccio-Fonseca, L.C. (2005) *Erotic Development: Sexual Deviancy and Technology*. Invited

Presentation at the 8th Annual Training Conference of The California Coalition on Sexual Offending, San Diego, CA.

Miccio-Fonseca, L.C. (2006a) Family Lovemaps: Challenging the Myths Related to Multiple Paraphilias, Denial and Paraphilic Fugue States. *ATSA Forum.*

Miccio-Fonseca, L.C. (2006b) *Multiplex Empirically Guided Inventory of Ecological Aggregates for Assessing Sexually Abusive Children and Adolescents (19 and Under): MEGA.* San Diego, CA: Author.

Miccio-Fonseca, L. C. (2006c) *Multiplex Empirically Guided Inventory of Ecological Aggregates for Assessing Sexually Abusive Children and Adolescents (19 and Under: MEGA: Manual and Rating Booklet).* San Diego, CA: Author.

Miccio-Fonseca, L.C. (2007) Challenging the Myths about Sexual Disorders: Understanding the Role of Bio-Physio Processes, Family Lovemaps and Paraphilic Fugue States. In Prescott, D.S. (Ed.) *Knowledge and Practice: Challenges in the Treatment and Supervision of Sexual Abusers.* Oklahoma City, OK: Wood n' Barnes.

Miccio-Fonseca, L.C. and Rasmussen, L.A. (2006a) Empirical Support for *MEGA.* In Miccio-Fonseca, L.C. *Multiplex Empirically Guided Inventory of Ecological Aggregates for Assessing Sexually Abusive Children and Adolescents (19 and Under: MEGA: Professional Manual and Rating Booklet).* San Diego, CA: Author.

Miccio-Fonseca, L.C. and Rasmussen, L.A. (2006b) *Implementing MEGA, A New Tool for Assessing Risk of Concern for Sexually Abusive Behaviour in Youth Ages 19 and Under: An Empirically Guided Paradigm for Risk Assessment: Revised Version.* Available from Www.Ccoso.Org.

Miccio-Fonseca, L.C. and Rasmussen, L.A. (2007) Assessing Predatory Sexually Violent Behaviour in Older Adolescent Males: Implementing *MEGA:* A New Risk Assessment Tool for Youth 19 and Under.

Miner, M. (2002) Factors Associated with Recidivism of Juveniles: An Analysis of Serious Juvenile Sex Offenders. *Journal of Research on Crime and Delinquency,* 39: 4, 421–36.

Money, J. (1986) *Lovemaps: Clinical Concepts of Sexual/Erotic Health and Pathology, Paraphilia and Gender Transposition in Childhood, Adolescence and Maturity.* New York: Irvington.

Money, J. (1988) *Gay, Straight and In Between.* New York: Oxford University Press.

National Association of Social Workers (1999) *Code of Ethics of The National Association of Social Workers.* Washington, DC: Author. Retrieved November 6, 2007 From: Http:// Www.Socialworkers.Org/Pubs/Code/ Code.Asp

Office of Juvenile Justice and Delinquency Prevention (2006) *Statistical Briefing Book.* Retrieved November 6, 2007 From: Http:// Www.Ojjdp.Ncjrs.Gov/Ojstatbb/Nr2006/ Downloads/NR2006.Pdf

Perry, G.P. and Orchard, J. (1992) *Assessment and Treatment of Adolescent Sex Offenders.* Sarasota, Fl: Professional Resource Exchange.

Pithers, W.D. et al. (1998a) Caregivers of Children with Sexual Behaviour Problems: Psychological and Familial Functioning. *Child Abuse and Neglect,* 22: 2, 129–41.

Pithers, W.D. et al. (1998b) Children with Sexual Behaviour Problems: Identification of Five Distinct Child Types and Related Treatment Considerations. *Child Maltreatment,* 3: 4, 384–406.

Prentky, R. et al. (2000) An Actuarial Procedure for Assessing Risk in Juvenile Sex Offenders. *Sexual Abuse: A Journal of Research and Treatment,* 12: 2, 71–93.

Prentky, R. and Righthand, S. (2003) *Juvenile Sex Offender Assessment Protocol-II (J-SOAP-II) Manual.* Office of Juvenile Justice and Delinquency Prevention, Juvenile Justice Clearinghouse. Retrieved November 6, 2007 From: Http://Www.Csom.Org/Pubs/ JSOAP.Pdf

Prentky, R., & Righthand, S. (2004). *Juvenile Sex Offender Assessment Protocol II (J-SOAP-II) Manual.* Retrieved October 30, 2005, from http://www.forensicexaminers.com/jsoap.pdf

Rasmussen, L.A. (1999a) Factors Related to Recidivism among Juvenile Sexual Offenders. *Sexual Abuse: A Journal of Research and Treatment,* 11: 1, 69–85.

Rasmussen, L.A. (1999b) The Trauma Outcome Process: An Integrated Model for Guiding Clinical Practice with Children with Sexually Abusive Behaviour Problems. *Journal of Child Sexual Abuse,* 8: 4, 3–33.

Rasmussen, L.A. (2001) Integrating Cognitive-Behavioural and Expressive Therapy Interventions: Applying the Trauma Outcome Process in Treating Children with Sexually Abusive Behaviour Problems. *Journal of Child Sexual Abuse,* 10: 4, 1–29.

Rasmussen, L.A. (2004) Differentiating Youth with Sexual Behaviour Problems: Applying a

Multidimensional Framework when Assessing and Treating Subtypes. *Journal of Child Sexual Abuse*, 13: 3, 57–82.

Rasmussen, L.A. and Cunningham, C. (1995) Focused Play Therapy and Non-Directive Play Therapy: Can they be Integrated? *Journal of Child Sexual Abuse*, 4: 1, 1–20.

Rasmussen, L.A. and Miccio-Fonseca, L.C. (2007a) Empirically Guided Practice with Young People who Sexually Abuse: A Risk Factor Approach to Assessment and Treatment. In Calder, M.C. (Ed.) *Children and Young People who Sexually Abuse: Taking The Field Forward.* Lyme Regis: Russell House Publishing.

Rasmussen, L. and Miccio-Fonseca, L. (2007b) Paradigm Shift: Implementing *MEGA*, A New Tool Proposed to Define and Assess Sexually Abusive Dynamics in Youth Ages 19 and Under. *Journal of Child Sexual Abuse*, 16: 1, 85–106.

Rich, P. (2006) *Attachment and Sexual Offending: Understanding and Applying Attachment Theory to Juvenile Sexual Offenders.* Chichester: John Wiley and Sons.

Righthand, S. et al. (2005) Factor Structure and Validation of the Juvenile Sex Offender Assessment Protocol (J-SOAP) *Sexual Abuse: A Journal of Research and Treatment*, 17: 1, 13–30.

Rosenbaum, A., Geffner, R. and Benjamin, (1997) A Biopsychosocial Model or Understanding Relationship Aggression. In Geffner, R., Sorenson, S.B. and Lundberg-Love, P. (Eds.) *Violence and Sexual Abuse at Home: Current Issues in Spousal Battering and Child Maltreatment.* New York: Haworth.

San Diego County Sex Offender Management Council (2003) *Standards for the Treatment of Sexually Abusive Youth: Approved by the San Diego County Sex Offender Management Council.* Retrieved February 27, 2005 From: Http://Www.Sdsomc.Com/Images/Juv_Tx_Standards.Pdf

Schram, D.D., Milloy, C.D. and Rowe, W.E. (1991) *Juvenile Sexual Offenders: A Follow-Up Study of Reoffence Behaviour.* Unpublished Manuscript.

Williams, G.J. and Money, J. (1980) *Traumatic Abuse and Neglect of Children at Home.* Baltimore, MD: The Johns Hopkins University Press.

Worling, J.R. (2004) The Estimate of Adolescent Sexual Offence Recidivism (ERASOR): Preliminary Psychometric Data. *Sexual Abuse: A Journal of Research and Treatment*, 16: 3, 235–54.

Worling, J.R. and Curwen, T. (2000) Adolescent Sexual Offender Recidivism: Success of Specialised Treatment and Implications for Risk Prediction. *Child Abuse and Neglect*, 24, 965–82.

Worling, J.R. and Curwen, T. (2001) *The ERASOR: Estimate of Risk of Adolescent Sexual Offence Recidivism.* Toronto, ON: Sexual Abuse Family Education and Treatment Program, Thistletown Regional Center for Children and Adolescents, Ontario Ministry of Community and Social Services.

# CHAPTER 4

# Sharp Practice: The Sexually Harmful Adolescent Risk Protocol (SHARP)

*Graeme Richardson*

## Introduction

This chapter details the conceptual, empirical, and pragmatic construction of The Sexually Harmful Risk Protocol (SHARP). The protocol is presented as representing sharp practice, that is, when devoid of legal connotations, providing evidence based, clear, concise, pragmatic, and safe guidance to the hard working practitioner under pressure. *Occam's Razor* encapsulates the logical principle that underpins sharp practice. That is:

> One should not increase, beyond what is necessary, the number of entities required to explain anything.

Practitioners, like nature, prefer simplicity. If simpler models explain the phenomenon, then let's base our practice on simpler models. Let's not complicate things for ourselves, and more importantly for our clients, especially when they are children and young people. In relation to sexually harmful behaviour exhibited by children and adolescents, *Occam's Razor* tells us that:

- *sexually harmful behaviour will be strongly associated with sexual development, and*
- *sexual development will be strongly associated with general development.*

Simple really! Beyond this appealing simplicity of logic lie the potential complexities of efficiently and accurately assessing multiple developmental domains, and the interplay between them, involved in the onset and maintenance of sexually harmful behaviour. In addition, there is the reality that many of these children and adolescents present with complex needs, which typically means multiple difficulties across several developmental domains. In light of this, we need to heed the words of Einstein when he said:

> Everything should be made as simple as possible, but not simpler.

In relation to evaluation and accuracy, we should also take into account his statement that:

> Not everything that counts can be counted and not everything that can be counted counts.

The SHARP is not about counting risk-need factors; rather it is about guiding the practitioner through the process of completing a developmental formulation of the young person's sexually harmful behaviour. Essentially the SHARP integrates a developmental perspective on the Risk-Need-Responsivity approach to offender assessment and rehabilitation (Andrews and Bonta, 2003) with an understanding of sexually harmful behaviour in children and young people informed by a case conceptualisation or case formulation perspective derived from clinical psychology and cognitive therapy (Eells, 2007; Persons, 1989).

The critical conceptualisation underpinning the SHARP is that sexually harmful behaviour is associated with and dependent upon the young person's sexual development. It is proposed that sexual development may be usefully categorised in terms of having been:

- *precocious/accelerated* (as in the case of sexualised pre-pubertal children),
- *delayed* (as in the case of adolescent males who have had no age appropriate experiences),
- *dysfunctional* (as in the case of sexual behaviour meeting non-sexual needs), and
- *deviant* (as in the case of deviant sexual arousal, interests, and preferences)

The SHARP's conceptualisation of sexual development emphasises the interplay between other areas of development and their potential impacts on sexual development in particular cases. The supporting conceptualisation underpinning the SHARP is related to the evaluation and functional classification of these various developmental domains in terms of *adjustment* as a catchall term, which means in practice:

- functioning,
- adaptation, and
- integration.

*Functioning* refers to skills and abilities; *Adaptation* refers to age and socially appropriate behaviours; and *Integration* refers to relationships and attachments. The resulting developmental formulation of sexually harmful behaviour directly informs case management practice.

## Overview

Heterogeneity or diversity characterises the field of the study of sexually harmful adolescents, in terms of:

- The behavioural characteristics of the sexually harmful behaviour (offence types).
- The psychosocial characteristics of the sexually harmful behaviour (motivations and reinforcements).
- The functional abilities of the young person pertaining to general psychosocial developmental tasks.
- The adaptation and integration achieved by the young person pertaining to interpersonal and social relationships.

This heterogeneity highlights both the importance of and the professional challenges associated with the task of assessment in this field. One approach to capturing this heterogeneity is to conceptualise it in terms of:

- risk
- need
- responsivity
- resilience

. . . or the *Risk, Need, Responsivity, Resilience Principle*. When following this principle the assessment becomes comprehensive and holistic, rather than restricted to risk factors known to be associated with sexual recidivism.

The Sexually Harmful Adolescent Risk Protocol (SHARP) is a research guided protocol; it guides the professional practice of the risk, need, responsivity, resilience assessment of sexually harmful adolescents. It guides practitioners' evaluations of the risk that the young person is considered to present, but does not take the judgement out of their hands by making the decision for them by means of a numerical scoring system. It is not intended to 'simply' predict the risk for sexual recidivism and therefore does not limit itself to the assessment of risk factors that research has shown to be associated with sexual re-offending. Consequently, it is consistent with the widely accepted Structured Professional Judgement approach to risk assessment, which defines the latest risk assessment protocols in the field of violence and sexual violence (Hart et al., 2003; Kropp, Hart and Belfrage, 2005; Kropp, Hart and Lyon, 2006; Kropp et al., 1999; Webster et al., 1997). It is also consistent with the Risk, Need, Responsivity Principle, which underpins the latest risk assessment protocols in the field of general criminality (Andrews, Bonta and Wormith, 2004). In fact, the Structured Professional Judgement approach combined with the Risk, Need, Responsivity Principle is at the heart of the SHARP.

As well as these technical approaches to risk assessment cited above, also at the heart of the SHARP is the young person in the context of his general development and progress through his adolescence. This shifts the focus on to developmental domains critical to the young person's psychosocial functioning, interpersonal and social adaptation and interpersonal and social integration. Consequently, the SHARP is not an actuarial assessment protocol that prioritises static (historical) and unchangeable factors, rather it emphasises the young person's developmental context (which is quintessentially dynamic as it is a process of personal adaptation and change), their current functioning and adaptation across the primary domains of adolescent development and dynamic risk, need, responsivity factors. It represents a developmentally sensitive comprehensive assessment of the young person and their sexually harmful behaviour and a holistic approach to risk, need, responsivity evaluation. A holistic and comprehensive assessment that centres on the young person's global adolescent development allows the practitioner to understand sexually harmful behaviour, rather than simply describe it. A developmentally informed understanding is achieved through the process of risk formulation, which the SHARP guides the practitioner through. This risk formulation is utilised to inform the case management process, which incorporates the process of risk projection, its rationale being to help formulate more insightful and potentially more effective case management planning and decision-making.

The SHARP does not produce a probability of reconviction and does not profess to be able to accurately predict sexual re-offending. However it does guide the practitioner through the process of case management. Specifically, it informs and guides *risk management* (interventions that target risk-specific factors) and *harm reduction* (interventions that target risk-related or need factors). The SHARP accommodates potential changes in risk status or classification over time, by seeking to monitor and evaluate the impact of case management interventions on risk, need, responsivity targets, that is, intervention-adjusted risk status/classification, by means of risk reviews or re-assessments. Consequently, the SHARP is an instrument designed to facilitate multi-agency and multi-professional collaboration and co-ordination in the practice of risk management and harm reduction in an individual young person. The SHARP also guides the practitioner through the identification of imminent risk (acute dynamic risk factors) for sexually harmful behaviour to inform acute supervision and monitoring strategies and interventions. It includes the assessment of responsivity factors and resilience or protective factors, which are identified to monitor and enhance case management planning and harm reduction strategies.

## Terminology

Developmentally sensitive and appropriate language and terminology are used. Several of the risk domains refer to different aspects of the young person's overall development and current adjustment within a developmental context. The term 'sexually harmful' is used to refer to sexually inappropriate, sexually abusive or sexually offending behaviours and to refer to the young person who has committed a sexual offence or who has perpetrated sexually abusive behaviour but not received a criminal conviction. The primary purpose of the risk protocol is to inform and improve 'risk management' and 'harm reduction' interventions by means of an evidence based, systematic approach to 'case management'. Case management is the overall management of the behaviour and the young person in the pursuit of public protection/victim

protection and is intended to be a multi-agency and multi-professional enterprise. Case management is comprised of risk management strategies and interventions, which explicitly target and impact on immediate risk for sexually harmful behaviour and harm reduction interventions, which target criminongenic and non-criminongenic needs and are rehabilitative or therapeutic in nature.

## The young person

The SHARP was constructed and developed to assess sexually harmful behaviour and the young person who exhibited that behaviour. Its practice remit is that it is intended for males aged from 12 to 19 years, who are in the developmental stage of adolescence. It is appropriate for young people diagnosed with a learning disability or a psychiatric disorder. It assists the assessment of all types of sexually harmful behaviour. It is appropriate for young people in community settings and in secure settings. The young person may have received a criminal conviction for a sexual offence or may be awaiting a sentencing hearing. Alternatively, the young person may be subject to Child Protection procedures. Consequently, it is intended for both Criminal Justice (criminal law) and Social Service (civil law) statutory assessment tasks.

## Targeted agencies and services

The SHARP is intended to be utilised and operationalised by the range of agencies and services that are involved in the assessment and case management of sexually harmful young people. These include:

- The Youth Offending Service in the UK.
- Juvenile Justice Services in North America.
- The Probation Service (in relation to mandatory public protection services, such as Multi-Agency Public Protection Arrangements in the United Kingdom.
- The Police Service (also in relation to mandatory public protection services).
- Social Services in the United Kingdom and Child Welfare Services in North America (in relation to mandatory child protection and child sexual abuse services).
- The secure estate institutions, such as, young offender prisons in the United Kingdom,

juvenile correctional facilities in North America and secure child care institutions.

- Forensic child and adolescent mental health services provided within prison or correctional and secure care establishments, in-patient secure hospitals facilities and outpatient health services.

## Targeted professionals

The SHARP is intended to be utilised and operationalised by the range of professional groups who are involved in the assessment or case management of sexually harmful young people. These include:

- Youth Offending Service staff in the United Kingdom.
- Juvenile Justice Services staff in North America.
- Probation officers who provide mandatory public protection services.
- Police officers who provide mandatory public protection services.
- Social workers who provide mandatory child protection or child sexual abuse services.
- Prison or correctional psychologists and psychiatrists.
- Psychologists and psychiatrists who work into secure care facilities.
- Forensic and clinical psychologists who are attached to Youth Offending Services and Juvenile Justice Services.
- Mental health practitioners who work into criminal justice services.
- Child and adolescent psychiatrists and psychologists who provide mental health assessments and consultation services for other agencies or projects who provide services for sexually harmful young people.
- Forensic child and adolescent psychiatrists and forensic child and adolescent psychologists working in forensic mental health services for young people.

## The fundamentals of assessment

The SHARP adheres to the fundamental principles of assessment in the human services, namely:

- Standardised and structured evidence based practice.

- Developmentally appropriate and sensitive assessment targets and procedures.
- Encompassing the diversity of sexually harmful behaviours and young people who sexually harm.
- Assessment directed risk management.
- Assessment directed harm reduction interventions.
- Regular re-assessment and re-evaluations of risk, need and responsivity.

## Structured Professional Judgement approach

The SHARP adopts and adheres to the Structured Professional Judgement approach to risk assessment, which means that:

- It reflects evidence based practice.
- It is structured in its approach.
- It is comprehensively documented in terms of its format and presentation.
- It guides the practitioner through the whole process of the assessment.

This SPJ approach provides practice advantages for both the practitioner and the service or agency. The advantages for the practitioner include:

- Relevant and pertinent information is collected and utilised.
- The risk assessment process is explicitly documented.
- It is indicated when to seek specialist input from other agencies or professions.
- It informs the production of a case management plan.
- It informs the production of a risk management and harm reduction intervention plan.
- It highlights the need for monitoring the effectiveness of planned interventions and for regular reviews.

The advantages for the service or agency include:

- It provides an empirically derived evidence base to the practice adopted by the service or agency.
- It provides a documented approach to risk assessment and management.
- It enables more competent practitioners.
- It provides a more defensible practice.

• It provides a more efficient and effective service.

## Risk, Need, Responsivity Principle

An assessment protocol based on the *Risk, Need, Responsivity Principle* (see Andrews and Bonta, 2003) provides the structured framework for the seamless progression from assessment to case management, including risk management and harm reduction interventions to contain or minimise risk and meet unmet needs, in a service delivery context consistent and compatible with best practice in the field and is responsive to the nature of the young person's sexually harmful behaviour and his personal characteristics (including functional abilities and difficulties).

### Risk/need

The SHARP provides for the assessment of 50 factors (see Appendix 1), which are either risk or need or responsivity factors. Simply, risks need to be contained or minimised and needs need to be met. Risks and needs are regarded as intertwined and effective case management requires that both are targeted and addressed.

### Responsivity

The SHARP facilitates adherence to the responsivity principle, which refers to the nature and extent of the professional responses to the young person. Responsivity refers to the marrying of risk/need profiles with the nature and extent of professional interventions. Responsivity incorporates two related areas:

1. *General responsivity* (the characteristics of the interventions or level of service provided to the young person and to the victim/public in terms of protection from sexual harm).
2. *Individual responsivity* (the characteristics of the individual young person).

#### Level of service

On the one hand, adherence to responsivity ensures that the most intensive and restrictive case management interventions and most intensive treatment interventions are reserved for high-risk-high-need individuals. The level of service provided in terms of the provision of services from different agencies and different professions, the duration and intensity of those services, the range of those services and degree and nature of specialisation provided by those services is consistent with the assessed risk or need profile. Services include those that provide risk management interventions (including surveillance, impose restrictions and monitor conditions and compliance) and those that provide harm reduction interventions, that is (interventions to remediate functional deficits and enhance the young person's development) including highly specialised interventions in relation to child and adolescent psychiatric disorders and dysfunctional or deviant sexual functioning.

#### The individual young person

Adherence to responsivity ensures that interventions are cognisant of and compatible with the personal characteristics of the individual young person in terms of his age, developmental maturity, personality, cognitive abilities, psychosocial functioning and his motivation and compliance with professional staff and interventions. The practitioner needs to assess and respond to any identified responsivity factors specific to the individual young person. This will guide the approach of staff and the service in terms of how interventions are devised and delivered in practice.

#### Resilience (protective) factors

In addition to risk, need and responsivity, the SHARP incorporates Resilience or protective factors. This is consistent with the other child and adolescent risk protocols, such as the Structured Assessment of Violence Risk in Youth (SAVRY: Borum, Bartel and Forth, 2002). For some time, the child and adolescent mental health literature has identified resilience factors, which mitigate the harm caused to children by adverse childhood life events and experiences, such as neglect, abuse and trauma. Resilience generally refers to several domains:

• The child's inherent resources and strengths.
• Support from the child's family.
• Wider networks of social support.

The presence of resilience factors may indicate greater potential for pertinent professional interventions to facilitate more appropriate and healthy general development, which may impact on risk reduction. In addition, the literature on young offenders has identified protective factors that interrupt criminal career trajectories. Risk management and harm reduction strategies and interventions are likely to be more effective if they utilise resilience factors and consolidate or enhance protective factors. The SHARP provides for the assessment and recording of resilience or protective factors, which are then utilised in the case planning and management sections of the SHARP.

## Conceptual underpinnings

The conceptual underpinnings of the construction of the SHARP may be summarised in terms of six areas of knowledge. These are:

1. Child and adolescent general development.
2. Empirically derived knowledge about risk assessment.
3. Clinically derived knowledge about risk assessment.
4. Theoretically derived knowledge about risk assessment.
5. Empirically derived knowledge about the structured professional judgement approach.
6. Empirically derived knowledge about the risk, need, responsivity principle.

Clinically derived knowledge pertaining to the author's professional experiences has highlighted the critical importance of sexual development during childhood and adolescence and how it is influenced and shaped by five parallel areas of child and adolescent development, namely:

1. Social development.
2. Emotional development
3. Personality development.
4. Psychological or mental health develonpment, and
5. Cognitive development.

## Developmental perspective

The SHARP was shaped around child and adolescent development and known influences and factors that impede or divert a healthy trajectory in adolescent development. The overall approach reflects developmentally sensitive practice. This developmentally sensitive approach refers to:

- The young person's sexually harmful behaviour.
- Their developmental stage.
- Their wider developmental needs.

Pertinent childhood and adolescent disorders are considered. A developmental perspective is sensitive to transient psychosocial deficits and difficulties that may play an influential role in the aetiology and onset of sexually harmful behaviour. It also embraces the range of physiological, personal, interpersonal and social changes that are characteristic of the life stage of adolescence and on this basis it is generally optimistic about a young persons' ability to control and change his sexual behaviour. In relation to the construction of a risk, need, responsivity protocol for adolescents, it is contended that there should be more dynamic risk factors relative to static risk factors. In addition, dynamic factors associated with psychosocial development should be regarded as 'modifiable' dynamic, rather than 'stable' dynamic as classified in the adult literature. This acknowledges the greater potential to modify personality and psychosocial variables in young people, which may be more ingrained and fixed in adults.

## Developmental formulation

The SHARP integrates a developmental approach to risk-need-responsivity assessment and case management with a case conceptualisation or case formulation of the young person's sexually harmful behaviour. This approach is designed to provide the practitioner with a developmental formulation and a developmental case management plan. The process involves the following sequential stages:

1. A developmental formulation of risk-need-responsivity factors
2. A developmental formulation of the young person's sexually harmful behaviour
3. A developmentally informed and sensitive risk management plan
4. A developmentally informed and sensitive rehabilitation/treatment plan

To achieve the above the SHARP assists the practitioner in the evaluation of the following developmental areas of functioning:

- Social development
- Emotional development
- Personality development
- Sexual development
- Cognitive development

From an assessment perspective, the SHARP assists the practitioner in the completion of the following:

1. A comprehensive assessment of sexually harmful behaviour
2. A psycho-social assessment
3. A psycho-sexual assessment

In addition, the SHARP assists the practitioner in determining the impact of mental health difficulties on the young person's general development and his sexual development. This will involve collaboration with a mental health practitioner to access any existing psychiatric or psychological evaluations, or referral for a current mental health evaluation.

Armed with all this information the SHARP assists the practitioner in the evaluation of the compound adverse impact of difficulties in individual developmental domains on the young person's sexual development, then arrive at a case formulation opinion on the associations between the young person's sexual development and adjustment and his sexually harmful behaviour. The structure of the SHARP then provides guidance on how to translate a developmental formulation into pragmatic case management decision making in terms of risk management and rehabilitation interventions.

### The inter-relationships between developmental domains

From the perspective of developmental psychology, the different domains of the child's or young person's development are inter-related and inter-dependent. For example, cognitive and emotional development impact on the child's social development, as does the child's personality development. Similarly, a psychiatric disorder or mental health difficulties will have consequences for the young person's social development. The SHARP emphasises the inter-relatedness and inter-dependence of cognitive, emotional, personality and social development on the one hand and sexual development on the other hand. In the author's practical experience, sexually harmful behaviour in young people has for the most part been found to have been associated with delayed or dysfunctional development in these associated areas of child and adolescent development. The SHARP refers to these as functional developmental domains. Specifically, difficulties in cognitive, emotional and personality development find expression in problematic interpersonal and social relationships. Hence the primary developmental domain associated with sexual development becomes social development. This conclusion is premised on the inter-relatedness and inter-dependence of social and sexual development, given that healthy sexual development and expression of sexuality is dependent upon competent social functioning, healthy interpersonal and social relationships and interpersonal attachments.

### Social and sexual development

Social development is central to adolescence. Social identify, peer relations, peer acceptance and approval are core developmental tasks that pre-occupy adolescents. In addition, a unique and equally critical area of change during the teenage years is associated with sexual development. Physical changes and development necessitate adjustment by the young person to their emerging sexuality. Sexual development is relational, in that, sexual understanding, sexual exploration and sexual expression require interpersonal interactions and relationships, followed by acquired interpersonal intimate attachments. This sequential process of moving closer towards more intimate attachments with peers requires experience, skills and self-confidence in terms of opposite sex peer interactions (as is the case for heterosexual adolescents). Consequently, sexual development and adjustment are intimately associated with and dependent upon, functional social development, successful social adjustment and social integration. Social competency and social integration are therefore closely allied to successful sexual competency and sexual integration.

This stage of transition, known as adolescence, may be problematic, even for teenagers who have not experienced adverse childhood experiences or childhood difficulties in terms of their cognitive abilities and or mental health. A young person may experience significant difficulties in terms of their social development, which may result in social adjustment and integration difficulties. These difficulties may be associated with temperamental and personality characteristics (such as severe shyness), cognitive deficits, mental health difficulties, problematic peer relations, or lack of opportunities to socialise with other young people. For those young people who have experienced significant difficulties in terms of their social adjustment and integration, this may leave them vulnerable to sexual adjustment and sexual integration difficulties due to the dependency of successful sexual development on successful social development. Therefore, a developmental perspective has the potential to inform a risk, needs, responsivity formulation (holistic and comprehensive understanding) of the young person's sexually harmful behaviour. The SHARP seeks to assist the practitioner in determining a formulation unique to adolescents and one which differentiates them from their adult counterparts, by emphasising that social competency deficits, social adaptation difficulties and social exclusion may led to sexual competency deficits, sexual adaptation difficulties and sexual exclusion. Consequently, the SHARP seeks to identify and specify the combination of deficits, maladaptations and exclusions in both the social and sexual developmental domains in order to produce a risk, needs, responsivity formulation to inform case management interventions.

## Personality and sexual development

A young person's personality development may be classified in terms of being either adaptive and functional or maladaptive and dysfunctional. Emerging personality difficulties or dysfunction in adolescence may be described in terms of a combination of adaptive and maladaptive personality traits and their associated behaviours. Young people with personality dysfunction are more likely to experience significant, recurrent and long-standing difficulties in terms of relating to other people and in their interpersonal and social relationships. They are more likely to be emotionally labile and impulsive, which are emotional developmental factors that can impede the development of self-regulation (self-control

and self-management) and they are less likely to be able to adequately cope with the demands and stressors associated with everyday life. Similarly to the social developmental domain, difficulties in healthy development are most clearly seen in terms of functional impairments in the young person's interpersonal and social behaviour. Consequently, the SHARP emphasises the potential adverse impact of dysfunctional personality development upon social development and consequently upon sexual development. It stresses the importance of a comprehensive assessment of personality development, including emerging personality dysfunction or disorders, in order to identify risks and needs related to maladaptive personality functioning. In terms of differential diagnosis, several clinical disorders in childhood and adolescence share symptoms with emerging personality dysfunction. These are:

- Attachment disorder.
- Conduct disorder.
- Mixed disorder of emotion and conduct.
- Social anxiety or phobia.
- Asperger's syndrome.

## Child and adolescent psychiatric disorders and sexual development

In addition to emerging personality dysfunction, the SHARP includes the assessment of the separate category of psychopathology in terms of the young person's mental health status, which although independent of the other developmental domains, is considered to have the potential to exert an adverse impact upon the course of these developmental domains. In terms of risk, need, responsivity evaluation the symptomatology associated with a particular psychiatric disorder may be directly associated with the aetiology of the sexually harmful behaviour, or may be the cause of other functional impairments, which are more directly associated with the onset of sexually harmful behaviour. As with the other developmental functional impairments, psychopathology reflects a potentially modifiable dynamic risk factor, one which will require focused interventions, specifically psychiatric and psychological interventions to treat and manage the disorder by alleviating the symptomatology and remediate any associated functional impairments, such as in the areas of emotional and social functioning. Different child and adolescent disorders will vary in terms of their dynamic nature, that is, their responsivity to treatment and their prognostic course over the life span of the young person. Some disorders have a cyclic prognosis, involving a sequence of relapses over time, while other conditions, such as the pervasive developmental disorders, are lifelong disorders, in that they are not curable, where the goal becomes to improve the young person's functioning, adaptation, integration and hence their quality of life. Consequently, the SHARP directs the practitioner's attention to the potential adverse impact of psychiatric disorder or mental health difficulties on the young person's interpersonal and social development, again seen most acutely in terms of functional impairments in interpersonal and social functioning, adaptation and integration.

### Functional impairments and sexual development

In terms of adolescent sexual development there are only two potential outcomes:

1. Normal healthy sexual functioning.
2. Maladaptive (including harmful) sexual functioning.

Normal healthy sexual functioning incorporates functional abilities (skills and abilities), adaptation (interactions and relationships) and integration (intimacy) in relation to the interpersonal and social contexts in which sexuality and sexual behaviour are rooted. Maladaptive sexual functioning, on the other hand, reflects functional impairments and negates healthy sexual adaptation (absent or dysfunctional interactions and relationships) and integration (absence of intimacy). There will be several different pathways leading to maladaptive sexual functioning and these will be associated with different aetiologies for sexually harmful behaviour and reflect the heterogeneity or diversity known to exist in populations of sexually harmful adolescents. These various pathways will be characterised by functional impairments in the different domains of child and adolescent development, cognitive, emotional, social, personality and sexual. Functional impairments may be associated with psychosocial functioning or psychiatric disorders/mental health difficulties. In this developmental model, adolescent sexual development may become

maladaptive because of impaired functioning in any of the developmental domains, and, of course, because of abnormal or unhealthy development of the child or adolescent's sexuality itself (as in the case of the sexually abused prepubertal child). Consequently, functional impairments in whatever developmental domain represent modifiable dynamic risk factors, with some proving more or less modifiable than others. All will require focused remedial interventions in order to render them truly dynamic, that is, alterable. In terms of risk evaluation, so long as the functional impairments identified as associated with sexually harmful behaviour remain intact, the risk for future sexually harmful behaviour will remain viable. In addition, the number of functional impairments across the range of developmental domains and the severity of these impairments, will strongly indicate the level of risk/need. Consequently, these functional impairments and their severity reflect an inherent propensity for sexually harmful behaviour (once sexually harmful behaviour has been exhibited) and need to be targeted by harm reduction interventions.

## Conceptualisation of risk and the risk assessment process

The SHARP's conceptualisation of risk and the risk assessment process that it guides the practitioner through incorporates the following:

- Risk factors (individual factors).
- Risk process (risk trajectory).
- Risk types (typologies associated with both sexually harmful behaviour and the young person's functioning, adaptation and integration).
- Developmentally guided risk evaluation.
- Risk based on sexual development.
- Risk level (ascribing low, moderate, high ratings).
- Risk calculation.
- Risk formulation.
- Risk classification.
- Risk projection.

### Risk factors (individual factors)

Risk factors are the common currency of risk assessments and risk evaluations. They are selected specifically in relation to a particular type of criminal behaviour, such as sexual offending. They typically pertain to:

- The offence behaviour
- The offender
- The victim
- The contextual or social environment

They are selected on the basis of the available empirically derived risk literature and ideally, they should be empirically associated with recidivism. In relation to certain criminal offending, particular risk factors are considered to be more significant in terms of recidivism. For instance, deviant sexual arousal and antisocial orientation or lifestyle are considered to be very significant in relation to violent sexual offences. In a practical risk evaluation sense, these critical risk factors carry additional weight from a structured professional judgment approach. Notwithstanding this, typical risk assessment guides do not ascribe differential weightings to particular risk factors. The risk factors included in a risk assessment guide should be both, firstly, empirically valid, in that they have been shown to be associated with repeated sexual offending and secondly, practically useful, in that they are broad enough to inform case management decision-making in terms of risk management and harm reduction planning.

The SHARP differentiates six types of risk factors:

1. Static risk factors.
2. Dynamic risk factors.
3. Aetiological risk factors.
4. Sustaining risk factors.
5. Acute risk factors.
6. Critical risk factors.

## Static risk factors

Static risk factors refer to factors that are:

- Historical in nature.
- Unchangeable (in terms of reducing).
- Permanent.

They are typically previous experiences and behaviours. As they are assumed to be static, they will continue to have the same influence on the practitioner's evaluation of risk at different points in time. An example would be previous

childhood sexual abuse. However, some static risk factors are changeable in terms of increasing from one risk assessment to another over a period of time. For example, previous convictions for sexual offences may increase in number or increase in severity following a previous risk assessment. Static factors have been regarded as more relevant to the task of risk prediction rather than the task of case management.

## Dynamic risk factors

Dynamic risk factors refer to factors that are:

- Characteristics or features of an individual's personality and interpersonal and social functioning.
- Characteristics or features of an individual's sexuality and sexual functioning.
- The individual's mental health status and cognitive functioning.
- Modifiable.

As such, they will not continue to have the same influence on the practitioner's evaluation risk at different points in time. An example would be denial of sexually harmful behaviour. However, the degree to which some dynamic risk factors are modifiable is questionable, for example, sexually deviant interests or psychopathic traits. Also, the time and effort necessary to bring about positive changes are likely to vary for different dynamic risk factors, for example personality dysfunction in comparison to social skills deficits will require more intensive therapeutic efforts, more specialist interventions, over a longer period of time. Dynamic factors have been regarded as more relevant to the task of case management and are often treatment targets.

## Aetiological risk factors

Aetiological risk factors are those factors known to be associated with the onset of sexually harmful behaviours. In this simple sense, they may be regarded as causal risk factors. The literature indicates that the onset of sexually harmful behaviour is the consequence of the interplay between multiple factors. Not one single factor has causal authority or priority. Consequently, several aetiological risk factors are likely to be present in any single case. An example of one such factor is childhood sexual victimisation. In the literature, these risk factors may also be referred to as distal or predisposing risk factors. The literature is less categorical about the association between aetiological risk factors and sexual recidivism.

### Sustaining risk factors

Sustaining risk factors are those factors known to be associated with persistent risk for the commission of a sexual offence. They are present at all times, but may vacillate between been active or inactive in terms of their influence on the individual young person. Some or all are likely to co-exist with acute risk factors during the 'build up' phase to a sexual offence. An example is frustration about an absence of sexual experiences. In the literature, these risk factors may also be referred to as proximal or maintaining or perpetuating risk factors. Some of these risk factors are known to be associated with sexual recidivism.

### Acute risk factors

Acute risk factors are those factors known to be associated with the immediate commission of a sexual offence. They are highly relevant to the evaluation of imminent risk. The time scale allows for the consideration of a 'build up' phase to the offence, which may be as long as several months or as short as a few hours. Acute risk factors are considered in an environmental context, which includes access to a potential victim and opportunity to commit the offence. An example would a situation where a young person is asked to baby sit a child, he is alone with the child and he watches a sexually explicit TV programme with the child sat next to him. In the literature, these risk factors may also be referred to as precipitating risk factors. Some of these risk factors are known to be associated with sexual recidivism.

### Critical risk factors

The identification of these various categories of risk: static, dynamic, aetiological, sustaining and acute, enables the formulation of a temporal approach to the assessment of risk, which is consistent with the risk trajectory approach. It may also facilitate the identification of critical risk factors that are more relevant to the young person as a developing individual and to his current circumstances and more pertinent to his immediate and medium term future, including his future circumstances. These critical risk factors are therefore more relevant to the task of case management. They are determined by the practitioner and therefore they are consistent with and facilitate the structured professional judgement approach to risk evaluation.

### *Risk process (risk trajectory)*

The literature on childhood delinquency and juvenile criminality has identified various developmental pathways or trajectories towards chronic criminal behaviour and serious and violent criminal behaviour. These pathways or trajectories are characterised by common patterns of conduct problems and offending behaviours and are associated with predictable criminal careers (Loeber and Farrington, 1998). The utility of this approach is that it can help discriminate between:

- Juvenile offenders who persist in their offending into adulthood and those who desist in their adolescent years.
- Serious and violent juvenile offenders and those minor and non-violent juvenile offenders.

This approach identifies risk factors, but considers them in the context of behavioural patterns over time. Consequently, serious antisocial behaviour is conceived of in terms of a sequential progression from conduct problems to serious criminality over a course of time, typically from childhood through to adolescence. These temporal and sequential factors allow the charting of childhood and adolescent antisocial behaviour and the identification of a process of escalation in and establishment of harmful antisocial behaviour. The SHARP seeks to adopt a similar approach in relation to sexually harmful behaviour to assist the risk assessment process, specifically in terms of the potential to differentiate a transient trajectory for sexually harmful behaviour from a persistent trajectory for sexually harmful behaviour. This approach may also be used to determine an escalating pattern of sexually harmful behaviour and to estimate the likely end point in that escalating pattern, that is, the potential severity of the behaviour. Consequently, the higher the predicted trajectory in terms of persistence and severity, the higher the risk status or classification ascribed. The SHARP integrates the projected trajectory of the individual's sexually harmful behaviour into the risk formulation and informs the process of risk projection (see below).

## Risk types (typologies)

The relevant literature describes different groups of sexually harmful adolescents differentiated on the basis of the nature of their sexually harmful behaviour or characteristics in terms of their personal, interpersonal and social functioning. These groupings are variously referred to as sub-types, typologies, or taxonomies. The relationship between different sub-types and sexual recidivism has not been adequately investigated, but no correlation between sub-types and recidivism has yet been found. A promising study by Worling (2001), found two sub-groupings, defined on the basis of personality characteristics, had significantly higher recidivism rates than other sub-groups. These two higher risk groups were defined by more disturbed personality profiles, which may be framed in terms of greater need in relation to their personality development. Notwithstanding the paucity of relevant research, from a pragmatic perspective, the practice of considering risk for repeated sexual offending in relation to particular sub-types of young people may assist the risk evaluation process. The SHARP contends that consideration of typologies is likely to assist the process of risk formulation when they:

- differentiate victim characteristics
- differentiate the motives and reinforcements that underpin the sexually harmful behaviour
- differentiate the nature and severity of cognitive, emotional, social and personality functional impairments
- differentiate mental health disturbance

The SHARP itself provides the practitioner with the means by which to assess several typologies, which are used in the risk formulation process. These pertain to the following SHARP domains:

- Domain 1: Sexually harmful behaviour
- Domain 2: Antisocial behaviour
- Domain 3: Adverse life events
- Domain 4: Sexual development and adjustment
- Domain 5: Social development and adjustment
- Domain 6: Emotional development and adjustment
- Domain 7: Personality development and adjustment
- Domain 8: Mental health difficulties
- Domain 9: Cognitive development and adjustment

## Developmentally guided risk evaluation

As part of the process of evaluating risk, the SHARP provides a developmentally informed guide, whereby risk level or classification is allied to the young person's assessed level of developmental functioning in the area of their interpersonal and social relationships. The SHARP considers functional impairments in interpersonal and social relationships to be critical to the onset and persistence of sexually harmful behaviour. This guide in relation to psychosocial functioning is as follows:

### Low risk

Close to normal psychosocial functional development and age appropriate psychosocial functioning, adjustment and integration. Sexually harmful behaviour is associated with inept or inappropriate expressions of normal sexual interest and drive. Psychosocial development and functioning are within normal limits and age appropriate.

### Moderate risk

Developmental delay and associated cognitive-emotional-social deficits have resulted in impaired psychosocial functioning, adjustment and integration. Sexually harmful behaviour is associated with cognitive-emotional-social deficits, social adjustment difficulties and or social exclusion.

### High risk

Characterised by the presence of significant developmental psychopathology, this reflects pervasive and severe functional difficulties and/or highly dysfunctional sexual development. Both of these result in severely impaired emotional functioning, psychosocial functioning, social maladjustment and social exclusion. Sexually harmful behaviour is associated with:

- personality psychopathology
- symptoms of a psychiatric disorder
- dysfunctional sexual functioning
- deviant sexual functioning

## Risk based on sexual development

As described above, the SHARP emphasises sexual development and its critical importance to the onset and maintenance of sexually harmful behaviour. This developmental model poses three critical assessment questions, which the SHARP seeks to assist the practitioner in answering:

1. What influences or factors impede normal healthy sexual development?
2. What influences or factors distort normal healthy sexual development?
3. What influences or factors deviate or pathologise normal healthy sexual development?

These three questions related to three variations in developmental difficulties in the area of sexual development and reflect three levels of severity or level of risk. To compliment the developmentally informed guide in the area of interpersonal and social relationships as described above, the SHARP also provides a developmentally informed guide whereby risk level or classification is allied to the young person's assessed level of developmental functioning in the area of their sexuality and sexual expression. This guide in relation to sexual functioning is as follows:

### Low risk

Impeded sexual development, where sexually harmful behaviour is associated with inept or inappropriate expressions of normal sexual interest and drive.

### Moderate risk

Dysfunctional sexual development, where sexually harmful behaviour is associated with psychosocial deficits, interpersonal and social adjustment difficulties, social exclusion. This is likely to be associated with difficulties relating to opposite sex peers (for heterosexual adolescents) or an absence of opportunities for age appropriate sexual exploration and expression (for heterosexual and homosexual adolescents).

### High risk

Pathological sexual development, where sexually harmful behaviour is associated with:

- the expression of negative emotions
- personality psychopathology
- symptoms of a psychiatric disorder

- dysfunctional sexual functioning
- deviant sexual functioning

### Ascribing risk level

The SHARP follows the widely accepted differentiation of risk level into three categories: 'low', 'moderate', 'high' and provides such a designation for each of the 50 risk, need, responsivity factors. Whereas most existing risk assessment instruments categorise risk level based on whether the risk factor is absent, partially present or categorically present, the SHARP provides differential descriptions for each risk, need, responsivity factor to aid the practitioner's judgment when categorising it in terms of low, moderate, or high. This is achieved by behavioural descriptions or by concrete examples of the actual risk, need, responsivity factor.

### Risk calculation

Risk calculation is based on the absence, presence and judged level for the 50 risk, need, responsivity factors that comprise the SHARP. The accepted formula is that the greater number of risk, need responsivity factors that are present and at a high level designation, the greater the risk for the continuation of the previously identified sexually harmful behaviour, including the potential for an escalating pattern of sexually harmful behaviour. Also, the greater the number of dynamic risk, need, responsivity factors that are present means that the case management process will have to be more intense and more diverse. An important caveat is that particular risk, need, responsivity factors found to be present and deemed to be at a high level may override the overall calculation of risk, need, responsivity factors. In this sense, these particular factors are considered by the practitioner to carry more weight and thereby have greater importance in the final process of risk evaluation, termed risk classification. This is consistent with the structured professional judgment approach.

### Risk formulation

In clinical psychology and cognitive therapy it is common practice to derive a case formulation or conceptualisation of the client's presenting problems in order to generate a treatment plan. A formulation is a theoretically and empirically informed understanding of the client's condition and related difficulties. This formulation guides subsequent therapeutic interventions. Similarly, a risk formulation is a coherent and broad understanding of the risk level of the young person. It incorporates all the risk, need, responsivity factors, which are present including their designated level of severity and seeks to provide some understanding of the associations and interplay between them. It emphasises the process of interactions between these various factors and seeks to provide the practitioner with an understanding of the likely outcome of these multiple interactions and their cumulative influences on risk for future sexually harmful behaviour. The SHARP contends that a risk formulation will assist in conceptualising risk in a more sophisticated way:

- providing the young person with an explanation and understanding of their sexually harmful behaviour and their potential for further harmful behaviour
- evaluating overall risk level or classification
- producing feasible risk projections (informed descriptions of possible future sexually harmful behaviours)
- case management planning, with an emphasis on harm reduction interventions as part of this planning

The first phase of the risk formulation process is based on the presence and level of risk, need, responsivity factors (risk calculation) on the one hand, and, on the other hand, knowledge and the estimated significance of the young person's life history and life experiences in the developmental context of their level of functioning (adaptive or maladaptive) in each of the five functional developmental domains of the SHARP. The second phase of the risk formulation process utilises and integrates information derived from the following components of the SHARP:

- Risk process (risk trajectory)
- Risk types (risk typologies)
- Developmentally guided risk evaluation
- Risk based on sexual development

Professional judgement guided by the structure and content of the SHARP is at the heart of this formulation process.

## Risk classification

A pragmatic professional expectation of risk assessment protocols is that of risk classification (if not prediction). A traditional means of evaluating risk for sexual re-offending is to classify or categorise the overall risk that the young person is considered to pose in terms of 'low', 'moderate' or 'high' risk for sexual re-offending or recidivism. Some practitioners are cautious about the certainty with which risk for re-offending may be accurately predicted. Nevertheless, criminal and civil court proceedings, along with professionals from the criminal justice, health and social services agencies often request and expect practitioners to provide them with an overall estimation of risk in such terms. In the SHARP, risk classification is the process whereby the practitioner ascribes an overall risk level to the individual young person. Risk classification brings together the assessment processes of risk calculation and risk formulation. In so doing, the practitioner's judgment is informed by empirical knowledge and by case specific knowledge about the individual young person and their particular type of sexually harmful behaviour. Consequently, case management decisions may be derived from a more dynamic and interpretative assessment process.

The SHARP follows tradition by adopting the three categories: 'low', 'moderate' and 'high' when ascribing overall risk status to the young person. However, the SHARP contends that it is important to clarify the meaning of risk classification when referring to 'low', 'moderate' and 'high' categories. It differentiates 'risk' in terms of repeating sexually harmful behaviour from the severity of sexually harmful behaviour. In relation to point one, the estimated risk for future sexually harmful behaviour is based on what is known about the nature and extent of the sexually harmful behaviour at the time of the assessment. In relation to point two, it is necessary to categorise this sexually harmful behaviour in terms of severity, based on the actual and anticipated harm caused to the victim. The concept of risk types (including sexually harmful behaviour typologies) is utilised to assist in this determination. Therefore it does not make practical sense to talk about a 'high risk offender'. It does make sense to talk about a 'high risk' for repeated sexual offending of a particular type and it does make sense to talk about 'high risk' sexually harmful behaviour based on the nature and extent of the harm caused to the victim(s). Consequently, we could have a case where risk for future offending behaviour is 'high', alongside a 'low' risk category of behaviour based on degree of harm caused, for example indecent exposure. In addition, the risk assessment may usefully seek to estimate risk for increased severity, or an escalation in the harmfulness of sexual behaviour in the future. The concepts of risk process (risk trajectory), risk types (risk typologies) and risk projection are utilised to assist in the categorisation of risk in terms of future severity.

### Risk projections

Risk projection is a process that explicitly and directly informs case management planning and in particular risk management strategies and interventions. The risk projection process itself is informed by the preceding risk formulation process and the understanding and information gained from the particular risk formulation. The practitioner utilises the risk formulation to arrive at a series of relevant and feasible projections of future high or imminent risk situations leading to further acts of sexually harmful behaviour. These projections may include a variety of situational contexts, different potential victims or victim types, different acts or types of sexually harmful behaviour and an escalating pattern of sexually harmful behaviour to include serious interpersonal violence. These projections are detailed descriptions of possible future sexual offences that are specific and concrete in their detail. The risk projection process incorporates the following steps:

1. *Projected environmental contexts*: locations, situations, circumstances and opportunities related to increased potential for sexually harmful behaviour
2. *Projected victim selection*: named victims, potential victims and likely victim characteristics
3. *Projected interpersonal contexts*: interpersonal relations with potential victims, interpersonal relations with people known to or related to potential victims and interactions with potential victims
4. *Projected victim approach behaviour*: legitimate reasons to have contact with potential victims, manipulating opportunities

to have contact with potential victims, grooming behaviours, coercive and dominating relationship with potential victims and interpersonal violence towards potential victims

5. *Projected sexually harmful behaviour*: the same as previous sexually harmful behaviour, a variation of previous sexually harmful behaviour, different from previous sexually harmful behaviour, an escalation in the use of interpersonal violence and an escalation in the seriousness of the sexually harmful behaviour
6. *Projected behavioural contexts*: alcohol misuse, illicit drug misuse, misuse of pornography, misuse of the internet to contact other internet users and attempts to contact previous victims
7. *Projected functional decomposition*: reduced adaptive functioning in the functional developmental domains, reduced interpersonal and social integration, social isolation, reduced problem solving ability, increased impulsiveness, reduced self-regulation of interpersonal and social behaviour, reduced self-regulation of emotions, increased psychological and emotional disturbance, preoccupation with sexually deviant or sexually harmful behaviours, reduced self-regulation of sexual behaviour, uncontrolled hypersexuality, relapse of a psychiatric disorder
8. *Projected stressors*: interpersonal conflicts, breakdown in interpersonal relationships, loneliness, sexual frustration, worry, agitation, resentment, anger, low mood, lack of social supports and absence of professional supports.

This risk projection approach is consistent with Scenario-based-risk assessment utilised in the adult risk protocol, the Risk for Sexual Violence Protocol (RSVP: Hart et al., 2003). Consequently, the SHARP is a compatible risk assessment protocol, which is able to directly inform the completion of the RSVP in a case when a young person commits a sexual offence as an adult.

## Protocol construction

The SHARP protocol was constructed on the foundations of the following information:

- the published literature on adolescent studies of sexual recidivism

- the published literature on adolescent studies of particular risk factors associated with sexual recidivism
- the published literature on the characteristics and needs of sexually harmful young people
- the published literature on responsivity factors in populations of juvenile offenders and adult sexual offenders
- the published literature on resilience pertaining to sexually harmful adolescents
- published protocols for assessing risk for sexual violence in both adolescent and adult populations
- the professional consensus in the field as identified in books, conference presentations, professional communications and organisations, such as the Association for the Treatment of Sexual Abusers, The National Adolescent Perpetrator Network and the National Organisation for the Treatment of Abusers
- the relevant clinical experience of the author (1987 to 2008)

## Rationale and goals

The SHARP is all about the provision of services to the young person in the context of serving and promoting victim and public protection. Consequently, the SHARP is not an end in and of itself; rather it is intended to be a means to an end. To this end, the protocol has two inter-related goals: these are practice delivery goals and service delivery goals.

The practice delivery goals are:
- a comprehensive and holistic assessment of sexually harmful adolescents
- identify a cluster of risk factors
- identify a cluster of needs
- identify responsivity factors
- identify resilience factors
- ascribe a risk level to the identified risk, need, responsivity factors
- ascribe an overall risk level to the young person
- guide risk containment and management planning
- guide treatment planning
- re-assess risk, need, responsivity, resilience factors and risk level over time
- pre and post intervention assessments to evaluate risk management and harm reduction outcomes

The service delivery goals are:
- standardisation of assessment services across the criminal justice, mental health, social services and education agencies and the voluntary and private sectors
- multi-agency and multi-professional collaboration and co-ordination
- service delivery compatibility across different agencies and institutions
- continuity of professional practice and service delivery across different service delivery setting and different agencies
- multi-agency and multi-professional service delivery development and improvement

These practice and service delivery goals pertain to two fundamentally related areas of practice, which constitute the overarching practice of case management:

1. Risk management (risk reduction interventions) of sexually harmful behaviour to target opportunity for immediate risk, and
2. Harm reduction (treatment and other remediation interventions) that focuses on the functional abilities and psychosocial adaptation and integration of the young person to target propensity for future risk

The fundamental principles underpinning the SHARP in practice, in the furtherance of effective case management, that is, victim and public protection, are assessment-directed risk management interventions and assessment-directed harm reduction interventions.

## Assessment and case management process

The assessment of risk, need, responsivity and resilience and case management components of the SHARP are regarded and presented as a single process. Consequently, the SHARP consists of various inter-related documents designed to guide the practitioner through the risk, need, responsivity, resilience assessment process and structure the recording of relevant information. It also provides documentation to link the assessment findings with case management planning and guide the practitioner through the case management process itself. These documents consist of:

- a manual
- a coding sheet
- a scoring sheet
- a semi-structured interview booklet
- a self-report questionnaires booklet
- an information record booklet
- a risk formulation booklet
- a risk projection booklet
- a case management booklet
- a risk reduction intervention progress record

## Continuity across agencies, services, institutions and practitioners

It is contended that when different agencies, services, institutions and professional groups adopt a common assessment approach and protocol, it promotes inter-agency, inter-service and multi-profession collaboration, decision-making, planning and delivery of interventions. In so doing, it enables a systematic multi-agency and multi-professional means of reviewing risk over time, during the course of which different agencies, services, institutions and professionals may have been involved with or responsible for the young person. For example, by using the same assessment protocol within the secure estate (prison, correctional, secure social care and secure hospital institutions) and within the community based juvenile justice services (youth offending services and probation services in the United Kingdom and juvenile justice and probation services in North America) consistency and continuity between custodial and community-based services may be achieved in terms of risk assessment, risk management and re-assessment of a young person who has served a custodial sentence and then been released into the community under supervision conditions. In addition, it provides consistency and continuity across criminal justice, health, social services, education and voluntary and private agencies.

## Origins

In 1995 the author devised 'The Risk Matrix', which consisted of 26 risk factors. It was based on the available literature (North American) and clinical experience working at the Kolvin Clinic, an outpatient adolescent forensic mental health service in Newcastle, England. This risk assessment was part of a document written by

clinical staff from the Kolvin Clinic entitled *Assessing Risk in Sexually Abusive Young People*, which was published by the Derwent Initiative (Graham, 1995). The Risk Matrix was a two stage assessment of risk, the first stage was completed by professionals from social services and juvenile justice services and the second stage was completed by clinical staff from the Kolvin Clinic. Its goals were to promote inter-agency assessments of risk and the identification of young people requiring specialist intervention services from the adolescent forensic mental health service. In 2003, the author revised the Risk Matrix to include 31 risk factors, revision based on direct clinical experience over the years from 1995. In 2005 the original 1995 Risk Matrix was subject to research in terms of its ability to identify high risk adolescents who went on to commit further acts of sexually harmful behaviours (Christodoulides, Richardson, Graham, Kennedy and Kelly, 2005). The results showed that the Risk Matrix was unable to discriminate sexual recidivists from non-recidivists based on official criminal conviction data (20 per cent re-conviction rate). However, it was able to distinguish sexual recidivists from non-recidivists based on professional reports from a variety of agency sources (46 per cent re-offending rate). Since 2003 the Risk Matrix was further revised, updated and developed in to its current format and renamed the SHARP.

## Review of existing risk assessment protocols

During the development of the SHARP a comprehensive review of both adult and adolescent risk assessment instruments and protocols was undertaken. This was done as part of the extensive literature review that was conducted to provide the SHARP with a solid evidence base.

### Adult

The following fifteen actuarial and structured professional judgement risk assessment instruments or protocols were reviewed:

- The Rapid Risk Assessment for Sexual Offense Recidivism (RRASOR) (1997)
- The Sexual Violence Risk-20 (SVR-20) (1997)
- The Sex Offender Risk Appraisal Guide (SORAG) (1998)

- The Static-99 (1999)
- The Sex Offender Need Assessment Rating (SONAR) (2000)
- The Vermont Assessment of Sex Offender Risk Manual: Research Edition (VASOR) (2001)
- The Structured Risk Need Assessment (SARN) (2002)
- The Static-2002 (2003)
- Minnesota Sex Offender Screening Tool – Revised (MnSOST-R) (2003)
- The Violence Risk Scale – Sexual Offender Version (VRS-SO) (2003)
- The Risk for Sexual Violence Protocol (RSVP) (2003)
- The Adult Sex Offender Assessment Protocol (A-SOAP-II) (2005)
- The Risk Matrix 2000 (2007)
- Acute 2007
- Stable 2007

### Adolescent

The following five actuarial and structured professional judgement risk assessment instruments/protocols were reviewed:

- The Juvenile Sex Offender Assessment Protocol – II (J-SOAP-II) (2003)
- The Estimate of Risk of Adolescent Sexual Offense Recidivism (ERASOR) (2001)
- Juvenile Sexual Offense Recidivism Risk Assessment Tool – II (JSORRAT-II) (2005)
- Juvenile Risk Assessment Tool: Assessment of Risk for Sexual Re-offending (J-RAT.V3) (2007)
- Multiplex Empirically Guided Inventory of Ecological Aggregates for Assessing Sexually Abusive Children and Adolescents (MEGA) (in press)

### *Review of base rates for adolescent sexual recidivism*

Base rates in terms criminal behaviour refer to the known reconviction rates for a particular type of crime for a particular population group. Therefore, determining the base rates for adolescent sexual recidivism involves reporting on studies of sexual recidivism to provide an overall picture of the known base rates for sexual recidivism for studied adolescent sexual offenders and abusers. This base rate is necessary in order to ground the risk evaluation of the young person in empirical evidence pertaining to known reoffending rates. The SHARP contends

that one critical reason behind this process is to sensitise the practitioner or assessment team to the relatively low base rates reported in the literature and so engender a systematic and proportioned approach tempered by appropriate caution. This is to avoid over simplistic evaluations of risk and overzealous interventionist responses to that perceived risk. Hence the identification of base rates from recidivism studies is done irrespective of the methodological weaknesses inherent in the studies; differences across the individual studies in terms of how they define recidivism and does not distinguish treated groups from untreated groups. When differential recidivism rates are provided for treated and non-treated groups, the highest recidivism rate is quoted, which is, in fact, always for the non-treated group. This is to inform the practitioner about the highest reported recidivism rates.

During this review the following studies were excluded for not being recidivism studies, but often erroneously cited as being recidivism studies. As can be seen, they reported high re-offending rates:

| Studies | Sexual recidivism rates |
|---|---|
| • Awad and Saunders (1991) | 40% |
| • Becker et al. (1986) | 79% |
| • Fehrenbach et al. (1986) | 57.6% |
| • Groth (1977) | 75% |

These studies were descriptive retrospective studies reporting the characteristics of groups of juvenile sexual offenders. They were not reporting recidivism based on a follow-up methodology. Rather they merely defined recidivism as the young person having a history of previous sexual offences, sexually abusive behaviour or prior arrests for a sexual offence *prior to the study*.

An extensive literature review of 56 recidivism studies, including three meta-analytic studies, was completed (see Appendix 2). The range of percentage sexual recidivism was from nought per cent to 46 per cent. *The mean base rate for sexual recidivism was almost 13 per cent.* Consequently, the SHARP begins from the empirical position that on average across different populations of juvenile sexual offenders/sexually harmful young people only 13 out of 100 will commit a further sexual offence once identified and processed by criminal justice or other agencies.

## Review of risk factors associated with recidivism

The SHARP also reviewed thirty-six published studies of adolescent sexual recidivism, which identified 49 individual risk factors that were correlated with sexual recidivism (see Appendix 3). The purpose was to identify and incorporate critical risk factors that had some empirical credibility (defined as having empirical support from multiple independent studies) for inclusion in the risk assessment protocol so to improve the utility of the protocol in terms of being able to identify high risk adolescents. The most supported risk factors were:

- Previous sexual offences (supported by 11 studies)
- Sexual preference for children (supported by 10 studies)
- Previous non-sexual offences (supported by 9 studies)
- Multiple victims (supported by 8 studies)
- Stranger victim (supported by 8 studies)
- Antisocial/delinquent history (supported by 7 studies)
- Male victim (supported by 6 studies)
- Younger aged perpetrator at onset of sexually harmful behaviour (supported by 5 studies)
- Victim of sexual abuse (supported by 5 studies)
- Impaired social functioning (supported by 5 studies)
- No or incomplete offence-specific treatment interventions, which includes unresponsiveness to offered treatment (supported by 5 studies)
- Child victim/significant age between victim and perpetrator (supported by 5 studies)

## Review of risk and need related factors

Adolescent studies of relevance to each of the risk or need related domains were reviewed. This crucially included those five domains that focus on the young person's developmental needs, psychosocial functioning and adjustment and mental health status. For example, the SHARP reviewed all available literature pertaining to the presence of personality dysfunction in populations of sexually harmful adolescents (see Richardson, 2005, 2007).

## Review of conceptualisations of risk

Theories and conceptualisations of risk for sexual recidivism in both the adult and adolescent fields

were reviewed. For example, the model of risk proposed by Ward and Beech (2004).

## Review of approaches to case management

Current approaches to risk management and harm reduction conceptualised as case management were reviewed. The critical practice position adopted is the integration of the integral practices of risk assessment and case management. This has been referred to as 4th generation risk assessment (see Andrews and Bonta, 2003). The exemplar of this approach is the Level of Service Case Management Inventory (LS/CMI: Andrews, Bonta and Wormith, 2004) in the field of general criminal offending and also the Risk of Sexual Violence Protocol (RSVP: Hart et al., 2003) in the field of adult sexual offending.

## Professional experience and consensus

The SHARP incorporates the dominant professional positions and views, that is conceptual, theoretical and practical knowledge published and communicated by specialist academics and practitioners working in the field. This knowledge is derived from published books, book chapters, conference presentations, position statements by international professional organisations (such as the Association for the Treatment of Sexual Abusers, ATSA) and the author's personal communications with other professionals in the field. The SHARP is also significantly influenced by the author's practice, which amounts to 20 years practical experience working with sexually harmful adolescents.

## Consistency with other risk assessment protocols

Risk assessment practice in the adult field has led to the development of suites of risk assessment protocols that share the same conceptual, empirical and practice principles. This provides the practitioner with a number of compatible risk assessment protocols that focus on different criminal behaviours. The exemplar of this approach is the following suite of protocols:

1. The HCR-20: Assessing Risk for Violence (Webster et al., 1997)
2. The Risk of Sexual Violence Protocol (RSVP) (Hart et al., 2003)
3. The Risk of Spousal Violence (SARA and B-SAFER) (Kropp et al., 1999; Kropp et al., 2005)

4. The Stalking Assessment and Management (SAM) (Kropp et al., 2006)

The SHARP is consistent with this suite of assessment protocols and may be usefully used with adolescents who may then be subsequently assessed as young adults using the RSVP (eg sexual recidivists). The SHARP is also consistent with the Youth Level of Service Case Management Inventory (Hoge and Andrews, 2002) and may be usefully used in conjunction with this instrument to evaluate adolescents who are also general or persistent offenders and who may subsequently be assessed as young adults using the Level of Service/Case Management Inventory (Andrews, Bonta and Wormith, 2004).

### Consistency with other child and adolescent risk assessment protocols

The approach adopted by the SHARP is also consistent with the Structured Assessment of Violence Risk in Youth (SAVRY, Borum, Bartel and Forth, 2003) and the Early Assessment Risk List for Boys (EARL-20B, Augimeri et al., 2001). The SHARP may usefully be used in conjunction with the SAVRY with those adolescents who also have a history of interpersonal violence/violent sexual offences. In addition, the SHARP incorporates the assessment of psychopathic traits and is consistent with the Psychopathy Checklist: Youth Version (PCL: YV Forth, Kosson and Hare, 2003) and Antisocial Process Screening Device (Frick and Hare, 2001). When used in conjunction with these assessment instruments, the SHARP is useful for the evaluation of psychopathic sexually harmful adolescents.

### The manual

The manual follows the following format:

- the risk or need domain
- the risk or need factor in that domain
- an inclusion rationale for the risk or need factor
- published research evidence supporting the risk factor
- professional consensus based on practical experience as exemplified in published risk assessment instruments
- specified low risk criteria for each risk or need factor
- specified moderate risk or need criteria
- specified high risk or need criteria

- assessment guidance on how the practitioner goes about adequately assessing each risk or need factor, including recommended sources of information and assessment procedures
- recommended assessment instruments and measures that are widely available
- cross referencing to other SHARP documentation, including the semi-structured interviews, self-report questionnaires, recording booklets and case management booklet
- guidance on completing and scoring the SHARP coding and scoring sheets
- guidance on the production of a risk or need formulation
- guidance on formulating a risk management plan
- guidance on formulating a harm reduction plan

### SHARP domains

The term 'domain' refers to a distinct area under which a cluster of related risk factors are grouped. The SHARP consists of twelve such domains. These are categorised in terms of their nature:

- Domain 1 (sexually harmful behaviour) and Domain 2 (antisocial behaviour) pertain to the young person's known sexually harmful and criminal behavioural histories.
- Domain 3 (adverse life experiences) pertains to the young person's known history of maltreatment and victimisation.
- Domain 4 (sexual development and adjustment) pertains to a very detailed psycho-sexual evaluation of the young person's sexual functioning, adaptation, and integration.
- Domain 5 (social development and adjustment), Domain 6 (emotional development and adjustment), Domain 7 (personality development and adjustment), and Domain 9 (cognitive development and adjustment), all pertain to the young person's child and adolescent development and functioning.

These are termed 'functional developmental' domains, because they refer to functional impairments, maladaptation, and difficulties in terms of social integration. Similarly:

- Domain 8 (mental health difficulties) is also a functional domain in that it directly refers to the young person's psychological functioning or mental health status, and severe developmental disorders.

- Domain 10 (general self-regulation and level of independence) pertains to the young person general level of self-regulation in terms of their overall lifestyle functioning, and their level of independent functioning in the context of chronological appropriateness.
- Domain 11 (environmental risks) explicitly refers to risk opportunities in the primary systems making up the young person's social network of contacts with potential victims, these being family, neighbourhood, and school or college.
- Domain 12 (Motivation and Compliance) pertains to the young person and their family in relation to compliance with risk management arrangements, and their active participation in planned risk reduction interventions.
- Based on a simplistic classification in terms of risk, need, and responsivity, Domains 1, 2, 3, and 11 correspond to risk, Domains 4, 5, 6, 7, 8, 9, and 10 correspond to need, and Domain 12 corresponds to responsivity. Regarding the classification of risk factors as either static or dynamic, Domains 1, 2, and 3 reflect static risks, while Domains 4, 5, 6, 7, 8, 9, 10, 11 and 12 reflect dynamic risks.

### Sexually harmful behaviour

Domain 1 guides a detailed assessment of the young person's sexually harmful behaviour or behaviours in terms of eight assessment areas that fully describe the harmful or behaviour (see Richardson et al. 1995). This facilitates the determination of the severity or seriousness of the pattern of behaviour. It also facilitates the determination of the typological characteristics of the behaviour in terms of victim characteristics (see Richardson et al. 1997), which assists in the formulation of an offence typology that is used with other subsequent typologies to inform the process of risk formulation. Domain 1 then guides the assessment through two further assessment areas in the identification of emerging, established or escalating patterns of sexually harmful behaviours, which assists the practitioner in determining a trajectory of sexually harmful behaviour over time since onset, referred to as the risk process.

### Antisocial behaviour

Domain 2 incorporates three assessment areas and guides the assessment of the young person's antisocial or delinquent behaviours, history of property- and person-centred (non-sexual aggression and violence) offending and misuse of or dependency on alcohol or illicit substances. This domain assists the practitioner further in the process of risk type in that it identifies young people whose sexually harmful behaviour is accompanied by generalised antisocial and criminal behaviour, including violent behaviour, which suggests that their sexual offending is integral to, or associated with an antisocial orientation and lifestyle.

### Adverse life experiences

Domain 3 incorporates four assessment areas and guides the assessment of the young person's experiences of victimisation both within the family and outside of it, from both adults and peers. This history of victimisation includes physical and sexual abuse and peer victimisation in the form of bullying and interpersonal violence. This domain also guides the assessment of inappropriate vicarious exposure to sexual abuse or sexual violence in terms of experience of witnessing such acts.

### Sexual development and adjustment

Domain 4 incorporates twelve assessment areas and guides the assessment of:

- the young person's sexual development and adjustment
- their emerging sexuality
- the psychological components of their sexually harmful behaviour

This is achieved through the assessment of:

- unmet sexual needs
- sexual learning experiences (either appropriate or inappropriate)
- sexual identity, sexual orientation
- sexual interests and preferences
- pornography use
- social competencies and integration with members of the opposite sex
- experiences of dating and sexual exploration in mutual peer relationships (heterosexual or homosexual)

- attitudes and beliefs associated with sexually harmful behaviour
- motivation associated with the onset and maintenance of sexually harmful behaviour
- the nature of reinforcement gained from sexually harmful behaviour

The assessment of these areas provides a detailed psycho-sexual evaluation of the young person.

This approach enables the evaluation of sexually harmful behaviour in the context of the young person's sexual development and adjustment and their emerging sexuality. This domain produces additional information in terms the motivational and psychological characteristics of sexually harmful behaviour, from which to derive a motivational and psychological typology. This complements the typological information derived from Domains 1 and 2.

## Social development and adjustment

Domain 5 incorporates four assessment areas and guides the assessment of the young person's social development and adjustment. It includes social competency, which refers to social skills and effective social functioning and incorporates an affective component, that is anxiety associated with social and especially peer interactions and relationships. It then assesses social integration, which refers to social adaptation in terms of socialising opportunities and experiences, involvement in recreational activities and the extent and quality of peer relationships (same-sex and mixed-sex peer interactions). This focuses on peer acceptance, peer rejection, social exclusion and isolation. This domain enables the determination of the relationships between sexually harmful behaviour and the young person's social development, in terms of his functioning and integration and thereby provides additional information by which to gain typological insights into the young person's sexually harmful behaviour. This is achieved by distinguishing social immaturity from social delinquency. In essence, social immaturity refers to an established pattern of child-oriented socialising, whereas social delinquency refers to an antisocial peer-oriented pattern of socialising. Social immaturity characterises a young person who socialises with younger children rather than their peers. It incorporates the developmental perspective of teenagers who are socially immature who are functioning at a

pre-adolescent level in terms of their social relationships. Their social immaturity may be a consequence of peer relationship difficulties, including peer rejection and subsequent social exclusion. As they develop, they may feel more comfortable socialising with children, establish friendships with them and through this process of age inappropriate socialisation develop an emotional identification with children rather than peers. This social development type is associated with sexually harmful behaviour against pre-pubertal children, usually because unmet sexual needs associated with post puberty are met through the sexual abuse of children. In this instance, this Domain is closely linked to Domain 4 (sexual development and adjustment). In contrast, social delinquency refers to a young person who socialises with an antisocial or delinquent peer group and lives an antisocial or unconventional life style. This young person may be vulnerable or prone to irresponsible acts when encouraged by these peers or prone to irresponsible acts in order to gain peer group acceptance or status. This refers directly to the risk for committing rape of a peer-aged or adult female victim, whereby the young person who believes that sexual activities are important for gaining peer acceptance and status, but who lacks the skills or opportunities to gain sexual experiences with a consenting female peer, meets his unmet sexual need and social needs for male approval through sexually harmful behaviour. In this instance this domain is closely linked to Domain 2 (antisocial behaviour). This domain produces additional information in terms of a social functioning typology, which distinguishes sexually harmful behaviour associated with social immaturity from that linked to social delinquency. It therefore complements Domains 1 and 2.

## Emotional development and adjustment

Domain 6 incorporates four assessment areas and guides the assessment of the young person's emotional development and adjustment. Emotional regulation refers to the young person's capacity (willingness and ability) to regulate or control their emotions. The assessment focuses on negative emotions, such as anger, anxiety, fear, loneliness and their psychological components, such as hostility, resentment, revenge, worry and sadness. It guides the determination of emotional dysregulation, that is the inability to effectively control and cope with these emotions in non-antisocial and non self-defeating ways. Emotional regulation is important because it underpins self-management over emotionally driven behaviours. Emotional dysregulation is associated with a lack of self-control over emotionally driven behaviours and deficiencies in self-management. This is particularly pertinent to sexually harmful behaviour that is motivated by negative emotions and their psychological components, which is regarded as a motivational sub-type and one that indicates possible personality disturbance. Consequently, this domain adds to the potential information pertaining to sub-types of sexually harmful behaviour and therefore to the process of identifying risk types.

Empathy refers to the capacity to feel and exhibit empathy towards other people. It incorporates:

- an affective component (fellow feeling or sympathy)
- a cognitive component (perspective taking)
- a behavioural component (helping or comforting behaviours)

It is subdivided into general empathy for any other person and victim empathy for the victim of the young person's sexually harmful behaviour. The capacity to form empathy is associated with having experienced positive child-parent attachments. Empathy and the capacity for positive attachments with other people are critical in the development of subsequent peer friendships and intimate (sexual partner) relationships. Functional impairments in empathy are pertinent to sexually harmful behaviours, given that healthy and appropriate sexual expression occurs in the relational context of social and interpersonal encounters and the establishment of intimate relationships. Empathy for victims is associated with risk reduction interventions.

Emotional immaturity refers to delayed emotional functioning, which is likely to impede peer relations in terms of acceptance and integration, and therefore prevent peer friendships. It incorporates a lack of readiness for more mature interpersonal relationships, which are critical to the establishment of opposite sex or more intimate attachments and relationships. Emotional immaturity may prevent interpersonal mobility, whereby the young person is prone to associate with and form attachments with developmentally inappropriate younger children. Attachment difficulties refer to more general difficulties forming functional relationships and attachments with people in general, not just peers. Difficulties in terms of forming attachments are likely to seriously impede sexual development given sexual expression and sexual maturity are both dependent on the formation of intimate relationships.

## Personality development and adjustment

Domain 7 incorporates two assessment areas and guides the assessment of the young person's personality development and adjustment. It incorporates emerging personality difficulties conceptualised with reference to psychiatrically defined personality disorders emerging and beginning to establish themselves in the developmental stage of mid to late adolescence. Significant personal difficulties or emerging personality disorder are known to significantly impair interpersonal and social behaviours and relationships. These functional impairments are pertinent to sexually harmful behaviours, given that healthy and appropriate sexual expression occurs in the relational context of social and interpersonal encounters and relationships. Research has identified several types of personality difficulties in groups of young people who sexually harm others (see Richardson et al. 2004; Richardson, 2005; Richardson 2007; Vizard et al., 2004; Vizard et al., 2007). Further, this domain includes the evaluation of psychopathic traits as formally evaluated using published measures of psychopathy. Psychopathy ratings are included in this domain because psychopathic traits and measures of psychopathy are associated with persistent rule breaking, callousness, which is the polar opposite to empathy, persistent and serious antisocial and general criminality, including violent behaviour, and with sexual recidivism, especially involving sexual violence. This domain is closely linked to Domain 2 (antisocial behaviour). It also provides further information from which to derive typologies related to personality dysfunction. It thereby complements the typological information derived from Domains 1, 2, 4, 5 and 6.

## Mental health difficulties

Domain 8 incorporates two assessment areas and guides the assessment of the young person's mental health status and any emerging or established mental health difficulties. Mental health difficulties are conceptualised in terms of psychiatrically defined childhood and adolescent psychiatric disorders. The assessment includes childhood and adolescent psychiatric disorders and particular symptoms and functional deficits associated with these disorders. There is no empirical evidence to indicate that childhood and adolescent psychiatric disorders, in and of themselves, are associated with the aetiology or onset of sexually harmful behaviours. From a developmental perspective, such disorders may be pertinent to the onset of sexually harmful behaviour by exerting two indirect, adverse influences on the young person's overall development. Firstly, a disorder may have adversely affected the normal developmental processes and healthy developmental trajectory of the young person, thereby causing or contributing to functional impairments in one or several developmental domains, such as cognitive, personality, emotional, or social development. This then impedes normal and healthy developmental progress and results in developmental delays and immaturity. Secondly, particular symptoms or functional deficits associated with the presence of a specific disorder may have an adverse impact on the young person's self-control, emotional regulation and ability to effectively manage their behaviour. This is especially pertinent to sexually harmful behaviour when symptoms or deficits impede self-control over sexual impulses and sexual expression, or when they result in sexual disinhibition, or when they result in hypersexuality, which is an intense and persistent state of sexual arousal. Increased risk may be associated with the presence of co-morbid disorders, especially when they are multi-axial in nature, such as the presence of a mental illness along with a personality disorder, or the presence of a pervasive developmental disorder with a mental illness. Such co-morbidity is likely to reflect greater risk because they represent greater need in terms of the intensity and duration of psychiatric and psychological care and interventions. This domain in particular requires specialised psychiatric and psychological assessments from psychiatry and psychology professionals, which will involve Child and Adolescent Mental Health services (CAMHS) or Forensic Child and Adolescent Mental Health services (F-CAMHS). This domain excludes

personality difficulties or emerging personality disorder, as these are technically not childhood or adolescent psychiatric disorders. Instead these are included in Domain 7 (personality development and adjustment). This domain produces additional information in terms of a functional typology based on the presence and nature of mental health disorders/difficulties and their association with the young person's sexually harmful behaviour. In so doing it complements Domains 1, 2, 4, 5, 6 and 7.

## Cognitive development and adjustment

Domain 9 incorporates two assessment areas and guides the assessment of:

- intellectual ability and cognitive deficits, which incorporates global learning disability and specific cognitive deficits, such as attention and executive functioning deficits; and
- social-cognitive processing deficits, such as impulsivity and interpersonal problems solving deficits.

This domain assesses the degree to which intellectual and cognitive deficits impair judgement, verbal reasoning, planning, consequential thinking, problem solving, interpersonal communication, and social functioning.

## General self regulation and level of independence

Domain 10 incorporates two assessment areas and guides the assessment of:

- the young person's capacity for general self-regulation incorporating how they are able to cope with and effectively manage current life stressors, and
- their level of independence defined in terms of their capacity for age appropriate independence in their daily living environment and activities.

This domain assesses the degree to which self regulation deficits impair general daily behaviour and functioning, including following rules and routines, and meeting personal and social obligations, and the level of independence attained by the young person in terms of daily living skills and their sense of personal autonomy compared to their chronological age. This domain excludes emotional dysregulation, which is assessed in Domain 6.

### Environmental risks

Domain 11 incorporates three assessment areas and guides the assessment of the young person's potential access to previous victims, vulnerable individuals, potential victims of sexual harm and situational opportunities to commit further acts of sexually harmful behaviour. Potential access and opportunities are evaluated in three critical ecological systems in the young person's life, namely:

- the family environment, which includes contact and relationships with all family members, relatives and their family members
- the neighbourhood locality, which includes social and recreational activities, peer contacts and relationships and other associations with individuals in the locality
- the school environment, which includes travel to and from school, structured and unstructured activities on the school premises and contacts and interactions with other pupils and teaching staff

This domain explicitly informs case management planning and decision-making and the immediate environmental management of risk and so the prevention of harm.

### Motivation and compliance

Domain 12 incorporates two assessment areas, one in relation to the young person's parents or adult carers and close relatives, and the other in relation to the young person. This domain guides the assessment of:

- acceptance of the commission of sexually harmful behaviour.
- acknowledgement that this behaviour indicates the presence of developmental difficulties and related needs.
- acceptance that there is a risk of further acts of sexually harmful behaviour.
- commitment to co-operate and comply with case management interventions, including services to meet the young person's (and the family's, if appropriate) unmet needs and with strategies and interventions to reduce or prevent risk (including specialist treatment).

- promoting and maintaining motivation to prevent further sexually harmful behaviour.

This domain explicitly informs case management planning and decision-making in terms of the responsivity of the family and young person in terms of compliance with agency and professional interventions designed to prevent further sexual harm.

## Summary

So what is SHARP practice? The SHARP provides a highly structured and evidence-based assessment protocol for the evaluation of sexually harmful young people aged between 12 and 19 years. It represents an holistic and comprehensive assessment, not merely an assessment of those risk factors known to be associated with sexual recidivism in adolescent populations. From a specialised perspective pertaining to the field of adolescent sexual offending, the SHARP incorporates heterogeneity and evaluates diversity in terms of (1) the form and expression of sexually harmful behaviour and (2) the life experiences, developmental maturity, psychosocial characteristics, functional competencies in the areas of interpersonal and social relationships, social integration and the mental health status of the young person. SHARP practice, therefore, is responsive by responding differently to the young person's development in terms of functioning, adjustment and integration and to their sexually harmful behaviour in terms of its motivation (or motive), its expression and its reinforcing properties. From a technical perspective, the SHARP adheres to firstly, the Structured Professional Judgement approach, which currently dominates the professional practice of risk assessment for violent and sexual offending behaviours and secondly, the risk, need, responsivity principle approach, which currently dominates the field of the assessment and rehabilitation of criminal behaviours. Both these approaches complement one another and represent best practice. The SHARP also incorporates the resilience principle. SHARP practice is consistent with, and compliments, existing best practice in the fields of offender risk assessment and rehabilitation. From a developmental perspective, the SHARP emphasises the importance of assessing and understanding sexually harmful behaviour in the context of the young person's previous child development progress and current adolescent development in five functional developmental domains:

- sexual development
- social development
- emotional development
- personality development
- psychological/mental health development

The SHARP also conceptualises risk and need in terms of the inter-dependence of these functional developmental domains and evaluates how progress and maturity in social development and in personality development exerts a significant influence on the young person's sexual development. Developmental progress or the lack of it is evaluated in terms of three related functional areas:

- functional ability (skills and competencies)
- adjustment (behavioural and psychological)
- integration (interpersonal and social relationships)

SHARP practice conceptualises different forms and expressions of sexually harmful behaviour in terms of deficient coping with sexual developmental maturity and related tasks, or maladaptive coping with sexual developmental maturity and related tasks, as opposed to adaptive sexual development and adjustment. From a service delivery perspective, the SHARP seeks to encourage and facilitate the implementation and delivery of effective 'human services' in the pursuit of victim protection, public protection and rehabilitation of the young person. The SHARP reflects current best practice in the criminal justice field, where the assessment and case management of risk, need and responsivity factors are one and the same integrated practice. SHARP practice promotes and facilitates a multi-agency and multi-professional service delivery model of practice and assessment-directed case management, both of which are dependent on the application of the same assessment and case management protocol. Currently, in the adult fields of offender assessment and rehabilitation and criminal justice service delivery, we have several exemplary models of practice, which SHARP practice has learned from, is consistent with, and compliments. These are:

- The Level of Service Case Management Inventory (LS/CMI: Andrews, Bonta and Wormith, 2004).
- The Risk for Sexual Violence Protocol (RSVP: Hart et al., 2003).
- The Scottish Executive Risk Management Authority, which has published standards and guidelines for risk assessment and risk management practices across the Scottish criminal justice system to facilitate standardised and effective delivery of services (see Risk Assessment and Management of Serious Violent and Sexual Offenders: A Review of Current Issues, 2002; Risk Management Authority Standards and Guidelines for Risk Assessment, 2006; Risk Management Authority Risk Assessment Tools Evaluation Directory, 2007).

## Appendix 1 Sharp Coding Sheet

# SHARP    *Sexually Harmful Adolescent Risk Protocol*

Name...................................................................... Reference Number.............................................
Date of Birth.............../................./.................    Sex:    M    F    Date of Test............./................/.................
Referral Source........................................................................................................................
Rater....................................................................................................................................

### Domain 1:    SEXUALLY HARMFUL BEHAVIOUR

| 0 | 1 | 2 | | |
|---|---|---|---|---|
| 0 | 1 | 2 | 1. | Situational Dynamics of Sexually Harmful Behaviour |
| 0 | 1 | 2 | 2. | Victim Characteristics |
| 0 | 1 | 2 | 3. | Age Difference between Abuser and Victim |
| 0 | 1 | 2 | 4. | Location Where Sexually Harmful Behaviour Occurred |
| 0 | 1 | 2 | 5. | Severity of Sexually Harmful Behaviour |
| 0 | 1 | 2 | 6. | Nature of Aggression Used During Sexually Harmful Behaviour |
| 0 | 1 | 2 | 7. | Onset and Duration of Sexually Harmful Behaviour |
| 0 | 1 | 2 | 8. | Frequency of Sexually Harmful Behaviour |
| 0 | 1 | 2 | 9. | Escalating Pattern of Sexually Harmful Behaviour |
| 0 | 1 | 2 | 10. | Established / Emerging Pattern of Harmful Sexual behaviour |

### Domain 2:    ANTI-SOCIAL BEHAVIOUR

| 0 | 1 | 2 | 11. | History of Violent Behaviour / Criminal Convictions |
|---|---|---|---|---|
| 0 | 1 | 2 | 12. | History of Delinquency / Criminal Convictions |
| 0 | 1 | 2 | 13. | Substance Misuse / Dependency |

### Domain 3:    ADVERSE LIFE EXPERIENCES

| 0 | 1 | 2 | 14. | History of Childhood Sexual Victimisation |
|---|---|---|---|---|
| 0 | 1 | 2 | 15. | History of Childhood Physical Victimisation |
| 0 | 1 | 2 | 16. | Exposure to Sexual Abuse / Sexual Violence |
| 0 | 1 | 2 | 17. | Peer Victimisation |

### Domain 4:    SEXUAL DEVELOPMENT AND ADJUSTMENT

| 0 | 1 | 2 | 18. | Unmet Need for Sexual Contact / Experience with a Peer |
|---|---|---|---|---|
| 0 | 1 | 2 | 19. | Motive Underpinning Sexually Harmful Behaviour |
| 0 | 1 | 2 | 20. | Nature of Reinforcement from Sexually Harmful Behaviour |
| 0 | 1 | 2 | 21. | Pornography Misuse / Dependency |
| 0 | 1 | 2 | 22. | Sexual Learning Experiences |
| 0 | 1 | 2 | 23. | Sexual Fantasies |
| 0 | 1 | 2 | 24. | Sexual Preferences |
| 0 | 1 | 2 | 25. | Sexual Orientation   / Relations with Same- Sex peers |
| 0 | 1 | 2 | 26. | Cognitive Rules Underpinning Sexually Harmful Behaviour |
| 0 | 1 | 2 | 27. | Attitudes and Beliefs Underpinning Sexually Harmful Behaviour |
| 1 | 1 | 2 | 28. | Heterosocial Competency / Relations with Opposite-Sex Peers |
| 0 | 1 | 2 | 29. | Heterosexual / Dating Experiences |

# SHARP   *Sexually Harmful Adolescent Risk Protocol*

## Domain 5:   SOCIAL DEVELOPMENT AND ADJUSTMENT

| | | 0 | 1 | 2 |
|---|---|---|---|---|
| 30. | Social Competency | 0 | 1 | 2 |
| 31. | Social Integration | 0 | 1 | 2 |
| 32. | Social Immaturity | 0 | 1 | 2 |
| 33. | Social Delinquency | 0 | 1 | 2 |

## Domain 6:   EMOTIONAL DEVELOPMENT AND  ADJUSTMENT

| | | 0 | 1 | 2 |
|---|---|---|---|---|
| 34. | Emotional Dysregulation | 0 | 1 | 2 |
| 35. | General / Victim Empathy Deficits | 0 | 1 | 2 |
| 36. | Emotional Immaturity | 0 | 1 | 2 |
| 37. | Attachment Difficulties | 0 | 1 | 2 |

## Domain 7:   PERSONALITY DEVELOPMENT AND ADJUSTMENT

| | | 0 | 1 | 2 |
|---|---|---|---|---|
| 38. | Emerging Personality Disorder | 0 | 1 | 2 |
| 39. | Psychopathy Rating | 0 | 1 | 2 |

## Domain 8:   MENTAL HEALTH DEVELOPMENT AND ADJUSTMENT

| | | 0 | 1 | 2 |
|---|---|---|---|---|
| 40. | Childhood & Adolescent Psychiatric Disorders | 0 | 1 | 2 |
| 41. | Childhood & Adolescent Psychiatric Symptoms and Deficits | 0 | 1 | 2 |

## Domain 9:   COGNITIVE DEVELOPMENT AND ADJUSTMENT

| | | 0 | 1 | 2 |
|---|---|---|---|---|
| 42. | Intellectual Disability and Cognitive Deficits | 0 | 1 | 2 |
| 43. | Social-Cognitive Information Processing Deficits | 0 | 1 | 2 |

## Domain 10:   GENERAL SELF REGULATION & LEVEL OF INDEPENDENCE

| | | 0 | 1 | 2 |
|---|---|---|---|---|
| 44. | General Self-Regulation and Coping Deficits | 0 | 1 | 2 |
| 45. | Level of Independence | 0 | 1 | 2 |

## Domain 11:   ENVIRONMENTAL RISKS

| | | 0 | 1 | 2 |
|---|---|---|---|---|
| 46. | Family Environment and Opportunities for Sexually Harmful Behaviour | 0 | 1 | 2 |
| 47. | Neighbourhood Environment and Opportunities for Sexually Harmful Behaviour | 0 | 1 | 2 |
| 48. | School Environment and Opportunities for Sexually Harmful Behaviour | 0 | 1 | 2 |

## Domain 12:   MOTIVATION AND COMPLIANCE

| | | 0 | 1 | 2 |
|---|---|---|---|---|
| 49. | Family Acceptance / Compliance / Responsivity | 0 | 1 | 2 |
| 50. | Young Person's Manageability / Treatability / Responsivity | 0 | 1 | 2 |

# Appendix 2 Adolescent Sexual Recidivism Studies

| Study | Sexual recidivism rate (%) |
| --- | --- |
| Knopp, 1985 | 3 |
| Smith and Monastersky, 1986 | 14 |
| Heinz et al., 1987 | 7 |
| Smets and Cebula, 1987 | 5 |
| Khan and Lafond, 1988 | 9 |
| Becker, 1990 | 8 |
| Ryan and Miyoshi, 1990 | 9 |
| Khan and Chamber, 1991 | 8 |
| Schram et al., 1991 | 10 |
| Steiger and Dizon, 1991 | 12 |
| Bremer, 1992 | 11 |
| Mazur and Michael, 1992 | 0 |
| Lab, Shields and Schondel, 1993 | 4 (no treatment group) |
| Rubenstein et al., 1993 | 37 |
| Boyd, 1994 | 11 |
| Brannon and Troyer, 1995 | 16 |
| Broadhurst and Loh, 199 | 7 |
| Auslander, 1998 | 8 |
| Sipe, Jensen and Everett, 1998 | 10 |
| Walker, 1998 | 5 |
| Alexander, 1999 (meta analysis) | 7 |
| Hagan and Gust-Brey, 1999 | 16 |
| Rasmussen, 1999 | 14 |
| Langstrom and Grann, 2000 | 20 |
| Prentky et al., 2000 | 4 |
| Worling and Curwen, 2000 | 18 (no treatment group) |
| Borduin et al., 2001 | 42 (no treatment group) |
| Gretton et al., 2001 | 15 |
| Shapiro et al., 2001 | 8 |
| Hagan et al., 2001 | 20 |
| Worling, 2001 | 11 |
| Hecker et al., 2002 | 11 |
| Langstrom, 2002 | 30 |
| Miner, 2002 | 8 |
| Waite et al., 2002 | 4 |
| Allan et al., 2003 | 10 |
| Kraszlan et al., 2003 | 10 |
| Seabloom et al., 2003 | 8 (no treatment group) |
| Wieckowski et al., 2003 | 4 |
| Nisbet et al., 2004 | 25 |
| Christodoulides, Richardson et al., 2005 | 20 (criminal convictions) 46 professional reports |
| Edwards et al., 2005 | 16 (no treatment group) |
| Epperson, Ralston et al., 2005 | 13 |
| Heilbrum, Lee and Cottle, 2005 | 14 |
| Waite et al., 2005 | 5 |
| Hickey et al., 2006 | 5 |
| Parks and Bard, 2006 | 6 |

| | |
|---|---|
| Richardson (unpublished) | 24 |
| Reitzel and Carbonell, 2006 (meta-analysis) | 13 |
| Caldwell, 2007 | 7 |
| Clift, Gretton and Rajlic, 2007 | 6 |
| Martinez et al., 2007 | 13 |
| Rojas and Gretton, 2007 | 12 |
| Kemper and Kistner, 2007 | 4 |
| Hendriks and Bijleveld, 2008 | 11 |
| Viljoen et al., 2008 | 8 |
| **Number of studies** | **56** |
| **Range of recidivism rates** | **0–46** |
| **Mean sexual recidivism rate** | **12.4** |

## Appendix 3 Adolescent Risk Factors Studies

| Risk factors associated with sexual recidivism | Empirical support |
|---|---|
| Previous sexual offences | Kahn and Chambers, 1991 |
| | Langstrom, 2002 |
| | Langstrom and Grann, 2000 |
| | Schram et al., 1991 |
| | Worling and Curwen, 2000 |
| | Nisbet et al., 2004 |
| | Epperson et al., 2005 |
| | Rombouts, 2005 |
| | Poole et al., 2000 |
| | Morton 2003 |
| | Santman 1998 |
| Duration of sexual offending history | Hecker et al., 2002 |
| | Epperson et al., 2005 |
| Committed a sexual offence while on a probation or supervision order | Epperson et al., 2005 |
| Number of different type of offence locations | Epperson et al., 2005 |
| Two or more victims in the index offence | Langstrom and Grann, 2000 |
| Abuse involved penetration | Miner et al., 1997 |
| Multiple victims | Langstrom, 2002 |
| | Langstrom and Grann, 2000 |
| | Rasmussen, 1999 |
| | Worling, 2002 |
| | Epperson et al., 2005 |
| | Rombouts, 2005 |
| | Christodoulides et al., 2005 |
| Stranger victims | Ageton, 1983 |
| | Smith and Monastersky, 1986 |
| | Langstrom, 2002 |
| | Lee, Cottle and Heilburn, 2003 |
| | Heilbrun, Lee and Cottle, 2005 |
| | Rombouts (2005) |
| | Poole et al., 2000 |
| | Morton, 2003 |
| Previous non-sexual offences | Kahn and Chambers, 1991 |

| | |
|---|---|
| | Boyd, 1994 |
| | Nisbet et al., 2004 |
| | Epperson et al., 2005 |
| | Rombouts, 2005 |
| | Morton 2003 |
| | Poole et al., 2000 |
| | Santman 1998 |
| Younger-aged perpetrator | Khan and Chambers, 1991 |
| | Heilbrun et al., 2005 |
| | Lee, Cottle and Heilbrun, 2003 |
| | Santman (1998) |
| | Nisbet et al. (2004) |
| Multiple separate offences | Langstrom, 2002 |
| | Nisbet et al., 2004 |
| Early onset conduct disorder | Rasmussen, 1999 |
| | Hagan et al., 1994 |
| Sexual offence in a public location | Langstrom, 2002 |
| | Langstrom, Grann and Lindblad, 2000 |
| | Epperson et al., 2005 |
| Childhood victimisation | Worling, 2001 |
| Multiple female victims | Rassmussen, 1999 |
| Acquaintance victim | Heilbrun et al., 2005 |
| | Lee, Cottle and Heilbrun, 2003 |
| | Poole et al., 2000 |
| Male victim | Langstrom and Grann, 2000 |
| | Langstrom, Grann and Lindblad, 2000 |
| | Smith and Monastersky, 1986 |
| | Poole et al., 2000 |
| | Morton, 2003 |
| Victim of sexual abuse | Rubenstein et al., 1993 |
| | Khan and Chambers, 1991 |
| | Epperson et al., 2005 |
| | Rasmussen (1999) |
| | Redlak (2003) |
| Victim of physical abuse | Epperson et al., 2005 |
| | Rombouts, 2005 |
| Early sexual experience | Rubenstein et al., 1993 |
| Child victim | Boyd, 1994 |
| Use of verbal threats | Kahn and Chambers, 1991 |
| Offence preceded by play, grooming, deception or enticement | Epperson et al., 2005 |
| Denial of sexual offence | Epperson et al., 2005 |
| Blames victim | Kahn and Chambers, 1991 |
| Justifying sexual abuse | Schram et al., 1991 |
| Delinquent peer group | Ageton, 1983 |
| Impaired social functioning | Knight and Prentky, 1993 |
| | Worling, 2001 |
| | Langstrom and Grann, 2000 |
| | Kenny et al., 2001 |
| | Christodoulides et al., 2005 |
| Sexual preference for children (male and female) self-report; therapist rating; PPG | Worling and Curwen, 2000 |
| | Kenny et al., 2001 |
| | Schram et al., 1991 |
| | Khan and Chambers, 1991 |

| | |
|---|---|
| | Clift, Gretton and Rajlic, 2007 |
| | Rombouts, 2005 |
| | Hunter and Figueredo 1999 |
| | Morton 2003 |
| | Redlak (2003) |
| Impulsive/antisocial behavioural history | Knight and Prentky, 1993 |
| | Prentky et al., 2000 |
| | Waite et al., 2005 |
| | Park and Bard, 2006 |
| | Morton, 2003 |
| Poor community adjustment | Prentky et al., 2000 |
| History of intrafamily violence | Boyd, 1994 |
| Severe difficulty relating to siblings | Epperson et al., 2005 |
| History of delinquency | Boyd, 1994 |
| History of physical violence | Ageton, 1983 |
| Earlier onset sexual offending | Kahn and Chambers, 1991 |
| | Langstrom, 2002 |
| | Heilbrun, Lee and Cottle, 2005 |
| Unstable family home | Miner et al., 1997 |
| | Redlak (2003) |
| | Christodoulides et al., 2005 |
| Truancy | Schram et al., 1991 |
| Special educational needs | Epperson et al., 2005 |
| Cognitive distortions | Schram et al., 1991 |
| Social isolation | Langstrom and Grann, 2000 |
| | Kenny et al., 2001 |
| | Morton 2003 |
| No or uncompleted offence specific treatment | Borduin et al., 1990 |
| | Worling and Curwen, 2000 |
| | Heilbrun et al., 2005 |
| | Epperson et al., 2005 |
| | Lee, Cottle and Heilburn, 2003 |
| Psychopathy scores | Gretton et al., 2001 |
| | Park and Bard, 2006 |
| Diagnosed with a self-regulatory disorder (ADD, ADHD, Impulse Control Disorder, Conduct or Oppositional Defiant Disorder) | Epperson et al., 2005 |
| Physical separation from biological or adoptive parent prior to age 16 years | Epperson et al., 2005 |
| No or uncompleted mental health treatment | Epperson et al., 2005 |
| Non-contact index sexual offence | Rombouts, 2005 |
| | Lee, Cottle and Heilbrun, 2003 |
| | Hunter and Figueredo 1999 |
| Significant age difference between victim and perpetrator | Hendriks and Bijleveld, 2008 |
| Female victim outside the offenders family | Hendriks and Bijleveld, 2008 |
| **Number of Risk Factors** | **49** |
| **Number of Studies** | **36** |

## References cited in chapter

Andrews, D.A. and Bonta, J. (2003) *The Psychology of Criminal Conduct* (3rd ed.). Cincinnati, OH: Anderson Publishing.

Andrews, D.A., Bonta, J.L. and Wormith, J.S. (2004) *Level of Service/Case Management Inventory* (LS/CMI): *An Offender Assessment System*. Mental Health Systems Inc. 3770 Victoria Park Avenue, Toronto, On M24 3M6

Association for the Treatment of Sexual Abusers (ATSA) www.atsa.com

Augimeri, L.K., Koegl, C.J., Webster, C.D. and Levene, K.S. (2001) *Early Assessment Risk List for Boys: Version 2* (EARL-20B). Child Development Institute, Toronto, Canada. www.childdevelop.ca

Awad, G.A. and Saunders, E.B. (1991) Male Adolescent Sexual Assaulters: Clinical Observations. *Journal of Interpersonal Violence*, 6: 4, 446–60.

Becker, J.V., Cunningham-Rather, J. and Kaplan, M.S. (1986) Adolescent Sexual Offenders: Demographics, Criminal and Sexual Histories, and Recommendations for Reducing Future Offences. *Journal of Interpersonal Violence*, 1: 4, 431–45.

Borum, R., Bartel, P. and Forth, A. (2002) *Manual for the Structured Assessment of Violence Risk in Youth: Version 1.1* (SAVRY), University of South Florida, Florida.

Christodoulides, T.E., Richardson, G., Graham, F., Kennedy, P.J. and Kelly, T.P. (2005) Risk Assessment with Adolescent Sex Offenders. *Journal of Sexual Aggression*, 11: 1, 37–48.

Eells, T.D. (2007) *Handbook of Psychotherapy Case Formulation* (2nd Ed.). Guilford Press. England.

Fenrenbach, P.A., Smith. W., Monastersky, C. and Deisher, R.W. (1986) Adolescent Sexual Offenders: Offender and Offence Characteristics. *American Journal of Orthopsychiatry*, 56, 225–33.

Forth, A., Kossen, D. and Hare, R.D. (2003) *The Hare Psychopathy Checklist-Youth Version* (PCL YV), Multi-Health Systems Inc., New York.

Frick, P.J. and Hare, R.D. (2001) *The Antisocial Process Screening Device* (APSD). Toronto: Multi-Health Systems, Inc.

Graham, (1995) *Assessing Risk in Sexually Abusive Young People*. The Derwent Initiative, The Derwent Series, UK.

Groth, A.N. (1977) The Adolescent Sexual Offender and His Prey. *International Journal of Offender Therapy and Comparative Criminology*, 21, 249–54.

Hart, S.D., Kropp, P.R., Laws, D.R., Klaver, J., Logan, C. and Watt, K.A. (2003) *The Risk for Sexual Violence Protocol: Structured Professional Guidelines for Assessing Risk of Sexual Violence* (RSVP). Burnaby, BC: Simon Frazer University, Mental Health, Law and Policy Institute. [ISBN 1-895553-52-0]. Proactive Resolutions Inc. [ISBN 0-9738840-0-2]. www.proactive-resolutions.com

Hickey, N., Vizard, E., McCrory, E. and French, L. (2006) Links Between Juvenile Sexually Abusive Behaviour and Emerging Severe Personality Disorder Traits in Childhood. Home Office, Department of Health and National Offender Management Service.

Hoge, R.D. and Andrews, D.A. (2002) *Youth Level of Service/Case Management Inventory: User's Manual*. Toronto, ON: Multi-Health Systems.

Kemshall, H. (2002) Risk Assessment and Management of Serious Violent and Sexual Offenders: A Review of Current Issues (2002) Scottish Executive Social Research. [ISBN 0-7559-3450-4]. www.scotland.gov.uk/socialresearch

Kropp, P.R., Hart, S.D. and Belfrage, H. (2005) *Brief Spousal Assault Form for the Evaluation of Risk* (B-SAFER). Proactive Resolutions Inc. [ISBN 0-9738840-0-2]. www.proactive-resolutions.com

Kropp, P.R., Hart, S.D. and Lyon, (2006) *Stalking Assessment and Management* (SAM). Proactive Resolutions Inc. www.proactive-resolutions.com

Kropp, P.R., Hart, S.D., Webster, C.D. and Eaves, D. (1999) *Spousal Assault Risk Assessment Guide* (SARA). Toronto: Multi-Health Systems, Inc.

Loeber, R. and Farrington, D.P. (1998) *Serious and Violent Juvenile Offenders: Risk Factors and Successful Interventions*. Thousand Oaks, CA: Sage.

National Adolescent Perpetrator Network (NAPN). www.kempe.org

National Organisation for the Treatment of Abusers (NOTA). www.nota.co.uk

Persons, J.B. (1989) *Cognitive Therapy in Practice: A Case Formulation Approach*. New York: W.W. Norton.

Richardson, G. (1995) Risk Evaluation: Stage 1, 51–4 and Risk Evaluation: Stage 2, 73–5. In Graham, F. (Ed) *Assessing Risk in Sexually Abusive Young People*, The Derwent Initiative, The Derwent Series, UK.

Richardson, G, (2005) Early Maladaptive Schemas

in a Sample of British Adolescent Sexual Abusers: Implications for therapy. *Journal of Sexual Aggression*, 11: 3, 259–76.

Richardson, G. (2007) Emerging Personality Disorders in Sexually Harmful Young People (pp. 65–95). In Calder, M.C. (Ed) *Working with Children and Young People who Sexually Abuse: Taking the Field Forward*. Lyme Regis: Russell House Publishing.

Richardson, G. (unpublished) Criminal Recidivism in a British Sample of Sexually Abusive Adolescents.

Richardson, G., Graham, F., Bhate, S.R. and Kelly, T.P. (1995) A British Sample of Sexually Abusive Adolescents: Abuser and Abuse Characteristics. *Criminal Behaviour and Mental Health*, 5, 187–208.

Richardson, G., Kelly, T.P., Bhate, S.R. and Graham, F. (1997) Group Differences in Abuser and Abuse Characteristics in a British Sample of Sexually Abusive Adolescents. *Sexual Abuse: A Journal of Research and Treatment*, 9: 3, 239–57.

Richardson, G., Kelly, T.P., Graham, F. and Bhate, S.R. (2004) A Personality-based Taxonomy of Sexually Abusive Adolescents derived from the Millon Adolescent Clinical Inventory (MACI). *British Journal of Clinical Psychology*, 43, 285–98.

Risk Management Authority, St James House, 25 James Street, Paisley, PA3 2HQ, Scotland. www.rmascotland.gov.uk

Risk Management Authority Standards and Guidelines for Risk Assessment (2006) Risk Management Authority, Paisley, PA3 2HQ, Scotland. www.rmascotland.gov.uk

Risk Management Authority Risk Assessment Tools Evaluation Directory (2007) Risk Management Authority, Paisley, PA3 2HQ, Scotland. www.rmascotland.gov.uk

Vizard, E., Hickey, N. and McCrory, E. (2007) Developmental Trajectories Associated with Juvenile Sexually Abusive Behaviour and Emerging Severe Personality Disorder in Childhood: 3-year study. British Journal of Psychiatry, 190 (suppl. 49) s27–s32.

Ward, T. and Beech, R. (2004). The Etiology of Risk: A Preliminary Model. Sexual Abuse: *A Journal of Research and Treatment*, 16: 4, 271–84.

Ward, T., Polaschek, D.L.L. and Beech, A.R. (2006). Theories of Risk. In Ward, T., Polaschek, D.L.L. and Beech, A.R. *Theories of Sexual Offending*. (pp. 197–210) John Wiley & Sons Ltd.

Webster, C.D., Douglas, K.S., Eaves, D. and Hart, S.D. (1997) *HCR-20: Assessing Risk for Violence, Version 2*, Burnaby, BC: Simon Frazer University, Mental Health, Law and Policy Institute. [ISBN 0-86491-157-2]

Worling, J.R. (2001). Personality-Based Typology of Adolescent Male Sexual Offenders: Differences in Recidivism Rates, Victim-selection Characteristics, and Personal Victimization Histories. *Sexual Abuse: A Journal of Research and Treatment*, 13: 3, 149–66.

## References cited in Appendix 2: Adolescent Sexual Recidivism Studies

Alexander, M.A. (1999) Sexual Offender Treatment Efficacy Revisited. *Sexual Abuse: A Journal of Research and Treatment*, 11, 2, 101–16.

Allan, A., Allan, M.M., Marshall, P. and Kraszlan, K. (2003) Recidivism among Male Juvenile Sexual Offenders in Western Australia. *Psychiatry, Psychology and Law*, 10: 2. 359–78.

Auslander, B.A. (1998) An Exploratory Study Investigating Variables in Relation to Juvenile Sexual Offending. Unpublished Doctoral Dissertation. Florida State University, Tallahassee.

Becker, J.V. (1990) Treating Adolescent Sexual Offenders. *Professional Psychology: Research and Practice*, 21, 362–5.

Borduin, C.M. and Schaeffer, C.M. (2001) Multisystemic Treatment of Juvenile Sexual Offenders: A Progress Report. *Journal of Psychology and Human Sexuality*, 13, 25–42.

Boyd, N.J. (1994) Predictors of Recidivism in an Adolescent Sexual Offenders' Population. Unpublished Doctoral Dissertation, University of Wisconsin-Madison.

Brannon, J.M. and Troyer, R. (1995) Adolescent Sex Offenders: Investigating Adult Commitment-Rates Four Years Later. *International Journal of Offender Therapy and Comparative Criminology*, 39: 4, 317–26.

Bremer, J.F. (1992) Serious Juvenile Sex Offenders: Treatment and Long-term Follow-up. *Psychiatric Annals*, 22nd June, pp. 326–32.

Broadhurst, R. and Loh, N. (1997) *Careers of Sex Offenders: The Probabilities of Re-arrest*. Paper presented to the Australian Institute of Criminology Second National Outlook Symposium, March, Canberra, Australia.

Caldwell, M.F. (2007) Sexual Offense Adjudication and Sexual Recidivism among Juvenile Offenders. *Sexual Abuse: A Journal of Research and Treatment*, 19: 2, 107–13.

Christodoulides, T.E., Richardson, G., Graham, F., Kennedy, P.J. and Kelly, T.P. (2005) Risk

Assessment with Adolescent Sex Offenders. *Journal of Sexual Aggression*, 11: 1, 37–48.

Clift, R.J.W., Gretton, H.M. and Rajlic, G. (2007) The Relationship between Deviant Arousal and Sexual Recidivism in Adolescent Sex Offenders. In Calder, M.C. (Ed.) *Working with Children and Young People who Sexually Abuse: Taking the Field Forward* (pp. 96–102) Russell House Publishing.

Edwards, R., Beech, A., Bishopp, D., Erickson, M., Friendship, C. and Charlesworth, L. (2005) Predicting Dropout from a Residential Programme for Adolescent Sexual Abusers using Pre-treatment Variables and Implications for Recidivism. *Journal of Sexual Aggression*, 11: 2, 139–55.

Epperson, D.L., Ralston, C.A., Flowers, D. and De Witt, J. (2005) *The Juvenile Sexual Offense Recidivism Risk Assessment Tool – II* (JSORRAT-II), Iowa State University, USA. [dle@iastate.edu] http://www.psychology.iastate.edu/faculty/epperson/jsorrat-ii-download.htm

Gretton, H.M., McBride, M., Hare, R.D., O'Shaughnessy, R. and Kumka, G. (2001) Psychopathy and Recidivism in Adolescent Sex Offenders. *Criminal Justice and Behavior*, 28: 4, 427–49.

Hagan, M.P. and Gust-Brey, K.L. (1999) A Ten-Year Longitudinal Study of Adolescent Rapists Upon Return to the Community. *International Journal of Offender Therapy and Comparative Criminology*, 43: 4, 448–58.

Hagan, M.P., Gust-Brey, K.L., Cho, M.E. and Dow, E. (2001) Eight-year Comparative Analyses of Adolescent Rapists, Adolescent Child Molesters, other Adolescent Delinquents, and the General Population. *International Journal of Offender Therapy and Comparative Criminology*, 45: 3, 314–24.

Hecker, J., Scoular, J., Righthand, S. and Nangle, D. (2002) *Predictive Validity of the J-SOAP over 10-plus Years: Implications for Risk and Assessment*. Paper presented at the Annual Conference of the Association for Treatment of Sexual Abusers, Montreal, Quebec, Canada.

Heilbrun, K., Lee, R.J. and Cottle, C.C (2005) Risk Factors and Intervention Outcomes: Meta-analyses of Juvenile Offending. In Heilbrun, K., Goldstein, N.E.S. and Redding, R.E. (Eds.) (2005) *Juvenile Delinquency: Prevention, Assessment, and Intervention* (pp. 111–133) New York: Oxford University Press, Inc.

Heinz, J.W., Gargaro, S. and Kelly, K.G. (1987) *A Model Residential Juvenile Sex Offender Treatment Program: The Hennepin County Home School*. Safer Society Press, Brandon, VT.

Hendriks, J. and Bijleveld, C. (2008) Recidivism among Juvenile Sex Offenders after Residential Treatment. *Journal of Sexual Aggression*, 14: 1, 19–32.

Hickey, N., Vizard, E., McCrory, E. and French, L. (2006) Links Between Juvenile Sexually Abusive Behaviour and Emerging Severe Personality Disorder Traits in Childhood. Home Office, Department of Health and National Offender Management Service.

Kahn, T.J. and Chamber, H.J. (1991) Assessing Re-offense Risk with Juvenile Sexual Offenders. *Child Welfare*, 70, 333–45.

Kahn, T. and Lafond, M.A. (1988) Treatment of the Adolescent Sex Offender. *Child and Adolescent Social Work*, 5, 135–48.

Kemper, T.S. and Kistner, J.A. (2007) Offense History and Recidivism in Three Victim-age-based Groups of Juvenile Sex Offenders. *Sexual Abuse: A Journal of Research and Treatment*, 19: 4, 409–24.

Knopp, F.H. (1985) *The Youthful Sex Offender: The Rationale and Goals of Early Intervention and Treatment*. Syracuse, NY: Safer Society Press.

Kraszlan, K. (2003) Recidivism among Male Juvenile Sexual Offenders in Western Australia. *Psychiatry, Psychology and Law*.

Lab, S.P., Shields, G. and Schondel, C. (1993) An Evaluation of Juvenile Sexual Offender Treatment. *Crime and Delinquency*, 39: 4, 543–53.

Langstrom, N. (2002) Long-term Follow-up of Criminal Recidivism in Young Sex Offenders: Temporal Patterns and Risk Factors. *Psychology, Crime and Law*, 8, 41–58.

Langstrom, N. and Grann, M. (2000) Risk of Criminal Recidivism among Young Sex Offenders. *Journal of Interpersonal Violence*, 15: 8, 855–71.

Martinez, R., Flores, J. and Rosenfeld, B. (2007) Validity of the Juvenile Sex Offender Assessment Protocl – II (J-SOAP-II) in a Sample of Urban Minority Youth. *Criminal Justice and Behavior*, 34: 10, 1284–95.

Mazur, T. and Michael, P.M. (1992) Outpatient Treatment for Adolescents with Sexually Inappropriate Behavior: Program Description and Six-month Follow-up. *Journal of Offender Rehabilitation*, 18: 3/4, 191–203.

Miner, M.H. (2002) Factors Associated with Recidivism in Juveniles: An Analysis of Serious Juvenile Sex Offenders. *Journal of Research in Crime and Delinquency*, 39: 4, 421–36.

Nisbet, I.A., Wilson, P.H. and Smallbone, S.W. (2004) A Prospective Longitudinal Study of Sexual Recidivism among Adolescent Sex Offenders. *Sexual Abuse: A Journal of Research and Treatment*, 16: 3, 223–34.

Parks, G.A. and Bard, D.E. (2006) Risk Factors for Adolescent Sex Offender Recidivism: Evaluation of Predictive Factors and Comparison of Three Groups based upon Victim Type. *Sexual Abuse: A Journal of Research and Treatment*, 18: 4, 319–42.

Prentky, R., Harris, B., Frizzell, K. and Righthand, S. (2000) An Actuarial Procedure for Assessing Risk with Juvenile Sex Offenders. *Sexual Abuse: A Journal of Research and Treatment*, 12: 2, 71–93.

Rasmussen, L.A. (1999) Factors Related to Recidivism among Juvenile Sexual Offenders. *Sexual Abuse: A Journal of Research and Treatment*, 11: 1, 69–85.

Reitzel, L.R. and Carbonell, J.L. (2006) The Effectiveness of Sexual Offender Treatment for Juveniles as Measured by Recidivism: A Meta-analysis. *Sexual Abuse: A Journal of Research and Treatment*, 18: 4, 317–440.

Richardson, G (unpublished) Criminal Recidivism in a British sample of Sexually Abusive Adolescents.

Rojas, E.Y. and Gretton, H.M. (2007) Background, Offence Characteristics and Criminal Outcomes of Aboriginal Youth who Sexually Offend: A Closer Look at Aboriginal Youth Intervention Needs. *Sexual Abuse: A Journal of Research and Treatment*, 19: 3, 257–83.

Rubinstein, M., Yeager, C.A., Goodstein, B.A. and Lewis, D.O. (1993) Sexually Assaultive Male Juveniles: A Follow-up. *American Journal of Psychiatry*, 150: 2, 262–5

Ryan, G. and Miyoshi, T. (1990) Summary of Pilot Follow-up Study of Adolescent Sexual Perpetrators after Treatment. *Interchange*, 10: 1, 6–8.

Schram, D.D., Milloy, C.D. and Rowe, W.E. (1991) *Juvenile Sex Offenders: A Follow-up Study of Reoffense Behavior.* Washington Institute for Public Policy, Urban Policy Research and Cambie Group International.

Seabloom, W., Seabloom, M.E., Seabloom, E., Barron, R. and Hendrickson, S. (2003) A 14 to 24 Year Longitudinal Study of a Comprehensive Sexual Health Model Treatment Program for Adolescent Sex Offenders: Predictors of Successful Completion and Subsequent Criminal Recidivism. *International Journal of Offender Therapy and Comparative Criminology*, 47: 4, 468–81.

Shapiro, J.P., Welker, C.J. and Pierce, J.L. (2001) An Evaluation of Residential Treatment for Sexually Aggressive Youth. *Journal of Child Sexual Abuse*, 10, 1–21.

Sipe, R., Jensen, E.L. and Everett, R.S. (1998) Adolescent Sexual Offenders Grown Up: Recidivism in Young Adulthood. *Criminal Justice and Behavior*, 25: 1, 109–24.

Smets, A.C. and Cebula, C.M. (1987) A Group Treatment Program for Adolescent Sex Offenders: Five Steps toward Resolution. Child Abuse and Neglect, 11: 2, 247–54.

Smith, W.R. and Monastersky, C. (1986) Assessing Juvenile Sexual Offenders Risk for Reoffending. *Criminal Justice and Behavior*, 13, 115–40.

Steiger, J.C. and Dizon, C. (1991) *Rehabilitation, Release and Re-offending: A Report on the Criminal Careers of the Division of Juvenile Rehabilitation Class of 1982.* Olympia, WA: Juvenile Offender Research Unit, Department of Social and Human Services.

Viljoen, J.L., Scalora, M., Cuadra, L., Bader, S., Chavez, V., Ullman, D. and Lawrence, L. (2008) Assessing Risk for Violence in Adolescents who have Sexually Offended: A comparison of the J-SOAP-II, J-SORRAT-II, and SAVRY. Criminal Justice and Behavior, 35: 1, 5–23.

Waite, D., Pinkerton, R., Wieckowski, E., McGarvey, E.L. and Brown, G.L. (2002) *Tracking Treatment Outcome among Juvenile Sexual Offenders: A Nine-year Follow-up Study.* Paper presented at the Annual Conference of the Association for Treatment of Sexual Abusers, Montreal, Quebec, Canada.

Waite, D., Keller, A., McGarvey, E.L., Wieckowski, E., Pinkerton, R. and Brown, G.L. (2005) Juvenile Sex Offender Re-Arrest Rates for Sexual, Violent Nonsexual and Property Crimes: A 10-year Follow-up. *Sexual Abuse: A Journal of Research and Treatment*, 17: 3, 313–31.

Walker, G. (1998) *Victoria: A World Leader in Working with Teen Sex Offenders.* Department of Human Services, Victoria, Australia. Internet resource: www.dhs.vic.gov.au

Wieckowski, E., Waite, D., Pinkerton, R., McGarvey, E.L. and Brown, G.L. (2003) Sex Offender Treatment in a Juvenile Correctional Setting: Program Description and Nine-year Outcome Study. Unpublished presentation.

Worling, J.R. (2001) Personality-Based Typology of Adolescent Male Sexual Offenders: Differences in Recidivism Rates, Victim-selection Characteristics, and Personal

Victimization Histories. *Sexual Abuse: A Journal of Research and Treatment*, 13: 3, 149–66.

Worling, J.R. and Curwen, T. (2000) Adolescent Sexual Offender Recidivism: Success of Specialised Treatment and Implications for Risk Prediction. *Child Abuse and Neglect*, 24: 7, 965–82.

# References cited in Appendix 3: Adolescent Risk Factors Studies

Ageton, S.S. (1983) Sexual Assault among Adolescents. Lexington, MA: Lexington Books.

Borduin, C.M., Henggeler, S.W., Blaske, D.M. and Stein, R.J. (1990) Multisystemic Treatment of Adolescent Sexual Offenders. *International Journal of Offender Therapy and Comparative Criminology*, 34: 2, 105–14.

Boyd, N.J. (1994) Predictors of Recidivism in an Adolescent Sexual Offenders' Population. Unpublished Doctoral Dissertation, University of Wisconsin-Madison.

Christodoulides, T.E., Richardson, G., Graham, F., Kennedy, P.J. and Kelly, T.P. (2005) Risk Assessment with Adolescent Sex Offenders. *Journal of Sexual Aggression*, 11: 1, 37–48.

Clift, R.J.W., Gretton, H.M. and Rajlic, G. (2007) The Relationship between Deviant Arousal and Sexual Recidivism in Adolescent Sex Offenders. In Calder, M.C. (Ed.) *Working with Children and Young People who Sexually Abuse: Taking the Field Forward* (pp. 96–102). Lyme Regis: Russell House Publishing.

Epperson, D.L., Ralston, C.A., Flowers, D. and De Witt, J. (2005) *The Juvenile Sexual Offense Recidivism Risk Assessment Tool – II* (JSORRAT-II), Iowa State University, USA. [dle@iastate.edu] http://www.psychology.iastate.edu/faculty/epperson/jsorrat-ii-download.htm

Gretton, H.M., McBride, M., Hare, R.D., O'Shaughnessy, R. and Kumka, G. (2001) Psychopathy and Recidivism in Adolescent Sex Offenders. *Criminal Justice and Behavior*, 28: 4, 427–49.

Hagan, M.P., King, R.P. and Patros, R.L. (1994) Recidivism among Adolescent Perpetrators of Sexual Assault against Children. *Journal of Offender Rehabilitation*, 21 1, 127–37.

Hecker, J., Scoular, J., Righthand, S. and Nangle, D. (2002) *Predictive Validity of the J-SOAP over 10-plus Years: Implications for Risk and Assessment*. Paper presented at the Annual Conference of the Association for Treatment of Sexual Abusers, Montreal, Quebec, Canada.

Heilbrun, K., Lee, R.J. and Cottle, C.C. (2005) Risk Factors and Intervention Outcomes: Meta-analyses of Juvenile Offending. In Heilbrun, K., Goldstein, N.E.S. and Redding, R.E. (Eds.) *Juvenile Delinquency: Prevention, Assessment, and Intervention* (pp. 111–33). New York: Oxford University Press, Inc.

Hendriks, J. and Bijleveld, C. (2008) Recidivism among Juvenile Sex Offenders after Residential Treatment. *Journal of Sexual Aggression*, 14: 1, 19–32.

Hunter, J.A. and Figueredo, A.J. (1999) Factors Associated with Treatment Compliance in a Population of Juvenile Sexual Offenders. *Sexual Abuse: A Journal of Research and Treatment*, 11, 49–67.

Kahn, T.J. and Chamber, H.J. (1991) Assessing Re-offense Risk with Juvenile Sexual Offenders. *Child Welfare*, 70, 333–45.

Kenny, D.T., Keogh, T. and Seidler, K. (2001) Predictors of Recidivism in Australian Juvenile Sex Offenders: Implications for Treatment. *Sexual Abuse: A Journal of Research and Treatment*, 13: 2, 131–48.

Knight, R.A. and Prentky, R.A. (1993) Exploring Characteristics for Classifying Juvenile Sex Offenders. In Barbaree, H.E., Marshall, W.L. and Hudson, S.M. (Eds.) *The Juvenile Sex Offender*, (pp. 45–83). New York: Guilford Press.

Langstrom, N. (2002) Long-term Follow-up of Criminal Recidivism in Young Sex Offenders: Temporal Patterns and Risk Factors. *Psychology, Crime and Law*, 8, 41–58.

Langstrom, N. and Grann, M. (2000) Risk of Criminal Recidivism among Young Sex Offenders. *Journal of Interpersonal Violence*, 15: 8, 855–71.

Langstrom, N., Grann, M. and Lindblad, F. (2000) A Preliminary Typology of Young Sex Offenders. *Journal of Adolescence*, 23, 319–29.

Lee, R.J., Cottle, C.C. and Heilburn, K. (2003) The Prediction of Recidivism in Juvenile Sexual Offenders: A Meta-analysis, cited in Worling J.R. and Langstrom, N. Assessment of Criminal Recidivism with Adolescents who have Offended Sexually: A Review. *Trauma, Violence and Abuse*, 4: 4, 341–62.

Miner, M.H., Siekert, G.P. and Ackland, M.A. (1997) *Evaluation: Juvenile Sex Offender Treatment Program*, Minnesota Correctional Facility – Sauk Centre (Final report – Biennium 1995–1997). Minneapolis, MN: University of

Minnesota, Department of Family Practice and Community Health, Program in Human Sexuality.

Morton, K.E. (2003) Psychometric Properties of Four Risk Assessment Measures with Male Adolescent Sex Offenders. Unpublished Masters thesis, Carlton University, Ottawa, Canada.

Nisbet, I.A., Wilson, P.H. and Smallbone, S.W. (2004). A Prospective Longitudinal Study of Sexual Recidivism among Adolescent Sex Offenders. *Sexual Abuse: A Journal of Research and Treatment*, 16: 3, 223–34.

Parks, G.A. and Bard, D.E. (2006) Risk Factors for Adolescent Sex Offender Recidivism: Evaluation of Predictive Factors and Comparison of Three Groups based upon Victim Type. *Sexual Abuse: A Journal of Research and Treatment*, 18: 4, 319–42.

Poole, D., Liedecke, D. and Marbibi, M. (2000) Risk Assessment and Recidivism in Juvenile Sexual Offenders: A validation study of the Static-99. Austin: University of Texas, School of Social Work.

Prentky, R., Harris, B., Frizzell, and Righthand, S. (2000) An Actuarial Procedure for Assessing Risk with Juvenile Sex Offenders. *Sexual Abuse: A Journal of Research and Treatment*, 12: 2, 71–93.

Rasmussen, L.A. (1999) Factors Related to Recidivism among Juvenile Sexual Offenders. *Sexual Abuse: A Journal of Research and Treatment*, 11: 1, 69–85.

Redlak, A. (2003) An exploratory Meta-analysis of the Predictor Variables of Juvenile Sex Offenders who Sexually Recidivate. Unpublished doctoral dissertation, California School of Professional Psychology, Fresno.

Rombouts, S. (2005). *Development of a Risk Assessment Checklist for Juvenile Sexual Offenders: A Meta-Analytic Approach*. Unpublished PhD. School of Psychology, Faculty of Health Science, Griffith University, Brisbane, Australia, available from www.4gu.edu.au8080/adt-root/uploads/approved/adt-QGU20070123.151237/public/02whole.pdf

Rubinstein, M., Yeager, C.A., Goodstein, B.A. and Lewis, D.O. (1993) Sexually Assaultive Male Juveniles: A Follow-up. *American Journal of Psychiatry*, 150: 2, 262–5.

Santman, J. (1998) A Taxonomic Model of Juvenile Sexual Offender Recidivism. Unpublished doctoral dissertation, California School of Professional Psychology, California.

Schram, D.D., Milloy, C.D. and Rowe, W.E. (1991) *Juvenile Sex Offenders: A Follow-up Study of Re-offense behavior*. Washington Institute for Public Policy, Urban Policy Research and Cambie Group International.

Smith, W. R. and Monastersky, C. (1986) Assessing Juvenile Sexual Offenders Risk for Re-offending. *Criminal Justice and Behavior*, 13, 115–40.

Waite, D., Keller, A., McGarvey, E.L., Wieckowski, E., Pinkerton, R. and Brown, G.L. (2005) Juvenile Sex Offender Re-Arrest Rates for Sexual, Violent Nonsexual and Property Crimes: A 10-year follow-up. *Sexual Abuse: A Journal of Research and Treatment*, 17: 3, 313–31.

Worling, J.R. (2001) Personality-Based Typology of Adolescent Male Sexual Offenders: Differences in Recidivism Rates, Victim-selection Characteristics, and Personal Victimization Histories. *Sexual Abuse: A Journal of Research and Treatment*, 13: 3, 149–66.

Worling, J.R. (2002) Assessing Risk of Sexual Assault Recidivism with Adolescent Sexual Offenders. In M.C. Calder (Ed.) Young People Who Sexually Abuse: Building the Evidence Base for Your Practice. Lyme Regis: Russell House Publishing.

Worling, J.R. and Curwen, T. (2000) Adolescent Sexual Offender Recidivism: Success of Specialised Treatment and Implications for Risk Prediction. *Child Abuse and Neglect*, 24: 7, 965–82.

## Risk assessment protocols cited

### *Adult*

**The Rapid Risk Assessment for Sexual Offense Recidivism (RRASOR)**
Hanson, R.K. (1997) *The Development of a Brief Actuarial Scale for Sexual Offense Recidivism*. User Report No. 1997-04. Ottawa: Department of the Solicitor General of Canada. [Www.sgc.gc.ca]

**The Sexual Violence Risk –20 (SVR-20)**
Boer, D.P., Hart, S.D., Kropp, P.R. and Webster, C.D. (1997) *Manual for the Sexual Violence Risk – 20. Professional Guidelines for Assessing Risk of Sexual Violence*. Burnaby, British Columbia: The Mental Health, Law, and Policy Institute, Simon Fraser University.

**The Sex Offender Risk Appraisal Guide (SORAG)**

Quinsey, V.L., Harris, G.T., Rice, M.E. and Cormier, C. (1998) The Sex Offender Risk Appraisal Guide (SORAG), In *Violent Offenders: Appraising and Managing Risk*. Washington, D.C.: American Psychological Association.

**The Static-99 (1999)**
Hanson, R.K. and Thornton, D.M. (1999) *Static-99: Improving Actuarial Risk Assessment for Sexual Offenders*. Ottawa, Canada: Department of the Solicitor General of Canada (Corrections Research User Report 199-02).

**The Sex Offender Need Assessment Rating (SONAR)**
Hanson, R.K. and Harris, A.J.R. (2000) *The Sex Offender Need Assessment Rating (SONAR): A Method for Measuring Change in Risk Levels* (User report No. 2000-1). Ottawa: Corrections Research, Department of the Solicitor General of Canada. [www.sgc.gc.ca]

**The Vermont Assessment of Sex Offender Risk Manual: Research Edition (VASOR)**
McGarth, R.J. and Hoke, S.E. (2001) *The Vermont Assessment of Sex Offender Risk Manual: Research Edition*. Center for Sex Offender Management (CSOM). [www.csom.org.]

**The Static-2002**
Hanson, R.K. and Thornton, D.M. (2003) *Notes on the Development of Static-2002*. Ottawa: Department of the Solicitor General of Canada. [www.sgc.gc.ca]

**Minnesota Sex Offender Screening Tool – Revised (MnSOST-R)**
Epperson, D.L., Kaul, J.D., Huot, S.J., Hesselton, D., Alexander, W. and Goldmanm, R. (2003). *The Minnesota Sex Offender Screening Tool – Revised* (MnSOST-R), Minnesota Department of Corrections, USA. [www.doc.state.mn.us]

**The Risk for Sexual Violence Protocol (RSVP)**
Hart, S.D., Kropp, P.R., Laws, D.R., Klaver, J., Logan, C. and Watt, K.A. (2003) *The Risk for Sexual Violence Protocol: Structured Professional Guidelines for Assessing Risk of Sexual Violence* (RSVP). Burnaby, BC: Simon Frazer University, Mental Health, Law and Policy Institute. [ISBN 1-895553-52-0]. Proactive Resolutions Inc. [ISBN 0-9738840-0-2]. www.proactive-resolutions.com

**The Structured Assessment of Risk and Needs (SARN)**
Thornton, D. (2002) Constructing and Testing a Framework for Dynamic Risk Assessment.

*Sexual Abuse: A Journal of Research and Treatment*, 14: 2, 139–3.
Webster, S.D., Mann, R.R., Carter, A.J., Long, J., Milner, R.J., O'Brien, M.D., Wakeling, H.C.and Ray, N.L. (2006) Inter-rater Reliability of Dynamic Risk Assessment with Sexual Offenders. *Psychology, Crime and Law*, 12: 4, 439–52.

**The Violence Risk Scale – Sexual Offender Version (VRS-SO)**
Wong, S.C.P., Olver, M.E., Nicholaichuk, T.P. and Gordon, A. (2003) Saskatoon, Saskatchewan, Canada: Regional Psychiatric Centre and University of Saskatchewan.

**The Adult Sex Offender Assessment Protocol (A-SOAP II)**
Prentky, R.A. and Righthand, S. (2005) *The Adult Sex Offender Assessment Protocol: Manual*. Bridgewater, MA: Justice Resource Institute.
Olver, M.E., Wong, S.C.P., Nicholaichuk, T.P. and Gordon, A. (2007) The Validity and Reliability of the Violence Risk Scale-Sexual Offender Version: Assessing Sex Offender Risk and Evaluating Therapeutic Change. *Psychological Assessment*, 19: 3, 318–29.

**The Risk Matrix 2000**
Thornton, D. (2007). *Scoring Guide for the Risk Matrix 2000*. 9/SVC February 2007 Version. Unpublished manuscript.

**The Stable 2007**
Hanson, R.K., Harris, A.J.R., Scott, T.L. and Helmus, L. (2007) *Assessing the Risk of Sexual Offenders on Community Supervision: The Dynamic Supervision Project* [2007–05]. Public Safety Canada. www.sgc.gc.ca

**The Acute 2007**
Hanson, R.K., Harris, A.J.R., Scott, T.L. and Helmus, L. (2007) *Assessing the Risk of Sexual Offenders on Community Supervision: The Dynamic Supervision Project* [2007–05]. Public Safety Canada. www.sgc.gc.ca

### Adolescent

**The Estimate of Risk of Adolescent Sexual Offense Recidivism (ERASOR)**
Worling, J.R. and Curwen, T. (2001) *The ERASOR: Estimate of Risk of Adolescent Sexual Recidivism* (Version 2.0). Toronto, Ontario, Canada: Safe-T Program, Thistletown Regional Centre.

**The Juvenile Sex Offender Assessment Protocol – II (J-SOAP-II)**

Prentky, R. and Righthand, S. (2003) *Juvenile Sex Offender Assessment Protocol – II (J-SOAP-II) Manual*: NCJ202316. The Office of Juvenile Justice and Delinquency Prevention's Juvenile Justice Clearinghouse.

**Juvenile Sexual Offense Recidivism Risk Assessment Tool – II (JSORRAT-II)**

Epperson, D.L., Ralston, C.A., Flowers, D. and De Witt, J. (2005) *The Juvenile Sexual Offense Recidivism Risk Assessment Tool – II (JSORRAT-II)*, Iowa State University, USA. [dle@iastate.edu] http://www.psychology.iastate.edu/faculty/epperson/jsorrat-ii-download.htm

**Juvenile Risk Assessment Tool (Version 3) J-RAT**

Rich, P. (2007) *The Juvenile Risk Assessment Tool.* Barre, MA: Stetson School. Retrieved from: www.stetsonschool.org/clinical_materials/assessment_tools/assessment_tools.html

**Multiplex Empirically Guided Inventory of Ecological Aggregates for Assessing Sexually Abusive Children and Adolescents (MEGA) (in press)**

Rasmussen, L.A. and Miccio-Fonseca, L.C. (2007) Empirically Guided Practice with Young People who Sexually Abuse: A Risk Factor Approach to Assessment and Evaluation. In Calder M.C. (Ed). *Working with Children and Young People who Sexually Abuse: Taking the Field Forward.* (pp. 177–200). Lyme Regis: Russell House Publishing.

## Suggested reading

Beech, A.R. and Ward, T. (2004) The Integration of Etiology and Risk in Sexual Offenders: A Theoretical Framework. *Aggression and Violent Behavior*, 10, 31–63.

Bonta, J. and Andrews, D.A. (2007) *Risk-Need-Responsivity Model for Offender Assessment and Rehabilitation.* Public Safety Canada. www.publicsafety.gc.ca/res/cor/rep/risk_need_200706-eng.aspx

Calder, M.C. (Ed.) (2007) *Working with Children and Young People who Sexually Abuse: Taking the Field Forward.* Lyme Regis: Russell House Publishing.

Caldwell, M.F. (2007) Sexual Offense Adjudication and Sexual Recidivism among Juvenile Offenders. *Sexual Abuse: A Journal of Research and Treatment*, 19: 2, 107–13.

Fortune, C-A. and Lambie, I. (2006) Sexually Abusive Youth: A Review of Recidivism Studies and Methodological Issues for Future Research. *Clinical Psychology Review*, 26, 1078–95.

Gerhold, C.K., Browne, D.K. and Beckett, R. (2007) Predicting Recidivism in Adolescent Sexual Offenders. *Aggression and Violent Behavior*, 12, 427–38.

Parks, G.A. and Bard, D.E. (2006) Risk Factors for Adolescent Sex Offender Recidivism: Evaluation of Predictive Factors and Comparison of Three Groups based upon Victim Type. *Sexual Abuse: A Journal of Research and Treatment*, 18: 4, 319–42.

Prescott, D.S. (2006) *Risk Assessment of Youth who have Sexually Abused: Theory, Controversy, and Emerging Strategies.* Wood 'n' Barnes Publishers.

Reitzel, L.R. Carbonell, J.L. (2006) The Effectiveness of Sexual Offender Treatment for Juveniles as Measured by Recidivism: A Meta-analysis. *Sexual Abuse: A Journal of Research and Treatment*, 18: 4, 401–21.

Worling, J.R. and Langstrom, N. (2003) Assessment of Criminal Recidivism Risk with Adolescents who have Offended Sexually: A Review. *Trauma, Violence and Abuse*, 4: 4, 341–62.

# CHAPTER 5

# The Core Assessment of Young Females who Sexually Abuse

*Susan L. Robinson*

*Assessment is an art; unfortunately there is no unique formula.*

(Saradjian and Hanks, 1996: 207)

## Overview

Sexually abusive behaviour committed by girls is an existing problem that has received insufficient attention. Consequently, there have been few treatment programmes or assessment tools specifically designed to meet the needs of this population. The existing models of treatment and assessment are based on working with males. These models originated from working with adult male incarcerated sex offenders and subsequently were adapted to meet the needs of residential and outpatient sexually abusive male youth. Because there were relatively few girls entering the system for sexual offending behaviour, few perceived a need to tailor programming to girls. Others assumed that the treatment and assessment would be the same. This belief, although slowly changing, remains prevalent today. In 2003, female juveniles accounted for two per cent of the 4,240 juvenile arrests for forcible rape and nine per cent of the 18,300 juvenile arrests for other sex offences (excluding prostitution) in the United States alone (Snyder, 2005). This amounts to 1,731 female juvenile arrests for sexual offending behaviour in one year. Further, there are many girls who are not charged for sex-offending behaviour but have been sexually abusive towards family members and instead, are under the supervision and monitoring of social services. Given the amount of girls entering the judicial or social services system for sexual abusing behaviour, assessment and treatment models specifically designed for female youth are necessary, ones that take into account female development and the dynamics of female juvenile sexual aggression.

While it is true that there are many commonalities among juvenile males and females who sexually abuse, there are gender differences that need to be considered. Because the development and socialisation process of females and males differs, the questions asked and information gleaned from the assessment process will, at times, be different. This chapter focuses on the development of a differential assessment for sexual offending female youth with the idea that such an assessment will further an understanding of the needs, issues, and risk factors unique to this population. In an effort to determine how the assessment process may diverge from one geared towards male sexual offending juveniles, this chapter examines differences between male and female development, and juvenile male and female sexual offending behaviour. The literature on female adolescent sexuality and aggression are also discussed in order to augment awareness of the areas warranting consideration in the assessment process of these girls. Furthermore, the current risk assessments and their applicability to juvenile females are explored. Risk factors specific to girls are discussed. Offered in the appendices, are an assessment guideline and a listing of some assessment tools that can be useful for this population.

## Literature review

Although a body of literature exists on female juvenile sexual aggression (Bumby and Bumby, 1997; Fehrenbach and Monastersky, 1988; Higgs, Canavan, Meyer, 1992; Hunter, Lexier, Goodwin, Browne, and Dennis, 1993; Johnson, 1989; Kubik, Hecker, and Righthand, 2002; Mathews, Hunter, and Vuz, 1997; Miccio-Fonseca, 2000; Ray and English, 1995; Scavo, 1989; Turner and Turner, 1994) there is an absence of information about assessment as it applies to this population. For example, in one chapter on female sexual abusers, the need for a comprehensive assessment of sexually abusive female adolescents is underscored, but it does not state how this comprehensive assessment should be conducted (Minasian and Lewis, 1999). The chapter further maintains the necessity for the development of assessment tools specific to females. Johnson

(1989) also noted a need to develop specific tools and risk criteria for assessing sexually abusive girls. Bumby and Bumby (1997) suggested that risk factors, which should be considered in the assessment and treatment of sexually abusing girls, include depression, suicidal ideation, anxiety, poor self-concept, and childhood sexual victimisation. Finally, Hunter and Mathews (1997) concluded that the assessment of both female sexual offending adults and young people should be conducted knowing that female sexual offending behaviour often occurs in a broader context of psychiatric and psychosocial impairments. They noted the lack of gender-specific assessment tools.

## Developmental considerations

In order to conduct a thorough assessment of a female who sexually abuses, it is important to understand some of the differences between male and female development. Female development is a relational development; that is, females tend to derive their identity through their relationships and connections with others (Brown and Gilligan, 1992; Gilligan, 1982; Gilligan, Lyons, and Hammer, 1990; Jordan, Kaplan, Miller, Stiver, and Surrey, 1991; Miller and Stiver, 1997). Surrey (1991) describes this development as 'self-in-relation.' Comparatively, research on male development indicates males tend to develop their identities through independence, separation, and autonomy (Erikson, 1950, 1968; Kohlberg, 1981; Levinson, 1978). Girls tend to be interpersonally oriented due to their relational development; boys have more of an instrumental orientation geared towards action and achievement. This relational development is important to nurture with girls for their overall mental health and sense of identity.

Another area where juvenile males and females tend to differ is in the way they manage their feelings. Girls are socialised to internalise their feelings more than boys. Harris, Blum, and Resnick (1991) discuss how adolescent girls engage in behaviours of 'quiet disturbance,' e.g., eating disorders or suicide attempts. Conversely, boys tend to externalise their feelings, which can lead to more overt aggressive behaviours and diagnoses that are consistent with an externalisation process, eg Conduct Disorder, Oppositional Defiant Disorder, Attention Deficit and Hyperactivity Disorder (Harris et al., 1991;

Leschied, Cummings, Van Brunschot, Cunnigham, and Saunders, 2000; Loeber and Stouthamer-Loeber, 1998; Perry, 1997; Perry, Pollard, Blakley, Baker, and Vigilante, 1995). Given this internalisation process, it is not surprising that depression is significant in the lives of female adolescents (Allgood-Merten, Lewinsohn, and Hops, 1990; Commonwealth Fund, 1997; National Center on Addiction and Substance Abuse [NCASA], 2003, Rutter, 1986). This is a striking gender difference – one that is twice as common in females – and found across cultures, unfolding during puberty and persisting throughout adulthood (Solomon, 2001). Problems with body image and eating disorders are also markedly higher for adolescent girls than boys (Commonwealth Fund, 1997).

Anger is one emotion that tends to be processed and manifested differently in males and females (Brown, 1998; Lamb, 2001; Lerner, 1988; Simmons, 2002). The cultural script teaches girls that anger is not acceptable. Girls are 'supposed' to be 'sugar and spice and everything nice.' Because of this unrealistic expectation, many girls learn to deny, suppress, and hide their anger. Simmons (2002) maintains that because our culture disallows the overt expression of conflict for girls, they learn to release anger in alternative ways. Research indicates that adolescent girls are more likely to adopt indirect forms of aggression than adolescent boys (Bjoerkqvist, Lagerspetz, and Kaukiainen, 1992; Bjoerkqvist, Osterman, and Kaukiainen, 1992; Owens and MacMullin, 1995). Indirect aggression is defined as covert behaviour that does not involve direct confrontation, such as gossiping or spreading a rumour. Similarly, relational aggression is readily used by adolescent girls; this is also a covert form of aggression but it specifically uses relationships as weapons and harms others by damaging relationships (Crick and Grotpeter, 1995; Cummings, Leschied, and Heilbron, 2002; Simmons, 2002). Forms of this aggression include rumour spreading, the silent treatment, name-calling, backbiting, exclusion, manipulation, and nonverbal gesturing. Male aggression is often physical in nature; relational aggression is psychological and threatens what is most important to girls and their development – relationships. It threatens affiliation and connection and it is effective because of girls' fears of abandonment, rejection, and isolation.

Self-confidence is another area of gender difference. As girls mature into their high school years, their self-confidence decreases; yet for boys, it increases (American Association of University Women [AAUW], 1995; Orenstein, 1994). In the Commonwealth Fund Survey of the Health of Adolescent Girls (1997) only 39 per cent of girls demonstrated a high level of confidence. Those at greatest risk for this self-confidence loss are Caucasian, Hispanic and Asian-American girls. African-American girls are more likely to sustain their confidence as they mature (Sadker and Sadker, 1994).

A loss of voice, the loss of a pre-adolescent authentic self, and the development of a false self are discussed in the literature on female adolescence (Brown and Gilligan, 1992; Gilligan, 1982; Hancock, 1989; Pipher, 1994; Shandler, 1999; Stern, 1991). Pipher (1994: 19) regards female adolescence as a time when girls 'crash and burn in a social and developmental Bermuda Triangle'. Stern (1991) refers to a 'disavowing' of the self that occurs during this life stage. Freud (as cited in Stern, 1991: 105) observed female adolescence as a 'fresh wave of repression.' It is from this loss of self and voice that girls develop a chameleon identity as a result of sociocultural scripts that direct them to be desirable, liked, and fit in; girls acting in this manner can easily become what they perceive others want them to be. This is one way girls protect themselves from relationship loss and rejection. The unfortunate result, however, is that they may eventuate weakly constructed identities since their identities change depending upon who they are with and what environment they are in.

Additionally, substance abuse differs among adolescent males and females. The groundbreaking study, *The Formative Years: Pathways to Substance Abuse Among Girls and Young Women Ages 8–22* (NCASA, 2003) found that the reasons for and risk factors underlying teenage female substance abuse greatly differ from those of teenage males. Depression, suicidal ideation, physical and sexual abuse, early puberty, and dieting and eating disorders increase the likelihood of substance abuse, as do frequent moves and times of transition (eg from middle school to high school). Further, girls often use substances to mitigate stress and depression, lose weight, increase confidence, or enhance sex. In contrast, boys typically use drugs for heightened social status and sensation seeking. Girls are more likely to use and abuse prescription painkillers, stimulants, and tranquillisers. Females are also predisposed to

medical problems as a result of substance abuse. According to the National Clearinghouse for Alcohol and Drug Information (2001) girls who regularly smoke marijuana are at a higher risk for infertility problems and raised testosterone levels. Alcohol abuse also causes menstrual and fertility problems for girls, and may impede adolescent maturation. Substance abusing girls are at greater risk for unwanted and unprotected sex, unwanted pregnancies, and sexually transmitted diseases.

## The cultural sexual script

Perhaps one of the greatest areas of difference between female and male adolescence has to do with the sociocultural scripts each gender receives pertaining to sexuality. The literature on adolescent female sexuality speaks of rigid gender constructions, societal pressures, and the silencing of female sexuality (Fine, 1988; Lamb, 2001; Thompson, 1990, 1995; Tolman, 1991, 1994, 1999, 2001, 2002; Wolf, 1997). The overwhelming conclusion emanating from this work is that adolescent girls are largely unaware of, and unsure about, their sexuality. However, attaining sexual subjectivity is an adolescent developmental task (Tolman, 2002). Sexuality for teenage girls is often hidden and ignored; it becomes buried underneath scripts of how girls are taught to behave. And girls often learn to pleasure boys before they learn how to pleasure themselves. A girl's body remains her own unexplored territory; she learns the topography of her body largely through her interactions with the opposite sex (Farber, 2002). In this respect, learning about her sexuality becomes an afterthought, secondary to pleasing her partners. As Wolf (1997: 70) writes, during female adolescence sex becomes a 'performance for the benefit of boys'. In other words, female adolescents become sexually accommodating. Girls become objects and fail to be the sexual subjects of their own lives. They want to be wanted (Young-Eisendrath, 1999) and are willing to become objects because their self-worth may become dependent upon the degree to which they are successful at being objects for the opposite sex.

Additionally, it is through an unawareness of their own anatomy and arousal that girls subordinate their needs and act dishonestly (eg by feigning pleasure) to please their partners.

Many teenage girls sacrifice their right to achieve an orgasm or their right to request further exploration and stimulation to learn what feels good (Tolman, 2002). It is incongruent that many girls do not learn to take ownership over their sexual selves and desires, yet they perceive themselves as responsible for what occurs in their sexual relationships, and will blame themselves for not performing sexually 'good enough' to keep their romantic partner interested. One client of this author's described her perspective on this by stating, 'Girls must know how to do everything while having sex or it is their fault.'

Our culture also teaches girls that being 'good' is equal to being sexually passive. This sanctioned script purports that girls should not appear sexually demanding or too knowledgeable; rather, they should be desirable, not desiring (Tolman, 2002). This supposition to act inexperienced and naïve prevents girls from developing negative reputations. Girls who show sexual initiative, drive, and confidence are often viewed as 'sluts,' whereas the same attributes for males are primarily seen as acceptable, expected, and normal. The script that girls should be inexperienced makes it difficult for girls to navigate their own desires. They have no compass guiding their sexual rights. Masturbation, for example, is still something that is rarely discussed among girls; consequently, many girls are left feeing guilty, abnormal, or dirty after masturbating, which results in diminished pleasure. Not only is female adolescent sexuality dampened due to fears of negative labelling, but also because of fears of male sexual aggression. If girls hide their sexuality, they believe they may be able to protect themselves from becoming possible targets of male sexual violence. Despite this sexually passive script, many girls learn to appear abundantly aware of their sexuality and use it to their advantage to attain power over and manipulate the opposite sex. However, this does not mean that these girls have healthy sexual subjectivity. They may still lack awareness about their own sexuality, but are acutely cognisant how to look good and 'fake it' to get what they want.

The final result of the overall silencing of female adolescent sexuality is that a girl who has desire, may perceive herself as deviant (Lamb, 2001: 58). And as Lamb concludes, 'Sexual shame drives girls to do such things in closets and behind closed doors'. By examining the literature on female adolescent sexuality, clues may be rendered to explain how these gendered pressures and expectations relate to female sexual aggression. The question is: What can female adolescent sexuality tell us about female adolescent sexual aggression, and what implications does this have for the assessment of a sexually abusive female adolescent? This will be discussed in the section addressing juvenile females' motivations for sexual offending behaviour.

## Pathways to female aggression

Another important area to understand for assessment purposes is the developmental pathways to female aggression. Assessment includes determining the pathway for each sexually abusive female juvenile. The underlying pathway is then considered in the development of individualised treatment needs and goals.

Victimisation is a prominent pathway for the development of female delinquent behaviour. Acoca and Dedel (1998: 116) maintain, 'victimisation is *the* critical dynamic underlying girls' involvement in crime and other problem behaviours'. In their study, 92 per cent of the girls reported experiencing emotional, physical, and/or sexual abuse. Odgers (2005) study of 125 adolescent females incarcerated in a correctional facility, found only a few girls (N=4) without victimisation histories. The majority of the girls reported experiencing severe forms of victimisation by peers, maternal figures, and romantic partners. 46 per cent of the girls had histories of sexual abuse; 45 per cent were the victims of domestic violence. Experienced psychological trauma by mothers was predictive of physical aggression by the girls. Further, trauma can lead to compromised self-regulation and increased aggression. A diagnosis of Post-traumatic Stress Disorder (PTSD) leads to high distress levels and low self-restraint (Cauffman, Feldman, Waterman, and Steiner, 1998) and therefore, increases the risk of behavioural problems and offending behaviours. Not surprisingly, the rate of PTSD is higher for incarcerated female delinquents than incarcerated male delinquents. Cauffman et al. (1998) found that their sample of incarcerated juvenile females were 50 per cent more likely than incarcerated juvenile males to exhibit current PTSD symptomatology. Similarly, Brosky and Lally

(2004) in their sample of 76 court-referred females and 76 court-referred males between the ages of 12–18, found that females had significantly higher rates of trauma and a higher prevalence of PTSD symptoms than their male counterparts. Interestingly, research indicates females are more vulnerable to the development of PTSD. When faced with assaultive violence, females experience a larger number of PTSD symptoms than males; the lifetime prevalence of PTSD is approximately twice as high for females than for males; and the duration of symptoms for females is four times longer than in males (Davis and Breslau, 1998).

Depression is viewed as a more significant pathway for delinquency in girls than it is for boys (Obeidallah and Earls, 1999). Leschied et al. (2000) found that young, depressed girls were nearly four times more likely to be aggressive than boys. The relationship between female depression and aggression has been replicated in other studies as well (Paikoff, Brooks-Gunn, and Warren, 1991; Zoccolillo and Rogers, 1991). Further, Leschied, Cummings, Zerwer, and Saunders (2002) concluded that in contrast to male aggression, the development of female aggression is accompanied by depression, suicidal ideation, and generalised anxiety disorders. Zoccolillo and Rogers (1991) concluded that for females, depression and anxiety disorders often coincide with conduct disorder and antisocial personalities. Many girls involved with the criminal justice system evidence mental health disturbances and at a higher rate when compared with males (Cauffman, 1998). These mental health disturbances appear to be an integral link to their manifestation of delinquent behaviours.

Family stress, criminal behaviour within families, and high levels of family conflict are also viewed as influential to the development of female delinquent behaviours. The presence of criminal behaviours among family and extended family members has a greater influence on the development of a negative trajectory and antisocial values in girls than boys (Chamberlain and Moore, 2002; Cloninger, Christiansen, Reich, and Gottesman, 1978). Another study concluded that a history of family violence was correlated to girls' aggression and that psychosocial variables may be more closely linked to aggression in females than in males (Day, Franklin, and Marshall, 1998). Wood, Foy, Goguen, Pynoos, and James (2002: 125) concluded that 'Family

dysfunction appears to serve as a critical pathway to violent and criminal behaviour among females, more so than among males'. Additionally, poor relationships with parents (Funk, 1999) particularly mothers (Levene, Augimeri, Pepler, Walsh, Webster, and Koegl, 2001) and a lack of caregiver continuity (Levene et al., 2001) also appear to correlate more to female delinquency than boys. Associations with delinquent peers seem to play less of a role in the development of delinquent behaviours for girls than boys (Liu and Kaplan, 1999; Mears, Ploeger, and Warr, 1998; Moffitt, Caspi, Rutter, and Silva, 2001). Further, Levene et al. (2001) note that disliked girls are at high risk for developing antisocial behaviours. Aggressive girls, given their lack of compliance with gender norms and stereotypes, are even more likely than boys to experience peer ostracism. Because female development is relationally based, the impact of interpersonal difficulties (eg social isolation, peer rejection, family conflict) appears to be more pervasively negative for girls. When the relational development of girls is compromised, psychopathology can develop.

There are also studies indicating that girls require a higher number of risk factors for aggression to develop (Cloninger et al., 1978; Mannuzza and Gittelman, 1984). Regarding female adolescent sex offending behaviour, Mathews et al. (1997: 194) conclude, 'biological and socialisation factors create a higher threshold for the externalisation of experienced developmental trauma in females than males'. Additionally, females are less socialised to condone and engage in aggressive behaviours, but more socialised towards nurturing and maintaining the peace. Males tend to have more normative beliefs supporting aggression and antisocial behaviour (Huesmann and Guerra, 1997; Huesmann, Guerra, Zelli, and Miller, 1992). Girls then, that view aggressive and antisocial behaviours as normative are at an increased risk for the development of these types of behaviour.

Also important to understand for assessment purposes is the gender paradox that has been described by Loeber and Keenan (1994). Although boys are more often diagnosed with conduct disorder and attention deficit and hyperactivity disorder (ADHD) a girl who is diagnosed with either has a poorer prognosis in terms of psychiatric outcomes. Szatmari, Boyle, and Offord (1989) found that girls diagnosed with Attention Deficit Disorder were more likely than boys to develop Conduct Disorder. Similarly, Cohen (1996) found that a diagnosis of Conduct Disorder in girls was more likely to lead to the development of personality disorders.

Given the importance of this gender paradox in the pathway of female aggression, it is imperative to be cognisant of the different manifestations of ADHD and conduct disorder in girls and boys for assessment purposes. Researchers argue that girls with ADHD have been under identified because the symptom presentation in girls typically reflects inattention rather than the overt behavioural problems more often exhibited among boys (Biederman, Faraone, Mick, Williamson, Wilens, Spencer, Weber, Jetton, Kraus, Pert, and Zallen, 1999; Gaub and Carlson, 1997). Peer rejection, social isolation, difficulties with forming and maintaining relationships, and a lack of involvement in activities have also found to be problematic in girls having ADHD. Biederman et al. (1999) found that 45 per cent of girls with ADHD also exhibit comorbid diagnoses such as disruptive behaviour disorders, mood disorders, anxiety disorders, and substance abuse. Moreover, males with Conduct Disorder will exhibit confrontational behaviours such as fighting and stealing, yet girls with this diagnosis are more likely to engage in less confrontational behaviours such as lying, prostitution, substance abuse, running away, and truancy (American Psychiatric Association, 2000).

## Protective factors for girls

Being female is, in and of itself, a protective factor. Being male is one of the strongest predictors of delinquent and antisocial behaviour (Mears et al., 1998; Rowe, Vazsonyi, and Flannery, 1995). There is no denying that males are more inclined to engage in criminal behaviour (Baron-Cohen, 2003; McElvaine, 2001) and the yearly arrest and incarceration rates reflect this. Additionally, many protective factors for girls relate to their relational development. Levene et al. (2001) note, through their examination of various studies, that a positive relationship with an adult outside a girl's immediate family, eg a teacher-child relationship, is a significant protective factor for girls. Flansburg (1991) also noted that a girl's self-esteem could increase given one non-exploitive relationship with an adult. Likewise, a healthy relationship with one's mother is a protective factor for girls (Harris et

al., 1991) as well as having close friends (Werner and Smith, as cited in Levene et al., 2001). As Gilgun (1990) states, 'The underlying factor of protective mechanisms is human relationship' (p.180). Interestingly, girls have the advantage with protective factors given their socialisation: Girls learn to identify and express their feelings more so than boys; adults support the expression of feelings in girls; and, emotional expressiveness is the single most important protective factor (J. Gilgun, personal communication, June 15, 2003).

Problem-solving abilities have also been noted as a protective factor for girls (Keltikangas-Jaervinen and Pakaslahti, 1999). Additionally, academic success and a positive orientation towards school are considered protective (Jessor, Van Den Boss, Vanderryn, Costa, and Turbin, 1995; Office of Juvenile Justice and Delinquency Prevention [OFFDP], 1998). Finally, in citing studies by Heimer and Perry et al., Levene et al. (2001) note that the acceptance of gender normative beliefs and definitions is a protective factor specific to girls. It may also be that girls who do not lose their ability to voice and assert themselves during adolescence, when so many girls forfeit their voice for passive social constructions, are also better protected from developing negative trajectories because they are honest and congruent with themselves and their self-esteem stays intact. Other protective factors to be aware of in the assessment of juvenile females are those also noted in the literature to be helpful for males: resilience, an ability to self-soothe (self-regulation) a positive sense of self, and the capacity to envision a positive future (Gilgun, 2001).

Empathy and the ability to engage in perspective taking is a powerful mitigating force to the development of abusive behaviours (Miller and Eisenberg, 1988, Ryan, 1998, 2003). Girls have the advantage with this protective factor since empathy is more often modeled to them (Zahn-Waxler, Cole, and Barrett, 1991) beginning at an early age. Girls' socialisation process often dictates they consider their actions on others to maintain their relational bonds. Miller and Stiver (1997) assert that a girl who empathises will be less likely to engage in behaviour that causes harm to others or her relationships. Likewise, guilt is viewed as a protective factor. Research indicates that female adolescents tend to experience feelings of guilt more so than males, especially about antisocial or rude and insensitive behaviour (Bybee, 1999). This guilt process appears to have an inhibitory effect on the commission of delinquent behaviours.

## Differences between juvenile male and females with sexual offending behaviour

Although there have been a few comparative studies conducted on female and male sexual offending juveniles, it is important to understand that these findings are preliminary and should not be considered conclusive due to the limitations of these studies (ie small sample sizes, a reliance on self-reporting, possible clinician bias, and the use of non-randomised sampling procedures). Nevertheless, evaluators and treatment providers should be aware of these suggested differences during the assessment process, otherwise they may fail to recognise dynamics that are unique and important to female juvenile offending behaviour. Perhaps the most consistent and striking finding for sexually abusive female juveniles is the high rates of victimisation they have experienced compared to sexually abusive juvenile males (Bumby and Bumby, 1997; Kubik et al., 2002; Mathews et al., 1997; Miccio-Fonseca, 2000; Ray and English, 1995). Ray and English found that girls exhibited higher rates of sexual abuse histories than boys (94 per cent versus 85 per cent). Mathews et al. (1997) found from their sample that 77.6 per cent of sexually abusive girls reported sexual abuse histories, compared to 44.3 per cent of sexually abusive boys. In Bumby and Bumby's comparison study between 18 juvenile sex offending females and males, 100 per cent of the girls had been sexually abused versus 63 per cent of the boys. Miccio-Fonseca found that 72 per cent of sexually abusive females had sexual abuse histories, compared to 50 per cent of sexually abusive males.

Sexually abusive girls are also more likely than boys to be abused at younger ages (Mathews et al., 1997; Miccio-Fonseca, 2000). Mathews et al. found that 64 per cent of the girls were abused prior to the age of 5, compared to 25.8 per cent of the boys. The median age that girls were sexually abused in Howley's study (2001) was 3.8; for Hunter et al.'s study (1993) the age was 4.5. Many sexually abusive girls have been sexually abused by more than one perpetrator (Bumby and Bumby, 1997; Howley, 2001; Hunter et al., 1993; Kubik et al., 2002; Mathews et al., 1997). In Kubik et al., the mean number of perpetrators for girls was 4.83 versus 1.75 for boys. In Mathews et al., the mean number of perpetrators for girls was 4.5

versus 1.4 for the boys. In Howley's study, 74 per cent of the girls had been abused by two or more perpetrators. Hunter et al. found that the mean number of perpetrators for girls was 5 (ranging from 2 to 7). Also reflecting the severity of sexual abuse in these girls' lives, Kubik et al. found that 75 per cent of the girls had been victimised three or more times versus 20 per cent of the boys. 71.4 per cent endured anal or vaginal penetration, compared to 22.2 per cent of the boys. In Mathews et al., 72.5 per cent of the girls reported being the victim of force and aggression versus 45.2 per cent of the boys.

Regarding other forms of abuse, Ray and English (1995) found that sexually abusive girls were more likely to have experienced multiple types of abuse (94 per cent vs. 86 per cent). Mathews et al. (1997) found that 60 per cent of the sexually abusive girls in their study had histories of physical abuse, compared to 44.9 per cent for the boys. Howley (2001) found that 82 per cent of the girls had histories of physical abuse and 71 per cent had experienced general neglect. 75 per cent of the girls in Bumby and Bumby's (1997) sample had physical abuse histories; 42 per cent had experienced emotional and physical neglect.

For sexually abusive girls whose development has been disrupted by trauma, their ongoing development takes an arduous course, and comorbid diagnoses become unwelcome guests. Females, more so than males, are more likely to develop mental health disturbances as a result of trauma (for a discussion, see Cauffman et al., 1998) and are six times more likely to develop PTSD (Giaconia et al., as cited in Cauffman et al., 1998). In the Commonwealth Fund Survey of the Health of Adolescent Girls (1997) girls with abuse histories were approximately twice as likely as to drink alcohol than non-abused girls. They were more likely to have used drugs, and more likely to have engaged in behaviours characteristic of eating disorders, ie binging and purging (32 per cent versus 12 per cent). They were twice as likely to have low self-confidence (57 per cent versus 27 per cent). Girls with abuse histories also tend to be psychosomatic and have issues about their body (Commonwealth Fund, 1997). Perry (1997) and Perry et al. (1995) have found that girls will often adapt to trauma by resorting to dissociation, whereas boys adapt to trauma primarily through hyperarousal. Because many sexually abusive girls have extensive trauma histories, diagnoses such as Post-traumatic Stress Disorder, depression, anxiety, and eating disorders are more the norm than not. Likewise, self-destructive behaviours, especially cutting and suicidal gestures are common.

Specific to sexually abusive girls, Hunter et al. (1993) found that 80 per cent of girls in their sample received prior mental health services. Bumby and Bumby (1997) found that 83 per cent of the girls in their sample had received prior mental health treatment, 83 per cent had histories of depression, 58 per cent had histories of drug use, and 75 per cent abused alcohol. Females abused drugs at a higher rate than the males in their comparison study. Kubik et al. (2002) found that 50 per cent of their sample of sexually abusive girls had a diagnosis of PTSD, compared to only 9.1 per cent of sexually abusive boys. Regarding suicidal ideation, many sexually abusive girls have histories with this (Bumby and Bumby, 1997; Hunter et al., 1993; Mathews et al., 1997; Miccio-Fonesca, 2000). Bumby and Bumby found that 58 per cent of their female sample attempted suicide. In Hunter et al., 60 per cent of their girls had a history of suicide attempts or ideation. Mathews et al. also noted suicidal behaviours in a subgroup of girls. Finally, in Miccio-Fonesca's study, 44 per cent of the females versus 15 per cent of the males had attempted suicide and interestingly, 50 per cent of the females had come from families where someone had attempted suicide versus only eight per cent of the males.

Sexually abusive girls are also known to participate in other forms of delinquent behaviour. Stealing, truancy, and running away are not uncommon (Bumby and Bumby, 1997; Howley, 2001; Hunter et al., 1993; Ray and English, 1995). In Bumby and Bumby's sample, 33 per cent of them had been arrested for stealing, 58 per cent had histories of running away, and 58 per cent had histories of truancy. In their latter comparison study, sexually abusive girls had higher truancy rates than the sexually abusive boys. Hunter et al. found that 60 per cent of the girls had previously runaway. In Howley's study, 49 per cent had histories of running away and 39 per cent had engaged in truancy. Ray and English found higher rates of stealing and truancy among girls than boys in their study.

Girls tend to sexually abuse at younger ages than boys (Howley, 2001; Johnson, 1989; Ray and English, 1995). In Ray and English, 50 per cent of the girls were 12 years old or younger when they offended, yet only 30 per cent of the boys were. Howley found that the average age of a girl's first offence was 10.65 and 30 per cent of the girls

offended prior to the age of 10. Johnson's (1989) study consisted of girls who perpetrated between the ages of 4 to 12.

Girls that sexually abuse often lack positive female role models (Mathews, Hunter and Vuz, 1997). It is not coincidental that many mothers of sexually abusive girls have a history of displaying poor sexual boundaries and discussing their sexual problems with their daughters. Johnson (1989) found that many of the mothers of girls in her sample had been victims of domestic violence and sexual abuse, and/or had substance abuse issues. Overdependency, enmeshment, and role reversals were common in the mother-daughter relationships. Likewise, Turner and Turner (1994) found that the mother-daughter relationships in their sample were characterised by enmeshment, malevolent attachments, and abandonment. In some cases, the girl was in a parentified role and was the mother's caretaker. In this author's experience, few female sexually abusing females display healthy relationships with their mothers. The girls have typically experienced real abandonment or have perceived that their mothers emotionally abandoned them. In some cases, the mother sacrifices her own daughter to maintain an unhealthy relationship with a male partner who sexually molests the daughter. Given the importance of the same sex parent to role model for their child, and the significant deficits apparent in many of these mother-daughter relationships, the mother-daughter relationship is an important facet of the assessment process.

Sexually abusive female juveniles are also viewed differently than sexually abusive male juveniles. Whereas male juvenile sexual aggression is seen as more 'typical' (because male adolescents are often viewed as being overpowered by their sexual impulses) females committing sexual offences are often regarded as victims who are acting out their own victimisation and therefore in need of help for their victimisation issues, or as psychiatrically ill requiring psychiatric intervention (Allen, 1990). Furthermore, girls are less likely than boys to enter the criminal justice system for sexual offending behaviour (Ray and English, 1995). This is due, in part, to an overall denial of the criminal justice system to acknowledge that juvenile female sexual offending behaviour exists because it defies the traditional belief that females are protectors, not abusers. A gender bias is particularly prevalent with sexual offences perpetrated on peers: Although girls may sexually harass or abuse peers, they are far less likely than boys to be adjudicated for sexual offending on peers. Conversely, female juveniles, who are labelled as 'bad' girls for defying sociocultural scripts that espouse how 'good' girls ought to sexually behave, may be punished for overt defiance. Historically, female juveniles have more often than boys been adjudicated for status offences for sexual transgressions (Chesney-Lind, 1997). Similarly, girls committing sexual offences are not only violating victims, but are violating traditional female sexual roles; this may result in stiffer sentences for some girls who are made examples of by the criminal justice system.

Additionally, because there is more documented sexual abuse committed by males and more sexually abusive boys are involved in the criminal justice system, girls with sexual offending behaviours often feel isolated and alone. A sexually abusive girl may initially believe she is the only girl that has offended. She may perceive herself as 'bad' because she has not acted in a manner consistent with how girls are taught to behave. Because of this, the internalisation of shame appears higher for girls who sexually offend (Robinson, 2002). Similarly, parents of a sexually abusive girl may experience more shame and embarrassment over their daughter's behaviour and are less likely to understand how their daughter could have engaged in such behaviour. Accepting sexual abuse has occurred can be a greater difficulty for these parents. Parents of sexually abusive girls are also more likely to blame their daughter's behaviour as a result of known or unknown sexual victimisation.

Attachment disturbances are also evident among sexually abusive girls and are important to be aware of for assessment purposes. Bartholomew (1990) developed a four-category model of attachment styles based on a positive and negative view of self and others. Although adolescents, given their identities are still developing, may not clearly fit into one of these categories, traits can be discerned and for some, attachment styles appear to be in place. Two of these four attachment styles seem particularly relevant to sexually abusive juvenile females: preoccupied and fearful. These two styles can culminate into destructive relational patterns. The preoccupied attachment style is characterised by a negative view of self and a positive view of others. Female over-dependency and abusive relationships are possible outcomes for those possessing this attachment style. This author has found that female juveniles who sexually abuse tend to be more dependent in their relationships than boys. They are more likely to enter dysfunctional, chaotic, and abusive intimate peer relationships. Moreover, their dependency keeps them from leaving abusive relationships because of their fear of abandonment and loneliness. For some sexually abusive girls, as is true for adult females who sexually offend, their dependency may also be linked to their sexual offending behaviour because of an inability to assert themselves for fear of losing a relationship. Likewise, a negative view of self and others denotes a fearful attachment style whereby the person is socially avoidant and fearful of intimacy. Because females are more often the victims of abuse (ie sexual), female juveniles seem more likely to adopt a fearful attachment style than males. Males are more inclined to adopt a dismissive attachment style (Bartholomew and Horowitz, 1991). It is also from these two attachment styles that females frequently act as chameleons. Although the chameleon presentation often occurs among female adolescents for reasons described earlier, chameleon identities also develop as a result of trauma and such an identity is characteristic of sexually abusive girls. A chameleon presentation reflects hypervigilance, a symptom of Post-traumatic Stress Disorder, and is a coping strategy utilised to optimise survival. It is a means of ensuring safety by blending into abusive environments rather than standing out or 'rocking the boat,' so to speak.

There are other notable differences. Girls are more likely to sexually abuse someone they know, most often in the context of caretaking (Bumby and Bumby, 1997; Fehrenbach and Monastersky, 1998; Margolin, 1991; Mathews et al., 1997). Girls tend to abuse family members (Johnson, 1989) and are less likely to abuse strangers (Mathews, et al., 1997). Additionally, girls appear more likely to resort to caretaking and altruistic cognitive distortions to justify their behaviour and will explain their offending behaviour as an act of altruism due to their caretaking nature. For example, one of this author's clients reported that her reason for offending was to prepare her sister for being sexually abused by their stepfather. Another girl stated her sexual contact with her sister was her way of fulfilling a motherly role by helping her sister overcome masturbation: 'I thought if she lays on top of me, I can ask her why. I wanted to help the situation and that's why I put her on top of me.' A few studies also indicate that females tend to use less force or violence than males when sexually abusing (Matthews, 1993; Ray and English, 1995) and are less likely to perpetrate act of rape (Ray and English). Moreover, it is rare for female juveniles to force others to sexually abuse with them. This is a dynamic that occurs more often with male offenders and many adult female offenders fit into the typology of a male coerced (Mathews, Matthews, and Speltz, 1989, 1990) or male accompanied offender (Syed and Williams, 1996).

## Juvenile females' motivations for sexual offending behaviour

The reasons for and motivations behind sexual offending among males and females may also differ. Traditionally, the male model of sex offending behaviour has viewed sexual aggression as stemming from a need to have power and control and/or be sexually gratified. However, research on adult and juvenile sex offending females indicates that females do not abuse as often for sexual reasons as males (Connor et al., as cited in Hunter and Mathews, 1997; Davin, 1999; Dunbar, 1999; Finkelhor and Russell, 1984; Johnson, 1989; Mathews et al., 1990; O'Connor, 1987; Saradjian and Hanks, 1996; Turner and Turner, 1994). Johnson found that few, if any, of the preadolescent girls in her study were seeking sexual satisfaction, orgasm, or sexual pleasure. Howley (2001) also concluded that sex-offending behaviour was more often about anger for girls than sexual curiosity or stimulation. This difference perhaps reflects the notion that female sexual response is based less to a sexual act itself and more to the context and quality of a relationship, or the imagination of a sexual relationship (Hales, 1999; Ellis and Symons, 1990). This is the reason for an interesting gender difference: romance novels being the domain of females versus pornography being more the domain of males. With this said, it is also true that sexual arousal can play a role in sexual offending behaviour for girls. Unfortunately, there is a lack of physiological measurements to assess sexual arousal in sexually abusive girls and it also appears that

girls are less likely to disclose sexual arousal due to a lack of awareness of their sexuality and arousal response, in addition to scripts that teach them to deny their sexuality.

Although sexually abusive males may abuse as a reaction to their own sexual victimisation (or at least in part) the correlation between victimisation and sexually abusive behaviour appears stronger for sexually abusive females. Particularly relevant to a girl's sexually abusive behaviour is whether or not she previously disclosed her own history of victimisation and if so, if her disclosure resulted in support and assistance, or invalidation and rejection. Johnson (1989) found that all the girls in her sample had sexual abuse histories and none of these girls had supportive and positive experiences disclosing their own histories of abuse. The development of female juvenile sexual offending behaviour then, often appears to stem from an environmental context unsupportive and disbelieving of a girl's own sexual victimisation. For some girls, sex offending may be a way to get someone to notice that they have been sexually abused as a response to a caretaker's failure to protect and believe them. For example, one client described her offence as a cry for help; she wanted someone to stop her mother's boyfriend from sexually assaulting her. Although she had previously told her mother, her mother failed to intervene because she did not believe her daughter's disclosure.

Given the relational development of females, female sex offending may be a form of relational aggression (Lamb, 2001; Leschied et al., 2000; Loeber and Stouthamer-Loeber, 1998; Simmons, 2002). Although by definition sexual offending behaviour is not the kind of conduct categorised as relational aggression, it is aggression, and it is relational in that the behaviour may be a way to attempt to connect with a particular person (not necessarily the victim) or disconnect from a relationship (Robinson, 2002). Salzman (1990) noted that when the attachment system is compromised in girls, the sexual system becomes a substitute venue to form attachments. For some sexually abusive girls, sexual aggression then, becomes their means to connect. Similarly, Moretti, Dasilva, and Holland (2004: 42) further confirm that aggression in girls, more so than boys, 'more frequently reflects a coercive strategy to engage others and maintain their availability and responsiveness'. Turner and Turner (1994: 17) viewed juvenile female sexual aggression as a way to maintain relationships and noted that all the girls in their sample were 'striving to establish relationships'. They additionally maintained, 'It is from the relationship aspect of victimisation that a female may commit abuse. That is, identifying with one's aggressor, taking on his or her characteristics, is a way of staying in the relationship' (p. 16). They also hypothesised that girls sexually abused as one avenue to differentiate themselves from their enmeshed, victim-identified mothers. Johnson (1989) and Turner and Turner (1994) both found that for some girls, their sexual offending behaviour appeared to be a reaction to their mothers' victimisation stance and over dependency on their daughters. Other girls simply describe sex offending as a means of finding a connection with someone. One client maintained, 'I was lonely and wanted someone to be sexual with me. I wanted to feel close to someone and be touched.' Another stated, 'I felt lonely and angry . . . If I did this then I would be closer to them and less lonely.' Additionally, a different client said, 'I abused so . . . I could feel that someone cared and loved me.'

This author has found a strong correlation between real or perceived maternal loss and offending behaviour. In some instances, the girl's offending is a way to express anger towards her mother. For example, one client stated that part of her motivation to sexually abuse her younger siblings was because of 'not feeling loved by mother . . . I chose them because they were taking all the attention away from my mom. I was jealous of them.' Howley (2001) also found anger to be a motivating factor in approximately 60 per cent of her sample of 66 juvenile females; consistent with this author's experience, Howley found the anger was primarily directed towards the girls' main caretakers. Similarly, other girls offend to elicit the attention they believe has been insufficient from their mothers; consequently, offending becomes a tool to re-establish the mother-daughter relationship. One client said, 'I wanted my mom to pay more attention to me than the boys.' Another stated, 'I wasn't getting enough attention . . . If I get these kids alone and I do something bad with them then maybe my mom will pay more attention to me instead of her boyfriend.' This is not to negate the role or attachment to fathers, however, the attachment or lack of attachment to the mother appears much more significant in the lives of these girls because of the importance the maternal attachment has in the development of their identities. Likewise, for boys, the attachment and relationship to their fathers may play a more crucial role as an antecedent variable to sexual aggression.

It is important to note that the language used for describing the motivations behind sex offending has historically neglected attachment and relational dynamics despite the research that has been conducted in this area (Marshall, Hudson, and Hodkinson, 1993; Ward, Hudson, Marshall, and Siegert, 1995). It may be that male sexual offending is significantly more relational than clinicians have previously believed, however, because treatment providers have traditionally looked through a lens of power and control, other explanations have been overlooked. Although relational dynamics are present in male sexual aggression, perhaps due to their relational orientation, females are better able to describe their behaviour in relational terms.

Because one of the primary differences between juvenile males and females has to do with the different sociocultural scripts and subsequent pressures they receive, it is important to assess for each sexually abusive girl, if and to what extent these sociocultural influences relate to her offending behaviour. Is female adolescent sexual aggression a reaction to, and rejection of, the cultural script that teaches girls to suppress and hide their own sexuality, and place the sexual needs of males above their own? How many sexually abusive girls reject the current construction of female adolescent sexuality and adopt alternative avenues (ie sexual abuse) to explore their sexuality and sexual orientation? This author proposes that for some girls, sexually abusive behaviour may be a rejection of cultural norms that teach girls to be silent and unaware of their own sexuality.

For example, a girl who sexually offends may be claiming experiential knowledge of her own body, needs, and desires, on her own terms. She may be defying the passive construction of female sexuality, refusing to subordinate her desires, trying to take ownership of her sexuality and find her own pleasure, and rejecting the compulsory heterosexuality script (Rich, 1984) albeit at the expense of a victim. One client described her reason for offending by stating, 'I could learn more about sex in my own terms.' Another client described her reason for sexual offending as a means to explore her sexual identity. Peers at school were referring to her as a lesbian and teasing her. She was not sure if she was at the time, but she certainly did not want to have sexual contact with female peers, leaving her more open to ridicule and exclusion. Her decision to sexually abuse two boys for whom she babysat, was a way for her to see if she could be sexually aroused by males. Moreover, many girls are worried about being labelled a slut if they appear too sexually desiring, therefore, for some sexually abusive girls who victimise a younger child, they may be engaging in such behaviour to avoid getting labelled a slut by their peers. Furthermore, since many girls learn to be submissive in their interpersonal relationships, perhaps sexual abuse for some is a means to attain the more traditional view of sexual aggression: power and control. It can also become a means for girls to protect themselves from exploitation, particularly for those with sexual victimisation histories. One client described her sexual aggression by stating: 'I will not be a victim or place myself in a position to be victimised.' Her choice was to be the victimiser instead; that way she did not have to worry about being used or treated as an object.

The assessment of any girl with sexual offending behaviour should include asking her about her motivation to offend and what it was a means to achieve. For example, it may have been a means to establish or injure a relationship, express buried anger, learn about her sexuality and be in control over her body, protect herself from being victimised, or a combination of the above. Remembering that sexual abuse rarely occurs from a single motivation but instead a combination of various factors is important so that each one can be adequately addressed in treatment.

## Considering preliminary typologies

Typologies can be useful to determine the etiology of and motivations underlying sexual aggression. Further, typologies assist in the identification of treatment needs and goals. Therefore, distinguishing which typology may be applicable to a sexually abusive juvenile female is one aspect of the assessment process. But given the lack of research conducted on girls, this is a difficult task. Research has been conducted to classify adult and adolescent sexually abusive males (Hunter, Figueredo, Malamuth, and Becker, 2003; Knight and Prentky, 1990, 1993). There have also been categories developed for adult female offenders (Faller, 1995; Mathews,

Matthews, and Speltz, 1989; McCarty, 1986; Saradjian and Hanks, 1996) however, these categories are primarily based on descriptive data and have lacked the scientific rigor of studies conducted on males. Even fewer studies have attempted to develop typologies for sexually abusive juvenile females (Mathews, Matthews, and Speltz, 1990; Mathews et al., 1997). Mathews et al. (1990) describe female adolescents as falling into three basic groups: intergenerationally predisposed offenders, experimenters and exploiters, and male coerced offenders. The intergenerationally predisposed offender was a typology initially generated from working with adult females (Mathews, Matthews, and Speltz, 1989). These girls tend to have extensive sexual and physical abuse histories. They most often abuse relatives. The abuse tends to be repetitive and compulsive. Their reason for offending is significantly linked to their abuse histories and is abuse reactive in nature. These girls are often reenacting their childhood sexual abuse trauma; their offending behaviour is similar to the behaviour perpetrated on them, and the age of their victims may be similar to the age they were when sexually victimised. Girls fitting into this typology have a multitude of deficits including poor boundaries, weak ego strength, and low self-esteem. They are described as more likely to abuse females, however, the gender of the victim is often determined by opportunity. Intergenerationally predisposed girls comprise the majority of sexually abusive juvenile females. The second group, experimenters and exploiters, are girls that offend often while babysitting on a male child on one occasion. They tend to be naïve and have not yet engaged in sexual behaviours with peers, nor do they feel safe to explore their sexuality with peer-aged males. They lack social skills and confidence in social settings.

Like the intergenerationally predisposed offender, their third typology, the male-coerced offender, was developed through their work on adult females (Mathews, Matthews, and Speltz, 1989). In their 1990 study, only three adolescent females fit into this typology from their sample of 20 adolescent girls and one of those three was actually coerced to offend by a female peer, not a male. Similar to male-coerced adult females, girls fitting into this typology may be dependent, unassertive, and lack self-esteem. Caution should be used in applying this typology to an adolescent female given the small number of girls falling into this group making the reliability of this subgroup more questionable than the others described. Second, by definition, the notion of a male-coerced offender diminishes a girl's responsibility in sexual offending; it may be that she was not coerced but rather an equal participant who maintains she was forced in order to minimise or justify her culpability. The study conducted by Mathews et al. (1997) consisting of 67 adolescent sexually abusive females, did not identify any girls fitting into this category. This author has identified a few girls who sexually offended due to peer-influence. They most likely would not have sexually abused on their own accord; instead, they needed the influence of others in a specific situation to offend. One client, for example, was dared by two peer-aged males to perform oral sex on a younger male. She was not coerced into doing so, nor did she describe complying to their wishes; she made a choice to abuse and was a willing participant in the offence. Another client sexually abused one of her best friends with another girlfriend (who served as a peer group leader) and a few boys. The client wanted to 'fit in' with this peer group leader and often followed her lead. Without this situation, it is highly unlikely she would have engaged in sexually abusive behaviour.

Mathews et al. (1997) did not develop typologies but rather, described three subgroups of girls in their sample from outpatient and residential treatment settings based on offence dynamics, background variables, and psychological profiles. Girls fitting into the offence dynamic subgroup (a small subgroup) most closely resemble those girls in the experimenter/exploiter typology in the aforementioned study. These girls offended on a single or few occasions with non-related children most often while babysitting. Their behaviour was motivated by sexual curiosity. They exhibited many strengths and lacked individual psychopathology. These girls did not have abuse histories or come from disturbed family backgrounds. From this author's perspective, girls fitting into this subgroup would also consist of those described earlier as defying sociocultural scripts; these are girls that are attempting to learn about sex and their sexuality without the pressure to behave in accordance with sexual norms. Blockage may also be a motivating factor for their offending behaviour (Finkelhor, 1984).

The subgroup of girls based on background variables consisted of approximately one-third of the outpatient girls in their sample. These girls are described as having mild to moderate levels of individual psychopathology. Additionally, histories of maltreatment and impaired family systems were noted. Most of these girls displayed personality strengths and appropriate social skills for their age, but they lacked sexual experiences with peers. They offended due to being triggered by their own sexual abuse histories; their offending was similar to the manner in which they were abused.

The final subgroup of girls, based on psychological profiles, were girls with moderate to severe levels of individual and/or family psychopathology (approximately half of their sample). The girls in this subgroup endured severe abuse and neglect. The abuse they perpetrated was often extensive and repetitive. Many of them had comorbid diagnoses of depression, anxiety, conduct disorder, or post-traumatic stress disorder. They exhibited attachment and empathy deficits. These girls also had a tendency of coping with their abuse histories through their own sexualised presentations and behaviours. Some had deviant sexual arousal patterns.

Girls fitting into these last two subgroups are similar to the predisposed girls described in Mathews et al. (1990). This author has also found a similar subgroup in her work and would add that many of these girls have an inchoate or disorganised identity. Additionally, this author has also worked with some girls who appear to fit into the experimenting/exploiting typology but also have a history of sexual abuse. However, their sexual abuse histories are not as severe or extensive as girls fitting into a typology of predisposed offending. Furthermore, their primary motivation to offend appears to be sexual curiosity. Their sexual offence does not seem to be triggered by their own victimisation; their abuse history may be one contributing factor but it is not the most significant.

In conclusion, there is far more research needed in the development of female adolescent typologies. What can be discerned thus far is that the majority of young females who sexually abuse appear to be predisposed in some way due to extensive histories of abuse. They tend to have significant interpersonal and individual deficits, and comorbid diagnoses. A second subgroup reflects girls who are experimenting on or exploiting younger children due to their own naiveté, peer blockage, and lack of sexual confidence. Opportunity is the key to their offending behaviour, which often occurs in the context of babysitting. There also appears to be another subgroup of girls who are influenced by their peers and would not sexually offend without this situational influence.

When assessing a sexually abusive juvenile female, it is important to remember sexually abusive girls (like boys) are a heterogeneous group and clinicians should not be over eager to classify them, nor should typologies be used to label adolescents. Given that there needs to be far more research conducted in order to develop valid and reliable typologies for juvenile females, listening to the narratives these girls share during the assessment and treatment process, can help further an understanding of their behaviour and be beneficial in the future development of typologies.

### The current state of (and dilemmas associated with) female risk assessment

An empirically validated risk assessment designed specifically for sexually abusive girls has not yet been developed. Thus far, research on the recidivism of young people who sexually abuse have either not included females (Hagan and Cho, 1996; Sipe, Jensen, and Everett, 1998; Smith and Monastersky, 1986) or have included relatively few (Kahn and Chambers, 1991; Lab, Shields, and Schondel, 1993; Rasmussen, 1999; Worling and Curwen, 2000). Lab et al.'s study (1993) included 151 males and 1 female. Rasmussen's study was based on 167 males and 3 females. The ratio of males to females in Kahn and Chambers' study based on 221 participants, was 20 to 1. In Prentky, Harris, Frizzell, and Righthand's study (2000) of 96 juvenile sexual offenders, there was no mention of females being included in their sample or the possible differences in risk among females and males who offend. The one exception to this scant juvenile female representation is the more recent work of Prentky, Dube, Pimental, Cavanaugh, and Latham (2004) which includes a sample size of 135 girls and 585 boys. This study will be discussed later in this section. Because of the under-representation of female juveniles in the studies of juvenile sexual reoffence, the current juvenile risk assessment tools, such as the J-SOAP-II (Prentky and Righthand, 2003) which is only intended for sexually abusive boys from age 12–18, and the ERASOR (Worling and Curwen, 2001) have been developed based on studies

primarily consisting of male participants and thus, have questionable applicability to females. The fact female juveniles have been underrepresented is understandable given the higher numbers of males adjudicated for sexual offending behaviour, however, in developing risk assessments it is not accurate to presume that the risk factors correlated with male sex offending recidivism are the same for females. It stands to reason that gender differences in development, socialisation processes, and the manifestation of aggression (including sexual) need to be considered when designing a risk assessment protocol.

It is concerning, then, that clinicians are left utilising risk assessments based on male offending to their female clients, especially when there is evidence that strongly suggests a need for female assessment. Although Simourd and Andrews (as cited in Leschied et al., 2000) concluded that male risk factors for delinquency are important to female delinquency, Funk (1999) determined that not only do female risk factors differ from those of males, but a risk assessment designed specifically for females predicts female recidivism more than twice as well as one designed for both sexes. Although many of the risk factors for males appear to be applicable to females, such as having numerous victims, this author contends we do not yet have enough information on female juvenile offending to assume these factors equally apply to both sexes.

Furthermore, risk assessment appears to have limited utility when it comes to females. One reason is because females are less likely to recidivate than males (Salekin, Rogers, Ustad, and Sewell, 1998). This is, in part, due to the differing developmental course of aggression between females and males (Lewis, Yeager, Cobham-Portorreal, Klein, Showalter, and Anthony, 1991; for a discussion, see Odgers, Moretti, and Reppucci, 2005). Lanctot, Emond, and Le Blanc (2004) found in their longitudinal study that participation in violence substantially decreases as adjudicated girls enter adulthood. The variety of violent behaviours also decreases with age. In their study, girls in mid-adolescence had the highest variety of violent behaviour: 31 per cent of adjudicated females in the sample engaged in at least five types of violent behaviour during this developmental phase. At the beginning of adulthood, only four per cent had similar behavioural diversity. They suggest that the substantial decrease in violence and criminality during girls' transition to adulthood may be explained by the unfolding of new social roles, eg becoming a parent, joining the work force, cohabitating with a partner. The decrease in female delinquency as girls enter into adulthood has been replicated in other studies as well (Lanctot and Le Blanc, 2002; Pajer, 1998).

Specific to sexual offending, Cortoni and Hanson (2005) in examining sexual recidivism among adult females with a sample size consisting of 380 female sexual offenders, found statistically significant differences in recidivism rates over a five-year average follow-up period between males and females. The sexual recidivism rate for female sexual offenders was only one per cent; male sexual recidivism is roughly 13–14 per cent. The rate of female violent recidivism (including sexual) was 6.3 per cent; comparatively, for males it is approximately 25 per cent. The rate of any female recidivism (including violent and sexual) was 20.2 per cent, yet adult male recidivism is considered to be 36–37 per cent. Cortoni and Hanson (2005: 12–3) recommended that evaluators need to be more concerned about the risk of non-sexual rather than sexual recidivism for females. They further noted, 'the substantial difference in recidivism rates suggests that risk tools developed on male sexual offenders are unlikely to apply to females. Simply extrapolating from the male sexual offender literature to assess risk in female sexual offenders is likely to lead to invalid risk appraisal and unintended consequences'. More appropriate female risk factors, for example, would include problematic relationships, emotional dyscontrol, and substance abuse.

Risk assessments also appear to have compromised utility due to the low base rates of female offending, in addition to the fact that risk assessment instruments are not yet designed to capture or predict familial violence and relational abuse. Females are less likely to target strangers; rather, the targets of female violence are often those with whom they have close interpersonal relationships, eg children and intimate partners (Moretti et al., 2004). Odgers, Schmidt, and Reppucci (2004: 199) state: 'If violence risk prediction is the goal, the low base rate of the types of violence that are recorded in traditional risk assessment studies among women makes accurate prediction difficult if not impossible . . . Several key factors related to the types of relationally based violence that women are more likely to engage in are missing from current

assessment schemes'. Similarly, juvenile females are more likely to aggress against family members, intimate partners, or members of their peer group (Odgers et al., 2004: 204). Regarding juvenile females, they assert: 'There is a low probability that these girls will go on to commit the types of non-familial violence that traditional risk assessment instruments were designed to predict. The low base rate of future serious and violent official offending among female adolescents makes accurate prediction difficult if not impossible'. They conclude that they 'cannot empirically or ethically justify their use due to the obvious limitations in our knowledge regarding risk assessment for girls and the serious decisions that may be made based on these assessments' (p. 206). Their subsequent article (2005) produced similar findings that there is no evidence to support the use of risk assessment for violence prediction in girls. Instead, female juvenile risk assessment may be more suitable to predict negative adult outcomes (Odgers et al., 2004).

This assertion is based on research noting poor adult outcomes for delinquent female juveniles and for girls diagnosed with Conduct Disorder. Moffit et al. (2001) found that girls with Conduct Disorder during childhood and adolescence had poor outcomes as adults including significant mental health disturbances (depression, anxiety, psychosis, suicidality) repeat victimisation experiences/domestic abuse, acts of physically assaultive behaviour towards partners in the act of self-defence, as well as medical problems. Zoccolillo and Rogers (1991) found considerably poor outcomes among their sample of 55 adolescent girls diagnosed with Conduct Disorder: some experienced early pregnancy, some died violent deaths, the majority dropped out of school, many were rearrested, and several sustained traumatic injuries. Lewis et al. (1991) in their study of 21 female delinquents who were then followed-up seven to twelve years later, found that most of them were impaired neuropsychiatrically. Suicidal ideation, alcoholism, drug addiction, violent relationships, high mortality rates, and an inability to care for their own children characterised the lives of these women. Unlike their comparative sample of males, it was the neuropsychiatric conditions that marked their adult functioning, not criminality.

We are then left with the question: What risk assessment instruments are available to use on female adolescents? And, what can risk assessments used on adult females offer to juvenile females? Currently, the Psychopathy Checklist – Revised (PCL-R) and Psychopathy Checklist – Youth Version (PCL-YV) are widely used as the gold standard for risk assessment and evaluation. Unfortunately, the validity of this evaluative tool is problematic with females. For example, although the Psychopathy Checklist Revised (PCL-R) has been found to predict risk in adult males (Salekin, Rogers, and Sewell, 1996) and it is often used on adult females, the predictive value for recidivism for adult females is poor. Salekin et al. (1998) found that the PCL-R did not yield predictive validity for females and 'identifying female psychopaths for the prediction of recidivism resulted in high false-positive and false-negative rates (p. 125).' The behavioural criteria do not serve as strong predictors for recidivism, although the personality criteria have more potential in this regard. Similarly, Vitale and Newman (2001: 128) conclude: 'If clinicians were using the PCL-R for the sole purpose of predicting specific outcomes for any particular woman in these areas, they would be doing so without empirical evidence of the predictive power of the PCL-R in such domains . . . Thus, we caution against the premature use of the instrument to make important decisions based upon PCL-R ratings'. They also determined that PCL-R ratings are not associated with poor treatment amenability. Likewise, Verona and Vitale (2006: 431) concluded, 'The PCL-R does not do as well in predicting violence and is not associated with childhood conduct problems and aggression in women'. These findings indicate that the PCL-R does not adequately reflect the expression of criminality in females (such as violence against family members and the neglect of children). The first study to provide an extensive evaluation on the utility of the Psychopathy Checklist-Youth Version with female juveniles (Odgers, 2005) mirrored the results from studies on adult females; that is, the PCL-YV was not predictive for future offending behaviours. However, the likelihood of general reoffending was significantly increased based on prior victimisation experiences. Experienced physical abuse and psychological abuse perpetrated by a girl's mother increased the odds of recidivism. Victimisation by a girl's mother predicted recidivism, but victimisation by a girl's father was not statistically significant.

It appears then, that a history of non-sexual victimisation can increase general recidivism risk.

High levels of experienced physical and emotional abuse, and neglect are pervasive in the childhoods of sexually abusive girls (Bumby and Bumby, 1997; Howley, 2001; Kubik et al., 2002; Mathews et al., 1997; Ray and English, 1995, Turner and Turner, 1994). When compared to boys, these histories tend to be more severe. Ray and English (1995) found that girls outnumbered boys as having experienced multiple forms of abuse in their childhoods. The extensive role modelling of aggression and the impact sustained from numerous trauma insults may make the offending behaviour even more intractable for girls with these histories and play a determining role in future offending behaviours. Funk (1999) found that an abuse history had a much stronger correlation to re-offending for girls than boys. Therefore, a history consisting of high levels of multiple forms of abuse (sexual and non-sexual) could be an important risk factor for girls.

Similarly, two studies, one by Sepsi and another by Shields (cited in Bonta, Pang, and Wallace-Capretta, 1995) found an association between sexual abuse and recidivism among female juvenile offenders. Mailloux (1999) also found that women who reported physical and sexual abuse histories committed a greater frequency and variety of self and other directed violent behaviours. Based on studies conducted thus far, and as previously explained, sexual trauma is a prominent feature among sexually abusive girls (Bumby and Bumby, 1997; Fehrenbach and Monastersky, 1988; Howley, 2001; Hunter et al., 1993; Johnson, 1989; Kubik et al., 2002; Mathews et al., 1997; Miccio-Fonseca, 2000; Ray and English, 1995; Turner and Turner, 1994). For many girls, the association between their victimisation histories and sexual perpetration is significant. A history of sexual abuse appears to serve a criminogenic need for females that also may correspond to recidivism.

Given the pronounced comorbid conditions among delinquent girls (Loeber and Keenan, 1994; see Odgers et al., 2004; Odgers et al., 2005; Wood et al., 2002) it is irrefutable that these conditions predispose girls to risky behaviours, and can serve as a pathway to further offending behaviour. Leschied et al. (2000) found that aggressive girls often have psychiatric diagnoses of depression, anxiety, and adjustment disorders, and have higher rates of suicidal ideation than boys. Depression has been strongly associated with aggressive behaviours in females (Leschied et al., 2000; Obeidallah and Earls, 1999; Zoccolillo and Rogers, 1991). Significantly higher levels of depression among girls when compared to boys were also evident in Wood et al.'s (2002) study. Depression is especially notable among sexually abusive girls. Depression and anxiety, for example, were common in Johnson's sample (1989) of pre-adolescent sexually abusive girls. Post-traumatic stress disorder also has some validity as a predictive factor and will be discussed below.

A history of suicide or suicidal ideation also appears to be a strong predictor of risk specific to females (adult and juvenile). Two studies on incarcerated adult females (Bonta et al., 1995; Blanchette and Motiuk, as cited in Blanchette and Motiuk, 1997) found an association between a history of self-injury and recidivism. Chamberlain and Moore (2002) found a significant difference with suicide attempts in histories of girls and boys with antisocial behaviour: 64 per cent of the girls versus three per cent of they boys had previously attempted suicide. Odgers et al. (2004: 16) assert that based on prior research 'suicidal behaviours may be considered as a marker for distinct types of psychological maladjustment and as a risk factor for future violence towards self and others'. As previously mentioned, suicidal histories are relatively common among sexually abusive girls.

Another risk factor worth examining for girls is early maturation. Levene et al. (2001) describe sexual development as a risk factor specific to girls. As they describe, girls with early sexual maturation are predisposed to negative body image, concerning social affiliations and involvements with older boys, and substance abuse. Precocious sexual behaviour may occur leading to sexual victimisation and/or a tendency for these girls to define themselves through their sexuality and success at attracting the opposite sex. Although early sexual maturation appears to correlate to the development of negative behaviours, the role it plays specifically in girls' sex offending behaviour has not yet been studied. Nevertheless, this author suggests that early maturation may correlate to female juvenile sex offending behaviour. Many girls who mature early experience peer ostracism and rejection, and their peer group may not be developmentally ready to engage in sexual exploration. Although young physically mature girls may not be developmentally prepared for sexual involvements, because their bodies are already developed, they often inappropriately believe that they are emotionally prepared (or at least

should be) for sexual contact. Therefore, the lack of sexual opportunities with their peer group – or blockage as described by Finkelhor (1984) – could lead to developing their own opportunities to explore their sexuality. Many girls go to older boys or men; other girls may explore their sexuality given access to younger children.

Furthermore, given the relational development of girls, if the avenues to engage in the normal course of relational development are blocked and impaired, these impairments could impact girls in such a way to increase their risk for negative behaviours. For example, an absence of a healthy same sex role model or parent appears to pertain to a girl's risk to re-offend. Like many boys who sexually offend, many sexually abusive girls tend to lack a functional and stable same sex parent. Since a healthy relationship between a girl and her mother is a protective factor for developing some forms of mental health disturbances (Harris et al., 1991) the lack of a healthy relationship with a girl's mother or female caregiver could increase risk. In this regard, negative female role modelling is a compromising influence that provides a catalyst for the development of disturbing behaviours. As previously noted, Odgers (2005) study showed that victimisation by a mother was predictive of recidivism. Tremblay, Nagin, Seguin, Zoccolillo, Zelazo, Boivin, Perusse, and Japel (2004) also found that maternal perpetration related to a development of aggressive behaviours. Levene et al. (2001) further substantiate the importance of the mother-daughter relationship in the development of an antisocial trajectory for girls. The caregiver-daughter interaction is a risk factor identified for girls (Levene et al., 2001) and is a distinguishing difference from the risk factors noted for boys (Augimeri, Koegl, Webster, and Levene, 2001). Although fathers are, of course, paramount to their daughter's upbringing and general well being, and a deprivation of this relationship can also lead to behavioural disturbances, the maternal contribution tends to be more significant because of the same sex influence, as well as the fact that many sexually abusive girls are raised by single parent mothers. It is not surprising that Mathews et al. (1997) found that poor female role modelling and an notable absence of support were present in many of the lives of the sexually abusive girls in their sample. Turner and Turner (1994) as well as Johnson (1989) also revealed discordant and enmeshed mother-daughter dynamics in their studies on sexually abusive girls. Sexual victimisation by a female aggressor may also be a factor worth examining for risk. In Mathews et al. (1997) girls were three times more likely than boys to have been sexually abused by a female. In Hunter et al. (1993) 60 per cent of the girls that offended were sexually abused by females. Howley (2001) also found that many of the girls in her sample had been molested by females. Perhaps girls who are sexually abused by females are at a heightened risk to repeat the behaviour due to the impact that the same sex modeling of such behaviour has on their burgeoning identity.

A Juvenile Female Risk Assessment for Sexual Abuse (JFRA-SA) was recently proposed based on clinical experience and the literature on female delinquency and sexual abuse (Robinson, 2006). It should be viewed as a starting point in the development of a gender-specific risk assessment for girls by noting factors worthy of further research (some of which have already been discussed). The risk assessment should not be used to predict recidivism but instead for determining treatment needs and goals, as the recent research has encouraged. Any suggestion of future risk would need to include a clear caveat. Additionally, Prentky et al.'s (2004) work also serves as a place to further our understanding of risk factors specific to girls. Their research examined the relationship between the J-SOAP and sexual aggression by gender and age. The predictive risk factors for girls included: Post-traumatic Stress Disorder, Attention Deficit and Hyperactivity Disorder, a history of multiple changes in living situations, conning and manipulative behaviour, juvenile antisocial behaviour, the total number of victims, and the level of sexual aggression.

A history of multiple changes in living situations, depending on how this factor was specifically defined, may be consistent with a history of inconsistent care giving, as listed on the JFRA-SA. Research describes the risk potential resulting from multiple changes and moves for girls. In Chamberlain and Moore's study (2002) the girls involved in the criminal justice system ($n = 42$) averaged 3.9 out of home placements; comparatively, the boys averaged 1.3. Rutter and Wolkind (as cited in Cloninger et al., 1978) found that early removal from the family and residential care was pathogenic for girls. A similar finding was not rendered for boys. The involvement with multiple caregivers and the losses associated with changing caregivers can disrupt a girl's

attachment (especially given their relational development) thus posing a developmental risk and creating a negative trajectory. The negative sequelae associated with a compromised relational development supports the legitimacy of this risk factor. Another risk factor, total number of victims, is also consistent with Funk's (1999) finding that a history of person-related offences increased the risk of re-offending for female delinquents, whereas the total number of prior offences was determined to be a risk factor for boys. Because girl's are socialised more towards covert aggressive behaviours (indirect and relational aggression) rather than overt physical assault, girls that engage in assaultive behaviour towards others may be more predisposed for delinquent behaviours than males (Cloninger et al., 1978) which could correspond to increased risk.

Prentky et al. (2004) found post-traumatic stress disorder to be a predictive risk factor; the diagnosis of PTSD is also listed on the JFRA-SA. As previously noted, PTSD leads to high distress levels and low self-restraint, and increases the risk of behavioural problems and offending behaviours (Cauffman et al., 1998). Not surprisingly, PTSD is far more common among juvenile incarcerated females due to the disabling impact it has on their emotional regulation. Wood et al. (2002) found high rates of PTSD symptomatology among the females in their sample: 52 per cent compared to 28 per cent of their male comparison sample. Unsurprisingly, many sexually abusive girls meet the criteria for PTSD (Bumby and Bumby, 1997; Hunter et al., 1993; Kubik et al., 2002). The robust relationship between victimisation and perpetration among many sexually abusive girls is striking.

Prentky et al. (2004) also determined that juvenile antisocial behaviour and conning and manipulative behaviour were predictive risk factors for girls. However, modifying the description of antisocial behaviour to better encompass the manifestation of female antisocial behaviour is warranted. Stealing, substance abuse, running away, truancy, lying, manipulation, conning, and relational aggression exemplify female antisocial behaviour and these criteria apply to many sexually abusive girls. Relational aggression represents one of the more harmful dimensions of female aggression, yet descriptions of delinquency and antisocial behaviour have typically not included this expression of female behaviour. Cummings et al. (2002) found a correlation between relational and direct aggression in girls. Henington, Hughes, Cavell, and Thompson (1998) also found that the use of relational aggression was predictive of overt aggression in girls. Finally, Odgers and Moretti (2002) proposed that among high-risk girls, relational aggression provides the contextual background for more serious aggressive acts to occur. Therefore, a better risk factor for girls may be a history of relational aggression, or at the very least, female juvenile antisocial behaviour should include the criterion of relational aggression. Relational aggression was considered in the development of the EARL-21G for pre-adolescent girls (Levene et al., 2001) and also appears applicable to adolescent females.

Factors in Prentky et al.'s study (2004) that were not found to be predictive included: multiple types of offences, an arrest before the age of 16, Conduct Disorder, caregiver instability, exposure to domestic violence, and impulsivity. It is interesting that Conduct Disorder was not predictive given the research outcomes on girls with this disorder, however, this non-predictive finding may relate to the fact that there is a gender bias with this diagnosis (girls are less often diagnosed with CD despite their symptomatology) and the criteria do not adequately capture female behaviour as well as it does for males (Zoccolillo, 1993; Zoccolillo, Tremblay, and Vitaro, 1996). Criteria for Conduct Disorder, ie use of a weapon, physical cruelty to animals, armed robbery, fire setting, and mugging (American Psychiatric Association, 2000) are behaviours more commonly associated with males. In Kubik et al.'s study (2002) only 9.1 per cent of the sex-offending girls were given the diagnosis of Conduct Disorder, yet nearly half of the boys (45.5 per cent) were diagnosed with this condition. The item, multiple types of offences, was not found to be a predictive risk factor, however, this non-predictive finding mirrors Funk's (1999) study that a total number of prior offences was a risk factor for boys, not for girls. Multiple types of offences reflect the more overt aggression committed by males. Examples as listed on the J-SOAP-II include: kidnapping, assault causing bodily harm, property offences such as burglary, criminal trespass, and arson, serious motor vehicle offences, and violation of a protection/restraining order. The fact that it was not found to be predictive for females is understandable.

Finally, exposure to domestic violence was not predictive in Prentky et al.'s study (2004) perhaps because of the reality that girls who witness domestic violence, especially if their mothers are the victims, identify with their mothers and are more likely to become victims themselves. Instead, family dysfunction, conflict, and exposure to criminal behaviour among family members may be more predictive for girls. Research is abundant in this area. Henggeler, Edwards, and Borduin (1987) found that families of female delinquents tended to be more conflictual than those of males and that females appeared to be more susceptible to the disorganising influence of family conflict. Chamberlain and Moore (2002) found that 43 per cent of the mothers of delinquent girls in their sample had been convicted of a crime, compared to 22 per cent of the mothers of delinquent boys. 63 per cent of the girls' fathers had a crime conviction versus 22 per cent of the boys' fathers. 75 per cent of the girls had at least one parent convicted of a crime, compared to 41 per cent of the boys. They concluded that girls came from 'families that were extremely chaotic and distressed, even compared to the highly distressed families of juvenile justice-referred boys' (p. 94). Lastly, Funk (1999) found higher levels of family problems among female delinquents than males (males had more delinquent peer associations).

A final consideration: evidence of sexual preoccupation is a risk factor on the J-SOAP-II. Examples of this include: 'excessive preoccupation with sexual urges or gratifying sexual needs . . . paraphilias (exposing, peeping, cross-dressing, fetishes, etc.); compulsive masturbation; chronic and compulsive use of pornography . . .' (Prentky and Righthand, 2003: 15). The ERASOR (Worling and Curwen, 2001) also notes deviant sexual interests and obsessive sexual interests/preoccupation with sexual thoughts as risk factors. However, as noted earlier, research suggests that female sex offending is less about deviant sexual interests, arousal, and sexual preoccupation (Davin, 1999; Dunbar, 1999; Finkelhor and Russell, 1984; Howley, 2001; Johnson, 1989; Saradjian and Hanks, 1996; Turner and Turner, 1994). In their work with adult female offenders, Sardajian and Hanks (1996: 144) concluded that the use of sexual fantasy was 'less extensive and universal' than for male sex offenders. Many of the women in their study actually had low sexual drives further suggesting that for many females, their motivation to offend is not primarily sexual gratification. Moreover, paraphilias are not as common among females.

The sex ratio among paraphilias is estimated to be 20 males for each female; the one exception is sexual masochism (American Psychiatric Association, 2000). (Although it should also be noted that females are given more latitude to expose themselves and female exhibitionism is not necessarily viewed as a problematic or abusive behaviour requiring intervention.) In addition, females are less likely to use pornography, especially in an excessive manner. Marshall and Eccles (1993: 133) discuss the fact that deviant sex and pornography remain a male terrain and suggest the difference in socialisation is the reason: Western culture promotes values and stereotypes that lead to the development in adolescent males to adopt a 'sexualised view of the world,' thereby leading to predatory and sexually aggressive behaviour towards females. Yet there is also evidence that males are more biologically predisposed to visual stimuli and response due to testosterone levels (Blum, 1997). Consequently, these risk descriptors (sexual preoccupation, deviant sexual interests, or multiple paraphilias) do not appear to be as valid for sexually abusing female juveniles; it simply does not exemplify female sexual offending as well as it does for males. However, it does seem suitable to note sexual preoccupation as a risk factor for girls but with alterations in the description. Evidence of masturbation to victimisation experiences may correlate more with female sexual recidivism. Trauma re-enactment is pronounced among sexually abusive girls; some girls masturbate to their own victimisation experiences, which can ignite a motivation to offend. Girls who also have a high sexual drive, and engage in sex as a primary coping strategy to mitigate pain, feel complete, and experience momentary connection, may also be at an increased risk. Finally, despite the fact it is less evident in girls, obviously girls with deviant sexual interests and arousal could be at a heightened risk.

Although there are differences in male and female risk factors, many of those listed for males appear to be congruent with female sexual aggression. The J-SOAP-II lists the quality of peer relationships as a risk factor and the ERASOR includes a lack of intimate peer relationships/social isolation as a risk factor. Given female relational development, these risk factors have great significance for girls. Bumby and Bumby (1997) found that 75 per cent of girls in their sample were socially isolated and all but one girl had peer difficulties at school. In Johnson's (1989) sample, the girls had few, if any, peer relationships. Additionally, an internal motivation to change, an item on the J-SOAP-II, seems equally applicable to girls, as does a sexual trauma history, remorse and guilt, and empathy. Some risk factors listed on the JFR-SA include: a history of sexual victimisation, a history of person-related offences, Depressive Disorder, Post-traumatic Stress Disorder, evidence of sexual subjectivity, emotional expressivity, attachment style, attitudes reflecting non-normative beliefs, and investment in school. Despite the current awakening focus on female juvenile risk assessment, the development of such tools remains in its infancy. Further research and larger sample sizes are required to better determine the predictive value of risk items. For now, female risk assessments can be a useful evaluation tool to determine treatment needs, but any attempt to designate a risk for future behaviour must be viewed with significant caution.

## Conclusion

The purpose of this chapter has been to increase awareness of the needs and issues specific to female sexually abusive youth. It is through an awareness of the differences between male and female juveniles, that a thorough assessment on juvenile females can be conducted thereby informing and guiding the treatment of sexually abusive girls. The assessment process should be guided by an understanding of female development and sexual behaviour; without this, the assessment procedure may miss important dynamics and characteristics specific to females requiring treatment attention. Since assessment has historically been conducted through the lens of male sex offending behaviour, it is time to assess through the lens of female development and sexual behaviour. It is from such an approach that specific tools and treatment methods will be developed for these girls. This is a work in progress. And much work is needed in the development of assessment tools for sexually abusive girls. It is this author's hope that further research on sexually abusive juvenile females will be conducted to promote our understanding of this population and improve current treatment approaches to better suit this growing and unique population.

## Appendix 1 A Guideline for Female Assessment

Because there is a lack of assessment tools that have been developed for female juveniles with sexual abuse behaviours, there is a greater reliance on self-report (Hunter and Matthews, 1997). When assessing sexually abusive juvenile females, much of the assessment process will reflect similar questions posed to juvenile males, however, below are questions that may be help guide the assessment process of a juvenile female. These questions are based on the literature on female adolescent development and sexual offending and can help to identify a girl's clinical needs. This is by no means an exhaustive list and is a guideline to alter as desired.

1. Offending behaviour:

- What was her victim selection: stranger, family member, acquaintance? How many victims?
- What was her relationship to her victim? If she knew her victim, how would she describe their relationship (ie close, distant)?
- How did she gain access to her victims? Was she in a position of trust, ie caretaking, or other?
- What was her motivation for offending? Examine cultural scripts which may influence offending motivation, offending behaviour as a form of relational aggression, dependency issues, trauma re-enactment, or sex as a means of attachment (sex=love). Was it an expression of anger or a way to learn about her sexuality?
- What are her cognitive distortions? Does she exhibit altruistic/caretaking justifications for offending?
- Does she exhibit guilt, remorse, shame, or empathy for her offending behaviour? Is there evidence that she is feigning empathy?
- What is her pathway to offending behaviour (ie depression, victimisation, early maturation, criminal activity among family members, etc.)?
- Which typology seems to match her behaviour (ie predisposed, experimenting/exploiting, peer influenced)?

As with the assessment of boys, other areas to pay attention to include: the degree of premeditation or impulsivity; the relationship of offending to sexual arousal; the level of coercion; the severity of the offence and duration of behaviour; and the level of denial.

2. History of maltreatment (physical, sexual, emotional abuse or neglect):

- What kind of maltreatment did she experience?
- Has she witnessed marital violence?
- Has she been raised in an environment of criminal activity or substance abuse?
- Is there role modelling of aggression by a female perpetrator in her history?
- Are there multiple perpetrators?
- What was her relationship to her perpetrators? What words does she use to describe the relationship (ie close, damaged, untrusting, loving, caring)?
- How young was she when abused? What was the duration?
- Did she disclose abuse? If so, was there a positive or negative outcome to disclosure?
- How has the abuse affected her? What negative messages has she incorporated into her identity (ie thinking the abuse was her fault; thinking she is damaged goods; believing she deserved to be abused; or, believing she must have liked the abuse due to a sexual arousal response)?

3. History of conduct disordered behaviour or relational aggression:

- Does she have a history of lying? About what types of things?
- To what extent does she lie? Does it seem characterological?
- Does she have a history of stealing? If so, what would she steal?
- What other forms of negative behaviours have occurred, eg fighting, vandalism, or false reporting.
- Has she engaged in relational aggression, ie backbiting, gossiping, hurtful rumours, shunning previous friends, malicious behaviour towards female peers? To what extent?

4. Relational development, female identity, and attachment styles:

- Are relationships important to her?
- Is there evidence of healthy and supportive relationships (reciprocity, mutuality)?
- What are her current peer and intimate relationships like?
- Has she experienced any abusive relationships? If so, is she in one now?
- What is her family constellation?
- What are the family dynamics?

- What are the strengths and weaknesses of her family system?
- Does she have close relationships with extended family members?
- What are the dynamics of the mother-daughter relationship? What is her previous and current relationship like with her mother?
- Does she have healthy or unhealthy female role models?
- What is her view of females?
- What is her view of self?
- Is her identity inchoate, formulated and stable, or disorganised and incoherent? Does she easily change her identity based on whom she is with and what she perceives others want her to be, ie 'chameleon' identity?
- What is her attachment style (negative or positive view of self and others)?
- Is she overly dependent? Or, does she refuse to depend on anyone?
- Is her ability to trust impaired?
- What kind of boundaries does she have (non-existent, walled, or healthy)?
- To what extent does she use others to get her needs met?
- Is her external presentation congruent with her internal presentation? Does she protect herself from vulnerability by acting tough?

5. Sexual functioning, body image, and health:

- Does she describe herself as having low or high sexual desire?
- Is she sexually experienced, promiscuous, sexually naïve, or inexperienced?
- Is there evidence of a trauma bond pairing sexual victimisation and arousal, or other deviant sexual interests and behaviours?
- Does she take ownership of her sexuality or is she sexually passive and allow herself to be the object of others?
- Is she aware of her sexuality and sexual orientation?
- How does she feel about her sexuality? Does she have a positive or negative view of sex? Is there evidence of sexual shame? Does she perceive herself as sexually inadequate?
- Does she define herself by her sexuality and desirability?
- Is she sexually knowledgeable? (For example, does she know where to find her clitoris? Does she know about female sexual response and orgasms? Is she informed about birth control?)

- What is her sexual experience? Have her sexual experiences (other than her offending behaviour) been positive, negative, or both? What kinds of sexual exploration has she engaged in? For example, while it is often not spoken about, it is fairly common for girls to practice having sex with other girls; it provides them with a 'rehearsal' in preparation for contact with boys. Has she engaged in practicing behaviours with other girls? How did it feel?
- How many consensual and non-consensual sexual experiences has she had?
- What is her reproductive health? Has she had any pregnancies, abortions, or miscarriages? Has she had any sexually transmitted diseases?
- Does she have any sexual dysfunctions?
- Does she place herself in unsafe sexual situations where she is victimised? Has she done so previously?
- Does she engage in unprotected sex? If so, why?
- Does she own and use birth control?
- Does she have a desire to get pregnant? Has she previously lied about being pregnant? If so, why?
- When did she begin menstruating? What stages of puberty has she reached?
- What is her body image? Does she feel positively or negatively about her body? Does she view herself as overweight?
- Does she have any history of medical problems? Any current problems?
- Has she ever taken naked or provocative photos of herself and posted them on the Internet? What was her motivation?

As with boys, examine any prior exposure and use of pornography, sexual involvement in chat rooms, and formal sexual education.

6. Mental health issues and internalisation:

- Has she received any prior mental health treatment or been psychiatrically hospitalised?
- Are there current or prior mental health problems, such as, depression, dissociation, anxiety, low self-esteem, suicidal ideation or attempts, self-mutilation, substance abuse, eating disorders, hypercriticism, perfectionism, Post-traumatic Stress Disorder, hygiene, recklessness, or compulsive exercise?
- Does she meet the criteria for ADHD or Conduct Disorder? (Be mindful that the

manifestation of these disorders can be different in girls.)

- How does she manage her anger? Was she taught that anger was not an acceptable feeling to have or express?
- How does she manage other difficult feelings, ie shame, sadness, fear? Pay attention to forms of internalisation as well as externalisation.

As with boys, other areas to assess include: the kinds of defence mechanisms utilised (primitive or highly adaptive); the level of self-esteem; the degree of ego strength; and, the ability to self-regulate and self-soothe.

7. Academic functioning:

- Does she have a history of school behavioural problems, eg fighting, stealing, talking back to teachers and disrespecting authority? Has she ever been suspended or expelled?
- Does she have a history of truancy?
- Has school been an area of success?
- What is her attitude toward learning?
- Does she have any diagnosed or possibly undiagnosed learning problems?
- Does she have difficulties with concentration or inattention?

8. Assets and protective factors:

- Is she able to voice herself and assert herself appropriately?
- What are her problem-solving abilities?
- Does she possess a healthy and genuine confidence in herself?
- Is she emotionally expressive?
- Is she able to empathise and entertain various perspectives?
- Does she have healthy support systems and relationships in place?
- Does she have a positive relationship with her mother? Who does she have as positive female role models?
- Does she have a connected and healthy family system?
- Does she have close friendships? Does she engage in relational reciprocity?
- Does she accept gender normative definitions and beliefs?

9. Risks and deficits:

- Is there unprocessed trauma and PTSD reactivity?

- Is there caregiver loss or abandonment?
- Does she have a negative or abusive relationship with her mother?
- Are there family members involved with criminal activity that serve as role models to her?
- Does she have a stressful or abusive family system?
- Has she witnessed family violence?
- Does she exhibit an inability to voice and assert herself?
- To what extent is there evidence of relationship instability or disconnection?
- Has she experienced social rejection and peer exclusion?
- Does she reject female normative definitions and beliefs?

Many other strengths, protective factors, risks, and deficits are similar for male and female youth. These facets can be determined by examining whether or not a youth has the following: secure attachment, resilience, intellectual abilities, areas of competence, affect regulation, impulse control, an ability to delay gratification, emotional expressiveness, pro-social interests or talents, self-soothing and self-care strategies, an ability to envision a positive future, and, a sense of hope. Finally, the assessment process for any sexually abusive youth would not be complete without a review of offence reports and the victim's account; other pertinent aspects of a developmental history (prenatal care, developmental milestones, early medical traumas, brain injuries etc.); treatment amenability; and, the evaluation of risk factors that could specifically lead to recidivism.

## Appendix 2 Existing Tools

The following are some of the existing tools that may be helpful during the assessment process for a sexually abusive female juvenile.

1. *Adolescent Dissociative Experiences Scale* (A-DES; Armstrong, Putnam, and Carlson, 1997): This 30-item scale for 10–21 year olds, measures an adolescent's use of dissociation which is helpful given the extent and severity of sexual abuse in the histories of girls with sexually abusive behaviours. Available from: Sidran Institute, 200 E. Joppa Rd., Suite 207, Towson, MD, 21286. Online: www.sidran.org

2. *Clinical Assessment Package for Client Risks and Strengths* (CASPARS; Gilgun, 1999): The CASPARS includes five instruments that are used to assess a child's assets and risks in different domains: Emotional Expressiveness, Family Relationships, Peer Relationships, Sexuality, and Family's Embeddedness in the Community. The instruments have been found to have high reliability and validity. Although these tools are not gender specific, the benefit of these tools is that they determine the client's strengths needing to be increased and risks needing to be decreased throughout treatment. Information and instruments available online at ssw.che.umn.edu/faculty/jgilgun/caspars.htm

3. *Child Behaviour Checklist and Youth Self-Report* (CBCL/6–18 and YSL; Achenbach): The Child Behaviour Checklist, consisting of 118 items, is designed to assess social competence and behaviour problems for children ages 6–18. There is a profile specific to girls. The Youth Self-Report is for ages 11–18. Online: www.aseba.org.

4. *Early Assessment Risk List for Girls* (EARL-21G; Levene et al., 2001). This tool was specially designed for girls up to the age of 12. The purpose is to assess a girl's risk for future antisocial behaviour. Available from: Earlscourt Child and Family Centre, 46 St. Clair Gardens, Toronto, Ontario, M6E, 3V4, Canada. Phone #: 416–654–8981. Online: www.earlscourt.on.ca.

5. *Little's Aggression Inventory* (Little, Brauner, Jones, Nock, and Hawley, 2003). This tool is used to differentiate overt and relational aggression. It has six subscales: pure overt, overt relational, overt instrumental, pure relational, reactive relational, and reactive instrumental. For further information see: Little, T. D., Brauner, J., Jones, S. M., Nock, M. K., and Hawley, P. H. (2003). Rethinking aggression: A typological examination of the functions of aggression. *Merrill-Palmer Quarterly*, 49, 343–369.

6. *Massachusetts Youth Screening Instrument* (MAYSI-2; Grisso and Barnum, 2003): This self-report instrument is designed to identify adjudicated 12–17 year old youths who may have mental health needs. It is a quick, user-friendly instrument consisting of 52 questions. This is a gender sensitive tool: There are 7 scales for boys and 6 scales for girls. Available online from Professional Resource Press: www.prpress.com.

7. *Multiphasic Sex Inventory* II JF (adolescent female form) (MSI II JF; Nichols and Molinder): This instrument is specifically geared to sexual offending girls and is used to examine their sexual characteristics. It can also be utilised to assess treatment progress. It has not yet been standardised on juvenile females. It is a paper and pencil test that takes approximately 90 minutes to complete and requires a 7th grade reading level. Online: www.nicholsandmolinder.com.

8. *Personal Sentence Completion Inventory* (Miccio-Fonseca, 1997): This is a flexible tool to assess sexual development that consists of open-ended sentence stems. Available through Safer Society Press, PO Box 340, Brandon, Vermont, 05733. Phone: 802-247-3132. Online: www.safersociety.org.

9. *Piers Harris Self-Concept Scale* (Piers-Harris 2; Piers and Herzberg, 2003): This self-concept scale is used for children ages 7–18. It is a 60-item self-report measure that can be completed in 10–15 minutes. It requires at least a second grade reading level. Available online from Psychological Assessment Resources: www.parinc.com.

10. *Polygraph examinations*: Specific-issue, sexual history disclosure polygraphs, and maintenance examinations are often used for assessment and monitoring purposes in offence-specific therapy (Colorado Sex Offender Management Board, 2002; Cross and Saxe, 2001). Although the pros and cons of such an exam needs to be weighed with those girls with severe trauma histories (due to the potential for a trauma response and a significant emotional cost) polygraphs have become a standard of offence-specific therapy in many places.

11. *Relationship Questionnaire* (Bartholomew and Horowitz, 1991): This self-report instrument is used for adolescents and adults. Clients rate themselves on a 7-point rating scale in response to four short paragraphs depicting attachment styles. Available in: Bartholomew, K., and Horowitz, L. M. (1991). Attachment styles among young adults: A test of a four-category model. *Journal of Personality and Social Psychology*, 61(2) 226–244.

12. *Reynolds Adolescent Depression Scale* (RADS-2; Reynolds, 2002). This is a 30 item self-report measure for 11–20 year olds that can be completed in 5–10 minutes. Available online from Psychological Assessment Resources: www.parinc.com.

13. *Sexual Attitudes Scale* (Craig, Follingstad, Franklin, and Kalichman, 1988). A measure initially designed for men, the wording was changed so it could be used for females. It may be appropriate for older adolescent females. This 19-item scale was designed to differentiate sexually coercive from non-coercive individuals. Available in: Anderson, P. B., and Struckman-Johnson, C. (Eds.). (1998). *Sexually Aggressive Women: Current Perspectives and Controversies.* New York: The Guilford Press.

14. *Trauma and Attachment Belief Scale* (Perlman, 2003). This is a self-report measure developed for 9–18 year olds to assess cognitive schemas. It can assist in identifying a client's interpersonal patterns and the effects of trauma on their sense of safety, trust, esteem, intimacy, and control. The assessment tool consists of 84 items and is appropriate for those who have at least a third grade reading level. Available online from Western Psychological Services: www.wpspublish.com.

15. *Trauma Symptom Checklist for Children* (TSCC; Briere, 1996). This checklist for 8–16 year olds includes 54 items to measure Post-traumatic Stress and other psychological sequelae of traumatic events. It takes 15–20 minutes to complete. There are *female profile forms.* Available online from Psychological Assessment Resources: www.parinc.com.

# References

Acoca, L. and Dedel, K. (1998) *No Place to Hide: Understanding and Meeting the Needs of Girls in the California Juvenile Justice System.* Oakland, CA: The National Council on Crime and Delinquency.

Allen, C.M. (1991) *Women and Men who Sexually Abuse Children: A Comparative Analysis.* Brandon, VT: Safer Society Press.

Allgood-Merten, B., Lewinsohn, P.M. and Hops, H. (1990) Sex Differences and Adolescent Depression. *Journal of Abnormal Psychology,* 99: 1, 55–63.

American Association of University Women (1995) *How Schools Shortchange Girls – The AAUW Report: A Study of Major Findings on Girls and Education.* New York: Marlowe and Company.

American Psychiatric Association (2000) *Diagnostic and Statistical Manual of Mental Disorders, Text Revision – DSM-IV-TR.* 4th edn. Washington, DC: American Psychiatric Association.

Anderson, P.B. and Struckman-Johnson, C. (Eds.) (1998) *Sexually Aggressive Women: Current Perspectives and Controversies.* New York: The Guilford Press.

Armstrong, J.G. et al. (1997) Development and Validation of a Measure of Adolescent Dissociation: The Adolescent Dissociative Experiences Scale. *The Journal of Nervous and Mental Disease,* 185: 8, 491–7.

Augimeri, L.K. et al. (2001) *Early Assessment Risk List For Boys, EARL-20B (Version 2)* Toronto, ON: Earlscourt Child and Family Centre.

Baron-Cohen, S. (2003) *The Essential Difference: The Truth about the Male and Female Brain.* New York: Basic Books.

Bartholomew, K. (1990) Avoidance of Intimacy: An Attachment Perspective. *Journal of Social and Personal Relationships,* 7, 145–78.

Bartholomew, K. and Horowitz, L.M. (1991) Attachment Styles among Young Adults: A Test of a Four-Category Model. *Journal of Personality and Social Psychology,* 61: 2, 226–44.

Biederman, J. et al. (1999) Clinical Correlates of ADHD in Females: Findings from a Large Group of Girls Ascertained from Pediatric and Psychiatric Referral Sources. *Journal of The American Academy of Child and Adolescent Psychiatry,* 38, 966–75.

Bjoerkqvist, K., Lagerspetz, K.M. and Kaukiainen, A. (1992) Do Girls Manipulate and Boys Fight? Developmental Trends in Regard to Direct and Indirect Aggression? *Aggressive Behaviour,* 18, 117–27.

Bjoerkqvist, K., Osterman, K. and Kaukiainen, A. (1992) The Development of Indirect and Aggressive Strategies in Males and Females. In Bjorkqvist, K. and Niemela, P. (Eds.) *Of Mice and Women: Aspects of Female Aggression* (51–64) New York: Academic Press.

Blanchette, K. and Motiuk, L.L. (1997) *Maximum-Security Female and Male Federal Offenders: A Comparison.* Retrieved February 2,

2004, From: Http://Www.Csc-Scc.Gc.Ca/Text/Rsrch/Reports/R53/R53e_E.Shtml

Blum, D. (1997) *Sex on The Brain: The Biological Differences Between Men and Women.* New York: Penguin Books.

Bonta, J., Pang, B. and Wallace-Capretta, S. (1995) Predictors of Recidivism among Incarcerated Female Offenders. *The Prison Journal*, 75: 3, 227–93.

Briere, J. (1996) *Trauma Symptom Checklist for Children (TSCC): Professional Manual.* Lutz, FL: Psychological Assessment Resources.

Brosky, B.A. and Lally, S.J. (2004) Prevalence of Trauma, PTSD and Dissociation in Court-Referred Adolescents. *Journal of Interpersonal Violence*, 19: 7, 801–14.

Brown, L.M. (1998) *Raising Their Voices: The Politics of Girls' Anger.* Cambridge, MA: Harvard University Press.

Brown, L.M. and Gilligan, C. (1992) *Meeting at the Crossroads: Women's Psychology and Girls' Development.* New York: Ballantine Books.

Bumby, K.M. and Bumby, N.H. (1997) Adolescent Female Sexual Offenders. In Schwartz, B.K. and Cellini, H.R. (Eds.) *The Sex Offender: Vol. 2. New Insights, Treatment Innovations and Legal Developments.* Kingston, NJ: Civic Research Institute.

Bybee, J. (1999) The Emergence of Gender Differences in Guilt during Adolescence. In Carlston, D.E (Ed.) *Social Cognition, Vol. 17.* Purdue, IN: Purdue University Press.

Cauffman, E. et al. (1998) Posttraumatic Stress Disorder among Female Juvenile Offenders. *Journal of The American Academy of Child and Adolescent Psychiatry*, 37: 1 1209–17.

Chamberlain, P. and Moore, K.J. (2002) Chaos and Trauma in the Lives of Adolescent Females with Antisocial Behaviour and Delinquency. In Greenwald, R. (Ed.) *Trauma and Juvenile Delinquency: Theory, Research and Interventions.* New York: The Haworth Maltreatment and Trauma Press.

Chesney-Lind, M. (1997) *The Female Offender: Girls, Women and Crime.* Thousand Oaks, CA: Sage.

Cloninger, C.R. et al. (1978) Implications of Sex Differences in the Prevalence of Antisocial Personality, Alcoholism and Criminality for Familial Transmission. *Archives of General Psychiatry*, 35, 941–51.

Cohen, J. (1996) Childhood Risks for Young Adult Symptoms of Personality Disorder: Method and Substance. *Multivariate Behavioural Research*, 31, 121–48.

Colorado Sex Offender Management Board (2002) *Standards and Guidelines for the Evaluation, Assessment, Treatment and Supervision of Juveniles who have Committed Sexual Offences.* Denver, CO: Colorado Department of Public Safety.

Commonwealth Fund (1997) *The Commonwealth Fund Survey of the Health of Adolescent Girls.* Retrieved July 19, 2000, From Http://Www.Cmwf.Org/Programs/Women/Factsheet.Asp

Cortoni, F. and Hanson, R.K. (2005) *A Review of the Recidivism Rates of Adult Female Sexual Offenders.* Ottawa, ON: Correctional Service of Canada. Available online: From Http://Www.Csc-Scc.Gc.Ca

Crick, N.R. and Grotpeter, J.K. (1995) Relational Aggression, Gender and Social-Psychological Adjustment. *Child Development*, 66, 710–22.

Cross, T.P. and Saxe, L. (2001) Polygraph Testing and Sexual Abuse. The Lure of the Magic Lasso. *Child Maltreatment*, 6: 3, 195–206.

Cummings, A.L., Leschied, A.W. and Heilbron, N. (2002) Assessing Relational and Direct Aggression in Adolescent Girls. In Cummings, A.L. and Leschied, A.W. (Eds.) *Research and Treatment for Aggression with Adolescent Girls.* Queenston, ON: The Edwin Mellon Press.

Davin, P.A. (1999) Secrets Revealed: A Study of Female Sex Offenders. In Davin, P.A., Hislop, J.C. and Dunbar, T. *The Female Sexual Abuser: Three Views.* Brandon, VT: Safer Society Press.

Davis, G.C. and Breslau, N. (1998) Are Women at Greater Risk for PTSD than Men? *Psychiatric Times*, 15: 7 Retrieved January 30, 2004, From Http://Www.Psychiatrictimes.Com/P980765.Html

Day, H., Franklin, J.M. and Marshall, D.D. (1998) Predictors of Aggression in Hospitalised Adolescents. *Journal of Psychology*, 132: 4, 427–34.

Dunbar, T. (1999) Women who Sexually Molest Female Children. In Davin, P.A., Hislop, J.C. and Dunbar, T. *The Female Sexual Abuser: Three Views.* Brandon, VT: Safer Society Press.

Ellis, B.J. and Symons, D. (1990) Sex Differences in Sexual Fantasy: An Evolutionary Psychological Approach. *Journal of Sex Research*, 27: 4, 527–56.

Erikson, E.H. (1950) *Childhood and Society.* New York: W.W. Norton.

Erikson, E.H. (1968) *Identity: Youth and Crisis.* New York: W.W. Norton.

Faller, D.C. (1995) A Clinical Sample of Women who have Sexually Abused. *Journal of Child Sexual Abuse*, 4: 3, 13–31.

Farber, S.K. (2002) *When the Body is a Target: Self-Harm, Pain and Traumatic Attachments.* Northvale, NJ: Jason Aronson.

Fehrenbach, P. and Monastersky, C. (1988) Characteristics of Female Adolescent Sexual Offenders. *American Journal of Orthopsychiatry,* 58: 1, 148–51.

Fine, M. (1988) Sexuality, Schooling and Adolescent Females: The Missing Discourse of Desire. *Harvard Education Review,* 58: 1, 29–52.

Finkelhor, D. (1984) *Child Sexual Abuse: New Theory and Research.* New York: The Free Press.

Finkelhor, D. and Russell, D. (1984) Women as Perpetrators: Review of the Evidence. In Finkelhor, D. *Child Sexual Abuse: New Theory and Research.* New York: The Free Press.

Flansburg, S. (1991) *Building a Self: Teenaged Girls and Issues of Self-Esteem.* Washington, DC: Women's Educational Equity Act Publishing Center.

Funk, S. (1999) Risk Assessment for Juveniles on Probation: A Focus on Gender. *Criminal Justice and Behaviour,* 26: 1, 44–68.

Gaub, M. and Carlson, C.L. (1997) Gender Differences in ADHD: A Meta-Analysis and Critical Review. *Journal of The American Academy of Child and Adolescent Psychiatry,* 36: 8, 1036–46.

Gilgun, J.F. (1990) Factors Mediating the Effects of Childhood Maltreatment. In Hunter, M. (Ed.) *The Sexually Abused Male: Vol. 1. Prevalence, Impact and Treatment,* Lexington, MA: Lexington Books.

Gilgun, J.F. (1999) CASPARS: New Tools for Assessing Client Risks and Strengths. *Families in Society,* 80, 450–9.

Gilgun, J.F. (2001) Protective Factors, Resilience and Child Abuse and Neglect. *Healthy Generations,* 2: 1, 4–5.

Gilligan, C. (1982) *In a Different Voice: Psychological Theory and Women's Development.* Cambridge, MA: Harvard University Press.

Gilligan, C., Lyons, N.P. and Hammer, T.J. (Eds.) (1990) *Making Connections: The Relational Worlds of Adolescent Girls at Emma Willard School.* Cambridge, MA: Harvard University Press.

Grisso, T. and Barnum, R. (2003) *Massachusetts Youth Screening Instrument – Version 2 (MAYSI-2): User's Manual and Technical Report.* Sarasota, FL: Professional Resource Press.

Hagan, M.P. and Cho, M.E. (1996) A Comparison of Treatment Outcomes between Adolescent Rapists and Child Sexual Offenders. *International Journal of Offender Therapy and Comparative Criminology,* 40, 113–22.

Hales, D. (1999) *Just Like a Woman: How Gender Science is Redefining What Makes Us Female.* New York: Bantam Books.

Hancock, E. (1989) *The Girl Within.* New York: Fawcett Columbine.

Harris, L., Blum, R.W. and Resnick, M. (1991) Teen Females in Minnesota: A Portrait of Quiet Disturbance. In Gilligan, C. Rogers, A.G. and Tolman, D.L. (Eds.) *Women, Girls and Psychotherapy: Reframing Resistance,* Binghamton, NY: Harrington Park Press.

Henggeler, S., Edwards, J. and Borduin, C. (1987) The Family Relations of Female Juvenile Delinquents. *Journal of Abnormal Child Psychology,* 15(2) 199–209.

Henington, C., Hughes, J.N., Cavell, T.A. and Thompson, B. (1998) The Role of Relational Aggression in Identifying Aggressive Boys and Girls. *Journal of School Psychology,* 36: 4, 457–77.

Higgs, D.C., Canavan, M.M. and Meyer, W.J. (1992) Moving from Defense to Offence: The Development of an Adolescent Female Sex Offender. *The Journal of Sex Research,* 29: 1, 131–9.

Howley, D. (2001) *A Descriptive Study of Sexually Abusive Female Juveniles in Residential Treatment.* Workshop Presented at The National Adolescent Perpetration Network Annual Conference, Kansas City, Missouri.

Huesmann, L.R. and Guerra, N.G. (1997) Children's Normative Beliefs about Aggression and Aggressive Behaviour. *Journal of Personality and Social Psychology,* 72, 408–19.

Huesmann, L.R. et al. (1992) Differing Normative Beliefs about Aggression for Boys and Girls. In Bjorkqvist, K. and Niemela, P. (Eds) *Of Mice and Women: Aspects of Female Aggression.* New York: Academic Press.

Hunter, J.A. and Mathews, R. (1997) Sexual Deviance in Females. In Laws, R.D. and O'Donohue, W. (Eds.) *Sexual Deviance: Theory, Assessment and Treatment.* New York: The Guilford Press.

Hunter, J.A. et al. (2003) Juvenile Sex Offenders: Toward the Development of a Typology. *Sexual Abuse: A Journal of Research and Treatment,* 15: 1, 27–48.

Hunter, J.A. et al. (1993) Psychosexual, Attitudinal and Developmental Characteristics of Juvenile Female Sexual Perpetrators in a Residential Treatment Setting. *Journal of Child and Family Studies,* 2, 317–26.

Jessor, R. et al. (1995) Protective Factors in Adolescent Problem Behaviour: Moderator

Effects and Developmental Change. *Developmental Psychology*, 31, 923–33.

Johnson, T.C. (1989) Female Child Perpetrators: Children who Molest other Children. *Child Abuse and Neglect*, 13, 571–89.

Jordan, J.V. (1991) *Women's Growth in Connection: Writings from the Stone Center*. New York: Guilford Press.

Kahn, T.J. and Chambers, H.J. (1991) Assessing Reoffence Risk with Juvenile Sexual Offenders. *Child Welfare*, 70, 333–45.

Keltikangas-Jaervinen, L. and Pakaslahti, L. (1999) Development of Social Problem-Solving Strategies and Changes in Aggressive Behaviour: A 7-Year Follow-Up from Childhood to Late Adolescence. *Aggressive Behaviour*, 25: 4, 269–79.

Knight, R.A. and Prentky, R.A. (1990) Classifying Sexual Offenders: The Development and Corroboration of Taxonomic Models. In Marshall, W.L., Laws, D.R. and Barbaree, H.E. (Eds.) *The Handbook of Sexual Assault: Issues, Theories and Treatment of the Offender*. New York: Plenum.

Knight, R.A. and Prentky, R.A. (1993) Exploring Characteristics for Classifying Juvenile Sex Offenders. In Barbaree, H.E., Marshall, W.L. and Hudson, S.M. (Eds.) *The Juvenile Sex Offender*. New York: The Guilford Press.

Kohlberg, L. (1981) *The Philosophy of Moral Development*. San Francisco: Harper and Row.

Kubik, E.K., Hecker, J.E. and Righthand, S. (2002) Adolescent Females who have Sexually Offended: Comparison with Delinquent Adolescent Female Offenders and Adolescent Males who Sexually Offend. *Journal of Child Sexual Abuse*, 11: 3, 63–85.

Lab, S.P., Shields, G. and Schondel, C. (1993) Research Note: An Evaluation of Juvenile Sexual Offender Treatment. *Crime and Delinquency*, 39, 543–53.

Lamb, S. (2001) *The Secret Lives of Girls: What Good Girls Really Do: Sex Play, Aggression and Their Guilt*. New York: The Free Press.

Lanctot, N. and Le Blanc, M. (2002) Explaining Adolescent Females' Involvement in Deviance. *Crime and Justice: An Annual Review*, 29, 113–202.

Lanctot, N., Emond, C. and Le Blanc, M. (2004) Adjudicated Females' Participation in Violence from Adolescence to Adulthood. In Moretti, M.M., Odgers, C.L. and Jackson, M.A. (Eds.) *Girls and Aggression: Contributing Factors and Intervention Principles*. New York: Kluwer Academic/Plenum.

Lerner, H.G. (1988) *Women in Therapy*. New York: Harperperennial.

Leschied, A.W. et al. (2002) Correlates of Aggression with Adolescent Girls. In Cummings, A.L. and Leschied, A.W. (Eds.) *Research and Treatment for Aggression with Adolescent Girls*. Queenston, ON: The Edwin Mellen Press.

Leschied, A. et al. (2000) *Female Adolescent Aggression: A Review of the Literature and the Correlates of Aggression* (User Report No. 2000-04) Ottawa: Solicitor General Canada.

Levene, K.S. et al. (2001) *Early Assessment Risk List for Girls, Earl-21G (Version 1 – Consultation Edition)* Toronto, ON: Earlscourt Child and Family Centre.

Levinson, D. (1978) *The Seasons of a Man's Life*. New York: Alfred A. Knopf.

Lewis, D.O. et al. (1991) A Follow-up of Female Delinquents: Maternal Contributions to the Perpetuation of Deviance. *Journal of The American Academy of Child and Adolescent Psychiatry*, 30: 2, 197–202.

Little, T.D. et al. (2003) Rethinking Aggression: A Typological Examination of the Functions of Aggression. *Merrill-Palmer Quarterly*, 49, 343–69.

Liu, X. and Kaplan, H.B. (1999) Explaining the Gender Difference in Adolescent Delinquent Behaviour: A Longitudinal Test of Mediating Mechanisms. *Criminology*, 37, 195.

Loeber, R. and Keenan, K. (1994) The Interaction between Conduct Disorder and its Comorbid Conditions: Effects of Age and Gender. *Clinical Psychology Review*, 14, 497–523.

Loeber, R. and Stouthamer-Loeber, M. (1998) Development of Juvenile Aggression and Violence: Some Common Misconceptions and Controversies. *American Psychologist*, 53: 2, 242–59.

Mailloux, D.L. (1999) *Victimisation, Coping and Psychopathy: Associations with Violent Behaviour among Female Offenders*. Unpublished Manuscript, Carleton University.

Mannuzza, S. and Gittelman, R. (1984) The Adolescent Outcome of Hyperactive Girls. *Psychiatry Research*, 13, 19–29.

Margolin, L. (1991) Child Sexual Abuse by Nonrelated Caregivers. *Child Abuse and Neglect*, 15, 213–21.

Marshall, W.L. and Eccles, A. (1993) Pavlovian Conditioning Processes in Adolescent Sex Offenders. In Barbaree, H.E., Marshall, W.L. and Hudson, S.M. (Eds.) *Juvenile Sex Offending*. New York: Guilford Press.

Marshall, W.L., Hudson, S.M. and Hodkinson, S. (1993) The Importance of Attachment Bonds in the Development of Juvenile Sex Offending. In Barbaree, H.E., Marshall, W.L. and Hudson, S.M. (Eds.) *Juvenile Sex Offending*. New York: The Guilford Press.

Mathews, R. Matthews, J.K. and Speltz, K. (1989) *Female Sexual Offenders: An Exploratory Study*. Orwell, VT: Safer Society Press.

Mathews, R., Hunter, J.A. and Vuz, J. (1997) Juvenile Female Sexual Offenders: Clinical Characteristics and Treatment Issues. *Sexual Abuse: A Journal of Research and Treatment*, 9: 3, 187–200.

Mathews, R., Matthews, J. and Speltz, K. (1990) Female Sexual Offenders. In Hunter, M. (Ed.) *The Sexually Abused Male: Vol. 1. Prevalence, Impact and Treatment*. New York: Lexington Books.

Matthews, J.K. (1993) Working with Female Sexual Abusers. In Elliott, M. (Ed.) *Female Sexual Abuse of Children*. New York: The Guilford Press.

McCarty, L. (1986) Mother-Child Incest: Characteristics of the Offender. *Child Welfare*, 65: 5, 447–58.

McElvaine, R.S. (2001) *Eve's Seed: Biology, the Sexes and the Course of History*. New York: McGraw Hill.

Mears, D.P., Ploeger, M. and Warr, M. (1998) Explaining the Gender Gap in Delinquency: Peer Influence and Moral Evaluations of Behaviour. *Journal of Research in Crime and Delinquency*, 35, 251–66.

Miccio-Fonseca, L.C. (1997) *Personal Sentence Completion Inventory: User's Guide*. Brandon, VT: Safer Society Press.

Miccio-Fonseca, L.C. (2000) Adult and Adolescent Female Sex Offenders: Experiences Compared to other Female and Male Sex Offenders. *Journal of Psychology and Human Sexuality*, 11: 3, 75–88.

Miller, J.B. and Stiver, I.P. (1997) *The Healing Connection: How Women Form Relationships in Therapy and in Life*. Boston, MA: Beacon Press.

Miller, P.A. and Eisenberg, N. (1988) The Relation of Empathy to Aggressive and Externalising/Antisocial Behaviour. *Psychological Bulletin*, 103, 324–44.

Minasian, G. and Lewis, A.D. (1999) Female Sexual Abusers: An Unrecognised Culture. In Lewis, A.D. (Ed.) *Cultural Diversity in Sexual Abuser Treatment: Issues and Approaches*. Brandon, VT: Safer Society Press.

Moffitt, T.E. et al. (2001) *Sex Differences in Antisocial Behaviour: Conduct Disorder, Delinquency and Violence in the Dunedin Longitudinal Study*. Cambridge: Cambridge University Press.

Moretti, M.M., Dasilva, K. and Holland, R. (2004) Aggression from an Attachment Perspective: Gender Issues and Therapeutic Implications. In Moretti, M.M., Odgers, C.L. and Jackson, M.A. (Eds.) *Girls and Aggression: Contributing Factors and Intervention Principles*. New York: Kluwer Academic/Plenum.

National Center on Addiction and Substance Abuse at Columbia University (2003) *The Formative Years: Pathways to Substance Abuse among Girls and Young Women, Ages 8–22*. New York: Author.

National Clearinghouse for Alcohol and Drug Information (2001) Retrieved November 10, 2001, From Http://Www.Health.Org/Govpubs/

O'Connor, A. (1987) Female Sex Offenders. *British Journal of Psychiatry*, 150, 615–20.

Obeidallah, D.A. and Earls, F.J. (1999) *Adolescent Girls: The Role of Depression in the Development of Delinquency*. Washington, DC: US Department of Justice.

Odgers, C.L. (2005) *Violence, Victimisation and Psychopathy among Female Juvenile Offenders*. University of Virginia.

Odgers, C.L. and Moretti, M. (2002) Aggressive and Antisocial Girls: Research Update and Future Research Challenges. *International Journal of Forensic and Mental Health*, 2, 17–33.

Odgers, C.L., Moretti, M.M. and Reppucci, N.D. (2005) Examining the Science and Practice of Violence Risk Assessment with Female Adolescents. *Law and Human Behaviour*, 29: 1, 7–26.

Odgers, C.L., Schmidt, M.G. and Reppucci, N.D. (2004) Reframing Violence Risk Assessment for Female Juvenile Offenders. In Moretti, M.M., Odgers, C.L. and Jackson, M.A. (Eds.) *Girls and Aggression: Contributing Factors and Intervention Principles*. New York: Kluwer Academic/Plenum.

Office of Juvenile Justice and Delinquency Prevention (1998, October) *Guiding Principles from Promising Female Programming: An Inventory of Best Practices*. Washington, DC: Author.

Orenstein, P. (1994) *Schoolgirls: Young Women, Self-Esteem and the Confidence Gap*. New York: Harperperennial.

Owens, L.D. and MacMullin, C.E. (1995) Gender Differences in Aggression in Children and Adolescents in South Australian Schools. *International Journal of Adolescence and Youth*, 6, 21–35.

Paikoff, R.L., Brooks-Gunn, J. and Warren, M.P. (1991) Effects of Girls' Hormonal Status on Depressive and Aggressive Symptoms over the Course of One Year. *Journal of Youth and Adolescence*, 20, 191–215.

Pajer, K.A. (1998) What Happens to Bad Girls? A Review of Adult Outcomes of Antisocial Adolescent Girls. *American Journal of Psychiatry*, 155, 862–70.

Perry, B.D. (1997) Incubated in Terror: Neurodevelopmental Factors in the 'Cycle of Violence.' In Osofsky, J.D. (Ed.) *Children, Youth and Violence: Searching for Solutions*. New York: Guilford Press.

Perry, B.D. et al. (1995) Childhood Trauma, the Neurobiology of Adaptation and 'Use-Dependent' Development of the Brain: How 'States' Become 'Traits.' *Infant Mental Health Journal*, 16: 4, 271–91.

Piers, E.V. and Herzberg, D.S. (2003) *Piers-Harris 2: Piers-Harris Children's Self-Concept Scale*, 2nd Edn. Los Angeles, CA: Western Psychological Services.

Pipher, M. (1994) Reviving Ophelia: Saving the Selves of Adolescent Girls. New York: Ballantine Books.

Prentky, R. and Righthand, S. (2003) *The Juvenile Sex Offender Assessment Protocol-II (J-SOAP-II) Manual*. Retrieved January 16, 2004, from Http://Www.Ncjrs.Org/Pdffiles1/Ojjdp/202316.Pdf

Prentky, R. et al. (2004) Risky Behaviours in Abuse Reactive, Sexually Coercive Children and Adolescents: Base Rates and Trends across Three Developmental Epochs and Risk Implications. Paper presented at The 23rd Annual Meeting of The Association for the Treatment of Sexual Abusers, Albuquerque, New Mexico.

Prentky, R. et al. (2000) An Actuarial Procedure for Assessing Risk with Juvenile Sex Offenders. *Sexual Abuse: A Journal of Research and Treatment*, 12: 2, 71–93.

Rasmussen, L.A. (1999) Factors Related to Recidivism among Juvenile Sexual Offenders. *Sexual Abuse: A Journal of Research and Treatment*, 69–85.

Ray, J.A. and English, D.J. (1995) Comparison of Female and Male Children with Sexual Behaviour Problems. *Journal of Youth and Adolesence*, 24: 4, 439–51.

Reynolds, W.M. (2002) *Reynolds Adolescent Depression Scale*. 2nd Edn, Lutz, FL: Psychological Assessment Resources.

Rich, A. (1982) *Compulsory Heterosexuality and Lesbian Existence*. Denver, CO: Antelope Publications.

Robinson, S. (2002) *Growing Beyond: A Workbook for Sexually Abusive Teenage Girls*. Holyoke, MA: NEARI Press.

Robinson, S. (2006) Adolescent Females with Sexual Behaviour Problems: What Constitutes Best Practice. In Longo, R.E. and Prescott, D.S. (Eds.) *Current Perspectives: Working with Sexually Aggressive Youth and Youth with Sexual Behaviour Problems*. Holyoke, MA: NEARI Press.

Rowe, D.C., Vazsonyi, A.T. and Flannery, D.J. (1995) Sex Differences in Crime: Do Means and Within-Sex Variation have Similar Causes? *Journal of Research in Crime and Delinquency*, 32, 84–100.

Rutter, M. (1986) The Developmental Psychopathology of Depression: Issues and Perspectives. In Rutter, M., Issard, C. and Reads, P. (Eds.) *Depression in Young People: Developmental and Clinical Perspectives*. New York: Guilford Press.

Ryan, G. (1998) The Relevance of Early Life Experience to the Behaviour of Sexually Abusive Youth. *The Irish Journal of Psychology*, 19: 1, 32–48.

Ryan, G. (2003) Hindsight: Cause for Change or Respite from Fear? *Journal of Sexual Aggression*, 9: 2, 125–33.

Sadker, M. and Sadker, D. (1994) *Failing at Fairness: How Our Schools Cheat Girls*. New York: Touchstone.

Salekin, R.T., Rogers, R. and Sewell, K.W. (1996) A Review and Meta-Analysis of the Psychopathy Checklist and Psychopathy Checklist-Revised: Predictive Validity of Dangerousness. *Clinical Psychology: Science and Practice*, 3, 203–15.

Salekin, R.T. et al. (1998) Psychopathy and Recidivism among Female Inmates. *Law and Human Behaviour*, 22: 1, 109–28.

Salzman, J.P. (1990) Save the World, Save Myself: Responses to Problematic Attachment. In Gilligan, C., Lyons, N.P. and Hammer, T.J. (Eds.) *Making Connections: The Relational Worlds of Adolescent Girls at Emma Willard School*. Cambridge, MA: Harvard University Press.

Saradjian, J. and Hanks, H. (1996) *Women who Sexually Abuse Children: From Research to Clinical Practice.* New York: John Wiley and Sons.

Scavo, R.R. (1989, February) Female Adolescent Sexual Offenders: A Neglected Treatment Group. *Social Casework: The Journal of Contemporary Social Work,* 114–7.

Shandler, S. (1999) *Ophelia Speaks: Adolescent Girls Write about Their Search for Self.* New York: Harperperennial.

Simmons, R. (2002) *Odd Girl Out: The Hidden Culture of Aggression in Girls.* New York: Harcourt.

Sipe, R., Jensen, E.L. and Everett, R.S. (1998) Adolescent Sexual Offenders Grown Up: Recidivism in Young Adulthood. *Criminal Justice and Behaviour,* 25, 109–24.

Smith, W.R. and Monastersky, C. (1986) Assessing Juvenile Sexual Offenders' Risk for Reoffending. *Criminal Justice and Behaviour,* 13, 115–40.

Snyder, H.N. (2005) *Juvenile Arrests 2003.* Washington, DC: Office of Juvenile Justice and Delinquency Prevention, US Department of Justice.

Solomon, A. (2001) *The Noonday Demon: An Atlas of Depression.* New York: Touchstone.

Stern, L. (1991) Disavowing the Self in Female Adolescence. In Gilligan, C., Rogers, A.G. and Tolman, D.L. (Eds.) *Women, Girls and Psychotherapy: Reframing Resistance.* New York: Harrington Park Press.

Surrey, J.L. (1991) The 'Self-In-Relation': A Theory of Women's Development. In Jordan, J.V. et al. (Eds.) *Women's Growth in Connection: Writings from the Stone Center.* New York: The Guilford Press.

Syed, F. and Williams, S. (1996, December) *Case Studies of Female Sex Offenders in The Correctional Service of Canada* [On-Line]. Available: Http://Www.Csc-Scc.Gc.Ca/Sexoff/Female/English/Female-09.Htm

Szatmari, P., Boyle, M. and Offord, D.R. (1989) ADHD and CD: Degree of Diagnostic Overlap and Difference among Correlates. *Journal of The American Academy of Child and Adolescent Psychiatry,* 28, 865–72.

Thompson, S. (1990) Putting a Big Thing Into a Little Hole: Teenage Girls' Accounts of Sexual Initiation. *Journal of Sex Research,* 27, 341–61.

Thompson, S. (1995) *Going All The Way: Teenage Girls' Tales of Sex, Romance and Pregnancy.* New York: Farrar, Straus and Giroux.

Tolman, D.L. (1991) Adolescent Girls, Women and Sexuality: Discerning Dilemmas of Desire. In Gilligan, C., Rogers, A.G. and Tolman, D.L. (Eds.) *Women, Girls and Psychotherapy: Reframing Resistance.* Binghamton, NY: Harrington Park Press.

Tolman, D.L. (1994) Daring to Desire: Culture and the Bodies of Adolescent Girls. In Irvine, J.M. (Ed.) *Sexual Cultures and the Construction of Adolescent Identities.* Philadelphia, PA: Temple University.

Tolman, D.L. (1999) Female Adolescent Sexuality in Relational Context: Beyond Sexual Decision Making. In Johnson, N.G., Roberts, M.C. and Worell, J. (Ed.) *Beyond Appearance: A New Look at Adolescent Girls.* Washington, DC: American Psychological Association.

Tolman, D.L. (2001) Female Adolescent Sexuality: An Argument for a Developmental Perspective on the New View of Women's Sexual Problems. In Kaschak, E. and Tiefer, L. (Eds.) *A New View of Women's Sexual Problems.* Binghamton, NY: Haworth Press.

Tolman, D.L. (2002) *Dilemmas of Desire: Teenage Girls Talk about Sexuality.* Cambridge, MA: Harvard University Press.

Tremblay, R.E. et al. (2004) Physical Aggression during Early Childhood: Trajectories and Predictors. *Pediatrics,* 114, 43–9.

Turner, M.T. and Turner, T.N. (1994) *Female Adolescent Sexual Abusers: An Exploratory Study of Mother-Daughter Dynamics with Implications for Treatment.* Brandon, VT: Safer Society Press.

Verona, E. and Vitale, J. (2006) Psychopathy in Women: Assessment, Manifestations and Etiology. In Patrick, C.J. (Ed.) *Handbook of Psychopathy.* New York: Guilford Press.

Vitale, J.E. and Newman, J.P. (2001) Using the Psychopathy Checklist-Revised with Female Samples: Reliability, Validity and Implications for Clinical Utility. *Clinical Psychology: Science and Practice,* 8: 1, 118–32.

Ward, T. et al. (1995) Attachment Style and Intimacy Deficits in Sexual Offenders: A Theoretical Framework. *Sexual Abuse: A Journal of Research and Treatment,* 7: 4, 317–35.

Wolf, N. (1997) *Promiscuities: The Secret Struggle for Womanhood.* New York: Random House.

Wood, J. et al. (2002) Violence Exposure and PTSD among Delinquent Girls. In Greenwal, R. (Ed.) *Trauma and Juvenile Delinquency: Theory, Research and Interventions.* New York: Haworth Press.

Worling, J.R. and Curwen, T. (2000) Adolescent Sexual Offender Recidivism: Success of Specialised Treatment and Implications for Risk Prediction. *Child Abuse and Neglect*, 24, 965–82.

Worling, J.R. and Curwen, T. (2001) The 'ERASOR' (Estimate of Risk of Adolescent Sexual Offence Recidivism – Version 2.0) Thistletown Regional Centre: SAFE-T Program.

Young-Eisendrath, P. (1999) *Women and Desire: Beyond Wanting to be Wanted*. New York: Harmony Books.

Zahn-Waxler, C., Cole, P.M. and Barrett, K.C. (1991) Guilt and Empathy: Sex Differences and Implications for the Development of Depression. In Garber, J. and Dodge, K.A. (Eds.) *The Development of Emotional Regulation and Dysregulation*. Cambridge: Cambridge University Press.

Zoccolillo, M. (1993) Gender and the Development of Conduct Disorder. *Development and Psychopathology*, 5, 65–78.

Zoccolillo, M. and Rogers, K. (1991) Characteristics and Outcome of Hospitalised Adolescent Girls with Conduct Disorder. *Journal of The American Academy of Child and Adolescent Psychiatry*, 30, 973–81.

Zoccolillo, M., Tremblay, R. and Vitaro, F. (1996) DSM-III-R and DSM-III Criteria for Conduct Disorder in Preadolescent Girls: Specific but Insensitive. *Journal of The American Academy of Child and Adolescent Psychiatry*, 35, 461–70.

# CHAPTER 6

# The Assessment of Young People with Learning Disabilities who Sexually Harm Others

*Rachel Fyson*

## Introduction

The inclusion of a separate chapter concerning the assessment of young people with learning disabilities who sexually abuse has the aim of providing useful background information for professionals who may find themselves working with these particular young people. As such, the chapter is both essential reading and an unnecessary diversion: essential because of the increasing awareness that young people with learning disabilities make up a significant proportion of all young people who sexually harm others; a diversion because the assessment and risk management of such young people is fundamentally no different from that of other young abusers.

> *As a group, individuals categorised as having 'mental retardation' are at-risk for a number of co-occurring factors that, individually or in combination, might explain an increased statistical risk for sexual offences. These factors include increased risk for having been sexually abused, lack of sexual knowledge, limited opportunities for appropriate sexual expression, or simply being more likely to be caught.*
>
> (McCurrey et al., 1998: 23)

There is, as yet, no definitive answer to the question of whether young people with learning disabilities are more likely or less likely than their non-learning disabled peers to sexually harm others. Young people are known to be the perpetrators of somewhere between one quarter and one third of all recorded sexual offences in the UK (Home Office Statistical Bulletin, 2005 and 2006; Cawson et al., 2000; Grubin 1998; Glasgow et al., 1994) a proportion which rises to almost two-thirds when figures for police cautions and reprimands, rather than just court convictions, are included in the analysis (Erooga and Masson, 2006). Within this population of young people who sexually harm others, there is a significant over-representation of young people with learning disabilities. Although young people with learning disabilities who sexually harm others have much in common with their non-learning disabled peers, there may also be some significant differences between the two groups. More importantly, professionals who come across young people with learning disabilities who sexually harm others will need to adopt approaches to assessment and case management which recognise the significance of impairments to cognitive and social functioning which are associated with learning disabilities, whilst not allowing these to be used as an excuse for the harm which has been caused to others.

This chapter will start by presenting some of the research evidence which supports the assertion that learning disabilities are more prevalent within clinical populations of young people who sexually harm than they are within the general population. It will then move on to examine more closely how the term 'learning disability' is currently defined; how practitioners can begin to determine whether a particular young person does or does not have a learning disability; and to explore the social and sexual development of young people with learning disabilities. It will conclude with a description of some of the assessment frameworks currently used in the UK for the assessment of young people who sexually harm; a critique of their use with young people with learning disabilities; and an overview of some key issues for non-specialist practitioners who may find themselves working with such young people.

## Prevalence of learning disabilities amongst populations of young people who sexually harm others

> *One of the key changes in the response to adolescent sexual aggression over the past decade is a rapid increase in the number of young people with learning disabilities being identified and referred for intervention.*
>
> (Hackett, 2004: 44)

The reason for this sudden increase in the number of young people with learning disabilities being identified as sexual abusers is at present unclear, although it is unlikely to represent a sudden change in behaviours amongst this group of young people (Balogh et al., 2001). However, the fact that young people with learning disabilities are, for whatever reason, significantly over-represented amongst clinical populations of young people who sexually harm cannot be doubted.

Overviews of the literature on young people who sexually harm others have consistently identified learning disabilities and poor school achievement as common characteristics (DoH, 2006; Erooga and Masson, 2006; Hackett, 2004; Lovell, 2002; Bailey and Boswell, 2002; Vizard et al., 1995). A number of empirical studies undertaken in the UK have confirmed these observations. In 1996 a prevalence survey of juvenile sexual offending in Oxfordshire reported that 58.1 per cent of the individuals identified were of 'below average ability' (James and Neil, 1996). Given that in a normal distribution one would expect to find 50 per cent above and 50 per cent below average ability, this indicates a significant, but not overwhelming, over-representation of young people with learning disabilities amongst populations of young people who sexually abuse.

Other studies, however, have found a far greater over-representation of learning disabilities – particularly those based on studies of young people who sexually harm others who had been referred to clinical services or other specialist treatment. A retrospective analysis of young people referred to an adolescent forensic unit because of their sexually harmful behaviour reported that learning disabilities were indicated in 45 per cent of cases (Dolan et al., 1996); this included 38 per cent who were categorised as having mild learning disabilities, 5.8 per cent who had moderate learning disabilities and 1.6 per cent with severe learning disabilities. An analysis of referrals to a specialist assessment and treatment facility for young people who sexually harm (Manocha and Mezey, 1998) found that one third (33.3 per cent) were poor academic achievers, including one fifth (19.6 per cent) who had a formal diagnosis of learning disability. Another specialist service reported that half of the referrals they received related to young people with some degree of learning disability (O'Callaghan, 1998); and an evaluation of a

therapeutic community for young men who sexually harm others found that fully 80 per cent of those who completed the therapeutic programme had been assessed as having mild, moderate or serious learning disabilities (Boswell and Wedge, 2002). More recently, a survey of UK services for young people who sexually harm others (Masson and Hackett, 2003 and 2004) reported high rates of learning disability amongst juvenile sexual offenders known to youth offending teams; over half of these teams (53 per cent) estimated that at least one quarter of the juvenile sexual offenders with whom they worked had mild or moderate learning disabilities, and a further 18 per cent of teams reported even higher proportions of learning disability within juvenile sex offender programmes.

The figures cited in the above studies suggest that the prevalence of learning disabilities amongst populations of young people who sexually harm others is far higher than the prevalence of learning disabilities amongst the general population, which is estimated at 25 per 1,000 population – or 1.2 million people in England (DoH, 2001). However, several authors have urged caution in the interpretation of such findings, pointing out that studies based on clinical samples or on referrals to specialist treatment services are not necessarily representative of general populations of young people who sexually harm others (Hackett, 2004; Balogh et al., 2001; O'Callaghan, 1999; Hoghughi, 1997). Research shows that professionals who work with children and young people often feel that they lack the skills or knowledge to work with young people who sexually harm others (Ladwa-Thomas and Sanders, 1999). More particularly, there is evidence to suggest that, where sexually harmful behaviour is indicated, professionals working in both child protection and youth offending teams lack confidence in their own abilities to work effectively with these young people if they also have a learning disability (Fyson, 2007a; Fyson, 2005; Vail 2002). This may therefore make child protection and youth offending professionals more likely to refer a young person with learning disabilities on to more specialised services, whether or not this is warranted by the behaviours exhibited or other risk factors. Other authors have further suggested that young people with learning disabilities are more likely than other juvenile sexual offenders to be diverted away from the criminal justice system and into treatment facilities (Gilbey et al., 1989; O'Callaghan, 1999).

There are other factors, however, which suggest that the over-representation of learning disabilities amongst populations of young people who sexually harm may be both actual and expected. In particular, attention must be paid to the complex links between disability and abuse. Although there is not a simple, direct or linear relationship between experiencing abuse as a child and going on to sexually harm others (Freidrich, 1998) it is known that prior experiences as victims of abuse and neglect are common amongst populations of young people who sexually abuse others. Research indicates that whilst between one quarter and one third of these young people have themselves been victims of sexual abuse (Manocha and Mezey, 1998; Dolan et al., 1996; James and Neil, 1996) an even greater proportion have experienced physical abuse, emotional abuse and neglect (Bentovim and Williams, 1998; Dolan et al., 1996; James and Neil, 1996). The fact of a connection between being a victim of abuse and becoming a perpetrator of sexual abuse is important, even if we do not yet fully understand the precise dynamics of the relationship. This finding is particularly important in relation to young people with learning disabilities who sexually abuse others because it is well-established that children and young people with disabilities are more likely than non-disabled children to experience abuse of all kinds (HM Government, 2006; Westcott and Jones, 1999; Sullivan and Knutson, 1998 and 2000; NSPCC, 2003; Kelly, 1992); that disability is associated with longer durations of abuse (Westcott and Jones, 1999); and that disability is associated with less active interventions from statutory child protection services following disclosure of abuse (Cooke and Standen, 2002; Cooke, 2000). It is therefore reasonable to suppose that the over-representation of young people with learning disabilities amongst populations of young people who sexually harm others is connected to, amongst other things, the higher levels of victimisation amongst this group.

The limited number of published studies which have specifically examined the experiences of young people with learning disabilities who sexually harm others have noted very high rates of previous victimisation. For example, Fyson (2007a, 2005) found that 13 out of 15 of the young people with learning disabilities in her sample had either disclosed abuse or were believed by

professionals working with them to have been abused (because, for example, they had lived with a schedule one offender), figures which included 3 young people who had been placed in foster care following abuse within the birth family. Balogh et al. (2001) noted that, of 22 young people with learning disabilities known to have been perpetrators of sexual abuse, 16 had previously been victims of sexual abuse; this included five female perpetrators, all of whom had previously been victims. Based on the same sample of admissions to a psychiatric service, Firth et al. (2001) explored the experiences of young people with learning disabilities who sexually abused others in more detail. They found that 'perpetrators could be distinguished by whether they had suffered sexual abuse alone, sexual and physical abuse, or neither' (ibid, p. 244) and their findings suggest that a history of physical abuse, with or without a history of sexual abuse, was associated with the sexual abuse of younger victims.

## Characteristics of young people with learning disabilities who sexually harm others

There are a great deal more similarities than differences between young people with and without learning disabilities who sexually harm others. As noted above, both groups are more likely than non-abusers to have experienced both physical and sexual abuse. They are also similarly likely to have personal histories which involve family dysfunction and neglect (Sternac and Sheridan, 1993; O'Callaghan, 1998; McCurrey et al., 1998); intimacy deficits (Barbaree et al., 1998); and attachment insecurity (Smallbone, 2005). Whilst there are also some identifiable differences between the two groups which are worth exploring it must be remembered that these are *group* differences, which may or may not be evident in relation to any *particular* young person.

Relatively little research has yet been undertaken which has sought to shed light on the distinguishing characteristics of young people with learning disabilities who sexually harm, but those few which have done so have produced a remarkably consistent pattern of findings. The following three signifiers are the clearest areas of difference between young learning disabled and non-learning disabled abusers:

1. *Gender of victim*

   Gilbey, Wolf and Goldenberg (1989) were the first authors to note that adolescents with a learning disability appeared to be less discriminating in their choice of victim than non-learning disabled abusers. Their study of adolescents referred to a specialist psychiatric service found that adolescents with a learning disability had offended equally against male and female victims, and that in 30 per cent of cases there had been victims of both gender. More recent studies (Balogh, 2001; Tudiver and Griffin, 1992) have found a similar lack of gender preference amongst young people with learning disabilities who sexually abuse, a finding which has also been evident in studies of men with learning disabilities who sexually abuse (Thompson and Brown, 1997).

2. *Nuisance behaviours*

   In the same seminal study, Gilbey et al. (1989) also noted that although learning disabled and non-learning disabled young abusers were equally likely to have committed serious sexual assaults, those with a learning disability were significantly more likely to have exhibited acts classified as non-contact nuisance behaviours – including voyeurism, exposure of genitals and public masturbation. Fyson (2007a and 2005) likewise noted high levels of sexually inappropriate behaviour between pupils in special schools, but this only very seldom developed into behaviours which might constitute a sexual offence.

3. *Impulsivity*

   Both the findings with regard to gender of victim and those which relate to nuisance behaviour suggest that young people with learning disabilities may have a greater tendency than other young abusers to act on impulse rather than in a premeditated manner. A number of authors have suggested that impulse plays a significant role in the abusive acts perpetrated by young people with learning disabilities, not least because this is a characteristic which is also known to be associated with poor social skills (Hackett, 2004; Timms and Goreczny, 2002; O'Callaghan, 1998 and 1999; Sternac and Sheridan, 1993; Tudiver and Griffin, 1992).

## Defining 'learning disability'

One of the many factors which make working with young people with learning disabilities so challenging is the lack of clarity over the term 'learning disability' itself. This has arisen in part because ongoing attempts to avoid labels which stigmatise have resulted in relatively rapid changes in nomenclature. Terms such as 'idiot', 'imbecile' and 'moron' which, in living memory, were used as meaningful medical categories are now understood as offensive and insulting terms of abuse. Until the 1980s the term 'mental handicap' was commonly used in the UK, but has since fallen out of favour.

### Social and educational definitions of learning disability

The most established current (non-medical) definition of learning disability is that found in the *Valuing People* White Paper, which set out the Government's plans for improving services to children and adults with learning disabilities (DoH, 2001). It states that:

> *Learning disability includes the presence of:*
> - *A significantly reduced ability to understand new or complex information, to learn new skills (impaired intelligence).*
> - *A reduced ability to cope independently (impaired social functioning).*
> - *Which started before adulthood, with a lasting effect on development.*
>
> *This definition encompasses people with a broad range of disabilities. The presence of a low intelligence quotient, for example an IQ below 70, is not, of itself, a sufficient reason for deciding whether an individual should be provided with additional health and social care support. An assessment of social functioning and communication skills should also be taken into account when determining need. Many people with learning disabilities also have physical and/or sensory impairments. The definition covers adults with autism who also have learning disabilities, but not those with a higher level autistic spectrum disorder who may be of average or even above average intelligence – such as some people with Asperger's Syndrome.*
>
> *'Learning disability' does not include all those who have a 'learning difficulty', which is more broadly defined in education legislation.*
>
> (DoH, 2001: 14)

The above definition is not simple or straightforward, but it does help by stating the two factors which need to be present for an individual to be assessed as having some degree of learning disability – ie impaired intelligence *and* impaired social functioning. It also alludes to some of the confounding factors which can make inter-professional communication prone to misunderstandings; in particular, it precludes 'learning difficulty' from being used as a synonym for 'learning disability'. In this definition, a 'learning difficulty' is a problem which affects a specific area of learning and would therefore include conditions such as dyslexia (difficulties with learning to read or interpret words, letters and other symbols) and dyscalculia (difficulties with understanding and interpreting numbers) which are specific disorders that do not affect global intelligence or broader social functioning.

In professional parlance, however, the distinction between learning disability and learning difficulty is less clear, not least because, although in adult care the term 'learning disability' is used most often by services that provide social care and support, some authorities have chosen instead to call themselves 'learning difficulty' services. This is because 'learning difficulty' is the term preferred by many self-advocacy groups, who argue that this 'is a label which doesn't hurt us' (People First, 2004). Use of the term 'learning difficulty' therefore has a strong political credibility, and this has led to its adoption by some special schools as a descriptor of their pupils. In mainstream education, however, 'learning difficulties' are still usually understood to refer to dyslexia, etc. It is therefore vital that whenever a young person is described as having 'learning difficulties' that practitioners check whether or not this implies the presence of a learning disability.

A further note of caution must also be added for those seeking further information from internet sources. In a reversal of the situation in the UK, the term 'learning disability' is normally used in the United States to refer to specific conditions such as dyslexia. It is therefore advisable to use the term 'intellectual disability' for searching the internet as, at the time of writing, this term is the most widely understood and accepted internationally.

### Medical definitions of learning disability

The definition of learning disability cited above rejects the idea that psychometric measurement of intelligence, resulting in an IQ (intelligence quotient) score, can be used to determine the presence of a learning disability. However, such tests are still commonly used by psychiatrists and psychologists, particularly in cases where the criminal justice system requires 'evidence' of a

person's cognitive functioning. Chapter 9 by Craig, Stringer and Hutchinson provides a detailed analysis of IQ testing and other psychometric tests which can be used to evaluate both an individual's cognitive and social functioning. Many of the tests to which they refer have versions which are designed for use with children and young people aged under 18. For example, an adapted version of the Wechsler Adult Intelligence Scale (WAIS) has been developed for use with children and is known as the Wechsler Intelligence Scale for Children (WISC). The resulting IQ scores are often used as a convenient shorthand by which to indicate an individual's cognitive abilities, with the average IQ being 100 and the presence of a learning disability being indicated when the IQ score falls below 70.

In the UK, psychometric tests of this kind can only be administered by qualified psychiatrists or clinical psychologists, who will interpret WISC scores in light of 'all relevant information about an individual child's life and circumstances' (Weiss et al., 2006: 1). In theory, therefore, psychometric tests can provide an assessment of both intellectual abilities and social adaptation or social functioning. However, it should be noted that there has been ongoing debate concerning exactly what such tests measure (see, for example, Richardson, 2002) and their ability to accurately measure the extent of individual learning disability. Particular attention has been paid to the fact that people from some black and ethnic minority communities and people from lower socio-economic groups consistently perform less well than those of Caucasian descent and those from higher socio-economic groups.

Since the term 'learning disability' is used as a catch-all for such a wide range of abilities, it is nevertheless useful to have some way of indicating the comparative abilities of any individual. IQ is one such shorthand; as are the descriptors 'mild', 'moderate', 'severe', and 'profound'; and the concept of 'mental age'. The latter is a concept which has, rightly, fallen out of favour – implying as it does that people with learning disabilities are somehow childlike. However, 'mental age' may still be of some assistance in explaining to people new to this field the relative cognitive and social abilities of individuals in each category. This is notwithstanding the fact that adolescents and adults with learning disabilities will have had life experiences which mean that their knowledge,

**Table 6.1**   Degrees of learning disability

| IQ range | Descriptive category | Mental age | Outcome in terms of functional ability |
|---|---|---|---|
| 55–69 | mild learning disability | 9–12 years | Some problems in relation to educational attainment, but likely to be able to sustain employment and relationships in adult life |
| 40–54 | moderate learning disability | 6–9 years | Noticeable developmental delay during childhood but likely to be able to achieve some educational targets and to develop independence in relation to self care and communication. May require support to live or work outside the family home. |
| 25–39 | severe learning disability | 3–6 years | Limited ability to function independently and likely to require continuous support and/or supervision throughout life |
| 0–24 | profound learning disability | Below 3 years | Severe limitations in functional ability affecting all aspects of daily life, including self care, mobility and communication |

emotions and desires (eg for sexual relationships) can in no way be compared to that of a child.

With the above proviso, Table 6.1 is offered by way of summarising the various ways in which distinctions are commonly drawn between the differing degrees of cognitive and social impairment associated with learning disability.

## Identifying learning disability in practice

Most professionals who work with young people will, knowingly or unknowingly, come across young people with learning disabilities at some point in their career. In the past it was relatively straightforward to identify someone with a learning disability because they would have attended a special school and/or had a statement of special educational need. Nowadays, however, in many areas the majority of children and young people with learning disabilities attend mainstream schools and, furthermore, government policy is now seeking to minimise the use of statementing (DfEE, 1997; DfES, 2004) in order to reduce bureaucracy (Pinney, 2004). These shifts in policy make educational indicators increasingly unreliable as a basis for identifying young people with learning disabilities, particularly as Local Education Authorities (LEAs) vary in the extent to which they have embraced the policy of reducing statementing (Pinney, 2004). It is therefore important that all those who work with children and young people know their LEA's policy in relation to

statementing – and hence whether many or few young people with learning disabilities are likely to have a statement of special educational need.

Studies of young people who sexually harm indicate that many of those with a learning disability will not have received a formal diagnosis (Vail, 2002). For example, Masson and Hackett (2004) observed that although youth offending teams reported high rates of learning disability amongst juvenile sexual offenders, these figures were largely based on informal perceptions rather than formal, professional assessment and diagnosis by psychologists or psychiatrists. Similarly Fyson (2007a and 2005) noted that, amongst her 15 case studies of young people with learning disabilities who had shown sexually abusive behaviour, five were attending or had attended special schools, five had attended mainstream schools but had statements of special educational needs which identified the presence of a learning disability, and five were in mainstream schools without a statement – but neither school nor statementing appeared to bear much relationship to the degree of learning disability.

In many ways the fact that fewer young people are being socially stigmatised by being labelled as having a learning disability is to be welcomed (Ho, 2004; Klotz, 2004). Difficulties can arise, however, in situations where the learning disability may have contributed to a particular problem or where specialist services are required, as may be the case for young people with learning disabilities who have sexually harmed others (Fyson, Cooke and Eadie, 2003). In such instances, it is left to non-expert professionals to first notice that a young person may have a learning disability, to refer for professional diagnosis if necessary and to devise ways of working with the young person which are appropriate to their intellectual and social abilities. Identification in such circumstances is likely to be hampered by the fact that many people with mild learning disabilities are necessarily expert at hiding their impairment and 'passing for normal' (Simons, 2000; Edgerton, 1993).

## Social and sexual development of young people with learning disabilities

*The opportunities young people have available to them to explore their sexuality and develop relationships differ widely. For young people with learning disabilities these opportunities can be governed by a range of factors one of which is societal attitudes towards disability and sexuality.*
(Wheatley, 2005: 196)

The phenomenon of young people with learning disabilities, like other social issues, needs to be understood in light of the social context in which it arises. All young people growing up today are doing so in a world which bombards them with sexual imagery; it is undoubtedly true that because of their cognitive impairments young people with learning disabilities will find it harder than many of their peers to distinguish between advertising and reality, fantasy and socially acceptable behaviour. However, in addition to the difficulties which arise directly from their impaired intellectual and social functioning, young people with learning disabilities also have to cope with living in a social world which often devalues or demonises their sexuality, leaving little space for the development of 'ordinary' sexual relationships.

Although the groundbreaking work of Ann and Michael Craft (Craft and Craft, 1978) paved the way for an emerging consensus amongst professionals that people with learning disabilities should be afforded the same sexual rights as anybody else, this view has yet to gain full acceptance within wider society. Authors have continued to note that not only members of the general public, but also parents and carers often find it hard to accept that young people with learning disabilities will develop sexual desires as they pass through puberty and that it is

right that they should be able to express their sexuality and engage in sexual relationships (O'Callaghan, 1998; Craft, 1994 and 1987; Hattersley et al., 1987). Almost no research has been undertaken to explore what people with learning disabilities themselves think about sex and sexuality, although Heshusius (1987) reviewed a small number of ethnographic and/or participant observation studies which clearly showed that a majority of people with mild or moderate learning disabilities regarded sex as pleasurable, desirable and an essential part of life.

Negative societal attitudes towards disability and sexuality have arisen from powerful, yet contradictory, beliefs about people with disabilities in general and people with learning disabilities in particular (Priestly, 2003; Brown, 1994; Craft, 1987; Ryan and Thomas, 1987). On the one hand disabled people are regarded by many as asexual beings, 'eternal children' who should be protected from all sexual knowledge and prevented from engaging in sexual behaviours of any kind. This view is perhaps particularly prevalent amongst parents of children with more severe and profound disabilities, who may erroneously believe that sexual ignorance can protect their child from abuse. On the other hand is the equally powerful myth, originating from within the eugenics movement (which enjoyed popular support in the UK until after the Second World War) that people with learning disabilities possessed monstrous and abnormal sexual appetites, which must be suppressed.

Needless to say, these paradoxical beliefs have little basis in reality. In truth, the vast majority of people with learning disabilities will experience ordinary physical and sexual development, pass through puberty at the same age as their non-disabled peers and experience the same desires for both friendships and sexual relations. There are a number of chromosomal and neurodevelopmental disorders which result in either failure to reach physical sexual maturity (for example, Klinefelter's Syndrome, Prader-Willi Syndrome and Turner's Syndrome) or precocious puberty (see Siddiqui et al., 1999) but these are relatively rare conditions which affect small numbers of individuals. Any differences in socio-sexual development between young people with and without learning disabilities are therefore largely due to the different social expectations placed upon them. These differences are likely to be more pronounced when the learning disability is severe or profound and less pronounced for young people with mild or moderate learning disabilities. However, those with mild and moderate learning disabilities may be more likely than less able youngsters to engage in behaviours which cause harm to others for a number of reasons, including being under less strict supervision and being more influenced by peer pressure (Wheatley, 2005).

## Sex education

Many of the problems encountered by young people with learning disabilities are exacerbated by the fact that many have received only limited and insufficient sex education (Hackett, 2004; O'Callaghan, 1998 and 1999; Mansell et al., 1998). This is despite the fact that sex and relationship education (SRE) is a compulsory part of the educational curriculum in the UK and the fact that, in recent years, the availability of sex education resources which are designed to meet the needs of young people with learning disabilities has increased (Brook, 2007; Sex Education Forum, 2004a).

The problems arising from inadequate sex education may be particularly acute amongst young people with learning disabilities who have attended mainstream schools, where sex education classes are unlikely to have met their particular needs (Wheatley, 2005); and amongst young people who have attended pupil referral units (Sex Education Forum, 2004b). Young people who have attended special school as a consequence of their learning disability are likely to have received more comprehensive SRE. However, since these young people are also more likely to have severe or profound learning disabilities they may often find it difficult to translate what they have been taught in the classroom into everyday behaviours – particularly in situations where they are sexually aroused.

## Asperger's syndrome and autistic spectrum disorders

Although the definition of learning disability provided earlier specifically excludes people with Asperger's and other 'higher level' autistic spectrum disorders it nevertheless seems pertinent to allow some space for the consideration of autism-related influences within young people with learning disabilities who sexually harm others. Autism is a lifelong developmental disability, which is often referred to as consisting of a 'triad of impairments', the three elements being:

- *Difficulty in communicating.*
- *Difficulty in social relationships.*
- *A lack of social imagination and creative play.*
                    (National Autistic Society, 2007)

Autism affects a person's ability to communicate with other people and their ability to interpret the social environment; it is difficult for people with autism to form relationships with other people because they have little or no ability to understand other people's emotional states or to 'put themselves in someone else's shoes'. Repetitive patterns of behaviour and resistance to any change in routine are also common features of autism.

In many cases people with autism also have some degree of learning disability, but autistic traits can also be present in people with average or above-average IQ – in which case a diagnosis of Asperger's syndrome or 'high functioning' autism is usually given. People with Asperger's, unlike people with more severe forms of autism, usually have good verbal communication skills – although they may take words literally and struggle to understand idiomatic language (eg 'it's raining cats and dogs'). However, like others with autistic spectrum disorders, young people with Asperger's syndrome often exhibit obsessive behaviours and it is this aspect of the condition which may present problems in relations to sexual harm.

Anecdotal evidence suggests that young people with more severe forms of autism are particularly vulnerable to accusations of sexually abusive behaviour, much of which may not in fact be motivated by anything other than asexual sensory exploration, or ill-conceived attempts at communicating with others (Fyson, 2005). By contrast, young people with Asperger's, most of whom do not attend mainstream schools, may develop sexually harmful behaviours because 'they have difficulty judging the appropriateness of expressing a sexual behaviour in any given context' (Henault, 2006: 38) and, once established, such behaviours may become obsessive and extremely resistant to change. The high rate of dual diagnosis of Asperger's and ADHD (attention deficit hyperactivity disorder) (Gillberg et al., 2004; Gillberg and Billstedt, 2000; Clark et al., 1999) a condition strongly associated with impulsive behaviours, may be another factor which contributes to sexually harmful behaviours amongst this group.

Drawing on the work of others, Bailey (2002) suggests four reasons why young people with autism may find themselves overstepping social boundaries:

1. Social naivety which allows them to be easily led by others.
2. Distress and/or aggression following disruption of their routines.
3. Lack of understanding or misinterpretation of social clues.
4. The development of obsessions which result in criminal behaviour.

(adapted from Bailey, 2002)

There is a growing recognition that sexuality and sexual relationships is a social terrain which, because of the complex and fluid rules which govern such interactions, presents particular difficulties for young people with Asperger's (Henault, 2006, 2005, 2003). Although advice on sex education for this group of young people is beginning to emerge (Benson, 2007) working therapeutically with young people with Asperger's who have sexually harmed remains largely unresearched.

## Working with young people with learning disabilities who sexually harm others: assessment and therapeutic interventions

*Clearly management and treatment of these young people have to be planned in the light of careful assessment of their cognitive and social functioning so that, for example, treatment delivery attends to issues such as shortened attention spans, more experiential styles of learning and the need for careful use of language and repetition of messages.*

(Masson and Erooga, 1999: 8)

Any work undertaken with young people with learning disabilities who sexually harm others will, of necessity, have to take into account the degree of learning disability experienced by the individual concerned (see Table 6.1). Since learning disability is not an absolute or definitive category, but rather a relative assessment of

cognitive and social functioning as measured against population norms, there can be no absolute or definitive rules about how to approach assessment or therapeutic interventions. However, the following is offered as a starting point for considering those factors which may be of particular relevance when working with this sub-group of young people who sexually harm others.

### Background information and generic assessment tools

In the UK, most young people who sexually harm others who come to the attention of statutory services will be subject to child in need, child protection and/or youth justice assessments. Those who have entered the system via the child in need or child protection routes are likely to have undergone assessment under the *Framework for the Assessment of Children in Need and their Families* (DoH et al., 2000) whilst those who have entered the system via the youth justice route will have been assessed using the *Asset* framework (Youth Justice Board, 2000 and 2006). Whilst neither of these assessment frameworks offers an effective tool for assessing needs or risks associated with sexually harmful behaviour, both can provide background information which may be of use to professionals charged with undertaking more specific forms of assessment. However, these two assessment frameworks have been developed to serve rather different purposes and this should be borne in mind when utilising information drawn from them. It may also be worth noting that young people with learning disabilities are more likely than other young people who sexually harm to have been assessed under the *Framework for the Assessment of Children in Need and their Families*, since they are frequently diverted away from criminal justice systems (Fyson, 2007b; O'Callaghan, 1999; Gilbey et al., 1989).

Assessments undertaken under the *Framework for the Assessment of Children in Need and their Families* are used for both needs assessment and child protection purposes. Assessment is based on three distinct but inter-related domains, each of which is then further sub-divided into a number of critical dimensions:

1. *The developmental needs of children.*
2. *The capacities of parents or caregivers to respond appropriately to those needs.*

3. *The impact of wider family and environmental factors on parenting capacity and on children.*
(DoH et al., 2000: 17)

Because of its strong focus on the developmental needs of the child or young person, assessments undertaken using this framework should, in theory, be effective in assessing the impact that a learning disability has had on the young person's development and how this has, in turn, interacted with wider social and environmental factors – including social attitudes towards disability. In practice, of course, this will depend very much upon the skill of the individual carrying out the assessment. However, at the very least, such an assessment should provide some evidence of the strengths of both the young person themselves and of their family and social support system. Importantly, however, the framework has been criticised as being relatively ineffective at identifying issues relating to risk and abuse (Calder, 2001). This type of assessment would not offer sufficient depth in relation to risk and therefore should only be used in conjunction with other, more focused, assessments of sexually harmful behaviour.

By contrast *Asset* (Youth Justice Board, 2000 and 2006) which is used within Youth Offending Teams, is a structured assessment tool which aims to look at a young person's offences and identify contributory factors in order to develop effective interventions. The focus is therefore very much upon risk, albeit largely on risk of re-offending. A large-scale study of data generated using *Asset* revealed that one quarter of young offenders had special educational needs, of whom 60 per cent had been statemented (Baker et al., 2003). This suggests that this tool may be reasonably effective in identifying the presence of learning disabilities. However, it remains unclear whether this translates into effective assessment of the complex dynamics which arise between cognitive and social functioning, offending behaviours and environmental influences.

*Asset* requires assessors to consider a range of issues which together provide a 'core profile' of the young person, these being:

- Offending behaviour
- Living arrangements
- Family and personal relationships
- Education, training and employment
- Neighbourhood
- Lifestyle
- Substance use
- Physical health
- Emotional and mental health
- Perception of self and others
- Thinking and behaviour
- Attitudes to offending
- Motivation to change
- Positive factors
- Indicators of vulnerability
- Indicators of serious harm to others
(Youth Justice Board, 2006)

Several of these areas are very similar to those covered by the *Framework for the Assessment of Children in Need and their Families*. However, it should be noted that *Asset* is in part an actuarial tool – assessors are required to rank certain areas of risk on a scale of 1 to 4 and at the end of the process the scores are used to predict whether the young person will re-offend. For this reason the introduction of *Asset* to the youth justice system in 2000 led to considerable debate, particularly about the comparative merits and demerits of standardised bureaucratic approaches versus professional judgement (Baker, 2005). Even though *Asset* has been found to be 67 per cent accurate in predicting re-offending (Baker et al., 2003) the analysis does not indicate whether this statistic holds equally true for offenders with learning disabilities.

Although neither the *Framework for the Assessment of Children in Need and their Families* nor *Asset* should be used as the sole means of assessing young people with learning disabilities who sexually harm others, their value should not be dismissed. This is not least because the effective completion of either requires professionals both to establish a rapport with the young person and to make links with a variety of other professionals who may be able to contribute relevant information, including education and health services. These standard assessments may therefore provide a jumping off point for more detailed and targeted pieces of work.

## Assessment of (sexual) risk

In addition to the background information which generic social work and youth offending assessments are able to offer, assessments of young people who sexually abuse must offer a realistic appraisal of the likelihood that the sexually harmful behaviour will be repeated and whether it will escalate in seriousness. In comparison to assessments of adult sexual abusers, the assessment of young people who sexually harm may be more complex – this is because the risk that a young person poses is more dynamic, changing as the young person continues to develop and adapt, moves away from home and expands their social horizons (Epps, 1999). Such dynamic factors may be present to a greater or lesser extent in the lives of young people with learning disabilities, depending in large part upon their degree of learning disability. For example, a person aged 17 with moderate learning disabilities may (given the right opportunities) have greater scope than an average 17-year-old for further developmental progression, but at the same time may be less likely to enter employment or leave home because of the greater barriers they face in relation to attaining independence.

Assessment frameworks are designed to support professionals in their *systematic* evaluation of the risk which the young person presents to others and their attempts to balance such risks against any existing protective factors (Calder, 2001). At present, the assessment framework most widely-used in the UK is that developed by the AIM (Assessment, Intervention, Moving on) project in greater Manchester. The assessment framework itself is just one part of a comprehensive system for ensuring effective interagency working to identify and treat young people who sexually harm others (Morrison and Henniker, 2006); as such, it's focus is on identifying '. . . "strengths" and "concerns" rather than "risks"' (ibid: 37) in order that both the young person's behaviour and the context in which it occurred can be understood. Unlike *Asset*, AIM does not rely on actuarial elements, but seeks to place young abusers within a matrix, ranging from low concerns/high strengths – where low-level community-based interventions would be an appropriate response, through to high concerns/low strengths – where residential therapeutic facilities might be deemed necessary. Recent evaluation of the introduction of the AIM framework to youth offending services (Griffin and Beech, 2004) suggests that it is encouraging a more consistent response to sexually harmful behaviour amongst young people, but offers no insights into the particular needs of those with a learning disability. This is despite the fact that a version of the AIM framework has been designed specifically to meet the needs of this group (O'Callaghan, 2002, cited in Morrison and Henniker, 2006).

A number of more detailed psychometric tools have also been developed for use in assessing the risks posed by young people who sexually abuse others (Youth Justice Board, 2004; Hackett, 2004). However, it is important to note that none of these tests has yet been validated for use with young people with learning disabilities.

On a more general level, Vizard (2002) provides a useful summary of the overall structure that should be followed in the assessment of any young person who sexually harms others, proposing that there should be four key stages:

1. *The professional meeting*
2. *The assessment interview*
3. *The psychological assessment*
4. *The comprehensive report*

(Vizard, 2002: 187)

Of the above stages, the third is of particular note. Vizard argues that 'a full psychological assessment including cognitive assessment of every child and young person referred for assessment in specialist young abuser teams should be undertaken' (ibid: 192). This is because of the high incidence of learning disabilities within this population and the need to ensure appropriate management of risk; to provide information to courts on whether the young person is fit to plead; and to inform approaches to treatment.

These are all sound reasons for needing to identify the presence of a learning disability, but may require some explanation – not least because one might reasonably expect risk management and approaches to treatment to be equally relevant issues for non-learning disabled young abusers. At the most fundamental level, identifying the presence and extent of a learning disability is needed because the following issues need to be addressed:

1. Did the young person know, or could they reasonably have been expected to know, that they were harming someone else? This is the equivalent of, in a legal setting, establishing *mens rea* – ie establishing intention or knowledge of wrongdoing.
2. To what extent is the young person able to understand abstract concepts?
   - This may affect factual recall – for example dates, time, and number/frequency of events.

- It may also limit the usefulness of concepts such as the 'cycle of abuse', which in other cases might help a victim-abuser understand a pattern of events (Youth Justice Board, 2004).
- It may also limit the ability of the young person to generalise their learning from the specifics of a particular discussion.
3. How long does it take for new information to be absorbed? In many cases, people with learning disabilities are able to master quite complex ideas, but only after frequent repetition and reinforcement.

### Therapeutic interventions

There are no published empirical studies which provide clear evidence of how best to approach therapeutic interventions with young people with learning disabilities who sexually abuse, although a recent government review suggested that 'interventions should bear in mind the implications of shorter attention spans and learning based more on experience, thus requiring a more cautious use of language along with the repetition of messages' (DoH, 2006).

It is important to stress that the presence of a learning disability does not automatically mean that the young person should not be held accountable for their actions. Indeed, taking responsibility for the harm done to others may rightly be viewed as the first step in a young person starting to manage their own risk (McCarlie and Brady, 2005). In a therapeutic context, however, there is a need to have some understanding of how a learning disability may affect cognitions. For example, the idea that sexual abusers may often be 'in denial' at the start of the therapeutic process is common throughout the literature on both adult and juvenile abusers. However, the 'denial' exhibited by young people with learning disabilities may arise from a genuine misunderstanding of what constitutes appropriate sexual behaviour, or a lack of understanding of the concept of 'consent'. Therapists, and assessors, will therefore need to undertake careful groundwork to ensure that they share both vocabulary and conceptual understandings with the young person in question. This is undoubtedly part of the process with all young people who sexually harm, but in the presence of a learning disability this work will often be further confounded by the problem of acquiescence or 'choice bias'– that is, the

tendency of people with learning disabilities to agree with whatever is suggested (eg Therapist: 'You do understand what I'm saying, don't you?' Client with learning disability: 'Yes'). In general, all communication with people with learning disabilities should take into account not only the possibility of acquiescence, but also the need to avoid sentences with too many clauses (eg Don't ask: 'Tell me about the things you like and don't like, such as different subjects or different teachers, at school'; do ask 'Tell me about your school'); the need to avoid too many choices (eg Don't ask: 'Do you prefer tea, coffee, lemonade or orange juice?; do ask 'Do you drink tea?'); and the need to allow extra time for the person to think through their response.

In the past, it was often argued that people with learning disabilities were unable to benefit from talking therapies (Willner, 2005). However, there is now increasing acceptance that this is not the case and a number of studies have shown that young people with learning disabilities who sexually abuse others can benefit from therapeutic interventions (Lindsay et al., 1999; O'Callaghan, 1999; Boswell and Wedge, 2002) although therapeutic interventions with this group are likely to take longer to achieve positive outcomes. Professionals working at a less specialised level, for example in youth offending or child protection teams, will need to consider whether their approach is able to meet the particular needs of a young person with a learning disability. Programmes which are highly structured and inflexible, or which rely on group work, may have limited value (Fyson, 2007b).

Where referring on for specialist support is required, it may prove difficult to access services. There is evidence that some services are using the slow pace of progress with learning disabled clients as a reason to screen them out at the point of first assessment (Fyson, 2005). Overall, there are too few therapeutic services for young people who sexually harm which are willing and able to offer support to those with learning disabilities (Masson and Hackett, 2003; Vail, 2002; O'Callaghan, 1998) and some young people may need to travel in order to obtain the input they need. The benefit of more specialist professional support should therefore always be weighed not only against the risk which the young person may pose to others but also against the personal and relationship costs of moving far from home.

## Conclusion

Young people with learning disabilities who sexually harm others are a heterogeneous group. As with other young abusers, there are no known predictive factors which can help us determine, in advance, whether a particular young person will sexually harm another. Learning disability itself is not a predictive factor for sexually abusing others, although the impact of greater prevalence of previous abuse amongst the disabled population should not be underestimated. Learning disability is increasingly being identified as an 'issue' within our response to young people who sexually harm others for a variety of reasons, including over-representation; greater costs associated with lengthier interventions; and perceived lack of skills in working with this group of young people on the part of many professionals. However, there are more similarities than differences between young people with and without learning disabilities who sexually abuse. Assessments should take into account the presence of a learning disability, but not allow this to become the sole, or most significant, focus of attention.

## References

Bagley, C. (1992) Characteristics of 60 Children with a History of Sexual Assault against Others: Evidence from a Comparative Study. *The Journal of Forensic Psychiatry*, 3, 299–309.

Bailey, R. and Boswell, G. (2002) *Sexually Abusive Adolescent Males: A Literature Review*. (Monograph 4) Leicester: De Montfort University.

Bailey, S. (2002) Violent Children: A Framework for Assessment. *Advances in Psychiatric Treatment*, 8, 97–106.

Baker, K. (2005) Assessment in Youth Justice: Professional Discretion and the Use of *Asset*. *Youth Justice*, 5, 106–22.

Baker, K. et al. (2003) *Asset: The Evaluation of the Validity and Reliability of the Youth Justice Board's Assessment for Young Offenders*. London: Youth Justice Board www.yjb.gov.uk

Balogh, R. et al. (2001) Sexual Abuse in Children and Adolescents with Intellectual Disability. *Journal of Intellectual Disability Research*, 45, 194–201.

Barbaree, H., Marshall, W. and McCormick, J. (1998) The Development of Deviant Sexual Behaviours among Adolescents and Its Implications for Prevention and Treatment. *The Irish Journal of Psychology*, 19, 1–31.

Benson, S. (2007) *Sex Education and Children and Young People with an Autistic Spectrum Disorder*. London: National Autistic Society www.nas.org.uk

Bentovim, A. and Williams, B. (1998) Children and Adolescents: Victims who Become Perpetrators. *Advances in Psychiatric Treatment*, 4, 101–7.

Boswell, G. and Wedge, P. (2002) *Sexually Abusive Adolescent Males: An Evaluation of a Residential Therapeutic Facility*. Leicester: De Montfort University.

Brook, (2007) *Living Your Life: The Sexual Health Resource for Special Educational Needs*. London: Brook www.brook.org.uk

Brown, H. (1994) An Ordinary Sexual Life?: A Review of the Normalisation Principle as it Applies to the Sexual Options of People with Learning Disabilities. *Disability and Society*, 9, 123–44.

Calder, M.C. (2001) *Juveniles and Children who Sexually Abuse: Frameworks for Assessment*. 2nd Edn. Lyme Regis: Russell House Publishing.

Cawson, P. et al. (2000) *Child Maltreatment in the United Kingdom: A Study of the Prevalence of Child Abuse and Neglect*. London: NSPCC.

Clark, T. et al. (1999) Autistic Symptoms in Children with Attention Deficit Hyperactivity Disorder. *European Child and Adolescent Psychiatry*, 8, 50–5.

Cooke, P. (2000) *Disabled Children and Abuse*. Nottingham: Ann Craft Trust.

Cooke, P. and Standen, P. (2002) Abuse and Disabled Children: Hidden Needs? *Child Abuse Review*, 11, 1–18.

Craft, A. (1987) Mental Handicap and Sexuality: Issues for Individuals with a Mental Handicap, their Parents and Professionals. In Craft, A. (Ed.) *Mental Handicap and Sexuality: Issues and Perspectives*. Tunbridge Wells: Costello.

Craft, A. (1994) *Practice Issues in Sexuality and Learning Disabilities*. London: Routledge.

Craft, A. and Craft, M. (1978) *Sex and the Mentally Handicapped: A Guide for Parents and Carers*. revised edition. London: Routledge.

DfEE (1997) *Excellence for All Children: Meeting Special Educational Needs*. London: The Stationery Office.

DfES (2004) *Removing Barriers to Achievement: The Government's Strategy for SEN*. London: HMSO.

DoH (2001) *Valuing People: A New Strategy for Learning Disability for the 21st Century.* London: HMSO.

DoH (2006) *The Needs and Effective Treatment of Young People who Sexually Abuse: Current Evidence.* London: HMSO.

DoH, DfEE, Home Office (2000) *Framework for the Assessment of Children in Need and their Families.* London: HMSO.

Dolan, M. et al. (1996) The Psychosocial Characteristics of Juvenile Sexual Offenders Referred to an Adolescent Forensic Service in the UK. *Medical Science Law,* 36: 343–52.

Edgerton, R. (1993) *The Cloak of Competence: Revised and Updated.* Berkley, CA: University of California Press.

Epps, K. (1999) Looking After Young Sexual Abusers: Child Protection, Risk Management and Risk Reduction. In Erooga, M. and Masson, H. (Eds.) *Children and Young People who Sexually Abuse Others: Challenges and Responses.* London: Routledge.

Erooga, M. and Masson, H. (2006) Children and Young People with Sexually Harmful or Abusive Behaviours: Underpinning Knowledge, Principles, Approaches and Service Provision. In Erooga, M. and Masson, H. (Eds.) *Children and Young People who Sexually Abuse Others: Current Developments and Practice Responses.* 2nd Edn. London: Routledge.

Frank, G. (1983) *The Wechsler Enterprise: An Assessment of the Development, Structure and Use of The Wechsler Tests of Intelligence.* New York: Pergamon Press.

Freidrich, W. (1998) Behavioural Manifestations of Child Sexual Abuse. *Child Abuse and Neglect,* 22, 523–31.

Fyson, R. (2005) *Young People with Learning Disabilities who show Sexually Inappropriate or Abusive Behaviours.* Nottingham: Ann Craft Trust.

Fyson, R. (2007a) Young People with Learning Disabilities who Sexually Abuse: Understanding, Identifying and Responding from within Generic Education and Welfare Services. In Calder, M.C. (Ed.) *Working with Children and Young People who Sexually Abuse: Taking the Field Forward.* Lyme Regis: Russell House Publishing.

Fyson, R. (2007b) Young People With Learning Disabilities who Sexually Harm Others: The Role of Criminal Justice within a Multi-Agency Response. *British Journal of Learning Disabilities,* in press.

Fyson, R., Cooke, P. and Eadie, T. (2003) Adolescents with Learning Disabilities who show Sexually Inappropriate or Abusive Behaviours. *Child Abuse Review,* 12, 305–14.

Gilbey, R., Wolf, L. and Goldberg, B. (1989) Mentally Retarded Adolescent Sex Offenders: A Survey and Pilot Study. *Canadian Journal of Psychiatry,* 34, 542–8.

Gillberg, C. and Billstedt, E. (2000) Autism and Asperger Syndrome: Coexistence with Other Clinical Disorders. *Acta Psychiatrica Scandinavica,* 102, 321–30.

Gillberg, C. et al. (2004) Co-existing Disorders in ADHD: Implications for Diagnosis and Intervention. *European Child and Adolescent Psychiatry,* 13, 80–92.

Glasgow, D. et al. (1994) Evidence, Incidence, Gender and Age in Sexual Abuse of Children Perpetrated by Children. *Child Abuse Review,* 3, 196–210.

Griffin, H. and Beech, A. (2004) *Evaluation of the AIM Framework for the Assessment of Adolescents who Display Sexually Harmful Behaviour.* London: Youth Justice Board www.yjb.org.uk

Grubin, D. (1998) *Sex Offending against Children: Understanding the Risk.* London: Home Office.

Hackett, S. (2004) *What Works for Children and Young People with Harmful Sexual Behaviours?* Ilford: Barnardo's.

Hackett, S., Masson, H. and Philips, S. (2003) *Mapping and Exploring Services for Young People who have Sexually Abused Others.* Research Programme. YJB, NSPCC and NOTA.

Hattersley, J. et al. (1987) *People with Mental Handicap: Perspectives on Intellectual Disability.* London: Faber and Faber.

Henault, I. (2003) The Sexuality of Adolescents with Asperger Syndrome. In Willey, L. (Ed.) *Asperger Syndrome in Adolescence: Living with the Ups, the Downs and Things in Between.* London: Jessica Kingsley.

Henault, I. (2005) Sexuality and Asperger Syndrome: The Need for Socio-Sexual Education. In Stoddart, K. (Ed.) *Children, Youth and Adults with Asperger Syndrome: Integrating Multiple Perspectives.* London: Jessica Kingsley.

Henault, I. (2006) *Asperger's Syndrome and Sexuality: From Adolescence through Adulthood.* London: Jessica Kingsley.

Heshusius, L. (1987) Research on Perceptions of Sexuality by Persons Labelled Mentally Retarded. In Craft, A. (Ed.) *Mental Handicap and Sexuality: Issues and Perspectives.* Tunbridge Wells: Costello.

HM Government (2006) *Working Together to Safeguard Children: A Guide to Inter-Agency Working to Safeguard and Promote the Welfare of the Child*. London: The Stationery Office.

Ho, A. (2004) To be Labelled, or not to be Labelled: That is the Question. *British Journal of Learning Disabilities*, 32: 86–92.

Hoghughi, M. (1997) Sexual Abuse by Adolescents. In Hoghughi, M., Bhate, S. and Graham, S. (Eds.) *Working with Sexually Abusive Adolescents*. London: Sage.

Home Office Statistical Bulletin (2005) *Criminal Statistics 2004: England and Wales*. London: HMSO.

Home Office Statistical Bulletin (2006) *Crime in England and Wales 2005/6* London: HMSO.

James, A. and Neil, P. (1996) Juvenile Sexual Offending: One-Year Period Prevalence Study within Oxfordshire. *Child Abuse and Neglect*, 20: 477–85.

Kelly, L. (1992) The Connections between Disability and Child Abuse: A Review of the Research Evidence. *Child Abuse Review*, 1 157–67.

Klotz, J. (2004) Sociocultural Study of Learning Disability: Moving beyond Labelling and Social Constructionist Perspectives. *British Journal of Learning Disabilities*, 32, 93–104.

Ladwa-Thomas, U. and Sanders, R. (1999) Juvenile Sex Abusers: Perceptions of Social Work Practitioners. *Child Abuse Review*, 8, 55–62.

Lindsay, W. et al. (1999) Treatment of Adolescent Sex Offenders with Intellectual Disabilities. *Mental Retardation*, 37, 201–11.

Lovell, E. (2002) *'I Think I Might Need Some More Help With This Problem . . .' Responding to Children and Young People who Display Sexually Harmful Behaviour*. London: NSPCC.

McCarlie, C. and Brady, M. (2005) The Extra Dimension: Developing a Risk Management Framework. In Calder, M.C. (Ed.) *Children and Young People who Sexually Abuse: New Theory, Research and Practice Developments*. Lyme Regis: Russell House Publishing.

McCurrey, C. et al. (1998) Sexual Behaviour Associated with Low Verbal IQ in Youth who have Severe Mental Illness. *Mental Retardation*, 36, 23–30.

Manocha, K. and Mezey, G. (1998) British Adolescents who Sexually Abuse: A Descriptive Study. *The Journal of Forensic Psychiatry*, 3, 588–608.

Mansell, S., Sobsey, D. and Moskal, R. (1998) Clinical Findings among Sexually Abused Children with and without Developmental Disabilities. *Mental Retardation*, 36, 12–22.

Masson, H. and Erooga, M. (1999) Children and Young People who Sexually Abuse Others: Incidence, Characteristics and Causation. In Erooga, M. and Masson, H. (Eds.) *Children and Young People who Sexually Abuse Others: Challenges and Responses*. London: Routledge.

Masson, H. and Hackett, S. (2003) A Decade on from the NCH Report (1992): Adolescent Sexual Aggression Policy, Practice and Service Delivery across the UK and Republic of Ireland. *Journal of Sexual Aggression*, 9, 109–24.

Masson, H. and Hackett, S. (2004) The Extent and Nature of Work with Adolescents who have Sexual Behaviour Problems: Findings from a Survey of Youth Offending Teams in England and Wales. *Youth Justice*, 4, 160–77.

Morrison, T. and Henniker, J. (2006) Building a Comprehensive Inter-Agency Assessment and Intervention System for Young People who Sexually Harm: The AIM Project. In Erooga, M. and Masson, H. (Eds.) *Children and Young People who Sexually Abuse Others: Current Developments and Practice Responses*. 2nd Edn. London: Routledge.

National Autistic Society (2007) *What is Autism?* www.nas.org.uk

NSPCC (2003) *'It Doesn't Happen to Disabled Children' Child Protection and Disabled Children. Report of the National Working Group on Child Protection and Disability*. London: NSPCC.

O'Callaghan, D. (1998) Practice Issues in Working with Young Abusers who have Learning Disabilities. *Child Abuse Review*, 7, 435–48.

O'Callaghan, D. (1999) Young Abusers with Learning Disabilities: Towards Better Understanding and Positive Interventions. In Calder, M.C. (Ed.) *Working with Young People who Sexually Abuse: New Pieces of the Jigsaw Puzzle*. Lyme Regis: Russell House Publishing.

O'Callaghan, D. (2002) (cited in Morrison and Henniker, 2006) *AIM Initial Assessment of Young People with Learning Disabilities who Sexually Abuse Others*. Manchester: Greater Manchester Aim Project

People First (2004) *Who Are We?* Northampton: Central England People First. http://www.peoplefirst.org.uk/whoarewe.html

Pinney, A. (2004) *Reducing Reliance on Statements: An Investigation into Local Authority Practice and Outcomes*. London: DfES.

Priestly, M. (2003) *Disability: A Life Course Approach*. Cambridge: Polity.

Richardson, K. (2002) What IQ Tests Test. *Theory and Psychology*, 12, 283–341.

Ryan, J. and Thomas, F. (1987) *The Politics of Mental Handicap*. Revised edition. London: Free Association Books.

Sex Education Forum (2004a) *Sex and Relationships Education for Children and Young People with Learning Difficulties*. London: National Children's Bureau www.ncb.org.uk

Sex Education Forum (2004b) *Sex and Relationships Education in Pupil Referral Units*. London: National Children's Bureau www.ncb.org.uk

Siddiqui, S. et al. (1999) Premature Sexual Development in Individuals with Neurodevelopment Disabilities. *Developmental Medicine and Child Neurology*, 41, 392–5.

Simons, K. (2000) *Life on the Edge: The Experience of People with a Learning Disability who do Not Use Specialist Services*. Brighton: Pavillion.

Smallbone, S. (2005) Attachment and Insecurity as a Predisposing Factor for Sexually Abusive Behaviour by Young People. In Calder, M.C. (Ed.) *Children and Young People who Sexually Abuse: New Theory, Research and Practice Developments*. Lyme Regis: Russell House Publishing.

Sternac, L. and Sheridan, P. (1993) The Developmentally Disabled Adolescent Sex Offender. In Barbaree, H., Marshall, W. and Hudson, S. *The Juvenile Sex Offender*. New York: The Guilford Press

Sullivan, P. and Knutson, J. (1998) The Association between Child Maltreatment and Disabilities in a Hospital-Based Epidemiological Study. *Child Abuse and Neglect*, 22, 271–88.

Sullivan, P. and Knutson, J. (2000) Maltreatment and Disabilities: A Population-Based Epidemiological Study. *Child Abuse and Neglect*, 24, 1257–74.

Timms, S. and Goreczny, A. (2002) Adolescent Sex Offenders with Mental Retardation. *Aggression and Violent Behaviour*, 7, 1–19.

Thompson, D. and Brown, H. (1997) Men with Learning Disabilities who Abuse: A Review of the Literature. *Journal of Applied Research in Intellectual Disabilities*, 10, 125–39.

Tudiver, J. and Griffin, J. (1992) Treating Developmentally Disabled Adolescents who have Committed Sexual Abuse. *SIECCAN Newsletter*, 27, 5–10.

Vail, B. (2002) An Exploration of the Issue of Sexuality and Abusive Behaviour amongst Adolescents who have a Learning Disability. *Child Care in Practice*, 8, 201–15.

Vizard, E. (2002) The Assessment of Young Sexual Abusers. In Calder, M.C. (Ed.) *Young People who Sexually Abuse: Building the Evidence Base for your Practice*. Lyme Regis: Russell House Publishing.

Vizard, E., Monck, E. and Misch, P. (1995) Child and Adolescent Sex Abuse Perpetrators: A Review of the Research Literature. *Journal of Child Psychology and Psychiatry*, 36, 731–56.

Weiss, L. et al. (2006) WISC-IV Interpretation in Societal Context. In Weiss, G. et al. *WISC-IV Advanced Clinical Interpretation*. Burlington, MA: Elsevier.

Westcott, H. and Jones, P. (1999) Annotation: The Abuse of Disabled Children. *Journal of Child Psychology and Psychiatry*, 40, 497–506.

Wheatley, H. (2005) Sex, Sexuality and Relationships for Young People with Learning Disabilities. *Current Paediatrics*, 15, 195–9.

Willner, P. (2005) The Effectiveness of Psychotherapeutic Interventions for People with Learning Disabilities: A Critical Overview. *Journal of Intellectual Disability Research*, 49, 73–85.

Youth Justice Board (2000) *Asset*. London: Youth Justice Board.

Youth Justice Board (2004) *Professional Certificate in Effective Practice (Youth Justice: Young People who Sexually Abuse*. London: Youth Justice Board www.yjb.org.uk

Youth Justice Board (2006) *Asset – revised*. London: Youth Justice Board www.yjb.gov.uk

# CHAPTER 7

# The Core Assessment of Adult Male Sexual Offenders

*David I. Briggs*

The evaluation of sexual offenders tends to serve two purposes: the evaluation of risk and/or the management of such risk. This chapter has as its focus the assessment of adult male sexual offenders that frontline practitioners are likely to encounter. It is acknowledged at the outset that there will be inevitable overlap with other chapters in this text, specifically Craig et al. (the assessment of adults with a learning disability) and Collie et al. (the assessment of rape). No attempt is made in this chapter to address the issue of the evaluation of the internet misuser and the reader is referred to the chapter by Quayle on this subject.

To state the obvious, sexual offenders form an heterogeneous population. Some offenders are highly specific in the object of their attention and the nature of their abusive behaviour, others are less discriminating. The sexual offender population is characterised by diversity of age, intellect, race, culture, employment, education, sexuality, heritage and the like. The challenge when assessing the offender is to recognise the uniqueness of the individual; to allow our models and theoretical frameworks to support our understanding of the offender rather than squeeze our understanding of the offender to fit our preconceived ideas of the characteristics of this population. The quest is for understanding individual differences.

## The offence process

Much has been written about why men might commit sexual offences. There are theories which tend to emphasise single factors in the aetiology of the offending behaviour eg Laws and Marshall's conditioning theory (Laws and Marshall, 1990). Others tend to emphasise the influence of multiple factors on offending, eg Finkelhor's Precondition Theory (Finkelhor, 1984) Ward and Siegert's Pathways Model (Ward and Siegert, 2002) and Malamuth's Confluence Model of Sexual Aggression (Malamuth, 1996). We have

descriptive models of offending such as those depicting offence 'cycles' eg Salter, 1995; Wolf, 1985, or offence chains eg Ward et al., 1995. Further there have been attempts at synthesising information from different models, one of the more promising being Ward et al.'s 'Unified Theory of Sexual Offending' (Ward et al., 2006). It is beyond the scope of this chapter to present a detailed overview of the models mentioned above or others which have been published in the field. The reader is referred to Ward et al. (2006) for this purpose; their text not only provides a review of theorising about sexual offenders but also useful critiques of those models explored.

A simple description of the offence process as represented in Figure 7.1 might assist the frontline worker in gathering information to assist in risk assessment and risk management. The model of Figure 7.1 suggests there are developmental factors which have served to influence an individual's propensity to offend. The product of those developmental influences is a collection of relatively enduring traits, the most relevant to offending being a set of stable dynamic risk factors (the offender's criminogenic needs). It is suggested that the likelihood of an offence occurring is heightened by the presence of trigger events, so-called acute dynamic risk factors alongside opportunity to gain access to a potential victim. Conversely protective factors may serve to retard the likelihood of an offence occurring.

Whilst the framework outlined in Figure 7.1 is represented in linear fashion the reality is that of multiple feedback loops across the process. For example, if an offence occurs, is undetected and the victim makes no obvious complaint, the offender's beliefs about his behaviour (a dynamic risk factor) may be reinforced. Conversely a non-abusing partner (a protective factor) who makes clear the inappropriateness of adult-child sexual contact and who signals the likely victim effects may counter the offender's abuse supportive beliefs.

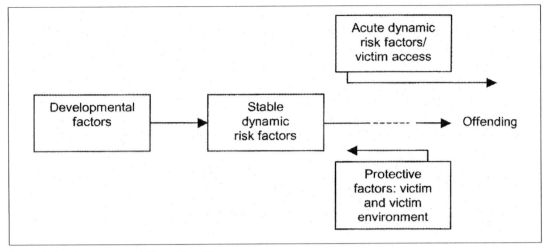

**Figure 7.1**  Linear representation of the offence process

## Developmental factors

When considering those factors that may have shaped the offender's proclivity to offending, some are not 'measurable' to the frontline worker. An individual's genetic makeup is an obvious example here. Other factors are more straightforwardly gained via a detailed personal history-taking of the offender, and using collateral information from significant others as well as historical documents such as medical and educational records. Simple questions to be explored here include:

- What did the offender learn about relationships, intimacy (sexual and non sexual), the expression of love, how to deal with conflict in relationships, who to trust, the nature of security and the value of children?
- What did the offender learn about how adults and children regulate their emotions, how problems are solved, the appropriateness or otherwise of alcohol/drugs as props to emotional support, how impulses are controlled and what are appropriate/inappropriate ways of meeting emotional needs?
- What did the offender learn about gender roles in society and in relationships, about adult-child sexual contact, about what happens to those who are sexually abused, about the effects of other sorts of victimisation eg neglect, physical maltreatment and psychological maltreatment?

- What did the offender learn about women and about children?
- What did the offender learn about various sexual acts including paraphilias, about the nature of sexuality, about sexual boundaries, about individual rights, about how sexual attraction can and should be displayed, about how an individual's needs and wants are met alongside the needs and wants of others?
- What did the offender learn about pornography and what makes for healthy/unhealthy sexual functioning, of how concerns about sexual functioning/sexuality are dealt with?
- What has the offender found to be a source of sexual arousal previously? What events might have served to shape the offender's preference for a partner? What are the offender's other preferences (eg in terms of the age, gender, race, culture, personality, body shape, dress of the partner). What paraphilias/fetishes enhance sexual arousal? What is the preferred duration/frequency of sexual activity with different sexual partners? What events may have reinforced or otherwise different sexual outlooks/interests? How have offence related sexual fantasies developed and been maintained?
- What victimisation experiences has the offender been subject to and how have these experiences shaped the offender's attitudes, thoughts, emotions and behaviour towards others, eg other offenders, victims, partners, those who have responsibility for protecting them?

- What messages did the offender gain from peers, the media and significant others in childhood as to what constitutes a healthy/acceptable relationship?
- What is known of the offender's early life experiences, in particular his attachment experiences and how might these have shaped his outlook on the world? What mental models of the world has the offender developed as a consequence?
- What primary 'human' goods are valued by the offender? How have these values developed and how has his offending met these goods, eg goods of:
  ○ striving for healthy living and functioning
  ○ mastering and achieving excellence in work and recreational activity
  ○ achieving a sense of autonomy and self directiveness
  ○ knowledge
  ○ creativity
  ○ pleasure and happiness
  ○ finding and making sense of a purpose in life
  ○ being part of a community
  ○ freedom from stress and emotional turmoil
  ○ friendships, including romantic and family relationships
  (For discussion of the relevance of 'human goods' to sexual offending the reader is referred to Ward and Fisher, 2006).
- What strengths does the offender possess, eg problem solving, empathy, sensitivity for others, humour, resilience?

As stated above the skill in working with sexual offenders is that of understanding individual differences. By taking a careful history from the offender using the questions above as a general guide, the frontline worker is in a position to develop a formulation of how factors have emerged and interacted to lead to the development of the offender's particular vulnerabilities.

## Stable dynamic risk factors

Essentially the questions above attempt to explore developmental factors within the linear model of Figure 7.1. It is suggested that these developmental influences shape the formation of the offender's unique character and his particular dynamic risk factors. Some of the most interesting

research in recent times has been that concerning our understanding of recidivism in sexual offenders and more specifically those factors that might be amenable to change and have association with reconviction risk. Ward and colleagues (Ward et al., 2006) have indicated four main groupings or domains of such 'dynamic' risk factors; attitudes supportive of abuse, difficulties in social functioning and intimacy, problems in self management and self regulation, and deviant sexual interests.

Mann and colleagues in the Autumn of 2006 presented a useful workshop to the ATSA Conference in North America linking the assessment of dynamic risk factors to treatment planning. Each domain was explored, defined and sub categorised. With Mann et al.'s framework in mind the following questions might be explored.

### *Domain One: Sexual interests*

#### Sub Factor: Sexual preoccupation

- Does the offender spend large amounts of time thinking about sex?
- Does the offender frequently and habitually engage in a wide range of sexual outlets?
- Does the offender spend a lot of time engaged in sexual acts and to the point where his lifestyle is unbalanced?
- Does the offender use pornography in an obsessive manner?
- Is the offender never satisfied with his sexual outlets?
- Is sex used as a way of dealing with tensions and unresolved emotions, ie as a form of self medication?
- Is sex non intimate and perfunctory yet frequent?

#### Sub Factor: Sexual interest in children

- Does the offender describe a sexual preference for children/pubescents (NB Mann et al. describe 'children' here as females age 12 and under, males 14 and under)?
- Are the offender's sexual daydreams predominantly of sexual contact with children?
- Is the content of the offender's masturbatory fantasy life or fantasies during love-making with age appropriate partners primarily focused on children or the paraphernalia of childhood?

- Does the offender sustain collections of child memorabilia/paraphernalia to stimulate sexual arousal?
- Does the offender describe sexual and romantic love for children?

## Sub Factor: Sexualised violence/preference for coercive sex

- Does the offender find coercive sex more sexually arousing than consenting sex? What is the offender's experience of/capacity for consenting sex?
- Is there evidence from the offender's history or more recent behaviour (including pornography usage) that his sexual arousal is triggered by cues of coercion rather than mutuality?
- Has the offender demonstrated evidence of an interest in sadism including bondage/ derogation of partners, eg in reports of his fantasy life, in his pornography usage, in his behaviour towards sexual partners?
- Has the offender evidenced other outlets for an interest in sexualised violence eg reading media reports of rape and sexual violence, attending trials of those charged with violent sexual acts, collecting scrapbooks of the paraphernalia of rape and sexual violence, retaining depositions, witness statements of those who have been sexually assaulted etc.?

## Sub Factor: Other offence related sexual interests

- Does the offender demonstrate any persistent, unusual sexual interest which has been satisfied through offending rather than consenting or legal sex?
- What fetishistic interests has the offender demonstrated or reported and how have these fetishistic interests been manifest in the client's behaviour?
- What paraphilic/fetishistic collections has or does the offender maintain?
- Is there evidence that the offender is prevented from expressing his fetishistic interests in legal ways?

## Domain Two: Distorted attitudes

(NB Mann et al. emphasise here that we are in the territory of generalised beliefs and deep seated 'schema' rather than specific cognitions).

## Sub Factor: Child abuse supportive beliefs

- Does the offender suggest that children are sexually knowing, enjoying talking about sex, as knowing a lot about sex, as non innocent, as having the ability to teach adults about sex?
- Does the offender suggest that children invite sex from adults, can lead adults astray, can flirt with adults and want sex with adults?
- Does the offender suggest that there is nothing wrong with sexual contact between children and adults, that most sexual contact between adults and children does not cause any harm, and/or that children can look after themselves?
- Does the offender perceive children or a specific child as a little adult?
- Is sex with children seen as something beneficial to the child?

## Sub Factor: Adversarial sexual attitudes

- Does the offender see sex as an arena in which he has to be dominant and his partner submissive?
- Is the offender motivated to ensure the conquest of sexual partners to the point where the partner's experience is disregarded?
- Is sex a vehicle for the offender to assume power within a relationship?
- Are women seen as adversaries and interactions between men and women, especially sexual interactions, seen as hostile?

## Sub Factor: Excessive sense of entitlement

- Does the offender show evidence of believing that his needs are more important than those of others?
- Does the offender believe his need for sex is more important than other considerations and the rights of others?
- Does the offender suggest that he is owed sex and/or deserves sex?

## Sub Factor: Women as deceitful

- What are the offender's beliefs about women? Are women viewed as essentially and fundamentally dishonest? Are women seen as provocative of men, users of men and manipulative in their interactions with men? Are women to be disbelieved? Are women seen as two-faced, ie saying one thing and meaning another?

(Mann et al. make clear here that the focus of these attitudes is women in general, that is, rather than hostility to men and women as a general trait).

### Sub Factor: Machiavellianism

- Does the offender display a callous outlook towards others? Is the offender calculating, confident, and assured in his belief that others are to be manipulated and that he has the skills to do it?
- Are fellow humans seen as inherently weak and vulnerable?
- Does the offender justify the use of others as the smart and logical thing to do?

### *Domain Three: Socio affective functioning*

### Sub Factor: Dysfunctional self evaluation

- Does the offender experience feelings of inadequacy including a belief that he is worthless, useless and inept?
- Does the offender have a fragile sense of his own worth which he boosts through delinquency?
- Does the offender display 'fragile narcissism' as evidenced by grandiose and inflated beliefs about himself?
- Does the client respond in inappropriately aggressive ways when the image he has of himself is being threatened or undermined?

### Sub Factor: Emotional congruence with children

- Does the offender find it easier to befriend children than adults?
- Does the offender meet his needs for companionship and closeness to others through children rather than adults?
- Is the offender 'as one' with children and himself in a way that he cannot be with adults?
- Does the offender experience a sense of romantic involvement with children?
- Is the offender's experience of relating to a child distorted by perceptions that he is a child or that the child is an adult?
- Does the offender have experience that children are accepting and understanding of him?

### Sub Factor: Lack of emotionally intimate relationship with adults

- Has the offender failed to sustain romantic and emotional intimacy with adults?
- Where the offender has sustained live-in relationships/marriage(s), have these been characterised by repeated tension, non-communication of emotional needs and repeated unfaithfulness?

### Sub Factor: Callous/shallow emotionality

- Does the offender struggle to experience and communicate emotions?
- Does the offender mis-label emotions and behave in ways that do not match what he says he is feeling?
- Is there a sense of the offender being unusually selfish, unempathic and indifferent to others?

### Sub Factor: Grievance thinking

- Does the offender behave in an aggressive manner when he perceives he has been wronged?
- Is the offender unusually vengeful in words and actions?
- Does the offender exhibit a mindset that others will try to wrong him?

### *Domain Four: Self management*

### Sub Factor: Lifestyle impulsiveness

- Does the offender exhibit widespread irresponsibility and stimulation-seeking behaviour, disorganisation, unrealistic long term goals and impulsivity?

### Sub Factor: Resistance to rules and supervision

- Does the offender evidence pervasive rule breaking eg violation of conditions/terms of formal Court orders, licence conditions, repeated violation of child protection agreements, eg persistent offending of whatever sort, irrespective of convictions?
- Does the offender miss appointments, fail to complete homework assignments, fail to notify the supervisor of essential activities/ information, routinely attend late for sessions, continually challenge the supervisor's agenda so as to avoid pertinent issues?

## Sub Factor: Poor problem solving skills

- Does the offender appear unable to break down the problems he experiences into manageable chunks?
- Does the offender struggle to think of a range of solutions to a problem and/or determine the best option to take?
- Does the offender struggle to anticipate where different courses of actions might lead and the consequences of those actions?
- Does the offender struggle to recognise that he has issues that might need dealing with before it is too late?
- Does the offender avoid dealing with problems which should be resolved?

## Sub Factor: Poor emotional control

- Is the offender emotionally labile?
- Does the offender have emotions that are triggered too quickly or too intensely proportional to the situation he is in?
- Does the offender sustain emotions long beyond their function?

# STABLE-2007

Whilst suggestions have been offered above of questions that might be used to explore stable dynamic risk factors, these have been based on one framework, that of Mann et al. Other researchers have been active in this field and have brought together research findings to develop instruments for the evaluation of dynamic risk factors. One of the most impressive of these has been drafted by Karl Hanson and Andrew Harris, the STABLE-2007 and its associated scale, the ACUTE-2007 (Hanson, et al. 2007).

The STABLE-2007 has been based on follow-ups of 997 sexual offenders from Canada, Alaska and Iowa. It consists of 13 items and produces reconviction risk estimates based on the number of stable dynamic risk factors present in the individual. It would not be appropriate to plagiarise the material of the STABLE-2007 here and those who would wish to use the instrument as a tool for predicting risk are advised to receive training in its use. Nevertheless when the instrument is examined, it is clear that the domains explored overlap with those of Mann et al. and indeed other researchers in the field:

- The STABLE-2007 notes that an offender's social network is one of the most well established predictors of criminal behaviour. The STABLE-2007 invites the assessor to determine those people who are likely to promote the offender's self control, offer emotional and practical support and promote pro-social values. The assessor identifies those who are relatively neutral influences, and also those people who may collaborate/encourage the offender towards offending or who may undermine the offender's efforts towards self control. (The STABLE-2007 provides a scoring system for evaluating the balance of these influences.)
- The STABLE-2007 explores evidence of the offender having experienced intimacy deficits, coding the offender's relationship stability.
- The offender's emotional identification with children is explored (subsumed under the heading of socio-affective functioning by Mann et al.) and also evidence of hostility towards women (cf the distorted attitudes domain of Mann et al.).
- The concept of general social rejection/loneliness is explored (offenders who frequently feel lonely and rejected, who have no social supports, and who have poor skills in attracting and maintaining close personal relationships attract concern here).
- The STABLE-2007 evaluates the risk factors of lack of concern for others, impulsivity, and poor cognitive problem-solving skills.
- Negative emotionality/hostility is explored. Those offenders who cling on to resentments and ruminate on even small setbacks, who ruminate on negative emotions/life events and who present with 'self-indulgent self-pity', as well as those who have 'irrational feelings of persecution' and 'chronic suspicion' are thought to be risky.
- The STABLE-2007 explores the domain of sexual self regulation, investigating three aspects in particular, namely sexual pre-occupations/sex drive, sex as coping and deviant sexual interests. The authors advise that these aspects tend to co-occur in sexual offenders.
*Sexual preoccupation* is characterised by behaviours such as excessive masturbation, a history of multiple sexual partners, regular use of prostitutes/sex industry workers, pornography collection, pre-occupation with sex crimes (own or others) and self reported

difficulties in controlling sexual impulses. *'Sex as Coping'* is described in the STABLE-2007 coding guide as sex being used as a 'self soothing activity – an attempt to mitigate or reduce unwelcome tension, anger, hostility or anxiety sates. It appears that a small proportion of sexual offenders use sexual expression as a stress management technique' (Hanson et al., 2007). *Deviant sexual interest* refers to the offender being aroused to objects, activities and/or people that are 'illegal, inappropriate or highly unusual'. These interests could include sexual interest in children, non consenting adults, voyeurism, exhibitionism, cross dressing, coprophilia and fetishism (Hanson et al., 2007).

• Finally, the STABLE 2007 examines the offender's co-operation with supervision. Offenders are considered risky if they are perceived to have disengaged with the workers, are seen to be manipulative, fail to attend appointments or do so late or at the wrong times, if they test the rules of supervision and if they do not accept the need to avoid risky situations.

Emphasis has been made within this chapter on the assessment of stable dynamic risk factors. Such assessment is seen as crucial for the front line worker as understanding of such traits is essential not only to the assessment of risk the offender presents, but it is also crucial to risk management. Whilst we cannot change static risk factors we can influence dynamic factors. Risk management in the ideal world will represent a combination of two activities – surveillance/monitoring/policing of the offender and treatment/attempts to address/contain dynamic risk factors, both stable and acute. Those who assess and manage sexual offenders must have fluency in recalling the detail of the four primary risk domains – offence related sexual interests, distorted attitudes, problems in socio-affective functioning and self management difficulties. Consideration of the balance of social influences on the offender's proclivity to offend is also necessary. Inevitably the language used to describe dynamic risk factors may vary according to the researchers concerned, but as can be seen from Figure 7.2 there is tremendous overlap here in the literature between constructs.

| Domain | Factors Mann et al. (2006) | Hanson et al. (2007) |
|---|---|---|
| **Sexual interests** | Sexual pre-occupation | Sexual pre-occupation |
|  | Sexual interest in children | Deviant sexual interests |
|  | Sexualised violence, preference for coercive sex | Deviant sexual interests |
|  | Other offence-related sexual interests | Deviant sexual interests |
|  |  | Sex as coping |
| **Distorted attitudes** | Child abuse supportive beliefs | |
|  | Adversarial sexual attitudes | |
|  | Excessive sense of entitlement | |
|  | Women as deceitful | Hostility towards women |
|  | Machiavellianism | Lack of concern for others |
| **Socio affective functioning** | Dysfunctional self evaluation | General social rejection/loneliness |
|  | Emotional congruence with children | Emotional identification with children |
|  | Lack of emotionally intimate relationships with adults | Capacity for relationship stability |
|  | Callous/shallow emotionality | |
|  | Grievance thinking | Negative emotionality/hostility |
| **Self management** | Lifestyle impulsiveness | Impulsive acts |
|  | Resistance to rules and supervision | Co-operation with supervision |
|  | Poor problem-solving skills | Poor cognitive problem-solving |
|  | Poor emotional control | |
| Other | | Significant social influences |

**Figure 7.2**  Descriptions of dynamic risk factors

## Acute dynamic risk factors

In our model of the offence process it is suggested that the likelihood of an offence occurring is heightened by the presence of trigger events, alongside access to a potential victim. For the frontline worker this indicates the need to understand the offender's current context. The worker will need to know the pattern of the offender's daily life – what he does, where he goes, who he meets and what he does with them, what hobbies/interests does he indulge in, the rhythm of the offender's week and so on. One of the more useful assessment activities here will be that of the offender keeping a detailed diary of each day's activity – the worker's role here is that of interrogating the diary and ensuring that time is fully accounted for. The worker should not rely on the offender's account here. Collateral information about the offender's activity and lifestyle should be sought, ideally from a range of sources (eg family members, employers, hostel staff, friends, health visitors, social workers and others). Hart et al. (2003) emphasise the importance of gathering case information from a number of sources, eg 'This principle recognises that perpetrators of sexual violence typically minimise or deny their sexual deviations and misbehaviours, and that over-reliance on a particular source of information – particularly uncorroborated statements made by an accused person in forensic contexts – can result in an evaluation that is incomplete and systematically biased'.

Research has progressed and our understanding of those factors which assist in the assessment of change in short term risk status has improved. Hanson and Harris (2007) have described acute dynamic risk factors which are implicated not only in sexual/violent recidivism but general recidivism. As with the evaluation of those stable dynamic risk factors described above, the frontline worker is referred to the instrument Hanson and Harris have developed to assist in the evaluation of the offender – the ACUTE-2007. Ideally they should access appropriate training in this tool if a more sophisticated analysis of the offender is required, or alternatively access the help of a co-professional who has received such training in this or similar instruments.

- The ACUTE-2007 notes that 'recidivism increases when the offenders have frequent and easy access to potential victims'. The assessor has to determine whether the offender is building his life/lifestyle to bring him into contact with a preferred victim group. The worker has to consider whether the pattern of the offender's life suggests he is grooming and mixing with potential victims. Alarm bells should ring for the assessor if the offender is being deceitful about his access to victims and/or if they evidence definite stalking and grooming behaviours.

- The ACUTE-2007 scores hostility as an acute risk factor, naming two particular factors to this construct ie general hostility towards women, and irrational and reckless defiance; this is hostility beyond their 'everyday' level of hostility (essentially we are looking for a marked change in behaviour here which may signal concern). Markers for hostility would include the offender expressing hostility towards women, making threats to the worker or others, being unusually argumentative when with people in various settings, involvement in fights, defiance in the face of helpful suggestions from others and angry rumination.

- The ACUTE-2007 suggests that sexual pre-occupation be considered an acute risk factor. Most importantly if the offender reports feeling out of control of his sexual urges or if he is engaged in 'high levels of impersonal sexual activity expressed with little or no effort to inhibit behaviour'. This is seen as very significant cause for concern and something for the assessor to act on. The assessor should be gathering evidence under this factor as to whether the individual is ruminating about sexual issues which then interfere with his life, whether he reports urges to act out sexually, whether he is exhibiting an increasing sex drive as indicated by increased/excessive masturbation, visiting sex industry workers, and the like, and whether deviant sexual interests are emerging eg in fantasy life, in discussion with others.

- The fourth acute dynamic risk factor emphasised by Hanson and Harris in the ACUTE-2007 is that of rejection of supervision. The assessor has to determine whether there is evidence of the offender working against them. The offender who continually misses appointments, who is manipulative and craves special favours, who lies and is non disclosive, who breaks rules and condition of licences/child protection agreements and who covers up information about potentially risky situations/behaviour is of concern here. Hanson and Harris suggest that we should be particularly concerned by some behaviours, for example if an offender attends sessions drunk or impaired, in possession of drugs or stolen property, if armed, or alternatively, if they have totally disappeared.

At the heart of the examination of such acute risk factors is the assessment of a shift in the offender's behaviour beyond the baseline of their stable risk factors towards circumstances and behaviour which put them closer to re-offending.

## Protective factors

In the linear model of Figure 7.1 it is suggested that the assessor also consider those factors which may help to reduce or retard risk. Whilst not exhaustive the assessor might consider the following:

- Is a clear relapse prevention plan in place to assist the offender, partner and others in the management of the offender's behaviour?
- In family settings is there a family safety plan in place to direct the offender's behaviour in the home/in respect of contact with potential victims?
- Are those who influence the offender (eg his partner, friends, close family members) fully aware of the offender's history, relapse prevention plan/family safety plan, the signs of sexual abuse, the nature of grooming behaviour, and the nature of both stable and acute dynamic risk factors?
- Are there strategies in place to monitor the offender, for example, unannounced home visits or calls?
- Are there clear multi-agency protection plans in place and are professionals who have contact with the offender sophisticated in their understanding of risk assessment, risk management and their professional responsibilities if they felt the offender was at risk?
- Does the offender have access to appropriate treatment including booster sessions as appropriate?
- Does the offender have an understanding of how to access help as appropriate if he felt he was at risk?

- Do those family members/friends who monitor the offender have access to appropriate professional support/guidance/updating?

## Assessment methodologies

In our attempts to increase the likely reliability and validity of assessments, multiple assessment methodologies are used.

The *client interview* is likely to remain the most fundamental assessment strategy. Whilst the information any interview yields is shaped by social desirability pressures and the willingness/ability of the interviewee to be honest about his actions and motives, nevertheless it is a crucial source of information on the offender. The interview is a *process* set within the *context* of a relationship with clear *objectives*.

The frontline worker interviewing the offender should have a clear sense of the process to be followed: the initial meeting with the offender (with attention being paid to the interview location); the explanation of the ground rules or rules of engagement (eg why the interview is being conducted, where information will be stored, who will have access to it, what other investigations are being conducted, how the offender can supplement information offered at a later date); the contracting with the offender participating in the interview; the information gathering stages; the closure of the interview.

The relationship with the offender is crucial. In sexual offender therapy it is observed that therapists who are empathic, genuine, rewarding, directive and non confrontational tend to enhance treatment responsivity (Marshall et al., 2003). Such is the level of shame, confusion, loss, stigmatisation and fear associated with sexual offending it is hardly surprising if offenders enter evaluations defensive, ambivalent or avoidant. It can be hypothesised that the characteristics above which relate to effective therapists are also important as characteristics of the effective assessor.

The relationship between the offender and interviewer can be enhanced by paying attention to the balance of support and challenge offered. If the client perceives the interviewer as offering both high levels of support alongside high levels of challenge he is more likely to assume an active, involved and purposeful stance. (Figure 7.3 reflects potential client behaviours as a function

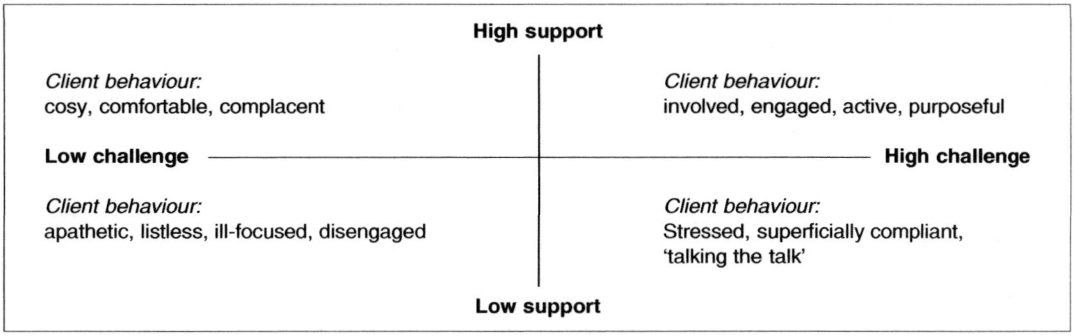

**Figure 7.3** Potential client behaviours during assessment as a function of worker support and challenge

of worker support and challenge). The interviewer can enhance the perception of support offered by explaining to the interviewee why questions are being asked, by paraphrasing responses and by checking with the interviewee that points have been understood, by maintaining a rhythm to the interview which matches the offender's attentional and intellectual capabilities, and by allowing the interviewee the opportunity to ask questions and seek clarification. Challenge can be sustained by the interviewer persisting with questions, by using open/socratic questioning techniques, by inviting the offender to explain discrepancies in their narratives when compared to collateral information, and by urging the offender to go beyond his accepted and 'safe' understanding of his abusive behaviour.

The objectives of the interview will reflect the purpose of the assessment, as stated above most typically concerned with risk assessment and/or risk management. It is good discipline for the interviewer to record objectives for the interview at the outset (eg 'to gather information as to antecedent events to the index offence, drawing on the offender's recollection of his thoughts, fantasies, behaviour and feelings beforehand') but to be clear as to how the information will be used (eg 'to determine whether there is a clear pattern to antecedent events to this man's offending when we analyse the index event alongside his past sexual offences').

Almost all assessments of the sexual offender by front line staff will include an interview with the offender and probably interviews with collateral informants such as partners, employers, and other family members.

Documents will be analysed, for example, depositions, witness statements from trials,

medical, social work, educational and occupational records, past evaluations, previous social enquiry/pre-sentence reports, probation/criminal justice records and institutional files. These investigations, alongside direct observations of the client's behaviour add to the tapestry of information gathered. Whilst it is argued that using multiple sources of information about the offender can add to the reliability and validity of our assessments it is also argued that the multi-professional assessment of clients enhances our practice.

There are some assessment methodologies which require particular and specialist training in their administration and interpretation. The use of physical measures is one such example, psychometric testing another.

Flak et al. (2007) have commented on the forensic assessment of deviant sexual interests. They describe psycho-physiological techniques which attempt to measure sexual responses to different stimuli. The penile plethysmograph (PPG) offers a measure of change in penile circumference or volume whilst the offender attends to different stimuli – typically visual and auditory stimuli which include sexual themes. Quinsey and Lalumier (2001) had provided an overview of the methodology of PPG evaluation and such was their confidence that they suggested 'there is a consensus that phalometric assessment is a necessary and, next to criminal history, probably the most important component of a comprehensive evaluation of child molesters'. The evaluation of sexual offenders via PPG continues, but attracts debate (eg Looman and Marshall (2005), Lalumiere and Rice (2007), Looman (2007). Flak et al. (2007) offer a measured overview of PPG evaluation, noting problems with the methodology. They signal that few reliability studies have been conducted; they raise the possibility of the offender faking responses; they note some offenders may simply be 'non responders'; and suggest that the method may be more useful with those who admit the offence rather than deny it. They note Freund and Watson (1991) 'child molesters convicted of a singular offence against one child responded equivalent to normal males indicating the non specificity of the instrument'.

Other physiological measures referred to by Flak et al. are the thermistor (see Kalmuss and Beech, 2005), pupilometry (Hess and Pelt, 1960), and electroencephalography (Waismann et al., 2003), none of which appear to have been developed and researched to the extent of the PPG and as such cannot be viewed as mainstream methodologies.

Flak et al. also refer to attempts to measure sexual interest through attention, viewing time and information processing measures. Viewing time assessments for example, are based on the assumption that there is a correlation between the time we attend to a stimulus and our interest in it. Typically in these assessments clients are asked to perform a task involving visual stimuli and the time the individual views the stimulus is recorded unobtrusively. One such device which has promise is called 'Affinity' (Glasgow et al., 2003). The stimuli used here are non-pornographic images. They are ranked and rated according to attractiveness whilst viewing time is measured covertly. Flak et al. have reported Holden's (2004) finding that Affinity was useful in discriminating child abusers who had abused adolescent males or pre-adolescent females.

Whilst it is unlikely that such physical assessment methods will be readily accessible to the majority of practitioners they are included in this chapter so that the reader is aware of developments in this field. It is more likely that practitioners will have come across the psychometric evaluation of offenders. Traditionally the province of psychologists, professionals from other disciplines now have access to training in particular tools and test batteries. At its heart the psychometric evaluation of an individual allows a comparison between the performance of that individual on the test concerned and the performance of a population of others who have completed the same test under similar conditions previously. Psychometric testing is often used in the evaluation of sexual offenders, and with the scope of psychometric testing being quite wide-ranging.

Intellectual assessment of the offender can guide an understanding of the offender's learning abilities and learning style. Attainment testing can guide our understanding of the offender's reading and literacy skills, including his ability to cope with written manuals and worksheets. Clinical instruments can provide evidence of mental health factors such as depression and personality difficulties which might be relevant to the client's ability to engage in treatment.

A particular application of psychometric testing is in the evaluation of so-called dynamic risk factors. Collie et al. (Chapter 11), in this volume, have commented on these issues. Earlier in this chapter reference was made to Mann et al.'s (2006) conceptualisation of stable dynamic risk factors and our suggestions as to questions that might explore these factors. Other researchers have also commented on such factors, eg Beech et al. (2003) Hanson and Harris (2007), Ward et al. (2006). Appendix 1 to this chapter sets out suggestions of psychometric instruments that are relevant to the evaluation of these risk factors.

In essence therefore, the front line practitioner is urged to call upon multiple sources of information when assessing the offender, whilst simultaneously paying attention to the relationship with the offender, the contracting of the assessment process, and the balance of support and challenge inherent in the relationship. Figure 7.4 below summarises the main assessment methodologies.

## Functional analysis

If the section on methodology above addresses the 'how' question of assessment, then what of the 'what' question?

As indicated at the outset of this chapter, a careful history of the offender is advised in order to learn of events that may have shaped his vulnerability to offending. A crucial task within assessment is an understanding of the offence itself which led to the offender coming into contact with agencies. Perkins (1991) has described a process of functional analysis. Essentially this approach structures the gathering of information about the 'index offence', those events which preceded it, and those which followed.

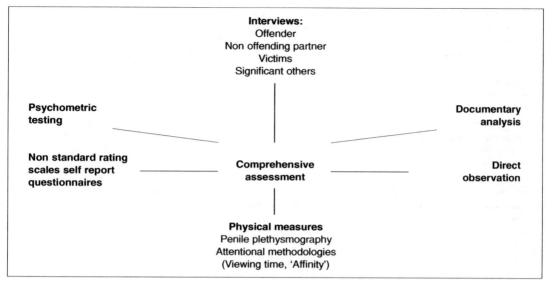

**Figure 7.4**   Assessment methodologies

| | Distal antecedent events | Proximal antecedent events | Offence events | Subsequent events |
|---|---|---|---|---|
| Behaviour | | | | |
| Thoughts | | | | |
| Feelings | | | | |
| Fantasies | | | | |

**Figure 7.5**   Skeleton for functional analysis

Perkins suggests that the offender's actions should be examined at different levels (see Figure 7.5 above). We are interested in what the offender did, his thoughts, his emotions and his fantasies at various stages of events. It can be useful to consider events which preceded the offence as either proximal (immediately preceding the offence) or distal (less immediate, eg days preceding). Using this approach the offender is asked to describe in detail what he did in the days prior to the offence and leading up to the day itself, including a detailed description of the moments prior to his committing the offence. The offence itself is then described in terms of what the offender did, followed by what the offender did in the moments, minutes and hours subsequently. The same stages are then described by the offender but with a focus on what he was thinking during the various stages. The questioning is then repeated to ask the offender about his feelings and emotions at each stage, followed finally by the exploration of the fantasies and daydreams the offender might have had throughout.

To complement the above, the worker should consider the questions that might assist in gathering information. The 5WF Model of McGuire and Priestley (1985) is simple and potentially effective. The letters here stand for 'who', 'what', 'when', 'where', 'why', and 'how'. The repeated use of such simple questions, whilst de-emphasising the 'why' question (as many offenders may not share understanding of causation or may speculate) is often helpful in the situational analysis of an abusive act. (More open-ended questions will be necessary when the client enters therapy and begins to reflect further on his actions).

## The assessment of offenders in denial

A special challenge facing front line workers is the evaluation of those sexual offenders exhibiting denial and minimisation of their offending and abuse histories. The subject of denial energises professional emotion as in many workers there is an implicit belief that offenders in denial of their offending are somehow particularly risky or resistant to treatment. We have to question both these assumptions.

At least two meta-analytic studies do not appear to support any strong link between denial of offending and reconviction risk for further sexual offences (Hanson and Bussiere, 1998; Hanson and Morton-Bourgon, 2004). Of these studies the more recent also suggests little obvious link between minimisation of offending and reconviction. Of course we have to question why this statistical association is not found. It may be that of the population of offenders who exhibit denial and minimisation, some are risky, for example those who exhibit psychopathic, callous traits and indifference to their victim. Denial for these individuals may simply be a facet of a self-serving protection mechanism designed to help these individuals avoid punishment and sanction. There may be another group of individuals however, who exhibit denial and minimisation but where those traits relate

much more to a sense of shame and remorse. Denial and minimisation may act here as a true psychological defence mechanism, serving to protect the individual from the disintegration of their well-being and self-worth. This latter group may not evidence any association between expressed denial/minimisation and reconviction if shame is serving to retard and control their deviant behaviour.

Needless to say our research efforts continue in this area. Nunes and colleagues in the summer of 2007 reported in the ATSA journal a paper under the intriguing title, 'Denial predicts recidivism for some sexual offenders'. It is perhaps worth citing the abstract here as an indication of their research findings:

> *Contrary to expectations, denial was associated with increased sexual recidivism among the low risk offenders with decreased recidivism among the high risk offenders. Post hoc analyses suggested that the risk item most responsible for the interaction was 'relationship to victims'. For incest offenders denial was associated with increased sexual recidivism, but denial was not associated with increased recidivism for offenders with unrelated victims. These interactions were substantially replicated in two independent samples (N=490 and N=73).*

Again perhaps this research highlights the need to consider individual differences. The skill and art of sex offender assessment lies in the quality of information gathering and formulation about the individual case.

Concerning the issue of the feasibility of treatment of men who exhibit denial, it was commonplace for those individuals who exhibited categorical denial to be excluded from treatment programmes. Programmers were also reluctant to accommodate those men who displayed extreme minimisation. (See Statement 28, Association for the Treatment of Sexual Abusers, 2005). There is some (albeit limited) suggestion in the clinical literature that offenders in denial can be worked with and positive outcomes achieved (Marshall et al., 2001). Needless to say this is very much territory for further exploration and research.

It is helpful for the worker evaluating offenders in denial to be clear what they are dealing with. Denial is multi-faced. The evidence for denial can vary according to the time of investigation, for example an offender may make admission of various behaviours just prior to sentence in the hope that this will secure a positive disposal; he may later retract those admissions (for example, when in custody). The offender may make admission to one worker but not another depending on the role of the worker or perceived characteristics of the worker.

The frontline worker is advised to consider the different manifestations of denial in the offender, bearing in mind these are not mutually exclusive. In essence these are:

- Categorical or absolute denial ('I didn't do it', 'I wasn't there').
- Denial of responsibility ('I did it but I was drunk', 'she got me so angry I couldn't control myself').
- Denial of facts ('I sat him on my knee and touched his thigh but I didn't touch his penis').
- Denial of intent ('it just happened').
- Denial of harm ('she didn't bleed', 'he still wants to be with me', 'she's grown up and had kids of her own').
- Denial of the likelihood of re-offending/re-abuse ('it was a one-off; it will never happen again').
- Denial of the frequency of offending ('I only did it twice though he says it went on for years').
- Denial of the sexual nature of the offence ('it was about love, I didn't have an erection').

The worker is also encouraged to consider what might motivate the offender's denial. Some of those in denial are fearful and anticipate aversive events if they were to make admissions, for example loss of a relationship, loss of family/friends, punishment, community retribution and hostility, guilt. Denial may be influenced by and 'modelled' on others, for example the suggestions made by the offender's defence team at trial by way of mitigation, contact with other offenders, including those who share group treatment and who minimise offending, and also workers who model minimisation via lukewarm and ill-focused, unchallenging questioning. Denial may be motivated by the offender gaining reward for non admission, for example a sense of power over the worker. Occasionally the offender may be ignorant of his intentions and the consequences of his behaviour. Finally, of course, the worker has to be alert to the possibility that the offender may not be in categorical denial – he may not have offended – however rare such a circumstance might be.

The assessment of denial in essence will call for the worker to compare the offender's statements and accounts with collateral information (eg victim statements) looking for discrepancies. Bearing in mind that denial is a dynamic and can change across time/circumstances of interrogation the worker would be advised to make sure that contemporaneous, ideally verbatim records of the offender's accounts be taken. (Whilst the scope of this chapter and text is not the treatment of the offender those interested in the management of denial may be interested to see treatment targets as recommended by Budrionis and Jongsma, 2003).

## Self care

To conclude this chapter a word must be said about the importance of self care. It has been suggested above that the successful assessment of offenders must focus on historical events, the influence of these on dynamic risk factors (both stable and acute) and those influences that may help contain the offender's proclivity to abuse. Note has been made that to increase the reliability and validity of our assessments multiple assessment methods should be employed and the importance of cross checking information via collateral sources of information has been emphasised.

All that is unlikely to be achieved properly however unless the assessor is emotionally robust and professionally well supported. This implies in the ideal world the need for clear line management, access to specialist consultancy, access to counselling or services which can help address how the work has and will impact on the worker, and informal support systems/ opportunity to meet with colleagues who undertake similar work. Furthermore, the work should be undertaken within clear organisational policies and procedures. The commitment should be to public/child protection whilst respecting a duty of care to those who carry out the work.

There are enough victims out there – we do not need to add the worker to the list of casualties.

## References

Abel, G. (1995) *The Abel Assessment of Sexual Interest*. Atlanta: Abel Screening.

Abel, G. and Becker, J. (1985) *The Sexual Interest Card Sort*. In Prentky, R. and Edmunds, S.

(1987) *Assessing Sexual Abuse. A Resource Guide for Practitioners*. Brandon: Safer Society Press.

Association for the Treatment of Sexual Abusers (2005) *Practice Standards and Guidelines for the Evaluation, Treatment and Management of Adult Male Sexual Abusers*. Beaverton, OR: ATSA.

Battle, J. (1992) *Culture Free Self-Esteem Inventories*. Austin: Pro-ed.

Beckett R.C. et al. (1994) *Community Based Treatment for Sex Offenders: An Evaluation of Seven Treatment Programmes*. London: Home Office.

Beech A.R., Fisher D. D. and Thornton D (2003) Risk Assessment of Sex Offenders. *Professional Psychology Research and Practice*, 34, 339–52.

Budrionis, R. and Jongsma, A.E. (2003) *The Sexual Abuser Victim and Sexual Offender Treatment Planner*. New Jersey: Wiley and Sons.

Bumby, K.M. (1986) Assessing the Cognitive Distortions of Child Molesters and Rapists: Development and Validation of the MOLEST or RAPE Scales. *Sexual Abuse: A Journal of Research and Treatment*, 8: 1, 37–54.

Burt, M.R. (1980) Cultural Myths and Supports for Rape. *Journal of Psychology and Sexual Psychology*, 38, 217–30.

Byers, E.S. and Heinlein, L. (1989) Predicting Initiations and Refusals of Sexual Activity and Cohabiting Heterosexual Couples. *The Journal of Sex Research*, 26, 210–31.

Check, J.V. (1985) The Hostility towards Women Scale. *Dissertation Abstracts International*, 45, 12. (Doctorial Dissertation, University of Manitoba, 1984).

Finkelhor, D. (1984) *Child Sex Abuse: New Theory and Research*. New York: Free Press.

Flak, V., Beech, A. and Fisher, D. (2007) Forensic Assessment of Deviant Sexual Interests: The Current Position. In Falshaw, L. and Rayment, L. (Eds.) *Issues in Forensic Psychology*. Leicester: British Psychological Society.

Freund, K. and Blanchard, R. (1982) Gender Identity and Erotic Preference in Males. In Davis, C.M. et al. (1998) *Handbook of Sexuality Related Measures*. Thousand Oaks: Sage.

Freund, K. and Watson, R.J. (1991) Assessment of the Sensitivity and Specificity of a Phallometric Test: An Update of Phallometric Diagnosis of Pedophillia. *Psychological Assessment: A Journal of Consulting and Clincial Psychology*, 3, 254–60.

Glasgow, D., Osborne, A. and Croxon, J. (2003) An Assessment Tool for Investigating Paedophile Sexual Interest Using Viewing Time: An Application of Single Case Research

Methodology. *British Journal of Learning Disabilities*, 31, 96–102.

Hall, E.R., Howard, J.A. and Boezio, S.L. (1986) Tolerance of Rape: A Sexist or Antisocial Attitude. *Psychology of Women Quarterly*, 10, 101–18.

Hanson, R.K., Gizzarelli, R. and Scott, H. (1994) The Attitudes of Incest Offenders: Sexual Entitlement and Acceptance of Sex with Children. *Criminal Justice and Behaviour*, 21: 2, 187–200.

Hanson, R.K. et al. (2007) *Assessing the Risk of Sexual Offenders on Community Supervision*. Ottawa Corrections Research, Public Safety Canada. (from www.ps-sp.gc.ca)

Hanson, R.K. and Bussiere, M.T. (1998) Predicting Relapse: A Meta Analysis of Sexual Offender Recidivism Studies. *Journal of Consulting and Clinical Psychology*, 66, 348–62.

Hanson, R.K. and Morton-Bourgon, K.E. (2004) *Predictors of Sexual Recidivism: An Updated Meta-Analysis*. Canada: Ottowa Public Safety and Emergency Preparedness.

Hart, S.D. et al. (2003) *The Risk for Sexual Violence Protocol*. British Columbia: Simon Fraser University.

Hess, E.H. and Polt, J.M. (1960) Pupil Size as Related to the Interest Value of Visual Stimuli. *Science*, 132, 349–50.

Hudson, W.W., Harrison, D.F. and Crosscup, P.C. (1981) A Short Form Scale to Measure Sexual Discord in Dyadic Relationships. *The Journal of Sex Research*, 17, 157–74.

Hughes, T. and Snell, W.E. Jr. (1990) Communal and Exchange Approaches to Sexual Relations. *Annals of Sex Research*, 3, 149–63.

Hurlbert, D.E. et al. (1994) Sexual Narcissism: A Validation Study. *Journal of Sex and Marital Therapy*, 20, 24–34.

Kalmus, E. and Beech, A.R. (2005) Forensic Assessment of Sexual Interest: A Review. *Aggression and Violent Behaviour*. 10, 193–217.

Lalumiere, M.L. and Rice, M.E. (2007) The Validity of Phallometric Assessment with Rapists: Comments on Looman and Marshall (2005). *Sexual Abuse: A Journal of Research and Treatment*, 19, 61–8.

Lawrence, K. and Byers, E.S. (1992) Development of the Interpersonal Exchange Model of Sexual Satisfaction in Long Term Relationships. *Canadian Journal of Human Sexuality*, 1, 123–8.

Laws, D.R. and Marshall W.L. (1990) A Conditioning Theory of the Aetiology and Maintenance of Deviant Sexual Preference and

Behaviour. In Marshall, W.L., Laws, D.R. and Barbaree, H.E. (Eds.) *Handbook of Sexual Assault: Issues, Theories and Treatment of the Offender.* New York. Plenum.

Looman, J. (2007) Response to Lalumiere and Rice: Further Comments on Looman and Marshall (2005) *Sexual Abuse: A Journal of Research and Treatment,* 19, 69–72.

Looman, J. and Marshall, W.L. (2005) Sexual Arousal in Rapists. *Criminal Justice and Behaviour,* 32, 367–89.

Lottes, I.L. (1988) Rape Supportive Attitude Scale. In Davis, C.M., Yarbes, W.L. and Davis, S.L. (Eds.)

Malamuth, N.M. (1996) The Confluence Model of Sexual Aggression: Feminist and Evolutionary Perspectives. In Buss, D.M. and Malamuth, N.M. (Eds.) *Sex, Power, Conflict; Evolutionary and Feminist Perspectives.* New York: Oxford University Press.

Malamuth, N.M. (1989) The Attraction to Sexual Aggression Scale. Part Two. *The Journal of Sex Research,* 26, 324–54.

Malamuth, N.M. (1989) The Attraction to Sexual Aggression Scale: Part One. *The Journal of Sex Research,* 26, 26–49.

Mann, R., Thornton, D. and Daniels, L. (2006) *Using the Structured Risk Assessment Model to Guide Treatment Planning.* Workshop to ATSA Conference, Chicago, 2006.

Marshall, W.L. et al. (2003) Process Variables in the Treatment of Sexual Offenders: A Review of the Relevant Literature. *Aggression and Violent Behaviour,* 8, 205–34.

Marshall, W.L. et al. (2001) Treatment of Sexual Offenders who are in Categorical Denial: A Pilot Project. *Sexual Abuse: A Journal of Research and Treatment,* 13, 205–15.

McGuire, J. Priestley, P. (1985) *Offending Behaviour, Skills and Strategies for Going Straight.* London: Betsford Academic.

Mosher, D.L. and Anderson, R.D. (1986) Macho Personality, Sexual Aggression and Reactions to Guided Imagery of Realistic Rape. *Journal of Research and Personality,* 20: 2, 77–94.

Nichols, H.R. Molinder, I. (1984) *Multiphasic Sex Inventory.* Tacoma WA: Nichols and Molinder.

Nunes, K.L. et al. (2007) Denial Predicts Recidivism in some Sexual Offenders. *Sexual Abuse,* 19: 2 91–106.

Perkins, D. (1991) Clinical Work with Sex Offenders in Secure Settings. In Hollin, C. and Howells, K. *Clinical Approaches to Sex Offenders and their Victims.* New York: Wiley.

Quinsey, V.L. and Lalumiere, M. (2001) Assessment of Sexual Offenders against Children. 2nd edn. Thousand Oaks: Sage.

Salter, A. (1995) *Transforming Trauma: A Guide to Understanding and Treating Adult Survivors of Child Sexual Abuse.* Thousand Oaks. CA: Sage.

Salter A. (1988) *Treating Child Sex Offenders and Victims: A Practical Guide.* California: Sage.

Snell, W.E. Jr., Fisher, T.D. and Walter, A.S. (1993) The Multidimensionality Sexuality Questionnaire: An Objective Self-Report Measure of Psychological Tendencies Associated with Human Sexuality. *Annals of Sex Research,* 6, 27–55.

Snell, W.E. and Popini, D.R. The 'Sexuality Scale'. An Instrument to Measure Sexual Esteem, Sexual Depression and Sexual Pre-Occupation. *The Journal of Sex Research,* 26, 256–63.

Spector, I.P., Carey, M.P. and Steinberg, (1996) The Sexual Desire Inventory: Development, Factor Structure and Evidence of Reliability. *Journal of Sex and Marital Therapy,* 22, 175–90.

Waismann, R. et al. (2003) EEG Responses to Visual Erotic Stimuli in Men with Normal and Paraphilic Interests. *Archives of Sexual Behaviour,* 32, 135–44.

Ward, T. and Fisher, D. (2006) New Ideas in the Treatment of Sexual Offenders. In Marshall, W.L. et al. *Sexual Offender Treatment: Controversial Issues.* Chichester: Wiley.

Ward, T. et al. (1995) A Descriptive Model of the Offence Chain for Child Molesters. *Journal of Interpersonal Violence,* 10, 452–72.

Ward, T., Palascheck, D.L. and Beech, A.R. (2006) *Theories of Sexual Offending.* London: Wiley.

Ward, T. and Siegert, R.J. (2002) Towards a Comprehensive Theory of Child Sexual Abuse: A Theory Knitting Perspective. *Psychology Crime and Law,* 9, 319–51.

Wolf, S.C. (1985) A Multifactor Model of Deviant Sexuality. *Victimology,* 10, 359–74.

# Appendix 1: Psychometric Evaluation of Dynamic Risk Factors

## Domain: Sexual interests

### Sub Factor: Sexual pre-occupation

Sexual Activity Questionnaire. Byers, 1989
The Sexuality Scale. Snell, 1989
Sexual Desire Inventory. Spector et al., 1996

### Sub Factor: Sexual preference for children

Abel Assessment of Sexual Interest. Abel, 1995
Clarke Sex History Questionnaire. Clarke, 1997
Multiphasic Sex Inventory. Nichols and Molinder, 1984
Abel and Becker Sexual Interest Card Sort. Abel and Becker, 1985

### Sub Factor: Sexualised violence

Revised Attraction to Sexual Aggression Scale. Malamuth, 1989
Aggressive Sexual Behaviour Inventory. Mosher and Anderson, 1986

## Domain: Distorted attitudes

### Sub Factor: Child abuse supportive beliefs

Children and Sex. Beckett et al., 1994
Abel and Becker Cognitions Scale. Abel and Becker. (In Salter, 1988)
Hanson Sex Attitude Questionnaire. Hanson et al., 1994

### Sub Factor: Adversarial sexual attitudes

Rape Myth Acceptance Scale. Burt, 1980
Rape Supportive Attitude Scale. Lottes, 1988
Rape Attitude Scale. Hall et al., 1986
Bumby Cognitive Distortions Scale. Bumby, 1997

### Sub Factor: Deceitful women

Hostility Towards Women Scale. Check, 1985

### Sub Factor: Sexual entitlement

Hurlbert Index of Sexual Narcissm. Hurlbert et al., 1994

## Domain: Social affective functioning

### Sub Factor: Dysfunctional self evaluation (inadequacy, delinquent pride, fragile narcissm)

Culture Free Self Esteem Inventory. Battle, 1992
The MultiDimensional Sexual Self Concept Questionnaire. Snell et al., 1993

### Sub Factor – Emotional congruence with children

Children and Sex. Beckett et al., 1994

### Sub Factor: Lack of emotionally intimate relationships with adults

The Sexual Relationship Scale. Hughes and Snell, 1990
Index of Sexual Satisfaction. Hudson et al., 1981
Interpersonal Exchange Model of Sexual Satisfaction Questionnaire. Lawrence and Byers, 1992

### Sub Factor: Callous shallow emotionality

PCL-R (Facet 2)

## Domain: Self management

### Sub Factor: Social deviance/lifestyle impulsiveness

PCL-R

# CHAPTER 8

# Assessment of Women who Sexually Abuse Children

*Hilary Eldridge, Ian Elliott and Sherry Ashfield*

## Summary

This chapter focuses on how to use knowledge from research and clinical practice to assess risk of harm and treatment needs of women who have sexually abused children. We will consider the difficulty inherent in identifying reliable protocols given the small numbers of women convicted and the consequent lack of data. We will propose what can be used, including a framework for assessment guidance specifically for female sexual offenders being developed with the University of Birmingham using data from Lucy Faithfull Foundation's clinical work. We will discuss assessment in practice, drawing from experience of running the programme devised by the Lucy Faithfull Foundation (Eldridge, Saradjian, Brotherston and Ashfield) with adaptations for use in custodial, hostel and community settings, and discuss how best to engage women in the assessment process.

## Part 1: The context: what is the actual scale of the problem?

'Cultural schema in any society that enable the majority of its citizens to feel psychologically comfortable are often maintained by a process of shared minimisation and denial. This is the means by which the long held "secret" of the sexual abuse of children by women has been ignored. Should this "secret" be explored and fully accepted then the seeming social security of having women as "sexually safe" primary carers and protectors of our children would be irretrievably damaged. Therefore, despite at least a century of knowledge pointing to a significant number of women engaging in sexually abusive behaviours towards children, it is still a phenomenon that has not been sufficiently accepted' (Saradjian, 2006: ix).

This problem persists in both the US and the UK. Denov (2001) comments that police and professionals had an informal yet well established way of seeing sexual assault with males as perpetrators and females as victims. Professionals regarded female sexual offending as less harmful than sexual abuse by men. Moreover they made efforts, either consciously or unconsciously to transform the female and her behaviour into more culturally acceptable notions of female behaviour. This ultimately led to denial of the problem.

Research available on female sex offending is far less extensive than that related to male offending. This is linked to the fact that very few women are actually convicted of sexual assaults: they form approximately 0.5 per cent of all sex offenders in prison and around one per cent of convicted sex offenders in England and Wales (Ford, 2006). Prevalence rates can be hypothesised from research into offender, victim and other populations. Bunting (2005) states that current understanding suggests that females may account for up to five per cent of all sexual offences against children. The low conviction rate may be partly because women commit fewer offences, but statistics are likely to be influenced by beliefs about females as abusers. Ford (2006) asks whether abuse by women is rare or just underreported. She adds that it is certainly significant: self-report studies find higher rates of female abuse than those relying on officially reported cases (Mendel, 1995). Denov (2003) also emphasises the disparity between official and self-report data. Information from survivors certainly indicates that although female abusers are in the minority, it is a larger minority than statistics suggest.

Self-report from adult male sex offenders in the UK shows a significant number identifying women as perpetrators. Rallings, Webster and Rudolph (2001) found that of 144 male offenders against adults who said they were sexually abused as children, 56 (39 per cent) said the perpetrator was a female, and of 401 male offenders against children who said they were sexually abused, 76 (19 per cent) cited a female perpetrator.

Children calling for help about abuse also identify female abusers. ChildLine figures for the year 2004 – 2005 revealed that overall 11 per cent of callers about sexual abuse were calling about a female abuser. Further breakdown of these figures indicated that three per cent of 6,538 girls calling about sexual abuse were calling about a female and that two per cent of the girls calling about a female abuser were calling about their mothers. Meanwhile, 35 per cent of the 2,099 boys calling about sexual abuse were calling about a female abuser and 17 per cent of the boys calling about a female were calling about their mothers (ChildLine, personal communication).

Saradjian (1996) notes that Finkelhor and Russell (1984) surveying the data then available, concluded that of all children who had been sexually abused the percentage of sexual contact by older females was about 20 per cent (range 14–27 per cent) for male children and about 5 per cent (range 0–10 per cent) for female children. (Finkelhor and Russell 1984: 179 cited in Saradjian 1996).

### Typologies of female sexual offenders

Saradjian's (1996) British study of female sexual offenders built on those of Matthews, Mathews and Speltz (1991) and Finkelhor et al. (1988). She identified that like their male counterparts, women offenders are a heterogeneous group who come from all walks of life. The three typologies most frequently discussed in the literature are the inter-generationally predisposed group who abuse their own young children and are often regarded as replicating their own childhood abuse; the woman who abuses adolescents of her preferred gender and sees herself as having an 'affair'; and the male coerced woman who is initially coerced into abusive behaviour, may cease offending after the departure of the coercive male or may develop her own independent pattern. Increasingly, the 'coerced' category is expanded to include male accompanied female offenders (Nathan and Ward, 2002). Vandiver and Kercher (2004) have identified a further group of women who engage in 'forcing behaviour', ie compelling prostitution, whose incentive appears to be primarily financial.

Societal denial of female sex offending leads to inadequate assessment and intervention with the women and a paucity of therapy for survivors of their abuse, even if they are heard and believed. However, professionals are beginning to recognise this problem and to ask for help in working with such women. Lucy Faithfull Foundation receives referrals from prison and probation staff wanting help with pre-sentence report writing, assessment, intervention, management and resettlement advice. Bunting (2005) found that Multi-Agency Public Protection Panels and Area Child Protection Committees felt that they lacked information about female sexual offenders and needed more effective ways of assessing and managing them.

## Part 2: Assessment protocols

The relatively small numbers of women coming to attention means that there is a lack of data about women's psychometric profiles, how they differ from women who commit non-sexual offences and from non-offending women; what factors link to re-offending and what should be targeted in treatment; treatment outcome and reconviction figures. Below, we consider options for development.

### Static risk assessment?

While many psychometric tools have been developed through work with male abusers, their validity and reliability with female sex offenders has not been adequately tested. The same is true for risk assessment instruments. As Aylward et al. (2002) state, 'actuarial risk assessment tools not validated on women are being used to assess risk'. The use of such tools can be dangerous in that results can be misleading and the level of risk over- or understated, with serious consequences for the women and for those victimised by them. One of the best-known and widely used actuarial tools for men is Risk Matrix 2000. Its lead author, David Thornton, clearly states in his guidance notes that RM 2000 should not be used with female sex offenders (Thornton, 2007). Static risk assessment protocols for women have not been developed due to small numbers, lack of previous convictions and lack of reconviction data. Whilst numbers continue to be small it is not practical to develop static risk assessment protocols for female sexual offenders.

### Can we use data from risk of reconviction studies on women who commit non-sexual offences?

In developing Lucy Faithfull Foundation's assessment programme we considered the available research on what is predictive of re-offending in female (non-sex) offenders. Clark and Howden-Windall (2000) describe a retrospective study of 195 female general offenders who were followed up after leaving prison in 1995. The women were representative of the female prisoner population regarding age and offence but the sample was weighted in favour of longer sentences.

The findings showed that factors significantly related to reconviction were criminal history variables, ie previous sentence, previous violent offence, early onset of offending. However, factors which were highly predictive of reconviction were familial factors, such as a problematic home life when growing up and lack of continuity of care. These were often exacerbated by being combined with lack of educational qualifications and substance abuse, which were also highly related.

We, Eldridge and Saradjian (2000), hypothesised that treatment for female sex offenders should address the effects of the women's background experiences on their attitudes and beliefs and their perceptions of how to meet their biosocial goals. Historical factors are fixed but are linked to changeable factors such as pro-offending attitudes, emotional loneliness, self-esteem and interpersonal skills deficits which can be targeted in treatment. Some dynamic risk factors for male sexual offenders may also be relevant for females. For example, poor self-management skills, fragile commitment to prevention of re-offending as well as sex offence specific problems such as deviant arousal, victim empathy deficits and social support for offending-related ideas (Correctional Services Accreditation Panel, 2003). Broad areas for treatment may therefore be similar to male offender programmes, but detailed targets, style and method of delivery must be responsive to the needs of female offenders and may be significantly different. For example, female sexual offending often takes place in the context of co-offending with males, so a treatment target may focus on this dynamic. Women who abuse their own young children alone frequently do this in the context of intimate child care, without any 'grooming', sometimes repeating what was done to them as children, so a treatment need may be to explore and make sense of this behaviour.

## Psychological tests for female sexual offenders?

In the UK, the Lucy Faithfull Foundation is collaborating with Richard Beckett, Head of Oxford Forensic Psychology Service, who is establishing a battery of standardised psychometric tests for female sexual abusers. The tests are based on the original battery of tests developed for use with male sexual offenders against children (Beckett, Beech, Fisher and Fordham, 1994). These tests include: locus of control (Nowicki); alcohol use (MAST); drug use (DAST); emotional loneliness (UCLA); general empathy (IRI); self-deception/impression management (Paulus PDS); social response inventory (Beckett adapted); self esteem (Thornton) and a sexual matters questionnaire. The Millon Clinical Multiaxial Inventory (Millon, 1994) has been added to the tests battery. The Victim Empathy vignettes have been designed with attention to the different female offender typologies identified by Saradjian (1996) and are developed individually for each woman referred for assessment. Provisional norms have been established for Beckett's Children and Sex Questionnaire and for the Victim Empathy Scales. Home Office funded work is to start in 2007 to fully standardise the measures on non-offending women and women convicted of non sexual crimes (Beckett, personal communication).

In a recent analysis of their data on female sexual offenders Beckett, Burke and Cotton (2006) found similar levels of socio-affective problems and levels of abuse related cognitions (cognitive distortions and victim empathy deficits) in both female and male child sexual abusers. Ring (2005) has recently normed the social competence measures on a community sample of non-offending women. The sexually abusive women were found to have significantly lower levels of self-esteem and assertiveness and higher levels of emotional loneliness and personal distress, and to have a more external locus of control than 'normal' women. When the dynamics of offending were considered, sole abusers were identified as having higher levels of pro-offending attitudes and less emotional congruence with children, while co-abusers demonstrated problems in assertiveness and personal distress.

### The development of a framework for assessing women who have sexually abused children

In order to more effectively assess risk of harm and tailor treatment appropriately, studies need to focus on what we can learn from women who sexually abuse children.

An investigation by Elliott, Eldridge, Ashfield and Beech (2007) examines potential risk factors, protective factors and treatment needs that are highlighted directly through the process of clinical intervention and assessment of female sex abusers with a view to finding out to what extent these factors may be prevalent within the population. To give this a coherent and theoretical basis, the investigation employs the Beech and Ward (2004) aetiological model of risk, together with an assessment of protective and treatment factors based on a framework originally developed by Carr (1999).

Preliminary work has been based on mining anonymised historical data that had not been collected initially with this purpose in mind. However, from the file data it has been possible to develop an extensive coding framework to analyse this information. This has already identified significant areas of interest and will form the basis of a multi-purpose guidance framework for therapists to use for their assessments in criminal justice and family court settings. This process will enable us to collect data from new contacts to increase the sample size and develop the tool.

Therapists will be trained to collect the relevant data and identify areas where there may be gaps or where further dimensions need to be considered. We propose to take this forward dynamically and hope to make the coding framework available for suitably trained practitioners beyond the Lucy Faithfull Foundation.

### The Beech and Ward (2004) aetiological model of risk

The Beech and Ward (2004) framework links contemporary theories of risk from the clinical and theoretical fields into a single comprehensive model, identifying four key aetiological domains of risk:

- Developmental factors.
- Vulnerability (trait) factors, which incorporate psychological vulnerabilities (dynamic factors) and historical markers (static factors).
- Contextual triggering factors.
- Acute (state) factors.

Although the overall model was not developed specifically for females, the broad domains provide a framework to understand human behaviour. Research and clinical practice with women indicates that the domains are relevant to them, although the specific factors within each domain may be different for males and females.

Beech and Ward (2004) suggest that early negative learning events in childhood development act as precursors to a number of psychological vulnerabilities that can lead to sexual offending. Beech and Ward state that some vulnerability factors play a causal psychological role in risk while others are 'historical' markers that may suggest the potential for a disorder. Beech and Ward define these vulnerabilities as *traits* and describe them as interacting with each other and converging together with trigger factors into offence-related acute psychological states. The psychological dispositions can be broadly categorised into four categories: interpersonal functioning, cognitive distortions, emotional self-management and deviant arousal.

Beech and Ward (2004) suggest that problems in interpersonal functioning can be categorised into three subsets: intimacy problems, inadequacy, and emotional identification with children. It is also proposed that (male) child molesters possess generalised beliefs that are supportive of offending behaviour. Ward and Keenan (1999) describe these as arising from a set of core schema that generate the cognitive distortions that are measured at surface level and break these schemata down into five implicit theories:

- children as sexual objects
- nature of harm
- entitlement
- dangerous world
- uncontrollability

In the Elliott et al. (2007) investigation, cognitive distortions have been categorised based on their relation to these five implicit theories. Problems with self-management are said to arise from inability to identify emotions or modulate any negative emotions and an inability to utilise social supports in times of distress. Finally, problems with sexual self-regulation and deviant arousal are based on the lability of sexual arousal and level to which sexual arousal can be modulated.

Trigger factors are conceptualised as contextual risk factors that interact with psychological vulnerabilities to generate states conducive to offending behaviour (Beech and Ward, 2004). In the Beech and Ward (2004) model the core underlying dispositions described above, when interacting with trigger factors, can lead to deviant sexual arousal, deviant thoughts and fantasies, a need for intimacy or control and positive or negative emotional states dependent on whether or not the offence behaviour is desired, creating higher levels of proximal risk. Using the broad Beech and Ward framework we analysed the file data to ascertain what developmental, trait, trigger and acute factors were present in female sexual abusers.

## *Strengths based assessment*

A further aim in the development of the assessment framework for use in clinical settings with women is to incorporate assessment of the women's strengths and ability to reduce their own risk, rather than simply focusing on their deficits. There has been increasing interest in the importance of understanding and harnessing the role of strengths, resilience and protective factors in helping individuals develop more positive lifestyles (Masten and Reed, 2005; Benard, 2006; Gilgun, 1999). A strengths-based approach allows not only for a comprehensive, balanced, more optimistic outlook for the offender, but also provides a positive emphasis to practice that is often associated with positive treatment effectiveness (Miller, Duncan and Hubble, 1997).

The Lucy Faithfull Foundation takes a strengths-based approach to treatment with the 'New Life' programme, highlighting the need to value and harness each woman's positive qualities and help her recognise that, although she has done harm, she is nevertheless a worthwhile human being capable of change (Eldridge and Saradjian, 2000). Ward, Polaschek and Beech, 2006, drawing on the work of Seligman and Csikszentmihaly (2000) emphasise the importance of a positive psychology approach which attempts to promote human welfare by concentrating on strengths. This approach has become an integral part of some widely used assessment protocols for young people (Gilgun, 1999; 2003; 2006; Print, Morrison and Henniker, 2001).

Elliott et al. (2007) assessed strengths based on a model developed by Carr (1999) for adolescent offenders and adapted for adolescent sexual offence behaviour by Bickley for Lucy Faithfull Foundation. This framework takes into account both personal and contextual protective factors, focusing on offence-specific issues, sexuality, social functioning and support, and self-management, and environmental conditions. The majority of these appeared to be relevant to female sexual offenders, however some of the factors were modified to place them in a female offender context, for example distinguishing between partner and family support.

## Method

The data was taken from referrals to the Lucy Faithfull Foundation for assessment in cases where there were legal findings, convictions and/or admissions involving the sexual abuse of children by women. An initial random selection of 13 files was analysed to inform the production of a preliminary risk factor coding framework outlining a number of risk factors in each specific Beech and Ward (2004) risk domain area, with space allowed for additional potential factors specific to each woman to be added. Subsequently, each file (including again the initial 13 files) was thoroughly examined using the coding framework.

## Sample

The sample data comprises 43 adult females who have been assessed on the basis of criminal convictions, family court legal findings and/or admissions relating to child sexual abuse. Twenty-four were referred via the criminal justice system and 19 were referred through non-criminal justice sources. Fourteen per cent of the sample had previous non-sexual, non-violent convictions, and none had previous violent convictions. Ages at which the known or alleged abuses began in the sample ranged from 18 to 42 years with an average age of 31.2 years. The average number of victims in the sample was 1.74. Of the 43 women in the sample, 44 per cent were alleged to have offended against male children, 40 per cent against female children, and 16 per cent against a combination of both male and female children. For those women for whom the data was available (n = 41) victim ages, recorded as the age at which the abuse began, ranged from six months to 15 years with an average age of 9.02 years. Fifty-one per cent of the women in the sample abused their own children, seven per cent abused other children within their family, 35 per cent abused children outside of the family, and seven per cent abused a combination of intra- and extra-familial victims.

The women in the sample were separated into four categories of offender typology:

- Lone offender (victim over 12 years) (n = 11)
- Lone offender (victim under 12 years) (n = 9)
- Male-associated (n = 18)
- Male-coerced (n = 5)

These typologies were based on those developed by Saradjian (1996) with an additional distinction between male-associated and male-coerced offences. Women who fell into one of these male-related categories were assessed in terms of the perceived levels of coercion described in their offending behaviours. Therefore if it was explicit in the file data that the woman was clearly forced into abusive situations by violent, often sadistic, partners she was placed in the male-coerced category rather than the male-associated category.

## Findings

In the following section we outline some of the more important findings, where the factor is present in over one-third (ie 34 per cent) of the sample, from the Elliott et al. (2007) investigation. Where proportions of the sample as a whole are reported they are given as percentages, but where we report proportions within groups we will report the actual numbers, given the smaller sizes of each group.

### Developmental factors

Parental relationships appear to be an important factor within this sample. Of the women, 49 per cent reported having a poor attachment to their primary caregiver and similarly, 51 per cent reported parental rejection and/or neglect during childhood. This was consistent across the four groups. Childhood abuse was also highly prevalent within the sample with 67 per cent of the sample reporting some form of emotional, physical and/or sexual abuse. Again, this was relatively consistent across the groups, though slightly more frequent in the lone perpetrator

(victim under 12) group where seven out of nine reported some form of previous abuse.

Forty-two per cent of the sample reported having been a victim of sexual abuse during their childhood. Of these, 10 had been abused solely by intra-familial perpetrators, four solely by extra-familial offenders and four by a combination of intra- and extra-familial offenders. Of the 10 women who were abused solely by intra-familial perpetrators, four were abused by a primary caregiver alone, three were abused by a non-caregiver such as a sibling, step-sibling or other family member, and three were abused by a combination of primary caregivers and other family members.

Interestingly, the lone offender (victim under 12) group were not only proportionally more likely to have been a victim of childhood sexual abuse (seven out of nine) they were also much more likely to have suffered from intra-familial abuse, with five out of those seven victims of sexual abuse in this group being the victim of solely intra-familial abuse.

### Vulnerability (trait) factors: Historical markers and psychological dispositions

When assessing adult male sexual offenders a key historical marker (static factor) is previous criminal convictions for sexual, violent and other types of offending. However, in the case of women these are found far less frequently. For example, in our sample just 14 per cent had previous non-sexual, non-violent convictions, none had previous violent offences and five per cent had previous convictions for sexual offences. Consequently, it is important to consider other markers such as findings of fact in the family courts, previous serious allegations and local authority concerns about risk to children. For example 16 per cent of the sample had been the subject of local authority concerns regarding possible sexual abuse. In addition, it is important to take account of psychological vulnerabilities and relevant historical markers for them.

Problems relating to interpersonal functioning were frequent within the sample. Eighty-one per cent reported low self-esteem, 79 per cent reported low confidence, 63 per cent reported low assertiveness and 86 per cent reported being socially isolated. These findings are also fairly consistent across all four groups, though there are a number of subtle group differences for other interpersonal factors. There was frequently a lack of empathetic concern for the victim reported in the lone offender (victim over 12) group (seven out of 11) and the male-coerced group (three out of five) in comparison to the other groups. Also, five out of 11 of the lone offender (victim over 12) group report a high level of emotional congruence with children, which is a high frequency compared to the sample as a whole (16 per cent).

There were a number of stable marker variables relating to interpersonal functioning frequently reported in the sample. Of the sample, 49 per cent reported a series of unstable previous relationships. Similarly, 74 per cent of the sample reported being in previous exploitative and/or abusive relationships, with all five of the male-coerced group reporting this factor. Interestingly, nine out of the 11 women in the sample who reported large age discrepancies in their current or previous relationships were from the male-associated group.

Ninety-three per cent of the sample displayed offence-supportive cognitions and these cognitive distortions reveal a number of subtle differences between the four groups. Of the sample, 72 per cent displayed cognitive distortions relating to viewing children as sexual beings, these distortions being especially common in the lone offender groups, with all 11 of the victim over 12 group and seven out of nine of the under 12 group demonstrating some distorted thinking of this kind. Here, the most common distortion relates to the offender imbuing the child with adult characteristics (44 per cent of the sample). Of particular interest, in the lone offender (victim over 12) group nine out of 11 displayed distortions regarding a child's ability to consent to sexual activity, five out of 11 reported a belief that abuse is either the child's fault or not always the adult's fault, and all 11 in this group reported imbuing a child with adult characteristics.

The majority of the sample (70 per cent) displayed cognitive distortions regarding the nature of harm. These distortions were particularly frequent among the lone offender (victim over 12) group, as seven out of 11 thought that their abuse was not harmful and six out of 11 suggesting that their victim experienced some level of enjoyment from the abuse. Also, six out of nine of the lone offender (victim under 12) group displayed some belief that sexual abuse was not harmful. Sixty-seven per cent of the women in the sample displayed cognitive distortions relating to entitlement. Interestingly, the women in the lone

offender groups frequently placed their own needs above the child's (six out of 11 in the victim over 12 group and five out of nine of the victim under 12 group) and the women in the male associated groups frequently placed their partner's needs above the child's (10 out of 18 in the male-accompanied group and four out of five of the male-coerced group).

Dangerous world and uncontrollable distortions were less common within the sample, except in the lone offender (victim over 12) group where five out of 11 reported feeling that a relationship with a child is easier and/or safer than with an adult, eight out of 11 blamed external factors for their offending behaviour, five out of 11 saw themselves as a victim.

Self-management and emotional self-regulation appeared to be a frequent problem highlighted in this sample, with 49 per cent of women reporting having problems dealing with negative emotions. Parenting issues seemed to be a concern, as 44 per cent of the sample reporting an inability to cope with their children, 60 per cent were said to have an inattentive or neglectful parenting style, and 37 per cent had been the subject of local authority concerns. The majority of those concerns were regarding actual sexual abuse or the risk of sexual abuse, neglect and emotional abuse of children, physical abuse of children and poor domestic conditions.

Very few sexual self-regulation factors were frequent within the sample. Only five per cent of the sample was found to have previous sexual offences. Interestingly, the four women who reported viewing relationships with children as the ideal sexual relationship were all in the lone offender (victim over 12) group. Also, eight out of 11 in the lone offender (victim over 12) group and five out of nine in the lone offender (victim under 12) group reported using grooming techniques as part of their offending behaviour, higher proportions than in the other two groups.

*Trigger factors*

Depression was frequently reported in the sample across all of the groups, with 42 per cent of the sample being prescribed anti-depressant medication at the time of their offence. A number of environmental trigger factors were also frequently reported. Of the sample, 53 per cent reported an unstable family life, which was consistent across all four groups. Relationship problems were also frequent in the sample, with

74 per cent reporting possessive and/or violent partners and 74 per cent reporting relationship problems. Perhaps unsurprisingly, a large majority of the women in the male-associated groups reported violent partners, with all five of the male-coerced group and 15 out of 18 of the male-associated group reporting a possessive or violent partner, compared with six out of 11 in the lone offender (victim over 12) group and six out of nine in the lone offender (victim under 12) group.

### Acute factors

Though few acute factors were reported within the sample as a whole there do appear to be subtle differences between the four groups concerning which factors are reported, specifically between the lone offender and male-related groups. Dysphoric mood states are reported by seven out of 11 of the lone offender (victim over 12) group and five out of nine of the lone offender (victim under 12) group compared with only three out of 18 of the male-associated group and none of the male-coerced group. Seven out of the 11 lone offender (victim over 12) group reported a need for intimacy and seven out of 11 reported a need for power or control as acute factors in their offending. Similarly, six out of nine of the lone offender (victim under 12) group reported a need for power or control. These compared with lower frequencies in the male-associated groups. The male-related groups seemed to report more environmental acute factors, for example 11 out of 18 in the male-associated group and three out of five of the male-coerced group reported a current partner who is either a Schedule 1 offender or has previous allegations of sexual abuse against a child, compared with much lower frequencies in the lone offender groups.

### Protective factors

Though the above discussion suggests a number of deficits displayed by female offenders, there are also positive protective factors displayed by the sample, which may be of great importance in the assessment of their risk and treatment needs.

In terms of offence-specific protective factors, 42 per cent of the sample displayed attitudes contrary to sexual offending behaviour, 72 per cent showed a raised awareness of offence

patterns, and 67 per cent showed an awareness of the consequences of offending. Effective social functioning skills were frequently observed within the sample, as 81 per cent of the sample was judged to have effective interpersonal skills and 67 per cent displayed pro-social attitudes and behaviours. Self-management skills were also apparent, with 37 per cent displaying adequate problem-solving and decision-making skills and 60 per cent identifying positive goals and interests. Contextual protective factors were also reported within the sample, with 44 per cent reporting a good level of social support and 93 per cent benefiting from effective supervision and monitoring.

Treatment system factors were also measured in the sample. Motivation towards assessment and treatment was frequent in the sample, with 79 per cent reporting a motivation to engage with these and 79 per cent being open about their offending behaviour during assessment. This may be related to the finding that 60 per cent of the sample reported a positive and consistent experience of intervention and good co-ordination between professionals was reported in 95 per cent of the cases.

### Summary of findings

There appear to be both a number of general risk factors and a number of more individualised risk factors frequent within this sample. Both the Beech and Ward (2004) model and Carr's (1999) protective factors also seem to present useful tools in understanding these factors, and identify a number of themes that appear to be frequent within a sample of female sexual offenders.

In terms of developmental factors, attachment problems and childhood abuse, particularly sexual abuse, appear to be frequently reported by female offenders. The psychological vulnerabilities section suggests that female offenders are characterised by low self-esteem, low confidence, low assertiveness and a lack of social support and interaction, and they seem to have problems managing both their own negative emotions and the stresses placed on them by parental responsibility.

They appear to hold similar cognitive distortions to male offenders, especially with regard to children as sexual beings, the nature of harm caused by sexual contact between adults and children, and adult entitlement to sexual contact. They do not, however, seem to be

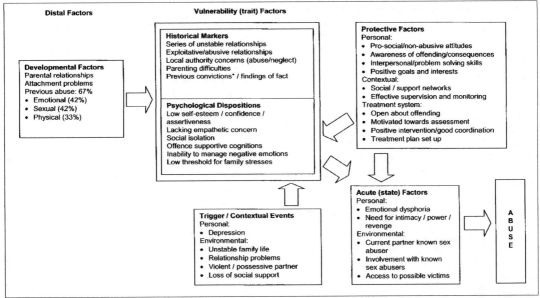

*Though these are infrequent within the sample they are still highly likely to constitute a serious risk variable. We have discussed in the chapter various reasons why these figures tend to be low for female offenders.

**Figure 8.1** An adapted version of the Beech and Ward (2004) model of risk, incorporating Carr's (1999) framework for protective factors, showing factors above a 34% (over one-third of the sample) in the Elliott et al. (2007) assessment of female sexual offenders

defined by deviant sexual interests, though this may be a function of the data sources in the present investigation. Further research into the effects of sexual arousal as a risk factor for female offenders is necessary to establish what sexual interests fuel the physiological sexual arousal that leads to high proximal risk.

These vulnerabilities appear to lead to acute risk through the intervention of a number of trigger factors, with relationship difficulties and family instability frequently reported within this sample. These trigger factors seem to push the women in the sample frequently into acute states of risk, particularly dysphoric mood states and states of personal need, both for intimacy and/or power and control that when coupled with sexual desire create states of proximal risk. It should, however, be noted that these factors are those most frequently reported and each individual will more often have her own particular combination of personal and contextual risk factors.

Each woman will also display a number of protective and strength factors that also need to be identified in the process of assessment. These women appear to have a range of social,

self-management and interpersonal skills that will be of great value to them in working towards an offence-free life. Though this would seem to conflict with our earlier findings regarding the problems these women appear to have in these areas, we would stress that this factor is based upon their behaviour during assessment with trained clinicians. Therefore we suggest that though the women appear to have these abilities they are not able to use them in the context of their day-to-day lives, for example alongside the presence of a domineering or violent partner. A number of women appear to display pro-social attitudes and have a knowledge of their offence-related behaviours and the consequences of offending, which suggests that they would be able to successfully engage in suitable treatment. If there is effective and positive intervention coupled with motivation and open communication between the women and their therapists, we can be optimistic about these women's ability to successfully manage their behaviour. Unfortunately, the lack of available resources for such work leaves many of the women vulnerable to future risk.

## Differences between the typologies

Though at first glance there do not appear to be great differences between the four identified typologies of female sex offenders, there do appear to be subtle differences that the model has assisted in highlighting.

One potentially important difference is the proportion of the lone offender (victim under 12) group that have themselves been the victim of child sexual abuse. Subtle differences are also notable in the types of cognitive distortions held by each group, for example the lone offender (victim over 12) group's generalised beliefs about children and sexuality, or the differences between the lone offender groups and the male-associated groups in terms of the prioritisation of their own, their partner's and their child's needs.

Certainly, there are also differences in terms of the acute risk factors that lead to offending behaviour, as the lone offender groups more frequently report personal acute factors, such as dysphoric mood states and personal unmet needs for intimacy and/or power and control, whereas the male-accompanied tend to report environmental acute factors such as their involvement with known sexual offenders. It seems that further work is needed into what personal needs are met by sexual offending behaviour for the male-accompanied group, whether it be approval, possibly even a level of power, within their relationships, or simply a need to avoid extreme violence.

## The value of the study

As the discussion shows, the investigation has highlighted a number of key themes for the risk assessment of female offenders. The research necessitated the development of an extensive coding framework with a firm theoretical basis, and retrospectively analysed existing data based on actual contact with the women.

The aim of the study was to highlight *potential* risk factors and create a framework that could be incorporated into the assessment of female sexual abusers to prospectively measure the prevalence of those factors in future samples and develop our knowledge of risk in this population. The assessment framework should be considered a preliminary guide to specific factors that have been identified in the clinical histories of female sexual offenders and should be used in conjunction with a thorough clinical assessment. It is a tool to aid the identification of deficits and strengths presented by a female sexual offender, the identification of which can feed into an assessment of risk and treatment need. We stress that it should not be used as a score-based risk assessment tool. Each woman should be assessed individually, taking full account of her personal circumstances.

The Elliott et al. (2007) study is exploratory. The data has not been subjected to formal multiple-marking and is mined from secondary sources, such as psychological and psychiatric reports: therefore there is a heavy reliance on the quality of those reports to ensure the quality of the data as well as the quality of self-report from the women themselves. Many of the factors, such as sexual interest or some cognitive distortions for example, rely on the women being completely open about their abusive behaviour. The sample size is small, which makes it difficult to translate these findings to a wider population of female sex offenders, though a sample of this size given the small size of the known population of female sexual offenders would be common to any study of this type.

The next stage will be to provide therapists with the preliminary coding framework and instructions on its use and allow them to incorporate it into their assessments of female sexual offenders to record data directly from new client contacts. This will allow for the development of the framework, with the therapists identifying areas where there may be gaps or areas where further consideration is necessary with the ultimate goal of creating a more comprehensive and dynamic tool for risk assessment guidance, as well as increasing the sample size.

# Part 3: More than a protocol – assessment in practice

To be effective, assessment must be an individualised and engaging process that considers the woman, her environment and those close to her, in the past, present and future. Critically, the needs of any children must be the first consideration.

In developing Lucy Faithfull Foundation's programme for women who sexually abuse children, we considered what research, especially that of Mathews, Mathews and Speltz (1991) and Saradjian (1996) and our own clinical practice indicate about the histories and motivation of female sex offenders, the range of their abusive behaviours, the techniques they use to gain victim compliance and prevent disclosure, and their patterns of offending.

In our programme, each woman undergoes an individual assessment to ascertain her treatment needs, risk factors that are particularly salient in her case, and her motivation to engage in therapeutic work. Based on the research, we hypothesised that the following may be key factors in combination in the aetiology of female sexual offending:

- Non-recognition of her responsibility for offending behaviour.
- Unresolved issues related to her own victimisation as a child and as an adult.
- Lack of empathy, either cognitive or emotional or both.
- Social isolation and poor ability to develop emotionally intimate relationships.
- Distorted views of children and the relationships between children and adults.
- Sexual arousal to children and aspects of childhood (not all cases).
- Poor self esteem and poor self efficacy.
- Poor capacity to deal with high levels of emotional arousal.
- Difficulty in recognising factors that precipitate sexual offending.
- Lack of protective factors.

In addition to assessing absolute risk and dangerousness, possible triggering factors and the risk the woman may present to children within certain contexts is considered. For example, what is the risk within a family setting, as a sole carer for her own children, as a babysitter, in a relationship with an abusive male? Any concerns must be communicated to the appropriate professionals who have the power to take action to protect children.

### Abusive solutions to unmet needs

Eldridge and Saradjian (2000) hypothesised that through her life experience a woman may have learned to fulfil unmet needs through the sexual assault of a child or young person. Haley (1990) proposes that any symptom, such as sexual offending, originates as an effective 'personal solution' to a problem or problems within the life of the perpetrator. Intervention with male sex offenders has focused mainly on stopping the

behaviour to solve the offending problem without sufficient consideration of what problems the offender is trying to solve by sexually offending. When faced with painful situations most human beings will revert to habitual methods of making themselves feel better and in the case of sexual offenders this can lead to re-offending.

For both men and women there are strong links between childhood experiences of pain, trauma and distorted and disturbed attachments and their expression in the sexual assault of a child (de Zulueta, 1993). Research carried out with 52 women who sexually abused children (Saradjian, 1996) and our long term clinical work with such women led to the conclusion that many do so because through their life experiences they have learned to meet their needs this way.

In order to help a woman stop sexually offending it is important to understand why and how she came to do so. There is no single reason why people sexually offend so a flexible model is needed to account for individual differences. The model used in the Lucy Faithfull Foundation programme is an eclectic one based on research into and clinical practice with women who sexually abuse children. It proposes that through her experiences the woman has learned that at least one of her basic human needs can be met by sexually abusive behaviours. She has also learned that it is somehow 'safer' or 'easier' for her to fulfil her needs in this way rather than via more appropriate means. Her life experience may also have led to thinking errors and empathy deficits that enable her to sexually abuse without experiencing prohibitively aversive emotions.

Thus, the assessment process involves gathering information to establish which needs the woman is attempting to meet by offending, why she believes that it is possible and acceptable for her to do this and what she needs to change in her life to reduce the risk that she will re-offend. Assessment should establish what treatment targets need to be set and how the woman can learn to meet her fundamental human needs in positive, non-abusive ways.

It is vital to collect information from available sources, including police statements, social work records, medical records, prison, probation and social services reports. However, in many cases there is very little external data and hence a great deal of reliance is placed on self-report. Consequently, it is important to elicit as much co-operation as possible without developing a collusive relationship.

### Engaging a woman in the assessment process

In training staff to use our assessment programme we emphasise the importance of an understanding and empathic approach. The following extract from our staff manual makes this point:

## Techniques and environments that facilitate engagement and fuller disclosure

In assessing a woman, consider that:

- She will probably not tell you everything she has done.
- She may not define some of her behaviours as sexual offending.
- She may have abused in conjunction with someone else.
- She is likely to exhibit beliefs and attitudes which justify or excuse her behaviour.
- She may have offence-related sexual fantasies.
- She has probably met some fundamental human needs and perceived needs through offending.
- She may be afraid of the consequences of (a) giving information, (b) changing.
- She will be fearful of the assessor's reaction to her.
- She is likely to feel extremely isolated in terms of (a) relationships generally, (b) as a female sex offender.

In the light of this, create a non-collusive but empathic therapeutic environment. The following are sensible ground rules for such an environment:

- We believe that with support you can make sense of how you came to be here.
- We want, with you, to create a safe, respectful environment for this work.
- We will need to share information from our work together with relevant colleagues.
- We'll help you ask yourself questions about what has happened and we'll support you in doing so.
- We believe change is possible but recognise that at this point you may need us to believe it for you.
- We know change is difficult and will take time and effort for all of us.

- We believe that you can make good choices and maintain a positive, offence-free life in the future.

Co-operation can be facilitated by:

- using language consistent with the level of understanding of the woman being assessed
- explaining the purpose of the assessment and what it entails
- acknowledging the difficulties of having to disclose to a stranger the most intimate details of her life
- stressing the advantages to the woman of disclosure in understanding: how she came to offend, how she can best be helped and how it can inform the help given to the victims
- encouraging her to see it as a start to sorting out difficult aspects of her life
- being honest with the woman; telling her the information you have already.

We teach assessors that no matter how the women present themselves, a significant barrier to disclosing offending behaviour can be shame, perhaps because they have so strongly deviated from societal norms for women. One helpful approach is for the assessor to place the woman's own experience within that of other women who have sexually offended. For example, rather than asking 'Do you have sexual fantasies?' say 'Some women describe having thoughts about children that make them feel aroused in some way, do you have similar thoughts?' 'What do you feel when you have these thoughts?' Many female sexual offenders genuinely cannot identify their own emotions due to emotional deprivation but may be able to describe the physical sensations they experience. They say things such as 'I feel tight inside', 'my heart races', 'I can't get my breath', 'I get so restless'.

Like anyone disclosing personally difficult material, the woman is likely to tell 'the tip of the iceberg', until feeling 'safe' with the listener. It is therefore important that the assessor does not display negative emotions such as shock, disgust or anger.

### Therapist style

The importance of a positive therapist style in engaging clients of both genders in the process of assessment and intervention is vital. An empathic, warm, rewarding therapist style has been shown to have a beneficial effect on male offenders' coping skills, perspective taking and relationship skills. (Marshall, Serran, Fernandez, Mulloy, Mann and Thornton (2003).

We propose that key components of therapist style that encourage positive responses include:

- warmth
- empathy
- reward
- respect
- compassion
- sensitive use of humour
- genuineness
- directiveness (but with flexibility)
- clear boundaries

## A shared venture toward an abuse-free New Life

A warm, empathic, respectful approach with clear expectations and ground rules is vital to a successful outcome. Ground rules include multi agency collaboration and case management and support that take account of any child protection issues as well as the needs of the woman. The assessment process will best facilitate identification of treatment need if it is a shared venture. Many of the women have experienced extensive abuse both as children and as adults. An 'abuse-free New Life' means not only a life free of abusing children but also free of being abused themselves.

From the beginning of assessment it is important to motivate the woman to engage in a positive way forward. This is highlighted in the following extract from the Staff Assessment Manual.

### Engagement

The purpose of the first meeting is to engage the woman in the assessment process. This is facilitated by explaining clearly the purpose of the assessment and outlining what areas will be covered and how the assessment will be used and who it will be shared with. Time should be allowed for the woman to raise questions and concerns and, where possible and appropriate, to receive answers.

In talking with the woman remember to:

### Listen

- Hear her version of events: it is important to her at this stage to present it in this way.
- Hear her concerns for physical/emotional safety.

- Recognise denial may be the best coping strategy she has now.
- Recognise she may not tell everything today.

### Question

- Use language she can understand.
- Use structured, sequential questions that allow for disclosure.
- Place the woman's experience within knowledge of other women who have offended.

In the early stages, the emphasis should be on *collecting information about beliefs and behaviours*. Later on self-challenge of pro-offending beliefs can be facilitated. Very early challenge of the woman's beliefs about the child's perspective or the amount of harm done may have the effect of preventing her giving further information.

Motivate the woman to engage in assessment by telling her right at the beginning that your intention is that the process will help her to find ways of improving her life from how it is at present and meeting her needs in new and positive ways: towards a New Life plan (see Eldridge and Saradjian: New Life Manual)*.

Our approach links strongly to the highly motivational 'Good Lives Model of Offender Rehabilitation', which asks therapists 'to develop an intervention plan that seeks to capitalize on offenders' interests and preferences and to equip them with the capabilities they need to realize their plan in the environment into which they are likely to be realized. Constraints relating to offenders abilities, the provision of resources, and the degree of support in their environments moderate the nature of such plans. The aim is to promote what goals are possible, taking into account each offender's unique set of circumstances . . . . We have been so busy thinking about how to get rid of sexual crimes that we have overlooked a rather basic truth: offenders want better lives not simply the promise of less harmful ones' (Ward, Mann and Gannon, 2007). In our view this truth needs to be acknowledged and built into interventions from the beginning of the assessment phase and emphasised throughout the work with each woman.

Our 'New Life Manual' was developed as a workbook directly from our clinical practice with female sexual offenders and provides anonymised, composite examples of other women's abusive patterns and self-management plans and encourages the reader to identify her own. Female sexual offenders often describe feeling isolated and bizarre. The manual offers them hope by helping them see that they are not alone and that other female abusers have succeeded in achieving an abuse-free life. The sample plans and the language used is drawn from clinical practice with the women themselves and much has been devised by them. Depending on individual need, sections of the manual are given to women during the assessment process, to help engage them in the journey toward creating a 'New Life'.

## Concluding thoughts

Criminal conviction and reconviction rates are very low for women who sexually abuse children. However, this does not mean that they do not pose a risk of harm to children. People carry their histories into their present and future, and many of these women have backgrounds in which they have been extensively abused and their needs have not been met. Their attitudes, beliefs and behaviours often reflect this, including choice of partners, which may lead to repetition of undetected abuse in a world in which women are seen as trusted caregivers.

The assessment and treatment of women who sexually abuse children is still in relative infancy. The positive side of this is that there is no excuse for repeating the mistakes that have been made with male offenders. The most important learning is that while identifying similarities and highlighting commonality we must assess and treat each woman as an individual with differing needs, circumstances and levels and contexts for risk of harm to children. We must also recognise the function of sexually abusive behaviour for her and how she can become motivated and empowered to meet her fundamental human needs in non-abusive ways. The role of appropriately individualised intervention is very important but resources are limited (Bunting, 2005). Lucy Faithfull Foundation hosts a special interest group with invitees from academia, clinical practice and policy-making. In this way we hope together to influence a national strategy and create positive change in these women's lives to prevent children from being harmed and to develop better lives for the women themselves.

## References

Aylward, A., Christopher, M., Newell, R.M. and Gordon, A. (2002) *What about Women who Commit Sex Offences?* Paper presented at the 22nd Annual Research and Treatment Conference of the Association for the Treatment of Sexual Offenders, St. Louis, MO.

Beckett, R. et al. (1994) *Community-Based Treatment for Sex Offenders: An Evaluation of Seven Treatment Programmes.* Home Office Publications Unit.

Beckett, R.C., Burke R. and Cotton S. (2006) *Predicting Risk with Female Sexual Abusers.* National Association for Treatment of Sexual Abusers (NOTA) Annual Conference, York. Available from the Author. Richard.Beckett@OBMH.Nhs.Uk

Beech, A.R. and Ward, T. (2004) The Integration of Etiology and Risk in Sex Offenders: A Theoretical Framework. *Aggression and Violent Behavior,* 10: 1, 31–63.

Benard, B. (2006) Using Strengths-Based Practice to Tap Resilience of Families. In Saleeby, D. *Strengths Perspective in Social Work Practice.* Boston, MA: Allyn and Bacon.

Bunting, L. (2005) *Females who Sexually Offend against Children: Responses of the Child Protection and Criminal Justice Systems.* NSPCC. London.

Carr, A. (1999) *The Handbook of Child and Adolescent Clinical Psychology: A Contextual Approach.* London: Routledge.

Clark, D. and Howden-Windall, J. (2000) A Retrospective Study of Criminogenic Factors in the Female Prison Population. London: HM Prison Service.

Correctional Services Accreditation Panel (2002–3) *Fourth Report from the Correctional Services Accreditation Panel.* London: Home Office.

Denov, M.S. (2001) A Culture of Denial: Exploring Professional Perspectives on Female Sex Offending. *Canadian Journal of Criminology,* 43: 3, 303–29.

Denov, M.S. (2003) The Myth of Innocence: Sexual Scripts and the Recognition of Child Sexual Abuse by Female Perpetrators. *Journal of Sex Research,* 40: 3, 303–14.

de Zulueta, F. (1993) *From Pain to Violence.* London: Whurr.

Eldridge, H.J. and Saradjian, J. (2000) Replacing the Function of Abusive Behaviours for the Offender: Remaking Relapse Prevention in Working with Women who Sexually Abuse Children. In Laws, D.R., Hudson, S.M. and

Ward, T. (Eds.) *Remaking Relapse Prevention with Sex Offenders: A Sourcebook.* Thousand Oaks: Sage.

Eldridge, H.J., Saradjian, J., Brotherston, S. and Ashfield, S. *Lucy Faithfull Foundation Assessment and Intervention Programme for Women who Sexually Abuse Children.* Birmingham: Lucy Faithfull Foundation.

Elliott, I.A., Eldridge, H.J., Ashfield, S. and Beech, A.R. (2007) *An Exploratory Investigation into Risk Factors, Protective Factors and Treatment Need in the Clinical Assessment Histories of a Sample of Female Sex Offenders.* Paper presented at the 5th Tools to Take Home Conference, Coventry, 24th April, 2007

Finkelhor, D. and Russell, D. (1984) Women as Perpetrators: Review of the Evidence. In Finkelhor, D. *Child Sexual Abuse.* New York: The Free Press.

Finkelhor, D., Williams, L.M. and Burns, N. (1988) *Nursery Crimes: Sexual Abuse in Daycare.* Thousand Oaks, CA: Sage.

Ford, H. (2006) *Women who Sexually Abuse Children.* Chichester: John Wiley and Sons.

Gilgun, J.F. (1999) CASPARS: Clinical Assessment Instruments that Measure Strengths and Risks in Children and Families. In Calder, M.C. (Ed.) *Working with Young People who Sexually Abuse: New Pieces of the Jigsaw Puzzle* (48–58) Lyme Regis: Russell House Publishing.

Gilgun, J.F. (2003) Working with Young People who have Sexual Behaviour Problems: Lessons from Risk and Resilience. Presented at G-MAP Conference *Working Holistically with Young People who Sexually Harm.* Bolton, UK, June 2003.

Gilgun, J. (2006) Children and Adolescents with Problematic Sexual Behaviours: Lessons from Research on Resilience. In Longo, R. and Prescott, D. (Eds) *Current Perspectives: Working with Sexually Aggressive Youth and Youth with Sexual Behavior Problems.* Holyoke, MA: Neari Press.

Haley, J. (1990) *Strategies of Psychotherapy* (2nd Edn). Rockville: Triangle Press.

Marshall, W.L. et al. (2003) Therapist Characteristics in the Treatment of Sexual Offenders: Tentative Data on their Relationship with Indices of Behaviour Change. *Journal of Sexual Aggression,* 9: 1, 25–30.

Masten, A.S. and Reed M-G. J. (2005) Resilience in Development. In Snyder, C.R. and Lopez, A.J. (Eds.) *The Handbook of Positive Psychology.* Oxford: Oxford University Press.

Matthews, J.K., Mathews, R. and Speltz, K. (1991) Female Sexual Offenders: A Typology. In

Patton, M.Q. (Ed.) *Family Sexual Abuse: Frontline Research and Evaluation.* Newbury Park: Sage.

Mendel, M.P. (1995) *The Male Survivor: The Impact of Sexual Abuse.* Thousand Oaks. CA: Sage.

Miller, S.D., Duncan, B.L. and Hubble, M.A. (1997) *Escape from Babel: Toward a Unifying Language for Psychotherapy Practice.* New York: W.W. Norton.

Millon, T. (1994) *Millon Clinical Multiaxial Inventory III.* Minneapolis, MN: National Computer Systems, Inc.

Nathan, P. and Ward, T. (2002) Female Sex Offenders: Clinical and Demographic Features. *Journal of Sexual Aggression,* 8, 5–21.

Print, B., Morrison, M., and Henniker, J. (2001) An Inter-Agency Assessment and Framework for Young People who Sexually Abuse: Principles, Processes and Practicalities. In Calder, M.C. (Ed.) *Juveniles and Children who Sexually Abuse: Frameworks for Assessment.* Lyme Regis: Russell House Publishing.

Rallings, M., Webster, S.D. and Rudolph, M. (2001) *The NOTA Intake Protocol: Characteristics of a Large Sample of Sexual Offenders.* Presented at NOTA Conference 12 Sept., 2001, Cardiff.

Ring, L. (2005) *Psychometric Profiles of Female Sexual Abusers: A Preliminary Analysis into the Differences between Sexually Abusive and Non-Offending Females.* The University of Birmingham.

Saradjian, J. (1996) *Women who Sexually Abuse Children: From Research to Clinical Practice.* Chichester: John Wiley and Sons.

Saradjian, J. (2006) Foreword. In Ford, H. *Women who Sexually Abuse Children.* The Lucy Faithfull Foundation.

Seligman, M.E.P. and Csikszentmihalyi, M. (2000) Positive Psychology: An Introduction. *American Psychologist,* 55, 5–14.

Thornton, D. (2007) Scoring Guide for Risk Matrix 2000.9/SVC. Available on: bham.ac.uk

Vandiver, D.M. and Kercher, G. (2004) Offender and Victim Characteristics of Registered Female Sex Offenders in Texas: A Proposed Typology of Female Sex Offenders. *Sexual Abuse: A Journal of Research and Treatment,* 16, 121–37.

Ward, T. and Keenan, T. (1999) Child Molesters' Implicit Theories. *Journal of Interpersonal Violence,* 14, 821–38.

Ward, T., Mann, R. and Gannon, T.A. (2007) The Good Lives Model of Rehabilitation: Clinical Implications. *Aggression and Violent Behavior.* 12, 87–107.

Ward, T., Polaschek, D. and Beech, A.R. (2006) *Theories of Sexual Offending.* Chichester: Wiley.

# CHAPTER 9

# Core Assessment of Adult Sex Offenders with a Learning Disability

*Leam A. Craig, Ian Stringer and Roger B. Hutchinson*

## Introduction

The past twenty years has witnessed great advances in the assessment and treatment of sexual offenders. However, while the literature has witnessed great advancement in the assessment of risk (Hanson and Thornton, 2000) psychological functioning and deviancy (Craig, Thornton, Beech, and Browne, 2007) theory (Ward and Siegert, 2002) and treatment efficacy (Hanson, Gordon, Harris, Marques, Murphy, Quinsey, and Seto, 2002) in non-learning disabled sexual offenders, the literature on the assessment and treatment of sexual offenders with learning disabilities has seen comparatively little research. Well controlled studies have found prevalence rates for individuals with learning disabilities to be slightly higher in offender populations than in the general population (Borthwick-Duffy, 1994; Lund, 1990; MacEachron, 1979). In a 10-month prospective study Barron, Hassiotis, and Banes (2004) followed 61 learning disabled offenders referred to specialist mental health and criminal justice services. Although not specific to sexual offenders, they found that offenders with learning disabilities begin offending at an early age, had a history of multiple offences, that sexual and arson offences were over-represented, and half re-offended at follow-up. In a sample of previous prison inmates with learning disabilities, Klimecki, Jenkinson, and Wilson (1994) reported a 34 per cent recidivism rate for sexual offenders over two years, and an 84 per cent of overall re-offending within the first 12 months. Indeed, learning disability might contribute to sexual related or aggressive behaviour in some individuals. It has been estimated that 6 per cent of the learning disability population have severe sexual aggression (Thompson and Brown, 1997) and that 41 per cent engage in challenging behaviours defined as 'sex related', of which 17 per cent had police contact and 4 per cent were convicted of sexual offences (McBrien, Hodgetts, and Gregory, 2002).

The true prevalence rate for sexual offenders with learning disabilities is unclear. Cooper (1995) estimates the prevalence of learning disability in the general population is 9 per cent, but 10 per cent to 15 per cent of all sex offences. Although in reality these differences are very small. Of offenders with learning disabilities, Gross (1985) estimates that between 21 per cent and 50 per cent had committed a sexual crime, whereas Walker and McCabe (1973) found that 28 per cent of 33 men with a learning disability detained under hospital orders had committed a sexual offence. It is important to note that the higher prevalence rate may to some extent be accounted for by the misinterpretation of behaviours. The increased visibility of offenders with learning disabilities, where the commission of their offences is often less sophisticated, increases the possibility of detection (see Craig and Hutchinson, 2005). Furthermore, of the studies comparing rates of sexual offending in learning disabled and non-learning disabled groups, it is not clear whether these groups were matched on educational level or other socio-demographic variables.

Compared to the literature on the assessment and treatment of non-learning disabled sex offenders, there is relatively little on the assessment and treatment of sex offenders with learning disabilities, and where studies exist these are usually restricted to case studies or small samples (eg Craig, Stringer, and Moss, 2006; Lindsay, Olley, Braillie, and Smith, 1999; Murphy, 1997; Rose, Jenkins, O'Conner, Jones, and Felce, 2002). However, this is an area of increasing interest to researchers and clinicians alike and a number of treatment programmes and psychometric procedures have recently been developed and standardised on sex offenders with learning disabilities. The aim of this chapter is to consider clinical and psychometric assessment procedures and to offer guidance to practitioners when working with sex offenders with learning disabilities.

## Defining learning disability

Before we consider the various assessment procedures that are currently available, it is important to first consider the clinical features of this client group and operational definitions of learning disability. Difficulties in assessing adaptive and social functioning have contributed to a tendency amongst clinicians to concentrate on assessment of intellectual functioning (Professional Affairs Board, 2001: 4). This assumes that provided significant impairment of intellectual functioning has been established, similar deficits in adaptive and social functioning are likely. The diagnosis of a learning disability is not solely related to low intellect. It is a mistake to overemphasise the role of intelligence quotient (IQ) as an indicator of appropriate treatment strategies, since IQ alone does not adequately describe a person's ability (Coleman and Haaven, 2001). Indeed, The British Psychological Society recommends that a classification of learning disability should only be made on the basis of assessed impairments of both intellectual functioning and adaptive and social functioning which have been acquired before adulthood. The Professional Affairs Board of The British Psychological Society document *Learning Disability: Definitions and Context* (2001: 4) was designed to clarify the ambiguity surrounding the use of different terminology (eg learning disability, mental retardation, mental handicap, mental subnormality, developmental disability) and the different definitions used to describe a learning disability. The document outlines the features that make up the definition of 'learning disability' as used within a health and social care context and identifies three core criteria for learning disability, all of which must be present for a person to be considered to have a learning disability:

- significant impairment of intellectual functioning
- significant impairment of adaptive functioning
- age of onset before adulthood.

The BPS document defines significant impairment of adaptive and social functioning as '. . . the individual requires significant assistance to provide for his/her own survival (eating and drinking needs, and to keep him/herself clean, warm and clothed) and/or with his/her social/community adaptation (eg social problem solving and social reasoning)' (p 6).

The American Psychiatric Association diagnostic criteria for mental retardation as described in the *Diagnostic and Statistical Manual of Mental Disorders* has changed little in the recently revised version (DSM TR, 2000: 47) and defines a learning disability as:

- significant sub-average intellectual functioning (IQ of approximately 70 or below) on an individually administered IQ test
- concurrent deficits or impairments in present adaptive functioning (ie the person's effectiveness in meeting the standards expected of their age and cultural group, in at least two of the following: communication, self-care, home living, social/interpersonal skills, use of community resources, self-direction, functional academic skills, work, health and safety)
- the onset before age 18 years.

The DSM-TR (2000) also defines the degree of disability as 'mild mental retardation' IQ range 50–55 to 70, 'moderate retardation' IQ range 35–40 to 50–55, and 'severe retardation' IQ range 20–25 to 35–40.

The Royal College of Psychiatrists (2001) report the term 'learning disability' is used synonymously with the term 'mental retardation' (*Classification of Mental and Behavioural Disorders – Clinical Description and Diagnostic Guidelines*, ICD-10-CDDG, 1992). However the *Diagnostic criteria for psychiatric disorders for use with adults with learning disability/mental retardation* (DC-LD, 2001) is a new classificatory system that has been developed in recognition of the limitations of the ICD-10 manuals and the DSM-IV (1994) and adopts the term 'learning disability', the diagnosis of which is dependent upon the person:

- having an IQ below 70
- continued impairment in adaptive behaviour/social functioning
- age of onset in the developmental phase (ie before the age of 18 years).

The DC-LD (2001) defines the degree of disability as 'mild learning disability' IQ range 50–69; mental age nine to under 12 years; 'moderate learning disability' IQ range 35–49, mental age six to under nine years; 'severe learning disability' IQ range 20–34, mental age three to under six years; and 'profound learning disability' IQ range less than 20, mental age less than three years. Importantly, the IQ range '70–79' is often referred to as 'borderline learning disability' however this term is not referred to in either the American Psychiatric Association (2000) or the DC-LD (2001) criteria.

The DC-LD criteria recommends that the diagnosis of a learning disability should be done in a hierarchical manner using the multiaxial system involving an assessment on several axes, each of which refers to a different domain of information that may help the clinician plan treatment and predict outcome:

- Axis I – refers to severity of learning disability.
- Axis II – refers to the cause of learning disability.
- Axis III – refers to psychiatric disorders.

DC-LD Level A – developmental disorders (includes autistic spectrum disorders etc.)

DC-LD Level B – psychiatric illness (dementia – Alzheimer's and Huntington's disease, schizophrenia, delusional disorders, anxiety and mood related disorders etc.)

DC-LD Level C – personality disorders

DC-LD Level D – problem behaviours (aggressive behaviour, self injury, sexually inappropriate behaviour, etc.)

DC-LD Level E – other disorders (disorders related to drug/alcohol abuse, gender identity, and disorders of sexual preference such as paraphilias including fetishism, paedophilia, exhibitionism, sadomasochism behaviours, and psychosexual developmental disorders).

From the DC-LD criteria, developmental disorders have been listed as a separate level in view of the recognition that the developmental disorder may not be the underlying cause of a person's learning disabilities (Axis II). For example, pervasive developmental disorders may coexist with syndromes such as Fragile X syndrome and Down's syndrome, and are not invariably associated with learning disabilities (p 13). The criterion distinguishes developmental disorders from psychiatric illness, although people with developmental disorders can develop co-morbid Axis II Levels B-D disorders. This can include brain damage, autism, learning disability or all three. Therefore, if a person presents with a learning disability this is the primary Axis I disorder and any other disorders should be diagnosed taking account of both Axis I and Axis II disorders.

The principle method for determining levels of intellectual functioning is via use of psychometric assessment. The most commonly used assessment is the Wechsler Adult Intelligence Scale, third version (WAIS-III Wechsler, 1999), from which intelligence quotients IQ can be calculated. The mean IQ score is 100 with a standard deviation of 15. A score of one standard deviation below the mean would correspond to an IQ of 85 or below, and two standard deviations below the mean would correspond to IQ of 70 and or below. In addition to using formal assessments of intellectual functioning, the ICD-10 and the Professional Affairs Board recommends the use of the Vineland Adaptive Behaviour Scales (VABS) (Sparrow et al., 1984) as an assessment tool to measure impairment of adaptive/social functioning. The VABS assesses the developmental level of learning disabled populations and provides an estimate of the person's developmental level in each of the three areas: communication, daily living skills and socialisation and a general estimate of developmental functioning based on the aggregate of these three scores. In general terms, individuals with learning disabilities are likely to experience a range of important cognitive deficits including: reduced capacity for and reduced speed of processing information; difficulties in learning new information; concrete thinking styles with difficulties in dealing with abstract information; difficulties with language; and limited education-based knowledge and skills. These deficits can be subdivided into six main areas (Mackinnon, Bailey and Pink, 2004). As a result assessment methods will need to be adjusted to take into account the individual's cognitive capacities.

## Clinical assessment

The purpose of assessment is to get as complete an understanding of an individual and their behaviour as possible. The more thorough the assessment, the more safe the management of the offender, and the more focused the treatment strategy (Mikkelsen, 2004). The assessment of sex offenders is fraught with difficulties (Carich and Calder, 2003). Lacking technology to access the mind, it is impossible to observe the many interactions of mental and social processes implicated in the generation of sexual behaviour such as attention and perceptions, judgement and decision-making, attitudes, values, beliefs, memories, mind maps, sexual preferences, orientation, fantasies, needs, drives and desires. Some of these processes are little understood by, or unknown to, the offender. Alternatively, some of these processes may be known, but the offender may use defence mechanisms and minimise, justify or deny their offending behaviours and underlying mental processes. Sexual offenders with learning disability add a further level of difficulty (Carich and Mussack, 2001). The experience of learning disability is difficult to comprehend for people who have 'normal' intellect. People with learning disability may think and learn differently and may master different adaptive skills such as effectively faking understanding. Similarities between disabled and non-disabled offenders have been noted (Haaven, Little and Petre-Miller, 1990) including the use of denial, limited coping skills and low self esteem.

The clinical assessment includes collecting valid information from the past and present life of the offender. Multifactoral research has consistently identified factors through developmental stages associated with criminal outcomes in adulthood (Herbert, 2003; Robins and Rutter, 1990), including intrauterine and perinatal, infancy, childhood, adolescence and adulthood. Having found all available relevant information from reliable sources, clinical decision-making is applied to generate functional analysis for the offending behaviour and treatment implications (Sturmey, 1996). Criminogenic historical factors and events experienced in the past are important as they may predispose a person to offend or re-offend. It seems reasonable therefore to draw up a list of factors commonly associated with offending and look for evidence of their presence in the offender's past and present life. Two paradigms are useful when conducting clinical assessments of adult sexual offenders with learning disabilities. One paradigm looks for indicators of developmental influences. Learning theories provide explanatory processes of how dysfunctional behavioural repertoires are acquired from influential others, such as parents, siblings and peers, through inconsistency, modelling, and shaping etc. (eg Bandura, 1973). A second paradigm using psychodynamic theory provides theoretical concepts and processes for offending behaviour, including motivational needs and gratification, and explanation for the role of emotions and their interactions with attitudes, values and beliefs, personality traits and sexuality (eg Andrews and Bonta, 1994;

Butcher, 1995). It also provides a framework to explain the acquisition of behavioural repertoires which develop in appropriate psychosocial environments via attachment theory (Bowlby, 1979; 1988; Howe, Brandon, Hinings and Schofield, 1999). Other psychodynamic concepts underpin other aspects of offender behaviour, for example defence mechanisms underpinning cognitive distortions.

## A semi-structured forensic interview

A clinical interview should include any and all relevant information from the person's history (through interview), current capacities (using psychometric measures) and current situation (through interview). Information should be gathered from all available sources: the client, family members, official records (criminal justice system, social/health/education services etc.). Differences, especially those between the client, family members, and official records, should be noted and where possible explained. The purpose is to identify any significant developmental influences (positive and negative). It may also be possible to find when and/or how problems started and associated triggers. The clinical interview will be guided by a number of questions including: Where does this behaviour come from, and does it have a developmental pathway? The most efficient way of extracting this information is using a semi-structured interview, containing factors, conditions and events identified by research. It is a requirement that a clinician is familiar with the client, the documents relevant to the assessment, and the relevant research literature. It is not possible to set out the entire field of knowledge here. The semi-structured interview can be organised into a number of significant areas of influence: early development, family home, family history, education history, employment history, criminal history, substance misuse, temper/violent history, accident/illnesses, psychiatric history, relationship history and sexual interests. A more detailed list of questions used to assess key aspects of an individual's personal history is in Appendix 1.

## Understanding the information

Many of these factors, conditions and events may be symptomatic of other problems, the presence of which does not invariably mean the client is asocial, antisocial or criminal. Rather, they may have dysfunctional psychology which may require sympathetic management, a matter of experience and clinical judgement. Often historical information is difficult to verify. Memories can fail or be repressed. In spite of this, a personal history can be useful, and is taken for two reasons. Firstly, to identify developmental conditions and influences that have shaped the client's early years and subsequent life, and secondly, to look for the presence of any past and current factors, conditions, events, and current attitudes, values and beliefs, which empirical research has identified as part of the developmental pathway for offending behaviours. As a rough rule of thumb, the more atypical factors are found, the stronger the indication the client has dysfunctional capacities or maladaptive behavioural repertoires. There is no certain, isomorphic relationship between psychological capacities or abilities as measured by existing psychometric technologies and offending behaviour. At best they may suggest cognitive, characterological or emotional patterns used in interactions, which may (or may not) contribute to thoughts, feelings or appetites antecedent to offending behaviour. A wide range of psychosocial factors, conditions and events have been associated with offending behaviours. In reality many, or few, may be found in the assessment of the individual. There are several patterns to look for in the information gathered and the following questions may help guide in the formulation and information gathering process.

### Identifying the problem

- What is the age of onset of problems?
- How frequently do they occur?
- Is there any evidence of escalation, increasing frequency or severity?
- Do the problems fall within or outside the 'normal' range?
- Are the problems symptomatic of psychological or mental health problems, or are they criminogenic?
- Is there a wide range of problems?
- What is their duration?

### Identifying the causes and influences

- What appear to be the causes of problems?
- Are they inherent in the abilities/capacities of the client? What indications are there the

behaviour may have been learned (acquired behaviours may be extinguishable)?
- Do they appear to have arisen from familial/social influences?
- What discrepancies are there between self report of the client and documents?
- Are there differences between the accounts of client and family members? Why?
- Are there any discrepancies between client's account of the current situation and other (eg official) accounts?
- Are there any discrepancies between the client's history, psychometric results, and account of the current situation and clinical impression during interview?
- Where there are discrepancies how might they have arisen?
- Whether or not there are discrepancies, do you estimate the client has been honest in their self report?
- How valid is the assessment?
- What are the legal contingencies acting on the client?
- Does the client have any knowledge of psychology or its assessment methodologies?

Knowledge of the literature will inform the evaluation of the information, provide an indication of the significance and functional relationship with offence behaviours.

### *Sexual deviancy*

Comprehensive assessment of sexual interests in people with learning disabilities remains dependent on very specialist services where practitioners have experience of both learning disability and forensic assessment. With offenders with learning disabilities, arousal preferences have been used to identify those with greater probability of re-offending. While this risk factor is well documented in recidivism studies for non-learning disabled sexual offenders (Hanson and Morton-Bourgon, 2005) there is a paucity of literature in this area for people with learning disabilities (O'Connor and Rose, 1999).

Although there are few measures designed to assess sexual deviancy on adult sexual offenders with learning disabilities, this does not lead to the conclusion that sexual preference should not be considered as a motivating factor in this client group (Tudway and Darmoody, 2005). The assessment of sexual preference in this client group is primarily limited to the clinical assessment of sexual interests and appetites (Swaffer, Hollin, Beech, Beckett, and Fisher, 2000). Physiological indices of arousal such as penile plethysmography (PPG) are widely used with non-learning disabled sexual offenders (Serin, Mailloux and Malcolm, 2001) and the indication of deviant sexual interest has been shown to be a good predictor of sexual reconviction (Hanson and Morton-Bourgon, 2005; Proulx, Pellerin, McKibben, Aubut, and Ouimet, 1997; Quinsey, Rice, and Harris, 1995). However, physiological assessment of deviant sexual interests has been criticised for being intrusive, lacking construct validity and standardisation and its accuracy as a risk predictor is questionable (Laws, 2003). A major source of criticism using this technology is the problem of faked responding where the ability to inhibit sexual arousal have been reported (Marshall and Fernandez, 2000). Tudway and Darmoody (2005) suggest issues relating to a lack of consistency in stimulus sets, poor discrimination abilities, and problems with regard to the nature and constitution of the populations in the studies using PPG that such measures may be problematic in learning disabled groups. An alternative to PPG technologies is that of 'reaction time' as a method of establishing sexual interest. As Tudway and Darmoody (2005) observe, this methodology exploits Singer's (1984) three-stage theory of sexual attraction in males in which the first stage is increased visual attention; the second stage is movement toward the desired object; and the third stage is resulting physiological arousal. Initial research results are promising (Abel, Huffman, Warberg and Holland, 1998) although it is not clear whether this procedure has been standardised on sexual offenders with learning disabilities.

An alternative approach to assessing deviancy in sexual offenders with learning disabilities was suggested by Craig, Moss and Hutchinson (2006). They assessed sexually inappropriate behaviour in the context of the developmental age in males with a learning disability and compared to a model comprising a four-group continuum of 'normal-to-deviant' sexual behaviour in children. The term 'normal' is used to describe behaviours that occur naturally throughout sexual development, as a result of biological and physiological changes. 'Abnormal' or 'pathological' are terms used to describe sexual behaviours that one would not expect to occur within the natural development. These kinds of

behaviours are indicative of a disturbance of the natural development (Araji, 1997). Craig, Moss and Hutchinson compared the inappropriate sexual behaviours by men with learning disabilities to a four group 'normal-to-deviant' continuum encompassing 'normal' to 'deviant' sexual behaviour in children as described by Johnson and Feldmeth (1993):

- Group 1, Normal Sexual Exploration or 'Sex Play', describes sexual behaviours, which may be considered as 'normal' for children to engage in, for example sex play or exposure with similar aged children, which is largely curiosity driven and with mutual involvement. When discovered, the response is one of shyness and embarrassment.
- Group 2, Sexually Reactive Behaviours, describes a wider range of behaviours where the focus on sexuality is 'out of balance' with their peer group; the child may approach a wider age range of children and also adults. The motivation would be anxiety reduction and non-coercive. When discovered the response may be one of surprise, upset, confusion or fear.
- Group 3, Extensive Mutual Sexual Behaviours, describes behaviours in which the child participates in a full range of adult sexual behaviours. There is an increased focus on sexual contact and the behaviour is likely to be planned, possibly with the use of coercion. The motivation may be a coping mechanism to decrease isolation, decrease boredom, stabilise sense of self, provide an attachment figure, decrease physiological arousal and sexual stimulation. When discovered the response may be one of denial and blaming other children.
- Group 4, Children Who Molest, describes sexual behaviours similar to those reported in Group 3 but here there is a greater use of threats, bribery or manipulation. There may also be a wider age range of targets; the behaviour is much more likely to be planned and blame attributed to the other child. Group 4 behaviours are also distinguished by feelings of anger, revenge and aggression as opposed to 'light-hearted' or confused feelings. This group are also more likely to engage in sexual behaviour with children who are younger than themselves compared to other groups who may engage in sexual behaviour with age-related peers. When discovered the response may be to

act out aggressively and angrily blame other children, and denial.

Significant differences were identified when comparing chronological and developmental ages, and between the categorisation of behaviour dependent upon whether a chronological or developmental context was used. Two groups of offender emerged. In one group, behaviour was assessed as being significantly less deviant when considered in the context of the individual's developmental level, indicating age appropriate behaviour in terms of a model of normal sexual development in children. In the second group, behaviour was identified as being deviant irrespective of the developmental level of the individual when compared to normal sexual behaviour exhibited by children of a similar developmental level. Under these circumstances, the clients in the first group would require social and personal education that facilitated developmental maturation and relationships training whereas the second group would require additional therapeutic input to address 'deviant appetites'.

# Psychometric assessment

There have been great advances in the assessment of non-learning disabled sexual offenders and a number of psychometric measures have been developed (Beech, Fisher and Beckett, 1998; Beech, Oliver, Fisher and Beckett, 2005). However, few of these have been standardised on sexual offenders with learning disabilities and it is not clear whether these measures are sensitive to subtle changes in cognitive shift in clients with learning disabilities (Craig, Stringer and Moss, 2006). Attempts have been made to 'adapt' these measures for sexual offenders with learning disabilities. Kolton, Boer and Boer (2001) argued that the Abel and Becker Cognition Scale (ABCS; Abel, Becker and Cunningham-Rathner, 1984), which measures cognitive distortions supportive of sexually assaultive behaviour by child molesters, may be too complex to be comprehended by offenders with learning disabilities. They modified the ABCS to increase its readability in an attempt to facilitate the valid assessment of the cognitive distortions of learning disabled offenders. Nevertheless, only a few measures have been specifically designed to assess sex offender attitudes in clients with

learning disabilities. Below we offer a summary of those measures specifically designed to assess functional ability and attitudes to sex offending in clients with learning disabilities.

## *Functioning and mental health assessments*

As part of a treatment study Craig, Stringer and Nagi (2007) recently evaluated the use of a range of psychometric measures used to assess various psychological constructs in sex offenders with learning disabilities. These measures included both screening measures (eg screening for suitability for cognitive-behavioural treatment) as well as core treatment measures (eg explicit targets for treatment such as victim empathy, cognitive distortions and sexual assault attitudes). In their treatment study, Craig et al. were able to demonstrate the positive effects of cognitive-behavioural treatment in sex offenders with learning disabilities as evidenced by post-treatment psychometric scores. Using the psychometric measures described below they found significant improvements in attitudes towards victims and significant reductions in attitudes relating to cognitive distortions and pro-sexual assault beliefs.

### Autism Assessment: The Diagnostic Criteria Checklist (Howlin, 1997)

The diagnostic criteria for the assessment of autism includes the assessment of three main areas: difficulties in social interaction (demonstrating feelings towards others, forming friendships, sharing activities and interests, and non-verbal communication), problems in verbal and non-verbal communication (including development of conversation, content/rate and form of speech, and use of language) and restricted repertoire of activities (including odd preoccupations, intense attachments to specific objects, restricted range of interests, following routines, and stereotyped body movements).

### The Mini PAS-ADD (Prosser, Moss, Costello, Simpson and Patel, 1997)

The Mini PAS-ADD interview is a protocol designed to provide a structured framework within which information on psychiatric symptoms in people with learning disabilities can be collected. The instrument has been designed to produce a reliable and valid record of the person's symptoms during the rating period. The schedule produces scores relating to the following areas: psychosis, expansive mood (hypomania), autism, depression, unspecified disorder, anxiety disorders, obsessive compulsive disorder. Scores in these areas, which exceed the scale thresholds, are assessed as being likely to present with an Axis 1 psychiatric disorder. Any score above the scale threshold indicates that the person should be referred for a comprehensive mental health assessment.

## The Vineland Adaptive Behaviour Scales (VABS) (Sparrow, Balla and Cicchetti, 1984)

The Vineland Adaptive Behaviour Scales is a semi-structured interview method and is designed to measure what the individual usually or habitually does and is divided into four domains: communication, daily living skills, socialisation and motor skills, the items of which are scored 0=no, 1=sometimes or partially and, 2=yes, usually. Scores can be compared to a range of different populations for which normative samples are available. Significant impairment of adaptive and social functioning is usually identified if scores fall at or below the third percentile range. The VABS assess the developmental level of learning disabled populations and provides an estimate of the person's developmental level in each of the three areas; communication, daily living skills and socialisation and a general estimate of developmental functioning based on the aggregate of these three scores. The communication domain assesses how able the person is to communicate with others within a variety of contexts (eg verbal, reading and writing skills). The daily living skills domain focuses on the skills required by a person to look after themselves on a day-to-day basis (eg their ability to cook, clean, cross roads safely, use public transport etc). The socialisation domain assesses the person's level of appropriate social interactions (eg turn-taking in conversations, ending conversations appropriately). The VABS was administered when an individual was referred for an assessment of risk. This assessment tool became standard procedure in 1999. The VABS provides a maximum developmental age of 18, at which point the person is assessed as adult and therefore in possession of the necessary skills in order to

function independently within a community setting. Administration takes place with the respondent most familiar with the behaviour of the individual being assessed, in the form of a semi-structured interview. When the Expanded Form is used, which comprises 577 items, administration must take place by a psychologist or other professional with a graduate degree. It takes approximately 1–1 ¼ hours to administer and scoring takes approximately a further 30 minutes.

## British Picture Vocabulary Scale (BPVS-II) (Dunn et al., 1997)

This protocol is designed to measure a subject's receptive (hearing) vocabulary for Standard English. It is therefore an achievement test since it shows the extent of English vocabulary acquisition. The test may also be viewed as a screening test of scholastic aptitude or as one element in a comprehensive test battery of cognitive processes. It is appropriate for people with serious impairments, especially aphasics and stutters. Results are presented in the form of 'age equivalent' language skills.

### *Sexual offender assessments*

Below is a brief summary of the psychometric measures currently available for assessing adult sexual offenders with learning disabilities. In comparison to non-learning disabled sexual offenders, few of the psychometric measures used for sexual offenders with learning disabilities have been empirically validated.

## Sexual Attitudes and Knowledge Assessment (SAK) (author unknown)

This protocol is designed to assess the subject's knowledge of sexual matters, sexual anatomy, and relationships across four domains: sexual awareness, assertiveness, understanding relationships, and social interaction. Participants are asked to respond to a series of questions, each accompanied by a picture. As few people were able to answer open-ended questions, the items were revised to 'yes or no' responses. The SAK can be used in several ways; to identify learning needs in individuals to determine the specific goals and strategies for group treatment; to complete pre- and post-treatment evaluations of a participant and assess programme effectiveness; and to design a one-to-one training programme for an individual. After scoring the assessment the clinician needs to carefully review the results in order to; identify concerns or knowledge deficits that may increase risk for sexual abuse or prevent the development of positive sexuality; and identify the strengths and positive aspects in the participant's attitudes, knowledge and skills.

## Questionnaire on Attitudes Consistent with Sexual Offenders (QACSO) (Lindsay et al., 1998; Broxholme and Lindsay, 2003)

This protocol is designed to measure cognitive distortions commonly expressed by sexual offenders across eight domains: rape and attitudes to women, voyeurism, exhibitionism, dating abuse, homosexual assault, offences against children, stalking and sexual harassment, and social desirability. The QACSO has been standardised on sexual offenders with learning disabilities, non-sexual offenders with learning disabilities, non-offenders with learning disabilities and mainstream males. The measure has been shown to discriminate sexual offenders with learning disabilities from non-offenders indicating particular cognitive distortions which facilitate offending behaviour in sexual offenders. The QACSO has adequate test retest reliability for all groups with the exception of 'rape' and 'attitudes towards women' for non-sexual offenders without learning disabilities. The measure has good internal reliability and construct validity. The QACSO can be used to assess individuals who have been identified as at risk of offending sexually and to reassess individuals who attend treatment to identify risk of re-offending. The measure can also be used for research purposes examining core themes and attitudes held by offenders (Broxholme and Lindsay, 2003). Internal consistency of each scale revealed alphas of around 0.8. On each of the scales, sex offenders scored significantly higher than other types of offender, non-offenders and a group of non-offending normal males. In addition to discriminating between groups, the assessment has been used to monitor treatment progress (Lindsay and Smith, 1998; Rose, Jenkins, O'Connor, Jones, and Felce, 2002). There is also some preliminary evidence that the QACSO may differentiate between offenders against children and offenders against adults, with the latter scoring significantly lower on the offences against children scale (Lindsay et al., 2005).

The QACSO has been shown to discriminate sex offenders with learning disability from non-offenders and between sex offender subgroups (rapists, dating abuse, homosexual assault and paedophilia) (Broxholme and Lindsay, 2003). The psychometric properties of the QACSO were recently cross validated in two studies (Lindsay et al., 2006). In Study 1, the responses of 12 sex offenders against adults were compared with those of 12 offenders against children. The six-scale version of the QACSO was administered including rape and attitudes to women, voyeurism, and exhibitionism, dating abuse, homosexual assault and offences against children. In Study 2, three groups of 10 participants each: offenders against adults, exhibitionists and offenders against children were compared on the seven scale version of the QACSO (stalking added). In both studies, the offenders against adults reported higher levels of attitudes consistent with sexual offending in the area of rape and attitudes to women. In both studies, offenders against children reported significantly higher levels of cognitive distortions in the area of offences against children. Both differences were in the predicted direction and there were no other significant differences on other sections. In general, all three groups reported higher levels of cognitive distortions than non-offenders.

## Victim Empathy (Beckett and Fisher, 1994)

This protocol is designed to assess a sexual offender's expression of empathy toward their victim. Score are expressed as percentages, where the higher the percentile score the lower the level of empathy expressed toward the victim. There is no empirical data available on this scale.

## Sex Offences Self-Appraisal Scale (SOSAS) (Bray and Forshaw, 1996)

This 20-item protocol is designed to assess attitudes known to be prevalent amongst sexual offenders using statements which form attractive excuses and are therefore likely to illicit agreement. As well as a total score, the scale also provides information on six domains: social desirability, victim blaming, denial, blame, minimisation and reality. The measures assess openness and objectivity, identifying levels of denial, blame or minimisation in relation to offending. Using a five point Likert scale, from 1 = strongly disagree, through to 5 = strongly agree, item responses are summed to give a total

SOSAS score, with higher scores relating to higher denial/distortions (range: 0–95). The scale has been shown to have good measures of internal consistency and a factor analysis revealed two distinct factors: denial of responsibility and denial of future risk (Williams, Wakeling, Webster, and Mann, 2006). It has also been shown to measure cognitive shift following intervention and distinguish between high and low risk groups.

## Adapted Relapse Prevention Interview (Beckett, Fisher, Mann, and Thornton, 1996)

This measure is an interview schedule designed for people with learning disabilities and can be used either at the point of assessment for group inclusion or within the first week of group attendance. It should be administered and scored by the person who has clinical responsibility for the treatment programme. The measure was originally developed for use in the Sex Offender Treatment Evaluation Project (Beckett, Beech, Fisher, and Fordham, 1994) as a research tool to measure to what extent individuals participating in treatment programmes were aware of their risk factors and risk situations. It is divided into questions that focus on awareness of risk factors and questions that focus on the use of appropriate strategies to avoid risky scenarios, escape from them, or if necessary, cope safely with them. The scoring guide ranges from 0 to 2, with 0 = the individual shows no understanding or refuses to recognise any risk, 1 = the individual does not refuse to recognise any risk and has some understanding of relapse prevention, and 2 = the individual has a clear and appropriate understanding of his offending, risk factors and relapse prevention concepts. The tool is able to distinguish between different areas of relapse knowledge and can inform on the effectiveness of a relapse prevention intervention. This scale is used in Her Majesty's Prison Service adapted treatment programme and has been shown to have a good measure of internal consistency and is very sensitive to treatment intervention (Williams, Wakeling, Webster, and Mann, 2006).

## Adapted Emotional Loneliness Scale

This scale is used in Her Majesty's Prison Service assessment battery and consists of 18 items measuring the participant's feelings of emotional loneliness. Adapted from the Russell, Peplan, and Cutrona's (1980) UCLA Emotional Loneliness scale, items measure an awareness of participants' own feelings. Respondents rate each item on a three point scale: yes, no and don't know. High scores equate to greater emotional loneliness (range 0–18). This measure is currently used in the adapted assessment battery in Her Majesty's Prison Service as a retrospective tool where participants are asked to think about 'how their life was six months prior to offending'. Although this scale showed good internal consistency it was not shown to be sensitive to treatment effects (see Williams, Wakeling, Webster, and Mann, 2006). It is suggested the scale could be used as part of a pre-treatment measure of emotional loneliness only to help inform clinical practice rather than a measure of cognitive shift.

## Sex Offenders Opinion Test (SOOT) (Bray, 1997)

The original Sex Offenders Opinion Test (SOOT) is a 28-item instrument measuring attitudes about victims of sexual offences in general. Of the 28 items, seven items measure lying with the remaining 21 items being scored using a five point Likert scale. Total scores relate to levels of distortions where higher scores relate to higher distortions about victims of sexual offences. The scale has been shown to have good measures of internal consistency and is sensitive to treatment effects. A factor analysis revealed two factors: factor 1 contained 15 items, which seemed to represent 'Deceitful Women and Children', and factor 2 contained 5 items, defined by 'Children, Sex and the Law' (Williams, Wakeling, Webster, and Mann, 2006).

## Adapted Self-Esteem Questionnaire

The Adapted Self-Esteem Questionnaire is an adapted version of Thornton's Brief Self-Esteem Scale (Thornton, Beech, and Marshall, 2004). The measure consists of 8 items used to evaluate levels of self-esteem. The items have been reworded using simpler phrasing and respondents rate items on a dichotomous yes/no scale. High scores relate to high self-esteem (range: 0–8). The measure is used by Her Majesty's Prison Service and has been shown to have good internal consistency and is sensitive to treatment effect with participants scoring higher post treatment, indicative of increased self-esteem.

# Risk assessment and sexual recidivism

## *Sexual recidivism rates*

Some studies suggest the sexual re-conviction rate is higher for sex offenders with learning disabilities compared to their non-learning disabled counterparts. Hodgins (1992) reports that offenders with learning disabilities are reported to be five times more likely to commit a violence offence, including rape and molestation, compared to non-learning disabled offenders. Klimecki et al. (1994) reported an overall re-offending rate of 41.3 per cent in previous prison inmates with learning disabilities at a two-year follow-up, and 34 per cent recidivism rate for sexual offenders. Day (1993, 1994) found that re-offending was more likely to occur in the first year following discharge and Klimecki et al. (1994) reported that 84 per cent of overall re-offending occurred within the first 12 months. However, Klimecki et al. noted that several individuals who had received prison sentences for sex offences were still incarcerated and were, therefore, unable to re-offend. More recently, in a review of treatment services for sexual offenders with learning disabilities (n = 62), Lindsay et al. (2002) found that four per cent of learning disabled sexual offenders re-offended within the first year and 21 per cent re-offended after four years. In a recent review of UK non-learning disabled sex offender follow-up studies, the mean sexual reconviction rate were five per cent at two years and six per cent at four years (Craig, Browne, Stringer and Hogue, 2008). Using Klimecki et al.'s (1994) re-offence rate of 34 per cent at two years, and Lindsay et al.'s (2002) re-offence rate of 21 per cent at four years, Craig and Hutchinson (2005) estimated the reconviction rate for sexual offenders with learning disabilities is 6.8 times that of non-disabled sex offenders at two years, and 3.5 times that at four years follow-up.

However, Lindsay et al. and Klimecki et al. used different definitions as indications of offending (ie 're-offending' and 're-offence', respectively) which may limit the extent to which the rates of recidivism of the two studies can be compared. Indeed, depending on which definition being used, and the method of recording offending behaviour, the base rate for sexual reconviction (six per cent) is less then the rate of sexual re-offending (seven per cent) which is less then the rate of sexual recidivism (16 per cent) in a sample of non-disabled sexual offenders (Falshaw et al., 2003). Further differences in samples may also account for the discrepancy in recidivist rates. Lindsay et al.'s study describes treatment provisions for sexual offenders with learning disabilities held within a community setting whereas Klimecki et al.'s study was based on offenders with learning disabilities held within a prison setting. Indeed, the methodological difficulties associated with measuring the prevalence of sexual offending by people with learning disabilities also apply when estimating the sexual re-conviction rate in this client group.

## *Risk assessment*

The predictive accuracy of clinical judgement and actuarial measures has been debated (Grubin, 1999) and although an actuarial approach is not without its critics (Litwack, 2001; Rogers, 2000; Silver and Miller, 2002), it is widely accepted that actuarial risk measures outperform clinical judgement (Bonta, Law and Hanson, 1996; Goggin, 1994; Grove, Zald, Lebow, Snitz and Nelson, 2000; Hanson and Bussière, 1996; Hanson and Morton-Bourgon, 2005; Harris, Rice and Cormier, 2002; Hood, Shute, Feilzer and Wilcox, 2002; McNeil, Sandberg and Binder, 1998) and the literature has witnessed a surge in empirically derived actuarial risk instruments designed to assess risk of violent and/or sexual offence recidivism. An actuarial scale consists of a list of risk factors which have been identified as being predictive of sexual reconviction. The items are scored dichotomously (present or absent) the sum of which translates into an overall level of risk of being reconvicted of a further sexual offence. The risk categories are low, medium or high risk, the higher the risk the greater the likelihood of being reconvicted of a sexual offence. Two of the more widely used and researched risk scales are that of the Rapid Risk Assessment for Sexual Offence Recidivism (RRASOR, Hanson, 1997) and the Static-99 (Hanson and Thornton, 2000). Based on a wide range of risk predictors drawn from the Hanson and Bussière's (1996) meta-analysis, a stepwise regression selected four risk items to be included in the RRASOR: prior sexual offences, age, victim gender and relationship to victim. Further analysis of RRASOR and the Structured

Anchored Clinical Judgement Scale (see Grubin, 1998) revealed that the two scales were assessing related but not identical constructs. It was argued that a combination of both scales would predict better than either original scale. Static-99 was created as a new scale (Hanson and Thornton, 2000) containing 10 items concerned with four broad categories associated with increased likelihood of committing further sexual offences: sexual deviance, measured by whether the offender has offended against males, ever been married and has committed a non-contact sexual offence; range of potential victim, measured by whether the offender offended against unrelated or stranger victim; persistent sexual offending, measured by the number of previous sexual convictions; and, anti-sociality as measured by current or previous non-sexual violence or four or more previous criminal convictions. While the predictive validity of Static-99 (Barbaree, Seto, Langton and Peacock, 2001; Craig, Beech and Browne, 2006; Craig, Thornton, Beech and Browne, 2007; Hanson and Morton-Bourgon, 2005; Hanson and Thornton, 2000; Hood et al., 2001; Nunes, Firestone, Bradford, Greenberg, and Broom, 2002; Sjöstedt and Långström, 2000; Thornton and Beech, 2002) and RRASOR (Barbaree, Seto, Langton, and Peacock, 2001; Hanson and Thornton, 2000; Hanson and Morton-Bourgon, 2005; Sjöstedt and Långström, 2000, 2002) have been established, it is not clear to what extent these measures can be applied to diverse populations such as offenders with learning disabilities. Indeed, in a cross validation study using the RRASOR and Static-99 on a sample of sex offenders with learning disabilities, Tough (2001) found that Static-99 may overestimate the risk.

Rogers (2000) argues that practitioners and actuarial researchers should consider the far-reaching effects of settings, referral questions and evaluation procedures when applying risk scales (pp 595). Bartosh, Garby, Lewis and Gray (2003) investigated the predictive validity of the Static-99, RRASOR, Minnesota Sex Offender Screening Tool-Revised (MnSOST-R, Epperson, Kaul and Hesselton, 1998) and the Sex Offender Risk Appraisal Guide (SORAG, Quinsey, Harris, Rice and Cormier, 1998). It was found that the effectiveness of each instrument varied depending on offender type. The Static-99 and SORAG were both significantly predictive of sexual, violent, and any recidivism for extrafamilial child molesters, and all four tests

were predictive of violent or any recidivism in this subgroup. For incest offenders, all four tests were at least moderately predictive of sexual recidivism, whereas the Static-99 and the SORAG were highly predictive of violent or any recidivism.

While the risk scales have encouraging predictive accuracy, the actuarial method compares similarities of an individual's profile to the aggregated knowledge of past events. This can have the effect of reducing the predictive accuracy of the scale when applied to an individual with characteristics that differ from the data cohort. Grubin and Wingate (1996) argue that empirical evidence from one population does not necessarily translate to another. Indeed, any comparisons between an individual's level of risk and 'base rate' data should be ignored unless all relevant characteristics between the offender and the sample base rate are shared (Cohen, 1981). Similarly, for behaviours with low base rates, prediction in ignorance of the relevant base rate can lead to error. When applied to behaviours amongst the population as a whole, predictions based upon data about infrequent events limited to small groups will lead to error. This error is exacerbated when meta-analytical methods are used to identify risk predictors. Given that the base rate for rapists (17.1 per cent) is higher than that of intrafamilial offenders (8.4 per cent) but less than that of extrafamilial offenders (19.5 per cent) (Hanson, 2002) it is therefore unclear to what extent actuarial measures can be used to generalise across sex offender sub-groups. For example, most actuarial risk measures include factors such as, number of previous criminal convictions, prior sexual convictions and prior non-sexual violence. However, as Green, Gray and Willner (2002) found, sexual offenders with learning difficulties were more likely to be convicted of a sexual offence if they had targeted children and males as victims. Those with differing victim characteristics were less likely to have been convicted and thus would not have a history of prior convictions. In these circumstances, actuarial measures may under-estimate the risk of those offenders diverted from the criminal justice system to mental health services.

Although Harris and Tough (2004) note that nobody has developed a reliable, static actuarial measure specifically for the population of people with learning disabilities, they argue there is no scientific reason to believe that static and stable factors that reliably predict risk for a normal offender will not reliably predict risk in offenders with learning disabilities. Harris and Tough have successfully applied the RRASOR to a sample of sex offenders with learning disabilities in an attempt to best direct services consistent with the risk principle (ie the most effective treatment resources target truly high-risk offenders). They also argue that until such times as empirical research proves otherwise, stable dynamic risk factors as recorded in the Stable-2000 (Hanson and Harris, 2000) scale should also be applied to sex offenders with learning disabilities in an attempt to manage dynamic risk. To some extent, this is consistent with Lindsay, Elliot and Astell (2004) who monitored 35 dynamic variables in a sample of 52 male sex offenders with learning disabilities followed-up over 12 months. They found that variables significantly correlated to evidence of re-offending were antisocial attitude, low self-esteem, lack of assertiveness, poor relationship with mother, allowances made by staff, staff complacency, poor response to treatment and offences involving violence. Some of these items are consistent with STABLE-2000. In terms of actuarial risk, Boer and colleagues (2004; 2006) also argue that RRASOR is more suited to assessing risk in sex offenders with learning disabilities as the scale does not ask questions relating to relationship, employment history, or non-sexual criminal histories. In validating the RRASOR on sex offenders with learning disabilities Tough (2001) found that the RRASOR provided a good estimate of overall risk for recidivism in this offender group. In addition to the RRASOR, Tough also developed a set of clinical guidelines for the design of intervention and management strategies for clients with learning disabilities.

## Assessment of Risk Manageability for Individuals with Developmental and Intellectual Limitations who Offend (ARMIDILO; Boer et al., 2004, 2006)

Although literature has witnessed great advances in the assessment and treatment of sexual offenders, much of this research has been primarily based on mainstream non-learning disabled offenders and there are relatively few descriptions of treatment studies or risk assessment systems designed and standardised on sexual offenders with learning disabilities. To bridge this gap in research, Boer and colleagues

(2004; 2006) recently developed a purely dynamic risk assessment system for sex offenders with learning disabilities. The ARMIDILO, used with an actuarial test and an appropriate structured clinical guideline is part of an assessment procedure which combines the assessment of risk and risk manageability in one assessment. The items in the ARMIDILO are distributed amongst staff/environment and client dynamic factors, both of which are further differentiated into stable and acute dynamic groups. Empirically-derived variables are related to an outcome measure (such as recidivism). The scale provides a structure for the data gathering process and data reporting, enhancing objectivity as much as possible. The scale provides likelihoods for re-offending within certain time-frames and allows easy comparison of any one offender to other offenders when using the same test. It also allows the test user to derive a treatment or management plan due to the inclusion of dynamic risk factors which can change. All items are as related to risk as they are to manageability in institutional or community settings. Each assessment will require the assessor to determine which variables are of most relevance to their client and determine which items is or is not indicative of elevated risk for the client. The items are mostly dynamic and have borrowed liberally from the STABLE (Hanson and Harris, 2004) and SONAR 2000 scales (Hanson and Harris, 2001). The ARMIDILO is divided into three steps: Step 1 considers the use of a static actuarial test for a baseline measure of risk. Boer (2006) argues the RRASOR has been shown to be an effective actuarial tool for use with sex offenders with learning disabilities (Boer, Tough, and Haaven, 2004). The risk level determined by the RRASOR provides a 'risk baseline' for risk or risk management assessments. This is an important piece of information as this risk estimate is 'static'. This actuarial risk estimate can serve as a decision factor in deciding treatment intensity level and supervision intensity level (higher risk, higher intensity, etc.). Step 2 looks at applying a structured guided assessment to risk using the Sexual Violence Risk-20 (SVR-20; Boer et al., 1997) or the Risk for Sexual Violence Protocol (RSVP, Hart, Kropp, Laws, Klaver, Logan and Watt, 2003) both systems being quite similar to each other (approximately 85 per cent content overlap, similar coding rules, risk level decision rules, etc). Boer argues there is more data to support the use of the SVR-20, with learning disabilities, non-learning disabled, mentally disordered and other client groups (eg Aboriginal). In the SVR-20, high, moderate, and low risk are defined in terms of treatment and supervision needs and the degree of need for a risk management plan. In the ARMIDILO, risk manageability is defined as the overall current dynamic risk manageability estimate, which is the offender's ability to manage his dynamic factors, adjusted by the individual's structured clinical risk estimate, and actuarial risk baseline (higher risk, less adjustment and vice versa). Step 3 considers the estimate of how manageable the client is with using the ARMIDILO risk items (see Table 9.1). Similar to other structured guidelines, Boer

suggests items may be scored for validation purposes: '+2' (a problem) '+1' (may be a problem) and '0' (neutral) or use 'yes', 'maybe', 'neutral', or 'no problem' when using the guideline for clinical purposes. Boer argues the items can also be conceptualised as protective factors, decreasing risk. Hence, an item could be scored '−2' – a definite protective factor, '−1' – a possible protective factor, whereas '0' remains neutral, or use 'definite protective factor (DPF)', or 'possible protective factor (PPF)', or 'neutral', when not a protective or risk increasing factor. The stable and acute risk factors are shown in Table 9.1.

The predictive accuracy of the ARMIDILO is yet to be determined, although the scale is likely

**Table 9.1** ARMIDILO Dynamic Stable and Acute Risk Items from Boer (2004)

| ARMIDILO risk items | | | |
| --- | --- | --- | --- |
| **Staff and environment items** | | **Client items** | |
| **Stable** | **Acute** | **Stable** | **Acute** |
| Attitude toward learning disabled clients | New supervisory staff | Attitude toward and compliance with (a) supervision and (b) treatment | Social support/ relationship changes |
| Communication among supervisory staff | Monitoring of client by staff | Knowledge of behaviour pattern, risk factors, and relapse prevention plan | Changes to substance abuse pattern |
| Client-specific knowledge by supervisors | Victim access | Sexual knowledge and self-management | Changes in sexual preoccupation |
| Consistency of supervision | Environmental changes | Mental health problems | Changes in emotional regulation |
| Environmental consistency | | Time management and goal-directedness | Changes in victim-related behaviours |
| | | Substance abuse | Changes in attitude/behaviour towards intervention |
| | | Victim selection and grooming | Changes in ability to use coping strategies |
| | | General coping ability and self-efficacy | Changes in routine |
| | | Relationship skills (a) intimate (b) others | Client-specific acute dynamic factors |
| | | Use of violence or threats of violence | |
| | | Impulsiveness | |
| | | Client-specific stable factors | |

to prove a useful method for structuring dynamic risk related information for sexual offenders with learning disabilities.

## Conclusions

This chapter reviews the core processes used when assessing sexual offenders with learning disabilities. Attention has been paid to the importance of building a clinical formulation of the problem behaviour using clinical interviewing techniques and understanding the functional relationship between the individual's psychological characteristics and offending behaviour. To assist with the clinical formulation of an individual's offending behaviour we also reviewed a number of psychometric measures used to assess various psychological constructs in sexual offenders with learning disabilities, including measures of cognitive distortions, emotional loneliness, self-esteem, victim empathy, and relapse prevention skills. The use of specific psychometric measures that have been standardised on sexual offenders with learning disabilities is a promising development in this field and will aid in the assessment and treatment of this client group. While it is encouraging that a number of measures have been developed specifically for sexual offenders with learning disabilities, these have yet to be independently validated and standardised. Although no actuarial risk assessment measures have been developed specifically for sexual offenders with learning disabilities, it is reasonable to make use of the risk assessments that have been validated on the general sex offender population where data exists where the scale has been used on this client group. However, the assessment of sexual preferences, attitudes, values and beliefs in people with learning disabilities who display sexually aggressive behaviour is complex and at present no particular measurement methodology is accepted universally within applied forensic practice. Such an assessment is likely to rely on a combination of clinical information and psychometric data.

## Appendix 1

Personal history questions used as part of a semi-structured interview to assess for capacities, developmental influences, attitudes, values and beliefs.

### Early development

1. Indications of complications during conception, pregnancy or birth (eg mother significantly ill or involved in accidents during pregnancy, alcohol or drug misuse during pregnancy, pre-term birth, low birth weight, anoxia at birth, etc.).
2. Indications of temperament as a baby. Information on ease or difficulty to care for as baby, feeding, sleeping, crying patterns, etc. Indications of early emotional or behavioural problems.
3. Information about developmental milestones and any indication of any abnormal delay in achieving developmental milestones, for example crawling (average 7 months; range within which achieved by most infants 5–11 months – consider 12–18 months or later delay); standing alone (average 11 months; range within which achieved by most infants 9–16 months; consider 17–24 months or later delay); walking alone (average 11–12 months; range within which achieved by most infants 9–17 months; consider 18–24 months or later delay); talking – first words (average 11–12 months; range within which achieved by most infants 8–18 months; consider 19–26 months or later delay).
4. Infancy illness, injuries, malnutrition, neglect – in particular, head injury; illnesses impacting on brain development (eg encephalitis, meningitis, epilepsy); severe malnutrition prior to age two; severe neglect and/or under-stimulation throughout first two years.

### Family home

The home life of the individual throughout their childhood and adolescent years.

1. What their home life was like in a general sense. Who was present at home?
2. Has the individual ever been in local authority care, in a foster home or children's home, if so, at what age, for how long, why, and their reaction?
3. Any indications of any material, emotional, physical or sexual abuse or neglect.
4. Whether there was any significant breakdown of the family structure during childhood or adolescence (eg parent divorcing, death of parent or sibling, being taken into care).

5. Approach to discipline within the family: presence of appropriate rules and boundaries; how rule breaking was dealt with; who did most of the discipline; was the discipline fair and consistent etc.?
6. Indicators of emotional or conduct problems.

### Family history

Information should be gathered in relation to all significant carers throughout childhood, for example parents, stepparents, other substitute carers. For each significant carer, information should be gathered about the following areas:

1. Their description of the person and relationship.
2. The amount and quality of care provided by that person.
3. History of substance use, criminal or psychiatric history of that person.
4. How did that person deal with problems and stress, including any indications of temper dyscontrol, violence, and over-control of emotions.
5. Current relationship and contact with that person.
6. Similar information should also be gathered about the individual's siblings.

### Education history

Information should be gathered about the individual's progression through the education system.

1. How old when first attended school?
2. How many schools attended? What was the reason behind changing schools, normal progression, behaviour problems, learning problems, moving house, being bullied?
3. Were the schools attended all mainstream schools? Did they attend any remedial classes, special schools, or receive any individual tutoring?
4. Were they ever 'statemented' as having special educational needs? If so, under what category and at what age?
5. When did they first go to school, any indications of school refusal?
6. What was their overall view of school? What was good/bad about it?
7. Information should be gathered about the individual's ability to form friendships at

school. How they related and got on with other pupils; were they ever the victim of or the perpetrator of bullying?
8. Information on how the individual got on academically at school.
9. Any problems learning to read or write.
10. Any problems keeping up with the pace of the lessons.
11. Any difficulties concentrating or attending for periods of time.
12. Indications of hyperactivity and level of interest in school and in learning.
13. Information on how the individual related to the teachers at school, any indication of hostility towards authority figures. Information on the individual's difficult behaviour at school, age of onset, frequency, severity, punishment received, effect of punishment, disruptiveness, rudeness to teachers, truancy, fighting, vandalism, fire-setting, lying, stealing, and cheating.
14. Has the individual ever been suspended or expelled from any schools? What age did they leave school?
15. What exams were taken and/or passed? How did this match their and others expectations? Do exams reflect their abilities?

### Employment history

Information should be gathered on the individual's record of employment since leaving school.

1. What kind of employment have they held?
2. What are the relative time periods that they have been in work and out of work?
3. Have they ever been sacked, when and why?
4. What has been their relationship with employers and work colleagues?
5. What is their current employment situation?
6. Is there any pattern to periods of employment? A few jobs, held for long periods? Many jobs of short duration?

### Criminal history

1. Age at first arrest, caution, conviction.
2. Number of convictions, type of offences, circumstances of offending, victim characteristics, age, gender, relationship to offender, motivation, and sentencing outcome.
3. Indication of escalation in offending.
4. Details of any violent and/or sexual offences.

5. Any offences of arson, kidnap, escape from custody or use of weapons (including possession and threat to use). Also give particular attention to any previous offences that are similar in nature to the index offence or behaviour of concern for which the assessment has been requested.

## Substance misuse

Information about any use of illegal substances, misuse of prescribed medication.

1. History of use of alcohol, pattern of use, periods of misuse, and indication of dependency.
2. History of use of street drug use, pattern of use, periods of misuse, and indication of dependency.
3. Information of any efforts to deal with any substance misuse problem.

## Temper/violence history

Information should be gathered regarding any history of temper dyscontrol and/or instrumental use of violence, and age of onset. Nature of violence, circumstances preceding violence or triggers, frequency, intensity, duration of violence.

1. Behaviour(s) – a description of what the violence entailed (eg pushing, slapping, hitting punching, biting, scratching, kicking, burning, shaking). Use of instruments/weapons. Injuries sustained, including specification of body area affected.
2. Triggers – a description of factors that appear to have acted as immediate or distal triggers to the behaviour.
3. Frequency – establish how many times and how often the individual acts violently. Be aware of any escalation over time.
4. Duration – for each violent incident, how long does the violent behaviour continue for? Be aware of any escalation over time.
5. Intensity – this related to the intensity of the violence used and the severity of the injuries sustained. Be aware of any escalation over time.
6. Target(s) – details about the victim of the non-accidental injury and other violence. Record age, gender, relationship to offender.

In addition to under-control of anger/temper, caution should be expressed towards individuals who tend towards over-control of emotions.

1. How are problems dealt with/reacted to?
2. Any indication of ruminating over problems, holding grudges, not reacting in any way and letting frustrations build up over long periods of time.
3. Where violence appears to be instrumental in nature, try to establish what the end-goals are.

## Accidents or illness (throughout lifetime)

Information should be gathered regarding whether the individual has a history of any serious illness or accidents resulting in head injury, concussion or especially unconsciousness (including self-inflicted injuries). If a person reports incident of serious illness or event leading to head injury, information should be gained on the following areas to assist in the clinical formulation: onset – year and age at which event occurred and injuries sustained; severity – concussion, hospitalisation (for how long, type of hospital, any follow up appointments); unconsciousness (for how long); amnesia (for how long); problems/differences noticed after the event; what problems continue today; what specialist input is ongoing.

## Psychiatric history

1. Does the individual have any formal history of psychiatric illness? Any formal diagnosis of mental illness, any prior contact with psychiatric or psychological services?
2. Any past or current symptoms indicative or neurotic or psychotic illness?
3. Any family history of psychiatric illness?
4. Is there any history of self-injurious behaviour?
5. Any history of past or present suicide thoughts or plans, statement of these plans or suicide attempts? Information should be gathered regarding the nature of these thoughts/attempts and the severity of current suicidal plans.

## Relationships

Information should be gathered regarding the pattern of significant relationships the individual has been involved in: age of onset, age and gender of partner, durations, seriousness, and problems encountered. The following questions may help guide the interview in this area:

1. How problems within the relationship were dealt with.
2. Presence of any relationship violence.
3. Whether it was a sexual relationship.
4. Presence of any sexual problems within the relationship.
5. Reason for relationship breakdown.
6. How the individual coped with and accepted the breakdown of the relationship.
7. How long was it before the next relationship began?

### Sexual history

Where relevant (eg where index behaviour is a sexual offence, any previous sexual offence, offences with a sexual element, or where concern has been raised currently or previously about deviant sexual behaviour) information should be gathered about the individual's sexual development.

1. Where education in sexual matters came from.
2. How they felt about sexual matters, age of onset of sexual interests, masturbation and sexual intercourse.
3. Sexual partners, number, age range, gender, other relevant characteristics.
4. Sexual interests, appetites and activities. Any fetishistic, atypical or deviant interests or appetites. Use of and nature of pornography.
5. Nature of current sexual fantasies? Frequency and intensity of sexual fantasies, masturbation and sexual activity.
6. Presence of any sexual dysfunction.

Information needs to be gathered about the nature of the index offence or behaviour of concern.

1. Description of what happened, in what circumstances, with whom, to whom and why.
2. Information needs to be gathered about the individual's current explanation for their behaviour; to what extent do they accept responsibility for their behaviour; their attitude towards it; whether they consider it a problem; their view of the victim; their insight into the need for help; and their current level of motivation to engage in intervention.

## References

Abel, G.G., Becker, J.V. and Cunningham-Rathner, J. (1984) Complications, Consent and Cognitions in Sex between Children and Adults. *International Journal of Law and Psychiatry*, 7, 89–103.

Abell, G.C. et al. (1998) Visual Reaction Time and Plethysmography as Measures of Sexual Interest in Child Molesters. *Sexual Abuse: A Journal of Research and Treatment*, 10, 81–95.

American Psychiatric Association (1994) Diagnostic and Statistical Manual of Mental Disorders, DSM-IV) Washington DC: American Psychiatric Association.

Andrews, D.A. and Bonta, J. (1994) *The Psychology of Criminal Conduct*. Cincinnati, OH: Anderson Publishing.

Ashman, L. and Duggan, L. (2003) Interventions for Learning Disabled Sex Offenders *The Cochrane Library*, Issue 1.

Bandura, A. (1973) *Aggression: A Social Learning Analysis*. Englewood Cliffs NJ: Prentice Hall.

Barbaree, H.E. et al. (2001) Evaluating the Predictive Accuracy of Six Risk Assessment Instruments for Adult Sex Offenders. *Criminal Justice and Behavior*. 28, 490–521.

Barron, P., Hassiotis, A. and Banes, J. (2004) Offenders with Learning Disability: A Prospective Comparative Study. *Journal of Learning Disability Research*, 48, 69–76.

Bartosh, D.L. et al. (2003) Differences in the Predictive Validity of Actuarial Risk Assessments in Relation to Sex Offender Type. *International Journal of Offender Therapy and Comparative Criminology*, 47, 422–38.

Beckett, R. et al. (1994) *Community-Based Treatment for Sex Offenders: An Evaluation of Seven Treatment Programmes*. London: Home Office. In Becket, R. and Fisher, D. (1994) *Victim Empathy Measure*. Unpublished.

Beckett, R. et al. (1996) Relapse Prevention Interview in Use for Offenders with Learning Disability. Unpublished.

Beech, A., Fisher, D. and Beckett, R. (1999) *Step 3: An Evaluation of the Prison Sex Offenders Treatment Programme*. London: HMSO. Available electronically from: Www.Homeoffice.Gov.Uk/Rds/Pdfs/Occ-Step3.Pdf.

Boer, D.P. (2006) Assessment of Risk Manageability for Individuals with Developmental and Intellectual Limitations who Offend (ARMIDILO) Presented at the 9th

Conference of The International Association for the Treatment of Sexual Offenders, September 6–9. Hamburg, Germany.

Boer, D.P. et al. (1997) *Manual for the Sexual Violence Risk-20 (SVR-20): Professional Guidelines for Assessing Risk of Sexual Violence*. Vancouver: The British Columbia Institute Against Family Violence.

Boer, D.P., Tough, S. and Haaven, J. (2004) Assessment of Risk Manageability of Intellectually Disabled Sex Offenders. *Journal of Applied Research in Intellectual Disabilities*, 17, 275–83.

Borthwick-Duffy, S.A. (1994) Epidemiology and Prevalence of Psychopathology in People with Mental Retardation. *Journal of Consulting and Clinical Psychology*, 62, 17–27.

Bowlby, J. (1979) *The Making and Breaking of Affectionate Bonds*. London: Routledge.

Bowlby, J. (1988) *A Secure Base: Clinical Applications of Attachment Theory*. London: Routledge.

Bray, D. and Forshaw, N. (1996) Sex *Offender's Self-Appraisal Scale. Version 1.1*. Lancashire Care NHS Trust/North Warwickshire NHS Trust. Unpublished.

Bray, D.G. (1997) *The Sex Offenders Opinion Test (SOOT)* North Warwickshire NHS Trust.

Broxholme, S. and Lindsay, W.R. (2003) Development and Preliminary Evaluation of a Questionnaire on Cognitions Related to Sex Offending for Use with Individuals who have Mild Intellectual Disability. *Journal of Intellectual Disability Research*, 47, 472–82.

Butcher, J.M. (1995) *Clinical Personality Assessment. Practical Approaches*. Oxford University Press.

Carich M.S. and Calder M.C. (2003) *Contemporary Treatment of Adult Male Sex Offenders*. Lyme Regis: Russell House Publishing.

Carich M.S. and Mussack S.E. (2001) *Handbook for Sexual Abuser Assessment and Treatment*. Brandon, VT: Safer Society Press.

Coleman, E.M. and Haaven, J. (2001) Assessment and Treatment of Learning Disabled Sexual Abusers. In Carich, M.S. and Mussack, S.E. (Eds.) *Handbook for Sexual Abuser Assessment and Treatment*. Vermont: Safer Society.

Cooper, A.J. (1995) Review of the Role of Two Anti-Libidinal Drugs in the Treatment of Sex Offenders with Mental Retardation. *Mental Retardation*, 33, 42–8.

Craig. L.A., Beech, A.R and Browne, K.D. (2006) Cross Validation of The Risk Matrix 2000 Sexual and Violent Scales. *Journal of Interpersonal Violence*, 21: 5, 1–22.

Craig, L.A., Browne, K.D., Stringer, I. and Hogue, T.E. (2008) Sexual Reconviction Rates in the United Kingdom and Actuarial Risk Estimates. *Child Abuse and Neglect: The International Journal*, 32, 121–38.

Craig, L.A. and Hutchinson, R. (2005) Sexual Offenders with Learning Disabilities: Risk, Recidivism and Treatment. *Journal of Sexual Aggression*, 11, 289–304.

Craig, L.A., Moss, T.E. and Hutchinson, R. (2006) Categorising Sexually Inappropriate Behaviour in Men with Learning Disabilities. Paper presented at the 15th Annual Conference, Division of Forensic Psychology, Preston, UK, June 20th.

Craig, L.A., Stringer, I. and Moss, T. (2006) Treating Sexual Offenders with Learning Disabilities in the Community: A Critical Review. *International Journal of Offender Therapy and Comparative Criminology*, 50, 369–90.

Craig, L.A., Thornton, D., Beech, A. and Browne, K.D. (2007) The Relationship of Statistical and Psychological Risk Markers to Sexual Reconviction in Child Molesters. *Criminal Justice and Behavior*, 34, 314–29.

Day, K. (1993) Crime and Mental Retardation: A Review. In Howells, K. and Hollin, C. (Eds.) *Clinical Approaches to the Mentally Disordered Offender*, Cambridge: John Wiley and Son.

Day, K. (1994) Male Mentally Handicapped Sex Offenders. *British Journal of Psychiatry*, 165, 630–69.

Epperson, D.L., Kaul, J.D. and Hesselton, D. (1998) Final Report on the Development of the Minnesota Sex Offender Screening Tool-Revised. Paper presented at the 17th Annual Conference, Association for the Treatment of Sexual Abusers. Vancouver, Canada.

Falshaw, L. et al. (2003) Assessing Reconviction, Re-offending and Recidivism in a Sample of UK Sexual Offenders. *Legal and Criminological Psychology*, 8, 207–15.

Goggin, C.E. (1994) *Clinical versus Actuarial Prediction: A Meta-Analysis*. Unpublished Manuscript, University of New Brunswick, St. John, New Brunswick.

Green, G., Gray, N.S. and Willner, P. (2002) Factors Associated with Criminal Convictions for Sexually Inappropriate Behaviour in Men with Learning Disabilities. *Journal of Forensic Psychiatry*, 13, 578–607.

Gross, G. (1985) *Activities of a Developmental Disabilities Adult Offender Project*. Olympia, WA.

Washington State Development Disabilities Planning Council.

Grove, W.M. (2000) Clinical Versus Mechanical Prediction: A Meta-Analysis. *Psychological Assessment*, 12, 19–30.

Grubin, D. (1998) *Sex Offending against Children: Understanding the Risk.* London: Home Office.

Grubin, D. (1999) Actuarial and Clinical Assessment of Risk in Sex Offenders. *Journal of Interpersonal Violence.* 14, 331–43.

Grubin, D. and Wingate, S. (1996) Sexual Offence Recidivism: Prediction Versus Understanding. *Criminal Behaviour and Mental Health*, 6, 349–59.

Haaven, J., Little, R. and Petre-Miller, D. (1990) *Treating Intellectually Disabled Sex Offenders.* Brandon, VT: Safer Society Press.

Hanson, R.K. (1997) *The Development of a Brief Actuarial Risk Scale for Sexual Offence Recidivism.* Ottawa: Department of The Solicitor General of Canada. Available electronically from: Http://Www.Sgc.Gc.Ca/Epub/Corr/E199704/E199704.Htm

Hanson, R.K. (2002) Recidivism and Age: Follow-Up Data from 4,673 Sexual Offenders. *Journal of Interpersonal Violence*, 17, 1046–62. Available electronically from: Http://Www.Sgc.Gc.Ca/Epub/Corr/Eage200101/Eage200101.Htm. (Cat No.: JS42-96/2001).

Hanson, R.K. and Bussière, M.T. (1996) *Predictors of Sexual Offender Recidivism: A Meta-Analysis.* Ottawa: Department of The Solicitor General of Canada. Available electronically from: Http://Www.Sgc.Gc.Ca/Epub/Corr/E199604/E199604.Htm

Hanson, R.K. and Bussière, M.T. (1998) Predicting Relapse: A Meta-Analysis of Sexual Offender Recidivism Studies. *Journal of Consulting and Clinical Psychology*, 66, 344–62.

Hanson, R.K. et al. (2002) First Report of the Collaborative Outcome Data Project on the Effectiveness of Psychological Treatment for Sex Offenders. *Sexual Abuse: A Journal of Research and Treatment*, 14, 169–94.

Hanson, R.K. and Harris, A. (2000) *The Sex Offender Need Assessment Rating (SONAR): A Method for Measuring Change in Risk Levels.* Ottawa, ON: Department of The Solicitor General of Canada.

Hanson, R.K. and Harris, A. (2004) *STABLE Scoring Guide. Department of Public Safety and Emergency Preparedness.* Ottawa, ON.

Hanson, K. and Morton-Bourgon, K.E. (2005) The Characteristics of Persistent Sexual Offenders: A Meta-Analysis of Recidivism Studies. *Journal of Consulting and Clinical Psychology*, 73, 1154–63.

Hanson, R.K. and Thornton, D. (2000) Improving Risk Assessment for Sex Offenders: A Comparison of Three Actuarial Scales. *Law and Human Behavior*, 24, 119–36. Www.Sgc.Gc.Ca/Epub/Corr/E199902/E199902.Htm).

Harris, G.T., Rice, M.E. and Cormier, C.A. (2002) Prospective Replication of the Violence Risk Appraisal Guide in Predicting Violent Recidivism among Forensic Patients. *Law and Human Behavior*, 26, 377–94.

Harris, A.J. and Tough, S. (2004) Should Actuarial Risk Assessments be Used with Sex Offenders who are Intellectually Disabled. *Journal of Applied Research in Intellectual Disabilities*, 17, 235–41.

Hart, S.D. et al. (2003) *The Risk for Sexual Violence Protocol (RSVP) – Structured Professional Guideline for Assessing Risk of Sexual Violence.* Simon Fraser University, Mental Health, Law and Policy Institute.

Herbert, M. (2003) *Typical and Atypical Development: From Conception to Adolescence.* Oxford: Blackwell.

Hodgins, S. (1992) Mental Disorder, Learning Deficiency and Crime: Evidence from a Birth Cohort. *Archives of General Psychiatry*, 49, 476–83.

Hood, R. et al. (2002) Sex Offenders Emerging from Long-Term Imprisonment – A Study of their Long-Term Reconviction Rates and of Parole Board Members' Judgements of their Risk. *British Journal of Criminology*, 42, 371–94.

Howe, D. et al. (1999) *Attachment Theory, Child Maltreatment and Family Support.* Hampshire: Macmillan.

Howlin, P. (1997) *The Diagnostic Criteria Checklist.* St George's Hospital Medical School.

Klimecki, M., Jenkinson, J. and Wilson, L. (1994) A Study of Recidivism amongst Offenders with a Learning Disability. *Australian and New Zealand Journal of Developmental Disabilities*, 19, 209–19.

Kolton, D.J., Boer, A. and Boer, D.P. (2001) A Revision of the Abel and Becker Cognition Scale for Intellectually Disabled Sexual Offenders. *Sexual Abuse: Journal of Research and Treatment*, 12, 217–19.

Laws, R. (2003) Penile Plethysmography: Will We Ever Get it Right? In Ward, T., Laws, D.R. and Hudson, S.M. (Eds.) *Sexual Deviance: Issues and Controversies.* Thousand Oaks, CA: Sage.

Lindsay, W.R., Elliot, S.F. and Astell, A. (2004) Predictors of Sexual Offence Recidivism in

Offenders with Intellectual Disabilities. *Journal of Applied Research in Learning Disabilities*, 17, 299–305.

Lindsay, W.R. et al. (2006) Response Patterns on the Questionnaire on Attitudes Consistent with Sexual Offending in Groups of Sex Offenders with Intellectual Disabilities. *Journal of Applied Research in Intellectual Disabilities*. 19, 47–53.

Lindsay, W.R. et al. (1999) Treatment of Adolescents with Learning Disabilities. *Mental Retardation*, 37, 201–11.

Lindsay, W.R. and Parry, C.J. (2003) Impulsiveness as a Factor in Sexual Offending by People with Mild Learning Disability. *Journal of Disability Research*, 47, 483–7.

Lindsay, W.R. and Smith, A.H. (1998) Responses to Treatment for Sex Offenders with Learning Disability: A Comparison of Men with One and Two Year Probation Sentences. *Journal of Learning Disability Research*, 42, 346–53.

Lindsay, W.R. et al. (2002) A Treatment Service for Sex Offenders and Abusers with Learning Disability: Characteristics of Referral and Evaluation. *Journal of Applied Research in Learning Disabilities*, 15, 166–74.

Lindsay, W.R. et al. (1998) The Treatment of Six Men With Learning Disabilities Convicted of Sex Offences. *British Journal of Clinical Psychology*, 37, 83–98.

Litwack, T.R. (2001) Actuarial versus Clinical Assessments of Dangerousness. *Psychology, Public Policy and Law*, 7, 409–43.

Lund, J. (1990) Mentally Retarded Criminal Offenders in Denmark. *British Journal of Psychiatry*, 156, 726–31.

MacEachron, A.E. (1979) Mentally Retarded Offenders: Prevalence and Characteristics. *American Journal of Mental Deficiency*, 84, 165–76.

Mackinnon, S., Bailey, B. and Pink, L. (2004) *Understanding Learning Disabilities: A Video-Based Training Resource for Trainers and Managers to Use with Staff*. Brighton: Pavilion.

Marshall, W.L. and Fernandez, Y.M. (2000) Phallometric Testing with Sexual Offenders: Limits to Its Value. *Clinical Psychology Review*, 20, 807–22.

McBrien, J., Hodgetts, A. and Gregory, J. (2002) Offending Behaviour in Services for People with Learning Disabilities in One Local Authority. Manuscript Submitted for Publication.

McNeil, D. and Binder, R. (1994) Screening or Risk of Inpatient Violence: Validation of an Actuarial Tool. *Law and Human Behavior*, 18, 579–86.

Mikkelsen, E.J. (2004) *The Assessment of Individuals with Developmental Disabilities who Commit Criminal Offences*. In Lindsey, W.L. and Sturmey, P. (Eds.) *Offenders with Developmental Disabilities*. Chichester: John Wiley and Sons.

Nunes, K.L. et al. (2002) A Comparison of Modified Versions of the Static-99 and the Sex Offender Risk Appraisal Guide. *Sex Abuse: A Journal of Research and Treatment*, 14, 253–69.

Professional Affairs Board. (2001) *Learning Disability: Definitions and Contexts*. Leicester: The British Psychological Society.

Prosser, H. et al. (1997) *Psychiatric Assessment for Adults with a Developmental Disability (Mini PASADD)* Hester Adrian Research Centre and The Institute of Psychiatry.

Proulx, J. et al. (1997) Static and Dynamic Risk Predictors of Recidivism in Sexual Offenders. *Sexual Abuse: A Journal of Research and Treatment*, 9, 7–27.

Quinsey, V.L. (1998) *Violent Offenders: Appraising and Managing Risk*. Washington DC: American Psychological Association.

Quinsey, V.L., Rice, M.E. and Harris, G.T. (1995) Actuarial Prediction of Sexual Recidivism. *Journal of Interpersonal Violence*, 10, 85–105.

Robins, L. and Rutter, M. (1990) *Straight and Deviant Pathways from Childhood to Adulthood*. Cambridge: Cambridge University Press.

Rose, J. et al. (2002) A Group Treatment for Men with Learning Disabilities who Sexually Offend or Abuse. *Journal of Applied Research in Learning Disabilities*, 15, 138–50.

Royal College of Psychiatrists (2001) *Diagnostic Criteria for Psychiatric Disorders for Use with Adults with Learning Disabilities/Mental Retardation (DC-LD)* London: Gaskell.

Russell, D., Peplan, C.A. and Cutrona, C.A. (1980) The Revised UCLA Loneliness Scale: Concurrent and Discriminant Validity Evidence. *Journal of Personality and Social Psychology*, 39, 472–80.

Singer, B. (1984) Conceptualising Sexual Arousal and Attraction. *The Journal of Sex Research*, 20, 230–40.

Silver, E. and Miller, L.L. (2002) A Cautionary Note on the Use of Actuarial Risk Assessment Tools for Social Control. *Crime and Delinquency*, 48, 138–61.

Sjöstedt, G. and Långström, N. (2000) *Actuarial Assessment of Risk for Criminal Recidivism among Sex Offenders Released from Swedish Prisons 1993–1997*. Paper presented at the 19th Annual Conference of The Association for the Treatment of Sexual Abusers; San Diego, CA.

Sjöstedt, G. and Långström, N. (2002) Assessment of Risk for Criminal Recidivism among Rapists: A Comparison of Four Different Measures. *Psychology, Crime and Law*, 8, 25–40.

Sparrow, S.S., Balla, D.A. and Chichetti, D.V. (1984) *Vineland Adaptive Behaviour Scales*. Minnisota: American Guidance Service.

Serin, R.C., Mailloux, D.L. and Malcolm, P.B. (2001) Psychopathy, Deviant Sexual Arousal and Recidivism among Sexual Offenders. *Journal of Interpersonal Violence*. 16, 234–46.

Sturmey, P. (1996) *Functional Analysis in Clinical Psychology*. Chichester: John Wiley and Sons.

Tough, S. (2001) *Validation of Two Standard Assessments (RRASOR, 1997; STATIC-99, 1999) on a Sample of Adult Males who are Intellectually Disabled with Significant Cognitive Deficits*. Master's Thesis. Toronto, ON: University of Toronto.

Thornton, D. and Beech. A.R. (2002) *Integrating Statistical and Psychological Factors through the Structured Risk Assessment Model*. Paper presented at the 21st Annual Research and Treatment Conference, Association of the Treatment of Sexual Abusers, October 2–5, Montreal, Canada.

Thornton, D., Beech, A. and Marshall, W.L. (2004) Pre-treatment Self-Esteem and Post-treatment Sexual Recidivism. *International Journal of Offender Therapy and Comparative Criminology*, 48, 567–99.

Tudway, J.A. and Darmoody, M. (2005) Clinical Assessment of Adult Sexual Offenders with Learning Disabilities. *Journal of Sexual Aggression*, 11, 277–88.

Tudway, J. (1990) *NOTA 1 Interview*. Unpublished.

Tudway, J. (1994) *Adapted Emotional Loneliness Scale*. Unpublished.

Walker, N. and Mccabe, S. (1973) *Crime and Insanity in England*. Edinburgh: University Press.

Ward, T. and Siegert, R.J. (2002) Toward a Comprehensive Theory of Child Sexual Abuse: A Theory Knitting Perspective. *Psychology, Crime and Law*, 8, 319–51.

Wechsler, D. (1999) *Wechsler Adult Intelligence Scale*. 3rd Edn. London: Psychological Corporation.

Williams, F.M. et al. (2006) A Clinical Evaluation of a Cognitive-Behavioural Treatment Programme for Sexual Offenders with Cognitive and Social Deficits. Manuscript Submitted for Publication.

World Health Organisation. (1992) *ICD-10 Classification of Mental and Behavioural Disorders: Clinical Descriptions and Diagnostic Guidelines ICD-10-CDDG*. Geneva: WHO.

# CHAPTER 10

# Assessment of Internet Sexual Abuse

*Ethel Quayle*

*You cannot have freedom of speech without the option to remain anonymous. Most censorship is retrospective, it is generally much easier to curtail free speech by punishing those who exercise it afterward, rather than preventing them from doing it in the first place. The only way to prevent this is to remain anonymous.*

(The Free Network Project)

The chapter begins with this rather contentious quote because it seems to say something about the tensions that exist in relation to the Internet between the ability to maintain freedom of speech and the need to protect people from harmful content or behaviour. Freenet is free software which makes it possible to publish and obtain information on the Internet anonymously. It is a decentralised peer to peer distributed data store aiming to provide electronic freedom of speech. Users contribute to Freenet by giving bandwidth and a portion of their hard drive for storing files. Unlike other networks, Freenet does not let the user control what is stored in the data store, and instead files are kept or deleted depending on how popular they are, with the least popular being discarded to make way for newer or more popular content. Files in the data store are encrypted to enable Freenet users to deny any knowledge of the content stored on their computers. Why is this an issue? Theoretically such a system would also allow illegal material, such as abusive images of children, to be shared with anyone, and makes Freenet ideal as an example of the problems of social control versus individual privacy (Godejord, 2007). This is not to suggest that Freenet is being used in this way, but illustrates the complexity of monitoring and policing the Internet, and the way it may support offending activities.

## Problems with definitions

As yet there is only a small literature that relates to Internet sexual abuse, and even less that has as its focus assessment. There is even confusion as to what constitutes Internet sexual abuse as while it is most frequently used in relation to people who commit sexual offences against children online, it could also be argued that it should include offences against any age group, such as cyberstalking (Adam, 2002). For the purpose of this chapter we are going to look at the former category, in part because it reflects a large number of individuals who are, in recent times, both evident in the criminal justice system and have a presence online as consumers. We can infer the latter due to the volume of abuse images clearly available online through media such as Web Pages (which are only one of the many sources). In 2007 the Internet Watch Foundation in the UK reported that, '. . . it has managed a 34 per cent increase in reports processed by its 'Hotline'. The reports led to the confirmation of 10,656 URLs, on 3,077 websites, containing potentially illegal child abuse content. 82.5 per cent of all the websites were apparently linked to the US or Russia, up from 67.9 per cent in 2005' (IWF, 2007).

Unlike other paraphilias, Internet sexual offenders cannot be easily diagnosed according to criteria set out in categorical models such as DSM (American Psychiatric Association, 2000) and we are largely limited by what people are observed to do in relation to the Internet. This includes: downloading illegal images from the Internet (which largely, but not exclusively relate to pictures of children); trading or exchanging such images with others; producing images through photographing children, or modifying existing images, and engaging in what has variously been called grooming, solicitation or seduction of children. As the law changes to try and keep pace with the opportunities that the Internet affords for offending activities, so do the definitions of behaviours and content that constitute what is illegal. For example, in the UK the Sexual Offences Act 2003 created an offence that included grooming, the purpose of which was to identify preparatory behaviour that could be criminalised before the offender had the opportunity to sexually abuse a child. The offence requires an offender to have met or communicated with a child on two or more occasions and subsequently to meet or travel to meet a child with the intention in either case to have sexual contact with a child (Gillespie, 2006). The legislation in part grew out of a series of high profile cases where an adult had used the Internet to 'groom' children for 'offline abuse'.

With regard to content, countries such as Japan both produce and consume cartoon representations of sexual activity related to children, which most western countries would describe as abusive. McLelland (2001) gives an interesting account of this, 'This means that images of a sexual nature, or references to sex, can appear in media that would be considered 'inappropriate' in Anglophone societies, such as comic books and animation aimed at young people ... Also, Japanese society has not traditionally made as severe a distinction between 'adult' and 'under-age' sexuality as has the West; in fact, Japan's rather narrowly interpreted obscenity laws which ... focus almost exclusively on the depiction of genitalia and pubic hair have encouraged sexualised depictions of children ... When Japan is described in Western reports as 'awash in child pornography' it is seldom pointed out that the vast majority of the images referred to are nothing more than highly figurative, unrealistic manga depictions of schoolgirls in their underwear. Moreover ... there is a genre parallel to rorikon that is immensely popular with Japanese women. Known as shootakon ... this genre of manga imagines graphic sexual interactions taking place between bishoonen (beautiful boys) ... and is potentially far more disturbing to Western sensibilities than is rorikon because it conjoins not heterosexuality but homosexuality with child sex'. However, while such material remains legal in many jurisdictions throughout the world (and a cultural norm in Japan) there is increasing pressure to make illegal content related to children that is either generated digitally (for example in Second Life) or through cartoons (Sipress, 2007, The Washington Post; National Offender Management Service, 2007).

It is important to acknowledge such challenges at the outset because it forces us to contextualise Internet sexual abuse as being situated in time and place. As legislation changes within, for example, the UK, we are likely to see many more people defined as sexual offenders, even though the content of the material obtained within that jurisdiction may have been produced in a country which deems it to be legal, if not acceptable. In

2006 the International Centre for Missing and Exploited Children produced a report on legislation within the 184 Interpol member countries and highlighted that 95 had no legislation which specifically addressed child pornography and 41 did not criminalise possession, regardless of intent to distribute (ICMEC, 2006). Even the term child pornography is contentious, because while it is a legal term in most countries, increasingly we see reference to abuse images in the literature (Taylor and Quayle, 2005).

Internet sex offenders are often referred to as paedophiles, and are often conceptualised as a homogenous group. Indeed, our stereotypes of this offender group are often reinforced by many of the educational campaigns aimed at keeping our children safe. In the context of diagnosis and sex offenders, Marshall (2007) has suggested that categorical models such as DSM (American Psychiatric Association, 2000) leave a lot to be desired and that a more useful approach would be to rate the features of each type of sexual offender along dimensions ranging from normal to seriously problematic. The advantages of using such a dimensional approach have been outlined in many areas other than sex offending (eg Bentall, 2006) and dominate current conceptualisations of 'normality'. Marshall (2007: 27) has argued that, 'Considering the problems of each client to be numerous, and to lie along definable dimensions, is likely to more accurately guide assessment (and risk assessment) and treatment, and should serve to circumvent the considerable difficulties (and likely failures) that arise from the 'one size fits all' approach to treatment ...' It is with this in mind that we might initially make a tentative attempt to describe some of these dimensions as they might apply to Internet sex offenders, as this structure may serve to act as a guide to clinical assessment (Quayle, 2008).

## Assessment dimensions

With regard to downloading images from the Internet, we need to initially establish:

- The content of the images, which relate to people who are under the age of 18, regardless of the age of sexual consent in the country of origin, or the country of access (ICMEC, 2006). Preferential content can be subdivided by:

predominant gender; age; racial group, and activities. As far as possible, the latter are best described using an objective measure eg COPINE Scale (Taylor, Holland and Quayle, 2001); Sentencing Advisory Panel, 2002). It is also important to look for evidence of the presence of pornographic material, which in itself may be legal or illegal (eg images depicting sado-masochistic practices or bestiality).

- The intensity of the behaviour (which is confirmation that it is purposeful rather than accidental) and might be assessed by the volume of images; the duration of the activity; its frequency, and the duration of sessions.
- The number of Internet behaviours/ applications used (adapted from O'Brien and Webster, 2007; Carr, 2004) which may include email; websites; peer to peer networks; newsgroups; IRC (Internet Relay Chat); ICQ (I Seek You); chat rooms; social networking sites; the storage medium used; the nature of image organization and cataloguing, and electronic attempts to hide activities.
- Self report evidence of sexual preoccupation, with reference to the frequency of masturbation to images, text and chat.

In a similar way, dimensions that relate to the trading or exchange of abuse images would include:

- The protocols used to effect image exchange, which may include email; websites; peer to peer networks; newsgroups; IRC; ICQ; chat rooms, and social networking sites.
- The exclusivity of exchange, evidenced through private networks or public fora.
- The intensity of the behaviour assessed through the volume of images traded; the duration of the activity, and its frequency.
- Any evidence of social engagement, both online and offline with others engaged in trading activities.

The production of abusive images clearly includes all of the above dimensions, as downloading, trading and producing are overlapping, rather than discrete categories. Of interest here would be:

- The content of the images produced, with regard to the gender, age, racial group of the children photographed as well as an objective description of the activities within the images.

- The nature of the photographer's relationship with child/children in the images. This may include someone in a parental role; other family member; a person having a position of trust, or stranger. It is important to also establish whether others were involved in the production of the images and whether these people were known to the child.
- The level of engagement of the child with the process of image taking (adapted from Taylor and Quayle, 2005) with reference to hidden photographs (images taken with a hidden or disguised camera which involves no physical contact with the child and where the child, and possible carer, has no knowledge that a photograph has been taken); as part of the sexual abuse of child (without the child's knowledge of being photographed); as part of the sexual abuse of a child (with the child's knowledge of being photographed) and as part of the sexual abuse of child with child's knowledge of being both photographed and actively engaged in the production and/or trading of the images themselves.
- The intensity of the behaviour, assessed through the number of children involved; over what period of time, and the number of images produced.
- The number of Internet behaviours/ applications used (as described above).

Child grooming/solicitation/seduction through the Internet is more difficult to define, as Gillespie (2006) has indicated that it is most commonly used to define behaviour that has as its end goal a contact offence with a child. However, we increasingly see reference to online activities that clearly involve the child in sexual behaviour, which may result in the child producing abusive images of themselves, but where no obvious attempt has been made to meet the child or children in question. An example of this might be the case of Adrian Ringland in the UK who used a Trojan to gain control of the child's computer and to frighten them into compliant behaviour that resulted in the production of images (BBC News Online, 2006). Dimensions to be assessed would take into account:

- The Internet protocols used as part of the grooming process (as described above).
- The ages of the children who were groomed.
- The gender of the children.

- The intensity of behaviour, as evidenced by the number of children contacted; the duration and frequency of the activity.
- The relationship with children, such as parental role; other family member; position of trust, and stranger.
- Online activities: befriending or grooming to gain the trust of a child; cybersex with a compliant victim restricted to online activity, and aggressive solicitation, which includes offline contact with the offender through regular mail, by telephone, or attempts or requests for offline contact that may result in the commission of a contact offence (Wolak et al., 2006) .
- Offline activities: contacting a child by phone/texting; writing to child/sending gifts; arranging to meet child without sexual activity taking place, and arranging to meet child with sexual activity taking place.

While much of this information is likely to be gained through an interview with the offender, it is important to acknowledge that most people accused of a crime have a vested interest in presenting themselves and their behaviour in the best light. Whether we see this simply as lying or a form of post-offence cognitive distortion, or even an adaptive reaction to a threatening situation, interviews do assume that there is a level of honesty in a person's response (Gannon et al., 2007). However, unlike questionnaires *per se*, it might be argued that a skilled interview enables a person to accurately assess and retrieve implicit belief structures about themselves and their actions. Clearly clinical assessment, particularly of risk, is weaker when the assessment is unstructured, unguided or used in isolation (Mandeville-Norden and Beech, 2006) and this is something that we will come back to later in this chapter. It is clearly of benefit to gain additional information from other sources, such as the person's partner and, where available, case notes. Where possible this should be supplemented by the forensic report, as one positive aspect of Internet sex crimes for the interviewer is the availability of information gained from images or text. In behavioural terms we might call this a permanent product and it does not rely on self report or even the ability to access and construct a coherent account. Wortley and Smallbone (2006) give an excellent guide to the gathering of forensic information related to 'child pornography', which may be of use to

practitioners working with offenders. In addition, the interview should include a detailed history of psychological and social development, as well as a sexual history. The interview should acknowledge that offending has a context as well as being part of a process (Quayle and Taylor, 2003).

Delmonico and Griffin (2008) have also indicated that an important part of the assessment process should include a global Internet assessment and describe the Internet Sex Screening Test (ISST) which has some empirical validation. The initial test was developed by Delmonico (1999) and consisted of twenty-five core items and nine general offline sexual compulsivity items. Delmonico and Miller (2003: 51–86) reported that a factor analysis yielded eight distinct subscales with low to moderate internal consistency reliability. These subscales included:

1. Online sexual compulsivity (continuation of online sexual activity, despite its offline consequences, repeated efforts to stop online sexual behaviour with little or no success, and excessive time spent preparing for, engaging in or recovery from online sexual experiences).
2. Online sexual behaviour: where there is a social context to the behaviour, or one which involves interpersonal interaction with others.
3. Online sexual behaviour which is isolated (surfing websites, downloading pornography).
4. Online sexual spending.
5. Interest in online sexual behaviour.
6. Non-home use of the computer (for sexual purposes).
7. Illegal use of the computer (downloading child pornography or exploiting a child online).

The final factor performs a brief screening for offline sexual compulsivity. These original 34 items have now been expanded to 117 items, which include a deception scale. The original shorter screening version is publicly available online at http://www.internetbehavior.com/ sexualdeviance. An individual's knowledge of Internet online behaviour can also be assessed using the Internet Assessment (Delmonico and Griffin, 2005) which is divided into two sections. The first measures Internet knowledge and behaviour and the second measures social, sexual and psychological aspects of Internet behaviour. The questions relate to six themes:

- Arousal (where they go and the content of materials or behaviours).
- Tech-savvy (how to better access and camouflage online sexual behaviour).
- Risk (the 'rush' related to the behaviour – an individual may increase the level of risk to achieve the same level of arousal).
- Illegal (those who have crossed the line into illegal behaviour).
- Secrecy (which may be used to hide extreme shame-based behaviours). Delmonico and Griffin (in press) suggest that it may be useful to identify these ego-dystonic behaviours early.
- Compulsive (behaviours that are compulsive, need-driven and ritualistic).

It is also important to think about the function of the behaviour for the individual. As the nature of the material and interactions have an obvious sexual content, it would be easy to make the assumption that their sole function is also to enable deviant sexual interest. However, it may be that there are multiple functions, such as facilitating online social relationships, collecting behaviour, as a form of self-administered 'therapy', and emotional avoidance (Quayle and Taylor, 2002; Sheldon, 2007). There is some evidence to support the function of emotional avoidance (Middleton et al., 2006; Sheldon, 2007; Quayle et al., 2006) and a possible explanation of this is provided by Marshall and Marshall (2000) who examined affective states and coping behaviour. These authors proposed that when in a state of negative affect, sex offenders are more likely to use sexual behaviours as a means of coping than are non-offenders, and this is reinforced and learned precisely because it is effective in reducing a state of negative affect (Howells et al., 2004). However, one criticism of using a model that focuses on function, rather than a traditional categorical model, is that emotional avoidance may be one of many functional categories, and does not account for all the cases where emotional avoidance is not an issue. More importantly, emotional avoidance may be the functional property of many topographically dissimilar behaviours, but it does not tell us why Internet pornographic images of children should be used, as opposed to any other behaviours (Quayle et al., 2008).

## Comparing populations

Accurately describing what offenders do (including private events such as thoughts and feelings) is an important part of the assessment. However, very often we are interested in how they compare with other populations. The most obvious comparative population is the offender who has committed a contact offence against a child. At present, there tends to be an assumption that in fact they are one and the same, and as Internet sex offenders are such a heterogeneous population (aside from gender and racial group) this is often going to be the case. Clearly sex offenders who have both committed a contact offence with a child or children and who then use child abuse images on the Internet are likely to have a lot in common with those who have sexually offended against a child in the offline environment. However, as yet there is surprisingly little data to support this.

Seto, Cantor and Blanchard (2006) investigated whether being charged with a child pornography offence was a valid diagnostic indicator of paedophilia, as represented by an index of phallometrically-assessed sexual arousal to children. Their results indicated that child pornography offenders had almost three times the odds of being identified as a paedophile phallometrically than offenders against children. Seto et al. (2006) suggested that child pornography offending is a stronger diagnostic indicator of paedophilia than is sexual offending against child victims. The results of this study pose a considerable challenge to us all. It may be that a parsimonious explanation is that as the stimulus material viewed was largely visual that it might have been highly salient for men who spent time on a regular basis viewing images and possibly masturbating to them.

Webb et al. (2006) compared Internet offenders with child molesters from probation caseloads across the Greater London (UK) area. Over an eight month period 210 offenders were assessed (90 Internet offenders). Both groups had experienced substantial levels of childhood difficulties, although child molesters were more likely to have been physically abused. A significantly higher number of Internet offenders had been in contact with the mental health services as adults, and had had significantly fewer live-in relationships. On the Hare Psychopathy Checklist, child molesters scored higher than Internet offenders, although the latter were reported as having significantly more problems with 'sexual self-regulation' than child molesters. The MCMI-III was used to examine personality and mental health, and there were no significant differences found between child molesters and Internet offenders, although child molesters scored higher on the social desirability scale.

In this study, 65 per cent of Internet offenders had had one life event or more in the 12 months prior to their arrest (related to financial and social issues, and personal health and sexual difficulties). Both groups presented with a more schizoid, avoidant and dependent profile, which the authors felt was suggestive of individuals who either retreat from interpersonal and social situations, sometimes fearing rejection and cutting themselves off emotionally, or individuals who place excessive reliance on their relationships with others in order to be able to cope. Webb et al. (2006) concluded that there might be different types of Internet offender groups, as suggested by their analysis. These results are interesting and are the first to examine specific personality and mental health variables, but the population is relatively small in each of the groups and it will be important to see if these results hold across a larger and more diverse sample.

The work of Sheldon (2007) attempted an examination of how far Internet offenders match conceptions of contact offenders. In this first study of its kind, sixteen Internet sex offenders, twenty-five contact offenders and ten mixed offenders were compared on a range of questionnaires exploring childhood and adult attachment, dispositional coping strategies, sexual fantasies and cognitive distortions. In addition, interview data was also used to examine the nature of Internet offending, the functions of child pornography and why Internet offenders did not pursue a contact offence with a child. Explanations for the latter included an emphasis on 'fantasy-contact', 'moral/ethical reasoning' and 'fear of consequences'. Comparing the populations, contact offenders were characterised by adverse childhoods (including sexual abuse); lengthy criminal records, and the use of emotionally oriented coping strategies. Internet sex offenders were more likely to be professionally employed; have more years in education; few criminal convictions; report some childhood difficulties and heterosexual sexualised play; high levels of paedophile fantasies and

cognitive distortions but few criminal convictions of any kind.

In this group paedophilic fantasies were related to sex play experiences and close themes between early childhood sexual experience and later adult abusive behaviour were evident. In relation to a separate population and within a psychodynamic framework, Wood (2007) has suggested that one feature of virtual sexual activity is the creation of a scenario loaded with meaning, which she described as a 'compelling scenario'. This often seems to encapsulate specific traumatic experiences and key object relationships from childhood and adolescence. This seems to have resonances with Sheldon's (2007) study, and she concludes that early sexualisation with other children may equally lead to sexually abusive behaviour in adulthood as childhood sexual abuse, and this is clearly an important area of investigation when interviewing an offender. The study also found some links between early abusive memories and later adult offending, and between early sex play experiences and later paedophilic thoughts. Within this study a specially constructed fifty-two item Sexual Fantasy Inventory was used. Sheldon (2007) suggested that the findings represent a dilemma for the fantasy literature, as in this study contact offending was associated with suppressed levels of girl (paedophilic) fantasy and brings into question any simple, direct model linking sexual fantasy to contact offending and contradicts the sexual preference hypothesis. This group of contact offenders appeared to have difficulty generating fantasy, and their fantasies had more confrontational non-contact content than did those experienced by Internet sex offenders (such as exposing their genitals to unsuspecting girls, where an important part of the fantasy was the response of the other person). Of relevance to this is Howitt's (2004) suggestion in relation to the need to commit a contact offence, 'The explanation might be that further offending may be a stimulus to fantasy rather than a consequence'. It would be tempting to speculate that for Internet sex offenders the fantasy is itself sufficient, but as yet there is little evidence to support this. It may be that Seto et al.'s (2006) study offers tentative support for this in that their non-contact offenders responded sexually much more to visual images than did contact offenders.

A further study comparing Internet sex offenders with non-Internet sex offenders was published by Bates and Metcalf (2007) using data generated by the Thames Valley Programme in the UK. The study sought to analyse the differences and similarities between the two groups using a battery of psychometric tests employed by the programme (Beech, 1998). These eight psychometric tests generate measures that can be divided broadly into three categories: offence specific; socio-affective and validity scales. Seventy-eight men were assessed, half of whom had a conviction related to a contact offence and half who had committed an Internet sex offence. Contact offences included offences against children and adults such as rape, indecent assault, indecent exposure and making obscene telephone calls. Two of the Internet sex offenders also had prior contact offence convictions.

In Bates and Metcalf's (2007) study, the overall rate of psychometrically derived 'high deviancy' was calculated by combining all of the differently weighted questionnaire scores. Their results suggested that overall rates of 'psychometric deviancy' were similar between the two groups (22.2 per cent of Internet sex offenders and 23.1 per cent of contact offenders). However, there were differences between the two groups. Using the Paulhus' Balanced Inventory of Desirable Responding (BIDR) contact offenders scored more highly on the self-deception subscale, while Internet sex offenders evidenced much higher scores on the Impression Management sub-scale (61.8 per cent of cases, as opposed to 39.5 per cent of contact offenders). The authors suggest that this may be highly suggestive of Internet sex offenders presenting themselves in an unrealistically positive way and it may also cast doubt on the validity of the psychometric test results for this group. They conclude that, '. . . psychometric scores should be treated with caution, and it is possible that greater psychological deficits than are currently identified are actually present for this group' (p 15). It is however, difficult to interpret the results presented within the study as no standard deviations are given and it is unclear whether this represents highly distorted scores for some offenders and not others.

Their overall psychometric scores suggested that Internet sex offenders showed higher self-esteem than contact offenders, but worse emotional loneliness. Levels of under-assertiveness were also marginally higher in the Internet sex offender group, but this group indicated much lower levels of external locus of control than did the contact offenders. Of interest

is that only 9.1 per cent of Internet offenders scored above the cut-off point on the emotional congruence scale, which measures the degree to which children are emotionally significant for the person, and on the victim empathy scale only 5.9 per cent were above the cut-off. Bates and Metcalf (2007) concluded that on this scale there were marked differences in the responses between the two groups. It would appear, however, that the levels of deviance shown by almost one quarter of Internet sex offenders derived from the socio-affective, rather than offence specific, category, but the largest difference was seen with the Impression Management Score. The authors suggest that this may be for a variety of reasons, such as the ambiguity about the nature of the offence and the possibility of being classed as a paedophile. Other explanations offered including the fact that higher education levels increase the capacity and need to 'fake good', as well as a greater investment in maintaining one's employment or social status.

The research by Bates and Metcalf (2007) is important as it explicitly compares the two populations in the context of entry into an accredited treatment programme. It also raises issues about how we conceptualise risk as, with reference to the elevated scores achieved by Internet sex offenders on scales measuring emotional loneliness, the authors state, 'This is of concern, bearing in mind that previous research into the Thames Valley Programme (Bates et al., 2004: 18) has identified that the emotional loneliness psychometric score was the only one that was statistically significant in differentiating recidivists from non-recidivists'. Emotional loneliness has also been associated with legal Internet pornography useage (Yoder et al., 2005). This brings us on to our next, and possibly most inconclusive area for assessment, which is risk.

## Risk assessment

Conroy (2006), in the context of risk management of sex offenders, draws our attention to the fact that a high risk of sexually re-offending is associated with a range of factors. Harris (2006) using the meta-analysis by Hanson and Morton-Bourgon (2004) summarised these as:

- The presence of sexual deviancy as measured by both phallometric assessment and deviant sexual preferences, measured by standardised tools. Sexual interest in children is a strong predictive factor in child molesters, although this is not the case with rape interest for rapists.

- The presence of an anti-social lifestyle and orientation, such as rule violation, poor employment history and reckless, impulsive behaviour.
- A range of additional factors established as having a moderate predictive value include:
  - age (younger offenders presenting a higher risk)
  - number of prior offences
  - single marital status
  - treatment failure
  - sexual preoccupations
  - intimacy deficits

Harris's (2006) publication is of interest as, in the context of actuarial approaches to risk assessment, it questions the validity of making case-level determinations on the basis of tools that have been derived solely from population-based probabilities. A case management approach would also use idiographic assessments, where decisions are based on case specific attributes related to circumstances presented during a particular point in time. This potentially moves the risk emphasis away from being prediction-oriented to being management–oriented. This seems similar to the approach advocated by Marshall (2007) which was discussed earlier in the chapter.

Two actuarial risk assessments commonly employed in the UK are Risk Matrix 2000 (Thornton et al., 2003) and Static-99 (Hanson and Thornton, 2000). Stage one of the Risk Matrix 2000 assessment included three static items (age at commencement of risk; sexual appearances and total criminal appearances). Offenders are allocated points and are placed in one of four categories (low, medium, high or very high). The second stage contains four aggravating factors ( a male victim, a stranger victim, non-contact sexual offences and lack of long-term intimate relationships). If two aggravating factors are present, the risk category is raised one level, and if all four are present the risk is raised two levels (Mandeville-Norden and Beech, 2006). Static-99 is based solely on static factors and there are ten items: prior sexual offences; prior sentencing occasions; convictions for non-contact sex offences; index non-sexual violence; prior non-sexual violence; unrelated victims; stranger victims; male victims; lack of long-term intimate

relationships and whether the offender is aged under twenty-five on release (or at present within the community). These instruments provide an estimation of long-term risk in a sex offender population and do not identify factors that may highlight more immediate risk of re-offending. It is also unclear as to their usefulness with Internet sex offenders and as yet there are few studies to inform the assessment of the probability that such an offender might go on to commit a further offence. The demographics of Internet use would also suggest that a younger age group are also more likely to use the new technologies (Livingstone and Bober, 2005) and are more likely to engage in risky and potentially criminal behaviour in relation to images (Carr, 2004). In the latter study of a New Zealand cohort of offenders, the largest group were teenagers and were therefore less likely to be in gainful employment (as opposed to education) and less likely to be in stable long-term relationships. In Middleton et al.'s (2006) study Risk Matrix 2000 was used with their sample of men convicted of an index offence of possessing and/or distributing images of child pornography, or the production, possession or distribution of pseudo-sexual images involving child pornography. Within this group 48 per cent were classified as low risk, 38 per cent medium risk and 17 per cent of high risk of reconviction.

The people within Middleton et al.'s (2006) sample also completed the standardised battery of psychometric tests used by the National Probation Service (Beech et al., 1999) and their results were somewhat different to those in Bates and Metcalf's (2007) study. Sixty per cent reported elevated scores on one or more of the psychometric indicators. Within this study, a large number of respondents recorded no problems with intimacy or dealing with negative emotions, no distortions in their sexual scripts and no cognitive distortions regarding the appropriateness of sexual contact with children, ' . . . and yet have displayed a delectation for online images depicting the sexual abuse of children'. These authors concluded that there is a population of Internet sex offenders, 'who do not share the psychological vulnerability typically displayed by sex offenders' (p 600). It is also of interest, given the results of Bates and Metcalf's (2007) study, that only a small number recorded high scores on the Personal Distress Scale and the Interpersonal Reactivity Index, which are measures for self-deceptive enhancement and image management. They did, however, show elevated levels of impulsivity, which the authors felt raised important questions about the possible level of risk posed by Internet sex offenders of future Internet offending, rather than the risk of contact sexual offences.

In many ways these questions are at the heart of our confusion about the measure of risk posed by people who used the Internet to commit offences. Risk of what? As we have seen, there are few studies to inform our understanding of risk with Internet sex offenders, and this is compounded by the different kinds of populations used (eg prison versus community), the time frame for the data collection (more recent accounts would suggest a greater availability of illegal images of children, through, for example peer to peer networks), the ways in which the data are gathered (telephone interviews, self-report questionnaires, re-conviction rates) and the lack of longitudinal data (Quayle, 2006).

What, for example, is the risk of becoming an Internet sex offender through exposure (accidental or purposeful) to illegal images of children? Galbreath, Berlin and Sawyer (2002) have suggested that clinicians are encountering cases where the presence of the Internet itself seems to have been the primary impetus for paraphilic behaviour, and Wood (2007) presents an argument that the Internet may 'fan the flames' of something that might otherwise have remained smouldering within the psyche. In one of the earlier case studies of Internet sex offenders (Quayle, Holland, Linehan and Taylor, 2000), an individual is described who appeared to have no prior history of sexual interest, fantasy or behaviour in relation to children. This question is of particular importance in relation to young people. Ybarra and Mitchell (2005) have indicated that those young people who report intentional exposure to pornography are also more likely to report delinquent behaviour and substance use in the previous year, along with clinical features of depression and lower levels of emotional bonding with care givers. Similarly Moultrie (2006), in one of the first studies of adolescent Internet offenders, found that within their sample of seven young people, two had also engaged in contact offences and five reported sexual arousal to the images of children that they had viewed.

A second risk is the commission of a similar, Internet-related sex offence, and as we have seen, this has been highlighted by Middleton et al.

(2006). One model that might inform our understanding of risk in relation to this is the research that has been done on Internet addiction (eg Carnes, Murray and Charpentier 2005; Delmonico, 2005) and helps to explain why it is commonly observed that Internet offenders go back online, sometimes even after they have been caught and are waiting conviction. However, another explanation may relate to the function that online activity has for the person – in simple terms, what 'needs' it appears to be meeting. It may seem very obvious that the function is largely a sexual one – people download images of children because they are sexually arousing and because they can masturbate to them. However, it does not explain why they need to go on engaging in risk-taking behaviour, when they have already secured material that possibly meets their unique sexual scripts and which can be used to fuel fantasy and arousal. Quayle and Taylor (2002) in their qualitative analysis of interviews with 13 men who had been convicted of various offences related to child pornography, suggested that there are in fact multiple possible functions: an aid to arousal and masturbation; collecting activity; as a way of facilitating social relationships; as a way of avoiding 'real life'; and on occasions as a form of self-administered 'therapy'. If the online activity was meeting needs that either could not be met elsewhere, or could no longer be met as the exclusivity of the behaviour had replaced other offline activities or social supports, then it is not surprising that there should be a strong compulsion to 'go back online' (Quayle, 2006). Webb, Craissati and Keen (2006) indicated that in their study 'Internet failures' (who went on to re-offend) fitted into two subgroups that posed a risk of *repeated* Internet offending, but not necessarily an escalation to contact sex offending.

Delmonico and Griffin (2008) give a good overview of assessments that can be used in relation to addictive or compulsive behaviours. Carnes, Delmonico and Griffin (2001) had suggested that problematic online sexual behaviours often exist in the presence of other addictive/compulsive behaviours, and that the Sexual Addiction Screening Test (Carnes, 1989) or Kalichman Sexual Compulsivity Scale (Kalichman and Rompa, 2001) can be useful. Daneback, Ross and Mansson (2006) suggest that three criteria can be used to screen compulsive behaviour: not being able to choose to engage in the behaviour; continuing to engage in the behaviour in spite of negative consequences, and obsession with the behaviour. The Kalichman Sexual Compulsivity Scale was originally developed by Kalichman et al. (1994) and had ten items which significantly correlated with loneliness, low self-esteem and low sexual self-control. Daneback et al. (2006) used this scale and found that those people with an elevated score subjectively reported having difficulties controlling their online sexual activities and that it was a problem in their lives. Within this study, 'sexual compulsives' were more likely to be male and be in a relationship.

A third potential area of risk is that of escalation to a further category of Internet sex offending. It would appear that at least for some offenders their behaviour is dynamic rather than static and shows movement through an offending process (Quayle et al., 2000; Wood, 2007; Sullivan and Beech, 2004). Quayle and Taylor (2003) generated a model of problematic Internet use that examined the role of cognitions and contextual cues which facilitated offending and were related to satiation of sexual arousal, processes of engagement with both collecting and communities, and the exploration of different online personas. This might also include movement through non-offending activities, such as accessing legal forms of pornography. A previous history of contact offences, personal circumstances and opportunity also appeared to be critical elements. What also may be of relevance here is research that relates to the role of individual differences. Shim, Lee and Paul (2007) discussed how research on antisocial disposition suggests that the more anti-social a person tends to be (eg the likelihood of violating social norms or pursuing deviant stimuli), the more likely he or she is to seek out and consume extreme forms of sexually explicit materials. These authors used a Sexual Opinion Survey Scale and a self report Psychopathy Scale to measure sexual and anti-social dispositions. Their results indicated that those high in sexual disposition were more likely to expose themselves to unsolicited pornography when they happened to come across it online. Those high in antisocial disposition were more likely to respond to images or links. Those high in both were more likely to expose themselves to extreme materials than all the others.

One final area of risk, and one which dominates work on risk assessment, is the likelihood of an Internet sex offender committing a contact sexual offence. This clearly relates to our definitions of Internet sex offenders, as those who have produced images are already likely to have committed a contact offence against a child (although this may not be the case in the commercial production of child abuse images). Much of the existing research predates the Internet. Marshall (2000) had suggested that there is not a causal link between viewing pornography and sexually offending behaviour, but that it can accelerate psychological processes, enhancing the cognitive distortions of offenders. Seto, Maric and Barbaree (2001) also felt that the evidence for a causal link between pornography use and sexual offending remained equivocal, and concluded that people who are already predisposed to offend are the most likely to show an effect of pornography exposure. Men who are not predisposed to offend were unlikely to show an effect, and if there was an effect it was likely to be transient. Seto and Eke (2005) examined the criminal histories and later offending activities of child pornography offenders. Of 201 adult male child pornography offenders, those with prior criminal records were significantly more likely to offend again in the same way during the follow-up period, and those who had committed a prior or concurrent sexual offence were the most likely to offend again, either generally or sexually. However, it is not clear from this study how many of the offenders had used the Internet to access child pornography. Finkelhor and Ormrod (2004) found only a modest association of general pornography crimes with child victimization. However, Wolak, Finkelhor and Mitchell's (2005) study of child pornography possessors arrested in Internet related crimes indicated that 40 per cent of their sample were 'dual offenders' who sexually victimized children and possessed child pornography. A very recent study by Vega and Malamuth (2007) attempted to examine the unique contribution of pornography consumption to men's sexually aggressive behaviour. Even after controlling for the contributions of risk factors associated with general anti-social behaviour and those used in confluence model research as specific predictors of sexual aggression, they found that high pornography consumption added significantly to the prediction of sexual aggression. This was due to its discriminative ability only among men classified (based on their other risk characteristics) at relatively high risk of sexual aggression. However, it is unclear how this research might relate to those who use child abuse images and the Internet.

## Dedicated assessments

There are very few studies that have specifically looked at the validity of assessments solely in the context of Internet sex offenders. O'Brien and Webster (2007) have suggested that there is a need to consider the transferability of assessment and treatment methods for men who access sexually abusive images of children on the Internet from that which has previously been generated in other areas of child sexual abuse. They argued that one of the major challenges in this area has to be the development of assessment tools that will enable effective discrimination between those involved in accessing child abuse images who represent little direct risk to others, and those who pose a real risk of committing a contact offence. Hammond (2004: 95) also suggested that, 'The fundamental question of whether such offenders may be qualitatively distinct from contact offenders, and the degree of overlap there is between them, depends on the collection and collation of data'. O'Brien and Webster's (in press) study describes the construction and preliminary validation of a measure of the attitudes and behaviours of convicted men whose offences related to child abuse images. An initial measure was constructed through the generation of items with reference to the emerging literature and was piloted with forty incarcerated Internet sex offenders. Phase two involved the validation of an improved version of the Internet Behaviours and Attitudes Questionnaire (IBAQ) with one hundred and twenty-three Internet sex offenders who were based in both the prison and the community.

The measure had good internal consistency and following factor analysis, a two-factor solution ('distorted thinking' and 'self-management') emerged from the attitudinal items. This was not influenced by social desirability and was able to discriminate those who disclosed the greater number of 'offending behaviours'. There were demographic differences between the two phases, with the men in phase one more likely to have been arrested as part of a 'ring'. The authors further analysed the distribution of Internet behaviours by low/high behaviour group, which indicated that engaging in certain behaviours related to a greater level of

Internet-related offending 'deviance'. These behaviours included accessing images using less common technologies; engaging in the trade of images; and engaging in more habitual behaviours relating to viewing, categorisation and masturbation. Similarly Wolak et al. (2005) suggested that those Internet offenders who had organized child pornography collections were more likely to have: in excess of 1000 images; to possess moving images; to have child pornography in non-computer formats; to have images of children younger than six; to have sophisticated computer systems; and methods to store or hide images. They also noted, however, that these people were not more or less likely to have sexually victimized children than were other child pornography possessors.

The aim of this chapter was to examine how we might adequately assess Internet sex offenders, but the reality is that we still know very little about this group and how comparable they are to those who commit offences against children in the offline world. It is apparent that there are similarities, but there are also differences, and as yet there is insufficient data for us to be able to make reasoned, rather than emotive, predictions about future behaviour. One final area that is worth consideration are the number of people who present to existing services, such as the helpline of STOP IT NOW, who feel concern about their thoughts and feelings towards children and who are looking for help. A number of these are people whose activities relate to Internet abuse images. Duff and Willis (2006) outlined the issues raised by the increasing number of clients who present to forensic services with a limited offence history but who have disclosed that they are at risk of sexually offending against children. While this study does not focus on Internet offenders as such, they raise important questions about the usefulness of current risk assessment approaches for understanding and developing treatment plans. They have suggested that in this population risk must be embedded within a psychological formulation that places the individual and their likelihood to offend within a descriptive context that includes an understanding of the nature of their disclosure and thus, potential triggers. They call such individuals 'offenders-in-waiting'. With the opportunities that the Internet and the new technologies afford for people to engage in highly problematic sexual behaviour, along with the proliferation of violent and sexualised content, it may be that there are many more 'offenders-in-waiting' than had previously been predicted.

# References

Adam, A. (2002) Cyberstalking and Internet Pornography. *Gender and the Gaze.* 4: 2, 133–42.

American Psychiatric Association (2000) *Diagnostic and Statistical Manual of Mental Disorders (DSM-IV-TR)* Washington, D.C.: APA.

Bates, A. and Metcalf, C. (2007) A Psychometric Comparison of Internet and Non-Internet Sex Offenders from a Community Treatment Sample. *Journal of Sexual Aggression*, 13: 1, 11–20.

Bates, A. et al. (2004) A Follow-Up Study of Sex Offenders Treated by Thames Valley Sex Offender Groupwork Programme, 1995–99. *Journal of Sexual Aggression*, 10, 29–38.

BBC News on line (2006) Available from: Http://News.Bbc.Co.Uk/2/Hi/Uk_News/England/Derbyshire/6133360.Stm.

Beech, A. (1998) Towards a Psychometric Typology for Assessing Pre-Treatment Level of Problems in Child Abusers. *Journal of Sexual Aggression*, 3, 87–100.

Beech, A.R., Fisher, D and Beckett, R.C. (1999) *An Evaluation of The Prison Sex Offender Treatment Programme.* Home Office. Available on-line: Www.Homeoffice.Gov.Uk/Rds/Pdfs/Occ-Step3.Pdf

Bentall, R. (2006) Madness Explained: Why we must Reject the Kraepelinian Paradigm and Replace it with a 'Complaint-Orientated' Approach to Understanding Mental Illness. *Medical Hypotheses*, 66, 220–33.

Carnes, P.J. (1989) *Contrary To Love.* Center City, MN: Hazelden Educational Publishing.

Carnes, P.J. et al. (2001) in *The Shadows of the Net: Breaking Free of on-line Compulsive Sexual Behavior.* Center City, MN: Hazelden Educational Materials.

Carnes, P.J., Murray, R.E. and Charpentier, L. (2005) Bargains with Chaos: Sex Addicts and Addiction Interaction Disorder. *Sexual Addiction and Compulsivity*, 12, 79–120.

Carr, A. (2004) *Internet Traders of Child Pornography and other Censorship Offenders in New Zealand.* New Zealand: Department of Internal Affairs.

Conroy, M.A. (2006) Risk Management of Sex Offenders: A Model for Community Intervention. *Journal of Psychiatry and Law*, 34, 5–23.

Daneback, K., Ross, M.W. and Mansson, S.A. (2006) Characteristics and Behaviours of Sexual Compulsives who Use the Internet for Sexual Purposes. *Sexual Addiction and Compulsivity*, 13, 53–67.

Delmonico, D.L. (1999) *Internet Sex Screening Test.* Available online from: http://www.sexhelp.com/isst.cpm

Delmonico, D.L., and Griffin, E.J. (2005) Sex Offenders on-line: What Clinicians need to Know. In Schwartz, B. (Ed.) *The Sex Offender: Issues in Assessment, Treatment, and Supervision of Adult and Juvenile Populations (Volume 5.)* Kingston, NJ: Civic Research Institute.

Delmonico, D.L., and Miller, J.A. (2003) The Internet Sex Screening Test: A Comparison of Sexual Compulsives Versus Non-Sexual Compulsives. *Sexual and Relationship Therapy*, 18: 3, 261–76.

Delmonico, D.L. (2005) Sexual Addiction and Compulsivity: Watching the Field Evolve. *Sexual Addiction and Compulsivity*, 12: 1–2.

Delmonico, D.L. and Griffin, E.J. (2008) Online Sex Offending: Assessment and Treatment. In Laws, D.R. and O'Donohue, W.T. (Eds.) *Sexual Deviance: Theory, Assessment, and Treatment*, 2nd Ed. N.Y.: Guilford Press, 459–85.

Duff, S. and Willis, A. (2006) At the Precipice: Assessing a Non-Offending Client's Potential to Sexually Offend. *Journal of Sexual Aggression*, 12: 1, 45–51.

Finkelhor, D. and Ormrod, R. (2004) *Child Pornography: Patterns from the NIBRS.* Washington, DC: US Department of Justice Programs, Office of Juvenile Justice and Delinquency Prevention.

Galbreath, N.W., Berlin, F.S. and Sawyer, D. (2002) Paraphilias and The Internet. In Cooper, A. (Ed.) *Sex and The Internet: A Guidebook for Clinicians.* New York: Brunner-Routledge.

Gannon, T.A., Ward, T. and Collie, R. (2007) Cognitive Distortions in Child Molesters: Theoretical and Research Developments over the Past Two Decades. *Aggression and Violent Behavior*, 12, 402–16.

Gillespie, A.A. (2006) Indecent Images, Grooming and the Law. *Criminal Law Review*, 412–21.

Godejord, P.A. (2007) Fighting Child Pornography: Exploring Didactics and Student Engagement in Social Informatics. *Journal for the American Society for Information Science and Technology*, 58: 3, 446–51.

Hammond, S. (2004) Assessing Internet Sex Offenders. In Calder M.C. (Ed.) *Child Sexual Abuse and The Internet: Tackling the New Frontier.* Lyme Regis: Russell House Publishing.

Hanson R.K. and Thornton, D. (2000) Improving Risk Assessment for Sex Offenders: A Comparison of Three Actuarial Scales. *Law and Human Behavior*, 24, 119–36.

Hanson, R.K. and Morton-Bourgon, K.E. (2004) *Predictors of Sexual Recidivism: An Updated Meta-analysis* (User Report 2004-2). Ottawa: Public Safety and Emergency Preparedness Canada. Available online from: www.psepc.gc.ca

Hanson, K. and Morton-Bourgon, K.E. (2005) The Characteristics of Persistent Sex Offenders: A Meta-Analysis of Recidivism Studies. *Journal of Consulting and Clinical Psychology*, 73: 6, 1154–63.

Harris, A.J. (2006) Risk Assessment and Sex Offender Community Supervision: A Context Specific Framework. *Federal Probation*, 70: 2, 36–43.

Howells, K., Day, A., and Wright, S. (2004) Affect, Emotions and Sex Offending. *Psychology, Crime and Law*, 10, 179–95.

Howitt, D. (2004) What is The Role of Fantasy in Sex Offending? *Criminal Behaviour and Mental Health*, 14, 182–188.

ICMEC (2006) *Child Pornography: Model Legislation and Global Review.* ICMEC.

Internet Watch Foundation (2007) 2006 Annual Report. Available on line from: Http://Www.Iwf.Org.Uk/Media/News.196

IWF (2007) Internet Watch Foundation Annual Report. Available online from: http://www.inf.org.uk/corporate/page.188.htm

Kalichman, S. and Rompa, D. (2001) The Sexual Compulsivity Scale: Further Development and Use with HIV-Positive Persons. *Journal of Personality Assessment*, 76, 379–95.

Kalichman, S.C. et al. (1994) Sexual Sensation Seeking: Scale Development and Predicting AIDS-Risk Behavior among Homosexually Active Men. *Journal of Personality Assessment*, 62, 385–97.

Livingstone, S. and Bober, M. (2005) *UK Children go On-line: Final Report of Key Project Findings.* Available on-line from: Http://Www.Lse.Ac.Uk/Collections/Children-Go-Online/Ukcgofinalreport.Pdf

Mandeville-Norden, R. and Beech, A. (2006) Risk Assessment of Sex Offenders: The Current Position in the UK. *Child Abuse Review*, 15, 257–72.

Marshall, W.L. (2007) Diagnostic Issues, Multiple Paraphilias, and Comorbid Disorders in Sexual Offenders: Their Incident and Treatment. *Aggression and Violent Behavior*, 12, 16–35.

Marshall, W.L., and Marshall, L.E. (2000) The Origins of Sexual Offending. *Trauma, Violence, and Abuse: A Review Journal*, 1, 250–63.

McLelland, M. (2001) Local Meanings in Global Space: A Case Study of Women's 'Boy Love' Web Sites in Japanese and English. *Mots Pluriel*, No. 19. Oct. Available on-line from: Http://Www.Arts.Uwa.Edu.Au/Motspluriels/MP1901mcl.Html.

Middleton, D. et al. (2006) The Pathways Model and Internet Offenders: An Investigation into the Applicability of the Ward and Siegert Pathways Model of Child Sexual Abuse with Internet Offenders. *Psychology, Crime and Law.* 12: 6, 589–603.

Moultrie, D. (2006) Adolescents Convicted of Possession of Abuse Images of Children: A New Type of Adolescent Sex Offender? *Journal of Sexual Aggression*, 12: 2, 165–74.

National Offender Management Service (2007) Consultation on Possession of Non-Photographic Visual Depictions of Child Sexual Abuse. Available on-line from Http://Www.Homeoffice.Gov.Uk/Documents/Cons–2007-Depiction-Sex-Abuse.

O'Brien, M.D., and Webster, S.D. (2007) The Construction and Preliminary Validation of The Internet Behaviours and Attitudes Questionnaire (IBAQ) *Sexual Abuse: A Journal of Research and Treatment*, 19, 237–56. Online From Http://Www.Icmec.Org/En_X1/Pdf/Modellegislationfinal.Pdf.

Quayle, E. (2008) Online Sex Offending: Psychopathology and Theory. In Laws, D.R. and O'Donohue, W.T. (Eds.) *Sexual Deviance: Theory, Assessment, and Treatment*, 2nd Ed. New York: Guilford Press, 439–59.

Quayle, E. and Taylor, M. (2002) Child Pornography and the Internet: Perpetuating a Cycle of Abuse. *Deviant Behavior*, 23: 4, 331–62.

Quayle, E. and Taylor, M. (2003) Model of Problematic Internet Use in People with a Sexual Interest in Children. *Cyberpsychology and Behavior*, 6: 1, 93–106.

Quayle, E., Vaughan, M. and Taylor, M. (2006) Sex Offenders, Internet Child Abuse Images and Emotional Avoidance: The Importance of Values. *Aggression and Violent Behavior*, 11: 1, 1–11.

Quayle, E., Holland, G, Linehan, C. and Taylor, M. (2000) The Internet and Offending

Behaviour: A Case Study. *The Journal of Sexual Aggression*, 6: 1/2, 78–96.

Sentencing Advisory Panel (2002) Offences Involving Child Pornography. Available on line from Http://Www.Sentencing-Advisory-Panel.Gov.Uk.

Seto, M. C. and Eke, A. (2005) The Criminal Histories and Later Offending of Child Pornography Offenders. *Sexual Abuse: A Journal of Research and Treatment*, 17: 2, 201–10.

Seto, M.C., Cantor, J.M. and Blanchard, R. (2006) Child Pornography Offences are a Valid Diagnostic Indicator of Pedophilia. *Journal of Abnormal Psychology*, 115, 610–15.

Seto, M.C., Maric, A. and Barbaree, H.E. (2001) The Role of Pornography in the Etiology of Sexual Aggression. *Aggression and Violent Behavior*, 6, 35–53.

Sheldon, K. (2007) *The On-Line Paedophile: A Comparison of the Demographic, Social, Criminal and Psychological Characteristics of Internet, Contact and Mixed Sexual Offenders*. Unpublished Thesis University of Loughborough.

Shim, J.W., Lee, S. and Paul, B. (2007) Who Responds to Unsolicited Sexually Explicit Materials on the Internet? The Role of Individual Differences. *Cyberpsychology and Behavior*, 10: 1 71–9.

Sipress, A. (2007) Does Virtual Reality Need A Real-Life Sheriff? Simulated Crimes Test Reach of Justice System. *The Washington Post*. Available on line from Http://Www.Concordmonitor.Com/Apps/Pbcs.Dll/Article?AID=/20070603/REPOSITORY/706030389/1013/NEWS03

Sullivan, J. and Beech, A. (2004) Assessing Internet Sex Offenders. In Calder, M.C. (Ed.) *Child Sexual Abuse and the Internet: Tackling the New Frontier*. Lyme Regis: Russell House Publishing.

Taylor, M. and Quayle, E. (2005) Abusive Images of Children. In Cooper, S. et al. (Eds.) *Medical, Legal and Social Science Aspects of Child Sexual Exploitation*. Saint Louis: GW Medical Publishing.

Taylor, M., Holland, G. and Quayle, E. (2001) Typology of Paedophile Picture Collections. *The Police Journal*, 74: 2, 97–107.

Thornton, D. et al. (2003) Distinguishing and Combining Risks for Sexual and Violent Recidivism. In Prentky, R. et al. (Eds) Understanding and Managing Sexually Coercive Behaviour. *Annals of The New York Academy of Sciences*. 989, 225–35.

Vega, V. and Malamuth, N.M. (2007) Predicting Sexual Aggression: The Role of Pornography in the Context of General and Specific Risk Factors. *Aggressive Behavior*, 33, 104–17.

Webb, L, Craissati, J. and Keen, S. (2006) *Characteristics of Internet Child Pornography Offenders: A Comparison with Child Molesters. Version 2: Follow Up Study*. Bracton Centre (Oxleas NHS Trust) and London Probation Area.

Wolak, J., Finkelhor, D. and Mitchell, K.J. (2005) *Child-Pornography Possessors Arrested in Internet-Related Crimes: Findings from the National Juvenile On-line Victimization Study*. Washington: National Center for Missing and Exploited Children.

Wolak, J., Mitchell, K. and Finkelhor, D. (2006) *On-line Victimization of Youth: Five Years Later*. Washington D.C.: National Center for Missing and Exploited Children.

Wood, H. (2007) Compulsive Use of Virtual Sex and Internet Pornography: Addiction or Perversion? In Morgan, D. and Ruszczynski, S. (Eds.) *Clinical Lectures on Violence, Perversion and Delinquency*. London: Karnac.

Wortley, R. and Smallbone, S. (2006) Child Pornography on the Internet. *COPS: Problem-Oriented Guides For Police*. US Department of Justice. Available on line at Http://Www.Ncjrs.Gov/App/Publications/Abstract.Aspx?ID=236113

Ybarra, M.L. and Mitchell, K.J. (2004) Youth Engaging in On-line Harassment: Associations with Care Giver-Child Relationships, Internet Use, and Personal Characteristics. *Journal of Adolescence*, 27, 319–36.

Ybarra, M. and Mitchell, K.Y. (2005) Exposure to Internet Pornography among Children and Adolescents: A National Survey. *CyberPsychology and Behaviour*, 8, 473–87.

Yoder, V.C., Vides III, T.B. and Amin, K. (2005) Internet Pornography and Loneliness: An Association? *Sexual Addiction and Compulsivity*, 12, 19–44.

# CHAPTER 11

# Rape Assessment

*Rachael M. Collie, Theresa A. Gannon, Lucy King and Tony Ward*

## Introduction

Rape of adult women is a highly prevalent crime (eg Myhill and Allen, 2002; Tjaden and Thoennes, 1998) that causes significant harm to the victim and great concern to society. Rape involves the penetration of the vagina or anus without legitimate consent. In the United Kingdom, for example, the legal definition of rape is *penile* penetration of the vagina, anus, or mouth, whilst vaginal or anal penetration by other objects is classified as *Assault by Penetration* (Sexual Offences Act, 2002). In practice, the term *rapist* is applied to individuals who have committed rape or attempted to do so against a victim above the age of legal consent for sexual relations (eg 16 years of age; Beech, Oliver, Fisher and Beckett, 2005). A significant proportion of rapes are perpetrated by partners, ex-partners, or acquaintances (Tjaden and Thoennes, 1998) and, undoubtedly, only a minority of all rapists are convicted. However, once identified, forensic and correctional services have the opportunity to prevent the recurrence of sexually aggressive behaviour through appropriate management and rehabilitation of those men at risk of re-offending. Also by identifying those men who pose lower risk, resources can be allocated more rationally to higher risk cases.

Assessment is the starting point of effective management and rehabilitation. The specific goals of assessment typically include:

- Determining an offender's likelihood of future sexual offending (and other serious crimes).
- Identifying an offender's rehabilitation needs, treatment amenability, and other salient issues important for risk management.
- Monitoring and evaluating an offender's progress.
  (Thakker, Collie, Gannon and Ward, in press)

In addition, assessments may be requested for specific legal considerations such as determining if an offender meets criteria for specific civil commitment or criminal sentences. These assessments all require a comprehensive psychosexual evaluation covering a range of domains using multiple assessment methods.

In this chapter we address what we consider to be the key issues in the assessment of rapists. We contend that assessment should be embedded within clear conceptual models of the etiological (causal) factors implicated in rape, the offence process, and designed to directly inform and support rehabilitation and risk management. The chapter is organised in two parts. In the first part we describe important rapist characteristics, the major etiological factors linked to the commission of rape, and offence pathways; highlighting the implications of these for assessment. In the second part we describe the assessment domains and methods included in a comprehensive assessment and outline various strategies for optimising the assessment process. We conclude by highlighting the implications of the Good Lives Model innovation in sex offender rehabilitation for assessment.

## Rapist characteristics, rape aetiology, and offence pathways

A good understanding of the relevant etiological and offence process theories ensures clinicians' assessments reflect contemporary knowledge of the causes of sexually aggressive behaviour and associated phenomenology. Although theories don't replace the need for clinical reasoning, assessment practices that are tightly linked to relevant theory helps guard against idiosyncratic assessment and conjecture about the causes and treatment needs of individuals who have offended. A good understanding of rape also helps clinicians be clear about what information is important for formulating the case and reduces the potential to spend large amounts of time gathering information without realising the salient issues.

Providing a comprehensive review of theories and research relevant to rape is outside the scope of this chapter and has been done well elsewhere (see Gannon and Ward, in press; Ward, Polaschek and Beech, 2005). However, in this section we highlight some important features of rapists and key aspects of rape theory that provides a framework for assessment. In particular we describe:

- Rapist characteristics and contrast these with child molesters and non-sexual offenders.
- The key aetiological factors specifically implicated in the commission of rape.
- Rape offence pathways.

## Rapist characteristics

In much of the literature, rape and rapists are subsumed within the broader category of sexual offending and offenders; a group that is, in reality, dominated by research on child molesters. Yet rapists differ from child molesters in several important ways, and in other ways are similar to non-sexual offenders. In terms of demographic characteristics, rapists tend to be like their general offending peers rather than child molesters. For example, they are often younger (Dickey, Nussbaum, Chevolleau and Davidson, 2002), early school leavers of lower socio-economic status (Bard, Carter, Cerce, Knight, Rosenberg and Schneider, 1987). Compared to child molesters rapists also tend to have engaged in more intimate relationships (Christie, Marshall and Lanthier, 1979) and demonstrate greater heterosocial competence (Dreznick, 2003). Although both rapists and child molesters report histories of sexual abuse, adverse familial relations (Dhawan and Marshall, 1996) and poor attachment experiences (Smallbone and Dadds, 1998; Ward, Hudson and Marshall, 1996) the specific impact of these adversarial experiences on attachment style may differ (Smallbone and Dadds, 1998). Notably, rapists are significantly more likely to be psychopathic, or hold psychopathic traits than child molesters (Abracen, Looman, Di Fazio, Kelly and Stirpe, 2006; Vess, Murphy and Arkowtiz, 2004; Firestone, Bradford, Greenberg and Serran, 2000).

Rapists are often likely to be criminally versatile. When assured confidentiality or polygraph tested, a significant proportion of rapists are shown to disclose offences against children as well as women (Abel, Becker, Cunningham-Rathner, Mittleman and Rouleau, 1988; Gannon, Beech and Ward, in press; Wilcox, Sosnowski, Warberg and Beech, 2005). Rape has also been associated with other inappropriate sexual behaviours, particularly exhibitionism (Simon, 2000; Stermac and Hall, 1989). As well as often having a more diverse pattern of sexual offending, a considerable number of rapists also hold convictions for non-sexual crimes (see Stermac and Quinsey, 1986; Weinrott and Saylor, 1991). For example, Simon (2000) found that rapists and violent offenders displayed significant diversity in their offence records in comparison to child molesters and held equivalent proportions of drug-related offences, theft, and burglary. Finally, recidivism studies show rapists tend to be as likely to recidivate non-sexually as sexually. Hanson and Bussière's (1998) meta-analysis of 61 recidivism studies found 22.1 per cent of rapists recidivated non-sexually over a four to five year period, whilst 18.9 per cent recidivated sexually.

Another important characteristic of rapists is their heterogeneity. A number of attempts have been made to develop classificatory taxonomies to help clarify the aetiology of rape and inform the design of treatment for subgroups with similar features. Perhaps the most notable instance is the work of Knight and Prentky (1990) who subdivided rapists along five primary motivating categories, namely *opportunistic, pervasively angry, sadistic, sexual non-sadistic, and vindictive rapists*. Beech et al. (2005) summarised these into three overall categories of rapist: those driven by *sexual urges* (ie opportunistic and sexual non-sadistic), those driven by *anger* (ie pervasively angry and vindictive) and those where sexual urges and aggression are fused (ie sadistic rapist). Although these distinctions appear useful for surface evaluations of rape aetiology, and are subject to ongoing evaluations, they are yet to lead to differential treatment or risk management of subgroups of rapists (Gannon and Ward, in press).

## Rape aetiology

A range of factors are implicated in rape and several comprehensive theories hypothesise the distal and proximal factors relevant to rape. Malamuth's *Confluence Model of Sexual Aggression* (Malamuth, 1986, 1996; Malamuth, Heavy and Linz, 1993) adopts an evolutionary stance to explain sexual aggression that distinguishes between *ultimate* (ie explaining why some mechanisms develop through our evolutionary history) and *proximate* causes (ie explaining how some mechanisms develop in a given person).

According to Malamuth (1996) evolution favoured differing mating strategies for men and women due to differential parental investment. Briefly, men's strategies include a preference for impersonal sexual encounters (ie *sexual promiscuity*) and use of sexual coercion when thwarted (ie *hostile masculinity*) to maximise reproductive success. More proximate causes of sexual aggression involve the confluence of several risk factors, namely: sexual arousal to rape, dominance motivation, hostility towards women, offence-supportive attitudes (eg rape myth acceptance), antisocial personality characteristics, and sexual experience (used to measure opportunity for sexual aggression). Malamuth contends that these risk factors are specific for aggression toward women but can also account for other adverse behaviours such as general dominance or controlling behaviour. Environmental factors, such as childhood experience and cultural values, are proposed to play an important part in either facilitating or inhibiting sexual aggression.

Marshall and Barbaree (1990; Marshall and Marshall, 2000) proposed the *Integrated Theory of Sexual Aggression* to explain general sexual offending (ie child molestation as well as rape). In brief, Marshall and Barbaree hypothesise that adverse experiences during childhood (eg physical or sexual abuse) creates vulnerability for subsequent sexual aggression via distorted internal working models of relationships, low self-esteem, and poor coping skills (self-regulation). When these vulnerabilities are paired with male pubertal hormonal activity they can compromise male adolescents' ability to inhibit aggressive impulses proposed to be instinctively associated with male sexual activity. Marshall and Barbaree suggest the presence of low self-esteem, for example, can make male adolescents vulnerable to adopting macho negative socio-cultural attitudes (eg viewing women as sexual objects) to enhance self-esteem which in combination with transient situational variables (ie affect, sexual arousal, intoxication) can trigger sexual aggression. Several aspects of Marshall and Barbaree's theory are empirically validated, perhaps most notably the hypotheses concerning intimacy deficits (Marshall and Hambley, 1996; Smallbone and Dadds, 1998).

Hall and Hirschman (1991) developed the *Quadripartite Model of Sexual Aggression* which implicated four main factors in rape: physiological sexual arousal; cognitive distortions; affective dyscontrol; and personality problems stemming from developmental experience. Hall and Hirschman hypothesise each factor characterises a subtype of rapist who is strongly motivated by that particular factor. For example, the driving motivational force behind rape by some offenders may be their cognition (eg beliefs about women, information processing distortions) or anger toward the victim. Even though all four factors are frequently present, one factor is hypothesised to be the primary motivating factor that can intensify the other risk factors and push a person over his *inhibitory threshold* (ie the combination of psychological and situational factors unique to that person that restrain sexual aggression).

Ward and Beech (2006; in press) have recently formulated the *Integrated Theory of Sexual Offending* (ITSO) by synthesising current knowledge of sexual aggression with biological, neuropsychological, and ecological theories of human behaviour. According to the ITSO, various combinations of three categories of causal factors produce the clinical problems generally hypothesised to lead to sexual aggression (ie self-regulation deficits, deviant sexual arousal, social and emotional difficulties, and cognitive distortions). These casual factors are biological (ie genetics and brain development), ecological (ie physical, social, cultural and personal circumstances) and neuropsychological (that is motivational/emotional, action/control and memory/perception systems). For example, one rapist's primary clinical problem (causal factor) may be his impulsivity (a problem in the action selection/control neuropsychological system) something that can be a product of brain injury during childhood (brain development) and that may be more evident during personally distressing and frustrating circumstances (ecological system).

### Offence pathways

The *Relapse Prevention (RP)* model has been the dominant approach to conceptualising the offence process and sexual recidivism of rapists over the last twenty years (for comprehensive review and critique see Laws, 2003, Laws, Hudson and Ward, 2000; Polaschek, 2003, Ward, 2000; Ward and Hudson, 1996). The RP model has been a core feature of rehabilitation and in many instances the organising framework for sexual offender programmes. According to the RP model, sexual offending is the end product of a cycle or sequence of psychological and situational events. These psychological and situational events can be described as a series of steps that involves *seemingly irrelevant decisions* (that is, subconscious purposive decisions) which lead to *high-risk situations*. Being in a high-risk situation undermines self-control which triggers a *lapse* in commitment to avoid offence related activities and the *problem of immediate gratification* (ie an inability to resist offending due to anticipation of its positive rewards). When a lapse occurs, the offender also experiences an *abstinence violation effect*; that is a series of negative emotions, expectations of failure, and ultimately, abandonment of his abstinence goal and an increased risk to re-offend. In summary then, the RP model of the offence process contends that sexual offending follows a predictable pattern that:

- unfolds over time.
- may be explained by a number of important concepts and principles.
- involves a regulation failure. In essence the RP model conceptualises offenders' relapse as the result of a failure to control impulses.

Despite the clinical appeal and wide adoption of the RP sexual offence relapse model, research with child molesters and rapists shows that sexual recidivism occurs not only because of self-regulatory failure (as depicted in the relapse process model) but also as a result of conscious and purposeful decision-making and planning by the offender (ie intact self-regulation; Laws et al., 2000; Ward, Louden, Hudson and Marshall, 1995; Webster, 2005). Hence, for some offenders the major problem is not disinhibition under conditions of negative affect and stress but basic values, beliefs and motivations that promote or neutralise sexual aggression.

Ward and Hudson (1998; 2000) developed the *Self-Regulation Model of Offending (SRM)* to account for the variety of offence pathways evident in sexual offenders' recidivism (see Ward and Hudson, 1998, 2000; and Ward, Bickley, Webster, Fisher, Beech and Eldridge, 2004 for comprehensive descriptions). The SRM contains four offence pathways representing different combinations of offence-related goals (ie avoidance or approach) and self-regulation styles (ie under-regulation, mis-regulation, and effective regulation). In brief, the *avoidant-passive* pathway

is characterised by the offender having a desire to avoid sexual offending but lacking sufficient coping skills to achieve this goal (ie an under-regulation style). The *avoidant-active* pathway is also characterised by the desire to avoid sexual offending but the offender uses ineffective or counter-productive strategies to control risk factors connected with offending (ie a mis-regulation style). The *approach-automatic* pathway is characterised by the desire to sexually offend but impulsive and poorly planned behaviour (ie an under-regulation style). Finally, the *approach-explicit* pathway is characterised by the offender having the desire to sexually offend and then using careful planning to achieve the sexual offence related goal (ie intact regulation style).

Studies validating the SRM with rape offenders highlight a number of important points for assessment. Yates, Kingston and Hall (2003) found all rapists could be reliability allocated to an offence pathway in the SRM, with most rapists exhibiting *approach* pathways. Approach goal sexual offenders demonstrated significantly higher risk of sexual recidivism on both a static and dynamic risk measure compared to offenders with avoidance goals. Webster (2005) also found most rapists in a known recidivist sample could be categorised to one of the four SRM pathways on both their original and subsequent sexual offence. The predominant pathway for this group was also the approach-explicit pathway, which is consistent with earlier speculation that sex offenders with approach-explicit offence pathways will be more difficult to treat than offenders with other pathways (Ward and Hudson, 2000).

In summary, the self-regulation model allows a more sophisticated evaluation of the series of offence processes that better reflects offenders' motivations, goals, and skills. In terms of assessment, the SRM facilitates the development of a more accurate and individualised picture of the offence process which in turn enables a more individualised treatment and risk management approach.

## Implications for assessment

Our review of rapist characteristics, etiological factors, and offence pathways highlights several important implications for assessment. First, assessment needs to be comprehensive to adequately capture the heterogeneity of rapists.

For example, rapists may present with different primary motivations for rape (eg anger, sexual; Hall and Hirshman, 1991; Knight and Prentky, 1990), differing self-regulation styles (Ward and Hudson, 1998, 2000) and approach or avoidance goals (Webster, 2005). Second, although somewhat variously described, rapists appear to have difficulties in several core problem areas: deviant sexual preferences (eg arousal to rape stimuli), antisocial cognition (for example cognitive distortions, negative socio-cultural attitudes, hostility toward women), socio-affective functioning (eg intimacy deficits, preference for impersonal sex) and self-regulation deficits (eg impulsivity, poor problem solving, poor coping skills). Personality problems are also implicated that involve a range of traits and symptoms that span across several areas. Of particular note, are antisocial and psychopathic personality traits. Third, several biological and developmental variables appear important predisposing factors that help explain how risk for rape was created, whilst a range of more proximal situational and contextual variables exacerbate or inhibit rape risk and thus appear particularly relevant for immediate assessments of risk.

A fourth major point is that although many individuals may experience one or two risk factors it is the coming together of risk factors that appears to dramatically increase the risk of rape. Another important hypothesis is that while many risk factors are likely to be present in an offender, some risk factors may play a stronger casual influence. For example, one risk factor may be primary and intensify or elicit other risk factors (eg antisocial and distorted cognition may be the primary problem that elicits use of coercion during sex). Thus, clinicians should guard against making default generalisations that *all* rapists are motivated by deviant sexual arousal (Lackie and de Man, 1997; Marshall, 2006a, 2006b) or that all risk factors are equally significant. Instead, assessment should attempt to identify the full range of mediating and moderating factors and formulate the relationships between these. Such individualised assessments are a necessary step for tailored and efficient treatment and risk management. Finally, rapists appear to be at as much risk, if not greater risk, of recidivating non-sexually as sexually. Hence, clinicians need to be clear about the purpose of their assessment, particularly what treatment needs and risk are to be evaluated (eg

serious offending and/or sexual offending). Obviously, general and violent risk assessment literature and assessment tools are relevant for complete assessments of rapists' risk of serious recidivism broadly defined.

## Assessment issues, domains and methods

A number of areas are covered in comprehensive assessment of rapists as outlined above. Assessments should be well structured and draw upon multiple sources of information including use of relevant, psychometrically sound assessment tools and collateral information (eg court and police documents, assessments from other professionals, and other pertinent information provided by family members). In this section we describe the offence process interview, psychosocial history interview, and assessment of the core problem areas implicated in rape including relevant psychometric instruments. We include a specific section on actuarial and structured clinical risk assessment measures. However, we first discuss issues related to optimising the clinical interview and veracity of offenders' self-report.

The clinical interview remains an important part of assessment. Factors necessary for effective interviewing in general clinical settings are equally important for interviewing with rapists (Towl and Crighton, 1996). Ideally, a good level of rapport is established early in the process (Shea, 1988) although with sex offenders a range of factors can undermine this objective. Most problematic is lack of genuine engagement from the offender. Reasons can include reluctance to discuss offending because of embarrassment about the nature of his offence, fear of potential legal repercussions if details about his offence history are disclosed, and general suspicion and hostility toward others particularly those working for forensic or correctional agencies. Thus, it is important to take sufficient time to explain the assessment purpose, process, and limits of confidentiality with offenders so they know and have time to consider exactly what they are agreeing to when they provide consent (Cowburn, 2005; Towl and Crighton, 1996). In addition, skilled clinicians can adapt their interviewing style to actively reduce clients' defences and respond to their concerns (Shea, 1988). Ward, McCormack, Hudson and Polaschek

(1997) for example, report that denial can be reduced by treating the offender as a whole person through respectful and empathic communication, framing the interview as an opportunity for unburdening (catharsis) and making a fresh beginning, and asking about known facts related to the offence before asking about the offence proper. Due attention to cultural issues is also important, such as managing cultural differences between the clinician and client that impede discussion of sexual matters.

Notwithstanding the importance of interviewing in a style that facilitates engagement and disclosure, it is unreasonable to expect a sexual offender to fully disclose his history of sexual offending in an initial assessment (Ward et al., 2004). Attention to an offender's impression management and malingering is also essential to gauge the veracity of his self-report (for a review see Rogers and Bender, 2003). An important clue to the presence of malingering is inconsistency in the information (Rogers and Bender, 2003; Weiner, 2003). For example, an individual may present very differently on two different psychometric tests that measure similar characteristics or there may be significant discrepancies between test results, behavioural presentation, or other sources of information from third parties. An offender's poor insight into his own difficulties, defensiveness, and difficulties comprehending assessment materials can also affect the accuracy of his self-report alongside impression management and deception.

## Psychosocial history

Gathering a clear psychosocial history is a standard component in any comprehensive psychological assessment and serves a number of purposes. Areas typically covered include family and relational history, educational and occupational history, sexual and social history, mental health and alcohol and drug history (including screening for head injury), medical history and criminal history. The psychosocial history contains valuable information about early distal and psychological vulnerabilities that predisposed the offender to commit rape, as well as more proximal psychological characteristics and situations that remain linked to their proclivity for future rape. The psychosocial history also provides an opportunity to assess the presence of more broad criminal behaviour and associated risk factors.

Ward et al. (2004) report that various themes are usually evident in offenders' histories that provide insight into an offender's general self-regulation style (under-regulation, misregulation, or intact regulation). These themes are particularly revealed by attention to offenders' reactions to significant life transitions (eg relationship break-ups, job changes) major disappointments, frustrations, and traumatic events. Offenders with an avoidant-passive offence pathway (ie avoidance goals and under-regulation style) are likely to present as feeling 'trapped', being unable to get their needs met, and having little sense of control over their own life. Offenders with an avoidant-active pathway (ie avoidant goals and a misregulation style) are more likely to express themes of being a capable and confident person who is confused, frustrated or angry when faced with a problem that they are unable to manage well themselves. In contrast, offenders with an approach-automatic pathway (ie approach goals and an under-regulation style) are likely to have a history of impulsive or opportunistic acts and a sense of entitlement to meet their own needs and wants regardless of the consequences. Finally, offenders with an approach-active pathway (ie approach goals and intact self-regulation) are likely to have lifestyles and interests that centre on sexual deviance, such as regular use of pornography, grooming, or current offending. Unlike the approach-automatic offenders, intact regulation will be demonstrated through evidence of delaying gratification, use of extensive planning, general self-regulation, and gaining satisfaction from these achievements.

## The sexual offence

Gathering a detailed understanding of the sexual offence and the context within which it was enacted provides information on the exact nature of the sexually aggressive behaviour, the offender's motivational and affective states and goals, and insights into the psychological and situational characteristics of the offender that are linked to his sexually aggressive propensity. The most recent or typical offence is usually selected to interview in detail. However, where an offender has committed offences over the same time period against multiple victims or has an extensive history of sexual offending, separate interviews can be conducted of different offences to ensure a comprehensive understanding of the offence processes (Ward et al., 2004; Webster, 2005).

Careful and targeted questioning about the thoughts, feelings, behaviours and events present in each phase of the SRM is the simplest way to proceed, and lends itself to mapping and then summarising the offence pathway. The nine SRM phases are:

- precipitating or triggering factors (individual and interpersonal influences)
- desire for deviant sex or associated activities
- offence-related goals established (ie avoidant or approach)
- attainment strategy selected (ie avoidant-passive, avoidant-active, approach-automatic, or approach-explicit
- high risk situation entered
- lapse (ie behaviour approximating or preceding sexual offending, such as deviant sexual fantasies)
- sexual offence committed
- immediate post-offence evaluation
- attitude to future offending.

## Deviant sexual preferences and behaviours

Key aspects of sexual preferences and behaviours that require assessment include a preference for sexualised aggression (eg fantasies and arousal to coerced or degrading sex), sexual preoccupation (eg repeated sexualisation of non-sexual situations, excessive fantasising about sex) and presence of any sexual dysfunction or paraphilia (eg exhibitionism, sadism) that is clearly related to the sexual offence. In addition to asking questions about sexual practices and behaviours in the psychosocial and offence interviews, self-report questionnaires provide offenders the opportunity to respond to quite personal questions in a less confronting manner. Questionnaires are also an efficient means of gathering a wide range of detailed information and allow normative comparisons. Instruments that are available include the *Multiphasic Sex Inventory* (Nichols and Molinder, 1984), *Sexual Experiences Survey* (SES; Koss and Oros, 1982), *Attraction to Sexual Aggression Scale* (ASA; Malamuth, 1989a and 1989b) and *The Multidimensional Assessment of Sex and Aggression*

(*MASA*; Knight, Prentky and Cerce, 1994). The *Sexual Self-Regulation Scale* (SSRS; Dickie, 1998) is also a self-report questionnaire that aims to measure general self-regulation in sexual relationships.

Although phallometry is a physiological measure that holds the promise of being an objective method of sexual interests that can circumvent the obvious limitations of self-report (eg denial and distortion), unfortunately there is little to suggest it is reliable (eg Barbaree, Baxter and Marshall, 1989) or valid with rapists (eg Fernandez and Marshall, 2003; Letourneau, 2002; Looman and Marshall, 2001). In fact, Marshall (2006a) recently concluded the routine use of phallometry in evaluations of sex offenders is *not* recommended. Further, whilst alternative techniques like viewing time are being developed and appear a promising measure of paedophilia (Gress, 2005; Laws and Gress, 2004) there is no evidence that this technique is useful in the assessment of *deviant* arousal in rapists (Letourneau, 2002).

## Pro-offending cognition

Beliefs, cognitive distortions, and attitudes are a central component of all theories of rape and the offence process. One of the major developments in the conceptualisation of cognition in sex offending is the application of schema-based cognitive theory to organise and understand the range of cognitive variables thought to be relevant. In brief, schemas are knowledge structures that contain cognitive content (for example beliefs, assumptions, attitudes, rules) that originate from early life experiences, and that guide information processing (and hence cognitive distortions). Ward (2000) proposed that sex offenders hold *implicit theories* (ie offence-supportive schema) which produce their conceptualisation of their victims (intended or actual) and facilitate their explanation and interpretation of their victims' and their own actions. Implicit theories contain general assumptions about the nature of peoples' individual psychological functioning (eg peoples' mental states and their relationship to each other and their behaviour) and specific beliefs about the motives, beliefs and desires of specific categories of people (such as women). They may also include idiographic beliefs about a particular victim. Implicit theories are thought to arise from adverse developmental experiences (that is they are explanatory theories) and exert an enduring influence throughout an individual's life. Ward and others (eg Mann and Shingler, 2006) argue that these schemas are the appropriate focus for treatment and management, rather than the individual beliefs, cognitive distortions, and attitudes that they generate.

Drawing from interview and questionnaire data with rapists, five implicit theories were hypothesised for rapists: *women are unknowable* (ie women are inherently different to men and cannot be understood readily by men), *women as sexual objects* (ie believing that women are sexually preoccupied and highly receptive to sexual advances), *women are dangerous* (ie, women are deceptive and malevolent), *entitlement* (ie beliefs centring around male supremacy and control) and *uncontrollability* (believing that actions cannot be controlled in the face of strong urges and impulses such as sexual arousal) (Polaschek and Gannon, 2004; Polaschek and Ward, 2002). Several studies have identified a range of rapists' schemas (Mann and Shingler, 2006) and these generally support these implicit theory themes. For example, Mann and Shingler summarised research that found evidence that rapists hold beliefs that promote hostile masculinity (Malamuth et al., 1993), a need for control (Myers, 2000, cited Mann and Shingler, 2006), suspiciousness (Malamuth and Brown, 1994), distrust of women (Myers, 2000, cited Mann and Shingler, 2006), a desire for vengeance, a need for respect, feeling damaged by others actions, and feeling controlled by past negative experiences (Mann, 2004, cited Mann and Shingler, 2006).

At present, there is no particular 'measure' of implicit theories. Instead clinicians need to assess and judge the presence and prominence of each implicit theory from a combination of sources (eg psychosocial and offence interview, administration of questionnaires, file review). Self-report questionnaires designed to assess offence-supportive attitudes and beliefs linked to rape that may be useful include the *Rape Myth Acceptance Scale* (RMAS; Burt, 1980), *Hostility Toward Women Scale* (HTWS; Check, 1985), *Hypermasculinity Scale* (Moshkin and Sirkin, 1984), the *RAPE Scale* (Bumby, 1996), the *Norwicki-Strictland Locus of Control Scale* (Norwicki, 1976) and the *Blame Attribution Inventory* (Gudjonsson, 1984).

## Victim empathy

Research indicates that sex offenders often have little empathy for their own victims but, excluding instances of psychopathy, do not necessarily have more general empathy deficits (Marshall, 2006b). These empathy deficits have recently been reconceptualised as arising largely from cognitive distortions about the nature of harm caused to victims (as well as potential difficulties recognising and identifying emotion in others; Marshall, 2001, 2006b). Thus, assessment of victim empathy overlaps with assessment of pro-offending cognition and emotional competence. Self-report instruments that are used for assessing empathy in rapists include the *Rape Empathy Scale* (RES; Dietz, Blackwell, Daley and Bentley, 1982) and the *Interpersonal Reactivity Index* (IRI; Davis, 1980).

## Social and emotional difficulties

A range of social and emotional difficulties may contribute to rape (Beech et al., 2005). For example, intimacy deficits may be satisfied through offending. Alternatively, lack of emotional intimacy can link to offending by removing the inhibition against offending that commitment to a relationship creates (Beech et al., 2005). Additional difficulties include feelings of social inadequacy (Beech, Fisher and Thornton, 2003) and patterns of hostility, suspicion, dominance, and so forth (Beech et al., 2005). A range of self-report inventories to assess general interpersonal and emotional characteristics are available in the general clinical psychology area. Measures that are often used with rapists include the *Fear of Negative Evaluation Scale* (Watson and Friend, 1969), *Social Avoidance and Distress Scale* (Watson and Friend, 1969), *Miller Social Intimacy Scale* (Miller and Lefcourt, 1982), *UCLA Loneliness Scale* (Russell, Peplau and Ferguson, 1978; Russell, 1996), *Buss-Durkee Hostility Scale* (Buss and Durkee, 1957), *Novaco Anger Scale* (NAS; Novaco, 1994) and the *Emotional Control Questionnaire* (EC2; Roger and Najarian, 1989).

## General self-regulation

Self-regulation involves processes that allow goal-directed behaviour to occur, and includes self-initiated, well-organised activity as well as self-control of urges or impulses (Ward, et al., 1998). Thus, impulsivity, poor problem solving, and poor emotional regulation (particularly anger) compromises self-regulation. Lifestyle impulsivity (ie well-established patterns of impulsive, irresponsible and antisocial actions and attitudes that do not support self-regulation) has been shown to predict rapists' recidivism (Knight and Prentky, 1990) and is one facet of psychopathic personality disorder (Cooke and Michie, 2001; Hare, 2003). Psychopathy should be measured using one of the psychopathy checklists (eg *Psychopathy Checklist-Revised; PCL-R*, Hare, 1991, 2003). A range of self-report personality questionnaires can also be used to assess features of emotional, social, and self-regulatory functioning (eg *Millon Clinical Multiaxial Inventory*; Millon, Davis and Millon, 1997).

In addition, problems with substances, particularly alcohol, are commonly reported in rapists (Marshall, 2001). Intoxication at the time of the offence may reflect chronic substance use difficulties or more situational use that compromises self-control. In some instances, offenders may purposefully use substances to augment the offence process and experience. A range of measures of substance use are available in the general clinical psychology area.

### Risk of re-offending

The purpose of risk assessment is to provide reliable and valid judgments about the *likelihood, seriousness,* and *imminence* of sexual harm occurring in the future by a particular offender either in absolute terms or relative to other offenders (Dvorskin and Heilbrun, 2001). In addition, identifying factors linked to risk that are potentially modifiable has become a central focus of treatment and risk management. Comprehensive assessment of sex offender risk should cover personal traits, historical variables, contextual antecedents, and also clinical factors (Beech et al., 2003). Three types of assessment cover these variables and potentially compliment each other: *functional assessments, statistical* or *actuarial* methods, and *clinically informed psychometrics* (see Beech et al., 2003).

Functional assessments are essentially standard clinical assessments which lead to a formulation of the predisposing, vulnerability, precipitating, and maintaining factors for an offender's rape. Actuarial assessments measure the statistical relationship between characteristics of offenders and the probability of an outcome (eg sexual recidivism). Actuarial assessments in the main

are shown and accepted to provide a more reliable and valid evaluation of the likelihood an offender will recidivate over medium to longer timeframes than pure clinical unstructured judgements (Dvorskin and Heilbrun, 2001). However, actuarial sex offender measures tend to predict general classes of outcomes (eg sexual recidivism, sexual and violent recidivism, any recidivism) and any further refinement about the seriousness of offence (eg exhibitionism vs. rape) requires assessment of past offending and clinical features of the case. Further, because actuarial sex offender measures tend to rely extensively on static (historic) risk factors (eg number and type of past offences, victim gender and age) these instruments don't provide useful information about treatment needs or changing risk status (Beech et al., 2003; Bonta, 2002; Craig, Browne and Stringer, 2004; Dvorskin and Heilbrun, 2001; Hanson, 2006). Due to such limitations, recent efforts to develop risk assessment models and instruments that include consideration of dynamic (changeable) and case specific factors are emerging (see Doren, 2006 for discussion).

In this section we review a selection of risk assessment measures designed to predict sexual recidivism. In most instances these instruments were developed on samples of offenders containing a large proportion of child molesters and smaller samples of rapists, therefore we highlight research with rapists where available.

### Static only measures

#### *Static-99* (Hanson and Thornton, 2000)

The Static-99 is a simple to use tool that is designed to assess the longer-term likelihood of sexual and violent recidivism in men already convicted of a sexual offence. The Static-99 contains 10 *historical* items shown to have empirical association with sexual recidivism (eg prior charges and convictions of a sexual nature) that are coded as either present or absent based predominantly on readily available official information (see Harris, Phenix, Hanson and Thornton, 2003 for latest coding information). The Static-99 produces a total score and assignment to a risk category (eg moderate-high risk). Probability estimates for scores and risk categories are given for five, 10, and 15 year periods. Hanson and Thornton (1999, 2000) reported the Static-99 had moderate predictive accuracy in development studies with predominantly child molesters, and other studies with rapist samples have found the Static-99 to perform similarly or better (Hanson and Thornton, 1999, 2000; Barbaree, Seto, Langton and Peacock, 2001; Sjöstedt and Långström, 2001; de Vogel, Ruiter, van Beek and Mead, 2004) although this is not universal (Craig, Beech and Browne, 2006).

## Sex Offender Risk Appraisal Guide (SORAG; Quinsey, Harris, Rice and Cormier, 1998)

The SORAG is a modification of the VRAG (*Violence Risk Appraisal Guide*; Quinsey et al., 1998). It has 14 items which include demographic information, criminal history and psychiatric diagnoses. Although shown to be equally effective in predicting violent and sexual recidivism as the Static-99 (Ducro and Pham, 2006; Nunes, Firestone, Bradford, Greenberg and Broom, 2002) in general the SORAG appears to predict violent recidivism more accurately than sexual recidivism (Ducro and Pham, 2006). Ducro and colleagues also note that the SORAG appeared more accurate when used with rapists than with child sex offenders, however, this finding requires replication. An assessment of psychopathy is required for one of the items on the SORAG. Thus, given the time required, Nunes et al. (2002) noted that the Static-99 is more efficient and better suited to briefer assessments.

## Risk Matrix 2000 (RM2000; Thornton et al., 2003)

The RM2000 also aims to predict sexual and violent (nonsexual) recidivism by sex offenders but is made up of two dimensions for these purposes: Risk Matrix 2000-Sexual and Risk Matrix 2000-Violent. The RM2000 uses static (historical) risk factors to produce an initial risk score and rating, which is then adjusted based on the presence of aggravating factors. The initial risk rating on the RM2000-Sexual, for example, is based on the presence and severity of age at commencement of risk, appearances for sexual crimes, and appearances for all crimes, and adjusted based on the presence of convictions for a contact sexual offence against a male, convictions for a contact sexual offence against a stranger, lack of long-term age-appropriate relationship, and conviction for a non-contact sexual offence. Research with samples of combined sex offenders has produced mixed

results. Thornton et al. (2003) found the RM2000 had moderate predictive validity with both sexual and violent recidivism and that it fared well compared to the Static-99. Although Craig et al. (2006) found the RM2000-Violent performed well, the RM2000-Sexual performed less well at predicting sexual recidivism than the RM2000-Sexual. Neither study disaggregated the samples into different types of sexual offenders.

## Minnesota Sex Offender Screening Tool-Revised (MnSOST-R; Epperson, Kaul, Huot, Goldman and Alexander, 2003)

The MnSOST-R was developed for the Minnesota Department of Corrections and contains 16 items examining a number of sexual offence variables, general criminality and antisocial behaviour, and demographic factors. The MnSOST-R has been criticised for its complex scoring procedure and lack of item relevance outside Minnesota (Beech et al., 2003). In addition, although shown in some studies to display moderate to good predictive validity (eg Epperson, et al., 2003; Langton, Barbaree, Hansen, Harkins, Seto and Peacock, 2002), Bartosh, Garby, Lewis and Gray (2003) reported that it failed to significantly predict sexual, non-sexual violent or any recidivism in rapists.

## Psychopathy Checklist-Revised (PCL-R; Hare, 1991, 2003)

Although not an actuarial (ie statistical) measure *per se*, the PCL-R can be used in an actuarial manner and is supported by an impressive body of research. The PCL-R is a 20-item clinician or researcher scored measure. Each item describes a prototypical characteristic or trait of psychopathy and is scored following a semi-structured interview with the offender and comprehensive review of file information (in research studies, scoring is sometimes based on comprehensive file review only). The PCL-R produces a total score and two factor scores (ie selfish, callous, and remorseless use of others, and chronically unstable and antisocial lifestyle). More recently, Hare proposed a four facet model of psychopathy whereby the two original factors are split into four, whilst Cooke and Michie (2001) have argued psychopathy is best conceptualised as having three factors (arrogant interpersonal style, deficient affective experience, and impulsive behavioural style) with antisocial behaviour being an outcome of psychopathy.

Psychopathic personality traits and disorder has important implications for risk assessment, treatment, and risk management (Hare, 2003; Hart, 1998). Psychopathic personality as operationalised by the PCL-R is shown to have a robust relationship with non-sexual violent recidivism and general recidivism in sex offenders; whilst the relationship to sexual recidivism is more ambiguous (see Hare, 2003; Knight and Guay, 2006). Knight and Guay (2006) concluded that when psychopathy does predict sexual recidivism, most research finds it is the impulsive-antisocial traits that are predictive. The combination of deviant sexual arousal and psychopathy has been found to be a more potent predictor of sexual recidivism in several (but not all) studies (Hare, 2003; Knight and Guay, 2006). The presence of psychopathic personality traits is also shown to make treatment more difficult (see Barbaree, Langton and Peacock, 2006; Hemphill and Hart, 2002; Serin, 1995).

## Dynamic measures

### Sex Offender Need Assessment Rating (SONAR; Hanson and Harris, 2001)

The SONAR aims to predict sexual recidivism in sexual offenders through measuring dynamic risk factors empirically linked to recidivism. An innovative feature of this instrument is the separation of dynamic risk factors into *stable-dynamic* and *acute-dynamic*. Stable-dynamic factors refer to an offender's psychological and situational characteristics that although potentially modifiable are slow to change across time (eg intimacy deficits, offence-supportive beliefs). Acute-dynamic risk factors are psychological and situational features that change rapidly (eg intoxication, being alone with a potential victim) and signal the imminence of offending. The SONAR also supports consideration of case-specific acute risk factors that are not included in the instrument, something which is extremely valuable for individualised risk management.

Hanson and Harris (2000) developed the SONAR on a relatively large sample containing equivalent numbers of rapists (n = 143), girl-victim child molesters, and boy-victim child molesters. They found all items significantly differentiated sexual recidivists from non-recidivists and the instrument had moderate predictive validity overall. Hanson and Harris

(2001) reported that with rare exceptions the same dynamic risk factors were found to be important for rapists as well as child molesters. Further development of the SONAR has seen separation of the scale into *Stable 2000* and *Acute 2000*; however, results about the performance of the revised scale are still pending.

### Sexual Violence Risk – 20 (SVR-20; Boer, Hart, Kropp and Webster, 1997)

The SVR-20 is a structured clinical guideline designed to predict the risk of sexual recidivism in adult sex offenders that contains both static and potentially dynamic predictors of sexual recidivism. The SVR-20 contains a list of 20 primarily empirically derived items organised into three domains: psychosocial adjustment, sexual offences, and future plans. The instrument includes consideration of case-specific factors formulated to elevate risk and a recent change score for each item to capture judgments about fluctuations in risk factors over time. Although the SVR-20 can be easily summed to produce a total score, structured clinical guidelines (unlike actuarial measures) require the assessor to make the final judgment about risk, giving consideration to all of the evidence. Compared to unstructured clinical judgements, structured clinical guidelines offer the promise of higher accuracy through use of empirically linked risk factors (Worling, 2004). In addition, they facilitate greater reliability and transparency in decision-making through the use of a systematic review. However, research to date about the predictive accuracy of the SVR-20 is mixed. Craig et al. (2006) found that the SVR-20 had moderate predictive validity with violent and general recidivism in sexual offenders but not sexual recidivism, whilst de Vogel and colleagues (de Vogel, et al., 2004) found that the SVR-20 total score and final risk judgment had high predictive validity with sexual recidivism.

### Risk for Sexual Violence Protocol (RSVP; Hart, Kropp, Laws, Klaver, Logan and Watt, 2003)

The RSVP (Hart et al., 2003) is a new set of structured clinical guidelines for assessing risk of sexual violence developed along the lines of the SVR-20 (Boer et al., 1997) but with several improvements (Garret, 2005). In brief, the RSVP combines review of static and dynamic risk factors with extensive case formulation designed to aid individualised treatment planning and risk management. However, to date little research investigating the validity of the RSVP is available.

## Polygraph

The use of the polygraph has always been controversial (Branaman and Gallagher, 2005) however, it has become more widely used to promote greater honesty and facilitate the validity of assessments with sex offenders over the last decade or so. Gannon, et al. (in press) reviewed the use of polygraph with sex offenders and concluded that evidence suggested it can motivate sex offenders to more accurately disclose about their sex offending and ongoing risk situations (eg English, Jones, Pasini-Hill, Patrick and Cooley-Towell, 2000; Heil, Ahlmeyer and Simons, 2003). For example, Heil et al. showed sex offenders admitted to many more previous sexual offences when questioned while polygraph tested. Nonetheless, research also shows that the reliability and validity of polygraph testing is generally low creating the problem of high rates of false positives (Stalans, 2004). Research with specific sex offender groups such as rapists is also lacking. In addition, there are a number of ethical issues associated with its use which need to be carefully weighed against any potential benefits and a number of practical issues related to availability, training and costs (Gannon et al., in press).

## *Concluding comments*

In this chapter we discussed what we consider to be key factors in the assessment of rapists to inform treatment planning, risk management, and monitoring and evaluating offenders' progress. We believe assessment ought to be tightly linked to contemporary aetiological and offence process theories, and reflect a good understanding of the unique and similar features of rapists compared with other groups of offenders. In this regard, several core problem areas are potentially implicated in rape which require careful assessment. Further, despite the wide use of the RP model in the assessment and treatment of sexual offenders, we noted its limitations in discriminating the various offence pathways of rapists. In contrast, the SRM represents an extensive reconceptualisation of the RP model that primarily relies on social cognitive theory for explanatory power, and most notably

enables thorough assessment of the diversity of offence pathways of rapists.

Our review highlighted a number of crucial issues for assessment. In relation to process, an interviewing style that facilitates early engagement and disclosure is crucial, given sex offenders' proclivity for a possible lack of genuine engagement, impression management and malingering. Clinicians also need to be vigilant to the difficulties in obtaining accurate information from offenders and not only draw upon clinical interview information, but also information from relevant assessment tools and collateral information from official sources, family and relevant others. Perhaps most notably is the need to use actuarial or structured clinical judgement assessment measures to assist in the prediction of sexual recidivism.

One observation about the current state of rape assessment is that most instruments have been developed on mixed samples of sex offenders that contain large proportions of child molesters. Although we sought to review measures that are suitable for use with rapists and highlight relevant research where available, clinicians need to carefully evaluate the appropriateness and limitations of assessment measures for rapists. This feature of the area also underscores the need for clinicians to avoid relying on generalisations about the nature of "sex offenders" when working with rapists. Indeed the heterogeneity of rapists means that literature on general and violent offending is also highly relevant for at least some rape offenders.

Innovations in the sex offender area also have implications for assessment of rape, particularly the emergence of the Good Lives Model (GLM) (Ward, 2002; Ward and Gannon, 2006) strengths-based approach to sex offender rehabilitation. The GLM is organised around the idea that all human activity is aimed at fulfilling certain basic needs and their associated goods. When an individual's primary human needs are met in one form or another, then he is said to have a 'good' life; that is, a life characterised by fundamental benefits such as sexual intimacy, friendship, physical health, autonomy, community connectedness and creativity. According to the GLM the core problem areas (or dynamic risk factors) associated with rape signal problems in the way a person seeks to meet his primary human needs. When combined with the SRM of the offence process, the GLM provides a deeper understanding of the goals being sought through offending (Ward and Gannon, 2006). For example, while two offenders may purposely approach sexual offending, one may be seeking the goal of autonomy (ie being able to exert control and exercise choice albeit in a dysfunctional manner) and the other sexual satisfaction (again, albeit in a harmful way). The GLM also allows for offending to be a direct means of meeting primary human needs, or alternatively as a result of frustration meeting these needs in otherwise legitimate ways that are more situationally or transiently based.

Thus, the GLM contrasts with deficit and problem based analyses of offending and instead encourages clinicians to focus on what offenders are actually seeking through offending and the relative influence of ecological variables. In turn, treatment planning involves thinking beyond treating problems and removing risk factors to considering what kind of life would be fulfilling and socially acceptable for clients and what internal and external capabilities and supports are needed to acquire and maintain this life. Although the implications of the GLM for assessment of rapists is yet to be fully realised, it clearly brings a new dimension where assessment of problems and risk occurs within broader questions about individuals' psychological and social functioning and well-being. Such an approach is intuitively appealing to many clinicians and holds the promise of providing a more positive, collaborative and engaging process with offenders that still seeks to address the causes of offending and promote safer communities.

# References

Abel, G.G. et al. (1988) Multiple Paraphilic Diagnoses among Sex Offenders. *Bulletin of The American Academy of Psychiatry and The Law*, 16, 153–68.

Abracen, J. et al. (2006) Patterns of Attachment and Alcohol Abuse in Sexual and Violent Nonsexual Offenders. *Journal of Sexual Aggression*, 12, 19–30.

Ackerman, S.J. and Hilsenroth, M.J. (2003) A Review of Therapist Characteristics and Techniques Positively Impacting the Therapeutic Alliance. *Clinical Psychology Review*, 23, 1–33.

Barbaree, H.E., Baxter, D.J. and Marshall, W.L. (1989) The Reliability of the Rape Index in a Sample of Rapists and Non-Rapists. *Violence and Victims*, 4, 299–306.

Barbaree, H., Langton, C. and Peacock, E. (2006) Sexual Offender Treatment for Psychopaths: Is it Harmful? In Marshall, W.L. et al. (Eds.) *Sexual Offender Treatment: Controversial Issues*. Chichester: Wiley.

Barbaree, H.E. et al. (2001) Evaluating the Predictive Accuracy of Six Risk Assessment Instruments for Adult Sex Offenders. *Criminal Justice and Behaviour*, 28, 490–521.

Bard, L. et al. (1987) A Descriptive Study of Rapists and Child Molesters. Developmental, Clinical and Criminal Characteristics. *Behavioral Sciences and the Law*, 5, 203–220.

Bartosh, D.L. et al. (2003) Differences in Predictive Validity of Actuarial Risk Assessment in Relation to Sex Offender Type. *International Journal of Offender Therapy and Comparative Criminology*, 47, 422–38.

Beech, A.R., Fisher, D. and Thornton, D. (2003) Risk Assessment of Sex Offenders. *Professional Psychology: Research and Practice*, 34, 339–52.

Beech, A., Fisher, D. and Ward, T. (2005) Sexual Murderers' Implicit Theories. *Journal of Interpersonal Violence*, 20, 1366–89.

Beech, A. et al. (2005) *STEP 4: The Sex Offender Treatment Programme in Prison: Addressing the Offending Behaviour of Rapists and Sexual Murderers*. England: Home Office.

Boer, D.P. et al. (1997) *Manual for the Sexual Violence Risk-20 Professional Guidelines for Assessing Risk of Sexual Violence*. Vancouver, BC: Institute Against Family Violence.

Bonta, J. (2002) Offender Risk Assessment: Guidelines for Selection and Use. *Criminal Justice and Behaviour*, 29, 355–79.

Branaman, T.F. and Gallagher, S.N. (2005) Polygraph Testing in Sex Offender Treatment: A Review of Limitations. *American Journal of Forensic Psychology*, 23, 45–64.

Bumby, K.M. (1996) Assessing the Cognitive Distortions of Child Molesters and Rapists: Developments and Validation of the MOLEST and RAPE Scales. *Sexual Abuse: A Journal of Research and Treatment*, 8, 37–54.

Burt, M.R. (1980) Cultural Myths and Supports for Rape. *Journal of Personality and Social Psychology*, 38, 217–30.

Buss, A.H. and Durkee, A. (1957) An Inventory for Assessing Different Kinds of Hostility. *Journal of Consulting Psychology*, 21, 343–9.

Check, J.P. (1985) *The Hostility Toward Women Scale*. Unpublished Doctoral Dissertation, University of Manitoba, Winnipeg, Canada.

Christie, M.M., Marshall, W.L. and Lanthier, R.D. (1979) *A Descriptive Study of Incarcerated Rapists and Child Molesters* (Report to The Solicitor General of Canada) Ottawa: Office of The Solicitor General.

Cooke, D.J. and Michie, C. (2001) Refining the Construct of Psychopath: Towards a Hierarchical Model. *Psychological Assessment*, 13, 171–88.

Cowburn, M. (2005) Confidentiality and Public Protection: Ethical Dilemmas in Qualitative Research with Adult Male Sex Offenders. *Journal of Sexual Aggression*, 11, 49–63.

Craig, L.A., Beech, A. and Browne, K.D. (2006) Cross-Validation of The Risk Matrix 2000 Sexual and Violent Scales. *Journal of Interpersonal Violence*, 21, 612–33.

Craig, L.A., Browne, K.D. and Stringer, I. (2004) Comparing Sex Offender Risk Assessment Measures on a UK Sample. *International Journal of Offender Therapy and Comparative Criminology*, 48, 7–27.

Davis, M.H. (1980) A Multidimensional Approach to Individual Differences in Empathy. *JSAS Catalogue of Selected Documents in Psychology*, 10, No. 85.

de Vogel, V. et al. (2004) Predictive Validity of The SVR-20 and Static-99 in a Dutch Sample of Treated Sex Offenders. *Law and Human Behaviour*, 28, 235–51.

Dhawan, S. and Marshall, W.L. (1996) Sexual Abuse Histories of Sexual Offenders. *Sexual Abuse: A Journal of Research and Treatment*, 8, 7–15.

Dickey, R. et al. (2002) Age as a Differential Characteristic of Rapists, Pedophiles, and Sexual Sadists. *Journal of Sex and Marital Therapy*, 28, 211–18.

Dickie, I. (1998) *An Information Processing Approach to Understanding Sympathy Deficits in Sexual Offenders*. Unpublished MA Thesis. Carleton University, Ottawa.

Dietz, S.R. et al. (1982) Measurement of Empathy toward Rape Victims and Rapists. *Journal of Personality and Social Psychology*, 43, 372–84.

Doren, D.M. (2006) Recidivism Risk Assessment: Making Sense of Controversies. In Marshall, W.L., Fernandez, Y.M., Marshall, L.E. and Serran, G.A. (Eds.) *Sexual Offender Treatment: Controversial Issues* (pp. 3–15). NY: Wiley.

Dreznick, M.T. (2003) Heterosocial Competence of Rapists and Child Molesters: A Meta-Analysis. *Journal of Sex Research*, 40, 170–8.

Ducro, C. and Pham, T. (2006) Evaluation of the SORAG and the Static-99 on Belgian Sex Offenders Committed to a Forensic Facility. *Sexual Abuse: A Journal of Research and Treatment*, 18, 15–26.

Dvorskin, J.A. and Heilbrun, K. (2001) Risk Assessment and Release Decision-Making: Toward Resolving the Great Debate. *Journal of The American Academy of Psychiatry and Law*, 29, 6–10.

English, K. et al. (2000) Department of Public Safety. *The Value of Testing in Sex Offender Management. Research Report Submitted to the National Institute of Justice*. Denver, CO: Division of Criminal Justice, Office of Research and Statistics.

Epperson, D.L. et al. (2003) *Minnesota Sex Offender Screening Tool – Revised (Mnsost-R): Development, Validation, and Recommended Risk-Level Cut Scores*. Technical Paper, St. Paul, MN: Minnesota Department of Corrections.

Fernandez, Y.M. and Marshall, W.L. (2003) Victim Empathy, Social Self-Esteem and Psychopathology in Rapists. *Sexual Abuse: A Journal of Research and Treatment*, 15, 11–26.

Firestone, P. et al. (2000) The Relationship of Deviant Sexual Arousal and Psychopathy in Incest Offenders, Extrafamilial Child Molesters, and Rapists. *Journal of The American Academy of Psychiatry and Law*, 28, 303–8.

Gannon, T.A. and Ward, T. (In Press) Rape: Psychopathology and Theory. In Laws, D. and O'Donohue, W. (Eds.) *Sexual Deviance: Theory, Assessment and Treatment*. 2nd Edn. NY: The Guilford Press.

Gannon, T.A., Beech, A.R. and Ward, T. (In Press) Polygraph and Risk Assessment. In Grubin, D. and Wilcox, D. (Eds.) *Polygraph in a Forensic Context*. Chichester: Wiley.

Gannon, T.A., Ward, T. and Beech, A.R. (2006) *Sex Offender Risk Assessment and The Polygraph: A Review*. Manuscript Under Review.

Garrett, T. (2005) The Risk for Sexual Violence Protocol (*RSVP*)-Structured Professional Guideline for Assessing Risk of Sexual Violence. *Journal of Sexual Aggression*, 11, 321–3.

Gress, C.L. (2005) Viewing Time Measures and Sexual Interest: Another Piece of the Puzzle. *Journal of Sexual Aggression*, 11, 117–25.

Gudjonsson, G.H. (1984) Attribution of Blame for Criminal Acts and its Relationship with Personality. *Personality and Individual Differences*, 5, 53–8.

Hall, G.C. and Hirschman, R. (1991) Toward a Theory of Sexual Aggression: A Quadripartite Model. *Journal of Consulting and Clinical Psychology*, 59, 662–9.

Hanson, R.K. (2006) Stability and Change: Dynamic Risk Factors for Sexual Offenders. In Marshall, W. et al. (Eds.) *Sexual Offender Treatment: Controversial Issues*. Chichester: Wiley.

Hanson, R.K. and Bussière, M.T. (1998) Predicting Relapse: A Meta-Analysis of Sexual Offender Recidivism Studies. *Journal of Consulting and Clinical Psychology*, 66, 348–62.

Hanson, R.K. and Harris, A. (2000) Where Should We Intervene? Dynamic Predictors of Sexual Offence Recidivism. *Criminal Justice and Behaviour*, 27, 6–35.

Hanson, R.K. and Harris, A.J. (2001) A Structured Approach to Evaluating Change among Sex Offenders. *Sexual Abuse: A Journal of Research and Treatment*, 13, 105–22.

Hanson, R.K. and Harris, A.J. (2001) *The Sex Offender Need Assessment Rating (SONAR): A Method for Measuring Change in Risk Levels*. Ontario: Department of The Solicitor General.

Hanson, R.K. and Thornton, D. (1999) *Static-99: Improving Actuarial Risk Assessments for Sex Offenders*. Ontario: Department of The Solicitor General.

Hanson, R.K. and Thornton, D. (2000) Improving Risk Assessments for Sex Offenders: A Comparison of Three Actuarial Scales. *Law and Human Behaviour*, 24, 119–36.

Hare, R.D. (1991) *The Hare Psychopathy Checklist-Revised*. Toronto, Canada: Multi-Health Systems.

Hare, R.D. (2003) *The Hare Psychopathy Checklist-Revised*. 2nd Edn Toronto, Canada: Multi-Health Systems.

Harris, A.J. and Hanson, R.K. (2004) *Sex Offender Recidivism: A Simple Question – 2004-03*. Ottawa. Department of The Solicitor General.

Harris, A. et al. (2003) *Static-99 Coding Rules: Revised 2003*. Ottawa. Department of The Solicitor General.

Hart, S.D. (1998) The Role of Psychopathy in Assessing Risk for Violence: Conceptual and Methodological Issues. *Legal and Criminological Psychology*, 3, 121–37.

Hart, S.D. et al. (2003) *The Risk for Sexual Violence Protocol (RSVP): Structured Professional Guidelines for Assessing Risk of Sexual Violence*. Burnaby, BC: Mental Health, Law, and Policy Institute, Simon Fraser University.

Heil, P., Ahlmeyer, S. and Simons, D. (2003) Crossover Sexual Offences. *Sexual Abuse: A Journal of Research and Treatment*, 15, 221–36.

Hemphill, J.F. and Hart, S. (2002) Motivating the Unmotivated: Psychopathic Offenders. In McMurran, M. (Ed.) *Motivating Offenders to Change: A Guide to Enhancing Engagement in Therapy*. Chichester: Wiley.

Knight, R.A and Guay, J-P. (2006) The Role of Psychopathy in Sexual Coercion against Women. In Patrick, C.J. (Ed.) *Handbook of Psychopathy*. NY: Guilford Press.

Knight, R.A. and Prentky, R.A. (1990) Classifying Sexual Offenders: The Development and Corroboration of Taxonomic Models. In Marshall, W.L., Laws, D.R. and Barbaree, H.E. (Eds.) *The Handbook of Sexual Assault* (pp. 23–52). NY: Plenum.

Knight, R.A., Prentky, R.A. and Cerce, D. (1994) The Development, Reliability, and Validity of an Inventory for the Multidimensional Assessment of Sex and Aggression. *Criminal Justice and Behaviour*, 21, 72–94.

Koss, M.P. and Oros, C.J. (1982) Sexual Experiences Survey: A Research Instrument Investigating Sexual Aggression and Victimisation. *Journal of Consulting and Clinical Psychology*, 50, 455–7.

Lackie, L. and De Man, A.F. (1997) Correlates of Sexual Aggression among Male University Students. *Sex Roles*, 37, 451–6.

Lalumière, M.L. et al. (2005) *The Causes of Rape: Understanding Individual Differences in Male Propensity for Sexual Aggression*. Washington, DC: American Psychological Association.

Langton, C.M., Barbarea, H.E., Hansen, K.T., Harkins, L., Seto, M.C. and Peacock, E.J. (2007) Reliability and Validity of the Static-2002 among Adult Sexual Offenders with Reference to Treatment Status. *Criminal Justice and Behaviour*, 34, 616–40.

Laws, D.R. (2003) Penile Plethysmography: Will we ever Get it Right? In Ward, T., Laws, D.R. and Hudson, S.M. (Eds.) *Sexual Deviance: Issues and Controversies*. Thousand Oaks, CA: Sage.

Laws, D.R. (2003) The Rise and Fall of Relapse Prevention. *Australian Psychologist*, 38, 22–30.

Laws, D.R. and Gress, C. (2004) Seeing Things Differently: The Viewing Time Alternative to Penile Plethysmography. *Legal and Criminological Psychology*, 9, 183–96.

Laws, D.R., Hudson, S.M. and Ward, T. (2000) *Remaking Relapse Prevention with Sex Offenders: A Sourcebook.* Thousand Oaks, CA: Sage.

Letourneau, E.J. (2002) A Comparison of Objective Measures of Sexual Arousal and Interest: Visual Reaction Time and Penile Plethysmography. *Sexual Abuse: A Journal of Treatment and Research,* 14, 207–23.

Looman, J. and Marshall, W.L. (2001) Phallometric Assessments Designed to Detect Arousal to Children: The Responses of Rapists and Child Molesters. *Sexual Abuse: A Journal of Research and Treatment,* 13, 3–13.

Looman, J. and Marshall, W.L. (2005) Sexual Arousal in Rapists. *Criminal Justice and Behaviour,* 32, 367–89.

Malamuth, N.M. (1984) Aggression against Women: Cultural and Individual Causes. In Malamuth, N.M. and Donnerstein, E. (Eds.) *Pornography and Aggression.* Orlando, FL: Academic Press.

Malamuth, N.M. (1986) Predictors of Naturalistic Sexual Aggression. *Journal of Personality and Social Psychology,* 50, 953–62.

Malamuth, N.M. (1989a) The Attraction to Sexual Aggression Scale: Part One. *Journal of Sex Research,* 26, 26–9.

Malamuth, N.M. (1989b) The Attraction to Sexual Aggression Scale: Part Two. *Journal of Sex Research,* 26, 324–54.

Malamuth, N.M. (1996) The Confluence Model of Sexual Aggression: Feminist and Evolutionary Perspectives. In Buss, D.B. and Malamuth, N.M. (Eds.) *Sex, Power, Conflict: Evolutionary and Feminist Perspectives.* NY: Oxford University Press.

Malamuth, N.M. and Brown, L.M. (1994) Sexually Aggressive Men's Perceptions of Women's Communications: Testing Three Explanations. *Journal of Personality and Social Psychology,* 67, 699–712.

Malamuth, N.M., Heavey, C.L. and Linz, D. (1993) Predicting Men's Antisocial Behaviour against Women: The Interaction Model of Sexual Aggression. In Hall, G.C. et al. (Eds.) *Sexual Aggression: Issues in Aetiology, Assessment and Treatment.* Washington, DC: Taylor and Francis.

Mann, R.E. and Shingler, J. (2006) Schema-Driven Cognition in Sexual Offenders: Theory, Assessment and Treatment. In Marshall, W.L. et al. (Eds.) *Sexual Offender Treatment: Controversial Issues.* Chichester: Wiley.

Marshall, W.L. (2001) Adult Sexual Offenders against Women. In Holin, C.R. (Ed.) *The Handbook of Offender Assessment and Treatment.* Chichester: Wiley and Sons.

Marshall, W.L. (2005) Therapist Style in Sexual Offender Treatment: Influence on Indices of Change. *Sexual Abuse: A Journal of Research and Treatment,* 17, 109–16.

Marshall, W.L. (2006a) Clinical and Research Limitations in the Use of Phallometric Testing with Sexual Offenders. *Sexual Offender Treatment,* 1, 03. Retrieved 13 Sep. from: Http://Www.Iatso.Org/Ejournal.

Marshall, W.L. (2006b) Diagnosis and Treatment of Sexual Offenders. In Weiner, I.B. and Hess, A.K. (Eds.) *The Handbook of Forensic Psychology.* 3rd Edn Hoboken, NJ: Wiley.

Marshall, W.L. and Barbaree, H.E. (1990) An Integrated Theory of Sexual Offending. In Marshall, W.L., Laws, D.R. and Barbaree, H.E. (Eds.) *Handbook of Sexual Assault: Issues, Theories and Treatment of the Offender.* NY: Plenum.

Marshall, W.L. and Hambley, L.S. (1996) Intimacy and Loneliness, and their Relationship to Rape Myth Acceptance and Hostility towards Women among Rapists. *Journal of Interpersonal Violence,* 11, 586–92.

Marshall, W.L. and Marshall, L.E. (2000) The Origins of Sexual Offending. *Trauma, Violence, and Abuse,* 1, 250–63.

Miller, R.S. and Lefcourt, H.M. (1982) The Assessment of Social Intimacy. *Journal of Personality Assessment,* 46, 514–8.

Millon, T., Davis, R. and Millon, C. (1997) *Millon Clinical Multiaxial Inventory III.* 2nd Edn MN: National Computer Systems.

Mosher, D.L. and Sirkin, M. (1984) Measuring a Macho Personality Constellation. *Journal of Research Personality,* 18, 150–63.

Myhill, A. and Allen, J. (2002) *Rape and Sexual Assault of Women: The Extent and Nature of the Problem: Findings from the British Crime Survey.* London: Home Office.

Nichols, H.R. and Molinder, I. (1984) *Multiphasic Sex Inventory.* Tacoma, WA: Authors (Available From Nichols and Molinder, 437 Bowes, Tacoma, WA 98466).

Nichols, H.R. and Molinder, I. (2000) *Multiphasic Sex Inventory II.* Tacoma, WA: Authors (Available From Nichols and Molinder, 437 Bowes, Tacoma, WA 98466).

Novaco, R.W. (1994) Anger as a Risk Factor for Violence among the Mentally Disordered. In

Monahan, J. and Steadman, H. (Eds.) *Violence and Mental Disorder: Developments in Risk Assessment.* University of Chicago Press.

Nowicki, S. (1976) *Adult Nowicki-Strickland Internal-External Locus of Control Scale. Test Manual.* Available from Nowicki, S. Jr., Atlanta: Department of Psychology, Emory University.

Nunes, K.L. et al. (2002) A Comparison of Modified Versions of the Static-99 and the Sex Offender Risk Appraisal Guide. *Sexual Abuse: A Journal of Research and Treatment*, 14, 253–69.

Polaschek, D.L. (2003) Relapse Prevention, Offence Process Models, and the Treatment of Sexual Offenders. *Professional Psychology: Research and Practice*, 34, 361–7.

Polaschek, D.L. and Gannon, T.A. (2004) The Implicit Theories of Rapists: What Convicted Offenders Tell Us. *Sexual Abuse: A Journal of Research and Treatment*, 16, 299–315.

Polaschek, D.L. and Ward, T. (2002) The Implicit Theories of Potential Rapists. What Our Questionnaires Tell Us. *Aggression and Violent Behaviour*, 7, 385–406.

Prentky, R.A. and Knight, R.A. (1991) Identifying Critical Dimensions for Discriminating among Rapists. *Journal of Consulting and Clinical Psychology*, 59, 643–61.

Quinsey, V.L. et al. (1998) *Violent Offenders: Appraising and Managing Risk.* Washington, DC: APA.

Rogers, R. and Bender, S.D. (2003) Evaluation of Malingering and Deception. In Goldstein, A.M. (Ed.) and Weiner, I.B. (Editor-In-Chief) *Handbook of Psychology, Volume 11, Forensic Psychology.* NJ: Wiley.

Roger, D. and Najarian, B. (1989) The Construction and Validation of a New Scale for Measuring Emotion Control. *Personality and Individual Differences*, 10: 8, 845–53.

Russell, D. (1996) The UCLA Loneliness Scale (Version 3): Reliability, Validity, and Factor Structure. *Journal of Personality Assessment*, 66, 20–40.

Russell, D., Peplau, L.A. and Ferguson, M.L. (1978) Developing a Measure of Loneliness. *Journal of Personality Assessment*, 42, 290–4.

Segal, Z.V. and Stermac, L.E. (1990) The Role of Cognition in Sexual Assault. In Marshall, W.L., Laws, D.R. and Barbaree, H.E. (Eds.) *Handbook of Sexual Assault: Issues, Theories, and Treatment of the Offender.* NY: Plenum Press.

Serin, R.C. (1995) Treatment Responsivity in Criminal Psychopaths. *Forum in Corrections Research*, 7, 23–6.

Sexual Offences Act (2002) Retrieved Jul 20, 2006, from http://www.opsi.gov.uk/ACTS/acts2003/20030042.htm

Shea, S.C. (1988) *Psychiatric Interviewing. The Art of Understanding.* Philadelphia: W.B. Saunders.

Sherman, S.J., Judd, C.M. and Park, B. (1989) Social Cognition. *Annual Review of Psychology*, 40, 281–326.

Simon, L.M. (2000) An Examination of the Assumptions of Specialisation, Mental Disorder, and Dangerousness in Sex Offenders. *Behavioral Sciences and The Law*, 18, 275–308.

Sjöstedt, G. and Långström, N. (2001) Actuarial Assessment of Sex Offender Recidivism Risk: A Cross-Validation of the RRAOR and the Static-99 in Sweden. *Law and Human Behaviour*, 25, 629–45.

Smallbone, S.W. and Dadds, M.R. (1998) Childhood Attachment and Adult Attachment in Incarcerated Adult Male Sex Offenders. *Journal of Interpersonal Violence*, 13, 555–73.

Stalans, L. (2004) Adult Sex Offenders on Community Supervision. A Review of Recent Assessment Strategies and Treatment. *Criminal Justice and Behaviour*, 31, 564–608.

Stermac, L.E. and Hall, K. (1989) Escalation in Sexual Offending: Fact or Fiction? *Annals of Sex Research*, 2, 153–62.

Stermac, L.E. and Quinsey, V.L. (1986) Social Competence among Rapists. *Behavioral Assessment*, 8, 171–85.

Thakker, J. et al. (In Press) Rape: Assessment and Treatment. In Laws, D. and O'Donohue, W. (Eds.) *Sexual Deviance: Theory, Assessment, and Treatment.* 2nd Edn. NY: The Guilford Press.

Thornton, D. (2000) *Structured Risk Assessment.* Paper presented at the Sinclair Seminars Conference on Sex Offender Re-Offence Risk Prediction, Madison, WI. (Videotape available from Www.Sinclairseminars.Com)

Thornton, D. (2002) Constructing and Testing a Framework for Dynamic Risk Assessment. *Sexual Abuse: A Journal of Research and Treatment*, 14, 139–54.

Thornton, D. et al. (2003) Distinguishing and Combining Risks for Sexual and Violent Recidivism. In Prentky, R.A., Janus, E.S. and Seto, M.C. (Eds) *Sexually Coercive Behaviour: Understanding and Management. Annals of The New York Academy of Sciences*, 989, 225–35.

Tjaden, P. and Thoennes, N. (1998) *Prevalence, Incidence and Consequences of Violence against Women: Findings from the National Violence against Women Survey.* National Institute of

Justice Centers for Disease Control and Prevention. Office of Justice Programs: US Department of Justice.

Towl, G.J. and Crighton, D.A. (1996) *The Handbook for Forensic Practitioners.* Routledge: London.

Vess, J., Murphy, C. and Arkowitz, S. (2004) Clinical and Demographic Differences between Sexually Violent Predators and Other Commitment Types in a State Forensic Hospital. *The Journal of Forensic Psychiatry and Psychology,* 15, 669–81.

Ward, T. (2000) Sexual Offender' Cognitive Distortions as Implicit Theories. *Aggression and Violent Behaviour,* 5, 491–507.

Ward, T. (2002) Good Lives and the Rehabilitation of Sex Offenders: Problems and Promises. *Aggression and Violent Behaviour,* 7, 1–17.

Ward, T. (2002) Marshall and Barbaree's Integrated Theory of Child Sexual Abuse: A Critique. *Psychology, Crime, and Law,* 8, 209–28.

Ward, T. and Beech, T. (2006) An Integrated Theory of Sexual Offending. *Aggression and Violent Behaviour,* 11, 44–63.

Ward, T. et al. (2004) *The Self-Regulation Model of the Offence and Relapse Process: A Manual. Volume 1: Assessment.* Available from Pacific Psychological Assessment Corporation.

Ward, T. and Gannon, T.A. (2006) Rehabilitation, Etiology and Self-Regulation: The Comprehensive Good Lives Model of Treatment for Sexual Offenders . *Aggression and Violent Behavior,* 11, 77–94.

Ward, T. and Hudson, S.M. (1996) Relapse Prevention: A Critical Analysis. *Sexual Abuse: A Journal of Research and Treatment,* 8, 177–200.

Ward, T. and Hudson, S.M. (1998) A Model of the Relapse Process in Sexual Offenders. *Journal of Interpersonal Violence,* 13, 700–25.

Ward, T., Hudson, S.M. and Marshall, W.L. (1996) Attachment Style in Sex Offenders: A Preliminary Study. *Journal of Sex Research,* 33, 17–36.

Ward, T. and Hudson, S.M. (2000) A Self-Regulation Model of Relapse Prevention. In Laws, D.R., Hudson, S.M. and Ward, T. (Eds.) *Remaking Relapse Prevention with Sex Offenders: A Sourcebook.* Thousand Oaks, CA: Sage.

Ward, T., Louden, K., Hudson, S.M. and Marshall, W.L. (1995) A Descriptive Model of the Offence Chain for Child Molesters. *Journal of Interpersonal Violence,* 10, 452–72.

Ward, T. et al. (1997) Rape: Assessment and Treatment. In Laws, D. and O'Donohue, W. (Eds.) *Sexual Deviance: Theory, Assessment and Treatment.* NY: The Guilford Press.

Ward, T., Polaschek, D.L. and Beech, A.R. (2005) *Theories of Sexual Offending.* Chichester, UK: Wiley.

Watson, D. and Friend, R. (1969) Measurement of Social-Evaluative Anxiety. *Journal of Consulting and Clinical Psychology,* 33, 448–57.

Webster, S.D. (2005) Pathways to Sexual Offence Recidivism following Treatment: An Examination of the Ward and Hudson Self-Regulation Model of Relapse. *Journal of Interpersonal Violence,* 20, 1175–96.

Weiner, I.B. (2003) The Assessment Process. In Graham, J.R. and Naglieri J.A. (Eds.) and Weiner, I.B. (Editor-In-Chief) *Handbook of Psychology, Volume 10, Assessment Psychology.* NJ: Wiley.

Weinrott, M.R. and Saylor, M. (1991) Self-Report of Crimes Committed by Sex Offenders. *Journal of Interpersonal Violence,* 6, 286–300.

Wilcox, D.T. et al. (2005) Sexual History Disclosure using the Polygraph in a Sample of British Sex Offenders. *Polygraph Journal,* 34, 171–83.

Worling, J.R. (2004) The Estimate of Risk of Adolescent Sexual Offense Recidivism (ERASOR): Preliminary Psychometric Data. *Sexual Abuse: A Journal of Research and Treatment,* 16, 235–54.

Yates, P.M., Kingston, D. and Hall, K. (2003, October) Pathways to Sexual Offending: Validity of Hudson and Ward's (1998) Self-Regulation Model and Relationship to Static and Dynamic Risk among Treated High Risk Sexual Offenders. Presented at the 22nd Annual Research and Treatment Conference of The Association for the Treatment of Sexual Abusers (ATSA) St. Louis, Missouri.

Yates, P.M. (2003) Treatment of Adult Sexual Offenders: A Therapeutic Cognitive-Behavioral Model of Intervention. *Journal of Child Sexual Abuse,* 12, 195–232.

# CHAPTER 12

# Mothers of Sexually Abused Children

*Martin C. Calder and Lynda Regan*

## Introduction

There is very little written on the role of the mother in sexual abuse cases, even less on a framework to guide practitioners in the task of assessing their needs at each stage of the child protection process, or on what components should be included in any 'ability to protect' assessment. It is an area that is often not addressed in Government guidance, thus workers are left to generate their own materials, this has led to practitioners formulating their own assessments based on their own levels of knowledge and skills in this area. We know that sexual abuse is an area that professionals often feel unclear and anxious about. It is an emotive area of work, it raises additional emotions and anxieties and can lead to assessments being built on stereotypical, pre-determined views. This approach can often disable workers and alienate mothers.

This chapter aims to consider the many complex issues involved, and seeks to offer a framework to undertake this type of assessment, in order to redress some of the current gaps in practice guidance in this area of work. It aims to provide a structure for helping mothers to move to a safer parenting position using an assessment-based programme and in the cases where this doesn't happen, this framework and process provides a clear format for evidencing conclusions reached. Undertaking this type of assessment should also provide information about the mother's commitment to the process and should indicate whether cooperation has been passive or active.

This chapter forms the basis of a more detailed book (Calder, Peake and Rose, 2001) from which a workbook has also been developed to further provide practitioners with all the tools needed for completing this type of assessment (Regan, 2006). These two books look in more depth at messages for professionals, more detailed exercises to elicit the required information, treatment issues, a review of the literature, causation, separate considerations for extra-familial abuse, and

detailed worksheets that will help to determine the most realistic outcome. However, this chapter alone offers some preliminary guidance and should go some way towards equipping workers when they are faced with assessing a mother in a situation of intra-familial sexual abuse.

'Mothers' are referred to throughout as the safe carer. This reflects the statistics in relation to child sexual abuse that clearly show perpetrators to be predominantly male. However, females can and do, sexually abuse children and therefore in some cases the safe carer may be male. This framework would be transferable in these cases.

This chapter also focuses on intra-familial abuse, where the perpetrator is a family member who, most often, has a parental role in relation to the child. This is a different scenario from extra-familial abuse where the perpetrator is from outside the family. This differentiation needs to be clear, as in cases of extra-familial abuse fathers will also be devastated by the situation, they will also need support and guidance and there would be different elements to any assessments undertaken, as issues of protection are not so complex as when sexual abuse occurs within the family setting.

## Engagement of the mother

Taking the time at the beginning of a worker's involvement with a mother, in order to understand her position and behaviours is absolutely crucial for two reasons:

- Helping the mother reach a position of support for her child is important to the child's recovery process.
- Having a reaction to traumatic news is a normal process.

We all have our internalised coping strategies that are automatic reactions. The speed at which we pass through the stages of shock will be different of each individual. For some it may be minutes or hours, for others it may be days or weeks. When in this position we need someone to help us to work through the stages, not judge us for them.

Therapeutic support to the safe carer can help them to come to terms with what has happened and to learn how to 'move forward'. Feedback from mothers involved in this process suggests that understanding some of the dynamics and processes is very important in helping them make some sense of the turmoil they experience. In my experience of working with mothers in this situation over a period of ten years, there are a number of frequently asked questions that occur, for example why my child, how could he do it to us, why do men sexually abuse children? Undertaking an assessment that also aims to inform the mother, may help her to understand some of these issues over time.

Berliner (1990) found that children said that the events that happened to them after disclosure did not matter as much as receiving support from their mothers. Therefore, if the mother is unable to give the support at the beginning of the process, the sooner she can be helped to move to this position the better for the child.

The accuracy and extensiveness of the assessment of the mother will depend on the ability of the worker to successfully engage the mother in the process (Print and Dey, 1992). This can often be facilitated by offering the mother a worker of her own with whom some degree of trust can be built. This helps to acknowledge that the mother also has issues that will be separate to those of her child and it is crucial that each of their needs be understood, in order to help to strengthen the relationship and ensure that the necessary protective factors are in place for the future:

*The purpose of the work is to empower them by recognising and developing strengths and thereby increasing their confidence to support and protect their children. This cannot be achieved if professionals merely mirror the behaviour of the abuser by making decisions about the child without involving the mother. If a mother is to increase her confidence and take responsibility for her child's welfare she must feel, and be, fully involved in planning for her child's future.*

(Print and Dey, 1992: 67–8)

For a fuller discussion of engagement issues the reader is referred to Calder (2001) and Regan (2006)

## Defining the initial and core assessments

The initial assessment of the mother is likely to be based on the child's disclosure, the known history of the family, the child's wishes and feelings, and the reactions of other family members. It is designed to establish whether abuse has occurred, the likelihood of future abuse, the degree of protection available, the necessity of legal intervention, and the placement needs of the child.

The core assessment should be part of a broader child protection plan, often agreed at child protection conference. It is likely to sit alongside assessments of the child's wishes and feelings, the same of any siblings, and with the perpetrator. It is imperative that the process of assessment is a two-way one: with the professionals providing the mother with support, understanding and information. This variation from the norm often requires new techniques which allow the mother to share their feelings and emotions as well as factual information. It is very important to assess a mother's ability to believe, support and protect the children. At no time, however, should the work with the mother, or her views, predominate over a consideration of the child's wishes and feelings and action deemed to be in their 'best interests'.

## Possible outcomes

The assessment process is likely to produce one of the following conclusions:

- The mother can protect and support the abused child (and siblings) and does not require further professional interventions (although some additional support around understanding sexual abuse may still be helpful and should be borne in mind).
- The mother understands the need to protect and support the abused child (and siblings) and is likely to do so, if provided with sufficient resources.
- The mother remains in a position of not believing the offences committed, but accepts the concerns of others and demonstrates clearly how she will act protectively 'just in case'. She is also willing to allow some external support networks to be put into place and may be willing to include the child in having

information and strategies to help them to keep safe.

- The mother is ambivalent. She accepts concerns of others, passively completes assessments but does not make significant changes or see the need to adopt protective strategies for the child. However, she agrees that the child's support and protection can be ensured by external sources, such as professionals, extended family etc.

  *This is a very difficult position for professionals because we know that sexual abuse is done in secrecy using strategies to groom the child and their 'safe' carer, therefore it is not something that is easy to detect.*

- The mother denies the abuse occurred, blames the child or is very dependant on the perpetrator, so is unable to adequately support or protect the child.

  *This invariably leads to the child's removal from the family.*

Recent experience tells us that many fall within the middle ground and this makes planning and decision making less clear, more anxious and more prone to legal intervention or challenge. This position is often fuelled by lack of criminal prosecution and conviction for recent offences, making clear and thorough assessments based on fact crucial to the process. Another all-too-common situation is where a previous allegation or conviction comes to light and the perpetrator has been living in a family, or has started a family in a different relationship, and the mother has not seen any evidence of sexual abuse or had any concerns about their partner's role in the family, often over a significant period of time.

## A working agreement

It is important that a written agreement be completed with the mother. This ensures she is involved in the process and understands the parameters, expectations and possible consequences of the work. In order to do this the worker also needs to be very clear about their own role, the frameworks they are using and the reasons for the assessment. Any written

agreement with the mother should be carefully negotiated and should enable her to exercise some control within the context of the child's best interests.

Some of the issues the worker needs clarity about are:

- Who has commissioned this piece of work (court, conference etc.)?
- What are the timescales?
- What is the assessment helping you to decide?
- Where will you meet, where does this woman feel safest?
- Does this woman have any learning difficulties, mental health problems, depression, drug or alcohol dependency, experience of domestic violence with this or previous partners?
- Is the woman a survivor of childhood sexual abuse themselves?
- Are there any issues around developmental levels, language, race, culture?
- Where will the information be shared?
- Do you have a way of ensuring the woman agrees with your written record of sessions, for example can she add her own comments to session notes?

For a more comprehensive discussion of these issues and a framework for an agreement the reader is referred to Regan, 2006.

Some of the issues to be clear about in relation to the mother are:

- the mother's feelings towards the abused child
- the mother's ability to understand the offences and their effects on the child, siblings and herself
- her ability to give appropriate emotional support to the abused child
- the mother's ability to protect the child (and siblings) from the perpetrator in particular
- the degree to which the mother is financially, emotionally, or practically dependent on the perpetrator
- the mother's support networks
- relevant issues from the mother's past, for example if she has been abused herself which may inhibit her abilities to support the child
- medical and social factors that might be relevant.

(Print and Dey, 1992: 68)

# Part One –
# Understanding the issues

## Impacts of disclosure on the mother (The effects of now 'knowing' about the abuse on the mother and the mother's distress to the disclosure)

Salter (1988: 56) maintains that for the mother the impact of the disclosure that her child has been sexually abused is like an *'emotional earthquake'*. Yet it is these women, even though they are in the midst of a crisis, on whom so much relies. They are the key person on whom depends their child's protection and recovery. They are crucial to the social services' ability to fulfil their statutory responsibilities to protect children whilst allowing them, if at all possible, to remain in their family (Walton, 1996).

When a mother is faced with sexual abuse, she faces simultaneous and overlapping tasks: assessing the accuracy of the information; determining the meaning of incest to her and her family; deciding what to do with the new information; and locating and using resources (Elbow and Mayfield, 1991).

The mother's behaviour following disclosure is important as it is often used to gauge their ability to protect/support their sexually abused child. Workers need to move beyond the outdated descriptive accounts of mothers as pathological and being unable to meet their child's needs because of their own unmet needs (Crawford, 1999). Although some mothers respond calmly and decisively, others exhibit symptoms of crisis such as shock, confusion and disbelief, any of which can limit their ability to take immediate protective action. Against this background, many take heroic actions to protect their children, which may well be overlooked by professionals, thus weakening the mother's support for the child. Many want to explore whether clues they have noticed are indicators of sexual abuse.

Professionals should not expect a 'new world' to spring fully developed and put into operation within moments of a disclosure just in time for the mother to fully support and protect her child victim. Rather, they should consider how they can help the mother as well as the victim to progress through the disclosure process.

Reactions to shocking news have been found to follow a predictable pattern of denial, anger, bargaining, depression and acceptance, and any

variation is one of degree rather than kind (Milner and Blyth, 1989). In relation to child sexual abuse, mothers will find that it is inextricably linked to their lives – both in terms of what might have happened to them in the past and what they might not have done; and in the future in terms of the need to do something for the children but balanced by a fear of the consequences if they get it wrong.

The emotional and behavioural impact on mothers mirrors what is experienced by the victims themselves. There is also a correlation between the level of distress in the child and that of the mothers (Massatt and Lundy, 1998). The emotions stirred up by sexual abuse have effects that can be both positive and negative. On the positive side, if the child is being abused, the mother's emotional reaction gets them started on the road to protection. On the negative side, the emotional reaction that is natural for any loving parent can cloud clear thinking and cause them to jump too quickly to conclusions (Myers, 1997). Emotions are not wrong or a sign of weakness although they can frequently be used against mothers. They are interpreted by judges and others (mostly men) as a sign of weakness, instability, and even hysteria or mental illness.

*The reactions of mothers to the sexual abuse may vary according to whether they have been sexually abused themselves. Irrespective of their own history, however, the reactions they have towards incest may well parallel those of the victims in many ways, as a consequence of living with a controlling and abusive husband. They may feel socially stigmatised, isolate themselves from extended family and friends, and even wish to leave their community of origin to avoid exposure.*

Dwyer and Miller (1996) applied the concept of 'disenfranchised grief' (Doka, 1989) to our understanding of the experiences of non-abusing mothers in incest families. They pointed us to the fact that the experiences of mothers and daughters are often intimately entwined, like 'hand and glove'. They argued that the complexity of this experience provides a powerful constraint to the recognition and resolution of grief. Those directly involved may struggle with confused and conflicting feelings; the need to take action in the face of disclosure may leave little room for reflection; and the number of people involved and the diversity of opinions held, can be traumatising in itself. Doka defined disenfranchised grief as '. . . *the grief that persons experience when they incur a loss that is not or cannot be openly acknowledged, publicly mourned, or socially supported. The concept . . . recognises that societies have sets of norms – in effect "grieving rules" – that attempt to specify who, when, where, how, how long, and for whom people should grieve'* (p4). He argues that grief may become disenfranchised for three reasons:

- The relationship between the grieved and the griever is not recognised. Grief at the loss of a relationship between family members is recognised and accepted. It is usually accompanied by a ritual such as a funeral. However, the act of sexual abuse is expected to invalidate the relationship between the perpetrator and other family members, and any expression of grief may be unacceptable both to the family and professionals. As such, no ritual exists after incest.
- The loss itself is not recognised as many argue the mother is better off without him. As such, the grief cannot be sanctioned by others, and the mother may be unable to recognise their own grief given their self-blame and shame.
- The griever is not recognised. This may well be the siblings or extended family members who are not seen as being directly involved in the abuse with the consequence that their own needs may be overlooked.

As a consequence of these, disenfranchising grief may complicate and exacerbate problems in coping with the loss, demonstrated through feelings of isolation, anger, self-blame, sadness, and fear. Dwyer and Miller (1996: 138) argue that 'these losses occur on many levels including: the loss of "family", both nuclear and extended; loss of innocence; loss of faith in themselves and their judgements; material losses such as homes, jobs/schools, and financial security; loss of dreams and hopes for the future, to name but a few'.

Once mothers accept that their children have been sexually abused they go through a succession of reactions similar to a complex grief reaction which may include denial, guilt, depression, anger and finally acceptance. This makes sense when one considers that the non-abusing mother's world has, at the very least, suffered a serious blow and may very well be dying.

Whilst the parallel experience of grieving a death may be useful, it also has its limitations. For example, sexual abuse is not, like death, a clearly defined event with an end and from which the

mother then recovers and returns to normal, but one which tends to have ongoing and unpredictable ramifications for years and years (Hooper, 1989). Hopkins and Thompson (1984) developed a 'reaction to loss' continuum. For losses at the 'highly acceptable' end of the continuum, society has established routine and ritualistic patterns of response – cards, expressions of sympathy, flowers, food, calls, extra attention – which legitimise the loss and grief and provide comfort for the bereaved and the giver. This is most evident in cases of 'normal' death and serious illness. Such clearly established recognition, acceptance and reaction patterns do not yet exist for the grief resulting from other types of losses – divorce, redundancy, suicide – although conventional forms of response to these losses are emerging. There are no generally recognised socialised responses to losses resulting from sexual abuse, which fall at the 'non-acceptable' end of the continuum.

### Responses to disclosure from the mother

Every mother will respond differently to the disclosure of sexual abuse of their daughter. There are, however, some common threads worth mentioning, which many will recognise to be similar to those of the primary victims.

### Shock

Shock is a common reaction to disclosure although it does vary in its intensity. It is often compounded by stress and anxiety, inducing confused and ambivalent feelings towards both the child as well as the perpetrator. This often renders decision-making by mothers impossible in the short term. It is important that workers do not dismiss the mother as being an un-protecting or an unfit mother, but rather they concentrate on helping her to meet her child's needs. This has the potential to encourage more informed and positive maternal responses. If this is not facilitated, then mothers can get 'stuck' in the process and never overcome denial. Since many mothers will be in a state of shock after learning of the sexual abuse, they are therefore unlikely to be able to make decisions and assume responsibility and it is unfair if workers expect them to do so.

### Denial

A mother's denial is to be seen as a normal and healthy reaction to this kind of news as it gives them time to assimilate the shock and build up the strength to deal with it. The problem comes if the mother does not move to the next stage of the reactive process. Many will move on as the reality niggles away but may slip temporarily into denial whenever they need to feel safe. For some, the denial is short-lived: within moments they accept the unpleasant reality and mobilise themselves to respond. These tend to be psychologically healthy mothers. For others, refusing to believe that the abuse could have taken place may persist for a longer time. Some are never able to acknowledge the abuse and resist all efforts to engage them in treatment. They never complete the process. Most, however, are able, with help, to support the child during the difficult process of resolving the sexual abuse situation.

Denial is likely to be expressed in a number of ways by mothers:

- denial that sexual abuse took place
- accepting that sexual abuse took place but denying that it was harmful to the child
- denial that there is a need for any external help to resolve the crisis
- that the partner was drunk
- that the child seduced him
- that he has been so stressed lately that he didn't know what he was doing, etc.

The extent of a mother's losses may become a compelling aspect of their denial. These being stated, workers cannot dismiss the link between denial and the children's safety. They need to use empathy as the most effective strategy for engaging the mother in this state.

Denial is the most acknowledged type of coping behaviour. The function of denial for mothers allows them to refuse to accept that abuse has really occurred. This allows her to remain in a passive position in order not to have to deal with the situation. Tinling (1990) sets out seven coping strategies:

1. Denial – Allows the mother to not to lose face or have to make decisions. Richardson and Bacon (1991) argue that there are different types of denial that are important to understand and these can be sub-divided into:
   - Benign denial: stems from a lack of basic information and the initial stages of shock and disbelief.
   - Transformed denial: arises from a distorted form of knowledge. It may be that a woman

has herself suffered abuse, which may or may not be part of her consciousness. Therefore the abuse of her child may be too painful for her to contemplate. It can also arise from a belief in misinformation put out by the media, therefore things like this don't happen to 'ordinary' people.
   - Malign denial: can be a form of concealment related to having some vested interest in promoting continued denial of the facts, such as a mother whose unresolved anguish allows her to defer choosing between her child or her partner.

2. Distortion – is similar to denial in achieving the same purpose, but involves being aware of the facts of the abuse while changing them to make them more acceptable to live with.

3. Delusions – serve to reinforce the person's logic. For example, the delusion of 'sin' and 'guilt' befits the 'martyr' and 'victim'. 'For mothers, this certainly entails the narcissistic striving of the mother to set herself up in a controlling position'.

4. Minimisation – involves playing down the abuse and attempts to make it less than it is, particularly with regard to the victim. This allows the mother to keep her reaction to a minimum.

5. Collusion – involves agreement between some, or all members of the family not to acknowledge what they know is really happening.

6. Negative confrontation – the mother may appear to believe and say the right things including confronting the perpetrator, but may then leave the children with him unsupervised.

7. Blame – shifting blame, such as the mother attributing blame to drink, or the child's seductiveness, rather than the perpetrator's behaviour.

## Anger

Mothers may then feel angry and want to blame the perpetrator, but they are often inaccessible for the expression of feeling. The perpetrator will often do anything to ensure they do not have a sexual conviction or sexual stain on their character. Mothers often end up selecting someone else to blame when faced with these issues. This may be the child, or the system. Anger is a common reaction of mothers – to the perpetrator, the child and the workers and it tends to be specific and triggered by a particular incident, person or object (Trotter, 1998). There may be anger towards the mother herself. For example, the child may be angry at the mother's failure to protect them, and they may be joined by members of the extended family as well as the professionals. A mother's anger is often associated with seeking a reason for why the abuse occurred. It can also manifest itself in depression, stress responses, etc. The person who the mother believes has caused the abuse will become the focus of her anger. This could be herself, the perpetrator or the child. Anger is legitimate, but it is how it is dealt with and expressed that is important. If it is expressed as revenge and she takes the law into her own hands, or uses her children as a tool against her partner, then it is inappropriate and may even place the children at greater risk.

When mothers respond to the disclosure with either denial or anger, this is simply their way of protecting themselves and is to be expected. They may feel betrayed by their partner as he has been living a lie by keeping the relationship with the daughter quiet, or they may feel angry and jealous of the daughter if they perceive her as a threat or rival. She will be confused because she wants to help the child on the one hand, but also maintain the relationship with the perpetrator on the other. Their feelings will not be changed or reversed overnight, and this often means that they will be faced with two sets of conflicting feelings. The mother may also be repulsed by the perpetrator and even hate him for the consequences of his behaviour. She may even feel she has failed as a wife. These are very powerful feelings that will often take some considerable time to resolve.

## Guilt

When anger expires, mothers may well enter the bargaining stage – 'maybe if . . .' Here, the range may be to do nothing as to do so might make it worse, to a fairly sophisticated rationalisation about limiting damage. Guilt is an inevitable maternal response to the discovery of child sexual abuse and may feature heavily in her initial responses and decision-making. For example, she may act to protect the child without reference to the personal implications, such as dealing with her own emotions, or more practical consequences such as where to live and how to support herself financially. Many mothers try to

conceal their own fears or confusion from others as well as from themselves, and this can have knock-on effects post-disclosure, for example being unable to confront any subsequent issues of pain. A mother's guilt will often be intensified if the abuse continued over a long period of time and she did not know about it. Once the mother learns of the child sexual abuse, this will lead to guilt either if they had their suspicions, or they did not know. They will relive any previous episodes of disbelief to the child. They will experience a continuing sense of loss, isolation and rejection as emotional accompaniments to the discovery. This will be aggravated if they have been isolated in the process of disclosure. They will often be faced with multiple, conflicting and changing versions of events and they may struggle to construct a single explanation. They will consider what they can remember of past events, with what they think they know about the perpetrator, to help them.

Guilt is a form of anger directed at oneself. This is most apparent when mothers believe that they should have known. The mother's feelings of guilt may be influenced by the child's age, the duration of the sexual abuse, and symptoms in the child which preceded the disclosure or discovery of the abuse. Mothers and daughters need to realise that every time they blame each other for the abuse, they absolve the perpetrator of their responsibility. Mothers with a history of sexual abuse themselves will have acute feelings of guilt thinking they should have recognised it happening.

Many parents of sexually abused children are racked with guilt. When a mother finds out that their child has been sexually abused, a thousand questions race through their mind, including: What is child sexual abuse? How common is it? How will I tell whether my child was abused? What will happen to them if they were abused? Who can I turn to for help? Will my child ever be normal again? What are the short- and long-term effects of child sexual abuse? Will my child grow up to be an abuser? Will my child blame me for the abuse? What could I have done differently? Why did I not see the signs that something was wrong? How could I let this happen to a child that I love so much? Why does my child still want to see the man who sexually abused her? Professionals need to facilitate the answering of these, and probably many other questions, if they are to equip the mother to help the child. They need to remind mothers that they did not commit the abuse, but rather are the ones trying to protect the child. Sexual abuse often occurs in secret and there are no witnesses. Mothers need to be cautioned against judging things retrospectively as hindsight is always a more exact science. They need to be reminded that they did nothing wrong. When they learned about the abuse, they took action. That is all that they can ask of themselves (Myers, 1997).

## Depression

Many then become overwhelmed, feeling helpless, inadequate and depressed, and this can lead to apathy and despair, and may lead to the mother's effectiveness as a mother being compromised and they become less able to respond to the distress of the child.

## Acceptance

The next stage might be an acceptance that the reality of sexual abuse is awful (and not passive resignation) and that it is difficult to tackle single-handedly.

## Other reactions

Sexual offences are something that families are *ashamed* of so the mother may choose to lead a double life to conceal the facts from others (Double, 1999). This is increasingly true in a culture that is adopting punitive attitudes towards the problem. The ensuing hysteria is something the mother and the remainder of her family have to deal with, often alone. Many experience overwhelming feelings of stigma and shame due to the nature of the offence, and mothers become dishonest to conceal the offence.

It is important not to interpret a mother's initial *hesitation* as her not wanting to protect her child. Once she has made the decision to protect her child, she may be faced with having to provide for the child alone. It is also important to assess the mother on the basis that they can only do their best with what they know at the time. We should work with them so that after the professional intervention, they emerge stronger and wiser.

The fact that the perpetrator may still be at large in the local community often instils *fear* into the mothers. Fear of their environment follows the discovery that nowhere is safe. The closer the mother's relationship with her child and partner, the greater the fear. This is important for professionals to understand so they do not slip into labelling the mother as uncooperative. They need to understand her fear of what has happened and what may happen next. This leads professionals to provide a context where the mother can assume a greater understanding and control over her life. Clear explanations are needed of each option and stage of the process to facilitate working through her fears, recognising that it will take some time.

## Grief and loss

Mothers may want to protect their child from loss of their father and this may be their motivating drive in keeping contact between father and daughter alive. This does not mean they are not anxious about this continuing relationship. Mothers do need to list all the losses they have experienced post-disclosure and this forms the basis for them understanding the complexities of grief and will help them map a strategy for resolution.

## Powerlessness

May come from a sense that events now control her life. She may feel that the situation will not go away and that things may not get better. There are a range of possible manifestations of this: rage, in an attempt to gain control, or apathy and withdrawal. Workers may want the mother to articulate those areas of her life where she does and does not have power to provide a framework within which her powerlessness can be explored. A schedule for successes can be set and reviewed quickly so positive strokes are provided. Workers need to be conscious of this dynamic when they are intervening. Partnership is the key rather than being 'told' what they must do (Ovaris, 1991).

Mothers described a range of *feelings* to match the devastation of disclosure, including sleep disturbances, psychological difficulties, difficulty in expressing their feelings, shame and embarrassment, letting their children down, an inability to trust, poor self-esteem, limited social skills, depression, inadequacy, frustration and ongoing distress (Trotter, 1998).

### Research findings

The mother's own behaviour at the time of disclosure may be related to the emotional stress brought on by the disclosure itself. Some mothers may experience shock and denial (Myers, 1985) and the symptoms may resemble those of post-traumatic stress (Timmons-Mitchell et al., 1996). Deblinger et al. (1994) found that those mothers who had been sexually abused as children may experience more severe symptoms at disclosure. Those who are overwhelmed by confusion and turmoil often find they persist over time (Hubbard, 1989) and it is important that professionals intervene quickly to help the mothers achieve a way of adapting and managing the abuse.

Burgess et al. (1977) reported that the reactions will vary according to the site of the abuse. For example, where the abuse takes place on 'home territory' that is considered to be 'safe ground', then the adults will have a stronger reaction, such as outrage, when that space is invaded. The authors identified several situations in which the mother was absent from the home: medical needs, recreation, errands, work, etc., showing that it is increasingly difficult to trust adults to care for and protect their children.

Those mothers who appear to be psychologically healthier at the beginning have more inner resources to draw on and can accept and be offered more appropriate support, will be better able to gain access to and express the full range of emotions necessary for the resolution of the crisis. Research does show that at disclosure, those mothers who have been sexually abused themselves displayed more distress than those who had not been sexually abused (Deblinger et al., 1994).

Manion et al. (1996) also found that the severity of distress was related to their own perceptions of themselves as parents, rather than to any variables about the abuse. The fact that many blame the mother rather than the perpetrator for the sexual abuse only compounds and complicates their reactions further.

Miller and Dwyer (1997) argued that there has been little recognition of the impact on mothers, and they would prefer them to be seen as *secondary victims*. Beyond the issues of grief and loss are the maternal suicide attempts as well as the ongoing psychological distress.

Fong and Walsh-Bowers (1998) found that all mothers reported feelings of helplessness and depression while they were dealing with the abuse. On the one hand, they were angry at their husbands for betraying them and hurting their daughters, but on the other hand they felt guilty for not knowing what happened and being unable to help their daughters to stop the abuse.

De Jong (1988) found that supportive mothers were more likely than non-supportive mothers to express anxiety about the effects that the experience would have on their children. Feelings of guilt, fear of repeat victimisation, and beliefs that friends or family members would not support them were more common in supportive mothers who noted emotional changes in themselves. Non-supportive mothers were often frustrated that the professionals were doing too much, whereas supportive mothers complained that they were doing too little.

De Francis (1969) suggested that the initial parental reaction to child sexual abuse may be either child-, self-, or perpetrator-orientated. Peters (1973) reported that the self-orientated reaction of the parent may be more common in household abuse. However, mixed feelings toward the perpetrator or external pressures not to file charges against a family member or friend may produce a perpetrator-orientated response.

Cohen and Mannarino (1996) found a strong correlation between parental emotional distress related to the abuse and treatment outcome in sexually abused pre-school children. It is possible that the strong relationship between parental emotional distress and child outcome measures were in part due to modelling, in that the child may learn fewer adaptive coping behaviours from a parent who is having difficulty coping with his or her own emotional distress. It is very likely that such a parent would be less emotionally and/or physically available to the child to provide needed emotional support. It is also possible that a biological factor may play a role in coping-style or capacity, such that the capacity to recover from emotional distress is in part genetically transmitted. This reiterates the importance of addressing parental distress in effective treatment for sexually abused pre-school children.

Salt et al. (1990) found that the actions a mother took in response to the abuse were strongly linked with their emotions. Those mothers who were more concerned about the child were also more likely to take protective action. Similarly, mothers who were angry were more likely to punish the child, possibly as they blamed the child for threatening her relationship with the perpetrator. They found that the mothers' attitudes and actions were shaped by their relationships with the perpetrators. Mothers were least protective and most angry and punitive toward the child when the perpetrator was not the natural father, but a step-father or boyfriend. This may be because they find it difficult to believe that a father would hurt his own child.

### Issues to consider

Workers need to acknowledge the extreme stress facing mothers at the point of disclosure and should not confuse her stress responses with how she behaved in the family whilst the incest was occurring. Mothers frequently apportion blame to themselves for the abuse, for example 'if only I had . . .', but this does not take account of the secrecy surrounding sexual abuse and the sophisticated *modus operandi* of the perpetrator. Mothers need to think through the consequences of self-blame when they need to be looking to move forward.

The mother will often face a flood of recurring memories for some considerable time after the abuse has come to light, as they are haunted by the story, and in particular how they may have prevented it. This is most noticeable where incest has occurred. These memories will strike at all times of day and in all places, such as shopping or driving, and strategies need to be constructed to deal with these when they arise, for example having a 24-hour contact agreement with a close friend.

Many mothers will consider the fact they should have known retrospectively, as do many professionals. This can affect their ability to recover and move on. It is not always true that time heals.

The mother is faced with a need to review the sequence of events to make sense of them. This process of review will include past knowledge of the child's behaviour problems, of the perpetrator's propensity to violence, the child's age and access to other sources of knowledge about sex, awareness of the reasons children find telling about sexual abuse difficult, and information from friends and public sources about sexual abuse in general. The mother may often make premature judgements in an attempt to protect their child, overlooking the need to attend to her grieving and the need for external support.

### Questions that need answering include:

- Can she work through her feelings of guilt/anger/shock/shame/denial?
- How quickly?
- How safe is the child while she does so?
- Does she understand that hers is a stress response?

There is no single formula for getting through the emotional tangle, although identifying an intelligent sounding board is recommended. The resolution of these reactions does not always pave the way to protective action, although support or pressure from outside authorities sometimes makes it easier for a mother to initiate and follow through with protective action. It can also make a mother's choices easier (Johnson, 1992).

It is also useful to consider what opportunities the woman has to process information and to understand the quality of her support networks. Does she have any significant attachment figures in her life? What are her coping strategies, for example, do you know how she responds to stress, who does she get support from, does anyone provide practical support, are her main support systems connected to the perpetrator and if so, what is their stance in relation to the allegations? Is she isolated or has she become isolated because of the current situation?

All of these things will have an impact on the mother and her ability to process information and manage practical day to day tasks at this time. It is important to understand these issues and it may be an area where she needs some additional support to enable her to function under the current circumstances.

## Consequences of disclosure for the mother

The last section highlighted the multiple processes that mothers will experience and those that they need to help the victims manage also. It is essential that every worker have some understanding about the imbalance between the negative and the positive consequences of accepting and working with the allegations for the perpetrator and his family. Figure 12.1 sets out the feared negative consequences of disclosure for all family members.

Mothers who are faced with a disclosure of sexual abuse have a great number of potential consequences: they have the impact of the sexual abuse itself to deal with; the choice between their partner or their children; the possible resurfacing of their own abuse; and the financial and

|  | Perpetrator | Mother | Child |
|---|---|---|---|
| 1. Legal | • Imprisonment | • Care order on child and other siblings | • Care order |
| 2. Family | • Marital separation<br>• Loss of children/restriction of contact<br>• Loss of support by other relatives | • Loss of partner<br>• Loss of child/ren<br>• Loss of co-parent<br>• Loss of support by other relatives | • Loss of father<br>• Loss of mother<br>• Loss of siblings<br>• Fear of not being believed<br>• Fear of retribution<br>• Fear of violence and punishment<br>• Fear of violence within the family<br>• Fear of perpetrator's and others' well-being (eg offender's threat of suicide) |
| 3. Psychological | • Suicide<br>• Guilt over effects<br>• Let down of partner<br>• Self respect<br>• Self-esteem and identity<br>• Own history of sexual abuse<br>• Fear of loneliness and isolation<br>• Inability to cope<br>• Inability to face addiction and tension relief through abuse | • Self-respect<br>• Let down of child<br>• Self-blame<br>• Having married a perpetrator<br>• Own history of sexual abuse<br>• Fear of loneliness and isolation<br>• Need to care without partner<br>• Desperation, fear, anger and loneliness | • Fear of being blamed<br>• Fear of being scapegoated<br>• Self-blame<br>• Fear of loneliness and isolation<br>• Loyalty<br>• Desperation, fear, anger and loneliness |
| 4. Social | • Reprisal<br>• Reputation<br>• Stigma<br>• Isolation<br>• Overcoming shame | • Reputation<br>• Stigma<br>• Isolation<br>• Problems of being a single parent | • Reaction of peers<br>• Treatment at school<br>• Loss of friends<br>• Behavioural changes, eg becoming beyond control<br>• Assumption of parenting role |
| 5. Financial and professional | • Loss of job<br>• Loss of earnings<br>• Loss of professional licence<br>• Loss of reputation | • Financial hardship and stress<br>• Effects on own work and professional career<br>• Legal expenses | • Doing part-time jobs to help (eg paper rounds) |

(adapted from Furniss, 1990: 245 and Wright, 1991)

**Figure 12.1**    The feared negative consequences of disclosure for all family members

associated consequences. They may feel they are to blame for the abuse. They also have to face the influx of professionals who will be watching them closely and making seemingly impersonal decisions. They will decide the disposition of the case and make decisions based on the mother's ability to make 'good' decisions and whether or not she colluded with the perpetrator. They will be recommending a series of assessments for the child victim, other children in the family, and

possibly herself. The mother will also be learning of the duration of protracted treatment (possibly years). She may face the prospect of the perpetrator being interviewed, possibly arrested and prosecuted, and that her child may have to testify in court. Should a custodial sentence be the outcome for the perpetrator, then the mother may be facing a significant loss of finances. This may result in her need to try and supplement her income, often via her extended family, or re-enter the workplace. This requires potential retraining and then she is faced with the difficult idea of safe childcare to facilitate this. This trust will clearly be at an all time low given the recent events.

The available information suggests that mothers continue to suffer from the consequences of the abuse for years after the disclosure. For many these remain invisible given the professional management of the situation. For example, those mothers who act 'appropriately' in protecting their children do not receive much follow-up, even though they may have lost practically (their partners, homes, income, support networks) and emotionally (their faith in people, their dreams for the future, and the loss of faith and trust in the world). In short, they put their lives on hold until the child is grown up (Dwyer and Miller, 1996). If a mother chooses her partner, then she faces a potential backlash from the professionals and she could lose her child and potentially her grandchildren. The perpetrator becomes her sole support, and this renders her isolated and lonely. While many may see the decision between child and partner as 'either-or', the mother may wish to support both. This option is rarely understood by the child or the professionals, who may push her to make a choice.

It is thus very important that we get the perpetrator, their families, as well as professionals, to look at any positive consequences of disclosure. These might include:

For the perpetrator:

1. An understanding of how their behaviour has developed as this is the start of repairing the damage and working at controlling any future repetition of their behaviour.
2. It allows the workers to identify and work on the most dangerous areas.
3. It shows the perpetrator they are able to accept responsibility for their behaviour and the need for change.

For the partner:

1. It allows them to make a more informed decision on the risk their partner poses and whether they are to continue with, or end the relationship.
2. It can encourage the perpetrator to complete the necessary work.

For the children:

1. It allows them to have a safe home environment.
2. It allows them to have their views regarding contact heard.
3. It allows them to have safe contact with their father.

It is important that the workers encourage the families they are working with to identify all the positive consequences of working on the sexual abuse, otherwise they will be overwhelmed by the negative consequences (Calder and Skinner, 1999).

### Research findings

Mothers often face loss at a number of levels: loss of self, loss of roles (as mother and wife) and loss of ideas about the future (for themselves and their family). The evidence suggests that anywhere between 40 per cent and 73 per cent of sexually abused children are removed from their homes post-disclosure (Hunter et al., 1990; Jaudes and Morris, 1990). The mother also has to manage the reality that many children blame themselves for this outcome, viewing removal as a form of punishment.

Homelessness is also a potential outcome for some families faced with an abrupt drop in income (see Shinn et al., 1991). Pellegrin and Wagner (1990) in their sample found that 58 per cent of mother's were working and 42 per cent were unemployed at the point of disclosure. They did not find that the unemployed mothers were more available to their daughters and being unemployed was associated with a greater probability of victim removal. They suggested that this may be due to their financial dependence on the spouse. Those of us who have never lived alone or been a single parent need to consider what an overwhelming prospect that is for the mother to contemplate. As such, it may seem easier to live with a 'child who lies' than to confront the issue of a partner who sexually abuses against children; or to accept minimisation and rationalisations from the perpetrator and believe that it will not happen again; or hope that now it is out in the open it will cease (Smith, 1995b). Most women do not have viable economic choices after the child has disclosed the sexual abuse, with many quitting their jobs to support their children's needs arising from the abuse or because they fear that their children will be abused again (Carter, 1993).

Mothers may face deteriorating mental health (McIntyre, 1981). A study by Goodwin (1981) suggests that following a child's disclosure, mothers are at increased risk of attempting suicide, whilst Bagley and King (1990) uncovered a range of mental health difficulties, including depression, anxiety attacks and engaging in acts of self-harm. They may also feel that they have failed in their duties as a wife, mother and a woman. De Jong (1988) found that some mothers required hospitalisation for somatic disorders.

Bagley and Naspini (1987) found that mothers of sexually abused children may also experience suicidal tendencies when their daughter reveals the abuse. Briere and Runtz (1986) studied 195 women seeking help from a community health centre and found that former child sexual abuse victims were more than twice as likely to have attempted suicide than non-abused clients. Factors of impaired self-esteem and self-blame; powerlessness, including vulnerability to depression; interpersonal dysfunction, and attempts to escape the abuse seemed to be important antecedents of self-destructive behaviour (Bagley and King, 1990). These issues are explored in more details in the social history section.

Mothers are frequently required to review their perceptions of significant others, including the child, the abuser and extended family members. This can be difficult and anxiety provoking, reflecting the reality that we tend to feel threatened and vulnerable when our beliefs are challenged (Engel, 1994).

### Issues to consider

Johnson (1992: 98) found that:

> . . . the coin of consequences for the mothers sometimes has two sides: punishment and betrayal on one side; relief, vindication, a way out, and new opportunities on the other. Crisis can be an opportunity for new growth and opportunities, and for some of the mothers this was true in terms of them individually. But when talking about their families, the consequences of the incest violated their illusions of family life.

## The mother's needs post-disclosure

> The field is beginning to realise that the needs of the non-abusing mother are as important as the needs of the children.
>
> (Massatt and Lundy, 1998)

Byerly (1992) set out the following list of needs experienced by mothers following disclosure:

- Someone to talk to, to express trust and belief in them, often for weeks or months afterwards.
- Someone to counsel them about their own incest, as the child's disclosure may have resurrected memories of their own abuse.
- To know what happened. This is essential as well as painful: they need to know the nature, the frequency, extent, the time and place, the child's feelings, etc.
- To know they weren't the first mother this had happened to so they are not alone, and can possibly meet and learn from shared feelings.
- To have a break from him. They need space away from the perpetrator in order to gain a perspective and consider their feelings about the relationship, etc.
- To be treated as a person; to have their feelings listened to seriously, to feel respected, to be acknowledged when they are present, etc.
- To regain control of their lives and minds: particularly in incest cases where they need to resume control over the day-to-day events and their personal thoughts.
- To obtain basic information on survival: to embrace new aspects of their lives, such as courts, police, treatment, etc.
- To understand how domestic violence and sexual abuse were related: and to understand they are separate issues that need to be addressed.
- To make basic life decisions: to move away, separate or divorce their husband, tell people, etc.
- To know the options regarding contact and custody: both in relation to their partner, but also if the child has been removed from home by the local authority.
- To know how their child/ren will react: as everyone will be affected to some degree by the trauma.
- To ensure this will not happen again: taking steps to safeguard the child from continued sexual abuse is important, such as no contact or supervised contact.

The needs of non-abusing parents can be neglected as professional responses focus on the children who have been abused, their siblings, and on the perpetrators of the abuse. In this sense, the professional response system is insensitive to the needs of women. However, both for the women's emotional survival and growth and so that they can provide appropriate parenting for their children, thereby reducing the need for their children to be removed from their care or remain there long-term, these women need the therapeutic opportunity to deal with their feelings about what has happened and to adjust to the major change that has taken place in their lives.

Initial intervention with the mother following disclosure needs to include a functional assessment of her need both for psychological support, and for concrete services such as interim safety, financial needs, and support in living independently (Byerly, 1985). The needs of the mother are often the same as the child: impaired self-image can be repaired through teaching women to recognise and respond to their own nurturing needs. Denial can be confronted as they learn to ventilate conflicting motivations and loyalties. Focus on universal dimensions can help shape reasonable expectations of their husbands and children. Practice in limit setting is required to overcome failures in establishing and enforcing limits. Anger needs to be recognised and validated, with appropriate outlets found (Bagley and King, 1990).

Walton (1996) found that help was not forthcoming from the child protection services for most of the mothers following the disclosure. The professionals concentrated on the needs for protection of the child, not the needs of the mother. Once workers impose a judgement on a non-abusing mother, they make decisions about what she needs and what she will do. In doing so, attempts may be made to make her fit the professional understanding and abilities. It might be more productive to approach her with the understanding that they know only some of what she has experienced, and this may then lead to the gathering of information required to make more informed decisions. Workers often have a temptation to 'know' why it happened which can override the objective of gathering information and understanding the uniqueness, needs and circumstances of the individuals involved (Ovaris, 1991).

Women in our society are expected to meet the needs of men and of children before their own needs. Orr (1995) pointed out that women develop differently to men and have a greater emphasis on continuity and connection with others rather than separation and autonomy. Indeed, women's sense of self becomes organised

around being able to make and then maintain affiliation and relationships. Thus, when a mother's self-worth comes from keeping the family together, the impact and consequences of sexual abuse can shatter her and make the meeting of her needs very difficult to achieve. Many experience disorganisation in their lives (internal and external) and struggle to keep things together. The disintegration of the family and loss of roles and relationships within the family can be disorientating. What is interesting is that at the point of disclosure, is that women are asked to make choices that will inevitable result in the dissolution of their family, and which thus opposes her socialisation. Many need to work through their feelings of being lost or confused to find out who they are and to get to know themselves better. Many mothers are ostensibly attempting to identify and then meet their own needs for the first time.

Following disclosure, many of the mothers become single parents. This often means that they are unable to cope with their children's needs given that so many of their own needs remained unmet. It is logical that in order to help the children, some attention must be paid to the mother's needs. More importantly, professionals need to ensure that they offer services that will fulfil the needs of the mothers as they see them, rather than as the professionals see them.

### Research findings

Mitchell (1985) identified that some mothers have suffered multiple forms of physical and emotional abuse from their male partners. They may require help themselves before they can move on to assist their children. For example, children do not need to be victims; they need help so they can move to becoming survivors. Mothers are an integral part of the creation of an environment where their experiences are acknowledged without stigma, suspicion, shame, guilt and fear. Unfortunately, this is often not a feature of professional intervention. Many writers have articulated the feelings of mothers in such situations who found themselves discounted and misunderstood. For example, Rivera (1988) found that mothers were often left to deal with the abuse alone. They also found that the court system was inadequate in securing justice and protection for victims, especially when the victims were under eight years of age. As such, no criminal charges were levelled, no prosecution undertaken, no conviction secured, and no admission of culpability made. Johnson (1992) argued that mothers were immobilised by the poor professional response, needing time alone to sort things out before they could take action. Whether the mothers sought help or not depended largely upon their feelings about the abuse, their sense of obligation, the social pressure they encountered, and the kind of resources available to them.

Salt et al. (1990) found that 50 per cent of the mothers in their sample were as pre-occupied with the effects on themselves as with those on the child. De Jong (1988) found that although some of the mothers appeared disturbed by their child's behaviour changes, many appeared more concerned about how they themselves were going to be able to cope with their own feelings and the responses of family, friends, and the agencies involved.

While the importance of family support for the sexually abused child is clear, there is some suggestion that children may benefit if their mothers are also receiving support. For example, Leifer et al. (1993) found a significant positive relationship between inadequate social support of the mother and the lack of maternal support to the child, as well as the increased likelihood of foster care placement for the child. Newberger et al. (1993) have explored the emotional functioning of mothers post-disclosure, and noted that they also should be identified as victims and provided with treatment. It is conceivable that the level of support the mother can provide is associated with their own emotional well being. Lipton (1997) explored the emotional distress of the primary caretakers of sexually abused children, as well as the relationship between maternal distress and the emotional well-being of her child. When comparing biological parents with foster or adoptive parents, she found that the biological caretakers were significantly more distressed; and that there was a significant positive relationship between the distress of the child and the distress of the caretaker. It may be that the marked differences in marital and economic status between the two groups could explain the variation in distress levels. By supporting the mothers, professionals might well create a mediating factor to the combined distress of the mother and the child.

It is well reported that mothers have extensive needs for support in the aftermath of abuse.

Humphreys (1995) explored the needs (and unmet needs) of mothers in the aftermath of child sexual abuse disclosure. She argued that the experience of the sexually abused child is highly dependent upon the support extended to the child's mother in the aftermath of abuse. Mothers identified the need for individual support and counselling to help them deal with their own crisis, particularly when their normal avenues of support were unavailable. This is acute in mothers from non-English speaking backgrounds. Disclosure of sexual abuse was experienced as undermining central beliefs about themselves, particularly in their role as parent. They were acutely aware that their ability to manage the crisis affected their children. Others found support through a self-help group where they met with mothers in similar situations. They spoke of a lack of support from their partners which manifested in different ways, particularly the different reactions to the disclosure. For example, men were far more likely to react with retribution against the perpetrator, and this became the source of conflict between the couples; as was their sexual relationship which was affected. This was exacerbated when the mothers wanted to talk through their feelings, and was magnified when the mother was blamed for the abuse by her husband. Overall, mothers needed ongoing support for themselves as individuals, couples and parents.

### Issues to consider

The mother has a crucial role to play in helping her abused child, and it is to them that the child will often turn for support, reassurance and future protection. Therefore workers need to provide mothers with the support, understanding and assistance that will help them to respond appropriately to their children. Furniss (1991) has noted that mothers are much more likely to become an ally for the child and the professionals if their own process of discovery is understood and facilitated.

Mothers need their own source of support and it is important to find a trusted adult who will not judge them and with whom they can talk things through. They need to be able to discuss honestly past and future risks and strategies for managing them. This requires that mothers become selective as they do not want the conversation disseminating in the local community. The problem will not simply disappear and if the mother tries to keep the problem contained within the family alone, then they remain vulnerable to the perpetrator's tactics of persuasion, and ultimately convincing themselves that the abuse did not happen, or that it has indeed stopped. However, mothers do need to remember that support from the extended family has the advantage that they have some knowledge of everyone involved, coupled with a slight distance from the situation, that does make it easier for them to be helpful (Smith, 1995b). Respite by looking after the children occasionally is also helpful.

Too often the professional response reinforces the reality that the needs of men and children come first and that mothers have no needs but to meet the needs of others.

Professionals need to slow the process down and lessen the trauma for women, giving them space to think. They need to create an environment where the mother can mobilise her own resources for recovery whilst shielding them from either a lack of support or conditional or cutting support. Mothers need some distance from the criticism and judgements of others whilst feeling they can regain a sense of control over their lives.

Smith (1994) pointed out that there is a need for mothers and workers to explore the available options in order to agree priorities for change.

## Perceived options or a 'no-win' situation?

A considerable amount of the literature points to the reality that no matter how hard mothers try or what they do, they are in a 'no-win' situation, and are still blamed for their actions and choices.

When a mother discovers or is told that her partner has sexually abused her child, she is faced with conflicting images of herself, her child, and the perpetrator. She will need to decide whom to believe, whom to continue a relationship with, and whom to maintain a loyalty to. It also leaves her having to sort though various options that may conflict with her view of marriage, parenting, and sense of competence as a wife and a mother. Unfortunately, professionals frequently want her to make life-changing decisions immediately upon discovery of the abuse. She must either separate from the perpetrator or lose her child; a difficult decision under the best of circumstances, but an

overwhelming one for someone in the throes of a situation that forces her to view her life in new ways (Elbow and Mayfield, 1991). Where social services alienate the mother in the investigation of the case, then they are increasing her vulnerability to pressure from the perpetrator. If the abuse is within the family, the mother is often left to make the choice about who to believe and stand by, and by implication, is taking sides against others. It is impossible to find some middle ground. Separating from the perpetrator requires resources that are often not immediately available. This concern about her material well-being may be re-interpreted as denial, greater loyalty to the perpetrator, or dependence upon him. This is unfair when incest is over-represented in low-income families (Julian and Mohr, 1979).

Beneath what may be a mother's disbelief or denial is the reality of what they will have to do, and this means making hard choices. Mothers may well be less able to initiate and follow through with protective action if they have to confront their husbands alone. Likewise, they may find it more difficult to move from disbelief and denial toward belief and acceptance and subsequent action without support and assistance of professional outsiders.

The mother may be very fearful that fully supporting the child will lead her to lose both her future security and her relationship with the perpetrator. This creates a dilemma of loyalty about whom to support and she may feel overwhelmed by confusion about what action, if any, to take. Burgess et al. (1978) looked at the social pressures and the psychological stress involved in making a decision about where to place one's loyalty post-sexual abuse. This is especially true in cases of incest. The question that the family must face is: should we be loyal to our child and react to the perpetrator as we would react to any perpetrator, basing this decision on our duty as community members to bring such a person to the attention of the law? The alternative to this choice is to make an exception for the family perpetrator and be loyal to the family ties rather than bring him to an outside group's attention. The family must choose one of the two courses of action.

There is a large personal cost for the women in making a decision that conflicts with a traditional notion of a 'good mother'. This decision places these women in conflict with the child protection system. The consequence of this conflict is that women are perceived as uncooperative and unable to protect their child.

Post-disclosure, mothers are required to reassess their marriage, although many expect this to only conclude with her decision to reject the man and support her child. This pressure from professionals comes from their benefit of experience and hindsight (of practice and research, which highlights how the perpetrator targets and grooms the situation) and they only view the male as a sexual perpetrator. The mother often sees things very differently. They may see the man as her partner and as a father. They are thus asked to consider the information against their history of being with them and these often conflict in every sense. Even when they hold their husband entirely responsible, they may be wracked by a sense of failure that they had chosen this individual. Many mothers are perplexed at why their choices are so difficult and they may be shocked that they still feel something for the man or find themselves unable to separate (Dwyer and Miller, 1996). However, this needs to be seen in the context that at a time in which they feel most vulnerable and uncertain, they are asked to be responsible and decisive.

Boulton and Burnham (1989) consider the process of social work intervention and the conditions that affect the response of the mother to that intervention (see Figure 12.2). It is always a legitimate question to ask, 'Who is responsible for the abuse?' However, enshrined within the question that often follows, 'Who will the non-abusing carer choose – their partner or their child?' There are inevitably assumptions by professionals about the women, based on their choice. The authors suggest that women who have low self-esteem, are poorly nurtured themselves, experience financial and environmental stress and/or are socially isolated, are inevitably more likely to have a greater need for the support their partners provide. Research into perpetrators would indicate that it is often families in this position that increase child vulnerability and attract potential perpetrators (Finkelhor and Baron, 1986.) The likelihood is that in being asked to choose, many women opt to continue their relationship with their partner in some way, either overtly or covertly. During the course of their work, Rose and Savage (2000) commonly heard professionals attach negative labels to these women. They have been described as collusive of the abuse, in denial, unfit mothers, minimising of the effects of the abuse, etc.

When professionals fail to recognise the feelings of the women and the context within which they are asked to make a choice, the assumptions about the 'sort' of mothers they are, appears to follow. The perceived hostile responses of professionals to women in this position often serve to strengthen the relationship between the women and their partners (where the women feel needed). The responses of workers to the women commonly took the form of the children's names being placed on the Child Protection Register as well as initiation of care proceedings. This action supported the concept of these carers as unsafe, and further entrenched the position of warring sides.

The social worker has the difficult job of helping the mother to overcome or contain her reactions to help her accept the need for a possible choice between child and the perpetrator; and to encourage her to maintain a benevolent and supportive attitude toward the child. It is important, and appropriate, to allow the mother a short period of time in which to collect herself and make a decision (Glaser and Frosh, 1988).

## Research findings

Hooper (1992) found that 40 per cent of women who discovered the sexual abuse in a clearly identifiable incident were those who decided to stay or reunite with their partners later. Of the five women faced with persistent denial from the perpetrator, 80 per cent had separated from the abusive men, although 40 per cent were not separated by their own choice.

Salt et al. (1990) found that the most difficult situation for mothers to deal with was a perpetrator who would not leave the child's home. When asked to do so, only 22 per cent of the mothers could make this demand on the perpetrator.

De Jong (1988) found that the child's parents or mother will frequently have mixed feelings about the perpetrator and may be pressured not to file charges by relatives or friends. The supportive mothers who did not press charges usually expressed concern about the stress of the legal proceedings on the children and themselves and the fear that the perpetrator might not be convicted. Overall, 17 per cent of the supportive mothers did not press charges, and 12 per cent of the non-supportive mothers did press charges. The latter group expressed a desire for the perpetrator to share the blame, although each

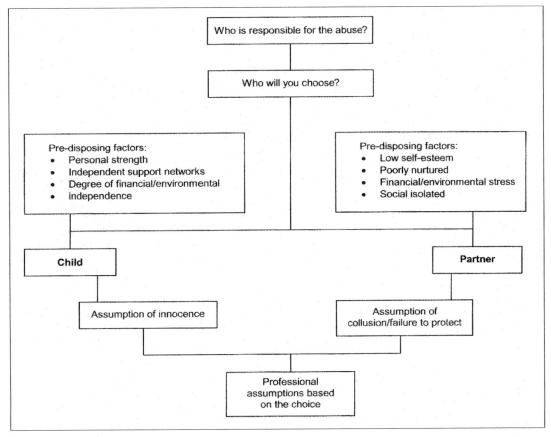

**Figure 12.2**  Who is responsible for the abuse? (Adapted from Bourton and Burnham, 1989, by Rose and Savage, 2000)

believed that the child had initiated or caused the contact.

Because of conflicting expectations, the victims and their families often find it difficult to decide whether or not to press charges against the perpetrator. The agony of making this decision is increased when he is a family member. Here, families are caught between two conflicting expectations: universalistic vs. particularistic. Should they be loyal to the child victim and treat the perpetrator as they would treat an assailant – thinking of their duty as citizens to bring such an offender before the law? Or should they be loyal to them and make an exception for him because he is a family member and let their duty to him as a particularistic individual prevail? They cannot honour both expectations, and the choice is often a difficult one (Burgess et al., 1977). In their sample, just over half resolved in favour of the

child. Even when a decision is made, this can be hard to bear, particularly if pressure is applied to reverse it, for example from the perpetrator's extended family. The low rate of action by the criminal justice agencies is often a factor in families' decisions. For example, Palmer et al. (1999) found that in only six per cent of the 384 cases in their sample was the perpetrator charged by the police, and he was only convicted in half of these cases (three per cent). This compared with 85 cases of children being removed from their homes due to the abuse and a further 17 per cent being removed for another reason.

McLurg and Craisatti (1999) found that in their sample 80 per cent of the partner's stayed together. In half of the families where they did so, the victim was the daughter of the alleged perpetrator and in one third of cases the victim was the step daughter of the alleged perpetrator.

Fong and Walsh-Bowers (1998) explored the responsiveness of mothers to father-daughter incest. Of the six women interviewed, half of the incestuous relationships occurred while the mother was still living with her partner (type A family) whereas the other half occurred after the women separated from their partner (type B family). For women from type A families, the disclosure of the abuse was complicated by the stability of family relationships. On the one hand, they were socialised to take the responsibility for keeping the family intact and helping their partners as well as their daughters to deal with the crisis. Because incest was an alien concept to them, they needed time to consider what to do. On the other hand, the professional system expects them to act immediately so as not to feed the view of them as either unfit mothers or as condoning the abuse. Type B families found that because their children were too young to be listened to seriously and the physical evidence was not considered sufficient to diagnose sexual abuse, their reports were not considered credible. When they tried to protect their daughters by denying the perpetrator access, they felt abused further by the court process, and the threat of contempt of court for failing to comply with judgements.

Sirles and Lofberg (1990) noted that mothers often have much to lose and little to gain by separating from their partners. In their research they found that the families that broke up were more likely to have young child victims and have additional problems with domestic violence. The child was likely to have revealed the abuse to the mother and was believed by her.

Wright (1991) explored the family effects of perpetrator removal from the home. Given that intervention and choices can have varied and unexpected consequences, it is important to state these to understand how the decisions on choice for the mother may be loaded. They uncovered a powerful picture of the emotional, structural and financial changes in the lives of all family members when the perpetrator is removed. They found two main themes: financial effects and structural effects. They expressed desperation, fear, anger, and hopelessness about their financial condition (which often predates the offender removal from home, but is aggravated by overwhelming treatment and legal expenses). This can impact on the children if they have to lose college education. Whilst mothers reported working long hours in multiple jobs just to make

ends meet, older children also took jobs of their own to help out financially. The ongoing psychological aspects of financial trauma need to be handled as any other trauma, particularly when affluent people have been demoted to joining lower classes.

Forty per cent of the adults believed that perpetrator removal had contributed to marital dissolution. They noted that boundary ambiguity (Boss and Greenberg, 1984) is a consequence of the situation they find themselves in. So when workers are trying to teach families about appropriate boundaries, couples are forced to experience a major boundary ambiguity situation – is the perpetrator 'in' or 'out'? Are they married or not? Are they a family or not? Another contributing factor to the marital dissolution may be the structure of the treatment programme if it calls for a logical, linear progression through individual issues, couple work and then family therapy. People do not live their lives linearly and relationships do not remain static or on hold while individual issues are resolved.

Hooper (1992) found that decisions to separate permanently from their partners were related to previously considering whether to leave on the grounds of domestic violence or earlier sexual abuse. This is a common pattern to women's response to domestic violence, recurring hopes and promises of reform, together with self-blame and the desire to make their marriages work, bringing women back until the relationship deteriorates still further. The sexual abuse became the 'last straw'.

### Issues to consider

Todd and Ellis (1992) explored the issue of divided loyalties following an abuse disclosure. Professionals with responsibility to protect children look very closely at a mother to inform their judgements about how the situation is best handled. Those who end their relationship with the perpetrator may be allowed to care for the child. Unfortunately, few women are able to immediately adopt such a position. Furthermore, any pressure to make a choice between the perpetrator and the child forces the mother into a corner, which is at best unhelpful, and at worst disastrous. Mothers need time and space in order to make decisions on anything. Workers have an important role in constructing an environment where women are enabled to express a whole range of changing feelings, There is also added guilt women feel at rendering their partner homeless if they 'choose' their daughter. The challenge for workers is how to assist women to meet their parental responsibilities without reinforcing the sense of blame and how to ensure that professional responsibility for responding to sexual abuse is not abdicated. The mothers in their study are testimony to their resourcefulness and capacity for trust that they retained some hope and belief in the possibility of embarking on new relationships in the future which would offer something positive both to their children and themselves.

One option open to workers is to try and introduce the mother to others who have had to endure the process previously, to facilitate informal avenues for identifying the choices to be made, with positives and consequences.

Smith (1995) noted that if a mother had options available to them and did not use them, or, worse, perceives no options and thinks sexual abuse is an inevitability which requires endurance skills rather than escape mechanisms, the prognosis is poor. However, if the mother believes the child, then the interventions should increase the options rather than persecute them for not perceiving those options in the first place.

## Relationship and co-operation with the agency (throughout the process)

There is a need to establish a good working relationship with mothers from the outset. Most women state that their first contact from social services shapes their relationship from then on. Parental willingness to co-operate with the process of child protection influences social workers' judgements. When it is forthcoming, children are perceived to be less threatened; conversely, uncooperative attitudes raise social workers' uncertainty about parental motivation towards their children. There is often the middle ground, where parents may be at odds with each other about whether to volunteer information, or may be prepared to go along with investigation of the allegedly abused child.

It is often difficult for mothers to co-operate closely with agencies whose intervention alienates them and subjects them to prescribed societal expectations. Many mothers have reported the services provided to be inadequate. For example, those mothers who were sent onto parenting courses were confused as to the

reasoning behind this and why the focus was on them. This appeared to be consistent with the view of women's responsibility being to protect the children.

Most mothers are willing to co-operate in the necessary assessment and treatment work once they trust that they are not being criticised or labelled for their confused and conflicting feelings.

### Research findings

It is important to accurately assess the family's level of co-operation with the work as this will have a direct correlation with the level of partnership proposed with the family, and the type of mandate needed. Co-operation will often fluctuate and will need to induce a more or less authoritative role from the workers in response to the presenting situation. This may occur when progress is slow or non-existent and a review of the plan is required.

Pellegrin and Wagner (1990) found that 40 per cent of the mothers in their sample attended appointments about 90 per cent of the time while 30 per cent attended less than 20 per cent of the time. Overall, 67 per cent of the mothers were deemed by the workers to be at least average in their compliance with the recommended plan. They noted that eliciting the co-operation of non-compliant or non-believing mothers was difficult to obtain. In these circumstances, the children were often removed from home as they could not be assured protection at home. This action confused the mothers as to what they were not co-operating with, the allegation or the removal. Workers also need to be alert to the reality that mothers of sexually abused children are not a homogeneous group, and thus a variety of techniques is needed as what works with one will not necessarily work with another. Resistance will be induced where workers try and fit the mother to the technique and not reverse this approach in the appropriate cases.

Gilgun (1984) argued that where the professionals assume that the mother knew of the abuse, then this is correlated with the source of maternal resistance to working with professionals. Conversely, where the professionals squarely placed the responsibility with the perpetrator, then they were more amenable to such an approach.

We know from *Messages from Research* (DoH, 1995) that plans made at conference do not necessarily mean they will be accepted or processed by the family. It is important to make a distinction between co-operation and compliance. Sayers (1995) noted that:

> . . . *our understanding of a mother's ability to protect is helped by carefully considering the extent to which she has taken seriously the child protection requirements of the agencies involved. However, we do need to think carefully about the extent to which the demands of the agencies on the mother are realistic. It would, for example, be unrealistic to expect that a mother could protect her child from a perpetrator who creates opportunities for contact with the child outside the home. We must ask ourselves whether the demands for protection that we make of the mother could be met by anyone, whatever their relationship with the child or however determined they are to ensure the child's safety and protection.*

Smith (1994) noted that it is difficult when a mother simply complies with the involvement (eg the removal from the home of the perpetrator is a professional and not a maternal decision).

Jones and Ramchandani (1999) explored the question 'how do professionals manage the dilemma of discovering whether a child is safe, while also not alienating potential carers, who may eventually work in partnership with the professional?' They found that the way in which a case is handled initially can affect the entire subsequent process. Where handled well and sensitively, keeping the non-abusing parent informed and involved, there can be a positive effect on the eventual outcome. Conversely, poorly handled initial contact can alienate both the child and carer, making later work more difficult. The variation in initial approach may reflect a worker's underlying beliefs about the way in which an investigation should be carried out. They found that some professionals approach parents on the basis of supportive acceptance, whilst others require parents to accept responsibility. The majority favour the latter. This has implications in the case of sexual abuse, where the wide range of parental reactions are often difficult to interpret accurately, particularly at the time when they were also considering placement issues. There is thus a wide difference in perspective between the parents and the professionals. Parents were typically shocked, frightened, or became withdrawn, whereas for the professional this was a 'routine' job. In these circumstances, professionals sometimes misjudged parental capacity to understand allegations or protect their children.

They found that parents retained a strong expectation of help despite the quality of the initial contact, showing that the prospect of working in partnership is not necessarily lost forever, particularly with mothers who remained open and receptive to advice given their predicament. Workers face the difficult task of balancing the need to obtain the non-abusing parent's commitment to help protect the child, while also being responsive to that parent's needs for understanding, information and psychological treatment. Fortunately many believe it possible to balance a supportive and accepting stance with one of encouraging parental responsibility, seeing them as a tension that can be maintained rather than a dichotomous choice.

Parents who were not kept well-informed were marginalised when they attended the initial child protection conference. They wanted professionals to consider all the family history and not just the sexual abuse in order to take decisions on the way forward. For example, issues of finances, supports, general parenting ability, previous domestic violence with its potential repercussions were all central to such decisions. Families have broad needs that require services and a focus in the assessment. Farmer (1993) has noted that the conference has an important role in ensuring the mother does not feel blamed as this can be a block to partnerships later. It has an important role in helping the mother become equal with the professionals.

Most clients value courtesy and respect, being treated as equals, as individuals and as people who can make their own decisions; they value workers who are experienced, well-informed and reliable, able to explain things clearly without condescension and who really listen; and they value workers who are able to act effectively and make practical things happen. Workers who deal with their clients in these ways empower them. This can become more difficult in some situations of child protection, where workers have considerable power, which makes the relationship inherently unequal.

## Issues to consider

With these points in mind, it is useful to have a framework for assessing the client's co-operation with the workers and tasks:

**1. Client is fully and actively involved in case planning, services and/or treatment**

- accepts and actively uses suitable services, including following through on tasks or on referrals to other service providers
- keeps appointments, makes self available as needed, and follows directions to best of their ability
- shows concern about impact of services or treatment; complains about inadequate service when warranted
- may not agree with everything suggested, but tries to be constructive in proposing alternatives
- when problems in co-operation develop, there tend to be extenuating circumstances.

## 2. Client is involved in planning and services, but lacks initiative and tends to hold back

- not as fully or actively involved in case planning or services as they could be. This maybe because client is rather disorganised or somewhat ambivalent about services
- accepts and uses suitable services, but doesn't always make best use of them, or drops them too early; follows through on referrals, but sometimes not in a timely manner
- makes appointments, but often postpones them and sometimes doesn't keep them at all
- may co-operate satisfactorily with services for other family members, but may co-operate less well with personal services focused on self
- tends to wait for caseworker to suggest and act, may complain without proposing alternative, but does accept advice.

## 3. Client is only minimally involved in planning and services

- passively resists co-operating or is argumentative at every stage
- may accept services verbally, but doesn't use them or follow through on referrals or tasks without constant prodding and direct assistance (eg has to be taken there every time, even though own transportation can be arranged)
- often has to be cajoled, coerced or 'chased after'
- makes appointments, but rarely keeps them; doesn't reschedule in advance, even if there are extenuating circumstances
- when services used, participates without much enthusiasm or at the minimum acceptance level
- but generally doesn't refuse to accept services, doesn't act consistently hostile, and doesn't actively sabotage services
- agency able to remain in contact with client.

## 4. Client rejects any involvement with agency

- actively or passively rejects any agency contact or involvement
- may refuse to accept any service, or actively sabotages services when persuaded or coerced into using any
- may threaten service providers, or otherwise discourage them from engaging client in service; may not accept even being 'led through' tasks; may have no reaction to admonitions or criticism at all.
- May display psychosomatic symptoms when confronted with need to act
- client may be very difficult to contact or retain in contact with.

(Magura et al., 1987: 27)

Jones and Ramchandani (1999: 25) set out some useful factors influencing a mother's co-operation with agencies:

- It is important to attempt to work in partnership with parents, especially with mothers who refer many, if not most, cases of suspected sexual abuse.
- Parents, and especially mothers, require clear information in an attempt to work as openly as possible, in order to keep them engaged in the process.
- Informing parents as swiftly and as completely as possible after children have been interviewed is necessary to enable trust to be maintained. Parallel sessions interviewing parents and children in tandem may prove useful.
- If conflict occurs between potentially jeopardising the partnership with parents and on the other hand fully protecting the child from harm, it is clear that the child's needs are paramount.
- Few specialists are currently involved and thus it may be useful to identify cases that need specialist help at an early stage.
- The early planning stage, following the initial referral, would be the most useful point to identify issues of race, culture, or language, which may require addressing.

Regan (2006) contains worksheets to use when considering a mother's commitment to the assessment process, with areas around motivation and ability to change being considered in conjunction with changes within the family, perpetrator and wider networks.

If the mother does alter her views or decisions at this stage of work, she will be very clear about why and it will be a decision she makes with knowledge and insight, as opposed to decisions she may feel have been made, or forced upon her, by others. Additionally, if the decision made is not to continue or resume the relationship, she is more likely to be able to distance herself emotionally and move forward from having had the opportunity to question and process information during the work undertaken.

## Openness regarding the sexual abuse

Because of the stigma attached to sexual abuse, families affected by it often do not want to share with others. They thus run the risk of becoming isolated and overwhelmed, even where they have believed the child and protected immediately. Many mothers will not want to broach the sexual abuse with family members for some time following the discovery or disclosure. Hesitant and tentative discussions are the norm. If this persists then it clearly places the child at greater risk. There is a need to try and replace secrecy with openness within the family as a whole, particularly if rehabilitation is being considered.

### Research findings

A mother's willingness to discuss the sexual abuse in the wider family may be dependent upon a number of factors. If she previously looked to them for support and guidance when any prior suspicions came to light, and they disbelieved, then this is unlikely to be replicated once substantiation has occurred. Trotter (1998) found that not all the mothers denied the reality of the abuse, but many of their families and friends disclaimed or rejected it to some extent or other. It was then very difficult to persuade them that the abuse had in fact happened. According to Berliner (1991) family members may also avoid imagining or thinking about what actually happened to reduce their own painful feelings. Unfortunately, this may lead to a lack of empathy for the child's experience and reinforce avoidance as a primary coping strategy.

Burgess et al. (1977) looked at how families decide whether or not to tell outsiders once the sexual abuse has been disclosed. Three possibilities exist: do nothing; handle it only as a family matter and tell no outsiders; or tell an outside group. Where the latter option is chosen, it prompts decisions being made by people often without any input from the victim. In their sample, nine of the 44 cases handled the matter as a family matter. Of these, two mothers explicitly severed family ties with the perpetrator's side of the family. In three cases, the perpetrators were lectured by another family member. In two cases the perpetrators were sent to live with the grandmother. In two cases, the offender continued to live in the same home as the child.

It is probable that many attempts to stop the sexual abuse by the mother do not come to the attention of the professionals. If these attempts fail, then they will probably work against the mother if the matter is eventually reported to the child protection agencies, as they may see her actions as denial or attempts to conceal the sexual abuse to protect the perpetrator. Elbow and Mayfield (1991) argued that the decision by the mother to report the matter requires considerable problem-solving skills on the mother's part. For example, she may be considering the impact of the process on the child even though it may appear that she is protecting the offender. It may be that she has been intimidated by threats of or actual physical abuse, thus fear and isolation may preclude both reporting and other attempts to limit the perpetrator's abuse of the child.

### Issues to consider

The mother of a newly disclosing incest victim must test out the extent to which she can rely on her own social network. Myer (1985) noted that this can be difficult when the family members may blame her for allowing the abuse, often reinforced by the intervening professionals. This is also linked to the escalation of stress for the mother if she cannot rely on the family in the short to medium term financially as well as emotionally and practically.

Most people do tend to cope with stressful life events within the family or within informal social networks before seeking help from formal service providers (Golan, 1981). They may even then turn first to the clergy or their doctor. Mothers will often weigh the efficacy of her own resources against the consequences or availability of external sources of help.

Engel (1994) explored how to break the news to the extended family. There is a need to acknowledge that the news will affect other family members, and that their immediate response may not be all the mother hoped for, for example they may respond with questions and doubt if not disbelief. Acknowledge that they will need time to absorb the information and process their feelings. Some will understand much more and provide the necessary support. It is thus important to consider how to elicit the latter response, and this may be through first approaching the family member the mother feels closest to.

There is a need to consider the motivation to tell: to force an alleged perpetrator to confess, to share it so they do not feel alone or to displace the responsibility for addressing the aftermath with someone else.

## Present attitude and relationship with the perpetrator

Faller (1988) has indicated the merits of exploring the mother's relationship with her partner. First, it is an indicator of the mother's overall functioning. Second, her information regarding the perpetrator can help the worker judge her level of dependence on him, his personality and functioning, and his treatment prognosis. Third, the worker may discover a pattern in the mother's relationships with men that are related to the dynamics of the sexual abuse and her prognosis for protecting her children. She also cautions workers to filter the information on the perpetrator provided by the mother depending on her reactions to the abuse, and in particular relating to her belief or disbelief of the allegations. For example, if she has decided to support her partner, she may well obscure his faults and lie about material related to the sexual abuse. Conversely, if she is supporting the child, then the information about the perpetrator may be very negative. It is more important therefore to explore her history of relationships. In doing so, workers should explore how the couple met, the length of time between meeting and sexual intimacy, the division of labour in the relationship, the quality of the relationship, good aspects versus bad ones, their sexual relationship, the partner's relationship with the children, any violence with her or the children, his work history, his use of drugs or alcohol, his involvement in criminal activity, and the reason they parted, if they have.

Loyalty is a highly valued feature of relationships, and is often understood to mean supporting and trusting a person at a time of adversity. The mother thus finds herself in a huge dilemma with incest, as being called upon to be loyal to one family member (her child) is at the cost of withdrawing her support from another (her partner). If the adult relationship remains in tact, then it is likely that the mother will show some semblance of commitment towards her partner.

The future relationship the mother chooses to have with the perpetrator is the litmus test of whether she will be able to offer her children any protection from further abuse. This often depends on the nature of the mother's relationship with the perpetrator. For example, offering protective action to the child and separation from the perpetrator usually presents relatively little difficulty if the perpetrator is a stranger to the family. The mother's protective abilities may similarly be mobilised if she learns of abuse of which she was previously unaware, for example, when the perpetrator was a family friend or is in a relationship with the child that exists relatively independently of the family.

The difficulties of ensuring protection for the child multiply as the perpetrator's emotional proximity to the family increases. This is particularly true when there is a close relationship between the mother and the perpetrator, leaving the mother with an extremely painful choice: break the relationship with the perpetrator or lose the child. This can be where the perpetrator is the partner or a valued relative, such as a grandfather. Only a minority of perpetrators agreed to leave the home as an expression of their responsibility for the abuse. Any mother that undertakes to exclude the perpetrator from the home will need considerable professional support to maintain the decision in the face of emotional and economic strains and stresses, and even threats of violence from the perpetrator and his family or friends (Glaser and Frosh, 1988). In cases where the perpetrator is the stepfather, the decision for the mother is complicated by the fact they have probably had a failed relationship already and are facing another one.

Mothers who are able to confront the perpetrator and are more able to exist independently from him are more likely to be able to effectively protect their children from further abuse. Those who are more dependent will require considerable external support to protect the child.

In response to the disclosure, the mother may become alarmed and distressed for her child and she may immediately feel very angry toward the perpetrator. She may have previously harboured suspicions, particularly if abused herself, possibly by the same man. The confirmation of her suspicions might lead to relief and enable her to pursue the protection of her child. When there is a continuing relationship between the mother and the perpetrator, the mother's natural first move will be to approach the perpetrator, who is likely to strenuously deny the abuse. This may lead to the mother gaining awareness of her pre-existing and now exceedingly uncomfortable position between the perpetrator and her child. The confusion and turmoil engendered in the mother by disclosure, particularly when faced by denial from the perpetrator, may lead the mother to disbelieve the child. Some mothers, themselves suspecting the abuse of the child, pursue their suspicions by questioning the child and the perpetrator. If the suspicions are confirmed, then outside help may be sought. Conversely, if the mother is deterred from pursuing help because of the consequences, then this becomes an obstacle to protecting her child (Glaser and Frosh, 1988).

Many mothers of sexually abused children may have been sexually abused themselves in childhood, and this may lead to them selecting emotionally inadequate partners (Cammaert, 1988) as a result of their low self-esteem. This can combine with their socialised role as being dependent on others and passive.

There is some controversy about the significance accorded to the mother's attitude towards the perpetrator and the apparent dependence by social services on them to protect children from sexual abuse. Whilst this is an important consideration, it should be considered alongside the perpetrator's willingness to address their behaviour as well as the child's ability to protect themselves. If the mother's position is considered in isolation, then it runs the risk of drawing the responsibility away from the perpetrator (MacLeod and Saraga, 1988). For many mothers, they simply maintain their relationship with their partner as a means of survival. Workers thus need to draw a careful line to facilitate the mother's participation in the process of assessment and determination of outcomes, without either holding women solely responsible for the safety of their children or blaming them for what has happened.

Women have increasingly been encouraged to separate from abusing partners to prevent sexually abused children being removed from home. However, such women have the right to remain with the sexually abusive partner, although this clearly challenges the traditionally held beliefs about safe parenting (Smart, 1997). There are ways in which the 'risk' presented by the continuing relationship between the women and their partners can be safely managed, and this can be seen as the best outcome for them in the longer-term. Experience has shown that if women feel pressurised into ending their relationships, the outcomes for children are rarely satisfactory and many continue the relationship, albeit in a clandestine way. For a fuller discussion around this area, please refer to the chapter on safe care by Rose and Savage, 1999.

Byerly (1992) set out some important factors for mothers to consider when making decisions about how and whether to maintain interaction with the perpetrator. They include:

- Proximity to the perpetrator can make them feel trapped, threatened or resentful, for example if the perpetrator is an immediate or extended family member. The mother needs to consider how to create and sustain space between them if desired.
- Emotional attachment is central to the mother's future relationship with the abuser, for example are they in love? What are their views about divorce? His willingness to undergo change and treatment? All of these take time. Where the mother wishes to remain with the perpetrator, they need to face issues such as re-establishing trust, sexual contact, openness, and a relationship based on equality (in terms of respect, shared responsibility, and privileges).
- Re-establishing sexual relationships with sexual perpetrators is often much more difficult than deciding to stay with him, and often takes time and counselling to achieve. This is often a part of the overall treatment package and needs to address how sexual boundaries and needs will be achieved and maintained.

### Research findings

Very little information is available regarding mothers who protect their children by leaving their partners but who do not go on to report the abuse to the authorities.

Todd (1989) found that the mothers' loyalties often remained with the perpetrator, whose needs predominated. This may be in part due to their history of abuse and their investment in their current relationship was often great. If the children have picked up on this, then they may well have accepted their subordinate role and acknowledged the importance of the adult union. In all the Sheffield cases, the mother could not escape the needs of the male partner. His triumph and control continues in that the child knows and understands that his or her disclosures have caused the devastation of the family. If this is the case, then reintroducing the perpetrator back into the home would present an unacceptable level of risk, and as such the safety of the child cannot be guaranteed.

For a mother to take action, she must feel strong enough to make a stand against the perpetrator, who is usually her male partner. Workers need to consider the co-existence of domestic violence with the sexual abuse, and how this impacts on the mother's choices. There is increasing evidence that domestic violence is more prevalent in sexually abusive families than in the general population (Truesdell et al., 1986) and thus workers need to acknowledge that any effective intervention will need to address the domestic violence before she can cope successfully with her child's victimisation (Dietz and Craft, 1990). Where the mother's partner tends to be violent, the mother's fear may compromise her ability to be supportive of a child who discloses. Even where her partner is not violent, a mother may be understandably reluctant to take action that may result in her partner being arrested, becoming alienated, or leaving the home. These inhibiting influences are reflected in the studies that show mothers are more likely to be supportive when they are no longer living with the perpetrator and that mothers who take action tend to divorce their partners (Faller, 1991).

Groth (1992) described two prominent patterns of husband-wife role relationships in incest families. The first is the aggressive-dominant husband, who occupies a dominant position in the family and chooses and marries a child wife. He maintains his power by keeping his wife and children economically dependent on him and socially isolated from relationships outside the family. The second pattern is the passive-dependent husband, who is more of a dependent, needy child and marries a

wife-mother. When the wife tires of fulfilling his excessive emotional needs and withdraws, the husband turns to his daughter, who is expected to take care of him. Johnson (1992) in her research found the relationship patterns were blurred and not as clear-cut as this. She found that the ways mothers defined and perceived their husbands as more powerful than themselves was much clearer. All the mothers in her sample described their husbands as men who asserted themselves as authoritarian heads of the household, and themselves as wives who were subject to that authority. But this did not mean they perceived themselves as fragile and powerless within all areas of their lives or that they were always passive or helpless in their responses to the different kinds of abuse they suffered.

Trepper et al. (1996) found in their sample that almost one-half (49 per cent) of the perpetrators and non-abusing spouses indicated a marital relationship in which extreme emotional separateness was the *modus vivendi*. An additional 40 per cent of couples displayed a moderate emotional separateness in their marital relationship. Only 11 per cent of these couples reported being more emotionally close than emotionally separate. The communication patterns of perpetrator and non-abusing spouses reflected estrangement between the two. Ninety per cent of perpetrators exhibited poor communication with their partner, that is, communication that was unclear, incongruent, and void of empathy. In fact, only 10 per cent of perpetrators displayed some effort to communicate effectively with their spouses. The majority of perpetrators (63 per cent) rated the alliance between themselves and their spouse as unhappy. Two-thirds of this group rated the relationship as very unhappy, whereas one-third rated their marital relationship as somewhat unhappy (that is more discontentment than contentment). The remaining one-third of perpetrators (38 per cent) ranked the relationship with their spouse as satisfactory, and none reported being happy in their marriage. However, two per cent of non-abusing parents classified the marital relationship as very happy although a quarter (26 per cent) viewed their marriages as satisfactory. 72 per cent of the non-abusing respondents appraised the couple's relationship as unhappy whilst 46 per cent of the total referred to their marital association as unhappy.

Massatt and Lundy (1998) found that the loss of the relationship with the perpetrator, whether through divorce, separation, or incarceration, and regardless of any history of physical and emotional abuse, came as a shock and a loss. They found that the number of non-abusing parents married to and living with the perpetrator dropped from 35 to two post-disclosure. The level of intimacy with him moved from 35.7 per cent reporting being 'not at all close in any way' before disclosure to 87 per cent reporting being 'not at all close in any way'.

Walton (1996) explored the issue of interpersonal role conflict for mothers between the perpetrator and the child. In this, the mother may well attempt to fulfil more than one role simultaneously and in so doing will find that they must satisfy multiple sets of expectations. Todd and Ellis (1992: 14) reported on children who had been sexually abused in the family and had been removed by the local authority. The mothers, on learning about the abuse, had decided to 'support and remain with (their) partner with the consequence that their children were admitted to care and in some instances expelled from the family completely'. They argued that the choice made by these mothers came as a result of forcing her to decide whom to support at such a time of emotional upheaval, placing her in an impossible position. In addition, the mother's isolation may be a critical factor in her management of events in that they may have to turn to the person whom they traditionally rely on for their support – the perpetrator.

Eaton (1993) highlighted the way in which perpetrators groom mothers as well as children, and Salter (1988) referred to the 'cognitive dissonance' to be reconciled by most mothers in order to believe their child and disbelieve their partner is enormous. Despite this, a significant proportion of mothers do find the time to make the choice of the child, with others requiring time and help to achieve the emotional and cognitive 'leap' of believing that their child has been sexually abused.

Dempster (1993) found that all 34 women in her sample took some action towards ending the abuse and protecting their children when they found out about the abuse. For some, this was done in the face of complete denial by the perpetrator, disapproval or even harassment from the perpetrator's friends, from relatives and sometimes even the surrounding community.

Sirles and Lofberg (1990) studied factors associated with divorce in cases of intra-familial child sexual abuse. They noted that the decision

about divorce is but one of the many and complex issues facing mothers. Often they have much to lose and little to gain by divorcing their husbands. In their sample of 128 incest cases, they found that 48 per cent ended in divorce. They identified significant relationships for the following variables:

- Age of the victim: with 72.7 per cent of the children being pre-school compared to 33.8 per cent who were teenage victims. This suggests that a protective bond exists between the mothers and their children.
- Who the abuse was revealed to: with 66.7 per cent of cases leading to divorce being reported initially to the mother, reducing to 33.3 per cent when reported to a friend and 34.5 per cent to a professional.
- The mother's reaction: 66.1 per cent were believed by their mothers compared to 33.9 per cent who were met with disbelief. Of those cases where the child was believed, 64 per cent of cases ended in divorce. In the majority of cases, the matter was reported to a professional agency immediately.
- A history of physical abuse of the mother was present in 68 per cent of the cases that ended in either separation or divorce, compared to 32 per cent that remained intact.
- Duration of the abuse: They found that victims whose families remained intact were abused for longer periods (m $=37.09$ months) than for families that broke up (n $=25.65$ months).

Overall, they found that there were differences between child sexual abuse cases that elected to stay together and those that divorce. Those who divorced had sufficient power and autonomy to take assertive action. They were not easily intimidated by their husband's physical abuse and threats of intimidation. They chose to place the protection of their child above the many negative consequences of separation.

Bagley (1995) found that mothers who had themselves been sexually abused often saw the marriage in unrealistic terms, as ideal relationships which contrasted with their unhappy childhood. Some of the women were also probably trapped in the cycle of learned helplessness. They rarely knew of the sexual abuse of their daughter, but often it was not difficult for their husbands to browbeat and deceive them. He noted that husbands of the mother group were on average 4.5 years older than their wives, significantly higher than the age difference of 3.1 years in the controls.

## Issues to consider

Some mothers wish their lives to return to how it used to be pre-disclosure. In order to achieve this, the mother may seek to normalise the perpetrator's behaviour by believing that his promises never to repeat the behaviour are valid; he is a good father in every other way; the impact of the abuse was not serious; or that herself or the daughter was responsible.

We need to explore the mother's current position regarding the perpetrator, bearing in mind his position regarding the abuse (admits, minimises or denies) and the tactics he will deploy when he now needs his partner more than ever before. For example, he may plead remorse and promise to change his ways as a means of blocking any information being provided to the professionals involved. This is necessary regardless of whether he continues to have contact with the child, because the crisis of the disclosure and of professional intervention may produce numerous changes in the non-abusing parent as well as in the perpetrator. For example, as the crisis of the disclosure recedes, the mother's previous, perhaps intensely held, feelings for the perpetrator may re-emerge. On the other hand, a mother may become more autonomous and less dependent in relation to him if he had been her father or cohabitee (Glaser and Frosh, 1988). If the mother and the perpetrator are to continue their relationship, in the context of rehabilitation, very careful work will be required.

## Questions to be asked

- What is expected of a mother who learns that her child has been sexually abused by a man whom she loved and trusted?
- It is very important that workers establish just how the couple met, in what circumstances, and how much he has groomed the mother. This can be reflected in how much her cognitive distortions mirror his. We also need to establish whether she has been abused by him sexually, emotionally or physically?
- What is her motivation for continuing her relationship with him?
- Where is her primary alliance – with the child or with the perpetrator? The less predictable or

less sympathetic the mother is to the child's interests, the greater the vulnerability of the child. The younger the child the greater the risk becomes.

- What is her complicity or non-complicity with the abuser post-disclosure?
- What are the mother's dilemmas?
- What do we as professionals need to offer practically?
- What do we need to understand ourselves?

Roberts (1992/3) argued that it is the notion of the couple as 'one', and the mother's fear of collapse at separation, which offers some clues to individual work with non-believing mothers. By giving them time to consider what qualities they find lacking in themselves and which they value in their partners, it is possible to convey clearly that their predicament is accepted and the reasons for their defensive behaviour understood. At a later stage, and at their own pace, they may also begin to assert themselves in the areas they regarded themselves as deficient, for example self-worth, setting limits, communication skills. They can become far less dependent upon their partner in those areas and much less likely to regard separation as losing a part of themselves. Coupled with the time to reflect upon their unenviable situation, and the provision of whatever practical help that is available, there can be at least some partnership and further exploration of the many confused and painful feelings they are experiencing (p269). We will not successfully convert all mothers to choosing their child and legal intervention to protect the child is often needed where the mother safeguards her adult relationship at all costs. A woman's allegiance to her partner may well be to avoid losing an important part of themselves, and, rather than acknowledge that she has misjudged her man, she will try all sorts of denials or strategies to put the most favourable interpretation on what has happened.

## Knowledge of the abuse taking place

One of the key debates in recent years has been whether or not the mother has known or suspected the sexual abuse of their child/ren. Historically, there was a strong belief that they *always* knew about it at some level (see Kempe and Kempe, 1978) although this is now beginning to give way to a recognition that they often did not. This is often because the sexual abuse takes place in their absence and the children are sworn or coerced into secrecy. Many children will go to great lengths not to let their mothers know (as well as others), although they often believe their mothers knew about the abuse when in fact they did not. Conversely, some children do not believe that their mother knew when in fact they did.

Friends may also insinuate that the mother must have known. Any insinuation from professionals that the mother is in some way to blame for what the perpetrator has done will deepen her emotional strife. Mothers caught in this tangled, dysfunctional web will find particular pain in such insinuations (Byerly, 1992).

There are some mothers who knew what was happening but were too intimidated or abused themselves to stop it. One mother who knew, slept with her child to protect her and put crackly paper under the bedroom door so she would wake when it opened. Workers do need to understand the devastating effect on mothers of learning of the sexual abuse. When the mother says 'I can't believe it' people think they are saying that they won't believe it. Mothers are either represented as collusive and offered no support, or else they are good mothers who believe in and protect the child so they are just left to get on with it. It is true that some children tell their mothers that someone has touched them and that the mothers don't believe or act to protect their children from further abuse. It is more common that the mother knows that something is wrong with her child but they are unclear about what that something might be.

Rickford (1992) noted that mothers of sexually abused children are frequently left alone to cope with assumptions of collusion. This may be coming from the child and only time and help will assist them in understanding that the mother did not know what was happening. As one mother indicated, 'She still hits and kicks me, and blames me. She said "You were cooking his dinner and let him come up and do the naughty things". She didn't realise that I didn't know'. Children see the mother as their protector, not the father or father-figure (Prendergast, 1991).

Todd (1989) in her sample in Sheffield found that that many of the youngsters had attempted to tell their mothers of the abuse. One had said 'Tell me if it happens again'. Another came home unexpectedly and found her daughter with the stepfather dressing in the bedroom. She claims

never to have known about the abuse. These cases show a profound level of denial by the mother, even when the evidence was overwhelming. In most of the cases, the mother put the perpetrator's needs first.

On occasions, the mother may have challenged the perpetrator about some of their behaviour (for example sharing a bath) only to be told they had the sexual hang-ups. One of the key problems is that suspicion is characterised by the inaccessibility of clear information about events conducted in secrecy, and uncertainty about the meaning of the information available.

In order to appraise a situation as potentially abusive, the mother must be sensitive to behavioural and/or mood changes or other clues. In some instances indicators are fairly clear, such as genital injury. In other situations the clues may be less obvious, such as atypical sexual curiosity. Professionals must remember that symptoms of incest are more apparent to professionals than to the public at large (discussed in detail in a later component). With the increasing trend towards male involvement in child care, it is unfair to blame the mother for this shared responsibility if something like sexual abuse occurs – particularly when Herman (1981) argued that this is likely to reduce such abuse. It is possible that denial may be a defence mechanism that protects mothers from confronting the emotional consequences of acknowledging that abuse is occurring, particularly if the mother was sexually abused herself. Mothers may also be overwhelmed by financial, marital, or other concerns and thus not notice clues that might be obvious under less stressful conditions.

There have been a number of lists developed to explain why it would have been difficult for a mother to know at the time their child was being sexually abused. These include:

- Most of the TV, videos, newspapers etc. tell us that sexual perpetrators are strangers or weirdos and monsters, not people you know.
- The perpetrator is usually someone known or trusted by you and would be the last person you would suspect.
- The perpetrator often manipulates the situation so they can give the 'love' and 'affection' to the child and prevents closeness between the mother and the children.
- The perpetrator often brings lots of presents and is seen as genuine in their care and concern for the children. This can easily deceive the

mother. A family may find themselves financially dependent on the abuser.

- The public is not provided with sufficient information which would alert them to the possibility of sexual abuse.
- The 'warning signs' (if they exist) are often non-specific signs of sexual abuse, for example stomach aches, nightmares, fears and phobias, that may put the thought in the back of your mind, but it is hard to see an overall picture. Also, the cause for these could be any number of things.
- The perpetrator may have a reasonable explanation for some of the child's behaviour and this may stop you looking for other reasons or cause you to lose faith in your own judgements or the explanation of the situation.
- The perpetrator may rationalise the child's behaviour so the mother loses faith in her own judgement.
- You may be a lone parent and there may be other children in the family. Lots of time and energy will therefore be taken up looking after lots of needs.
- You may have your own difficulties, for example recent bereavement, financial problems etc. and a change in a child's behaviour could be explained as due to these reasons.
- You may be blamed by the perpetrator for not satisfying him or being sick etc. This may make you feel like you have no power to change anything and the situation is your fault. The mother may lack self-esteem.
- The abuse will be well planned and hidden, highlighting that the perpetrator is aware that what they have done is wrong. It will be very difficult for you to detect. The perpetrator will go to great lengths to ensure that the child does not tell. Please refer to the later section on the *modus operandi* of the perpetrator and Calder (1999).
- The perpetrator may be violent and oppressive and it may be too frightening to speak about.
- Even if abuse is suspected, it may be hard to approach any professional about this for fear of what might happen.
- The perpetrator may control the mail and phone so it is impossible for you to communicate with others.
- In society, as a carer, you are not well listened to and your job is not always seen as worthwhile.
- There is limited support for carers who want to take their children away from abuse.

(Rose and Savage, 1995)

Peake and Fletcher (1997: 16–20) provided some stimulating debate around this subject, geared at helping mothers explore some ideas around the issue. They organise their section around three ideas: that sexual abuse of a child is always the responsibility of the perpetrator; it is never the fault of the child victims; and mothers rarely know at the time that their child is being sexually abused by someone they know and trust. In relation to this final point, these authors highlight four reasons that underpin this for most mothers:

- Children cannot tell about the sexual abuse: they are either too young or do not have the language to tell what is happening to them. They may also have been threatened, bribed or tricked by the perpetrator and may see no reason to tell their mother.
- Society has been slow to recognise that sexual abuse of children does occur and that the principal perpetrators are those close to them, not strangers. Society and not just mothers have defences that maintain that sexual abuse couldn't happen.
- There is no public education about child sexual abuse and its warning signs and thus mothers have no basis on which they could have known.
- Perpetrators are clever. They often groom the mother as well as the child, and the mother finds it difficult to accept that the person they know, need and trust so much has abused their child.

### Research findings

Whilst it has often been argued that mothers always know when a child is being sexually abused within the family, research more recently has been challenging this. For example, Jane Gilgun (1984) found that sexual abuse of one family member can take place for several years and no one but the perpetrator and the victim know about it.

Hooper (1989) found that all the sexual abuse in her sample was committed when the mother was not in the home. She suggested that it may be more productive, therefore, to explore the process of discovery (over time) rather than categorising women into those who did, and those who did not, know. There are many different levels of knowledge between total ignorance with no suspicions, through to full knowledge and understanding of the events. The level of knowledge depends on the available sources of information and on the coping strategies mothers adopt in response to the trauma discovery. Sources of information within the family include signs of distress in the child; observations of the perpetrator's or child's behaviour; the child telling directly or more often giving indirect and conflicting messages and the perpetrator confessing. Sources of information from outside the family might include the media or the experiences of family or friends. For the mothers, the discovery process was rarely straightforward and often chaotic, involving, for some, suspicions, confrontation and denial, conflict over the meaning of behaviour, self-doubt, and sometimes uncertainty about who the perpetrator was. Women may alternate between resisting the recognition of abuse for fear of the consequences and trying to gather proof and assess the evidence. This process may continue over months or years.

Disclosure can either be a specific, single event or a cumulative process over time. For example, Hooper (1992: 54) argued that discovery of the abuse is 'an active and interactive process which develops over time and has no clear beginning or end'. It may involve the mother and child only, or more commonly a range of others, both within and outside the family. It may involve a period of not knowing about the abuse, followed by a period of suspecting, followed by a period of knowing, or one or both of the first two stages may be omitted if the mother finds out fairly quickly after the abuse starts. The process is interwoven both with the woman's own response to loss and with decisions taken about family relationships and is not therefore a straightforward linear one. In some circumstances, suspicions can only be entertained where the mother has harnessed sufficient resources to address the possibility, particularly around her self-worth. The ability to confirm suspicions is dependent not only on the mother's motivation, but also on her interaction with both the child and the perpetrator, and the child's ability to confirm or refute (age and language issues). Where the child was unable to verbally confirm their suspicions, this impacted on the mother's ability to verify their concerns.

Hooper (1992: 54) found that many mothers spoke of not knowing, accompanied by reasons as to why they did not, as well as those who felt that something was wrong, and of suspecting

abuse, but needing their suspicions confirmed. There is a clear link between a mother's motivation to find out when compared with the losses accompanied with verification of sexual abuse. Some mothers did become pre-occupied with the need to find out and this contributed ultimately to their failure to protect. Many mothers may now consider statements that the victim has imparted at earlier points, and with the benefit of hindsight now believes them to have been an indirect or unspecific attempt at disclosure. Some mothers may have had their suspicions, but were unclear as to who the perpetrator might be.

In her sample, Hooper found that 66 per cent of the women where the perpetrator lived in the home, did not know of the abuse for a substantial period of time (ranging from one to five years). Within this group, 62 per cent found out in a sudden, clearly identifiable incident, although that was often followed by a period of reassessment, recurring confusion or ambivalence.

Kelly (1988) argued that women's responses to their own experiences of sexual abuse include 'forgetting and minimising', and they may employ similar strategies when their children are sexually abused. Such responses are better understood as coping strategies rather than as collusion with the abuse itself.

Breckenbridge and Berreen (1992) reported that between 40 and 60 per cent of workers believe that mothers 'know about' the incest. Their answers revealed that 10.3 per cent of them felt that a mother would know in most cases and 60.8 per cent felt that a mother would know in some cases. This means that overall 71.1 per cent of workers would have in their minds when dealing with a disclosure of incest, that mothers know – at least in some if not all cases. Whilst this does not equate with them being responsible for the abuse, it does lead to the view that they failed to act protectively towards the child. Conversely, some 28.9 per cent of workers believed that the mother would rarely know that incest was occurring before disclosure.

Johnson (1992) noted that there is considerable disagreement about how much a mother knows of the incest while it occurs. She found that some mothers in her sample suspected abuse (that is, had suspicions, especially if they had been victims of sexual abuse themselves) whilst others did not know (some may have been absent through work, or were unaware of the clues that might induce some concerns). She acknowledges that it is difficult for persons outside the incest family to believe that a mother does not know that her child is being sexually abused by her partner. Yet it is not a simple matter of whether the mother knew or did not know, consciously or unconsciously. Society expects mothers to be all-knowing about what goes on in the family and the home. Johnson found that 'there are complex explanations for why any mother may not recognise, see, acknowledge, interpret, understand, or know a multitude of things that happen to her children' (p25).

Other salient points from research have included that the perpetrator admitted to 22 per cent more sexual involvement than children disclosed (thus the mother would not have known about the true extent of the abuse previously (Terry, 1990); and gender differences did emerge in that there was a higher rate of disclosure among girls, although once boys had disclosed, they provided as much detail about alleged abuse as girls did (Devoe and Faller, 1999).

Bagley and Naspini (1987) found that in a sample of 44 mothers of sexually abused children only four had any knowledge that sexual abuse had taken place before the child disclosed and those four felt powerless to stop it. Thirty-eight of the women, when informed of the abuse, took immediate action to protect their children.

## The mother's role in the sexual abuse

### Active participant, 'turning a blind eye', or innocent bystander?

Whilst the role of the mother is repeatedly over-empathised, it can play a contributing role in some cases. Rejection, ridicule, defiance, infidelity, the withholding of sex, as well as other behaviours can trigger reactions in the perpetrator that increase the propensity to sexually abuse. Moreover, the desertion or absence of a partner and accompanying dynamics can enhance the risk for the sexual abuse of children (Faller, 1990).

Engel (1994: 116–18) set out the following ways in which opportunities may have been presented for the child to be sexually abused:

- By denying the child attention and affection: causing the children to be vulnerable to someone who could exploit their needs.

- By leaving the children unsupervised, or poorly supervised, for lengthy periods of time: often necessary for the perpetrator to groom the situation for the abuse.
- By leaving the children with caretakers who were abusive: even though the mother may have been unaware about the real risks, she may have been aware that they drank or were emotionally disturbed.
- By abusing the children herself: can lead to the children not learning to value themselves and this opens up the pathways for the perpetrator to ask them to do almost anything.
- By ignoring obvious signs of abuse and cries for help: this may be due to their own experiences of sexual abuse and their need to self-protect before having to take any action to stop the current abuse.
- By making the child feel that they would not be believed if they told: this may be a general message given to the child by the mother who has told the child they have exaggerated something or made it up.
- By showing other people that the children were not valued: by showing disdain for the children she implies they deserve what they get.
- By making the child feel that she could not, would not, protect them: maybe because the mother feels as helpless or as powerless as the child, thus making it impossible for her to do anything about the abuse.

There are cases where a non-abusing parent will have explicitly concealed the sexual abuse, and workers need to understand why, as there is still some potential to work with them later if they accept and believe the sexual abuse has taken place (Smith, 1995).

### Research findings

Dietz and Craft (1980) examined the attitudes of 200 child protection workers in Iowa about mothers in families where incest had occurred. They found that 87 per cent of the respondents believed that mothers gave their unconscious consent to incest and that 65 per cent believed that she was equally responsible. They also found that the professional attitudes were related to reading the professional literature. Indeed, this was moderately related to believing that mothers gave their unconscious consent to the abuse.

Faller (1991b) reported that, in a study of polyincestuous families, 38.8 per cent of her sample consisted of female abusers – mothers abusing with male partners. She states clearly that the possibility that a mother may be actively involved in sexually abusing her child cannot be overlooked. What should also not be overlooked is the fact that the mother will sense this, and her feeling that every move she makes will be scrutinised and judged will be intensified.

Scott and Flowers (1988) queried 24 adolescents and 26 adult female victims of father-daughter incest about their mothers' responses. Twenty-nine per cent of adolescent and 50 per cent of adult victims believed their mothers knew of the incest but failed to intervene. Maisch (1973) found that 12 per cent of mothers in their sample of 78 incest cases before the German courts knew of and tolerated an ongoing incestuous relationship and three per cent colluded with the incest.

## Questions that need answering include

- Was she involved?
- Was she coerced into involvement?

It is important to explore with the mother ways in which she can apologise to the child for anything that she did to set her up for the abuse (consciously or unconsciously) and then ways in which she can now support her. The child may well be angry with the mother for lots of reasons, such as failing to protect her, for looking the other way, for setting her up for the abuse, for blaming her, for nor listening when she tried to tell her, for not believing her, for remaining with the perpetrator, or for not providing her with the necessary love and attention she needed.

## Position regarding the child's disclosure

*Belief or disbelief? Stand by your man or your child?*

In this section, I will deal with the issue of maternal belief and support, given that they are inextricably linked.

### Belief

*The disclosure of incest differs from other family crises in that the mother is asked to believe something she may not want to believe, to interpret something that is at best difficult for her to comprehend, and to resolve the conflict*

*between her roles as central support figure to both her child and her male partner at a time when her own social, emotional, and economic supports may be at risk.*
(Everson et al., 1989)

Humphreys (1992) has persuasively argued that in terms of belief in her child's sexual abuse, the mother's response was characterised by fluidity and change. The mother could move between feelings of ambivalence, strong belief, and disbelief about the abuse. The fluidity in her belief was ongoing from the earliest stages of discovery and was expressed in the mother's attainment of a stance of belief in the disclosure and then further in the maintenance of that position. The vulnerability of the mother of the sexually abused child in the aftermath of disclosure is under-estimated by practitioners. There is a dearth of services for mothers commensurate with the crisis they experience, which indicates a failure to recognise their importance to the child victim and the fluid nature of belief. Understanding disclosure from the mother's perspective can be crucial as assumptions are often made about the mother's ability to believe, support and protect her child early in the investigation.

Mothers reported that the attainment of belief was inextricably linked to the process of disclosure and discovery. For some mothers disclosure was the end point of a long drawn-out process during which they had become increasingly concerned or suspicious about their children's behaviour. For others, disclosure was a 'bolt from the blue' for which they were completely unprepared. Regardless of the process of discovery, all mothers in this sample experienced a period in which they were unconvinced that the sexual abuse of their child has occurred. This may have been a period of five minutes while the evidence was placed before them or a more lasting state. Three mothers in this sample, at the end of the six-month period, could be said to have remained unconvinced that the abuse had occurred. However, each mother was left with some uncertainty.

All mothers also experienced periods of ambivalence in which they did not know whether to believe or disbelieve that the abuse of their child had occurred. This ambivalence took different forms for different women and included both emotional and cognitive aspects. For one group it was a time in which further evidence was gathered to support disclosure. For other mothers, the evidence was there and the disclosure made, however, the mother was not emotionally ready to confront the abuse.

Ambivalence does not only refer to *attaining* a stance of belief. Seven mothers in this sample said that they believed that the abuse had occurred. However, they had difficulty *maintaining* protection and support for the child. For five mothers, this was due to the perpetrator's continued influence in their lives whereby he would continue to deny the abuse, seek their love and support, promise to reform and generally undermined the mother-child relationship. Three other mothers, all victims of childhood sexual abuse, experienced a breakdown in the relationship with their daughters following disclosure. As the mother's relationships changed, her stance of belief that the abuse had occurred, or that the child was seriously affected or in danger, shifted.

Twenty-one of the twenty-two mothers also experienced a period at the other end of the continuum in which they were able to act congruently with the belief that the sexual abuse had occurred, and were able to communicate this to the child with protection and support.

This study showed that mothers throughout the sample period could move in either direction along the continuum from belief to ambivalence to disbelief and vice versa. Such movement suggests that the mother's perception of the event is not fixed and needs to be understood by practitioners who make judgements about the mother's position early in the assessment period. The process by which these changes occurred was complex, and experienced by women throughout the sample. The difficulties in sustaining a stance of belief, protection and support however, were much greater for women who were attached or who had ambivalent feelings towards the perpetrator who had been her partner prior to disclosure. This study indicated that three factors provided more powerful restraints to the mother's ability to comprehend that her child was being sexually abused. They were the power of the perpetrator over the child to keep the secret; the destruction of the communication between the mother and child that develops as a result of the imposition of the secret by the perpetrator; and the cleverness of the perpetrator in hiding his sexual abuse.

Without an admission of guilt and acceptance of responsibility, the path of the mother and the victim is doubly difficult. A particular problem is that the mother is left to judge whether the abuse has occurred or not.

Mothers also spoke of the emotional ingredients of 'belief' as against the more concrete elements mentioned in the previous section. It frequently occurred as a spontaneous, emotional reaction, a natural defence against traumatic news, and parallels the evidence in the literature about a person's initial response of denial in the face of death or grief. Mothers spoke of functioning on at least two different levels as a means of coping with their aversion to the traumatic news: the mother was cognitively saying 'no, it's not happening', while at the same time having feelings congruent with belief. The women reported that this lack of congruence did not cease after the initial shock had worn off. Because belief is a fluid notion, different levels of understanding operate simultaneously. The initial response was not necessarily an indicator of how women would behave towards their children later.

There is a consensus that human beings react with some similarity in situations of acute stress. Twenty-one of the twenty-two mothers testified to being numbed by the blow. Then, as the full impact of the situation was confronted they experienced a downward slump in behaviour wherein they felt confused, disorientated and helpless. After a period of disorganisation, they attempted to reorganise their lives using whatever mechanisms were available including denial, minimisation, active involvement in 'the fight', and/or finding new strengths and support with which to confront the problem.

This description exemplified important aspects of the mothers' response. However, two important qualifications stemming from the mothers' reported experience need to be made. First, mothers did not experience this crisis once, but could track many occasions both prior to (if they had witnessed a marked inexplicable change in their child's behaviour) and in the months and years following disclosure. Their experiences suggested that for many women it was a life transition dotted with a number of active crisis states, rather than a single point of intensive crisis. It thus resembles a long, grieving process as mothers come to terms with the many losses which child sexual assault has wrought in their and their children's lives. Second, crisis was not a linear state but, through the necessity to reorganise, was connected to the construct of belief in both its cognitive and emotional aspects.

Thus, each time stresses were placed on the mothers by either the perpetrator, the child, or the legal, economic and social consequences of the disclosure, the subjective state of the mother could be affected.

Humphreys found that a constellation of factors assisted mothers in the process of lifting the blind which had hidden the child's reality of sexual abuse from them. These factors included the age of the child, physical evidence of sexual abuse, police statements, past knowledge of the perpetrator's sexual deviance, the mother's own experience of child sexual assault, and professional and private support. As belief and support are not static states, these depicted areas are ones which may assist or restrain mothers in believing their child's disclosure. One factor in itself did not appear to be enough to confirm the mother's belief that abuse had occurred (reproduced with the kind permission of Cathy Humphreys).

There are a number of other factors relevant to the mother's response to any disclosure. These might include her relationship with the perpetrator; the nature of the child's relationship with the perpetrator; the power of the perpetrator in their life; the character of the intimate relationship between the mother and the perpetrator; the duration of the abuse; and the violation of trust. So, where mothers are powerless in their relationship with the perpetrator, they will respond to the disclosure with a proportionate sense of powerlessness. A good sexual relationship between the mother and the perpetrator can be a major restraint to women believing that sexual abuse could have occurred. The opposite is also true: mothers can find it easier to believe the disclosure if they know the perpetrator is sexually deviant in some way. Mothers may also be influenced by the child's age. Some mothers will not contemplate that their very young children had been abused, but tend to believe and sometimes blame older children.

There are some very clear obstacles to believing the child and these include: a parental history of abuse, which they promised would not happen to their child; a belief that they must terminate a relationship with the perpetrator once abuse is confirmed; excessive dependence on the perpetrator; or prior family rejection of the perpetrator, resulting in a situation where to believe is to accept family condemnation (Berliner, 1991). Where mothers have problematic relationships with their children and a lack of

'maternal protective behaviours', they are less likely to believe that abuse has taken place. This is even greater where there is a strong emotional tie between the mother and the perpetrator (Craig et al., 1989).

Faller (1990) argued that there are a number of dynamics which may influence a mother's willingness to believe: acknowledgement of shortcomings as a parent; acknowledgement of shortcomings as a spouse; the decision regarding leaving or staying with the perpetrator; facing the practical consequences of that decision; coping with professionals' intrusions. A mothers shock (or numbness) associated with the disclosure may also contribute to a mother's difficulties around believing (Byerly, 1985).

Mothers may find the allegations totally unbelievable to themselves: either because the acts described are beyond anything they could ever imagine one person doing to another or because they care about the person against whom the allegations are made so much that they cannot believe they would do such a thing.

It is important to remember that children rarely lie about sexual abuse, except to minimise their involvement. Much more often, they are afraid to tell or, when they do tell, they tend to downplay the actual abusive episodes. We need to remember that younger children usually provide less complete and less detailed testimony than older children, and there can be incomplete recall or a lack of clarity about frequency, dates, times, etc. Older children are often more aware of the power of such accusations, and can thus use them as instruments of manipulation. There are some cases where children do distort the truth in some fashion, sometimes exaggerating details or making up stories that indirectly express their anger or provide satisfaction to a third party, for example their mother in custody dispute cases (Hillman and Solek-Tefft, 1988: 47).

We should remember that accusations of sexual abuse are very difficult to make as they go against basic human loyalties and attachments. Children usually have great anxieties as to whether they will be believed and possibly fear the outcome if they are, such as the splitting up of the family and possibly being unwelcome. Older children may have an appreciation of the fact that 'the authorities' take such allegations seriously, and therefore that making an allegation is a way of drawing attention to their predicament or hurting somebody.

## Support

Rollins and Thomas (1979: 320) defined parental support as 'the behaviour manifested by a parent toward a child that makes the child feel comfortable in the presence of the parent and confirms in the child's mind that he is basically accepted and approved as a person by the parent'.

> *The construct of support is made up of both belief and protective action. Belief involves validation of the child's account, placing the responsibility on the adult rather than the child, and conveying an attitude of concern for the child. Protective action is defined in various ways but basically involves the mother backing up her belief by behaviours that protect the child from further abuse and aid in recovery, such as co-operating with the child protection services and criminal justice agencies, removing the child from perpetrator access, and seeking counselling for the child.*
>
> (Corcoran, 1998)

Humphreys (1992) differentiated professional from social support. She found that all the mothers required the help of professionals to confirm sexual abuse and to give appropriate information and encouragement to enable them to follow through with effective action. The importance of professional support is also illustrated by the mother's vulnerability to the perpetrator's definition of the situation when professionals withdrew the intensive involvement which was present during the initial investigation. This was particularly so in cases where mothers were emotionally involved with the perpetrator. The mother's position is crucial for many children, since they may feel that she is the only person who can 'give permission' for them to disclose. The mother may find herself in an impossible dilemma: Butler-Sloss (1988: 8) comments that 'in the conflict between her man and her child, the relationship with the man, the economic and other support which she receives from him may disincline her to accept the truth of the allegation'. The problem is worse when the child cannot say anything directly or clearly to the mother about sexual abuse. It will seem to be a choice between the word of the professional and the possible perpetrator.

In Humphreys' study, mothers who were acting with belief and protection towards their victimised children were in receipt of a greater level of personal and professional support than those mothers who were at the stage of being unconvinced or ambivalent. However, the relationship between support and belief is complex. Mothers in this sample who moved to a position of consistent belief and protection for the child were not attached to the perpetrator. They were therefore less constrained by the perpetrator's tactics and relatively speaking had greater assistance from friends and family. The three mothers who were unconvinced the abuse had occurred, either named the perpetrator as their major source of support, together with a network of friends and family who did not encourage the child, or they had no close emotional support. A problem for mothers was that the very nature of child sexual assault structured their isolation and ability to talk with others. They named factors, such as the perpetrator's tactics to isolate them, both prior and post disclosure; protection of the child's privacy; protection of close friends and family who might themselves already be very distressed at the disclosure; time constraints imposed by the necessity of working to support themselves; and lack of understanding by friends and family of the ambivalent feelings they may have towards the abuser.

Support has different dimensions and levels and appears to have measurable effects on the child's well-being. Most mothers respond with some support for children who disclose sexual abuse, although they frequently stop short of full support. One of the most commonly suggested adaptive responses is to convey a sense of belief in the child's report. It is also important that the mother conveys to the child that the abuse was completely the responsibility of the abuser instead of becoming angry at the child or blaming them for the event. Instead of emphasising the child's victim status, it is important to stress that the child is a survivor (Esquilin, 1987). It is helpful for mothers to respond in a matter-of-fact manner while continuing their routine, as well as reassuring the child that no lasting harm will result from their experiences. Other suggested reactions have included protecting the child from further harm, acknowledging the courage it took for the child to disclose, accepting the child's feelings about the event, and reinforcing the child's disclosure by praising him or her for 'doing the right thing' (Wurtele and Miller-Perrin, 1992).

In many cases the mother is not in a position to offer support for reasons not always considered or clearly understood. Frequently, maladaptive responses would be to doubt the veracity of the child's report or to deny that the abuse has occurred. Overreactions can also contribute to the child's sense of stigmatisation or feeling as though they are different from others or 'damaged goods'. Other inappropriate actions include over-protectiveness (for example restricting usual activities) which may have the paradoxical effect of making children more vulnerable to abuse by disrupting their lives and lessening their ability to control their environment (Regehr, 1990). In addition, mothers may be reluctant to touch child victims, which may reinforce their sense of being 'damaged goods.' Professionals should be encouraged to provide normal expressions of affection to prevent these negative outcomes and to reassure victims that normal affection is quite different than abusive touching. Roberts and Taylor (1993) found that some mothers minimised the abuse, failed to act, and either blamed or rejected the child. They also emotionally withdrew and were inactive. Children are affected adversely when confidants do not support them, particularly where it is perceived by the child as nothing can be done.

Everson et al. (1989) found that negative chain events are set in motion when professionals perceive low maternal support. Children with blaming or rejecting mothers are much more likely to be removed from their homes; this may entail testimony in the court, changing schools, and otherwise being removed from familiar activities and friends. Furthermore, any support a child may be receiving from important others, or simply from familiar routine may be undermined by removal from home.

### Research findings

Berliner and Conte (1995) found that the majority of children characterised the initial reaction as supportive (54 per cent). Twenty-six per cent reported a reaction of shock/surprise, while 15 per cent described upset/sadness, 11 per cent anger, eight per cent disbelief, and one per cent fear. Lyon and Kouloumpos-Lenares (1987) reported that though 70 per cent of the mothers believed in their children's sexual abuse, only 50 per cent responded with protective action, emotional support and co-operation with protective agencies. Another 26 per cent were appropriately protective in action by getting the perpetrator to leave the home, providing only

supervised contact, or making other child care arrangements. However, these mothers were also ambivalent, denying their children's need for treatment or additional support. Twenty-two per cent of the victims' mothers were non-protective. In this study, belief and action toward protecting the child were strongly associated. None of the non-believing mothers provided a protective response, while 58 per cent of the believing mothers were actively helpful.

### A continuum of protectiveness was developed by De Young (1994):

- High protective: the woman behaviourally responds to the disclosure or discovery of the incest by removing the perpetrator from the home; calling the police or social services; and bringing her daughter for medical evaluation.
- Medium protective: the woman behaviourally responds to the disclosure or discovery of the incest by verbally confronting her husband; talking with her daughter to gather details about the incest; and/or seeking advice from an appropriate professional.
- Low protective: the woman behaviourally responds to the disclosure or discovery of the paternal incest by seeking emotional support for herself, her daughter, and/or her husband from a person who is not a professional, and may include a member of the immediate or extended family, a friend, or a social acquaintance.
- Non-protective: the woman behaviourally responds to the disclosure or discovery of the paternal incest by doing nothing; physically withdrawing from, or leaving the family or home; refusing to co-operate with, or lying to professionals with investigation responsibility; and/or punishing her daughter.

From this schema, 10 per cent of the women were evaluated as high protective; 25 per cent were classified as medium protective; 25 per cent as low protective; and 40 per cent as non-protective.

Everson et al. (1989) evaluated parental reactions within two weeks of victim disclosure. Parental reactions toward 88 victims (aged six to 17 years) were determined by combining clinical ratings in three areas, including:

1. Emotional support (ranging from commitment and support of child, to threats, hostility, and abandoning the child psychologically).

2. Belief of the child (ranging from making a clear, public statement of belief, to totally denying that the abuse occurred).
3. Action toward perpetrator (ranging from actively demonstrating disapproval of their abusive behaviour, to choosing them over the child).

Where all three criteria were met, the mothers were believed to have offered full support to the child. Results indicated that 44 per cent of mothers were rated as providing consistent support, 32 per cent as ambivalent or inconsistently supportive, and 24 per cent were rated as non-supportive or rejecting. Maternal support was not related to victim characteristics (ie age, gender, race) or mother's educational level, but was related to the perpetrator's relationship with the mother. Mothers were most supportive of their children when the perpetrator was an ex-spouse and least supportive when the abuser was a current boyfriend, as the child's disclosure appeared to be more of a threat to her emotional and financial security. Mother's disbelief might also have been associated with the fact that all boyfriends denied the sexual abuse, compared to two-thirds of the ex-husbands. Most studies tend to support the finding that mothers have less of a problem with divided loyalty when the perpetrator is not a family member. Everson et al. (1989) found that maternal support was a primary predictor of overall psychological functioning for the child.

The circumstances of the disclosure may also be related to maternal reaction. For example, if a child told the mother about the abuse soon after it occurred rather than delaying for a period of time, the mother was more likely to be concerned and protective (Tufts, 1984). More specifically, when the child told the mother about the abuse, she was more likely to believe it when it was revealed to professionals first. The gender of the victim may well be important, with mothers being more protective of sons rather than daughters (Tufts, 1984).

Salt et al. (1990) found that the majority of mothers responded to the revelation of sexual abuse in a very appropriate manner. They expressed concern about the child's welfare and took appropriate steps to protect the child. They did find that for some mothers, their childhood histories affected how they responded after the disclosure. Those who reported having a poor relationship with either parent appeared to have less capacity to be concerned about their sexually abused daughters. Those mothers who did not protect their daughters seemed either to have experienced poor relationships with the maternal grandmothers or, as children, to have had mothers who were absent. Those mothers who described having poor relationships with their own parents were more likely to have their children removed from their care (Leifer et al., 1993).

It is important that workers do retain a strong understanding that some mothers do not believe and therefore do not support their children post-disclosure. Where mothers are less supportive, the children are at greater risk of removal (Pellegrin and Wagner, 1990). For professionals, the key question is whether this is a temporary or a permanent situation.

Leifer et al. (1993) studied various factors associated with supportive maternal behaviour toward sexually abused children and found that mothers who abused alcohol and who had limited social support were least likely to be supportive of their children. They also found a relationship between low maternal supportive behaviour and low child functioning. The mother's reaction to, and belief in, the child's report of the sexual abuse may be very important to the child, and may well constitute a protective factor that could minimise the negative effects of the abuse.

The mother's support is an important factor in the recovery process due to the need of the girl to be loved and accepted by her mother; as well as telling her it was not her fault, thus removing some of the perceived guilt. In this study, the mothers who acknowledged their own past childhood sexual abuse were perceived as more supportive than the mothers who reported that they had never been sexually abused. This has not always been the case. Friedrich (1990) found that mothers who were themselves victims of sexual abuse may be unable to support their own children because of their own unresolved sexual abuse issues. This may be explained by such factors as by responding in a manner similar to how they would have wished their own mothers to respond to them in a crisis. The results also show that the daughters perceived their mothers as less supportive than the mothers perceived themselves.

The research did identify similar perceptions of appropriate ways to show support, with the two most common themes being the need for the mother to believe the sexual abuse happened and the need for the mother to participate in the treatment process. The one area of disagreement centred on independence and space, with the adolescents wanting more of both, whilst the mothers thought this was just so they could have the total freedom to do what they want. This appears to be a consistent part of the developmental process where the mothers struggle to set limits and the adolescents strive for freedom.

### Issues to consider

This whole area is an important component when workers are looking for the way forward with a case, yet the expectations of mothers may differ slightly from the consideration applied for workers. Following Cleveland, professionals have been issued with very detailed guidance for the interviewing of child witnesses (Home Office, 1992) and this requires a very intensive training and accreditation programme. Mothers do not have this preparation although a great deal is expected of them, and they can be wrongly judged if they do not immediately espouse total belief with the child's disclosure. This is almost a case of double standards.

Signs that a mother has taken the abuse seriously include listening to what the child says about the impact of the experience, acknowledging the distress and pain for the child, placing responsibility for the abuse clearly with the adults involved, and taking all possible steps to ensure that the child is safe from further abuse by the same, or a different, perpetrator (Sayers, 1995).

A mother's response to the disclosure of sexual abuse appears to be influenced by many factors. Professional attention to the mother, however, can be limited and shaped by the fact that professionals feel intense pressure to quickly investigate and assess the situation for legal purposes and protection issues. Serious problems can arise when an initial maternal response is misunderstood and negatively interpreted by professionals with the authority to remove children from the home. It is questionable in this environment just how free a woman feels to respond in a fashion accurately reflecting her true emotional and mental state (Howard, 1993). In such a situation, assessment of her position with respect to belief or disbelief of the disclosure will be skewed at best, and is unlikely to strike at the

true source of her problems or achieve the desired goals. Moreover, if the mother senses blame, her energies may well be deflected from supporting the child to defending herself. This in turn has the potential to confirm professional suspicions and negative judgements.

Many mothers sense that something is not quite right but do not dream that sexual abuse might be the cause. Those that might suspect sexual abuse as the cause often convince themselves they are reading too much into the situation. After the sexual abuse has been disclosed, they often ask themselves how this could have happened to their child, where were they to allow it to happen, etc? Ask the mother what she did when she thought something was wrong with her child, and then what she did when she found out about the abuse.

### Questions that need answering include

- Did she believe straight away?
- Who had to tell her for her to believe it?
- Would she believe the child about further abuse?
- What does she think it would be helpful to know to keep her child safe/to know if her child is being abused?
- What did she do when she found out about the abuse?
- Why did she respond in a particular way?
- What could she have done differently?
- Why?

Sometimes hearing the child's account, particularly if she were not told directly, will help the mother conclude that sexual abuse has taken place. She can then tell the child that she had been told what they said and that she is glad about this and does believe them.

In assessing a mother's position, professionals need to consider whether the parent is minimising the extent of the abuse. This is understandable in the immediate crisis of discovery, but becomes less acceptable over time. More worrying are parents who disbelieve what the child has disclosed. In part, they may still be leaving open the possibility that, with additional information, they may believe the child's disclosure. This often needs to be the admission by the perpetrator or medical evidence or a criminal conviction. Where these are not available, workers need to actively help mothers try and make sense of conflicting information and in particular how to select the 'right' information. Using a child's statement can be helpful as it gives the mother the opportunity to come to terms with what the child has experienced. The same statement can then become the focal point of further work with the family.

Workers may want to adopt circular questioning to engage non-believing mothers into some areas of discussion. For example, they can be asked to think through what the child was alleging and consider what that experience may have been like. Why would they lie? It may also be appropriate for the mother to view the memorandum taped interview out of the presence of the child, and the transcript of the interview with the abuser (particularly where some partial admissions exist, or where there are known discrepancies and the mother will identify this and thus question any denial of the offences).

Craig et al. (1989) suggest that workers who work with mothers who do not believe the abuse has occurred, face feelings of helplessness, despair and frustration, yet they must go on to assess why the mothers are unable to do this. The important thing is not so much to establish why the mother failed to protect, but one of establishing the expectations of mothers as responsible parents.

Workers should always allow the mothers time and space to effect some change to their originating stance at the point of disclosure as reactions are often transitory.

It is important that workers discover what characteristics of the mother, her home situation and history, aspects of the abuse, or child characteristics determine her level of support for the child.

Rivera (1988) argued that given most mothers are confused post-disclosure, they need someone to guide them through the process without blaming them or making them feel guilty. The assessment process thus needs to be conducted without insinuating that the mother is somehow responsible for the abuse.

## Position regarding responsibility for the abuse (what am I responsible for?)

Several writers have tried to charge mothers with indirect responsibility for the abuse. For example, by failing to provide sexual gratification for their partners, mothers in incestuous families may indirectly foster father-daughter incest. A considerable amount of the early written material suggested that:

> When a mother withdraws from her family, her children and husband may turn to one another for support, practical assistance or comfort and the foundations of an incestuous relationship are laid. In other cases a man deprived of his conjugal rights may turn to the nearest available source of gratification – a dependent child.
>
> (CIBA, 1984: 9)

Justice and Justice (1979) have similarly portrayed mothers of abused children as 'frigid' and not wanting sex with their husbands. If you follow this line, then you will clearly attribute responsibility to mothers without assessing the individual cases.

In many cases, the responsibility for the sexual abuse is not focused for long on the perpetrator, and is often filtered quickly down onto the mother or the child, or both. Most mothers remain wedded to their responsibilities of maintaining the family and relationships even after the form of the family has changed (Orr, 1995). She found that there were many prescriptions for women post-disclosure – courts, counselling appointments, parenting courses – but very few for the men. The mothers also projected forward to assume the role of protectors of their grandchildren.

Mothers and daughters need to realise that every time they blame each other for the abuse, they absolve the perperator of their responsibility. Mothers are never responsible for the sexual abuse unless they actively or consciously encouraged it. It is important, however, that workers do not absolve mothers of their responsibilities, but rather bring their expectations and judgements into a realistic perspective.

Mothers need to be clear that the perpetrator alone is responsible for what they do. Perpetrators demonstrate each day an ability to control their behaviour in their work place and with others, so it follows that they must accept responsibility when they do not. However, next to denying the childhood sexual abuse entirely, the most common thing that perpetrators do is to make excuses for their behaviour (see Calder and Skinner, 1999, for a fuller discussion in this area). They may blame the child, the mother, or someone else. Often, even those who do admit to their actions, never actually accept responsibility for them.

As Sgroi (1982) has noted, the ability to be an effective ally for the child depends on allocating responsibility clearly to the perpetrator. Women should never be held accountable for someone else's behaviour nor should they have imposed on them unrealistic expectations about constant vigilance or ascribed to them the power to protect which they simply do not have. Yet we do have to consider what children have a right to expect within the family setting and this must include some measure of protection and nurture from their mother. The crucial issue is that women have some responsibility for protecting their children but all too often this is interpreted as sole responsibility (Todd and Ellis, 1992).

The issue of responsibility is a key one for mothers and this needs to be addressed quickly by workers. Mothers will often feel guilty about allowing the abuse to have happened in the first place and for allowing it to continue. They need to be told that the perpetrator has abused his position of power and responsibility by sexually abusing the child. It is the perpetrator who is responsible for cognitively distorting the child's behaviour as provocative, and the mother is often not responsible for what has happened. The mother may need to work through her feelings of guilt in order for her to shift responsibility for the abuse from herself to the perpetrator. This is important as it challenges her positive picture of the perpetrator and forces her to reassess her view of him, often with painful consequences.

Smith (1994) notes that the mother's position regarding the responsibility for the abuse is of less importance than her belief that it happened. Indeed, if she is able to discuss who is responsible for the abuse, then there is at least an acknowledgement that it has taken place. There are situations where the blame is targeted on the child and this is indicative of their likely removal from the family. The perpetrator often denies the abuse and their admission is a prerequisite for the mother attributing total responsibility to the perpetrator. The mother then needs to know how the perpetrator manipulated the situation to make it appear that the child was responsible for the sexual abuse.

Many child victims feel responsible for the abuse. Indeed, the perpetrator encourages this to increase the child's sense of entrapment that facilitates the continuation of the sexual abuse. The child's sense of responsibility can become distorted. They can feel overly responsible even for things that are clearly not their responsibility.

They may feel they are guilty and need to be punished (self-harm). If it is the child and not the perpetrator who is removed from the family home, then this further complicates the issue of responsibility. Many children also locate responsibility with their mothers and so a lot of work is needed to help them shift their view on this. The mother and the child are never responsible for the perpetrator's actions.

There needs to be a differentiation between responsibility for protecting the child and responsibility for or involvement in the abuse itself. A mother has five possible responsibilities towards her daughter:

- The mother did not know about the abuse: either because of her reactions to the disclosure or from circumstances in which the abuse took place. Mothers may have known nothing about the abuse because she was not in the home when it was taking place; she was caring for other children; the perpetrator ensured silence; it occurred in the context of normal family situations, such as bathing or putting to bed and each incident took a very short time and no-one else could possibly have known about it. Mothers are helped if the child states they believe that the mother did not know about the abuse.

- The mother suspected that sexual abuse was taking place but could not acknowledge it: some mothers pick up signals from their daughters that something is amiss, only to block or disregard the information. The mother may also doubt her perceptions, believing herself to be crazy for believing that such a thing could happen. The child who tried to tell her mother only to have the information ignored will conclude that her mother failed to protect her from further abuse.

- The mother knew of the abuse but did nothing to stop it: the child may have told the mother on more than one occasion, only to be responded to with disbelief, anger, or resigned acceptance. The child would conclude that the mother failed to protect her.

- The mother knew of the abuse and condoned it: the mother may even have set up the abuse by putting her in situations where she would be alone with the perpetrator, or by making her available for child prostitution or pornography. The child will blame her mother for failing to protect her, be very angry towards her, and struggle to understand her mother's behaviour.

- The mother sexually abused her: in which case the child will experience intense feelings of isolation and betrayal and feel that the mother has abdicated her maternal role. Few children disclose sexual abuse by their mother and they are likely to be met with greater disbelief.

(Hall and Lloyd, 1989)

Laing and Kamsler (1990) approach their work with mothers and children grounded in an appreciation of the perpetrator's central role in shaping the beliefs and perceptions of the mothers and victims and the issue of responsibility. Secrecy enables the perpetrator to avoid taking responsibility for the abuse, for its impact, and for the consequences for the rest of the family. A major ploy he uses to shift responsibility away from himself is to give the victim the message, either covertly or overtly, that the sexual contact is the child's fault. This shifting of responsibility from the perpetrator to the child creates a context in which the child will experience feelings of guilt and shame about the abuse, and these feelings will create a further barrier to her ability to overcome secrecy. In many instances, the perpetrator will go even further in his attempts to shift responsibility for his behaviour and seek to implicate the mother. This has the effect of the child becoming angry with the mother and even blaming her for the perpetrator's actions and her suffering. This shifting of responsibility by the perpetrator creates a situation in which the victim is encouraged to feel responsible for protecting the mother from learning the truth. The mother will be unaware of the ways in which the child has been coached by the perpetrator to keep secret what occurred. These tactics are likely to have a devastating effect on the mother-daughter relationship, creating division and mistrust.

## Research findings

Orr (1995) found that although the mothers were angry with the perpetrators, they also felt that it was their responsibility to help the perpetrators change.

Sirles and Franke (1989) found that the majority of perpetrator's (77.8 per cent) denied the abuse, thus potentially displacing the responsibility from them onto the mother. This may well be reinforced through the professional intervention.

Bagley and King (1990) noted that the question of responsibility versus blame is a common theme of the literature. Kroth (1979) found that women were able to resolve their own feelings very quickly in therapy, either accepting any responsibility for their role in a failing marriage or, in other cases, realising they were in no way responsible for the husband's actions. The complexity of this dilemma is clarified by understanding that people often tend to marry spouses with different but often complementary needs and problems. Both spouses may project concerns to distract themselves from their own pain, at the same time both need to prevent abandonment by the other partner and settle into an uneasy equilibrium, waiting for the other to change.

In an attempt to make sense of the involvement between fathers and daughters, mothers would often attempt to apply a logical explanation for what happened – they denied any accountability themselves. They did not acknowledge responsibility as they had not verbally sanctioned the behaviour, therefore they believed somehow that it was the daughter's fault. In the mothers' perceptions, the fathers responded sexually because the children made sexual overtures (Hubbard, 1989).

Hooper (1992) found that a key factor enabling women to leave abusive partners was a clear sense of the perpetrator's responsibility for the abuse. While mothers have often been observed to blame children for abuse, self-blame is also a problem. Hooper also identified several other issues which influence the degree of responsibility accorded to the perpetrator. Firstly, if the perpetrator is framed as being sick, then illness is seen as being beyond their control although they should assume responsibility for ensuring their recovery. Secondly, when the perpetrator indicates they would seek corrective (curative) help, they are accorded diminished responsibility and this can affect the woman's judgement of future options. The moral responsibility for the perpetrator 's actions (eg they are old enough to know right from wrong) is lost. This differs starkly from the mother who usually emphasises the responsibility by their own response, which can only be reviewed when the perpetrator has either accepted the responsibility or it has been firmly located with him. The latter does not always mean that the nature of the abuse is fully understood.

### Issues to consider

Get the mother to list all the responsibilities a parent has towards their children, for example protection from harm, caring for the children and allowing them to mature in a safe environment. Then get them to compile a list about the perpetrator, and compare the two to establish which responsibilities he met and which ones he abdicated (Hall and Lloyd, 1989). For example, perpetrators are well aware of the emotional needs of children, but they fail as a responsible adult by using this awareness to manipulate a child into sexual activity. This may challenge an idealistic view of the perpetrator which the mother has built up over time and this will allow her to formulate a more realistic and probably ambivalent view of him. It is important for the worker to remind the mother of the perpetrator's responsibilities when she lapses into self-blame.

## Definition of risk

Mothers need some definition of sexual abuse as a starting point so they have a reference point for the allegations. Some mothers may not correlate an incident as sexual abuse and they may need some time to reconsider whether the incident was indeed abusive. The length of this process will vary enormously depending on the individual. There are a number of potential areas for confusion: the relationship between pleasure and harm if the child appeared to enjoy the sexual contact; the significance of the power relationship between adults and children in defining abuse and the indirect relationship between harm and visible effects (Hooper, 1992: 78).

Defining risk is an important starting point in work with mothers. Wherever social workers 'intervene' with families, they start with a view about why they are there and what the best outcome could be. Achieving these outcomes can be relatively straightforward, for example where a child has been sexually abused by a stranger, the family believe and are sensitive to the needs of family members. The worker's view of the needs is most likely to be mirrored by the family's view and everybody is agreed about what needs to happen.

Alternatively the perception of the risk may not be immediately shared, for example a woman whose partner has offended outside the home, may view her own children as perfectly safe (Rose and Savage, 2000).

There is also a group of women who do take the decision to remain with their partners, the perpetrators. Whilst they would not be defined as traditional 'safe carers', neither were they the principal risk. They are women who need to learn to 'live with risk'. Rose and Savage helped them to develop an understanding that it is possible for some women to choose to continue their relationship, in some shape or form, with partners who are Schedule One offenders. In doing this, they can also remain carers of their children. Their belief remained that, if the 'risk' presented by the continuing relationship between the women and their partners could be managed safely for the children, then this was the best outcome for them in the longer-term.

The most significant confusion lay in workers failing to define with the women what the risk was, or where the differing responsibilities lay for managing the risk. The use of the child protection and court system only served to reinforce the position of fight rather than adding clarity to the plan. The final, and additional, task for the worker is to assess whether the suggested management of the risk is safe for the children. If it isn't, where this process has been followed it should be relatively easy to be clear about why not.

All the women accepted and agreed that putting the children's safety and well-being first was the most important thing. Equally, all the women agreed on some level that continuing a relationship with this man posed some risk (even if women were saying they felt sure he wouldn't re-offend within the family now, the women acknowledged they were often kept awake at night worrying about, 'What if?'). Once the risk to all family members had been named, the women were able to acknowledge that they were willing to accept this level of risk and move to developing ways of managing this risk.

Even in situations where involvement results in being unable to agree on a risk existing, the process of exploring this can enable women to gain some insight and information into why protective action was necessary. Rose and Savage found that the process of defining the risk was resolved much more quickly than they had imagined, with many of the mothers reaching a point by the third session where they were asking for more information and clarification in order to develop ways of managing their households. The conclusion for many was that they were dependent on the honesty of their partners and the focus then became one of developing rules for safe caring within their own situations, based on the assumptions that they would be unlikely to know prior to their partners re-offending. The enormity of trying to manage this risk was realised when the women began to think about their daily routine. For example, the simple task of bathing the children – the sounds alone may trigger the partner's distorted thinking without him being involved in the bathing itself.

## Research findings

Smart (1997) studied parents and professional perspectives in abuse situations. The study looked at the differences in information gathered from social work records and from interviews with families that had received protective services. Although factual matters were generally agreed, impressions and judgements were often different. In terms of continued risk to children, records noted more concerns than were acknowledged by parents. In follow-up interviews, researchers heard no parental reports of further abuse whereas official records showed that 19 per cent of families had received further services and another 18 per cent had been scrutinised following concerns for the child's welfare. Thus, social workers are more likely than parents to view the child as being 'at risk' and to regard preventative action as having been taken (Cleaver and Freeman, 1995).

## Issues to consider

What is her definition of sexual abuse?

Does the mother know how workers make informed estimates of perpetrator risk, so they are familiar with some of the risk situations? It is important that workers make this information available to mothers in a straightforward manner. Whilst Calder (1999) explores perpetrator risk in some detail, the following summary may be useful in discussions.

Assessing risk accurately is difficult when we know that perpetrators lack any distinct profile and there is an absence of longitudinal studies post-offence to accurately predict recidivism. The task is compounded further if the perpetrator is selective in the provision of information, or where the information derives solely from a single source.

Risk factors place the individual at risk to re-offend. They are guidelines only and not absolute predictors. A risk factor is defined as 'any experience, event, environmental influences/parameters, internal/external behaviour, historical factor, situations, that presents or enhances the offender's chances of re-offence. These may or may not be cycle behaviours and triggering events' (Carich, 1994).

In determining the risk a sexual perpetrator presents we need to consider the types of offences committed, sexual history, treatment history, and amenability to treatment. McGrath (1992) suggests that we focus on five factors, in order to look at perpetrator risk: probability of re-offence; degree of harm most likely to result from a re-offence; conditions under which re-offence is most likely to occur; likely victims of a re-offence; and the time-scale within which a re-offence is most likely to occur. These are dealt with below.

1. Perpetrator risk: cannot be exclusively defined by the nature of the problem for which the perpetrator has been referred when we are aware of potential cross-over of acts, the genders and ages of the victims, and the context of the offence, for example inside or outside the family. For example, Abel et al. (1985) also found that seventy-five per cent of recidivists crossed both age and sex in their choice of victims. The incest perpetrator has the lowest recidivism rates (although they are known to offend against more than one child) whilst untreated exhibitionists have the highest recidivism rates. The younger the incest victim, the higher the risk of re-offence (Williams and Finkelhor, 1992). Perpetrators who abused unrelated boys have higher recidivism rates than those who abused unrelated girls (McGrath, 1991) and the probability of recidivism rises with each offence. The degree of force is associated with an increased risk to re-offend, especially those who are sexually aroused by aggression. Deviant sexual arousal is also associated to recidivism. Repeated sexual crimes remain an important predictor of future behaviour. The sexual abuse may well not be the only concern that needs to be resolved before rehabilitation can be effected. Stermac et al. (1995) found that 55 per cent of incest perpetrators demonstrated non-sexual forms of violence and abuse within their homes. As such, issues of anger, power and control need to be addressed. A perpetrator's specific beliefs about his own behaviour is likely to be

predictive of future behaviour (Marshall and Eccles, 1991) as is their general attitude to sexual aggression (Segal and Stermac, 1990). Serin et al. (1994) found that psychopaths are at higher risk of re-offending than non-psychopaths; they re-offend sooner, and they are likely to become increasingly violent.

2. Harm from the offence: is again correlated with the use of weapons or force, and any escalation in the patterns of offending is significant.

3. Conditions associated with re-offending: embraces their response to the assessment, the degree of co-operation or compliance with any requests or conditions set down; the opportunity to access victims, either through family, friends or leisure interests, eg football coaching; the use of substances; availability of sexually stimulating material; level of mobility, for example through work leisure outlets such as train-spotting; and any anger related to job loss or restricted contact with their birth children.

4. Likely victims: through preference in previous offences, or as admitted by the perpetrator in the work to date.

5. When? Many perpetrators act when they have opportunity, or they actively create them. The degree of supervision the perpetrator receives from professionals and others, such as the family, will have a bearing on this point. In broader terms, research does suggest that the risks from sexual perpetrators against children is over a significant length of time and it is a myth that the risk reduces over time (particularly in the absence of treatment).

## Mother's relationship with her children

Hubbard (1989) defined the mother-daughter relationship as any thoughts or feelings about the relationship, description of the quality of the relationship, or any activities engaged in together.

Incest produces a crisis in a mother's relationship with her child. They have to deal with the anger of the children. The victim will have ambiguous feelings about the perpetrator: while they may have been afraid and disliked the sexual contact from the outset, there will have been dependence and usually affection for the perpetrator in other contexts. The threat from the perpetrator that maintained the child's secrecy may have been that the mother would become very angry and the family would have been destroyed. From the child victim's perspective, a mother removing the children from the home or forcing the father to leave will be a fulfilment of that prophecy. In this confusion and pain, the child may project anger onto the mother, especially if the incestuous father has presented himself as a victim of circumstances. In the mother's decisions and actions following disclosure of the abuse, the child will again feel powerless, further fuelling anger toward the mother. The mother is likely to feel that she is being challenged 'on all fronts' when this anger is expressed. In her own stress and frustration, she may retaliate 'in kind' only to chastise herself even more severely after the fact (Ovaris, 1991).

The child's relationship with the mother is a critical one, within which there may be difficulties predating the abuse and which will be compounded if the abuse was intra-familial and of long duration. This relationship may have a distant or a conflicting quality, which militated against disclosure and allowed the abuse to continue. The child may previously have tried unsuccessfully to tell her parent about the abuse, and anger about a perceived lack of protection may only emerge after disclosure. The mother may harbour feelings of resentment against the child for attracting the perpetrator, or for 'causing' a separation from him which has physical, emotional or economic consequences for the whole family (Glaser and Frosh, 1988). These authors advocate intervention which aims to help both mother and child to express their feelings, ensuring that the child is protected from excessive parental anger, while recognising the mother's predicament. Resolution requires the mother's open acceptance of the child's feelings, which may include some continuing fondness of the abuser. The mother's acknowledgement of their often inadvertent contribution to the child's emotional discomfort is part of the healing process. Bridging the distance that may have arisen between mother and child and enabling each to learn about and comprehend the feelings of the other is a process that can be substantially helped by the presence of two workers, each adopting a supportive position for one of the participants and attempting to avoid mutual recriminations. The principal professional goal is the restoration of the mother-child relationship and not meeting the mother's needs, which may well emerge and highlight the necessity for further individual support.

Because the mother may well be in acute shock post-disclosure, her availability for her children will be affected. Mothers who have been sexually abused themselves may have some difficulties relating to children. They may have lacked a good parenting model and they may have their own memories resurrected by the abuse, feeding their own neediness. They may turn to the child for support to deal with their distress, aggravating the child's sense of guilt about the abuse. They may also become over-protective of their children, for example keeping them in the house, not allowing them to do childhood things, ensuring the child has their body covered at all times. Over-protectiveness may be most pronounced in mothers who see characteristics of themselves in the child.

Emotional sensitivity can be affected by the mother if the child's reaction to the sexual abuse does not conform to expectations. If the child does not show distress and reject the abuser, then this is confusing for her. However, the mother should be careful not to condemn the perpetrator as a person as the child may well have confused feelings about him.

Mothers need to acknowledge the impact on the child's self-esteem and they need to expect an angry response. Whilst anger can be a legitimate and positive expression of emotion and necessary for the child's emotional growth, it can be misdirected onto the non-abusing carer if the perpetrator is not there ('kick the cat' syndrome). The mother has to understand that the child needs to be angry in order to trust again, and it is comforting to know that the child has a relationship with the mother which is worth being angry about. In time, the child may come to forgive the mother as they see her also as a mutual survivor. The child may well be angry with the mother for lots of reasons, such as for failing to protect her, for looking the other way, for setting her up for the abuse, for blaming her, for nor listening when she tried to tell her, for not believing her, for remaining with the perpetrator or for not providing her with the necessary love and attention she needed. In lots of ways, the child has to be given free licence to work through all of these things in order to release the anger.

Tinling (1990) noted that victims often hold bitter, confused feelings against the mother, even more intense than those they hold against the father. She reviewed victim accounts of sexual abuse to identify several distinctive characteristics of the mothers: that they are in conflict, have misplaced priorities, are chronic avoiders and perceived by victims as hopeless victims themselves. The victim often perceives the mother to have made destructive choices. The 'martyr' is the most commonly described type of mother by victims. Their goal is to attain nobility by silently enduring and suffering. The 'inadequate' mother, through her own default, gets others into her service. She manipulates her daughter into assuming her own responsibilities by her inability to deal with the overwhelming position she is in or has put herself in.

As many victims believe their mother to have been aware of their sexual abuse, they may well be angry towards them. They may believe the lies the perpetrator told the child about the mother so they would be disliked. They may even have tried to give out 'indirect' messages (acting out or withdrawal). In sum, they may feel the mother approved of what happened. Mothers have to work against feeling jealous towards their daughter as this serves the perpetrator's motives, and the child may well choose him if faced with a choice.

The response of adult caretakers to abused children is critical to the child's perception of the experience (Adams-Tucker, 1982). Having an opportunity to ventilate feelings about the abuse has been identified as central to the recovery process (Wyatt and Mickey, 1988). In this light, the mother's relationship with the child is going to be influenced by her reaction to the abuse disclosure or discovery.

Depression in either the child or the mother can lead to low levels of communication about anything. This lack of availability is often aggravated by a maternal preoccupation with personal survival where adult domestic violence (often to the point of repeated hospitalisation) is a feature of family life.

Mothers must be aware not to seek to apportion blame to others, particularly their children, for the sexual abuse and the grief that follows their loss of innocence.

Mothers have often been self-critical about their relationship with their children, compared with that of their partner. This can be the product of a close father-child relationship on the surface, but which can mask a grooming process.

## *Research findings*

Avery et al. (1998) discovered a frequently profound bitterness toward the non-abusing parent by survivors of intra-familial abuse. The negative feelings expressed were often more severe toward the non-abusing parent than toward the perpetrator. The mother may well need to understand the child's feelings, particularly if they expect anger at the perpetrator rather than the apparent attachment to him.

Burgess et al. (1977) pointed to the feelings child victims will experience post-disclosure and which need to be harnessed and understood by the mother if she is to enhance her relationship with the child. Perpetrators, if they are successful in gaining access to the child sexually, will continue to press for more activity with the child. For the perpetrator to keep his dominance and sexual control over the child, he must ensure that the secrecy of the behaviour is maintained. Thus, when the secret is disclosed, the tension surrounding the secret is broken and his power over the child is disrupted.

Gomes-Schwartz et al. (1990) considered the mother's relationship with the child. They formed four scales made up of ratings of the mother's relationship with the child: 'caring', meaning that the mother displayed love and concern for the child; 'depending', meaning maternal intrusiveness and reliance upon the child as a source of support; 'burdened', meaning the mother was not emotionally available; and 'hostile', meaning the mother was angry at the child and saw her as bad. Ninety-seven per cent of all mothers had moderate to high caring attitudes towards their children. Yet 43 per cent did show some tendency to be dependent on the child and 41 per cent felt burdened. They also found positive correlation between caring relationships and the level of concern and protection upon disclosure. Hostile relationships correlated negatively with concern and protection; they correlated positively with anger and with punishment toward the child upon disclosure. Burdened mothers tended to punish and be angry and not to protect. Depending mothers tended to express concern for themselves.

Fong and Walsh-Bowers (1998) found that almost all the mothers in their sample claimed that they had a better and closer relationship with their daughters after the disclosure.

Finkelhor (1984) found, in his sample of college women, that those who were at highest risk were the ones who said they were not close to their mother or received little affection from their mother. One hypothesis for this might be that when victimisation occurs, it alienates a girl from her parents, for example, because they have had to keep the abuse secret or because they felt betrayed by the failure of the parents to come to their support when they reveal it (Meiselman, 1978).

Rickford (1992) found that some women have great difficulty relating to the child physically – being unable to touch their child – and they need space to talk this through before looking at strategies to remedy this.

Meiselman (1978) found that three years after the incest had ended that 40 per cent of the victims continued to experience negative feelings towards their fathers, while 60 per cent were described as 'forgiving'. In contrast, 60 per cent of the mothers were definitely disliked by their daughters and only 40 per cent were regarded positively. Herman and Hirschman (1977) found that the daughters perceived their mothers as weak, helpless, and masochistic women who could barely care for themselves, let alone their children.

Hooper (1992) highlighted two purposes for the child directing their anger towards their mother. First, anger at the mothers enables girls partially to break their own identification with their mothers and hence with powerlessness, and to feel worthy of protection from abuse. Second, it is generally easier to direct anger at women than men.

Johnson (1992) identified two mother-daughter relationship patterns when talking to mothers: peer relationships and parent-child relationships.

1. Peer relationship patterns: fell into two patterns: pals and rivals. When pals, they would share sexual jokes and sex education together, advise on how to dress and wear make-up, and generally acted as 'one of the gang'. When rivals, their relationship was characterised by estrangement and misunderstanding rather than malice or jealousy. Both experienced a peer relationship with their daughters. While they may not be true role reversal, they saw their daughters in adult roles in the father-daughter relationship and themselves more as child-wives to their husbands. In both family configurations, the mother was outside the boundary around their husband and daughter.

2. Mother-daughter, parent-child relationship patterns: fell into two patterns: loving-close and strict-distant. In loving-close, both parents were overjoyed at the pleasure brought to them by the child, and this did not change as they got older. Indeed, they can view the child as mature and independent, but never parentified them or exchanged the parent role. The mother presents as more of a mother-wife than a child-wife and sees the daughter more as a peer to the husband than as an adult and herself as a mother to them both. In this family configuration the family boundary did not leave anyone outside, but enclosed all members in loving closeness. In the strict-distant, the mother is overprotective with her daughter because of her own childhood memories, fearing her daughter might do the same. The mother functioned here more as a mother-wife than as a child-wife and saw herself as a mother to both her daughter and her husband. She also saw her daughter as a child to her husband. In this family, the mother drew the boundary around herself and her daughter, leaving the father on the outside.

These findings confirm that mother-daughter relationships are complex. What is unclear is how the mothers' portrayals of family relationships compare or differ from other family members.

Todd and Ellis (1992) found an enormous complexity in the mother-daughter relationship. Mothers struggled with their ambivalence towards the child, their anger and need for the allegations to be untrue alongside the fearful prospect of losing their man, their child, or both. The fact that mothers were thrown into turmoil or immobilised by their experiences inevitably has serious consequences for the mother-daughter relationship. Daughters are engaged in strategies which will enable them to endure and survive their experiences. Mothers, on the other hand, have to negotiate a process of knowing and not knowing, of confronting the possibility that the man they married is molesting their child.

Wright (1991) found that there are consequences for the mother-daughter relationship when the perpetrator is removed from the home. They noted that one justification for removing him from the home is the hope that this will allow weak mother-daughter bonds to become stronger. Only two-fifths of the victims went on to establish healthier relationships with their mothers, with the remainder declining. They also found another change was the lack of control mothers experienced over their children. Where the mother and daughter had a history of strained or remote relationships and where mothers sometimes felt that they had something to make up to their daughters, maintaining effective parental control was difficult. In some cases, the male had been the disciplinarian in the family; in other cases the mother was too overwhelmed with financial and emotional stress to be firm whilst other mothers became stronger than ever before and children were reacting to this new strength. Another consequence was that some children assumed a parent role (mild or moderate).

### Issues to consider

Hall and Lloyd (1989) identified a number of issues for mothers and daughters (see Figure 12.3) which need to be acknowledged and then embraced in an agreed work programme.

The development of a trusting relationship with their mother is often the key to helping the child recover from their experience of sexual abuse. This can take many forms, such as the establishment of flexible and negotiated routines in the home that they feel comfortable with (and which encourage physical comfort, emotional security, love, affection and belonging, achievement and self-esteem, and self-actualisation) to working with professionals to provide future safety, supports outside the home and strategies for overcoming their trauma. Some agreements need to be reached about safety rules, such as it is never acceptable for the child to hurt themselves or others; it is important that family share with each other their whereabouts; and that it is never OK to keep secrets.

The ability of the mother to communicate with the child is central to achieving these goals, particularly since many victims are resistant to relationships, having experienced betrayal from the perpetrator. The crisis can provide the mother with the opportunity to engage with the child and connect with what they are experiencing, although it is also the time when they will feel most fearful about making a mistake. It can open the door to emotional vulnerability that allows the child to accept the connection with the mother.

Workers need to get some sense of the quality of the mother's relationship with each of her children, and any positive or negative feelings

| Mothers | Daughters |
|---------|-----------|
| Acknowledging that the abuse has occurred | Did she know about it? How could she not have known? |
| Feelings of guilt and failure to protect her child, of not being a good-enough parent | Why did she not see that something was wrong? What did she do/could she have done to stop it? |
| Vulnerability when confronted with the facts about the abuse | May want to protect mother from details of the abuse |
| Finds it difficult to cope with daughter's feelings | May want to protect mother so disguises her true feelings |
| Is she able to let her daughter know what it was like for her, especially in her relationship with the abuser? | May not want to hear. Finds it difficult to acknowledge mother's own difficulties |
| Mother may have been abused by the same man | Why didn't she protect me from him? She knew what he was like |

**Figure 12.3**   Issues for mothers and daughters

around. It is important to note whether the mother can see the child as an individual with needs separate from the mother's and to assess the accuracy of the mother's perception of the child by comparing it to their own and that of others (Faller, 1988b). Where the mother is unable to emotionally support the child at all, then a period of separation may be indicated until she can.

Brown (1998) argued that it is important for the mother to appreciate that her relationship with the child may need to develop over time; it is easy for the mother and the child to become stuck in their relationship. It may be that the abuse has left the mother less able to express physical affection. This can be hard for the child and can be experienced as a rejection and confirmation of the stigma borne. There will be layers of different emotions for both parties in this relationship and many aspects of the abuse and the role of the mother may need to be examined repeatedly too. Even where the child has disclosed to the mother, there may remain a residual tension about what has happened.

Workers may want to work with the child to enable them to tell their mother, thus increasing the availability of information, for example through a story or letter.

The mother and the children may need to set out a list of points describing how they see the mother-child relationship, the good and the bad, and how it may change for the worse or the better in the future. They then may move on to set out an action list of things they will change in the future, being realistic and setting small, attainable changes first.

The needs of both the children and the mother need to be listed as they often conflict and workers need to be alerted quickly to situations where they need to arbitrate and possibly conciliate.

Workers need to consider the answers to the following questions when talking with the mother and observing the mother and child together: what is the mother's response to the information around the sexual abuse? Is she angry with the perpetrator or the child? Does she believe that this could have taken place? What is her attitude towards the child? The mother's responses will help the worker assess the mother's relationship with the victim and her ability to perceive the child's needs, which will probably be very different to her own and those of the perpetrator.

## Knowledge of the effects of child sexual abuse on the victims – generally and specifically to their children (empathy)

Once a child is safe, the mother will want to know the short- and the long-term effects of the sexual abuse. Hooper (1989) found that many of the mothers in her sample were unaware about the effects of sexual abuse, leaving them with vague worries and little idea of how to help. Common questions from mothers will concern their children's sexual development, the impact on their current and future relationships with adults and other children, and the duration of current symptoms of stress (such as bedwetting and nightmares). Workers need to provide mothers with this information and also the stages of their child's recovery.

Although there is ample evidence about the *potential* negative impacts of sexual abuse on the victim, such victimisation does *not necessarily* have inevitable or massive impact on victims. There is no universal or uniform impact of child sexual abuse and no guarantee that any one person will develop any post-traumatic responses. Some children do not show any outward signs of harm or distress. The word asymptomatic is used to describe such children. In fact, up to 40 per cent of sexually abused children did not appear to have any of the expected abuse-related problems in several studies (such as Kendall-Tackett et al., 1993). This does not mean that the child is not suffering. Some children who keep the abuse 'bottled up' inside may become symptomatic at some future date.

It is important that we advise mothers of potential variance between the consequences on male and female victims. For some time, much of the information derived from work with female victims (set out below) and only in more recent times are we finding the particular issues that impact on the male victim (addressed later).

### Lessons for professionals

Workers need to have some understanding and awareness about the impact of socialisation on the possible presentation of boys, its effects on victims and thus indicators; the impact dimensions peculiar to male victims; the need to address their potential to become perpetrators; and the need to provide them with considerable time with, as well as written information about, others so they do not feel alone in their journey towards recovery.

## Theoretical models

For a full discussion of these, please refer to Chapter 1 of Finkelhor and Browne, 1988 (see References).

### *Issues to consider with mothers*

Whilst information on the impact of sexual abuse on children is important, workers need to establish whether the mother can empathise with her children. Victim empathy does not just

happen, it must be learned by the mother feeling deeply and paying very close attention to the real feelings of others.

Get them to think about things from their victim's perspective. Why did the perpetrator do what he did?

Get them to list the difficulties they might have as they work on developing empathy. What are the things about them, their feelings and attitudes, their circumstances and life situation right now that might be roadblocks to developing empathy?

The mother will probably need basic information about what is meant by sexual abuse, what is known about its effects, the way that children retract as part of the process, etc. in order to enable them to understand the situation and judge their response.

Get the mother to look at the effects of sexual abuse as set out in this component and get her to tick off or detail those that apply to her child, and herself if she is a victim of sexual abuse.

Get the mother to write an account of how the sexual abuse has affected the child, the siblings and herself.

## Siblings

Siblings are often a neglected group. It is important that professionals recognise how greatly the siblings, as secondary victims, are affected, in order that we may appreciate their need for, and use of survival strategies. Workers first need to establish the degree to which the siblings may have been aware of the sexual abuse. They may do this by talking with the children or by exploring their behaviour patterns previously and now. These may give some indication as to whether they were abused themselves or whether they may have witnessed the abuse. Both may result in the same range of responses.

It is important to establish whether a sibling has been the first to learn about the sexual abuse, and whether this was from the victim, or from an adult using them as a secondary mechanism of silence. If they are unaware, then the mother needs to be involved in telling them as this allows them to make some sense of the disruption as well as empowering them to act if the perpetrator acts inappropriately towards them – either in contact or if eventually returned to the family. Talking to the children has to be age-appropriate and in ways they understand, using terminology they are familiar with. It can the lead into useful discussions around secrecy, privacy and confidentiality (Smith, 1994).

If the perpetrator has moved out of the home whilst the situation is being investigated, there should be serious consideration given about telling them why in an age-appropriate fashion. There may be consequences to this in that the victim may be blamed. This is more likely where the mother has adopted this position. We cannot discount that the siblings also have been sexually abused but have chosen not to disclose such information at this stage. This can provide some insight into the strong reactions exhibited by siblings.

Siblings may well feel responsible or guilty concerning the abuse for several reasons: they knew what was going on and felt they should have told to stop the abuse continuing; they may have repeatedly breathed a sigh of relief when the victim was chosen rather than themselves; they may also have been jealous by the attention the abuser gave to the victim; or they may have been angry with the victim and felt that they deserved the abuse.

### Research findings

Anthony and Watkeys (1991) found that, of the siblings in their sample who were investigated because of residing with an alleged perpetrator or having a victim sibling, over half had been abused compared to eight per cent who had been harmed in the home of the alleged perpetrator. Overall, this may be considered as an indication that siblings of abused children must be treated as possible victims and as such included in the investigation and assessment.

Attention must be given to the needs of children within the family who may not have been sexually victimised, but who suffered the consequences of disordered family dynamics before and after revelation. For example, there may be problems about relating to each other, role reversals, collusion, secrets. The results for other siblings can be numerous. Rivalry and jealousy may result from all children in the family craving love and attention and not realising the price of special favours. Collusion may result when other children are socialised to be the next victim; or they may experience a combination of guilt and gratitude that they were not chosen. A climate of premature sexual stimulation within the family may result in the children being more susceptible to abuse by older persons outside the family (Bagley and King, 1990).

The other children in the family may feel different from the child who has been abused and perhaps begin to act distant, jealous (because the victim sibling is getting so much attention now) or otherwise differently than before. Depending on the age and knowledge of the other children, they may also exhibit confusion over what is happening. If they are very young, they may not grasp what has happened even if it is explained to them. If the siblings identify strongly with the victim they will exhibit traumatic responses similar to the victim. Talking to them and giving them appropriate information is important. They need to be updated as new events occur to help them understand why so much attention is focused on their sibling. They need to understand the need to be especially kind to the victim at this juncture (Byerly, 1992).

Monahan (1997) studied the attributions of incestuously abused and non-abused sisters. She explored the attributions of participants regarding the general sibling group, victim selection and non-selection, as well as attributions regarding jealousy, protection, and guilt within the sister relationship. She found that all participants harboured ambivalent feelings such as relief and then guilt for not being chosen for the abuse, and then anger at the targeted sister. Competition and antagonism were commonplace in a chaotic environment filled with distance, violence, and unpredictability. All participants presented clear perceptions of the family as dysfunctional and, very often, pathological. They articulated the following regarding the context of the abuse in their family:

- Attributions regarding context: siblings were often totally unaware of the nature of the abuse being endured. There were often reports of solidarity among the siblings even though it was unison against an unspoken enemy. Several participants remembered having their sister stand guard at the bed until she fell asleep in a valiant effort to protect her from her father.
- Attributions regarding victim selection: were related to factors such as parental perceptions of the child, inviting self-blame from many victims, compared to 'incest envy' from the non-abused siblings because of their 'special status'.

- Attributions regarding the sister relationship: all indicated that the incest had affected their sister relationship in some way, with many spending a great deal of time thinking about how much their relationship had suffered, and quite often, had spent just as much time trying to repair the sibling relationship. Each child had experienced the family in different ways. Whilst the normal development of a sibling will not be permanently disrupted, it is expected that a crisis will occur which will cause at least temporary cessation of normative experiences for the sibling. A non-abused sibling could be regarded as a secondary victim of the incest because while she was not directly abused, she may nonetheless learn that trusting men, or people in general, is not the safest thing to do. Additionally, she will learn which behaviours will keep her safe and which ones might subject her to possible abuse. The non-abused sibling, unlike her abused counterparts, was able to blame the perpetrator rather than themselves. While some of that blame was also projected at the abused sister, it can be viewed as a coping mechanism and therefore assisted the non-abused sister in rejecting a self-view as victim. It was noteworthy just how the non-abused women readily identified how and why they needed to take evasive action from their father and were able to identify and process the predatory styles of the male caretaker within their familial environments. They learned how to be assertive and how to sense danger. Several attributed their assertiveness or knowledge to remaining free from abuse. Many of the women, although motivated and optimistic about repairing the sister relationship, were also ambivalent demonstrating that the incest may have left its mark by making a supportive, trusting and functional adult relationship difficult at best.

Engel (1994) explored how siblings cope with the news of the abuse. Where the abuse has been allegedly perpetrated by someone they care about, denial may be the first response. The sibling may then have an investment in protecting the image of the perpetrator rather than in being there for the victim. Alternatively, the sibling may have been abused by the same person, in which case their response may be angry, anxious or upset. This could be aimed at the perpetrator, or if they have tried to block out their own abuse, towards the victim for reminding them of things they would have preferred to remain buried. The sibling may also have reasons for not wanting to believe the news: they may have known what was going on, but felt helpless to prevent it. This may induce feelings of helplessness, guilt, shame and inadequacy. They may experience some of these feelings as they are glad it happened to someone else and not themselves. Others resent the attention the abused child receives, feeling jealous towards them. This can create problems as the victim feels betrayed and abandoned, similar to siblings who refuse to believe or side with the perpetrator.

Fong and Walsh-Bowers (1998) found that mothers reported that siblings were also affected by the abusive relationship in different ways. Some children felt that because more attention was focused on the victim, they were left out; and as a result, mothers had to deal with the children's anger and disruptive behaviour. Other children sympathised with the victim and so were more willing to show emotional support.

Dwyer and Miller (1996) have noted that siblings may experience disenfranchised grief (see the earlier section on the 'effects of knowing' for a discussion of this concept). They found that many women perceive the interests of the child who has been abused as conflicting with those of other children in the family, who may still want and need their father. In these cases, the dictates of a 'good mother' are not easily defined.

Wright (1991) found that siblings were peripheral to the family as a whole. When they were talked about as important people, they were cherished for the roles they could fill, not for themselves. Despite this, the inclusion of siblings is important as they are undergoing enormous change and stress: they are losing their fathers, their mothers are changing, the whole world seems suddenly to be involved in the private lives of their families.

### Issues to consider

Professionals need to be sensitive and responsive to the needs and issues of children not involved in the incest directly and offer them support. They are *secondary victims* like their mother. They also need to be included in the healing or recovery process and assume the status of survivor. Siblings who are affected by the abuse will increase their demands on the parent.

Mothers will often seek advice about what to tell the children and the only basis of response is honesty and openness: *'children make up what they don't understand and they are especially vulnerable to the gossip or interpretations of others outside the immediate family'* (Ovaris, 1991).

It may take some time for siblings to work through the issues as they affect each individual, and this must be done at their own pace. Nobody should try to push them to face particular issues unless they are happy to do so. The sibling may well have experienced the abuse and family life very differently from the victim either by playing a different role in the family or by developing their own method of coping. Workers do need to consider whether there are preferred children in the family and what this means for them and for the other children, for example have they been scapegoated and marginalised?

Workers need to encourage siblings who have experienced sexual abuse by the same person to open up some dialogue in which they piece together their histories and childhood to enable some mastery to be gained over a lost past. Where the siblings are experiencing problems working together, then simple supportive opportunities need to be created, such as stating they care for each other even if they cannot offer what each needs at the present time. Siblings need to be careful not to accept any responsibility for not protecting the victim, not telling someone, feeling jealous of the attention the victim was getting from the perpetrator, or taking his side.

Mothers need to consider and devise strategies for managing and protecting siblings.

At some point, the siblings need to be forgiven for the feelings of responsibility for the abuse they have harnessed. For example, siblings may not have been responsible for the abuse, and may have been unable to stop it, but they still feel that they have failed the child victim.

# Part Two – Moving The Assessment Forward

## Knowledge of sexual offending behaviour: generally and specific to their partner

*The abusive adult understands children better than the rest of us. The child can come to depend on victimisation with terrible assurance, much more surely than our protection. It is the perfect fit between the child's needs and the adult's*

*desires that we must consider if we are to comprehend the incomprehensible and empower our interventions on behalf of the powerless.*

(Summit, 1990: 60)

Most people are only aware of sexual abuse through what they hear on TV or read about in newspapers. In these cases the perpetrators are often from outside the family and reporting tends to be sensationalist. When suddenly sexual abuse is something that has happened to their child within their family, there is a need to help them to understand some of the basic knowledge available on the issues and processes involved.

Unless a mother is helped towards some understanding, how can she even begin to make sense of what has happened to her child by someone she has most likely loved and trusted and, if she is not helped to do this, her ability to make clear decisions may be compromised through misunderstanding or lack of knowledge. Two of the most commonly asked questions by mothers the Cornerstone Project worked with over a period of ten years, were:

### 'Why my child?' and 'How can anyone do that?'

Mothers often ask many questions about the sexual perpetrator and which might include:

- How often is sexual abuse committed by strangers, and how often by people the child knows?
- How much sexual abuse is committed by fathers and step-fathers?
- How much sexual abuse is committed by teenagers?
- Do women sexually abuse children?
- Why do men sexually abuse children?
- What is paedophilia?
- Do sexual perpetrators have one or more victims?
- How do they get the trust of the child?
- What help do they need?
- What help is available?
- How can such help be accessed?
- Does treatment work?
- Can we ever live together again as a family? How? When?

This section will offer some basic information, which might help workers answer the mother's queries. Regan (2006) provides a set of pictoral worksheets combined with explanatory notes for undertaking this work with mothers.

## *Our current level of understanding*

It has taken some time to begin to shift the responsibility for the abuse from both the victim and the mother to the perpetrator, although there is still some way to go. There are many problems associated with a comprehensive knowledge base on child sexual abuse, not least the secrecy in which it is perpetrated, and the common invisibility of harm. Despite these problems, there is now a fairly broad knowledge base and level of insight with regards to how sexual perpetrators select their victims and perpetrate the abuse.

It is now generally agreed that there is a process to sexual offending and that perpetrators go through a number of stages prior to committing the offence (Finkelhor, 1984; Wolf, 1984). It is also known that individuals who perpetrate sexual offences against children plan their abuse and that they will undertake a variety of roles to enable them to gain access to potential victims. In certain circumstances this will involve 'targeting' women who are single parents. It is significant that perpetrators can target vulnerable children as well as mothers (eg single parents) and then groom them in order to gain access to the children. It is not difficult for a man who is intent on abusing children within his family to distance a child from its mother. His power in the family would allow him to effectively use physical or emotional threats. He may also 'groom' the child by offering special treatment or manipulate the child emotionally, for example telling the child that their mother would place her in care if she found out. Mothers should thus be regarded as vulnerable and in no way responsible. This is important as workers need to understand the continuing influence of the perpetrator on the mother and the children. For example, he is adept at denying responsibility for the abuse, displacing emotional responsibility and blame onto others in the immediate environment.

Most (but not all) perpetrators do have a cycle of behaviour which may go from masturbatory fantasy to contact with the victim. Each cycle is unique, which, if identified, allows work to focus on how it can best be interrupted and managed. Perpetrators can identify the points at which they are able to control and divert their thoughts and actions and consequently avoid offending.

Workers need to understand that the stages are not necessarily distinct and the sequence is not rigid: there is considerable overlap between the stages and smaller, repetitive cycles operate within the longer cycle. The length of the cycle may vary, and this is important as the frequency is an important indicator of risk. Perpetrators can travel through their cycle in a matter of hours, or it may take a few weeks or even years for others to reach the point of re-offending. The cyclical nature of the behaviour reinforces that it is continuous unless challenged.

Steven Wolf (1984) provided a theory of the cycle of offending which links factors known frequently to occur in the lives of individuals identified as sexually deviant. His paper builds on earlier research to suggest a comprehensive model to explain (in part) the development and maintenance of sexually deviant orientations. His hypothesis is that there exists a positive and increasing relationship between specific environmental and developmental experiences and the acquisition and maintenance of sexual deviance. He describes a multi-dimensional model linking factors known frequently to occur in the lives of individuals identified as sexually deviant and a learning model describing the relationship between inhibition and deviant arousal.

Wolf identified a category of 'potentiators' which simplistically relate early experiences of the perpetrator influencing their later attitudes and behaviour. The range of the latter includes witnessing sexual violence or abuse, family dysfunction, isolation, or a victim themselves of some kind of violence or abuse. He found that this group of perpetrators experienced significant abuse and deprivation at a rate approximately twice that of the general population. These potentiators seem to have a direct impact on the form of adult personality. These areas include low frustration, tolerance and poor social adjustment. They had a tendency to form interpersonal relationships that were shallow and lacking in true intimacy. They also commonly projected blame for whatever current difficulties they were experiencing. In terms of sexual preoccupation, Wolf noted that these individuals had developed a coping strategy for dealing with internally felt stress by translating it into sexual fantasy and behaviour. Under pressure the sex offender will give first in the weakest area of his personality membrane such as his sexuality.

Wolf then considered disinhibitors which he defined as transitory environmental factors or

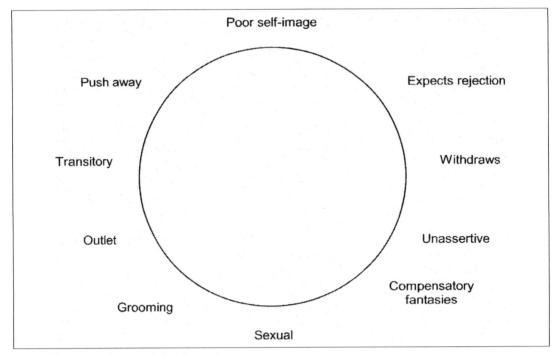

**Figure 12.4**  The offence cycle (Wolf, 1984)

internal states that act to lower the person's inhibitions against a specified behaviour. These have an important role in weakening the inhibition (social controls) against and strengthening the attraction to sexually deviant behaviour. Disinhibitors also have a role in terms of justification or rationalisation, which serve to further the individual's development and continuation of their sexual deviation.

Wolf also considers the role that sexual fantasy plays. Firstly, it acts as a disinhibitor towards the person being thought about. Secondly, it reinforces the attraction towards the behaviour, and finally it reinforces the rationalisations used in the fantasy which is the focus of masturbation. Fantasy acts to desensitise the perpetrator to the behaviour. The consistent repetition of the deviant theme in association with the pleasant sensations of sexual arousal and/or ejaculation serves to reinforce the attraction to the deviance so that the overall arousal and attraction to the deviant focus increases.

After the sexual fantasy the person may have to deal with a sense of guilt and embarrassment, so that a pattern of rationalisation is incorporated – a process known as 'cognitive distortion'. To the outsider such cognitive distortions amount to

unreal excuses, although to the perpetrator they are functional as they control the level of guilt and anxiety that the offender might otherwise experience as he repeats the abuse. Wolf points to how strong this belief system can be.

Wolf then looks at the addiction cycle, which has the advantage of being easily used in any direct work, and can be used for those who cannot read or write. Wolf developed the cycle of addiction after having looked both at the perpetrator's past history and his presenting behaviours.

Wolf''s cycle of offending can be expressed as shown in Figure 12.4.

This addiction cycle charts the entry level then all the points the perpetrator must go through in order to sexually abuse and then rationalise and continue their behaviour. The entry point of poor self-image is often related to their early life experiences and to a general dissatisfaction with their life. Indeed, Koester-Scott (1994) referred to the fact that perpetrators frequently present with a significantly disturbed developmental history; early feelings of emotional and social isolation, often combined with physical and sexual abuse which leads them to distort cognitively about themselves, others and the way in which the world operates. They often present in a state of 'victim posture'. They expect rejection, so they withdraw. They compensate through needs-fulfilment fantasies, which often have a sexual dimension or tone. This 'escape to sexuality' can be understood as a learned coping mechanism, which develops fairly early in life out of a realisation that sexual gratification is a way of displacing other more painful feelings. These belief systems form the beginning components of the 'offence cycle' as the offender develops a habit of using fantasy in order to manage emotional needs unmet because of a lack of connection with others. These fantasies serve as a cognitive rehearsal for deviant behaviour and may include aspirations of wealth, power, control and revenge. The escape to fantasy places the perpetrator in control and they then start targeting victims that match their deviant sexual interest. Indeed, if they fix their fantasy on a specific behaviour or individual it will increase the need for, or attraction to, that behaviour or individual. The result is that the fantasy begins to 'groom' the environment, as the perpetrator rehearses sexual behaviours and this reinforces their belief that the primary goal of sexual relations is to feel better about themselves. Behaviourally, compulsive masturbation often follows, as does the incorporation of rationalisation and justification to their fantasy. Although guilt and embarrassment follow (particularly relating to the possibility of being caught) it is quickly pushed away, and this is symptomatic of their general inability to take responsibility for themselves. They externalise responsibility and often promise never to do it again, although we need to note that they rarely learn from their mistakes. Since the perpetrator has not really changed and has been unsuccessful in applying discontinuation strategies they are again at step one and the whole process begins anew.

Finkelhor developed a multi-factor model to explain child sexual abuse by integrating a variety of single factor theories. It incorporates characteristics of the perpetrator, disinhibitors, the environment and the victim (see Figure 12.5). It operates at a high level of generality, thus allowing its use across a wide range of sexual perpetrators, whilst also encouraging analysis of the relative significance of the different factors in individual cases. It allows individual cases to be examined in detail, moving an offender on from asserting that his behaviour 'just happened' to an

understanding of the thoughts, feelings and conscious manipulation of people and events which he undertook before the offence could take place (Lancaster, 1996). Thus it emphasises that sexual abuse only takes place if the perpetrator already has sexual feelings towards the child and this firmly locates responsibility with the perpetrator. Finkelhor's model accounts for both familial and extra-familial child sexual abuse, and, although widely used, there remains a paucity of hard evidence to support the model or risk factors (Oates, 1990).

Finkelhor argues that all the known factors contributing to child sexual abuse can be grouped into four pre-conditions, which need to be met prior to the instigation of child sexual abuse. The four pre-conditions are:

1. *Motivation*: The potential perpetrator needs to have some motivation to sexually abuse a child. Thus, he will need to find children erotically and sexually desirable.
2. *Internal inhibitions*: They must overcome internal inhibitions that may act against his motivation to sexually abuse.
3. *External inhibitions*: They also have to overcome external obstacles and inhibitions prior to sexually abusing the child.
4. *Resistance*: Finally, they have to overcome the child's possible resistance to being sexually abused.

All four preconditions have to be fulfilled, in a logical, sequential order, for the abuse to commence. The presence of only one condition, such as a lack of maternal protection, social isolation or emotional deprivation is not sufficient to explain abuse.

## 1. Motivation to sexually abuse

Finkelhor argues that there are three functional components subsumed under the motivation to sexually abuse children:

- *Emotional congruence* in which sexual contact with a child satisfies profound emotional needs.
- *Sexual arousal* in which the child represents the source of sexual gratification for the perpetrator.
- *Blockage* when alternative sources of sexual gratification are not available or are less satisfying.

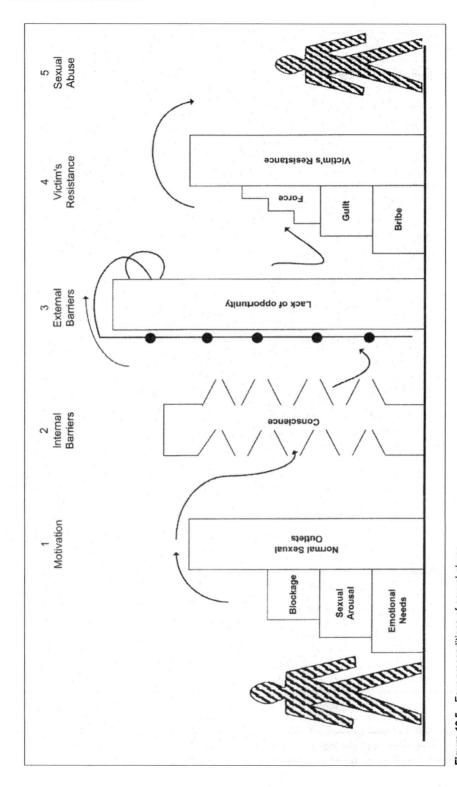

**Figure 12.5**   Four preconditions of sexual abuse

As these components are not actual preconditions, not all three need to be present for sexual abuse to occur. They are however important in explaining the variety of motivations perpetrators may have for sexually abusing children. The three components explain not only the instance of those who aren't sexually motivated but enjoy degrading victims by wielding power, but also the paedophile, and the sexually motivated perpetrator who looks towards children for variety, even though he has access to other sources of sexual gratification. In some instances elements from all three components may be present to account for whether the motivation is strong and persistent, weak and episodic, or whether the focus is primarily on girls or boys, or both.

## 2. Overcoming internal inhibitors

To sexually abuse, the perpetrator needs not only to be motivated but also to be able to overcome his internal inhibitions against acting on his motivation. No matter how strong the sexual interest in children might be, if the offender is inhibited by taboos then he will not abuse. Arguably, most people do have some inhibitions towards sexually abusing children. Disinhibition is not a source of motivation, it merely releases the motivation. Thus an individual who has no inhibitions against child sexual abuse, but who is not motivated, will not abuse. The second precondition aims to isolate the factors that account for how inhibitions are overcome and whether they are temporary or not. The element of disinhibition is an integral part of understanding child sexual abuse.

## 3. Overcoming external inhibitors

While preconditions one and two account for the perpetrator's behaviour, preconditions three and four consider the environment outside the perpetrator and child which control whether and whom he abuses. External inhibitors that may restrain the perpetrator's actions include family constellation, neighbours, peers, and societal sanctions, as well as the level of supervision that a child receives. Although a child cannot be supervised constantly, a lack of supervision has been shown in the clinical literature to be a contributing factor to sexual abuse, as has physical proximity and opportunity. External inhibitions against committing child sexual abuse may easily be overcome if the offender is left alone with a child who is not supervised.

## 4. Overcoming the resistance of the child

One limitation of much of the research literature is the failure to recognise that children are able to resist or avoid abuse. The focus in the clinical literature is on children who have been sexually abused ignoring those who, although approached, were able to avoid it or resist. The feminist argument proposes that insufficient attention is paid to the fact that children do have a capacity to resist. This capacity may operate in a very subtle, covert way, and does not necessarily involve overt protestations. Perpetrators may sense which children are good potential targets who can be intimidated and can be exhorted to keep a secret. They report that they can almost instinctively pick out a vulnerable child (and mother) on whom to focus their sexual attentions ignoring those who might resist. Frequently these children may not even be aware that they are being sexually approached or, indeed, resisting such advances.

Some of the risk factors that inhibit the capacity to resist include emotional insecurity and neediness, lack of physical affection, lack of friends, lack of support and interest from parents, age, naivety, and lack of information. Knowing which factors make children vulnerable is essential in formulating prevention programmes. Isolating behaviours that continue a risk, while emphasising those that enhance resistance or avoidance, can empower children to protect themselves. This is not to say that children who are not vulnerable do not get abused. Many children may be forced or coerced despite displaying resistance or avoidance behaviours. In such instances the factors overcoming a child's resistance has nothing to do with the child, or the child's relationship with the offender, but is the result of force, threat or violence. No matter how much resistance is manifested by the child, this may not necessarily prevent abuse.

Precondition four has three possible outcomes: the child may resist overtly by saying no and running away, or covertly by presenting a confident assertive demeanour which conveys a strong messages to the perpetrator not to attempt abuse for fear of detection or exposure; the child may resist but still be abused through the use of force or violence; or a child may resist but be overcome through coercion.

Acknowledging the child's capacity to resist or avoid abuse enhances our understanding of child sexual abuse. The notion that children can resist, albeit frequently covertly, is a positive one which could usefully generate more empirical research on the content of resistance behaviours and how these can be incorporated and adopted in the preventative programmes which aim to teach children how to avoid sexual abuse (Sanderson, 1990).

## Perpetrators: What they tell us

There are a growing number of papers which set out the findings of research into why sexual perpetrators commit sexual offences against children in their own words. These are essential developments in our understanding and are given some status as the respondents are frequently offered confidentiality, thus removing the fear of further consequences. Elliott et al. (1995) found:

## Selection of victims

The following selection characteristics used by sexual perpetrators:

- 42 per cent felt the child had to be pretty
- 27 per cent cited the way the child dressed was important
- 18 per cent reported being young or small was significant for them
- 13 per cent focused on innocent or trusting children
- 49 per cent reported an attraction to those who lacked confidence or had low self-esteem

Conte et al. (1989) interviewed a sample of adult sexual perpetrators who claimed a special ability to identify vulnerable children and to manipulate this vulnerability as a means of sexually using them. Vulnerability was defined in terms of children's status (eg living in a divorced home or being young) and in terms of emotional or psychological state (eg a needy child, a depressed or unhappy child).

This can be extended to include handicapped children, particularly those with a physical or learning difficulty, those in poor parenting situations who are not assertive or outgoing and who are trusting or withdrawn. Many claim that they can almost instinctively pick out vulnerable children and ignore those who might resist.

## Age of victim

Elliott et al. (1995) found that the child victim ranged from 1–18 years. The mean age of the youngest victims was 8.5 years: the mean age of the eldest victims was 13 years. 6.6 per cent also assaulted victims aged 19–45; one offender abused a 65 year old victim (p.583–4).

## Gender of victim

Elliott et al. (1995: 253) found that they generally had a preference for the gender of their victims: 58 per cent targeted girls, 14 per cent preferred boys, 28 per cent targeted both boys and girls.

## Relationship of victim to perpetrator

Sexual offences are often perpetrated by someone very familiar to the victim. Elliott et al. (1995) found that 46 per cent of the perpetrators felt that a 'special relationship' with the child was vital. They found that 66 per cent knew their victims. Most can be divided into three groups based on their relationship with the victim: family members, friends or acquaintances, and strangers.

- Family members: Waterhouse et al. (1993) found that 40 per cent of perpetrators were related to the victim. In their earlier research, Waterhouse and Carnie (1992) found that they were the natural father in 31 per cent of cases, step-fathers in 21 per cent of cases, and co-habitees in 11 per cent of cases. Kelly et al. (1991) found that close relatives (father figures, siblings, grandfathers, uncles and aunts) offended in 14 per cent of cases, compared to 68 per cent perpetrated by distant relatives, known adults and peers. Oates (1990) found that in 75 per cent of cases the perpetrator was known to the child and vice-versa. In 50 per cent of the cases, they were a member of the child's own family, whilst 50 per cent were trusted friends who had access to the children.
- Friends or acquaintances: Elliott et al. (1995) found that 66 per cent of perpetrators knew their victims through their families, friends or acquaintances, for example babysitting. Waterhouse et al. (1993) found that 60 per cent of the men in their sample were not biologically related to their victim.
- Strangers: The range of perpetrators unknown to the child pre-abuse ranges from 18 per cent

(Kelly et al., 1991) through 25 per cent (Oates,1990) to one-third (Elliott et al.,1995).

## Location of offence

Elliott et al. (1995) found that perpetrators often used more than one location to abuse children. Sixty-one per cent reported abusing in their own home compared to 49 per cent in the victim's home. Forty-four per cent reported abusing in public places such as toilets or parks, compared to 13 per cent in the homes of friends, six per cent in the vicinity of the perpetrator's home and four per cent in the car. It is highly significant that 48 per cent of them isolated their victims through babysitting.

## Strategies used

- offering to play games, teach them a sport or play a musical instrument
- giving bribes, taking them on outings, or giving them a lift home
- using affection, understanding and love
- telling stories involving lies, magic or treasure hunts
- asking a child for help (Elliott et al., 1995).

They found that 84 per cent used a strategy that had been previously successful, compared to 16 per cent who adapted theirs over time. Thirty per cent replayed their own experiences, whilst 14 per cent were influenced through pornography, television, films and the media.

## Types of offences

Elliott et al. (1995) found that all the perpetrators in their sample indecently assaulted their victims, sometimes in more than one way. Seventy-two per cent of them reported that this included masturbating the child and being masturbated by the child. Thirty-one per cent engaged in mutual oral sex and 57 per cent attempted or actually engaged in full sexual intercourse, either vaginal or anal. Eight per cent murdered or attempted to murder the child victim during or after the sexual assault. Eighty-five per cent committed the sexual acts with one victim at a time although the remaining five per cent had multiple victims present. Ninety-three per cent acted alone.

The first abusive action often involved one or two immediate sexual acts, such as sexual touching or genital kissing, whilst others desensitised the child by asking them to do something that would help them, such as undressing. The majority carefully tested the child's reaction to sex, by bringing up sexual matters or having sexual materials around, or by subtly increasing sexual touching. This 'normalised' sexual setting could be achieved by using sexually explicit videos, magazines or sexualised talking.

## The use of force

Perpetrators can use one or a combination of methods to secure a child's compliance. Elliott et al. found that 19 per cent used physical force with a child, 44 per cent used coercion and pursuasion and 46 per cent used bribery and gifts in exchange for sexual touches. Thirty-nine per cent were prepared to use threats or violence to control a resisting child. Sixty-one per cent used passive methods of control such as stopping the abuse and then coercing and persuading once again. Thirty-three per cent specifically told the child not to tell compared to 24 per cent who used threats of dire consequences, whilst 24 per cent used anger and the threat of physical force and 20 per cent threatened the loss of love or said the child was to blame. Sixty-one per cent were 'very worried' about the child disclosing.

The Waterhouse research reported on a wide range of means used to procure sex from naive children. Actual physical coercion and force was used in some 20 per cent of cases, verbal inducements or bribes in 14 per cent and coercion by verbal threats of violence in six per cent of cases. Margolin (1992) shattered the myth of the friendly and 'gentle' grandfather approaches reported earlier by Goodwin et al. (1983: 740) finding evidence of explicit threats and overt physical coercion. Conte et al. (1989) also noted that verbal threats are based on an understanding of the child and what will be an effective threat against them. Waterhouse et al. also recorded that most sexual abuse was severe. In 40 per cent of cases children were subjected to sexual manipulation of their genitals either beneath or above their clothing, vaginal intercourse occurred in 20 per cent of cases, whilst four per cent of the sample were subjected to oral sex, four per cent to sodomy, and five per cent to non-contact abuse. Conte et al. found that those relatively non-violent men in their sample had employed a range of coercive behaviours, for example conditioning through the use of reward and punishment and letting the child view violence towards their mother (p299).

## Crossover

Sexual offending can occur within and outside the family; with male and female victims, of varying ages and there can be a variety of sexually deviant behaviours. They are not always discrete or compartmentalised. Those perpetrators who are caught offending inside the family are potentially a threat to children living outside the family as a preference for that kind of behaviour develops (Wolf, 1984; Abel et al., 1987). It is important to provide such information as it is a central part of how professionals manage the perpetrator and assess risk. Most professionals assume a generalised risk to all children unless narrowed down through assessments.

### Research findings

- Abel and colleagues found that whilst there are clearly some men that only abuse inside or outside families, some 65 per cent of intra-familial perpetrators also abused outside the family.
- Research by Abel et al. (1987, 1988) has significantly influenced our approach to this group, as their work demonstrated that sexual perpetrators have a larger number of victims, acts, and multiple paraphilias than had previously been assumed. Few of the men were found to have a single paraphilia or to have only abused a single child. Indeed, extra-familial men were found to have an average of 19.8 victims (for those molesting a girl) and 150 victims (for those molesting a boy). The figures for incest perpetrators were significantly lower (approximately two victims). However, over half or more of them were noted to have abused outside their families, and 70 to 95 per cent were noted to have engaged in another paraphilia most commonly rape or exhibitionism.
- Earlier research (Abel, Mittleman and Becker, 1985) also established that many incest perpetrators who avowed no attraction to same sex children, disclosed a history of abusing children of both sexes and 44 per cent of them also revealed an astonishing number of child victims in addition to numerous other paraphilias. Abel and colleagues (1987) reinforced this cross over between different

sexually deviant behaviours. Indeed, they revealed that 23.3 per cent offended against both family and non-family members, 20 per cent offended against both sexes whilst 26 per cent offended against both sexes and 26 per cent used touching and non-touching behaviours.

- Freund and Blanchard (1986) also pointed out that those who have committed more than one type of sexual offence or deviation belonged to the group called 'courtship disorders': exhibitionism, voyeurism, obscene calls, toucherism and sadistic rape. Freund et al. (1983) found that 45 of the 86 exhibitionists, 11 of the 22 touchers, and 2 of the 7 voyeurs reported co-occurrence of these deviations. Abel, Becker, Cunningham-Rathner, Mittleman, and Rouleau (1988) investigated 561 male sexual perpetrators and found that at least 72 per cent of them (other than transsexuals) reported additional deviations.
- Day (1994) reported that mentally handicapped perpetrators are more likely than non-handicapped perpetrators to commit offences against both males and females, against both same-age and older victims, and are less likely to know their victims, to commit violence, or to commit penile penetration of the vagina.
- The principal implications of crossover relate to the number of children at risk, the possibility of an indiscriminate sexual arousal, as well as the practical difficulties surrounding where they live and whom they see.

### Issues to consider

Sexual abuse is not a random activity. It is overwhelmingly based within relationships where the perpetrator is in a trusted position of power and where the child is dependent, at least at times, on that person. The betrayal of loyalties by the perpetrator impacts on the mother who internalises the devastation of the betrayal, often leaving her truly damaged.

Workers need to explore how the perpetrator manipulated the situation and the mother's perceptions to facilitate the opportunity to abuse. The mother needs to understand how the perpetrator may have taught the child that the experiences they have undergone were normal and unimportant, and how the professionals will have advised them that they are significant and unusual. As such, the child has to adjust their viewpoint. The mother also needs to understand the processes by which the perpetrator has elicited victim loyalty: they often do not name their perpetrators.

Children who have been sexually abused will almost certainly have been told not to tell. Moreover, the perpetrators will have singled out the mother for exclusion. For example, threats will have been made about what will happen if they do tell, such as not being believed, being removed from the home, or their pets or friends being hurt. Mothers need to be aware of the chameleon-like nature of the perpetrator: they will be charming when they are in control but they can change dramatically when the allegations are made, becoming bullying and intimidating.

The men who sexually abuse children are not weird and bizarre strangers who suddenly appear in the lives of children, nor are they outcasts from their communities. Instead, these men are often known and trusted fathers, husbands, and relatives or 'respectable' neighbours and friends. The information from perpetrators themselves shows their behaviour to require motivation, intention, and planning. It is unfair to expect mothers to know when these trusted individuals pose a serious threat to the safety of their children. As the earlier research material has clearly indicated, they were unaware on most occasions that their children were being victimised. Perpetrators are adept at prevailing upon the children to keep the sexual abuse a secret from the mothers by just telling them to do so and, because of the unequal power relation between them, the children obey. They can also dissuade the children from telling their mothers by using bribery and threats. The perpetrator, by undermining the relationship between the mother and the child, is able to maintain the child's loyalty after the abuse.

Mothers and victims of sexual abuse are rarely aware about the compulsivity and repetitiveness of sexual abuse: their behaviour is not an accident that happens to perpetrators. It is not an illness that descends on them and then mysteriously passes. It is not a behaviour that necessarily gets better over time.

## The mother's role in the process (of further?) disclosure

The initial disclosure of a history of sexual abuse can come in a number of ways: from the child, possibly indicating that they are ready to address the secret; from the child already in therapy for some problem and having formed a trusting relationship with the helper; from medical evidence; from behavioural indicators; as a response to a direct question, or from some witness or other corroborating evidence.

The majority of children wish to tell their mother about the abuse, many do so, some repeatedly. The likelihood of, and circumstances leading to, a child telling her mother vary and are dependent upon several factors. The younger the child, the more likely the first disclosure is to be to the mother. Younger children may have greater difficulty in comprehending the abusive experience and the mother is usually the person to whom the child turns with physical soreness, etc. Younger children are also less likely to be fully aware of the negative consequences of disclosure and may disobey instructions by the abuser not to tell, impelled by their own developmentally appropriate inability to contain their anxiety. The more distant the relationship between the mother and the perpetrator, the more likely the child is to disclose to her mother. There are also identifiable categories who are less likely to disclose to their mothers. These include older girls who are aware of the consequences of disclosure, often feeling protective of their families in the face of predicted disruption to family life that disclosure will bring. In addition, sexually abusive relationships, which bring a degree of enjoyment for the girl are less likely to be disclosed to the mother where the abuse is not a member of the immediate family. The girl may be getting some of her own unmet needs within the family fulfilled outside of it. The associated guilt may further deter the girl from disclosing.

A child's reluctance to tell of abuse should never be attributed as a fault in the mother as this over-simplifies the difficulties of telling in sexual abuse cases. There are a number of reasons why children feel unable to tell:

- Children are dependent on adults for a lot of things, for example food, warmth, shelter as well as love, laughter and discipline etc. Children learn to look to adults to meet these needs as part of growing up.
- Children are taught to obey parents and adults, assuming power and authority over them as a right.
- The perpetrator is probably someone the child both likes and trusts. So they may want to protect them.

- The child may not understand that what is happening is wrong as the perpetrator may tell the child that this happens to all children.
- The perpetrator may make threats or bribes to the child or be violent. The child will therefore be too scared to tell because they believe something worse will happen or they will be punished.
- The child may not know or understand the consequences of telling or they may feel such guilt and shame that they cannot tell. This may be especially true if their body responded to the sexual stimulation.
- The child may think they have told and nothing happened. This will give or make stronger the message that the child is at fault or has done something wrong.
- Generally, adults are not good at talking openly about sex, sexuality and most of all sexual abuse. The child might therefore get the message that this is something that they cannot talk about.
- The child may be passive because they believe the perpetrator when he says that the sexual abuse is acceptable.
- The child may feel there is no use in telling. If the parents are rarely around or are preoccupied with their own lives, the child may think that their parents simply do not care about what happens to them.
- The child who is sexually abused may receive many rewards from the perpetrator, both in terms of presents and affection or attention. The child will not want this part to stop.
- They have a sense of loyalty or love for the perpetrator that makes it impossible for them to speak out against someone who is supposed to be protecting and caring for them.
- The child may not be getting love and cuddles and affection from other adults and so the abuse may be all the child receives in terms of these needs.
- The child may well fear the reactions of others, or has had unhelpful responses from people they have told before.
- The child may feel too much guilt and shame to tell anyone.
- They fear they will be blamed.
- They fear breaking up the family.
   (adapted from Engel, 1994; Hall and Lloyd, 1989 and Rose and Savage, 1995)

It is very important that mothers report the abuse once discovered. This is not a straightforward decision for many. Mothers' reports, as against those directly from children, are often viewed with particular suspicion (Humphreys, 1997). This has some origins in the professional perception of their culpability in the abuse (Hooper, 1989). A common reaction to learning about the abuse is to deny the need for outside help, feeling that the situation can be handled within the family unit. However, they must consider their sense of social responsibility to protect other children, desire for retribution, and fears that the court process will further traumatise the child (Regehr, 1990). The act of reporting sends a clear message to the child that what happened to them is very serious, must be stopped, and that the perpetrator needs to be punished or helped through legally-mandated treatment. To help them make the decision, mothers should be informed of the consequences of reporting and non-reporting, such as an inability to prosecute the perpetrator thereby allowing the risk to remain untreated. It also prevents treatment being available either for the child or the mother.

Any significant delay in responding to a disclosure can have the following effects: the child feels that her history of sexual abuse is too shocking or disgusting for her to be helped; she may feel rejected after plucking up the courage to tell; she may minimise/deny/retract that she has been abused; she may feel that her abuse is not serious enough to warrant attention; and there is the potential for self-injurious behaviour (Hall and Lloyd, 1989).

The disclosure clearly represents the beginning of the crisis for the mothers (discussed in detail in a later component) often aggravated further by the professional expectations that she will focus all her energies on the safety of her child. Many mothers do not have sufficient resources to do this immediately. Professionals also approach mothers suspiciously, rather than with an open mind, until the extent of their involvement can be ascertained. Such an approach is one of seeing them as guilty until proven otherwise. The professional intervention thus pushes the mother and child apart at a time when they most need to be together. It is not surprising that many mothers who know of the abuse struggle to take the next step of reporting it to the authorities.

### Research findings

Several studies show that fewer than half of victims tell anyone at the time of the abuse, and a large percentage never reveal the abuse until asked for research purposes. For example, Finkelhor (1990) found that only 40 per cent of both men and women had disclosed the abuse at the time it occurred, 24 per cent of women and 14 per cent of men told at a later time, and 33 per cent of women and 42 per cent of men had never told until the time of data collection.

Lawson and Chaffin (1992) found that disclosure was strongly associated with the attitude taken by the child's caretaker toward the possibility of abuse. Children whose caretakers accepted the possibility of abuse disclosed at a rate almost three and a half times as great as those whose caretakers denied any possibility of abuse. They noted that parental or caretaker attitude towards sexual abuse disclosure is not necessarily a discrete post-disclosure event, but may be explicitly or covertly manifest during or even prior to the disclosure itself. As such, it may influence not only post-disclosure adaptation, but also the child's decision to disclose or not to disclose. In their sample, they found that 63 per cent of children with supportive caretakers disclosed compared with only 17 per cent of children with unsupportive caretakers.

Howarth (1999) reported that statistics from Childline showed that 22 per cent of girls who disclosed sexual abuse told their mothers, compared to 43 per cent who told their friends, 12 per cent who told both parents and extended family, and three per cent who told social services. Howarth also noted that girls tend to be disclosing abuse at a much earlier stage than previously indicated, although there remains room for improvement in the one to five year age ranges. Furniss (1991) has noted that mothers are much more likely to become an ally for the child and the professionals if their own process of discovery is understood and facilitated.

Berliner and Conte (1995) found that according to the parents, in only 43 per cent of cases did their children directly tell them about the abuse. They noticed physical evidence (four per cent), behavioural change (11 per cent), or asked the child if anyone had touched them (10 per cent). In the remainder of cases, they learned about the abuse of their child through others. The children reported that they had told their mothers in almost half the instances (48 per cent) and their fathers first in five per cent of cases. The next largest category of first person told was a friend (17 per cent) while other relatives or professionals comprised the others to whom the children

reported. Relief was the emotion most often expressed about telling (69 per cent) with fear (16 per cent) sadness (seven per cent) and anger (three per cent) also mentioned. The majority of children characterised the initial reaction as supportive (54 per cent). Twenty-six per cent reported a reaction of shock/surprise, while 15 per cent described upset/sadness, 11 per cent anger, eight per cent disbelief and one per cent fear. The fact that many children did not report their experiences directly or did not tell their parents confirms that telling about the abuse is a difficult proposition.

Many children believe that their mothers were aware about their sexual abuse and this made it very difficult for them to disclose to their mothers. Palmer et al. (1999) found that 65 per cent of abuse survivors said that someone else knew about the abuse while it was happening. Only a minority (32 per cent) had disclosed to one or more persons while the abuse was occurring. The distribution was: disclosure to a non-abusive parent (41 per cent), another relative (32 per cent), a neighbour or friend (16 per cent), a professional (eight per cent), and others (three per cent). There were a range of reasons for non-disclosure: fear of the perpetrator (85 per cent); fear of negative reactions from family members (80 per cent); fear that no-one would believe them (72 per cent); belief that they deserved the abuse (62 per cent); and lack of awareness that the abuse was wrong or unusual (52 per cent). Most survivors reported that no effective help was forthcoming from their disclosure or from someone knowing about the abuse. Sixty per cent said it continued as before; 20 per cent said it became worse; 15 per cent said it stopped temporarily; and only five per cent said it stopped completely. The abuse stopped temporarily or completely 26 per cent of the time when mothers knew, compared to 16 per cent of the time when others knew. Children reported 'ignoring' behaviour on the part of families and of larger communities, aggravated when they thought that professionals appeared protective of the perpetrators. The child may also fear disclosing as they will lose the affection that the perpetrator has given them in the grooming process, and worse still, that they may not be believed. Gomes-Schwartz et al. (1990) found that the less loyalty the child feels towards the perpetrator, the more likely they are to tell, and they are least likely to tell when the perpetrator is a natural parent.

## Issues to consider

One of the greatest professional (never mind maternal) fears is that a child chooses to disclose sexual abuse to them. They feel unskilled, and disabled by the experience – even though they probably have detailed guidelines on how to deal with such a situation, and have someone else who can be called upon to deal with it. Panic can easily set in. Some will construct their own defences to divert the disclosure elsewhere.

The reactions of those who the child first tells will determine whether they feel encouraged to seek or accept further help. Indeed, the therapeutic work to overcome the effects of sexual abuse begins at this point. Positive responses to the child upon disclosure might include: acknowledging the difficulty of disclosing; relating the sexual abuse as linked to identified difficulties; offering immediate support; encouraging them to explore their feelings around the abuse; remaining calm and not showing any feelings of shock, disgust or distress. It is important to understand and impart the reality that the abuse is never the child's fault. It is equally often not the fault of the mother as she also may have been abused by the perpetrator.

Unfortunately, it can also end there if the disclosure is managed in an insensitive or intrusive way. Unhelpful reactions might include ignoring or minimising the effects of being sexually abused; showing an excessive interest in the sexual details; or appearing very angry, shocked or disgusted by the disclosure. Unhelpful comments might include 'It's in the past. Do try to forget about it'; 'That is not as bad as some sexual abuse that I have heard about'; 'It only happened a few times, so maybe there isn't really anything to worry about'.

By using the information about why children do not tell, get the child to share with their mother the difficulties they had in telling, and why. If the mother is a survivor of sexual abuse, then get her to do the same and some comparisons may sow the seeds of empathy.

Help the child to understand they were never wrong, for example, compare photographs of the perpetrator and the child and compare size, age and so on.

Mothers need to know that if the child disclosed to them, they did so for a reason, for example because mothers will believe what they are saying and will help them to sort it out. This does not negate the unexpected news when delivered and the process that follows.

## Questions that need answering

- Did the child tell the mother?
- How?
- Is there evidence of changes in their awareness and understanding of the process of disclosure?

## Position regarding self-protection work: what do their children know how?

Self-protection work does not refer to physical self-defence but rather to the complex of mental and behaviour skills that children of all ages employ to seek assistance in times of threat. The child's increased self-confidence will serve both healing and preventative functions (Orten and Rich, 1993). Whilst Regan (Chapter 13) provides us with a generic framework for body safety work, I will provide some specific guidance in context of this chapter.

A mother's first role in preventing any recurrence of harm is to permit their children to participate in a programme of self-protection. By teaching children strategies to avoid sexual abuse in no way implies that the child is any way responsible for the sexual abuse. It is a sad indictment on society today that they have to be prepared for such an event.

### Research findings

Palmer et al. (1999) found that there were a number of very real reasons why children did not disclose earlier than they did. These included the fact that they were unaware that the abuse was wrong or unusual, as well as fear of the perpetrator. The latter is not uncommon given the range of tactics deployed by the perpetrator, such as threats of harm to the child or other family members. Not knowing the abusive behaviour was wrong was a feature of many children. Their self-protection to this included not remembering, acknowledging or discussing the abuse. Some blocked it out completely. These authors found that preventative education to school-age children has a limited influence on their ability to respond to familial abuse, compared with the child's relationship with the perpetrator. First, abusive patterns in the family tend to begin so early for many children that the patterns would be established before the child's consciousness could be raised by a school programme. Second, respondents indicated that they were often inhibited by fears instilled by the perpetrators than by their own inability to perceive the abuse as wrong or unusual. To counter the strong influence of the family perpetrator, child education programmes could include survivors' experiences about how perpetrators blocked them from understanding and disclosing. Advance knowledge of typical rationalisations and methods of instilling fear, including death threats, may alert children and help them to recognise when they are being manipulated and to react in a self-protective way.

We know that relatively few parents opt to discuss child sexual abuse with their children (22 per cent to 60 per cent according to Wurtele and Miller-Perrin, 1992) and this may be because it is a difficult subject to discuss; the topic might frighten the child; the need for discussion has not occurred to the parent; the child is either too young for discussion, is in little danger of abuse, or is reluctant to discuss the topic; parents may lack the confidence in their own ability and this may be linked to a lack of knowledge, vocabulary, or materials.

Children may not recognise that they are being abused because they lack knowledge of social norms, and their awareness may be blocked by self-protective defence mechanisms. Perpetrators of sexual abuse often use a deceptive process of grooming, pressure for secrecy, and distortion of reality and morality, leaving the child confused about what happened (Berliner and Conte, 1990).

De Jong (1988) found that 31 per cent of the supportive mothers were not interested in counselling for their children, whereas nine per cent of non-supportive mothers sought such help for the child whom they had blamed for initiating the sexual contact with the perpetrators. De Jong argued that minimal counselling should include and address all the emotional, medical, social, environmental, and legal issues involved, as well as the treatment implications. At least one session with the entire family, including siblings, is recommended to clear the air and bring fears and concerns to the surface.

Elrod and Rubin (1993) reviewed the materials in relation to parental involvement in sexual abuse prevention education as well as establishing what parents know and need to know about child sexual abuse. They noted that parents are not typically given an opportunity to be involved in the planning of a children's curriculum on sexual abuse and often do not understand the issues or seriousness of the problem because of their own fear or lack of knowledge. These factors can lead to the parents denying their children access to important prevention information and increasing the susceptibility of children to sexual abuse and exploitation. In addition, if parents are not involved in prevention education for themselves, they may not perceive the reality or extent of sexual abuse or the need to be aware of the risks and the possibilities of prevention. Elrod and Rubin noted that most programmes on sexual abuse tend to target mothers. They found that the agreed topics for children's curriculum on prevention education for pre-schoolers included good/bad touches; how to tell if you are being abused; who to tell if someone abuses you; the importance of telling; abuse is not the child's fault; who abusers are; how to protect yourself; why abuse happens; what happens when you tell; what a child can do when they know someone else is being abused; and the likelihood of abuse happening to the child. The need for a professional involvement in the work was supported when they found that over half of the parents planned not to discuss several of the emotionally laden topics (such as who abusers are) although mothers planned to discuss significantly more topics than did the fathers.

## Issues to consider

Many children will be very angry with their mothers for failing to protect them sufficiently, and it is important that they be given the time and the space to work through this. Both the child and the mother could be asked to list all the reasons each of them are angry with each other, the perpetrator, and others (such as siblings and extended family members or professionals).

It may take considerable time for workers to get the trust of the victim or other children involved in the intervention process. Children may harbour feelings of guilt, shame and helplessness; and fear, disbelief, blame and rejection once more. The experience of sexual abuse by the child is surrounded by secrecy. It involves a misuse of power, betrayal of the child's trust, and compounds the child's helplessness and lack of control over the situation. Workers thus need to be very careful in exploring how they will engage the young person in the work as well as its content. Strategies might include being empathic, responding warmly, with interest and support, working at their pace, and respecting their right to remain silent about any issue, such as the detail of the abuse. It may take several months for a secure and trusting relationship to be forged and to allow any meaningful work to begin. We need to be aware that they may feel worse before they begin to feel better.

An initial disclosure of sexual abuse may only be the tip of the iceberg. Therefore, workers who are engaged in work with a child need to be aware about the possibility of subsequent disclosures, and in many cases, should actively facilitate them. In order to do this, they should use a range of materials so they have a choice of method of disclosure, for example writing, drawing or artwork, or talking face-to-face with the helper.

They should encourage disclosure by reminding them that by breaking their silence they will lose some of their pain. Workers do need to be mindful of the requirements of criminal courts if such disclosures are to lead to convictions, and they need to negotiate any self-protection work with the Crown Prosecution Service (CPS) so as not to prejudice any incomplete legal proceedings.

It is important that consideration is given to the role of the mother in the process, particularly since we know that mothers are important for clarifying concepts and applying their new knowledge in daily life. Mothers should be available for the child should they wish to disclose anything further in the future. In contrast, uninformed parents may not be able to answer questions, may contradict accurate information, and may not know how to correct any misconceptions their children may have (Adams and Fay, 1981).

Techniques and strategies to help children and young people avoid falling prey to perpetrators of sexual abuse must take into account a variety of factors. Children are sexually abused by young people in a range of different settings, usually by boys well known to them, such as brothers or family friends, but sometimes by complete strangers. The type of relationship between the perpetrator and the victim will influence the way in which the child is engaged in sexual activity. Thus, a perpetrator who has regular contact with the victim has the opportunity to persuade and

groom the victim, introducing the victim to sexual behaviour gradually as he gains the child's trust and confidence. This type of approach is frequently used by adult paedophiles and occasionally by experienced adolescent perpetrators, especially those who have themselves been groomed by adult perpetrators (Epps, 1997).

Some perpetrators, however, have no regular contact with children, or have made a conscious decision not to abuse children known to them, perhaps through fear of being caught. These men are more likely to prey on unfamiliar children, having no desire to engage victims in a longer-term relationship. Findings from community surveys show that boys are more likely then girls to be sexually abused outside of the home, especially boys from low income families who have also been subjected to physical abuse (Finkelhor, 1984). These stranger assaults are more likely to be accompanied by the use of threats, physical coercion and violence in an effort to force the child to participate in sexual activity. It is also likely that perpetrators of stranger assaults more often offend in an opportunistic way, not carefully planning the offence, and using excessive force in their desperation to engage the victim, perhaps with little thought as to the consequences. There is some evidence to suggest that perpetrators of sexual abuse are more likely to be reported to the police if they are strangers than if they are known to the victim (Finkelhor, 1979). It follows, therefore, that intra-familial assaults are least likely to be reported to the police (Finkelhor, 1984).

West (1991) recognises that some children are more vulnerable to abuse, especially those who have previously been abused. Victims of childhood sexual abuse sometimes exhibit sexualised and 'seductive' behaviours (Yates, 1982) making them vulnerable to further abuse by those adolescents and adults with a proclivity for sexually abusing children. Finkelhor (1988) refers to this effect as 'traumatic sexualisation', caused by premature and inappropriate sexual learning. Sexually abused children are often rewarded by their perpetrators with material goods, such as sweets and money, and may come to view sex as a way of manipulating people. According to Finkelhor (1988) children who have been abused under conditions of danger, threat and violence are especially likely to be traumatised.

Children are usually unaware of the distorted way in which perpetrators interpret their behaviour, and are therefore oblivious to the fact that they may be placing themselves at further risk.

Broadly speaking, two types of sexual abuse prevention programmes can be identified: those aimed at all children (primary prevention) and those targeted towards 'at-risk' children, including children who have already been abused (secondary and tertiary prevention). However, Elliott (1992) makes the important point that targeting specific children suggests that they are somehow responsible for their abuse or for being unable to stop it. Consequently she suggests that programmes should be aimed at all children, not just those that have been abused. In addition, programmes should aim to educate all parents and carers, raising awareness about the risks of sexual abuse, and encouraging the use of books and materials within the home which enhance self-protection. A range of books and videos are now available, aimed at different age groups. Many of these can easily be obtained through good bookshops and toyshops, or through charities such as KIDSCAPE. For example, 'Feeling Happy, Feeling Safe', written by Michele Elliott (1991) is aimed at ages three to seven. A brightly illustrated, colour picture book, it aims to teach children how to deal with bullies, how to keep safe, and how to react to advances by strangers and known adults.

Primary prevention programmes assume that all children are potentially at risk and will therefore benefit from self-protection strategies. Programmes usually provide classroom-based instruction for children of all ages on how to protect themselves from sexual assault and what to do if they experience actual or threatened abuse. Children are taught a variety of techniques, including how to distinguish between 'good' and 'bad' touching; how to be assertive, ranging from repeatedly saying 'no' to the use of self-defence techniques; and the importance of not keeping secrets. Most programmes aim to reduce the risk of abuse by changing the child's behaviour. By teaching children to avoid risky situations, to recognise inappropriate touching, to say no (if possible) when anyone tries to do something which makes them frightened or confused, to refuse to keep secrets, and to seek adult help, it may be possible to help children to avoid abuse.

Research suggests that boys exposed to prevention education programmes perceive themselves as less likely to be abused, perhaps because they feel more able to control potentially abusive situations (Dziuba-Leatherman and Finkelhor, 1994). However, doubts have been expressed about the ability of such programmes in preventing sexual abuse (Gilbert, 1988). Outcome research in this area is lacking and must be a priority for the future.

## Building better communication between the mother and the child

It is important that the mother is able to communicate with her child about what has happened on a number of levels:

- to affirm for the child that they were not to blame
- to provide a way for the child to talk about and sort out any confusions
- to confirm to the child that they will be kept safe
- to provide a way of communicating if the child is worried about anything in the future.

If there is a possibility that the family may reunite then a more comprehensive safety plan also needs to be in place with communication and a strengthening of the mother-child relationship being one of the key factors.

Considering some of the issues from the child's perspective will help to indicate the level of empathy the mother holds in relation to her child, and may indicate if additional work on this is needed. It would be useful to consider what the mother thinks about in relation to the specific issues concerning her child:

- what their experience was
- the strategies that were used
- what the child thinks and feels now.

what things the child might want or need to hear from mothers or from others (for example extended family members):

- They weren't to blame (for the abuse or the subsequent situation).
- You want them to be safe.
- They can talk to . . . if they have any worries in the future or if anyone does anything that they aren't sure about.
- You are sorry that you didn't know or weren't able to believe sooner.

What things mothers may want to say to their child:

- You love and believe them.
- You are sorry for the hurt and pain they have suffered.

We know that one of the strategies used by perpetrators is to isolate or distance the child from what may be a source of support. In many cases the relationship between the mother and the child is manipulated to develop tensions and conflicts, leading to loss (or perceived loss) of trust and emotional or physical availability of the mother. It is important that this relationship be re-established and that confidence be restored. Some mothers are able to do this instinctively whilst others are unable to speak about the child's experience without support to do so and are uncomfortable with the issues. Ways of developing communication about bodies, children's rights over their bodies and keeping safe are covered in more detail in Chapter 13.

## Ability to identify indicators in both the perpetrator and the children

Whilst it is important to educate mothers in the signs that may be indicators of sexual abuse, we need to also caution against overreactions which instigate a protective process which uncovers a false allegation. Symptoms of sexual abuse do not follow a set-pattern; there is no single behaviour or symptom or combination of behaviours or symptoms that always proves abuse, nor do all child victims display the same kinds of behaviour.

Every child is unique, and every abuse experience is unique (Myers, 1997). In some cases, there are no demonstrable changes in behaviour. Despite this, it is important to provide mothers with a framework to help them watch for any possible signs of abuse. In doing so, readers should refer back to the component on the effects of child sexual abuse on the victims and also acknowledge that it is impossible to detail all the possible behavioural changes and psychological symptoms in a book of this kind.

Several guidelines have been suggested which should help parents identify circumstances where they should be concerned:

- any radical change in behaviour, particularly where it is a dramatic change from their usual pattern of behaviour
- when any symptoms are chronic and fail to respond to the usual methods of management, then child sexual abuse should be considered

- any pattern of (three or more) symptoms and behaviours should indicate more likely harm or risk to the child
- the severity of the symptoms
- even where child sexual abuse is not proven from these, it should require an investigation for the cause of the behaviour.

(Wurtele and Miller-Perrin, 1992)

Mothers should document the changes and symptoms immediately in detail and in writing, along with when they first appear. They should note anything that might explain behaviour changes or psychological symptoms.

Mothers are often provided with information to alert them to the many behavioural indicators of child sexual abuse. These indicators have been established from victim accounts and with the benefit of hindsight. They are not always helpful checklists as they refer to behaviours fraught with value judgements and most children exhibit some of these behaviours at some point without necessarily being subjected to sexual abuse. Indeed, recent research shows that attempts to assess risk and dangerousness are in themselves risky (Clark et al., 1990). We must avoid the error of assuming that retrospective studies can be used to predict sexual abuse with any degree of accuracy. What mothers do need to be clear about is that the checklist is not the key feature, it is the picture which builds up around it which is important.

Given that there are often no distinct signs of sexual abuse, victims are often extremely hard to distinguish from any other children. Given that the essential human instinct is survival, it may be much better to identify signs of sexual abuse that we look for in survivors rather than victims. The least common survival method is disclosure that abuse has taken place. Brown (1998) has usefully set out the most obvious survival strategies utilised by children following the abuse:

- Forgetting: this might take the form of repressing the memory (either during or following the abuse), storing it in the subconscious as this may seem like the only way to continue to live. This is only a short-term strategy as it can create other difficulties, such as aspects of recall through smell or touch.
- Pretending: this can take the form of children fabricating an alternative and idealised picture

of their actual experience, for example seeing the perpetrator as the best parent in the world.

- Denying what has happened is a natural response combined with the awfulness of what has happened, the fear of the consequences of relating the abuse, and of telling what has happened.
- Distancing themselves physically from the perpetrator either by running away or staying with a friend's family is only a viable option for a few, particularly when the child is very young.
- Transcending is a psychological distancing, such as leaving their body throughout the abuse.
- Numbing allows the child to immunise the pain at both a physical as well as at an emotional level.
- Rationalising: includes excusing the behaviour of the abuser, for example 'they have their own problems.'
- Minimising plays down the importance and significance of the abuse, for example 'it wasn't that bad'.
- Justifying is rationalisation with accompanying self-blame, for example 'I deserved it'.
- Compartmentalising is where the child stores the abuse away from other aspects of life, freeing them to function well in other social settings, such as school.
- Striving for perfection: only by being the best will the child survive. They compensate for the abuse by creating outlets to escape from the abuse and this is seen in workaholics. The child may become obsessed with achieving success, academically, sporting, etc.
- Finding faith: here, the child looks for something more powerful (than the abuser) to place their trust in. Although this can be due to a belief that the abuse was justified and they are working to find forgiveness for their part in the abuse.

Any lists for recognising signs and indicators of sexual abuse should be used as a guide only. It is most likely that if sexual abuse is happening there will be a number of signs and indicators from all of the categories that have been present for quite some time.

When assessing indicators of sexual abuse, it is important to take into account the child's current development. For example, what may be appropriate behaviour for an older child, may indicate a problem for a younger child or vice versa. Sexual abuse may even stop growth at the developmental stage at which the abuse began. Many young people will regress to earlier developmental stages following abuse. They are seeking comfort, safety and reassurance from the adults around them, but have difficulty in re-establishing trust in relationships. Those who cannot function at the developmental level that corresponds with their chronological age will encounter a variety of difficulties in their daily life experiences. They may struggle to bond well with others. Many adults will interpret immature or uncooperative behavioural responses as a sign of unwillingness rather than inability and they will often respond harshly in return. Young people may then perceive themselves as failures when they are unable to meet the expectations of the adults around them, and their self-esteem suffers. Social problems develop as they encounter relationship difficulties with their peers: they may feel different from and inferior to others their own age; they may withdraw from social contact in shame or become aggressive, venting their anger and frustration; they may experience anxiety in situations that are competitive, or require them to measure themselves to standards of others; communication and problem-solving may be weak and present increased levels of frustration in expressing feelings and needs and in having needs met; there may be limited ability to show empathy or a caring attitude toward others; and any intolerance or indifference shown by other children can greatly heighten the anxiety of children and young people who long to belong or fit in with their peer groups (Croll, 1994).

Behaviours need to be assessed in the context of the child's total life situation and some questions that are helpful to ask include: 'what needs does this behaviour meet?' 'Is this behaviour developmentally appropriate?' 'Is there a pattern to this behaviour?' 'What other behaviours have been noticed?' 'How does the child understand the behaviour?'

### Normal sexual development, knowledge and behaviour

It is important for mothers to be clear about age-appropriate sexual behaviour, knowledge and development if they are to be able to differentiate the 'abusive' from the 'normal'. Hanks (1997) offered a very useful baseline from which to work.

### From birth to two years of age

| Sexual development | Sexual behaviour | Sexual knowledge |
| --- | --- | --- |
| • gender established<br>• newborns are capable of erect penis (male) and lubrication (females)<br>• physiology for arousal is present<br>• spontaneous penile erection | • erect penis<br>• recognition or experience of pleasurable feelings when touching genitals<br>• touching self, sometimes looking at and touching others | • limited language for body parts (including genitals) |

### From 2–6 years of age

| Sexual development | Sexual behaviour | Sexual knowledge |
| --- | --- | --- |
| • children grow<br>• boys testicles descend<br>• erections and lubrication for boys and girls | • Touch their own and other (peer) genitals<br>• look and play doctor, nurses, mum games with peers<br>• peer exploration<br>• masturbates self<br>• experiences pleasurable feelings<br>• interest in own faeces. Watches with interest when others use the toilet and bathroom<br>• mimicking having babies in their tummy<br>• rubs genitals, masturbates when uncomfortable, unhappy, tense, excited or afraid<br>• practices kissing | • language develops. They become more inquisitive and verbal about some functions; imitate without understanding; limited knowledge about childbirth and where babies come from. Know gender differences as they get older<br>• child asks about genitals, breasts, intercourse and will name body parts more accurately; using slang words for bathroom/toilet functions, genitals and sex<br>• little understanding of sex |

### From 6–12 years of age

| Sexual development | Sexual behaviour | Sexual knowledge |
| --- | --- | --- |
| • for some children of 8 or 9 years pubertal changes may begin<br>• some children are capable of childbirth<br>• menstruation, wet dreams, develop sexual fantasies | • masturbation in private<br>• shows guilt/embarrassment about sexual activities<br>• simulates intercourse, kissing, petting with peers<br>• may have actual intercourse without knowing consequences properly<br>• this age group cannot give informed consent | • language for genital parts<br>• increased knowledge of sexual behaviour and sexual language and slang (derived from media and peers)<br>• confused about sexual behaviour and causal effects<br>• unclear about intercourse and pregnancy |

### 'Normal' sexual behaviours in juveniles include:

| Joint activity with partner | Individual activity |
| --- | --- |
| • embracing and kissing<br>• close bodily contact<br>• fondling<br>• mutual petting and masturbation<br>• simulated intercourse<br>• intercourse | • masturbation<br>• highly eroticised fantasies<br>• 'wet' dreams |

**Figure 12.6   Normal sexual development, behaviour and knowledge in children and young people (Hanks, 1997)**

These indicators show the need to properly assess the age-appropriateness and behavioural appropriateness of the juvenile's sexual development and functioning. We then need to compare the sexual development alongside their physical, emotional, intellectual and social development and highlight any significant discrepancies between the two. On the basis of such an assessment we should be better able to distinguish between normal developmental sexual experimentation between age-mates and abusive experimentation which involves a pre-pubertal child; and abusive exploitation of a child by a juvenile who is sexually knowledgeable and is knowingly abusive; and sexual assault and violence (Richardson, 1990: 153).

Calder (1997) then went on to offer a framework for differentiating the 'normal' from the 'abusive' in young people:

- What is the age relationship between participants?
- What is the social relationship? In what context did the abuse occur? Are they related?
- What type of sexual behaviour is exhibited?
- What is the experience of the victim?
- How does sexual contact take place?
- How was the sexual activity revealed?
- How persistent is the sexual behaviour?
- Evidence of escalation
- Sexual fantasies
- What are the characteristics of the victims?

Johnson (1994) has produced 21 red flags in children's sexual behaviour that mothers might find useful:

1. The children engaged in the sexual behaviours do not have an ongoing mutual play relationship.
2. Sexual behaviours which are engaged in by children of different ages or developmental levels.
3. Sexual behaviours which are out of balance with other aspects of the child's life and interests.
4. Children who seem to have too much knowledge about sexuality and behave in many ways more consistent with adult sexual expression.
5. Sexual behaviours which are significantly different than those of other same-age children.
6. Sexual behaviours which continue in spite of consistent and clear requests to stop.
7. Children who appear to be unable to stop themselves from engaging in sexual activities.
8. Sexual behaviours which occur in public or other places were the child has been told they are not acceptable.
9. Children's sexual behaviours which are eliciting complaints from other children or adversely affecting other children.
10. Children's sexual behaviours which are directed at adults who feel uncomfortable receiving them.
11. Children (four years and under) who do not understand their rights or the rights of others in relation to sexual contact.
12. Sexual behaviours which progress in frequency, intensity or intrusiveness over time.
13. When fear, anxiety, deep shame or intense guilt is associated with the sexual behaviour.
14. Children who engage in extensive, persistent, mutually agreed upon adult-type behaviours with other children.
15. Children who manually stimulate or have oral or genital contact with animals.
16. Child sexualises non-sexualised things, or interactions with others, or relationships.
17. Sexual behaviours which cause physical or emotional pain or discomfort to self or others.
18. Children who use sex to hurt others.
19. When verbal or physical expressions of anger precede, follow or accompany the sexual behaviour.
20. Children who use distorted logic to justify their sexual actions (eg she didn't say 'no').
21. When coercion, force, bribery, manipulation or threats are associated with sexual behaviour.

Mothers who are aware of these frameworks and how children change developmentally over time, should be in a better position to identify any victims.

## Indicators in the perpetrator

It is very difficult to predict with any certainty those who will abuse and those who will not. There are, however, certain behaviours and personality characteristics that are common among men who sexually abuse children. These are warning signs, or red flags, that they may be more likely to sexually abuse a child. These indicators should not be singled out but seen in their entirety, as a unit (Engel, 1994). They include:

- poor impulse control
- low self-esteem
- selfishness and narcissism
- neediness and a tendency to make demands on the mother's time and attention
- timidity, lack of assertiveness, feelings of inadequacy, social awkwardness, poor social skills, difficulty developing adult social and sexual relationships
- alcohol abuse, alcoholism, and drug addiction
- history of being sexually abused as a child
- history of being abusive (physically, verbally, sexually) as an adult or older child
- history of mental illness
- dependent personality (unable to support oneself financially or emotionally).
- 'loves' to be with children, relates to children much better than adults, acts more like a child than an adult
- antisocial behaviour (does not believe in society's rules, has own set of rules that seem to accommodate his desires). Aggressive, abusive behaviour
- withdrawal into one's own world, an extremely active fantasy life
- inability to have a successful relationship with an adult woman
- overly sexed, preoccupied with sex, needs to have sex daily or several times a day, masturbates compulsively
- does not seem to have any limits when it comes to sex – anything goes (such as sadomasochism, wife swapping)
- overly involved in pornography: constantly reads porno magazines, watches porno movies
- exposure to and interest in pornography involving children
- showing more interest in the children than the mother
- sexual repression, moralistic behaviour, feeling guilty about sex
- sexual impotency or other sexual dysfunction with adult females
- need to feel powerful and controlling.

(Engel, 1994: 40–1)

Behaviour changes to be observed in the perpetrator when they return home include:

- starts to abuse alcohol or drugs
- stresses the impossibility of re-offending

- interested in pornography
- stresses the innocence of his sexual contact with children
- begins to minimise the impact of his past offending
- keeps leaving the house for no apparent reason
- lies in other areas of his life
- gets involved in youth activities
- wants to be left alone with the children
- changes noticeably in his sexual functioning
- discusses sexual issues in front of the children
- starts to use innuendos
- becomes paranoid and stresses the fact that you don't trust him.

(Wyre, 1987)

### Research findings

Hubbard (1989) found that many mothers believed they would recognise the signs in their own children. Without exception, this was not the case, although with hindsight there were clues which could have served as stimuli for the mothers to question what was occurring. As many of the clues went with no response and were avoided, it strengthened the mother's denial pattern and further dissociated themselves from their own sexual abuse.

### Issues to consider

What does she think it would be helpful to know to keep her child safe or to know if her child is being abused?

What would she notice if there was a risk to her child in the future?

Advise the mother that if the child has a number of indicators, then they should start asking questions of the child, rather than the perpetrator.

Mothers do need to be aware that they can often be confronted with contradictory messages from their child, which makes it very difficult to know how to respond. The child may describe something that suggests it is very distressing but they exhibit no signs of distress. These children have become adept at smothering their true feelings as a protective mechanism.

## General parenting

The issue of general parenting is important for a number of reasons. There is a correlation between a lack of confidence in their own parenting and a reduced awareness of risks for their children

(Hooper, 1992). There are a number of potential problems for those mothers who were either sexually or otherwise abused as children, particularly the lack of any good parenting model. Many mothers feel that they are inadequate parents for allowing the sexual abuse to take place.

The moment the professional agencies become aware of the alleged sexual abuse, the person who comes under the greatest scrutiny is the main carer, the mother. It seems a little unfair that at a time when she is preoccupied with the consequences of the disclosure she is required to make a super-human effort to be a model parent (Peake and Fletcher, 1997). This is often not the same for the perpetrator who may leave the home and not face up to the sexual abuse.

They may often find themselves referred for parenting courses or assertiveness training. We have to question the appropriateness of retraining them after they failed to prevent their partners from sexually abusing their child. It often appears that the women are slotted into pre-existing programmes open to professionals, rather than being tailored to this group or to individual cases.

The current practice of assessing risk centres around issues of parenting and the needs of the children. Many mothers think that this is the focus of the work from social services, particularly as they have received the message that remaining with their partner means that they are a bad parent. Mothers may become confused about what is expected of them if they are not prepared to change their decision. The consequence of this is that they feel isolated and can react with conflict and confrontation. This has the potential to result in stalemate. If this is perceived as non co-operation, it is possible that legal proceedings might be considered. The process thus confirms that they are inadequate parents (Rose and Savage, 1998).

## Research findings

Tamraz (1996) noted that non-abusing mothers are often reported to lack mothering skills. They may be characterised as detached and distant, or as over-attentive and over-involved. Some material contends that the mothers may never have received the mothering they needed in their childhood and accordingly lack the skills or the ability to provide their daughters with what they never had. They may go on to recreate their own childhood experience by repeating their own

mother's lack of protectiveness and so deprive their daughters of a strong sense of self, thereby facilitating incest.

In their exploratory study of parenting attitudes among women who were sexually abused as children, Cole and Woolger (1989) found that both incest victims and those abused by unrelated men had similar child-rearing attitudes regarding nurturance and control of their children, but that the incest victims had more stringent attitudes towards autonomy promotion. Their responses reflected a high interest in their children becoming self-sufficient as early as possible. As such, a possible indication of incest is that the victims distance themselves from the demands of parenting. The authors compared this with their practice experience when they found that mothers with a history of incest often reported positive attitudes towards child rearing, but often seemed hostile, resentful, and jealous when describing actual parenting situations. This raises a question as to whether the central problem is coping with the emotional demands of parenting or is an attitudinal problem. Many do not want to replicate the mistakes of their parents and most endorse the expectations of good parenting. Incest survivors may struggle most at times of acute emotional stress in parenting given that their history has taught them to flee from the feelings of inadequacy and confusion rather than moderate their feelings in ways that mothers typically do. Benedek (1959) has argued that confidence in one's own parenting is a protection against the inevitable frustrations of parenting.

Cole et al. (1992) examined the quality of the self-reported parenting experiences and practices of women who were incest victims as children, and compared them to families where alcohol but not sexual abuse was a feature. They found that incest survivors reported significantly less confidence and less sense of emotional control as parents than non-risk mothers. In addition, they reported significantly less support in the parental partnership with their spouses, and reported being less consistent and organised, and making fewer maturity demands on their children. Overall, being an incest victim as a child was related to their feelings of adequacy as parents.

## Issues to consider

Reder and Lucey (1995) explored the significant issues in the assessment of parenting. They provided a framework for the assessment of parenting under various headings/themes, each of which come together to provide an overall picture. They are set out below:

1. *The parent's relationship to the role of parenting*
   Does the parent provide basic, essential physical care?
   Does the parent provide age-appropriate emotional care?
   Does the parent encourage development of the attachment dynamic?
   What attitude does the parent have to the tasks of parenting?
   Does the parent accept responsibility for their parenting behaviour?
   Is the child expected to be responsible for their own protection?
   If there are problems, does the parent acknowledge them?
2. *The parent's relationship with the child*
   What feelings does the parent have towards the child?
   Does the parent empathise with the child?
   Is the child viewed as a separate person?
   Are the child's essential needs given primacy over the parent's desires?
3. *Family influences*
   What awareness and attitude does the parent have regarding their own parenting experiences?
   Is the parent able to sustain a supportive relationship with a partner?
   Is the child over-involved in the family's discordant relationships?
   How sensitive is the family to relationship stresses?
   What is the meaning of the child to the parent?
   What is the child's contribution to the parenting relationship?
   What attitude does the child have to their caretakers?
4. *Interaction with the external world*
   What support networks are available?
   What is the pattern of the parent's relationships with professional workers?
5. *The potential for change*
   What is the potential to benefit from therapeutic help?
   What responses have there been to previous offers of help?

These authors clearly believe that parenting is not a quality that someone does, or does not, possess, but is a relationship that responds to fluctuations in other relationships. The assessor needs to consider all such influences.

## Social and family history

### *Current family home environment*

The literature strongly supports the belief that incestuous families are dysfunctional families with multiple stressors. It is not typical for sexual abuse to occur independently of other aspects of family dysfunction. It occurs with greater frequency in homes disrupted by parental absence or separation, or in those in which standards of parental care are punitive, confused, and rejecting (Bagley and King, 1990). However, we must also remember that sexual abuse does occur in seemingly normal families, including the seemingly upright, religious and respectable ones. Judges, lawyers, doctors, school teachers, and social workers are all represented in the perpetrator population. Perpetrators are infrequently entirely bad parents. They have good sides too. Many children want the abuse to stop but they want to retain the good father as they love them when the abuse is not happening. Herman and Hirschman (1980) noted that when sexual abuse is carried out in the context of a caring relationship that almost all the victims expressed some warm feeling towards their fathers.

An assessment of current family functioning and level of support is needed to determine what kinds of supportive and therapeutic services mothers will need. Testa et al. (1992) hypothesised that children who did not disclose sexual abuse or who received negative support following victimisation were more likely to come from distressed families than those who are able to obtain support.

Workers need to consider the co-existence of domestic violence with the sexual abuse and how this impacts on the mothers' choices. There is increasing evidence that domestic violence is more prevalent in sexually abusive families than in the general population (Truesdell et al., 1986) and thus workers need to acknowledge that any effective intervention will need to address the domestic violence before the mother can cope successfully with her child's victimisation (Dietz and Craft, 1980). Nelson (1992) reported that in 40 per cent of divorces, women cite domestic violence as a factor. Ninety to ninety-seven per cent of domestic violence is from men to women.

Despite under-reporting, we do know that:

- One in four women experiences domestic violence in their lifetime and it is estimated that at any one time between one in eight/ten women will experience domestic violence.
- Every week two women in England and Wales are killed by their current or former partners.
- Domestic violence accounts for a quarter of all violent crime.
- UK figures suggest that between 40–60 per cent of separated, or divorced women experienced domestic violence.
- Women aged 16–29 are at greatest risk of experiencing domestic violence.
- Domestic violence often starts, or escalates during pregnancy.
- On average a woman will approach over ten different agencies before she receives an appropriate response and the help she needs.
- Domestic violence seriously impacts on women. It affects her physical health, mental health, and all other aspects of her life and the lives of her children.

(Rose, 2000)

Research tells us that child abuse is most likely to occur where abuse of mothers is present (Stark and Flitcraft, 1988) and that these mothers are the most likely to seek help to protect their children. Conclusions reached from research indicate that:

- Abused mothers do not usually come from disorganised or violent families of origin, casting doubt on the myth that family history predisposes women to domestic violence or their children to abuse.
- Mothers experiencing domestic violence are more punitively treated (ie their children are far more likely to be removed) than mothers not experiencing domestic violence, even when the abuse of the child is not physical.
- Professionals often fail to acknowledge the existence of abuse and its impact on women, at the same time as blaming them for the abuse of their children. Very often women are accused of 'failure to protect' when agencies are themselves failing to protect them.

The presence of other problems in the home needs to be explored. For example, Server and Janzen (1982) in a study of 48 incestuous families, found a 71 per cent rate of alcohol abuse and a 31 per cent rate of drug abuse. If denial exists in relation to these, then it will easily be extended to defend the sexual abuse.

Palmer et al. (1999) found that in their study of abuse survivors, only six per cent had experienced sexual abuse alone. Many had experienced a combination of different kinds of abuse: physical, emotional and sexual (45 per cent), physical and emotional (21 per cent), or sexual and emotional (17 per cent). This highlights the need to assess the family functioning broadly. They also found that the age of onset was very young: for physical abuse. 4.7 years; for emotional abuse, 6.3 years; and for sexual abuse, 6.3 years. The abuse tended to persist for many years. Emotional abuse had an average duration of 20.3 years, physical abuse 11.2 years, and sexual abuse 8.1 years. These findings were replicated in DeYoung's study (1994) where she found that many of the woman described having been sexually, physically and emotionally abused by their husbands.

Family dynamics may contribute to sexual abuse through improper supervision, poor choice of babysitters, inappropriate sleeping arrangements, and blurred role boundaries. Mothers who were themselves victims of sexual abuse may even set up their own children for abuse and then require additional help working through the prior unresolved incest experience before they can be supportive of their children (Goodwin et al., 1982).

About one in six British families is now headed by a lone parent, the vast majority of them women. The risks from babysitters are heightened in this group, particularly as they rarely have choices about whom they employ – especially as many are struggling on low incomes, and lack a support network of family or friends. Research tells us that perpetrators target single mothers to gain access to children (Nelson, 1992).

Hoagwood and Stewart (1989) reported on children's perceptions of family functioning in sexually abusing and non-sexually abusing families. They found that there were differences on three dimensions: problem-solving, roles, and general functioning. Sexually abused children were more likely to report poorer problem-solving skills in their families, more role confusion, and more general pathological functioning than children in the non-abused group. Differences in the problem-solving dimension is consistent with reports of chaotic family structure and concomitant dysfunction. The victim's feelings of isolation, anxiety and lack of support that many victims experience may also be reflected in this dimension. Difficulties in establishing and maintaining effective role boundaries often has a diagnostic significance regardless of whether the abuse is inside or outside the family. The greater overall dysfunction in families of abused children may reflect greater general unhappiness that the child victims experienced in their families. There were two differences between children sexually abused inside and outside the family: affective responsivity and affective involvement. Victims of intra-familial abuse reported more pathological affective responsivity and affective involvement within their family than those abused extra-familially. This shows that victims who are abused by a family member perceive more pathological affective intimacy and lack of emotional boundaries.

### Issues to consider

We will never know the true number of women who experience domestic violence as many women do not report violence to agencies for many reasons. These include the lack of awareness about, or access to available services; concern that agencies will not be sympathetic, sensitive or provide the help that is needed; fear of agencies having different agendas from their own, particularly with regard to their children; and fear of retribution from the perpetrator. Some women approach services but do not necessarily disclose violence as the source of their problems. For example, many women seek medical help and are not asked how their injuries were inflicted or by whom. Many women do disclose and still fail to get adequate, appropriate responses. If the opportunity for intervention is lost, violence may continue and women and children may be at significant risk.

Even after separation, women are at considerable risk from their former abusive partners. Contact with children is often used as an opportunity to further abuse women and children may be abused directly or indirectly by the man also. All women are vulnerable regardless of colour, race, nationality, ability, sexuality, lifestyle, class and income. However, women already experiencing oppression may find it more difficult to seek or access help. For example, black women, women with disabilities, women working in prostitution, will find additional barriers which agencies need to be aware of and work hard to remove if we are to safeguard the safety of all women and children.

Domestic violence between parents seriously compromises the protective capacities of both parents. Children can be frightened to let possible protectors know about sexual abuse for fear of the repercussions, both for themselves and for their mothers. If children have witnessed their father beating their mother, it is unlikely that they will perceive their mother as someone who could protect them. They are more likely to perceive her as a victim like themselves.

Where domestic violence and/or child abuse occurs in a family, it is important to examine the wider picture. It is important to be aware that violence continues after separation, often when women are most at risk and receive least support. This is also true where contact between violent fathers and their children occur.

It is important to ensure that questions about domestic violence are asked and framed in a non-blaming and sympathetic manner. The worker should explore the issues with the mother and from this develop an understanding of what risks there are for the child. The risks, both immediate and longer-term, should be discussed with the mother, including the need for protection of the child and how this can be achieved; who is responsible for providing this and what support can be given. Within this a view of the mother's immediate and longer-term capacity to understand the risks and to protect her child with support should be gained, including her awareness of the impact on the children. A safety plan should then be formed and agreed with the mother, reflecting the capabilities of the mother and the positive survival strategies that may already be in place.

Women living in situations of violence may be immobilised through shock or fear. Remaining in a violent relationship does not mean that the care and protection of the children is not a primary concern. Pressure to leave by professionals places the onus of responsibility for the violence on the woman. If a woman is not able to leave, she faces the possibility of being labelled a bad parent and of colluding with the violence. Thus begins the 'fight' with professionals at a time when information and time to assimilate this is most needed. Women in violent relationships may be acutely aware that leaving does not mean the violence will cease. Thus they may be constantly weighing up the safety issues on a day to day basis. Women will be employing complex strategies to avoid violence in the home. Mental ill health, alcohol and drug misuse can be a result of ongoing violence.

Women need to know they are not being judged by workers for the actions of their partners. It we can agree that the children's protection is a shared and primary concern, it is more likely that a creative solution can be found. In order for this to begin we need to believe women are not helpless victims.

We need to know who is living in the household and how family members are financially supported. This will help workers assess whether there was opportunity for sexual abuse, possible abusers (if unclear), other potential victims, the adequacy of the living situation, and how independent the mother is (or has the potential of becoming) of the alleged perpetrator (Faller, 1988c).

Mothers need to look at the dynamics in their families and to identify the power the perpetrator wielded.

## Family background

Faller (1988c) indicated that the family background can be quite useful in providing indicators of overall functioning, in understanding the dynamics of the sexual abuse and in making treatment plans. She advised that workers assess the discipline techniques of each parent, the nature of the relationship with each parent, and the relative closeness to each parent.

There are two major reasons for speaking with the mother about her family of origin and social network: to get some sense of what it was like for them growing up as well as wanting to assess the extended family and others as sources of social support. Many factors related to their upbringing may shed light on the dynamics of sexual abuse and predict prognosis. We need to find out what kind of people her parents were and how she experienced them, particularly if there is a history of little nurturing, significant trauma, and deprivation; physical or sexual abuse; a lack of intimacy or attachments; no reference to sex (so she grew up with little sexual knowledge), social isolation and the absence of social supports – particularly as social isolation can have several functions: it may facilitate, prolong, or be the result of sexual abuse.

### Research findings

Hanson and Scott (1996) researched the social networks of perpetrators and found that there is some evidence that they are likely to have friends and relatives who are also sexual perpetrators.

Salt et al. (1990) found that a significant number of mothers reported having indifferent to overtly hostile relationships with their maternal grandmothers. Testa et al. (1992) explored comparisons between women in treatment and a comparison group. They found that those in the treatment group were more likely to have been physically abused by one or both parents (62 per cent versus 35 per cent) to have had a parent with alcohol problems (56 per cent versus 34 per cent) and to be a member of a minority group (37 per cent versus 13 per cent). Treatment sample women came from families with lower socio-economic status and experienced more childhood family changes (such as divorce, remarriage, death) than women in the comparison group. Of the women who had been sexually abused, those in treatment were more likely to have experienced penetration (60 per cent versus 29 per cent) and exposure (83 per cent versus 69 per cent). They also experienced more sexually abusive incidents (31.82 versus 13.62).

Salt et al. (1990) found that mothers from lower social classes tended to be less protective of their children, more punitive, and less concerned for the child's welfare. Non-white mothers were more likely than white mothers to punish and blame the child for the abuse. These differences may be explained in part by the heightened stresses in the lives of poor families.

Trepper et al. (1996) examined the family-of-origin factors of both the perpetrator and the non-perpetrator in intact incestuous families. One third of perpetrators and their non-abusing partners acknowledged some form of abuse or neglect. The perpetrator was more likely to have experienced physical and emotional abuse compared to the non-abusing partner who was more likely to have experienced sexual abuse.

### Issues to consider

Child sexual abuse is intergenerational. That means that if one person in their family was sexually abused then the likelihood is that someone else was also. Does the mother know anyone else in the family who was sexually abused? Did anyone have a mental disorder, use drugs or alcohol, have a criminal record or have allegations made against them?

## Educational history

Faller (1988c) pointed to a mother's education as a good indicator of ability. A mother who reports she was the subject of a statement of special educational needs or was excluded from school or schools for long periods has clearly had difficulties in a major arena of childhood functioning.

It is important to establish their school performance and academic achievement; classroom behaviour; the presence or absence of problems within the school (relationships with peers and teachers, attendance and any activity whilst truanting, isolation, disciplinary, suspension or exclusion, bullying or bullied with staff and/or peers, etc.); interests in school; aptitudes and abilities; special educational needs or services (ability or behavioural); school changes (including reasons); and any significant events.

Information about her education tells workers a great deal about her overall functioning. School performance gives some information about her ability to persist at long-term goals and her self-discipline and self-esteem. The level of academic ability has a bearing on the type of assessment tools which can be used. Their school adjustment may offer some information about the development of peer relationships and their ability to relate to authority figures in a productive manner. As schooling is one of our first major life experiences to place demands on us to handle responsibilities, performance can be a useful predictor of subsequent difficulty or success in fulfilling life demands. Anyone who has failed at almost every major task is unlikely to benefit from any ongoing work.

### Research findings

Carter (1993) found that 38 per cent of the mothers in her sample had not completed high school, 38 per cent had and gone on to complete additional education, and 24 per cent had attended universities.

Deblinger et al. (1993) found in their sample that 28.3 per cent of mothers had completed at least some college; 35.4 per cent were high school graduates; and the remaining 36.4 per cent had not completed high school.

### Issues to consider

Questions to ask include:

- How did you feel when you started school?
- What was good about school?
- What was bad about it?
- Who were your friends at school?
- What did you do with them?
- What games or hobbies did you enjoy with other children?
- How did the teachers treat you?
- Did you enjoy schoolwork?
- Was any of it hard for you?
- What subjects did you like?
- What did your parents want for you in school?
- Did they want you to do well in sports, schoolwork, or religion?
- Were there changes in your living arrangements or family during secondary school years? Financial changes? Deaths? Moves?
- Did your feelings about school or achievements in school change in your secondary school years?
- What friends or activities were you involved with during your secondary school years?
- What kind of future job dreams or plans did you think about in your secondary school years?
- What were your goals?

(Schwartz and Cellini, 1995)

## Occupational history

Faller (1988) pointed to the work history as a further measure of the mother's overall functioning as well as being an indicator of her ability to act independently of the perpetrator. If she has a means of supporting herself, she will probably be more independent in other ways, including resisting his sexually abusive behaviour, extricating herself from the relationship with him, and supporting herself and the children. A history of employment commensurate with her skill level suggests to the worker that she can hold her own in the work arena.

### Research findings

Trepper et al. (1996) found that approximately half of the families in the study defined the highest level of parent's employment as skilled (47 per cent). Twenty-two per cent were classified as unskilled, 13 per cent were professional, and in 17 per cent of families both parents were unemployed. Two thirds of families reported a middle class income for the household with the majority of the remaining one third of families reporting low income.

Carter (1993) found that the work patterns of the mothers changed post-disclosure: with some mothers going from part-time jobs to no job at all; some taking part-time or full-time jobs when they had not been previously working; and others quitting to attend to their child's needs. Their options were limited and dictated by economic needs for survival. Mothers who decided to share the information of the sexual abuse at work largely received little or no emotional support or consideration.

Deblinger et al. (1993) reported that 52.5 per cent of the mothers in their sample reported that they had been employed at least sporadically during the last year, whereas 47.5 per cent were unemployed throughout the year.

### Issues to consider

Her working hours will give some indication about priorities and level of involvement in the family. Why does the mother work?

It is useful to obtain a record of her work history, including types of jobs, job performance, level of responsibility and employment stability, job satisfaction, relationships with colleagues and their ability to support themselves and their family. This information can throw light on their persistence, relationships, responsibilities and dependability – all keys to effective professional intervention and the creation of sustained change.

### Financial history

Financial history should include debts and assets. An individual's level of stability may be reflected in how they manage their finances. Furthermore, Faller (1988c) reported that over a quarter of cases of sexual abuse are marked with the onset of unemployment or some other factor that has an impact on self-esteem. It is therefore important to identify any such stresses which may contribute to the dynamics of child sexual abuse.

### Research findings

This has been partially covered in the earlier 'options' component. Carter (1993) found that the majority of two-parent families had incomes of over $40,000 per year, whereas the majority of single parents were living near the poverty line ($20, 411) with several mothers who were attempting to support their children on less than $10,000 per year. Most women do not have viable economic choices after the disclosure of the sexual abuse.

Deblinger et al. (1993) found that 36.7 per cent of the mothers in their sample reported annual family incomes greater than $20,000; 31.1 per cent between $10,001 and $20,000; and 32.2 per cent reported $10,000 or less.

### Health and medical history

Mothers in violent families frequently exhibit anxiety-related health problems prior to the discovery of child sexual abuse. Kinard (1996) noted that the detrimental impact of stress and inadequate social support on psychological well-being in adults has been well documented in research, with depression receiving the most attention as an outcome. The cumulative evidence suggests that inadequate social support is one of the strongest predictors of depression. Maternal deficiencies in social competence and interpersonal social skills may be the most important personality factors associated with the ability to develop and maintain social support networks. Indeed, deficiencies in these areas are likely to increase the risk of depression. Kinard explored this and found that at the first interview, mothers of abused children reported less perceived support from family and partners and greater depressive symptomatology than did mothers of non-abused children. The abuse and the non-abuse groups did not differ on perceived support from friends, neighbours, co-workers, or organisations. At the second interview one year later, the abuse and non-abuse groups continued to differ on family and partner support, but did not differ on competence. The depressive symptoms declined over time for mothers in the abuse group, although they remained higher than that of the non-abuse group. This may be due to improvements in family circumstances, to cessation of abuse, or to intervention services.

There are three reasons for exploring the mother's history for mental illness:

- Mental problems must be taken into account in assessing overall functioning. The longer the mental illness and the more severe its presentation, the poorer the treatment prognosis.

- Certain kinds of mental illness are indicative of poor object relations, and can affect the offender's ability to relate to children and partners.
- In a few cases, mental illness plays a key role in sexual abuse. For example, Finkelhor (1984) found that having an absent or ill mother was an important predictor of the likelihood of sexual abuse. Kaplan et al. (1988) found that the increased risk of parental depression in abusing families extends to mothers who were not the perpetrators of the abuse. Belsky (1984) concluded that the most important determinant of parenting skills is the parents' psychological well-being. Although low social support, lack of self-competence and depression have been noted as common characteristics of parents in abusing families, the links between them have seldom being examined. Trepper et al. (1996) found that 31 per cent of the mothers in incest families had some type of recognisable psychopathology. They were more likely to display a passive-dependent personality and to experience depression than was the offender or the victim. They also scored highly on seeing themselves as the victim, being introverted and having poor self-esteem.

Faller (1988c) notes that the mother's mental illness can have a range of functions. Occasionally a mentally ill parent who has some sexual dysfunction will develop delusions that her partner is sexually abusing the child. There are some circumstances where her mental illness may lead her to facilitate the sexual abuse. Another possibility is that the circumstances of the marriage and the sexual abuse may precipitate mental illness on the part of the mother. They may also be psychologically unavailable to others (partner and children). Where the mother needs periodic hospitalisation, she is physically unavailable to protect. Some mothers tend to focus on getting their own needs met and the needs of the child become secondary. The same techniques used for ascertaining the abuser's mental state can be used with the mother.

Depression can be a very disturbing and frightening experience. People often feel that depression descends on them from nowhere and feel powerless to understand or change that feeling. Whilst it can cause physical changes such as tiredness or loss of appetite, it is primarily a problem about feelings. For example, people may feel worthless, inferior, or unlovable; or they may feel negative about themselves in response to a particular event.

Newberger et al. (1993) found that a mother's level of depression may be an aspect of her emotional reaction to the disclosure of the sexual abuse itself. The findings regarding depression are important, because if chronic or recurrent, it may affect her post-disclosure ability to parent and protect her children. This is important when we know that depression in mothers is a significant predictor of children's subsequent functioning (Forchand et al., 1987).

Depressed mothers have been shown to report increased behavioural symptoms in their children (Deblinger et al., 1997). They may have less energy and tolerance than non-depressed parents and experience their children's behaviour as more symptomatic than they otherwise might. At the same time, distressed mothers may be less emotionally available for their children, thereby setting the stage for the development of increased child symptomatology.

Herman (1981) also found that over half of the incest survivors in her sample remembered that their mothers had had periods of disabling illness which resulted in frequent hospitalisations or in the mother's living as an invalid at home. Thirty-eight per cent of the daughters had been separated from their mothers at some time during their childhood either because their mothers were hospitalised or because they felt they could not cope with looking after their children. Depression, alcoholism and psychosis were among the most common problems that these mothers had.

Substance abuse may have a variety of functions in sexual abuse. Using either drugs or alcohol may cause the mother to lose her attractiveness to the abuser. She may not be sexually responsive to him because of her intoxication and this renders her unavailable to protect her children also. Drug use inevitably impacts upon the finances and she may involve herself in illegal activities to obtain money for drugs. This may extend to prostitution which also exposes the children to men who may exploit them.

Leifer et al. (1993) found that a maternal history of childhood abuse and of poor childhood attachment relationships were strongly associated with current maternal substance abuse. In turn, maternal substance abuse and dissatisfaction with current social supports were highly related to the lack of maternal support to the sexually abused child, and to a higher frequency of abuse incidents.

## Issues to consider

The task for professionals is to assess whether these mothers are capable of showing concern for their children and whether they have the potential to learn how to protect. If there are some promising indicators, such as the mothers feeling able to express concern for the child, then professional intervention of an intense nature may help them move on.

It is important that people set and keep to a routine which involves contact with people so they can begin to work with the positives around and explore how to learn to enjoy themselves again. Exercise is also a good stimulant.

The mother's recovery of mental health is an essential part and even preface to effective treatment, particularly since it has often been affected by the disclosure and then the subsequent intervention (Bagley, 1995).

## Interpersonal relationships

This section explores more than the mother's relationship with the perpetrator, covered in an earlier section. This section is designed to explore relationships with significant others and what this means for the mother in terms of networks and support.

Information about relations with significant others can be of benefit in understanding the dynamics and prognosis of sexual abuse. Interpersonal communication is a dominant human function, and many of our problems stem from our concerns over the way we relate to other people, and the manner in which they respond to us (Lazarus, 1976: 42). It is not surprising, therefore, that interpersonal relations are a central part of dealing with sexually abusing families.

Weiss (1974) identified six key areas which isolated people miss out on. They are: attachment, provided by close affectional relationships, which give a sense of security and place; social integration, provided by membership of a network of persons having shared interests and values; the opportunity for nurturing others, usually children, which gives some incentive for continuing in the face of adversity; reassurance of personal worth, which promotes self-esteem and comes both from those at home as well as from colleagues; a sense of

reliable alliance, which is obtained mainly from kin; and obtaining help and guidance from informal advisors when difficulties have to be resolved. Examples of the items include: at present, do you have someone you can share your most private feelings with (confide in) or not? Who is this mainly? Do you wish you could share more with them, or is it just about right the way it is? Would you like to have someone like this or would you prefer to keep your feelings to yourself?

Interpersonal dyadic relationships can be defined by three relatively independent dimensions: boundary, power and intimacy. Since the development of intimacy is a process, boundary and power cannot be isolated from any definition of intimacy (Waring and Reddon, 1983). A healthy intimate relationship is characterised by the capacity for constructive, respectful expression of positive and negative emotions. These expressions should be mutually acceptable and promote the psychological well-being of the individuals involved; their function is primarily to define boundaries, to communicate concern and commitment, to negotiate roles, and to resolve conflicts (Coleman, 1987a). Mothers with a history of being abused themselves have often lacked healthy role models, and boundaries between family members are too weak or too firm. The boundary difficulties resulting from these factors may lead to two distinct problems with intimacy: they may be needy, intrusive, enmeshed, or controlling resulting from a lack of clear boundaries between self and others, or the person may be avoiding and distancing, the outcome of boundaries too tightly drawn.

Intimacy is clearly important in establishing effective emotional and sexual relations with other adults (Brehm, 1992) and those who are able to develop it are seen to be warm and sincere; less aggressive, and better able to resist stress. Their relationships also provide them with a sense of security, emotional comfort, shared experiences, an opportunity to be nurturing plus a sense of self-worth (Marshall, 1995). Intimacy is a universal human characteristic. If thwarted in adult relationships, then sexual perpetrators may seek intimacy in other less appropriate ways. This failure to achieve intimacy leads to the experience of emotional loneliness, which causes considerable frustration.

## Research findings

Courtois (1988) found that incest survivors often lack friendships due to anger, mistrust, and a general devaluation of women, including themselves. Herman (1981) also noted that they favour men for their privileged position and resent woman for their powerlessness. Alexander (1992) suggested that they present with a consistent pattern of insecure attachment that interferes with their establishment of peer relationships.

Lubell and Peterson (1998) found that the closest relationships reported by incest survivors lasted an average of seven years less than those of the comparison participants. They also reported lower levels of interpersonal competence. Survivors of incest viewed their relationship with their mother as poor. They reported less satisfaction, less compatibility, less intimacy, more conflict, and less assurance in the continuity of these relationships. They spent less time with their mothers and desired even less contact with them than they had. They viewed their mothers as more isolated and lonely than the comparison groups. Perhaps this was due to the mothers being victims of sexual abuse themselves in their families of origin and/or experienced domestic violence in their current family environments. Perhaps they distanced themselves from others because they were reluctant to discuss their own experiences of incest or domestic violence. This finding contributes to understanding why mothers and daughters in families where incest occurred experienced poor interpersonal relationships – the family system was, and is, problematic.

## Issues to consider

Questions to be asked include:

- What is your partner like or what kind of a person is he?
- What about him pleases you?
- What displeases you?
- What kind of things do you do together? Do you enjoy these?
- Do you ever do things together without the children?
- Are there things about your partner you would like changed?
- Do you tell him things you don't tell anyone else?

- How do you show him when he pleases you or you are happy with him?
- How does he show you when you please him or he is happy with you?
- How does he know when you are displeased?
- How do you know when he is displeased?
- What do you have arguments about?
- Have you ever used physical force with each other? If yes, please describe.

(Faller, 1988c)

In exploring interpersonal relationships, we need to consider:

- the nature and quality of her relations with peers
- the nature, quality and duration of her friendships
- the kinds of friends they select as associates: are they susceptible to the influence of others?
- the nature and extent of social isolation, which may possibly indicate a more severe psychopathology
- whether the offender is active or passive in social relations, such as social interests, activities and memberships. Are they self-centred? Excessively controlling and competitive?
- the nature and stability in their relationships; obtain a relationship history, including the ages and sexes of the ex-partner's children.

The marital relationship needs to be specifically targeted for information, eliciting how they met their partners; how they were attracted to them; how long it lasted (if it has ended, why and when); how many serious relationships they had before they married; why they decided to marry; how their relationship changed after marriage; what were the good and bad parts of the marriage; did they or their spouses have other sexual relationships? Why? When? The number of children and their relationship with them; their attitudes and expectations regarding marriage; any history of rape, domestic violence, etc.; the quality of their relationships, their ability to see their spouse as a separate individual with their own needs, and the extent to which their descriptions correspond with information elicited from other sources. Marriage failures may reflect an inability to form lasting relationships, or to meet someone else's needs. How is her sexual relationship with her partner? Can they describe the kinds of sexual activity they engage in and their approximate frequency? How often do they engage in sexual activity? Has this relationship been more or less the same over the years or changing? Who initiates sex?

## Self-esteem

Self-esteem is defined as the way in which a person perceives themselves, values themselves and rates themselves in relation to other people (Briggs et al., 1998: 128).

If individuals grow up in a loving and supporting environment, then they learn to trust their own judgement; to feel 'safe' in the world; that they can be liked for themselves; that they can make their own decisions; that they are valuable; and that they deserve to be treated with love and respect.

When mothers have been sexually abused themselves or where their children have been sexually abused, their self-esteem may suffer as they learn that the world is a dangerous place where trusted people take advantage of them and use them for their own ends. This can lead to problems like not being able to say 'no' to people; always putting other people's needs first; not being able to make decisions; waiting to see what happens rather than making a choice; staying in bad relationships; and having a sense of no choices or control. Workers do need to create space to listen to mothers and assist in problem-solving that promotes their self-esteem.

Mothers' self-esteem is acutely affected by domestic violence and a controlling partner whose interaction is telling them what they can and cannot do as though they were children themselves.

Every mother will react differently to the disclosure of child sexual abuse linked to her personal characteristics and resources. Her self-esteem will affect and be affected by what she believes her alternatives might be in the presenting situation; how she perceives her relationship with the child and with the offender; what fears and losses she faces; what meaning she gives to the situation; and how she responds to therapeutic interventions (Ovaris, 1991: 14). These forces will become more apparent as the crisis evolves.

### Research findings

Bagley (1995) found that mothers and controls have identical levels of self-esteem. The most

likely reason for this is that the time mothers have spent in therapy has enabled them to develop normal levels of self-esteem, even though in the recent past they experienced crises which were associated with devastated mental health, depression, suicidal feelings and, in some cases, actual suicidal behaviour. Bagley argued that the longer the time that has elapsed since the revelation, the better the mother's self-esteem level is likely to be.

Cammaert (1988) found that many mothers in families where their child had been sexually abused had low self-esteem. This finding was echoed in the research of Leifer et al. (1993) and they found it was linked to the fact that 52 per cent of the mothers in the study had been sexually abused themselves.

Sgroi and Dana (1982) reported that low self-esteem is a common feature of mothers in incest families. An important task for workers is for them to attempt to rebuild self esteem as well as helping to mobilise support networks and providing practical advice to enable the mother to cope more positively with her own needs and those of her children. Hooper (1989) noted that a focus on self-esteem has important implications for intervention: attempting to reinforce women's performance in their family roles may produce guilt about the parts of their life that actually provide sources of autonomy and self-worth.

### Issues to consider

Most mothers experience some loss of self-esteem when their child is harmed. Low self-esteem is not the cause of the sexual abuse. *Self-esteem is an indicator of one's psychological resources and feelings of competence.* A lack of confidence in their ability to parent can make the simplest tasks seem very complex. Mothers often feel overwhelmed by the demands placed on them, which add to their perceived sense of failure. Mothers need to be given some permission to be overwhelmed and to talk through their feelings as they are experienced.

Mothers need to work on their thoughts and feelings about the abuse that will help them to feel better in themselves, thus encouraging self-esteem. They need to challenge any negative thoughts they have. For example, they may divide a piece of paper into negative thoughts and more positive thoughts. They then complete this task as though it was a diary, articulating the thoughts they have when they feel low. When you feel more positive, reflect on the thoughts and ask yourself whether this is very true or not, articulating counter-thoughts on the opposite side of the paper. You may want to do this with a friend or counsellor if there are more low moments than high ones at any given time. Another alternative is to simply keep to the positives and write a list of all the positive things about yourself, whether they be things you like about yourself or what you are good at. Reaffirm these to yourself as frequently as you feel is necessary.

Many mothers seek a speedy resolution to the problem and this can affect their self-esteem if they believe it is not possible and that this is her fault. Low energy levels and eroded self-esteem are not a good recipe for recovery. Indeed, a mother's self-esteem level will be critical to how she copes.

## Social skills

Social skills is a broad term used to describe a wide variety of behaviours and cognitive phenomena presumed necessary for effective functioning in social situations.

A lot of the literature on mothers of sexually abused children highlights their lack of self-esteem and social skills (Sahd, 1980). A woman's very sense of who she is may be sorely damaged by the discovery of sexual abuse, which challenges every aspect of her identity. She may question her judgement of the world, as her previous perceptions of reality, family relationships, partner and children are all thrown into turmoil (Hubbard, 1989).

### Research findings

Salt et al. (1990) found that 19 per cent of the mothers in their sample had serious problems in social interaction with others.

### Issues to consider

The interview itself can provide clues to the mother's social skills behaviours (verbal and non-verbal). Deficits may be indicated where they look away excessively, fail to listen, interrupt readily, lack social pleasantry, appear socially awkward, jump topics suddenly, become over-familiar with the worker or ask personal questions of the workers which are unrelated to the background relevant to the inquiry (Carich and Adkerson, 1995: 8).

Do they tend to be involved in insular activities? Do they value spending time with others? Has the influence of others been experienced primarily in negative or positive terms? Are there any differences in the way they describe interactions with children, same-sex adults and opposite-sex adults?

## Social support

Understanding the mother's support system is a central area of assessment as it may help in the understanding of the dynamics of the abuse; be of assistance in treatment planning; and aid in predicting prognosis. Indeed, social isolation can play a role in causing or prolonging sexual abuse. Conversely, if the mother does have a support system she will usually be better able emotionally to manage the abusive situation. In particular, she will probably be less dependent on the perpetrator and more able to seek out what is best for herself and her children.

It is not uncommon for the mother to lose extended family and support networks after the disclosure. This can happen even when they choose the child rather than their partner as they may not wish to burden others and they are often overwhelmed by shame and grief. Others may be shocked that friends or family may accuse them of over-reacting and rally to support the man. Conversely, others may see her grieving for someone believed to be undeserving as unacceptable and this can make it more difficult for her to gain the support needed to understand her own conflicting feelings.

There is often a need for an increased level of support following disclosure. This is important if the mother is to harness sufficient resources to cope with the presenting situation and look forward to protective strategies in the future.

We also need to be aware that where the mother herself has been the victim of physical and sexual abuse (particularly from her partner) then she may have great difficulty in asking for help, assuming rejection, disbelief and hostility; she fears regression when addressing the abuse due to any re-activation of the abuse, or the associated terror and despair; and she may have concerns over confidentiality, particularly if she remains in contact with the perpetrator.

### Research findings

Following the disclosure of sexual abuse, family members may become more socially isolated as contact with relatives and/or friends decreases or terminates entirely (MacFarlane and Bulkley, 1982). This is unfortunate since this is the time when the mother needs help in order to create some degree of stability in the family. It is always better when families work this problem out together. They too have to go through the same time-consuming, painful process before they can admit exactly what happened. As such, mothers may find that the extended family is believing and understanding about feelings one day, only to reverse their position the next. Mothers need to understand that other family members may have very good reasons for not wanting to believe. For example, they may not want to end their relationship with the perpetrator, or they may have had memories of their own abuse resurrected for them. This understanding on the part of mothers should lead to them allowing some space for the family to work through the issues as they affect individuals differently. In all families, the process of change remains an extremely difficult one to achieve. Over time families must learn different ways of communicating so that there is a lot more listening and a lot less blaming.

Immediate changes can take place in the relationships between the perpetrators and other members of the children's families when relatives, trusted friends, or neighbours were the perpetrators. Formerly friendly relationships disappeared. Many mothers were ostracised in and by their communities. In those families where the perpetrator was a relative, the disclosure of the sexual abuse invariably split families up as members took sides, leaving women whose social lives revolved around their families isolated. The most significantly lacking aspect for most mothers is the emotional support from significant others (Carter, 1993). The best support for mothers frequently came from female friends and sisters.

Fong and Walsh-Bowers (1998) reported that following disclosure, mothers tried to look for help from both formal and informal sources but were often disappointed. This may be linked to their physical and psychological health becoming affected. They found that whether the women received support from their extended families depended upon the depth of the previous relationships they had with them. Some women felt supported but others felt that their extended families would not want anything to do with such a family scandal and so they never tried to discuss it with them.

Trepper et al. (1996) found that families are vulnerable to incest because the members are socially isolated from the outside environment. Thirty-six per cent of the families in the study were described as extremely socially isolated with another 43 per cent identified as moderately socially isolated. Overall, three quarters of the families were more insulated from the social environment than not.

### Issues to consider

Child sexual abuse is an isolating and frightening experience for both children and women. Where mothers are offered their own worker, they often act more supportively towards their child and with less hostility to the professionals acting on behalf of the child.

There is a need to identify her supports and other means of validation in her life.

Workers need to explore the mother's relationships with her family, her partner's family, friends, work mates, neighbours and professionals. Has she been able to ask anyone to mind the children in the midst of the crisis? Who would she usually turn to if there is a crisis, such as needing to take one child to hospital? What has failed her to allow the abuse to take place, if anything? What can be mobilised to support the mother and child now, or in the future?

Many mothers identified isolation as a common factor with feelings of being unable to deal with all of the issues around the abuse. This often links to the mother needing something for themselves to cope as well as to offload. They need time out from the pressure and all the responsibilities. Many mothers feel that they have been let down by the agencies involved and the system and could rarely see any light at the end of the tunnel.

### Sexual history

Dual vulnerability: the mother's own history of sexual abuse

> *Non-offending mothers are not likely to seek help for resolving their childhood trauma until there is an external reason for doing so. This is due, at least in part, to a lingering belief that they were responsible for the abuse experienced in their childhood.*
>
> (Ovaris 1991: 60)

Hubbard (1989) defined a history of sexual abuse in mothers as any reference to sexual abuse experienced by the mothers, or the after effects of that sexual abuse, including references to the mothers' inability to establish intimate relationships with family members.

The possibility that the mother herself is a survivor of childhood sexual abuse cannot be overlooked. Many mothers will, when asked, identify incidents of sexual abuse in their own lives, and most will never have told anyone about it, may not have been supported if they did, and have probably not received adequate treatment. As such, they are probably still using coping strategies developed to contend with the original trauma. They may thus experience anxiety attacks, flashbacks, deepened depression, dissociation when confronted with the sexual abuse of their own child.

A classic response for many mothers to their own abuse is one of either forgetting or denying. It is not surprising, therefore, that they face huge dilemmas when they discover sexual abuse and they may choose against actively pursuing such information in relation to their children. Hooper (1989) sees these as coping strategies rather than collusion.

For some mothers, their history of sexual abuse has remained hidden, sometimes even to themselves, until an event in adult life brings the past to the surface. This can include the discovery that her child is being sexually abused by either the same perpetrator or another family member (such as her partner). Some factors which facilitate disclosure lie within the mother herself and include whether she has learnt to dissociate herself from the abuse as a child; the reactions of others to previous attempts to disclose as a child and as an adult; whether she has told anyone before; the extent of her recall of the abuse; her emotional reactions to the memories of the abuse; and whether she has had close relationships with non-abusive adults during childhood (Hall and Lloyd, 1989).

### Research findings

There is evidence that mothers who have been sexually abused experience greater distress than mothers who have not been abused (Kelley, 1990; Manion et al., 1996). It has also been noted that mothers of sexually abused children frequently have a history of sexual abuse and further, that this history interferes with their ability to deal with the current abuse of their children (Carter, 1993).

Cole et al. (1992) have also found a relationship between being an incest victim and reported

feelings of inadequacy as a parent, especially a lack of confidence and control. Furthermore, they also expressed higher expectations of themselves as mothers than did their non-abused counterparts. The authors suggest that problems coping with intense emotion induce withdrawal from immediate parenting situations, leaving children with less consistency and direction and mothers feeling overwhelmed or inadequate. The mother who is herself an incest survivor may feel an intensity to a greatly magnified degree and respond by emotionally withdrawing from the immediate situation. This is often *not* their final response to the disclosure.

Tinling (1990) argued that women who were abused sexually as children go on to marry child abusers and then become mothers of sexually abused children. Things are never that clear cut, but there is some evidence to show that sexual abuse histories can signal increased vulnerability to having children who are sexually abused. For example, a woman who has been sexually abused may feel uncomfortable with normal adult sexual relationships and choose a partner who does not make sexual demands upon her because his primary sexual attraction is to children. In addition, a woman who has a background of sexual victimisation may either not be as sensitive to risk situations as other woman and unwittingly place her children at risk, or conversely becomes over-protective and hyper-vigilant towards them.

Current research does indicate that a significant proportion of mothers in families where sexual abuse has occurred report having experienced sexual abuse during childhood. Faller (1989) examined the histories of mothers whose child had been sexually abused in the family, and found that 49.9 per cent of the sample recalled having sexually abusive experiences as children; whilst 42.2 per cent reported having experienced direct sexual victimisation.

Sroufe et al. (1985) found that women who suffered sexual abuse as children tended to behave in sexualised ways with their young male children, controlling them in seductive, over-intimate ways. Their relationship with their daughters was very different: they were distant and somewhat rejecting.

Bagley and King (1990: 168) found that half the mothers of abuse victims had experienced serious sexual abuse within their family, compared with 18 per cent of controls in comparable periods of family life. They hypothesised that these mothers failed to suspect sexual abuse as they had escaped their abusive homes by entering idealistically into new relationships which they assumed must inevitable be better. A combination of naïve optimism and continued powerlessness and subordination to male dominance had resulted in an emotional and cognitive framework which made it very difficult for them to understand what might be going on.

Burkett (1991) explored the links between a childhood history of childhood sexual abuse and current parenting behaviours of school-aged children. She found that there were blurred boundaries between parent and child subsystems with a greater percentage of self-focused rather than child-focused messages from abuse-history mothers. The children had clearly taken on board their parent's expectations that they take a leadership role in meeting the adult's needs for caretaking (role reversal). She identified two main parenting categories. The first category appeared to consist of women who struggle with depression, chemical abuse and despair. These women function marginally as parents, having little energy or emotional resources available for raising children. Women in this category are sometimes unable to provide their children with protection. These women could be called 'under-functioning' with regard to parenting. In the second category, mothers felt positive, excited, and enthusiastic about their parenting. These women were generally functioning better in various areas of life than those in the previous category. They had the energy and motivation to actively emphasise excellent parenting as a major personal goal, but seemed over-focused on their parental role and dependent on their children for emotional closeness. Many appeared to be caught up in a smothering, over-controlling kind of pseudo-nurturing. Women in both these categories were markedly more likely to meet their companionship needs through their children and rely on their children for emotional support than were comparison-group women.

Deblinger et al. (1994b) found that mothers with a history of sexual abuse felt more alone in the crisis than did mothers without a history. But, even with higher distress levels and feelings of aloneness, mothers with a history of abuse believed the allegations concerning their children and acted as advocates for their children to the same extent as mothers without such a history. They argued that a mother's history of sexual abuse is important, not because it is a risk factor for her child, but rather because it points to

critical issues to address in treatment, such as symptom distress and the sense of isolation. They believe that a maternal history of child sexual abuse should be included as a moderating variable in future investigations examining the effectiveness of interventions for sexually abused children and their parents.

Muram et al. (1994) explored the personality profiles of mothers of sexual abuse victims. They found that they did not display noteworthy psychopathology in any sphere. They were only marginally less outgoing than control mothers and nothing suggested that they were a markedly passive or apathetic group.

Newberger, Newberger and Gremy (1991) compared the psychiatric responses of women with and without sexual abuse histories to disclosures of their children's sexual abuse and to assess the relationship of these histories to the nature of the child's victimisation. They found that neither the duration nor the use of force in the child's abuse appeared to exert an effect independent of the mother's own abuse history. Whether the child's abuse was intra-familial also did not appear to contribute to the victimised mother's psychiatric responses. A marginal relationship was found, however, with the presence of intercourse in the child's abuse and the severity of the mother's psychiatric symptoms after 12 months. One specific aspect of the mother's own victimisation, its duration, was strongly associated with the nature of the children's abuse experience. The longer the mother's abuse the greater the likelihood that force would be used in the abuse of the child. They were unable to explain how the experience of child sexual abuse translates to the later vulnerability of women and their children. They did note, however, that it may be expressed as a panoply of troubles. These may include vulnerabilities in the domain of interpersonal relationships and with people who would be hurtful to herself and her children, and her incapacity to protect herself against them. In comparison to the children who were not sexually victimised in childhood, these women's children suffered abuses which were substantially more severe. This suggests that women and children may be vulnerable to domination by intrusive men, a *dual vulnerability*, which may be associated with the women's childhood victimisation experience. They proposed that from this set of connections that child sexual abuse in subsequent generations may be partly or largely explained by the enduring impacts of coercive control and powerlessness deriving from protracted abuse in the early years. Maternal powerlessness deriving from protracted abuse in childhood may be associated with later relationships of a coercive and intrusive nature. Support for such a formulation is suggested by the finding that the longer the mother's childhood abuse endured, the greater the likelihood that force would be used in the abuse of the child. Overall, the emotional burdens of a maternal history of child sexual abuse appear to be substantial, continuous, and connected to a child's vulnerability.

## The intergenerational nature of sexual abuse

The intergenerational model of child abuse has attracted considerable interest in the literature (see Buchanan, 1996). The transmission rate has ranged from seven per cent to 70 per cent in various studies. Belsky (1993) maintained that approximately one third of former victims become abusive parents themselves. The relationship between a parent's past history and current parenting behaviour is of particular interest in studying child sexual abuse given that most females are victims, yet most perpetrators are male. There has not been any research conducted that examines a connection between mothers who were sexually abused and the sexual abuse of their children.

Kreklowetz and Piotrowski (1996, 1998) explored how a mother's own sexual abuse influences her parenting perceptions and behaviour. The key findings included:

### Mothers' fears and protective behaviours

All the mothers described themselves as protective parents, with some describing themselves as 'overprotective'. The most frequently mentioned protection strategies were communication, education and information sharing. Mothers felt that the more information they could gain about parenting and the more open the communication channels were with their children, the more protected their daughters would be. Implicit in this strategy was a strenuous effort to promote good communication with their daughters. Mothers also supervised the contact with certain individuals and situations and developed safety plans. They withheld

contact with family members who refused to acknowledge the mother's own past abuse, and they stopped contact with their own abusers and the abuser of their child (if different). They felt they had less control over the child's safety outside of the home. Mothers developed 'monitoring behaviours' of their daughters both in the home as well as their social activities with peers. Mothers who perceived certain situations to be high risk expressed oncern about their daughter's safety (drinking, staying over at a friend's house). Most mothers agreed that their children were at greatest risk for harm when they were younger, smaller, and were less able to protect themselves. They made repeated reference to their child's physical size and suggested that their small stature left them more vulnerable to harm. Interestingly, some mothers even judged their daughter's age of vulnerability to be around the same age as when they themselves had been abused. In contrast, other mothers felt that very young children were at little risk, because they were easier to monitor closely. Finally, while some mothers acknowledged that their early adolescent daughters were now older and physically larger, the fact that they were more difficult to monitor closely contributed to maternal fears and anxiety that puberty was a high risk period for sexual abuse.

### Mothers' coping ability

Fourteen of the sixteen mothers described earlier periods during which they were emotionally and/or physically absent from their children, especially when they were pre-school aged or younger. These periods of illness, depression, heavy drinking, 'nervous breakdowns', or when they 'just couldn't function'.

### Parentification

All the mothers' current beliefs scored within the normal range, and half were not aware that parentified behaviour had taken place.

### Remembering their abuse

Many mothers began remembering their abuse during counselling. Those that did expended a lot of energy towards protecting their daughters. There is a potential, therefore, that mothers that have little or no recall of their own abuse may be at higher risk for the recurrence of incest. Mothers often became more confident after counselling, having worked on their own feelings from the past which had, in turn, opened the doors to communication between themselves and their children. Their self-estem had also improved.

## Effects on mothers' parenting and the influence of counselling

Mothers unanimously felt that their parenting had been affected by their past incest experience. These included repeating patterns; inability to experience emotional or physical closeness with their daughter, and pervasive anger and feelings of powerlessness as a parent. Most mothers found that resolving their abuse through counselling was instrumental in making them less fearful, less withdrawn, less depressed, and more actively protective of their daughters. This change in parenting focus points to the need to focus on survivors of sexual abuse prior to or early in their parenting years, and further work is needed to determine what factors play a role in this transition.

## Partner trust issues

Five of the seven women who were married or living with a partner expressed some ambivalence, worries, and concerns about trusting their partner and others.

Kreklowetz and Piotrowski found that no clear link has been made between a mother's own history of incest and her ability to protect her daughter from incest. They uncovered several strengths in the mothers' responses, which included having appropriate methods of protecting children, use of disciplinary methods other than corporal punishment, and having a clear understanding of the role of 'parent' and 'child'. The mothers usually displayed strong sensitivity to their children's needs.

McMillen et al. (1995) recorded four principal benefits of being sexually abused after interviewing 154 women. 46.8 per cent reported perceiving some benefit from child sexual abuse. 24 per cent felt they received quite a bit or a lot of benefit. 22.7 per cent felt they received a little or some benefit. 88.9 per cent also reported perceptions of harm. The reported types of benefit included protecting children, self-protection, increased knowledge of child sexual abuse, and having a stronger personality.

## Protecting children

29.2 per cent reported that they felt they were better able to protect children from being sexually abused as a result of being sexually abused themselves. Many mentioned general caution they take with their children. Others mentioned more concrete strategies used to protect children from abuse, such as teaching their children about child sexual abuse or controlling access to their children. Some women reported trying to keep an open, stronger relationship with their children in the hope that they would tell them if someone did try to touch them inappropriately.

## Self-protection

Women described themselves as less naïve, less trusting, more careful in their relationships, and trusting their instincts more.

## Increased knowledge of child sexual abuse

The knowledge women elicited from their own sexual abuse experiences seemed to be of two types: a general knowledge of sexual abuse and paedophilia; and increased empathy with victims of sexual abuse. This information sometimes led to self-protection or protection of children.

## Strength

Some women described themselves as being a stronger, better person and being much more self-sufficient.

These findings are important as they suggest that women may be empowered by their abuse experiences to take concrete actions to protect themselves and their children. There may be a trade-off between self-protection and satisfying adult relationships. A lack of trust in people (especially men) resulting in strained romantic relationships may be a common long-term consequence of child sexual abuse (Alexander, 1993).

Oates et al. (1998) studied whether mothers who were sexually abused in their own childhood are at increased risk of their children being sexually abused and to see if prior sexual abuse in mothers affected their parenting abilities. They found that sexual abuse in a mother's own childhood was related to an increased risk of sexual abuse occurring in the next generation, although prior maternal sexual abuse did not effect outcome in children who were sexually abused. They found that there was no significant difference of intra-familial sexual abuse occurring between those mothers who had, and those who had not, provided a history of being sexually abused themselves.

Cohen (1995) found that adult female survivors of sexual abuse were less skillful in their maternal function, particularly in role support, communication and role image than mothers who had not been sexually abused as mothers.

### Role support

She found that mothers who were incest victims function generally on a lower level than mothers who were not exposed to this trauma in their childhood. 'Indeed, the general plight of women who were incest victims, and the specific difficulties they experience as mothers, may well be linked to the past abuse. Incest and child sexual abuse is above all the betrayal of the child's trust and as such may hinder a victim's developing ability to protect others. In addition, these mothers may experience a constant fear that their children may also become victims, a fear which contributes to their seclusion. The past abuse may thus inhibit the victims from enlisting the support of husbands and friends in sharing child care responsibilities, leaving them overburdened and overextended with the unavoidable result of physical as well as emotional depletion'.

### Communication skills

Future difficulties in the mother's perceived role image can be traced to past sexual abuse and the family dynamics. Motherhood is a socially learned role and so past parentification and especially mother-daughter role-reversal and alienation may contribute to a general distortion of the psychological capacities for mothering, and also to future unrealistic perceptions and expectations regarding this role.

### Role image

Communication skills may be adversely affected by past sexual abuse and specifically linked to its secretive nature; the ensuing subjective experiences of the child victim are ones of isolation, inadequacy and guilt over the past abuse, and the adult women may continue to feel responsible for past occurrence as well as its continuation long after its cessation. The resulting reluctance, shame and fear of sharing her past abuse, coupled with 'learned submissiveness' in her family of origin, may well interfere with the mother's developing ability to communicate freely and openly, thus constricting her capacity in general, and eventually hindering open and spontaneous expression of feelings towards her children.

### Issues to consider

Mothers do need to be aware that having a history of sexual abuse themselves does not impact negatively on their capacity to protect. Rather, they should be more alert to the signs and indicators that their child is being sexually abused.

Mothers who remain in denial about their own abuse are not able to protect their children from the same or other perpetrators. They have such an investment in protecting themselves from their own memories that they cannot see the abuse or the indicators in their own children. There are issues for mothers who have faced up to their own abuse if this has not been in the context of therapy, as they may still have an investment in denying that the same thing is happening to their child and they also have to face up to their feelings about it.

### Questions

What are her survivor issues? Explore with the mother how she survived her childhood trauma and focus her attention on potential and actual strengths and previously used coping strategies; those that were successful and those that were not. Also explore any unresolved issues and assess how these may impact on her and the child's recovery. Unfortunately, by focusing on the weaknesses of her unresolved problems, the worker is most likely to engage the mother in treatment. Utilise her experience to focus on her ability to empathise with the child.

### Measuring change

As can be seen in this chapter, the issues involved in sexual abuse in relation to mothers are many and complex. If we are to try to make the best decisions possible, it is important to understand the individual's own experiences, knowledge, levels of ability and motivation to change. Only when all these components are put together in the

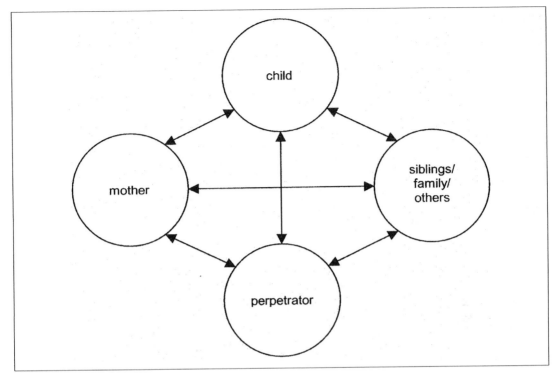

**Figure 12.7**    Family dynamics

context of the whole family system will we be anywhere near getting to a realistic conclusion about any ability to protect.

If the mother has decided to separate from the perpetrator and there is to be no further involvement with the family, then the key issues will be around rebuilding trust and confidence and developing some safer strategies for the future. If, however, reunification is the desired outcome, then it is crucial that changes are considered in all parts of the family as the various individuals form the dynamic family system of the child. In considering what progress has been made it may help to think in terms of:

- What information you already have – at this point.
- What gaps there still are, or that have become evident.
- What areas need revisiting – remembering that this type of assessment is a dynamic process and you are measuring how the mother has internalised, interpreted and put to use, the information covered into her parenting, values and attitudes.

Regan (2006) contains a process and worksheets to help workers collate and analyse the information gathered. It is important not to lose sight of the key issues involved. All information gathered should be considered in relation to how it relates to, or redresses, the dynamics that enabled the sexual abuse to occur. So, for example, has there been any change in the perpetrator accepting any responsibility for the abuse; has there been any reduction of isolation and secrecy; has the mother-child relationship become stronger; are the child's needs understood and prioritised; are there any realistic strategies being considered by the mother and the abuser in relation to roles and responsibilities for the future?

The most desirable pre-conditions for reunification involve changes in all parts of the family system as each person is inter-dependant within the family but with the primary emphasis being on the perpetrator accepting, at least some, responsibility for the offences. The framework for considering reunification is discussed in more detail in Chapter 14.

## Summary

This chapter has set out a detailed framework for assessing a mother's ability to protect in a way that encourages workers to think more about the knowledge and value base that structures their intervention style. There is a need to embrace more recent research and practice experience to inform an approach that considers impact, support and dilemmas facing the mothers when the sexual abuse is intra-familial in nature.

## References

Abel, G.G., Mittleman, M.S. and Becker, J.V. (1985) Sex Offenders: Results of Assessment and Recommendations for Treatment. In Ben-Aron, M.H., Hucker, S.J. and Webster, C.D. (Eds.) *Clinical Criminology: The Assessment and Treatment of Criminal Behaviour.* Toronto: M and M Graphics.

Adams, C. and Fay, J. (1981) *No More Secrets: Protecting your Child from Sexual Assault.* San Luis Obispo, CA: Impact Publishers.

Adams-Tucker, C. (1982) Proximate Effects of Sexual Abuse in Childhood: A Report on 28 children. *American Journal of Psychiatry,* 139: 1252–6.

Alexander, P.C. (1992) Application of Attachment Theory to the Study of Sexual Abuse. *Journal of Consulting and Clinical Psychology,* 60: 185–95.

Anthony, G. and Watkeys, J. (1991) False Allegations in Child Sexual Abuse: The Pattern of Referral in an Area where Reporting is not Mandatory. *Children and Society,* 5: 2, 111–22.

Avery, L., Massatt, C.R. and Lundy, M. (1998) The Relationship between Parent and Child Reports of Parental Supportiveness and Psychopathology of Sexually Abused Children. *Child and Adolescent Social Work Journal,* 15: 3, 187–205.

Bagley, C. (1995) *Child Sexual Abuse and Mental Health in Adolescents and Adults: British and Canadian Perspectives.* Aldershot: Avebury.

Bagley, C. and King, K. (1990) *Child Sexual Abuse: The Search for Healing.* London: Routledge.

Bagley, C. and Naspini, O. (1987) *Mothers of Sexually Abused Children.* Unpublished paper.

Belsky, J. (1993) Etiology of Child Maltreatment: Developmental-ecological Analysis. *Psychological Bulletin,* 114: 413–34.

Benedek, T. (1959) Parenting as a Developmental Phase. *Journal of the American Psychoanalytic Association,* 7: 389–417.

Berliner, L. (1990) Therapy with Victimised Children and their Families. *New Directions for Mental Health Services,* 51: 29–46.

Berliner, L. and Conte, J. (1990) The Process of Victimisation: The Victim's Perspective. *Child Abuse and Neglect,* 14: 29–40.

Berliner, L. and Conte, J. (1995) The Effects of Disclosure and Intervention on Sexually Abused Children. *Child Abuse and Neglect,* 19: 3, 371–84.

Boss, P. and Greenberg, J. (1984) Family Boundary Ambiguity: A New Variable in Family Stress. *Family Process,* 23: 535–46.

Boulton, A. and Burnham, L. (1989) Stand by your Man – or your Child? *Social Work Today,* 14th Sept: 20.

Breckenbridge, J. and Berreen, R. (1992) Dealing with Mother Blame: Workers Responses to Incest and Child Sexual Abuse. In Breckenbridge, J. and Carmody, M. (Eds.) *Crimes of Violence: Australian Responses to Rape and Child Sexual Assault.* North Sydney: Allen and Unwin.

Brehm, S.S. (1992) *Intimate Relationships.* (2nd ed) NY: McGraw Hill.

Briere, J. (1992) *Child Abuse Trauma: Theory and Treatment of the Lasting Effects.* Newbury Park, CA: Sage.

Briggs, D., Doyle, P., Gooch, T. and Kennington, R. (1998) *Assessing Men who Sexually Abuse: A Practice Guide.* London: Jessica Kingsley.

Brown, K. (1998) *Surviving Sexual Abuse.* Crowborough, E Sussex: Monarch Books.

Buchanan, A. (1996) *Cycles of Child Maltreatment: Facts, Fallacies and Interventions.* Chichester: Wiley.

Burgess, A.W., Holmstrom, L.l. and McCausland, M.P. (1977) Child Sexual Assault by a Family Member: Decisions following Disclosure. *Victimology,* 11: 2, 236–50.

Burkett, L.P. (1991) Parenting Behaviours of Women who were Sexually Abused as Children in their Families of Origin. *Family Process,* 30: 421–34.

Butler-Sloss, E. (1988) *Report of the Inquiry into Child Abuse in Cleveland.* London: HMSO.

Byerly, C.M. (1985) Mother Survival in the Incestuous Family. *Sexual Coercion and Assault,* 1: 11–3.

Byerly, C.M. (1992) *How to Survive the Molestation of your Child.* Kendall/Hunt Publishing Co.

Calder, M.C. (1997) *Juveniles and Children who Sexually Abuse: A Guide to Risk Assessment.* Lyme Regis: Russell House Publishing.

Calder, M.C. (Ed.)(1999) *Assessing Risk in Adult males who Sexually Abuse Children: A Practitioners Guide*. Lyme Regis: Russell House Publishing.

Calder, M.C. with Peake, A. and Rose, K. (2001) *Mothers of Sexually Abused Children: A Framework for Assessment, Understanding and Support*. Lyme Regis: Russell House Publishing.

Calder, M.C. and Skinner, J. (1999) A Framework for Comprehensive Assessment. In Calder, M.C. (Ed.) *Assessing Risk in Adult Males who Sexually Abuse Children: A Practitioners Guide*. Lyme Regis: Russell House Publishing, 65–158.

Cammaert, L. (1988) Non-offending Mothers: A New Conceptualisation. In Walker, L.E.A. (Ed.) *Handbook on Sexual Abuse of Children: Assessment and Treatment Issues* (pp.309–25). New York: Springer Publishing.

Carich, M.S. and Adkerson, D.L. (1995) *Adult Sexual Offender Assessment Packet*. Brandon, VT: Safer Society Press.

Carter, B. (1993) Child Sexual Abuse: Impact on Mothers. *Affilia*, 8: 1, 72–90.

CIBA (1984) *Child Sexual Abuse within the Family*. London: Tavistock/Routledge.

Cohen, J.A. and Mannarino, A.P. (1996) Factors that Mediate Treatment Outcome of Sexually Abused Pre-school Children. *Journal of the American Academy of Adolescent Psychiatry*, 34: 10, 1402–10.

Cohen, T. (1995) Motherhood among Incest Survivors. *Child Abuse and Neglect*, 19: 12, 1423–9.

Cole, P.M. and Woolger, C. (1989) Incest Survivors: The Relation of their Perceptions of Parents and their own Parenting Behaviour. *Child Abuse and Neglect*, 13: 1–8.

Cole, P.M., Woolger, C., Power, T.G. and Smith, K.D. (1992) Parenting Difficulties among Adult Survivors of Father-daughter Incest. *Child Abuse and Neglect*, 16: 239–49.

Coleman, E. (1987a) Chemical Dependency and Intimacy Dysfunction: Inextricably Bound. *Journal of Chemical Dependency*, 1: 1, 13–26.

Conte, J.R., Wolf, S. and Smith, T. (1989) What Sexual Offenders tell us about Prevention. *Child Abuse and Neglect*, 13: 293–301.

Corcoran, J. (1998) In Defence of Mothers of Sexual Abuse Victims. *Families in Society*, July–August.

Courtois, C.A. (1988) *Healing the Incest Wound: Adult Survivors in Therapy*. NY: WW Norton.

Craig, E., Erooga, M., Morrison, T. and Shearer, E. (1989) Making Sense of Sexual Abuse: Charting the Shifting Sands. In Wattam, C., Hughes, J. and Blagg, H. (Eds.) *Child Sexual Abuse: Listening, Hearing and Validating the Experiences of Children*. Harlow: Longman.

Crawford, S.L. (1999) Intra-familial Sexual Abuse: What we Think we Know about Mothers, and Implications for Intervention. *Journal of Child Sexual Abuse*, 7: 3, 55–72.

Croll, L. (1994) *Caring for Children and Young People who have been Sexually Abused*. Basildon, Essex: Breakthrough for Youth.

De Jong, A.R. (1988) Maternal Responses to the Sexual Abuse of their Children. *Pediatrics*, 81: 14–21.

Deblinger, E., Hathaway, C.R., Lippmann, J. and Steer, R. (1993) Psychosocial Characteristics and Correlates of Symptom Distress in Non-offending Mothers of Sexually Abused Children. *Journal of Interpersonal Violence*, 8: 155–68.

Deblinger, E., Lippmann, J., Stauffer, L. and Finkel, M. (1994) Personal versus Professional Responses to Child Sexual Abuse Allegations. *Child Abuse and Neglect*, 18: 8, 679–82.

Deblinger, E., Stauffer, L. and Landsberg, C. (1994b) The Impact of a History of Child Sexual Abuse on Maternal Response to Allegations of Sexual Abuse Concerning her Child. *Journal of Child Sexual Abuse*, 3: 3, 67–75.

DeFrancis, V. (1969) *Protecting the Child Victim of Sex Crimes Committed by Adults: Final Report*. Denver: American Humane Association, Children's Division.

Dempster, H. (1993) The Aftermath of Child Sexual Abuse: Women's Perspectives. In Waterhouse, L. (Ed.) *Child Abuse and Child Abusers*. London: Jessica Kingsley.

DeVoe, E.R. and Faller, K.C. (1999) The Characteristics of Disclosure among Children who may have been Sexually Abused. *Child Maltreatment*, 4: 3, 217–27.

DeYoung, M. (1994) Immediate Maternal Reactions to the Disclosure or Discovery of Incest. *Journal of Family Violence*, 9: 1, 21–33.

Dietz, C. and Craft, J. (1980) Family Dynamics of Incest: A New Perspective. *Social Casework*, 61, 602–9.

DoH (1995) *Child Protection: Messages from Research*. London: HMSO.

Doka K (1989) Disenfranchised Grief: Recognising Hidden Sorrow. Lexington, MA: Lexington Books.

Double, R. (1999) Hidden Victims. *Community Care*, 15–21 April.

Dwyer, J. and Miller, R. (1996) Disenfranchised Grief after Incest: The Experience of Victims/Daughters, Mothers/Wives. *Australian and New Zealand Journal of Family Therapy,* 17: 3, 137–45.

Dziuba-Leatherman, J. and Finkelhor, D. (1994) How does Receiving Information about Sexual Abuse Influence Boys' Perceptions of their Risk? *Child Abuse and Neglect,* 18: 557–68.

Eaton, L. (1993) Mother's Helpers. *Community Care,* 967, 16–7.

Elbow, M. and Mayfield, J. (1991) Mothers of Incest Victims: Villains, Victims, or Protectors? *Families in Society,* Feb. 78–85.

Elliott, M., Browne, K. and Kilcoyne, J. (1995) Child Sexual Abuse Prevention: What Offenders tell us. *Child Abuse and Neglect,* 19: 5, 579–94.

Elrod, J.M. and Rubin, R.H. (1993) Parental Involvement in Sexual Abuse Prevention Education. *Child Abuse and Neglect,* 17: 527–38.

Engel, B. (1994) *Families in Recovery: Working together to Heal the Damage of Child Sexual Abuse.* Los Angeles, CA: Lowell House.

Epps, K.J. (1997) Pointers for Carers. In Calder, M.C. *Juveniles and Children who Sexually Abuse: A Guide to Risk Assessment.* Lyme Regis: Russell House Publishing.

Esquilin, S.C. (1987) Family Responses to the Identification of Extra-familial Child Sexual Abuse. *Psychotherapy in Private Practice,* 5: 1, 105–13.

Everson, M., Hunter, W., Runyon, D., Edelsohn, G., and Coulter, M. (1989) Maternal Support following Disclosure of Incest. *American Journal of Orthopsychiatry,* 59, 197–207.

Faller, K.C. (1988) The Myth of the 'Collusive Mother': Variables in the Functioning of Mothers of Victims of Intra-familial Sexual Abuse. *Journal of Interpersonal Violence,* 3: 2, 190.

Faller, K.C. (1988b) Decision-making in Cases of Intra-familial Child Sexual Abuse. *American Journal of Orthopsychiatry,* 58: 121–8.

Faller, K.C. (1988c) *Child Sexual Abuse: An Inter-disciplinary Manual for Diagnosis, Case Management, and Treatment.* London: MacMillan.

Faller, K.C. (1989) The Role Relationship between Victim and Perpetrator as a Predictor of Characteristics of Intra-family Sexual Abuse. *Child and Adolescent Social Work,* 6: 217–29.

Faller, K.C. (1990) *Understanding Child Sexual Maltreatment.* London: Sage.

Faller, K.C. (1991) Possible Explanations for Child Sexual Abuse Allegations in Divorce. *American Journal of Orthopsychiatry,* 61: 86–91.

Faller, K.C. (1991b) Poly-incestuous Families: An Exploratory Study. *Journal of Interpersonal Violence,* 6: 310–22.

Farmer, E. (1993) The Impact of Child Protection Interventions: The Experiences of Parents and Children. In Waterhouse, L. (Ed.) *Child Abuse and Child Abusers: Protection and Prevention.* London: Jessica Kingsley.

Finkelhor, D. (1979) *Sexually Victimised Children.* NY: The Free Press.

Finkelhor, D. (1984) *Child Sexual Abuse: New Theory and Research.* NY: The Free Press.

Finkelhor, D. (1988) The Trauma of Child Sexual Abuse: Two Models. In Wyatt, G.E. and Powell, G.J. (Eds.) *Lasting Effects of Child Sexual Abuse.* Newbury Park, CA: Sage.

Finkelhor, D. and Browne, A. (1988) Assessing the Long-term Impact of Child Sexual Abuse: A Review and Re-conceptualisation. In Walker, L.E. (Ed.) *Handbook of Sexual Abuse of Children: Assessment and Treatment Issues.* NY: Springer-Verlag.

Fong, J. and Walsh-Bowers, R. (1998) Voices of the Blamed: Mothers' Responsiveness to Father-Daughter Incest. *Journal of Family Social Work,* 3: 1, 25–41.

Friedrich, W.N. (1990) *Psychotherapy of Sexually Abused Children and their Families.* NY: WW Norton.

Furniss, T. (1990) Dealing with Denial. In Oates, R.K. (Ed.) *Understanding and Managing Child Sexual Abuse.* Marrickeville: Harcourt Brace Jovanovich.

Furniss, T. (1991) *The Multi-professional Handbook of Child Sexual Abuse.* London: Routledge.

Gilbert, N. (1988) Teaching Children to Prevent Sexual Abuse. *The Public Interest,* 93: 3–15.

Gilgun, J.F. (1984) Does the Mother Know? Alternatives to Blaming Mothers for Child Sexual Abuse. *Response,* Fall.

Glaser, D. and Frosh, S. (1988) *Child Sexual Abuse.* London: MacMillan.

Golan, N. (1981) *Passing through Transitions.* NY: Free Press.

Gomes-Schwartz, B., Horowitz, J.M. and Cardarelli, A.P. (1990) *Child Sexual Abuse: The Initial Effects.* Newbury Park, CA: Sage.

Goodwin, J. (1981) Suicide Attempts in Sexual Abuse Victims and their Mothers. *Child Abuse and Neglect,* 5: 217–21.

Goodwin, J., Cormier, L. and Owen, J. (1983) Grandfather-Grand-daughter Incest: A Tri-generational View. *Child Abuse and Neglect*, 7: 163–70.

Groth, A.N. (1978) Guidelines for the Assessment and Management of the Offender. In Burgess, A., Groth, A.N., Holmstrom, L.L and Sgroi, S. (Eds.) *Sexual Assault of Children and Adolescents.* Lexington, MA: Lexington Books.

Hall, L. and Lloyd, S. (1989) *Surviving Child Sexual Abuse: A Handbook for Helping Women Challenge their Past.* Basingstoke: The Falmer Press.

Hanks, H. (1997) 'Normal' Psycho-sexual Development, Behaviour and Knowledge. In Calder, M.C. *Juveniles and Children who Sexually Abuse: A Guide to Risk Assessment.* Lyme Regis: Russell House Publishing.

Herman, J. (1981) *Father-Daughter Incest.* Cambridge, MA: Harvard University Press.

Herman, J. and Hirschman, L. (1981) Families at Risk of Father-Daughter Incest. *American Journal of Psychiatry*, 138: 967–70.

Hillman, D. and Solek-Tefft, J. (1988) *Spiders and Flies: Help for Parents and Teachers of Sexually Abused Children.* Lexington, MA: Lexington Books.

Hite, S. (1990) 'I Hope I'm not like my Mother'. *Women and Therapy*, 10: 13–30.

Hoagwood, K. and Stewart, J.M. (1989) Sexually Abused Children's Perceptions of Family Functioning. *Child and Adolescent Social Work*, 6: 2, 139–49.

Home Office (1992) *Memorandum of Good Practice.* London: HMSO.

Hooper, C.A. (1989) Alternatives to Collusion: The Response of Mothers to Child Sexual Abuse in the Family. *Educational and Child Psychology*, 6: 1, 22–30.

Hooper, C.A. (1992) *Mothers Surviving Child Sexual Abuse.* London: Routledge.

Hooper, C.A. (1992b) Child Sexual Abuse: Working with Mothers. *Childright*, 86.

Hopkins, J. and Thompson, E.H. (1984) Loss and Mourning in Victims of Rape and Sexual Assault. In Hopkins, J. (Ed.) *Perspectives on Rape and Sexual Assault.* London: Harper and Row.

Howard, C.A. (1993) Factors Influencing a Mother's Response to her Child's Disclosure of Incest. *Professional Psychology: Research and Practice*, 24: 2, 176–81.

Howarth, V. (1999) Presentation to Sex Offender Review Team Conference. York: Stakis Hotel, 28 June.

Hubbard, G. (1989) Mothers' Perceptions of Incest: Sustained Disruption and Turmoil. *Archives of Psychiatric Nursing* 3: 1, 34–40.

Humphreys, C. (1992) Disclosure of Child Sexual Assault: Implications for Mothers. *Australian Social Work*, 45: 3, 27–35.

Humphreys, C. (1995) Counselling and Support Issues for Mothers and Fathers of Sexually Abused Children. *Australian Social Work*, 48: 4, 13–9.

Hunter, W.M., Coulter, M.D., Runyan, D.K. and Everson, M.D. (1990) Determinants of Placement for Sexually Abused Children. *Child Abuse and Neglect*, 14: 407–18.

Jaudes, P. and Morris, M. (1990) Child Sexual Abuse: Who Goes Home? *Child Abuse and Neglect*, 14: 61–8.

Johnson, J.T. (1992) *Mothers of Incest Survivors: Another Side of the Story.* Indianapolis: Indiana University Press.

Jones, D.P.H. and Ramchandani, P. (1999) *Child Sexual Abuse: Informing Practice from Research.* Oxford: Radcliffe Medical Press.

Julian, V. and Mohr, C. (1979) Father-Daughter Incest: Profile of the Offender. *Victimology*, 4: 348–60.

Justice, B. and Justice, R. (1979) *The Broken Taboo.* NY: Human Sciences Press.

Kaplan, S.J., Pelcowitz, D., Salzinger, S. and Ganeles, D. (1988) Psychopatholgy of Non-violent Women in Violent Families. In Anthony, E.J, and Chiland, C. (Eds.) *The Child in his Family: Perilous Development: Child Raising and Identity Formation under Stress.* NY: Wiley.

Kelley, S.J. (1990) Parental Stress Response to Sexual Abuse and Ritualistic Abuse of Children in Day-care Settings. *Nursing Research*, 39: 25–9.

Kelly, L. (1988) *Surviving Sexual Violence.* Cambridge: Polity Press.

Kempe, R.S. and Kempe, C.H. (1978) *Child Abuse.* London: Fontana/Open Books.

Kendall-Tackett, K.A., Williams, L.M. and Finkelhor, D. (1993) Impact of Sexual Abuse on Children: A Review and Synthesis of Recent Empirical Studies. *Psychological Bulletin*, 113: 1, 164–80.

Kinard, E.M. (1996) Social Support, Competence, and Depression in Mothers of Abused Children. *American Journal of Orthopsychiatry*, 66: 3, 449–62.

Kreklewetz, C.M. and Piotrowski, C.C. (1996) *Towards a Theoretical Model of the Recurrence of Incest: Perspectives from Incest Survivor Mothers.*

Poster presentation to the 11th International Congress on Child Abuse and Neglect, August 1996, Dublin, Ireland.

Kreklewetz, C.M. and Piotrowski, C.C. (1998) Incest Survivor Mothers: Protecting the next Generation. *Child Abuse and Neglect*, 22: 12, 1305–12.

Kroth, J.A. (1979) Family Therapy Impact on Intra-familial Child Sexual Abuse. *Child Abuse and Neglect*, 3: 297–302.

Laing, L. and Kamsler, A. (1990) Putting an End to Secrecy: Therapy with Mothers and Children. In Durrant, M. and White, C. (Eds.) *Ideas for Therapy with Sexual Abuse*. Adelaide: Dulwich Centre Publications.

Lawson, L. and Chaffin, M. (1992) False Negatives in Sexual Abuse Disclosure Interviews: Incidence and Influence of Caretaker's Belief in Abuse in Cases of Accidental Abuse Discovery by Diagnosis of STD. *Journal of Interpersonal Violence*, 7: 4, 532–42.

Lazarus, A.A. (1976) *Multi-modal Behaviour Therapy*. NY: Springer Publishing.

Leifer, M., Shapiro, J.P. and Kassem, L. (1993) The Impact of Maternal History and Behaviour upon Foster Placement and Adjustment in Sexually Abused Girls. *Child Abuse and Neglect*, 17: 755–66.

Lipton, M. (1997) The Effect of the Primary Caretaker's Distress on the Sexually Abused Child: A Comparison of Biological and Foster Parents. *Child and Adolescent Social Work*, 14: 2, 115–27.

Lubell, A.K.N. and Peterson, P. (1998) Female Incest Survivors: Relationships with Mothers and Female Friends. *Journal of Interpersonal Violence*, 13: 2, 193–205.

Lyon, E. and Kouloumpos-Lenaris, K. (1987) Clinician and State Children's Services Worker Collaboration in Treating Sexual Abuse. *Child Welfare*, 67: 517–27.

MacFarlane, K. and Bulkley, J. (1982) Treating Child Sexual Abuse: An Overview of Current Treatment Models. *Journal of Social Work and Human Sexuality*, 1: 71–93.

Macleod, M. and Saraga, M. (1988) Challenging the Orthodoxy: Towards a Feminist Theory of Practice. *Feminist Review*, 28: 16–55.

Magura. S., Moses, B.S. and Jones, M.A. (1987) *Assessing Risk and Measuring Change in Families: The Family-risk Scales*. Washington, DC: Child Welfare League of America.

Maisch, H. (1973) *Incest*. NY: Stein and Day.

Manion, I.G., McIntyre, J., Firestone, P., Ligezinska, M., Ensom, R. and Wells, G. (1996) Secondary Traumatisation in Parents following the Disclosure of Extra-familial Child Sexual Abuse: Initial Effects. *Child Abuse and Neglect*, 20: 11, 1095–109.

Margolin, L. (1992) Sexual Abuse by Grandparents. *Child Abuse and Neglect*, 16: 735–41.

Marshall, W.L. and Eccles, A. (1991) Issues in Clinical Practice with Sex Offenders. *Journal of Interpersonal Violence*, 6: 68–93.

Massatt, C.R. and Lundy, M. (1998) 'Reporting Costs' to Non-offending Parents in Cases of Intra-familial Child Sexual Aabuse. *Child Welfare*, 77: 4, 371–88.

Mayer, A. (1983) *Incest: A Treatment Manual for Therapy with Victims, Spouses and Offenders*. Holmes Beach, Fl: Learning Publications.

McGrath, R.J. (1991) Sex Offender Risk Assessment and Disposition of Planning: A Review of Empirical and Clinical Findings. *Interpersonal Journal of Offender Therapy and Comparative Criminology*, 35, 4, 328–50.

McGrath, R.J. (1992) Assessing Sex Offender Risk. American Probation and Parole Association *Perspectives*, 16: 3, 6–9.

McIntyre, K. (1981) Role of Mothers in Father-daughter Incest: A Feminist Analysis. *Social Work*, 26: 462–6.

McLurg, G. and Craissati, J. (1999) A Descriptive Study of Alleged Sexual Abusers known to Social Services. *The Journal of Sexual Aggression*, 4: 1, 22–30.

McMillen, C., Zuravin, S. and Rideout, G. (1995) Perceived Benefit from Child Sexual Abuse. *Journal of Consulting and Clinical Psychology*, 63: 6, 1037–43.

Meiselman, K. (1978) *Incest: A Psychological Study of Causes and Effects with Treatment Recommendations*. San Fransisco: Jossey-Bass.

Mendel, M.P. (1995) *The Male Survivor: The Impact of Sexual Abuse*. Thousand Oaks, CA: Sage.

Miller, R. and Dwyer, J. (1997) Reclaiming the Mother-daughter Relationship after Sexual Abuse. *Australian and New Zealand Journal of Family Therapy*, 18: 4, 194–202.

Milner, J. and Blyth, E. (1989) *Coping with Child Sexual Abuse: A Guide for Teachers*. London: Longman.

Mitchell, A. (1985) Child Sexual Assault. In Guberman, C. and Wolfe, M. (Eds.) *No Safe Place: Violence against Women and Children*. Toronto: The Women's Press.

Monahan, K. (1997) Crocodile Talk: Attributions of Incestuously Abused and Non-abused Sisters. *Child Abuse and Neglect*, 21: 1, 19–34.

Muram, D., Rosenthal, T.L. and Beck, K.W. (1994) Personality Profiles of Mothers of Sexual Abuse Victims and their Daughters. *Child Abuse and Neglect*, 18: 5, 419–23.

Myers, J.E.B. (1997) *A Mother's Nightmare – Incest. A Practical Legal Guide for Parents and Professionals*. Thousand Oaks, CA: Sage.

Myers, M. (1985) A New Look at Mothers of Incest VIctims. *Journal of Social Work and Human Sexuality*, 47–58.

Nelson, S. (1992) Power failure. *Social Work Today*, 11 June.

Newberger, C.M., Gremy, I.M., Waternaux, C.M. and Newberger, E.H. (1993) Mothers of Sexually Abused Children: Trauma and Repair in Longitudinal Perspective. *American Journal of Orthopsychiatry*, 63: 92–102.

Newberger, E.H., Newberger, C.M. and Gremy, I. (1991) *Dual Vulnerability of Sexually Victimised Mothers and Sexually Victimised Children: A Longitudinal Study*. Paper presented to the 7th Annual Convention of the International Society for Traumatic Stress Studies, Washington, DC, Oct. 26th.

Oates, R.K. (Ed.) (1990) *Understanding and Managing Child Sexual Abuse*. Marrickville: Harcourt. Brace Jovanovich

Oates, R.K., Tebbutt, J., Swanston, H., Lynch, D.L. and O'Toole, B.I. (1998) Prior Childhood Sexual Abuse in Mothers of Sexually Abused Children. *Child Abuse and Neglect*, 22: 11, 1113–8.

Orr, T. (1995) *No Right Way: The Voices of Mothers of Incest Survivors*. London: Scarlet Press.

Orten, J.D. and Rich, L.L. (1993) A Model for Assessment of Incestuous Families. In Rauch, J.B. (Ed.) *Assessment: A Sourcebook for Social Work Practice*. Milwauke: Families International.

Ovaris, W. (1991) *After the Nightmare: The Treatment of Non-offending Mothers of Sexually Abused Children*. Holmes Beach, Fl: Learning Publications.

Palmer, S.E., Brown, R.A., Rae-Grant, N.I. and Loughlin, M.J. (1999) Responding to Children's Disclosure of Familial Abuse: What Survivors Tell Us. *Child Welfare*, LXXVIII: 2, 259–82.

Peake, A. and Fletcher, M. (1997) *Strong Mothers: A Resource for Mothers and Carers of Children who have been Sexually Sssaulted*. Lyme Regis: Russell House Publishing.

Pellegrin, A. and Wagner, W.G. (1990) Child Sexual Abuse: Factors Affecting Victims' Removal from Home. *Child Abuse and Neglect*, 14: 53–60.

Peters, J.J. (1973) Child Rape: Defusing a Psychological Time Bomb. *Hospital Physician*, 9: 46–9.

Porter, L.S., Blick, L.C. and Sgroi, S.M. (1982) Treatment of the Sexually Abused Child. In Sgroi, S.M. (Ed.) *Handbook of Clinical Intervention in Child Sexual Abuse*. Lexington, MA: DC Heath.

Prendergast, W.E. (1991) *Treating Sex Offenders in Correctional Institutions and Outpatient Clinics: A Guide to Clinical Practice*. NY: Haworth Press.

Print, B. and Dey, C. (1992) Empowering Mothers of Sexually Abused Children: A Positive Framework. In Bannister, A. (Ed.) *From Hearing to Healing with the Aftermath of Child Sexual Abuse*. London: Longman.

Reder, P. and Lucey, C. (1995) Significant Issues in the Assessment of Parenting. In Reder, P. and Lucey, C. (Eds.) *Assessment of Parenting: Psychiatric and Psychological Contributions*. London: Routledge.

Regan, L. (2006) *Helping Mothers Move Forward: A Workbook to Help Provide Assessment and Support to the Safe Carers of Children who have been Sexually Abused*. Lyme Regis: Russell House Publishing

Regehr, C. (1990) Parental Responses to Extra-familial Child Sexual Abuse. *Child Abuse and Neglect*, 14: 113–20.

Richardson, S. and Bacon, H. (1991) A Framework for Belief. In Richardson, S. and Bacon, H. (Eds.) *Child Sexual Abuse: Whose Problem?* Birmingham: Venture Press.

Rickford, F. (1992) You must have Known. *Social Work Today*, 23th Jan. 14–5.

Ringwalt, C. and Earp, J. (1988) Attributing Responsibility in Cases of Father-daughter Incest. *Child Abuse and Neglect*, 12: 273–81.

Rivera, M. (1988) Social Systems' Intervention in Families of Victims of Child Sexual Abuse. *Canadian Journal of Community Mental Health*, 7: 1, 35–51.

Roberts, J. (1992/3) Non-believing Mothers of Sexually Abused Children. *Practice*, 6: 4, 268–70.

Roberts, J. and Taylor, C. (1993) Sexually Abused Children and Young People Speak out. In Waterhouse, L. (Ed.) *Child Abuse and Child Abusers: Protection and Prevention*. London: Jessica Kingsley.

Rollins, B.C. and Thomas, D.L. (1979) Parental Support, Power and Control: Techniques in the Socialisation of Children. In Burr, W., Hill, R., Nye, F.I. and Reiss, I. (Eds.) *Contemporary Theories about the Family (volume 1)* NY: The Free Press.

Rose, K. (2000) *Practice Guidance on Domestic Violence.* Salford ACPC (unpublished)

Rose, K. and Savage, A. (1995) '*Who Cares?*' Kaleidoscope Project/ Salford Area Child Protection Committee.

Rose, K. and Savage, A. (2000) Living with Risk. In Wheal, A. (Ed.) *Working in Partnership with Parents.* Lyme Regis: Russell House Publishing.

Russell, D.E.H. (1984) *Sexual Exploitation: Rape, Child Sexual Abuse and Workplace Harassment.* Beverly Hills, CA: Sage.

Russell, D.E.H. (1986) *The Secret Trauma: Incest in the Lives of Girls and Women.* NY: Basic Books.

Ryan, G.D. (1991) Consequences for the Victims of Sexual Abuse. In Ryan, G.D. and Lane, S.L. (Eds.) *Juvenile Sex Offending: Causes, Consequences and Corrections.* Lexington, MA: Lexington Books.

Sahd, D. (1980) Psychological Assessment of Sexually Abusing Families and Treatment Implications. In Holder, W. (Ed.) *Sexual Abuse of Children: Implications for Treatment.* Englewood, CO: American Humane Association.

Salt, P., Myers, M., Coleman, L., and Sauzier, M. (1990) The Myth of the Mother as 'Accomplice' to Child Sexual Abuse. In Gomes-Schwartz, M. Horowitz, J.M. and Cardarelli, A.P. (Eds.) *Child Sexual Abuse.* Newbury Park, CA: Sage.

Salter, A.C. (1988) *Treating Child Sex Offenders and Victims: A Practical Guide.* Thousand Oaks, CA: Sage.

Sanderson, C. (1990) *Counselling Adult Survivors of Childhood Sexual Abuse.* London: Jessica Kingsley.

Sauzier, M. (1989) Disclosure of Sexual Abuse. *Psychiatric Clinics of North America,* 12: 445–71.

Sayers, T. (1995) Issues for and about the Non-abusing Parent. In Hollows, A. (Ed.) *Rebuilding Families after Abuse.* London: National Children's Bureau.

Scott, R.S. and Flowers, J.V. (1988) Betrayal by the Mother as a Factor contributing to Psychological Disturbance in Victims of Father-daughter Incest: An MMPI Analysis. *Journal of Social and Clinical Psychology,* 6: 1, 147–54.

Segal, L.E. and Stermac, L. (1990) The Role of Cognition in Sexual Assault. In Marshall, W.L.,

Laws, D.R. and Barbaree, H.E. (Eds.) *Handbook of Sexual Assault.* NY: Plenum.

Serin, R.C., Malcolm, P.B., Khanna, A. and Barbaree, H.E. (1994) Psychopathy and Deviant Sexual arousal in Incarcerated Sex Offenders. *Journal of Interpersonal Violence,* 9: 1, 3–11.

Server, J. and Janzen, C. (1982) Contraindications to Reconstitution of Sexually Abusive Families. *Child Welfare,* 61: 279–88.

Sgroi, S.M. (Ed.) (1982) *Handbook of Clinical Intervention in Child Sexual Abuse.* Lexington, Mass: Lexington Books.

Sgroi, S.M. and Dana, N.T. (1982) Individual and Group Treatment of Mothers of Incest Victims. In Sgroi, S.M. (Ed.) op. cit. 191–214.

Shinn, M., Knickman, J. and Weitzman, B. (1991) Social Relationships and Vulnerability to Becoming Homeless among Poor Families. *American Psychologist,* 46: 1180–7.

Sirles, E.A. and Franke, P.J. (1989) Factors influencing Others' Reactions to Intra-family Sexual Abuse. *Child Abuse and Neglect,* 13: 131–9.

Sirles, E.A. and Lofberg, C.E. (1990) Factors Associated with Divorce in Intrafamily Child Sexual Abuse Cases. *Child Abuse and Neglect,* 14: 165–70.

Smart, P. (1997) *Child Sexual Abuse: Non-abusing Parents Perspectives of Social Work Intervention.* Unpublished BA Research Project. University College, Salford.

Smith, G. (1994) Parent, Partner, Protector: Conflicting Role Demands for Mothers of Sexually Abused Children. In Morrison, T., Erooga, M. and Beckett, R.C. (Eds.) *Sexual Offending against Children: Assessment and Treatment of Male Abusers.* London, Routledge.

Smith, G. (1995) Assessing Protectiveness in Cases of Child Sexual Abuse. In Reder, P. and Lucey, C. (Eds.) *Assessment of Parenting: Psychiatric and Psychological Contributions.* London: Routledge.

Smith, G. (1995b) *The Protector's Handbook: Reducing the Risk of Child Sexual Abuse and Helping Children Recover.* London: Women's Press.

Sorensen, T. and Snow, B. (1991) How Children Tell: The Process of Disclosure in Child Sexual Abuse. *Child Welfare,* 70: 3–15.

Sroufe, L.A., Jacobvitz, D., Mangelsdorf, S., De Angelo, E. and Ward, M.J. (1985) Generational Boundary Discussion between Mothers and their Pre-school Children: A Relationship Systems Approach. *Child Development,* 56: 317–25.

Stark, E. and Flitcraft, H. (1988) Women and Children at Risk: A Feminist Perspective on Child Abuse. *International Journal of Health Services,* 18: 1, 97–118.

Stermac. L., Davidson, A. and Sheridan, M. (1995) Incidence of Non-sexual Violence in Incest Offenders. *International Journal of Offender Therapy and Comparative Criminology,* 39: 2.

Summit, R. (1983) The Child Sexual Abuse Accommodation Syndrome. *Child Abuse and Neglect,* 7: 177–93.

Summit, R.C. (1990) The Specific Vulnerability of Children. In Oates, R.K. (Ed.) *Understanding and Managing Child Sexual Abuse.* Marrickville: Harcooutt Brace Jovanovich.

Tamraz, D.N. (1996) Non-offending Mothers of Sexually Abused Children: Comparisons of Opinions and Research. *Journal of Child Sexual Abuse,* 5: 4, 75–99.

Terry, W.T. (1990) *Perpetrator and Victim Accounts of Sexual Abuse.* Paper presented at the San Diego Conference on responding to sexual maltreatment. San Diego, CA.

Testa, M., Miller, B.A., Downs, W.R. and Panek, D. (1992) The Moderating Impact of Social Support following Childhood Sexual Abuse. *Violence and Victims,* 7: 2, 173–86.

Timmons-Mitchell, J., Chandler-Holtz, D., and Semple, W.E. (1996) Post-traumatic Stress Symptoms in Mothers following Children's Reports of Sexual Abuse: An Exploratory Study. *American Journal of Orthopsychiatry,* 66: 3, 463–7.

Tinling, L. (1990) Perpetuation of Incest by Significant Others: Mothers who do not want to See. *Individual Psychology,* 46: 3, 280–97.

Todd, I. (1989) When There's Nowhere to Run. *Community Care,* 23th Sep. 18–19.

Todd, I. and Ellis, L. (1992) Divided Loyalties. *Social Work Today,* 25th June 14–5.

Tower, C.C. (1989) *Understanding Child Abuse and Neglect.* Boston: Allyn and Bacon.

Trepper, T.S/, Niedner, D., Mika, l. and Barrett, M.J. (1996) Family Characteristics of Intact Sexually Abusing Families: An Exploratory Study. *Journal of Child Sexual Abuse,* 5: 4, 1–20.

Trotter, J. (1998) *No-one's Listening: Mothers, Fathers and Child Sexual Aabuse.* London: Whiting and Birch.

Truesdell, D.L., McNeil, J.S. and Deschner, J.P. (1986) Incidence of Wife Abuse in Incestuous Families. *Social Work,* 31: 138–40.

Tufts New England Medical Centre, Division of Child Psychiatry (1984) *Sexually Exploited Children.* Unpublished manuscript.

Vander Mey, B.J. and Neff, R.L. (1986) *Incest as Child Abuse: Research and Applications.* NY: Praeger.

Walton, P. (1996) *Partnership with Mothers in the Wake of Child Sexual Abuse.* Social work monograph 154. Norwich: University of East Anglia.

Waring, E.M. and Reddon, J.R. (1983) The Measurement of Intimacy in Marriage. *Journal of Clinical Psychology,* 39: 53–7.

Waterhouse, L., Carnie, J. and Dobash, R. (1993) The Abuser under the Microscope. *Community Care,* 24th Jun, 24.

Weiss, R.S. (1974) The Provisions of Social Relationships. In Rubin, Z. (Ed.) *Doing unto Others.* Englewood Cliffs, NJ: Prentice-Hall.

West, D.J. (1991) The Effects of Sex Offences. In Hollin, C.R. and Howells, K. (Eds.) *Clinical Approaches to Sex Offenders and their Victims.* Chichester: Wiley.

Williams, L. and Finkelhor, D. (1992) *The Characteristics of Incestuous Fathers.* Unpublished manuscript: University of New Hampshire Research Laboratory.

Wolf, S. (1984) A Multi-factor Model of Deviant Sexuality. Paper at 3rd International Conference on Victimology. Lisbon, Nov.

Wright, S. (1991) Family Effects of Offender Removal from Home. In Patton, M.Q. (Ed.) *Family Sexual Abuse: Frontline Research and Evaluation.* Newbury Park, CA: Sage.

Wurtele, S.K. and Miller-Perrin, C.L. (1992) *Preventing Child Sexual Abuse: Sharing the Responsibility.* Lincoln: University of Nebraska.

Wyatt, G.E. and Mickey, M.R. (1988) The Support by Parents and Others as it Mediates the Effects of Child Sexual Abuse: An Exploratory Study. In Wyatt, G.E. and Powell, G.J. (Eds.) *Lasting Effects of Child Sexual Abuse.* Newbury Park, CA: Sage.

Wyre, R. (1987) *Working with Sex Abuse.* Oxford: Perry Publications.

Yates, A. (1982) Children Eroticized by Incest. *American Journal of Psychiatry,* 139: 482–5.

# CHAPTER 13

# Body Safety Skills

*Lynda Regan*

*A child may be able to learn some strategies for keeping safer, but children are dependant on adults. Children cannot and should not be expected to keep themselves safe.*

*Children are not able to understand adult motives and manipulations if the adult they are with is not a safe person.*

Working in the field of child sexual abuse highlights children's vulnerability on all levels. Children are by their very nature dependant on adults to meet their basic needs, one of which is to be protected. All children will have different experiences as they grow and progress towards adulthood. Child development theories tell us that adverse social relationships in childhood can affect a person's sense of well-being, self-worth, confidence, and ability to form satisfying conflict-free relationships in adulthood.

Sexual abuse can take many forms and may involve physical contact, for example indecent assault or rape, as well as non-contact activities that may involve taking indecent photographs, encouraging a child to behave in sexually explicit ways or watch sexually explicit material.

We know that child sexual abuse is an invisible form of abuse. It occurs in secrecy, there are rarely any witnesses and there are often no visible clues. However it is also a form of abuse that affects emotional, social and cognitive development processes that can subsequently impact on how children view themselves and how they relate to others.

It is important for children to gain a sense of safety, security and confidence in themselves and the world around them as they grow and develop. It is doubly important for children who have been sexually abused to be given opportunities to develop trust in themselves again, in their safe carer and any support networks they have.

If a child has also experienced other forms of abuse, such as neglect, poor parenting, emotional or domestic abuse, then sexual abuse adds yet another layer of confusion and distortion to their world. It is against this diversity of backgrounds, of experiences, levels of development and

understanding, that we seek ways to understand and respond appropriately to a child's needs.

Children are taught from an early age to trust, respect and accept adult authority, often without question especially if the adult is someone known to the child (and trusted by other adults in the child's life). Being obedient often equates with being good.

Children are incapable of understanding adult motives. A child may sometimes feel uncomfortable or unsure about something the adult does or says, but a child will not have the cognitive ability to understand the process or purpose of adult grooming strategies such as the use of tricks, bribes or subtle emotional manipulations that are used to gain affection, compliance and control. Consequently they have little defence against such tactics.

It would seem to follow that giving a child information about body safety in isolation from wider issues about trust, assertiveness, choices, feelings and without the support of a safe carer or network, then places responsibility for their future safety solely on the child's shoulders and this cannot be an acceptable position.

*Self-protection work is never a solution to a problem. It cannot make everything safe for a child. It can only be a starting point for identifying what each individual child needs from the safe adults around them.*

## Developing sexuality

Human sexuality is socially constructed and as such is influenced by both internal and external factors such as, country, culture (which may change over time), religion, family and community beliefs and traits.

*In the course of development from infant to adult in any society, individuals learn the current social rules which determine the sexual behaviour of men and women in their culture. These form a system of meaning which is made up of language, symbols and both explicit and implicit rules about behaviour. The developing individual becomes aware of how he or she is viewed within the sex and gender structure by other people of both sexes and thus becomes fundamental to his or her development and ideas of identity.*

(Ennew, 1986: 26)

The developing child becomes aware of their gender role from a very early age by the words and actions of adults around them.

A young child has no understanding of the social meanings of behaviours until it is given to them by adults through their reactions, attitudes, language, rewards or disapproval. Adults often feel that they face a moral dilemma when considering providing a child with information on sex and sexuality. Are children being protected from knowledge that may allow them to be safer, or by not giving information, are they being protected from what they may choose to do with that knowledge? Some of the questions often raised by adults I have worked with on these issues are:

- Is it putting ideas into a child's head?
- Is it better to preserve a child's innocence?
- If they are given information, will they want to use it? Will they become sexual?

Getting the balance right can seem to be a daunting task. *However any child who is uninformed is at risk because they have no notion that someone may want to hurt them and may have no notion of how to tell someone they need help.* As long as sexuality is seen as something distinct from other aspects of learning about growing into adulthood, developing relationships and communicating with each other, it retains the idea that it is solely about sex rather than about a development of ourselves emotionally, cognitively and physically.

The natural development of a child's sexuality is at the pace of the child and is not just about sex or gender, but is also about assertiveness, choices, feelings, and trust. It is in the formative years of childhood that many of our expectations about future relationships and how we get our needs met, are developed subconsciously from the people around us.

Children ideally need to have a safe parent/carer who can support them to learn and grow naturally. Someone who provides them with a protective environment within which the child can learn at their own pace about who they are in relation to the world around them.

We know that there are many strategies that perpetrators use in order to gain access to a child

and subsequently to gain the child's compliance. Children who have been sexually abused will have experienced distorted adult sexuality that they will not be able to fully understand and will have received confusing messages about sex, sexuality, relationships, boundaries and power.

## Why children need safety skills

- All children are vulnerable to sexual abuse.
- All children are powerless.
- Uninformed children trust all adults.
- Young children are incapable of assessing adults' motives.
- Children are taught that goodness equates with obedience to adults.
- Children are curious about their own bodies.
- Children are deprived of information about their own sexuality.
- Uninformed children do not realise that abusive behaviour is wrong.
- Sexual abuse is often presented as evidence of affection.
- Children are even at risk in their peer groups.
- Children are confused by sexual misbehaviour.
- Children are seldom encouraged to express their anxieties and fears.

(Briggs, 1995)

The above list highlights children's vulnerability and conversely, shows us what our work needs to address.

However this is only one aspect of what a child needs to be safe. Even with some extra knowledge and understanding, children will be unable to recognise some of the techniques abusive adults use to gain co-operation and it is both unrealistic and unfair to expect a child to take responsibility for their own safety.

For these reasons self protection work or safety skills work is only one part of the information children need to help them make some sense out of what happened, to unlearn some of the destructive patterns of responding in relationships generally, and to help keep themselves safer within effective and protective support systems.

What we do know is that adults often don't talk to children about unsafe touch, growing up, or keeping safe, in a mistaken attempt to protect the child from uncomfortable information. However, ignorance cannot protect a child, and neither can body safety skills work done in isolation. The safe adult needs to develop a way of talking to their child about feelings and emotions and to encourage them to problem-solve and to question things they are unsure about.

Current practice in relation to self-protection work would seem to have been developed from conceptual frameworks relating to some of the specific conditions we are aware of that allow sexual abuse to thrive, and a knowledge of impacts (see Chapter 4 for further details).

There are workbooks readily available in bookshops that provide useful aids to working with children on specific issues, such as good and bad touches, body awareness and body safety skills. However, these resources do not provide the whole of what the child needs.

It is important that this work is placed within a wider context of developing better communication with their safe carer and wider support network around the issues of feelings and emotions and having explicit permission to tell if they are unsure about anything.

When considering working with a child it is important to address the issue of timing. Undertaking body safety skills work following disclosure is not always appropriate. This may depend on whether there will be a court case and on the child's specific situation. Discussions will need to take place with any investigating police officers and the Crown Prosecution Service, to ensure that work being considered is done at the appropriate time, meets the child's needs and does not conflict with any possible court proceedings. Further clarity on this issue can be obtained by referring to the *Achieving Best Evidence Guidelines*.

## Therapy

Each child will need something different from the people around them following their experiences. Some children may need therapy in the form of psychological support or play therapy in order to explore their feelings and seek their own internal resolution about what has happened to them. Some children may want to undertake sexual abuse recovery work based on a more focused intervention, helping the child to understand some of the strategies used by perpetrators in order to help them make sense of why they were abused, to remove any feelings of guilt placed on them by the perpetrator, to develop some safety skills and to strengthen their support networks. Some children may just need to feel more in

control of their feelings and understand clearer boundaries, with others needing to feel secure and safe within their families. Each child's needs will be different and *not all children need or benefit from therapy*.

The majority of children can move forward providing their safe carer is able to support them appropriately. Therapy will only be meaningful if it is provided to children who need it and at the time they need it. This may be soon after disclosure or it may be some years on.

Sometimes it is more constructive to work with the safe carers to help them understand what sexual abuse is, how it happens and to help them to feel more confident in how to support their child. Often, having provided knowledge and support to work through their own issues, it can be possible to provide safe carers with the skills to help the child learn assertive body safety skills. Of course, this also facilitates a closer relationship between the carer and child, which is essential if the child is to feel safe and able to tell if anything else were to happen in the future.

When considering what support is needed, some key questions may be:

- **What is the cause of concern?** Not all children display problematic behaviours, but a child may need some support around understanding clear, safe boundaries and behaviours. This can often be done by their safe carer and is the start of developing a way of talking to the child about these issues, which is important for developing better communication around feelings and body safety, for the future.
- **Whose problem is it?** Is it the child's behaviours that are causing concern or is the safe carer unable to cope with what has happened and perhaps needs support and guidance to manage their own feelings and so be stronger for the child. If a child *is* displaying behaviours that are causing concern, are they ready to work on the issues or not? Sometimes a child may need to be given clear, consistent messages and support from their safe carer. This in itself may be enough to help the child understand that they are safe, their needs are prioritised, they are not blamed and to feel secure.
- **Is the child aware their carer has concerns?** Does the child know that others are concerned about them, and why. Does the child want some time (at this stage) to explore their own feelings, worries, confusions.

- **Is the child able to acknowledge what is troubling them?** In many cases the child's immediate worries can be around external issues, such as their friendships, getting into conflict or being bullied, becoming withdrawn or conversely, aggressive. These may be the issues they want support in solving in order to feel they are able to regain some control of their lives and emotions.

Only a small number of children go on to need therapy. These are the children who continue to show signs of emotional distress or confusions despite support offered by the safe carer or other professionals.

## Understanding the impacts of child sexual abuse

Child development theories tell us that adverse social relationships in childhood can affect a person's sense of well-being, self-worth, confidence, and ability to form satisfying, conflict-free relationships.

For children who have been sexually abused by someone they have known and trusted, if they aren't able to disentangle some of the distorted relationship patterns they have experienced, it can sometimes (but not in every case) have an impact on their adult relationships. This may present itself in having a lack of confidence or having some distorted views of how adults relate to each other. It may affect their expectations of what they deserve or how they relate to others.

During the grooming process (this is where the adult prepares the child for abuse without the child realising. For an understanding of this process the reader is referred to Chapter 1) children, receive distorted messages about trust, adults, relationships, sex/sexuality, giving and receiving affection, attention, boundaries and self-worth. The impacts are much wider than focusing on the physical sexual experience.

Once the child has spoken of the abuse, investigations have taken place and the child is placed with a safe carer (either within the immediate family or within the care system), there can be the assumption that they 'know' they are safe and as a consequence should be relieved, feel safe and be socially co-operative.

However, it is more common for destructive behaviours to emerge at times which can put further pressure on families and put placements at risks. It is often only when a child begins to feel safe from repeated abuse that they can start to process what has happened to them. It is like taking the top off a bottle off fizzy pop. All the feelings they have been trying to keep inside may well start to bubble over. This is the time that the child needs reassurance, patience and understanding from the adults around them. Things can and do get better.

It may help if the safe carer has some basic information about the emotional impact of sexual abuse on a child and be given an opportunity to reflect on how the child may have processed their experience. For example, if the abuser was a parent or carer the child may have experienced inner confusion and conflict.

It is important that the safe carer and other adults around the child are able to tolerate any disruptive behaviours and be consistent in their support and understanding of the child's experiences. This is not always easy as the safe carer may well be overwhelmed by what has happened. However, research tells us that the best prognosis for recovery is where a child is believed, protected and supported by their safe carer. In many cases, disruptive behaviours or levels of distress reduce over a short period of time.

### *Children who present sexualised behaviours*

The child may have learnt that to get attention you must give affection to an adult. This may lead to younger children behaving in sexual ways towards others that may lead to a misinterpretation of the child's behaviour when in reality their behaviour has been learnt and is a manifestation of inner distress and confusion.

It is this type of situation that is often distressing for the safe carer and other adults to manage. However, the child needs understanding and support at this point in order to learn that they have rights over their bodies, that what happened was not OK, and to learn that not all adults expect a child to behave in this way.

Providing clear, basic information to the safe carers on how to manage a child's behaviours may help them to understand how to begin helping the child to learn appropriate messages and boundaries.

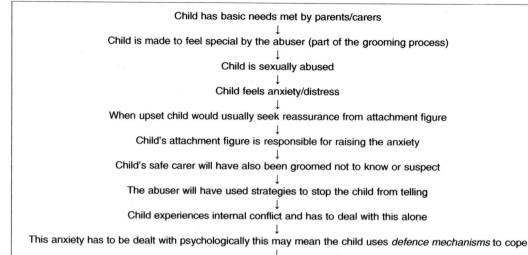

**Figure 13.1**   The grooming process

## Can young children learn personal safety skills?

In America where CSA prevention programmes are the strategy of choice used by communities to protect children, it is stated that 25 per cent to 35 per cent of all sexually abused children are under the age of seven years (Cupoli and Sewell, 1988; Eckenrode, Murish, Powers and Doris, 1988). There has been an ongoing debate about ages at which children can cognitively process information about CSA prevention concepts (Reppucci and Haugaard, 1989, 1993; Webster, 1993). Studies which compared responses of children from different ages groups found that older children knew more initially and learn more of the concepts than younger children (Laing, Bogat and McGrath, 1993; Nemerofsky, Carran and Rosenberg, 1994; Saslawsky and Wurtele, 1986). However recent research by Wurtele and Owens (1997), focusing on the effectiveness of a safety skills programme for pre-school age children, suggests that within a wider framework some children can increase their knowledge of body safety skills and translate this into practice. Their findings indicated that children who participated in the programmes demonstrated greater knowledge about sexual abuse and also improved their skills of recognising, resisting and reporting inappropriate touch requests.

Despite some measure of success with younger children understanding body safety and assertiveness skills at a basic level, there were a small group of children within the research who were unable to grasp prevention concepts and the one skill that was identified as being particularly difficult for young children to acquire was 'reporting', that is telling someone when something inappropriate had occurred.

These findings are encouraging on one level but also add a note of caution. They serve to remind us that children are only a part of their own prevention network and that they cannot protect themselves, by themselves. Also that knowledge evolves and so has to be built on as the child's understanding grows.

## Why disabled children are at higher risk of sexual abuse

Children with disabilities are at higher risk of sexual abuse than non disabled children. There are many reasons why this is the case, for example some children with learning disabilities may be more socially isolated than their peers. They may not be as assertive in their manner, or understand about their rights in relation to their bodies. It may also be more difficult to get a clear picture of their experience if they do tell if there are difficulties with memory recall in relation to time, place, sequence of events, and so on. Children with physical disabilities will have a range of different needs and levels of dependency. Some may have a variety of carers and may need help with personal care. For those children it may be hard to differentiate between who is safe and who isn't, what is abusive and what isn't.

Disabled children are often seen as needing protecting from information on bodies, growing up, sex and sexuality, as if these issues are not relevant to them. This approach heightens their vulnerability.

## Ethnicity, culture, religion, communities

Practitioners need to draw on their own and others' knowledge and skills, when working with children and families. It is important to consider issues in relation to culture, ethnicity, religion and community of each individual child and family as this may have an impact on what support is available, or how they will be affected within their wider social relationships. It is important to have an understanding of what sexual abuse will mean, not only for the child and the family individually, but also within their cultural norms; does it affect how the child is seen within their community; what additional support could the family expect to receive; may the family be excluded from certain places or occasions; are there implications for children by gender, and so on.

For each of the children and their families, the impact of sexual abuse will have a special significance in their lives. Some of the impacts will be common across all facets of society, some will bear specific relation to cultural, religious, community or ethnic norms.

It may be helpful for practitioners to make their own checklist of what additional information might be needed, some suggestions might be:

- How is sexual abuse viewed within the family/culture?

- What support can the young person expect from the family network?
- What support can the safe carer expect?
- What may be the response to the child/family/wider networks?
- Are there any implications because of the child's gender?
- Are there any issues for the child in the future?
- What supports are immediately available?
- Are there any child protection concerns?
- What may be the child/families biggest worries/fears?
- Are there financial/accommodation implications?
- Is the child likely to be able to get support from peers/school friends/teachers?

## Supporting children towards recovery

Research indicates that any child who is actively listened to; whose feelings and views are validated; who can learn to see the good within themselves and know that others see it too and experience some level of control in small situations will gain self-confidence and self worth and destructive behaviours will decrease.

It is important that the child's safe carer be helped to resolve their own confusion or lack of knowledge in order to help the child move forward in a positive way with insight and understanding. Whatever the plan of work is, the safe carer is a crucial element as it is within the day-to-day experience of life with family and friends that children will take their new knowledge. They can only do so if the safe adults around them make space for the changes and allow them to be.

If a safe carer has no information about body assertiveness work with the child, how do they encourage the child to practice this within the home? If they have no understanding of cycles of abuse, grooming methods or of how difficult it actually is for children to tell when something is happening, how can they support and encourage the child, how do they build on this in order to provide a support network to and for the child?

For additional information on how to support the safe carers and on what information they may need to receive the reader is referred to Appendix . . . *Who Cares?* booklet. This information was developed by project workers and is given to parents as a resource to help them understand some of the issues. It is used as a starting point to help them understand some of the processes, impacts and needs for the child and others. It also gives practical ideas for responding to and managing a child's behaviours following disclosure. For a fuller description of safe care, the reader is referred to Rose and Savage (1999) and Regan and Butterworth 2005.

## A framework to consider what work/support may be needed

If our intervention is to help the children we work with to be 'safer' in the future, we need to construct an individual framework from the knowledge we already have for each child, and then we must help the child take any new skills or information back into their family and wider relationships.

In a simplified form we can try to create our own 'menu' that considers each child's situation individually and which may allow us to target a more thorough support package for the child.

The menu should be constructed after considering:

- The circumstances that were present that allowed the child to be sexually abused.
- The impact on the child.
- The reasons why all children need safety skills.
- What current support networks the child has got.

Please refer to the Appendices at the end of this chapter for the worksheets.

If we focus on each of these areas in some depth we can effectively create our own checklist from which to begin to prioritise and shape our work with a child. It is important to complete the sheets from the knowledge you currently have. This may not be complete but it gives a starting point that can be added to and adapted as the work progresses or as further information becomes known. Below is a guide to help collate the information and to make sense of it in relation to a child.

### The circumstances that were present that allowed the child to be sexually abused (Appendix 1)

If we consider Finkelhor's (1984) four preconditions for sexual abuse we start to identify the specific circumstances for each child:

1. the presence of someone with a predisposition to sexually abuse a child
2. their ability to overcome their own internal inhibitors
3. creating opportunity (manipulating safe carers and the child)
4. overcoming the child's own resistance.

Without apportioning blame to anyone other than the perpetrator, focus objectively on the specific set of circumstances and identify where the distortions/manipulations occurred. If the safe carer and the child trusted the abusive adult there are dual issues about trust and responsibility that can yo-yo back and forth. How does the safe carer help the child to learn to trust appropriately again? (and who helps the safe carer?) What needs to happen to allow the safe carer to be able to check out with the child how they feel in other people's company in the future? What will issues of concern be? How will the child let the carer know they have some worries?

What were the child's own strengths (coping strategies)? What were the child's fears about telling? Who did they think would help/already knew? Were they protecting siblings?

From this information a picture may start to emerge about the focus of the work and who the work needs to be with. Individual work with the child around boundaries and trust for example, may be identified alongside the safe carers need to understand why someone would abuse a child and how they were both 'groomed'. For more detailed information in relation to work with safe carers please refer to Chapter 15).

### The impact on the child

*Effective treatment of the sexually abused child requires an understanding of the significant impact issues for the victim. Helping the child to overcome the effects of sexual victimisation is not easy; however, it is not impossible either. Unless the child victim is psychotic (fortunately a rare occurrence), the treatment goals will usually be a reflection of the impact issues.*
(Porter, Blick and Sgroi, 1982: 109)

When considering the impacts of sexual abuse on a child it is important to recognise that there is fluidity within the process. Children can be affected in different ways at different times and will move between identified areas dependant on individual internal and external factors, their own past experiences and the current support around them.

Allow yourself to focus on the 'here and now' for the child. How are they behaving; how does the child interact with carers, friends, wider networks; what concerns are people expressing about the child; what does the child think of the concerns expressed – regardless of actual behaviours, it is useful to get both the child and adult views to ensure that the child is aware that you will listen to their view of what is happening. This process may also be helpful in identifying whose problem it is.

For males there are some similar and some different issues to be considered. Please refer to the Worksheet for Males (Appendix 3) at the end of this chapter.

Refer to the appropriate worksheet and try to identify the issues presented from the knowledge you have about the child and the particular circumstances, for example:

- **Damaged goods syndrome** – is an amalgam of reactions. The child may believe that because there was pain there must be an injury, or that some part of them has been damaged and as time passes they may develop worries about whether they have healed; whether they will be able to have children; whether a partner will 'know' something has happened to them etc. They also highlight that externally, society's attitudes towards sexual abuse as sexuality may compound the view of sexual abuse as the 'damaged goods syndrome'.
- **Guilt** – it is widely recorded and accepted that all children who have been sexually abused carry feelings of guilt. It is suggested that this is experienced on three levels:
  - Responsibility for the sexual behaviour – children need to hear externally why they were not responsible and need help to understand their dependence and vulnerability at the time.
  - Responsibility for disclosure – given the secrecy and the deception, deceit and manipulation used by the perpetrator, it is more amazing that children ever have the courage to tell.
  - Responsibility for disruption – the child needs help to understand that the resultant effects on themselves, their family and siblings are the responsibility of the perpetrator and are not a response to the child's disclosure.
- **Fear** – of consequences, reprisals and threats coming true.

- **Depression** (sadness and loss) – children may exhibit signs of sadness, withdrawal, or may appear excessively tired, have repetitive 'illnesses'. Some children may act out their despair by self-harming.
- **Low self-esteem (and social skills)** – the abusive experience on a physical and emotional level may reinforce the child's notion that they are bad/unworthy and serves to undermine confidence and self-esteem.
- **Anger and hostility** – anger can either be acted out against 'safer' adults/peers, or more often is repressed to become problematic at some future time.
- **Trust** – a child who has been sexually abused by someone they trusted and cared for is likely to experience difficulty developing further trusting, mutually rewarding relationships.
- **Confusion** – a child may experience confusion because of the distortion of boundaries, trust and roles. If the abuser is also a parent or carer this confusion is magnified because the person causing the hurt is also the person the child is dependent on for their survival (food, shelter, clothes, warmth, protection, care etc).
- **Pseudo-maturity** – a child whose healthy sexual development has been prematurely interrupted may have confusion and conflict about sexual behaviours, boundaries, roles and expectations of theirs and other people's behaviours.
- **Self-mastery and control** – the child who has been sexually abused has been taught that they have no rights, no privacy and no power. Learning that they can be appropriately assertive, can have rights and can have rights over their own body, can help towards gaining some confidence, self-mastery and control.

List the impacts most significant for the child at this stage. You may also wish to note secondary issues that are currently 'bubbling under the surface' or which are present but (as yet) appear to have a lesser immediate impact. Think about who is identifying the issues, is it the child, their carer, or other person? Does the child want some support and what are the things they are struggling with the most?

We know from research that the impact on males include some of the same issues as for females but there are also some distinct differences. It is acknowledged in research that it is much harder for young men to disclose sexual abuse; that anger may be more overtly extreme;

or that depression and suicidal thoughts more intense. There are often fears around sexuality and some young males feel the need to over-compensate for their experience by 'proving' they are male; others may act out aggressively or sexually as they identify with the 'aggressor' as opposed to the 'victim'. For a fuller discussion of impact issues for males, the reader is referred to Calder in Chapter 1.

### The reason why all children need personal safety skills

Refer back to all the reasons why. We know that all these reasons are important for children, but which of these statements would seem to be a priority for the child you are working with? For example, we know that children who have been brought up to trust all adults are vulnerable because they may have learnt that being good equates with being compliant and obedient. If a particular child has been brought up in this way, they may need support to understand their rights over their own body, to develop appropriate assertiveness and to understand what they should be able to expect from an adult (care and protection) and what to do in situations where they feel uncomfortable or unsure.

### The child's current support networks

- Who is currently supporting the child?
- Who cares for the child, who does the child depend on, trust, tell how they are feeling?
- Who does the child go to if they are hurt or upset?
- Who offers support in wider settings (school, nursery, extended family) and who does the child relate to in these settings?
- Do they have a favourite auntie, uncle, teacher, neighbour, friends or parent?
- Consider who is there for the child when you aren't.
- What do their safe carers know about sexual abuse?
- How can they help to keep the child safe?
- How will the child test out new information and skills in their wider networks? Will the networks allow this to happen?
- What are the links that need strengthening to ensure this support (not everyone needs to know what has happened)?

In working with the child to help them keep safe in the future we also have a responsibility to promote and strengthen networks that will consolidate any new skills learned or information gained.

On learning new skills and information, to enable the child to use these when appropriate, the child needs to be able to take them into their main relationships with safe adults. In doing so the child may gain in confidence and may get back some notion of self-mastery and control. Involving the child's safe carer, or other trusted adult, is most likely to support the child to 'tell' of things that they feel unsure or unhappy about in the future. The work gives explicit messages to the child about their rights and needs and demonstrates that they will be listened to.

This in itself cannot wholly keep a child safe, but it does reduce the vulnerability of a child, which is a factor in the grooming process. Abusers target children they can control and children who are unlikely to be assertive or seek help.

It is worth considering that in all other forms of abuse, services are usually targeted at altering adult behaviours. Yet somehow within child sexual abuse there seems to have developed a notion of teaching the child in isolation to be responsible for their future safety. By taking this wider perspective we try to place responsibility at a more realistic level and acknowledge that the work with the child can really only have a chance of success if the child has a knowledgeable, protective safety network that they can access with confidence.

## A framework for direct work with a child

Once some of the immediate areas have been identified, workers can begin to plan their work with the child. It is important to acknowledge that the work discussed here is play work and this may also be termed direct work or short term focused intervention. It is *not* an in-depth therapeutic treatment programme.

The purpose of direct work as outlined in this context, is to explore alongside a child the impact of their experiences and untangle some of the confusion within themselves. If a child is exhibiting extreme behaviour, they may need a referral to a professional therapist or psychologist.

*At every age, direct work can be used to help strengthen current relationships, to understand the child's needs and perceptions, and to prepare him/her for transitions. However, when it comes to coping with the effects of earlier traumas and parental separations and losses, the child's cognitive abilities will strongly influence what can be accomplished.*

(Fahlberg, 1991: 334)

Any work with a child involves communication and takes on the same basic principles:

- **Every child's experience is unique and as such needs an individualised response.**
- **Some knowledge and understanding of child development is important.** Children's abilities and methods of communication vary according to age and stage of development (cognitive and social). There are added complexities for children who have a disability or who are from a different culture where there may be language differences or different cultural norms which would need to be understood at the planning stage.
- **An understanding of some basic principles in communicating with children.** Through play children may be able to communicate what they cannot express in words. Children are seldom comfortable with an interview type situation, their responses are often guarded and direct eye contact may feel quite oppressive to a child.
- **Communicating with a child is a dynamic process.** Our aim should be complete the task alongside the child, at their pace in a way that allows the child to feel accepted, gain insight into parts of their struggles, and to test out feelings and responses against new information/skills acquired during the process.
- **A child does not come to us in isolation.** The child has a family, safe carers, social networks and a history: their own ecosystem. If the child is to learn new information/skills and incorporate them into their life how will they do this, who needs to know, help and support the child in the process of change?
- **Is it appropriate to work with the child and safe carer together**, or to support the safe carer to work with the child themselves, offering support and guidance where needed?

Before starting any piece of work with a child we need a clear framework (see Figure 13.2 below). Plans may need to be adapted as work progresses and depending on what the child brings to the sessions, but without any frame of reference for the boundaries of the work, there is a danger that it will be unfocused, unclear and ultimately less helpful to the child.

## *Planning*

Issues to consider:

- **Time to plan and complete the work:** If you cannot commit to the sessions consider whether starting the work is appropriate. Often the children we work with have experienced rejection, loss, hurt and pain. Don't be another adult who lets the child down.
- **Clear and realistic aims:** A clear framework is essential to be able to stay on track. However, be adaptable and creative and notice what is important for the child in sessions.

Use the initial sessions to get to know the child. Ask the child to make a collage of things, such as themselves, their hobbies, best day, favourite things, etc; make clay models; play 'getting to know you' therapeutic-type board games. Initial sessions are about conveying a message to the child that they are important and you want to know more about them, their views, opinions, ideas, even if these are different to your own; that you enjoy spending time with the child, validating their 'self', acknowledging that they are worth being listened to.

A worker may have some ideas about session content and issues of relevance from the worksheets completed, but does the child share these or have their own agenda? Complete an Agreement with the child as outlined in detail below. This may take a session in itself, but is a useful reference point as the work progresses.

An Agreement allows you both to contribute to the planning and ensures the child understands fully what is happening. You may be able to agree with the child some of the issues to be covered, but remember to allow the child to take the lead in identifying their priorities. This may mean that if safe carers or others have a different agenda, the child's needs are heard and acted upon. The work will only be successful if it responds to the child's needs rather than the adults' agenda.

Be aware that some children have learnt to respond and survive within chaos. Some children 'flit' constantly from one topic to another. Whilst children sometimes need time to build confidence, others may use this as a distraction

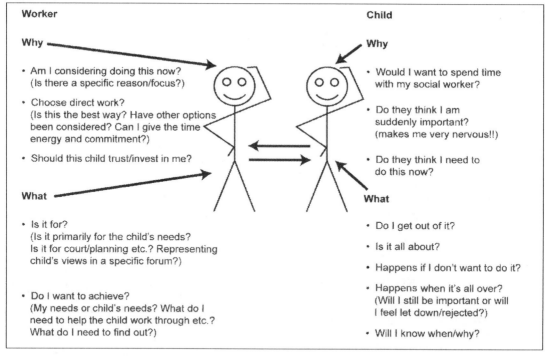

**Figure 13.2**   Some questions to ask before starting a piece of direct work

strategy. Having an Agreement to refer to can help. It may be possible to remind the child what has been agreed, with other issues being noted for consideration in later sessions. This way, the child feels 'heard' but may also be able to accept that some things can be addressed at a later stage.

*It is important to remember you cannot make right the whole of the child's confusion in one piece of direct work, but helping a child through one identified area allows them to also recognise that some parts of their lives are manageable and, with help to gain insight, they can regain some of their confidence, self-worth and self-mastery.*

Some ideas on addressing some of the common issues are included at the end of this chapter.

**Venue:** Where will the child feel comfortable and safe?

**Agreements**: Do children and young people always know why we are seeing them; what will happen when we see them; how long will we be seeing them for, when, where and how and what will happen afterwards? A useful way of addressing these issues with children and young people is through a written agreement. Given that this is most beneficial in the initial stages of work,

it can also be a 'tool' for establishing safety, trust and a working relationship.

To help the child have a sense of where sessions are up to:

– Make a calendar and cross off each session.
– Take the same number of marbles as the number of sessions to be held. Put these in a jar and each week take one out.

These techniques help a child to see clearly where the work is up to and how many sessions they have left.

### Other issues to consider

**Review the work:** Plan this into the work from the outset. It is useful to get regular feedback on sessions from the child. This could be done using a very short questionnaire. It is also useful to plan for a review half way through the work in order to check if the child is OK with the issues being covered, the pace of the work and to consider any outstanding issues.

This will give some indication if further sessions are likely to need planning for at the end of the current sessions. Even if further sessions

**1. Between who?**

**2. When?**    Weekly ☐
             fortnightly ☐   from 🕓 to 🕙
             monthly ☐

**3. Where?**

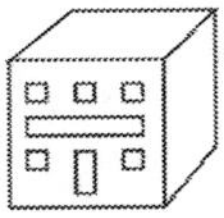

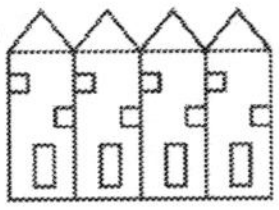

**4. Who will escort the child?**

**5. Where will the child's safe carer/others be while the session takes place?**

**6. Why are you there?**
  1. To look at any worries or troubles
  2. To talk about why _____
  3. To find a reason for _____

**7. What are 'the rules'?**
  – It's OK to say no
  – Don't have to talk about anything you don't want to
  – Don't have to stay
  – OK to be angry/sad/happy/loud/quiet
  – How will worker know if the child is any of the above and what is acceptable? For example, it is OK if the child gets angry/upset etc, but during the sessions we don't hurt ourselves or each other
  – Who the child can contact if they are unhappy about the work – complaints procedure information to child/parent

**8. Who will you be talking to about the sessions?**
Family members, Police, Courts, 'boss' in supervision, others, no one?

**9. Confidentiality**
Never agree to keep secrets. What will you agree to do, if a child indicates during sessions, that they or another child is being hurt or abused? For example, while we are doing work, if I feel that you or any other child is being hurt or is in danger, then I will tell someone so that we can help you/them to be safe. If I need to do this, I will tell you first and we can try to decide together what to do next.

**10. Case recordings**
Who gets to see the case recordings? Does the child get a copy, is there space for the child's comments and are they signed by both of you? Or do you put together a resource file for the child that they can keep at the end of the work to look back over at a later stage if they want to, or to share with their safe carer?

**11. Information needs to be given on the Data Protection Act** (*see Appendix XX for an example of a child friendly leaflet*)

**12. How long will the sessions go on for?**    ☐ forever
                                                ☐ 100 years
                                                ☐ 2 months
                                                ☐ 6 weeks etc.

**Figure 13.3** Components of an agreement might be:

are needed, keep to the original number, review the work again at the end and then plan additional sessions. This keeps clear boundaries around the work and ensures that the child understands from the beginning that the work must end at some point. Building in the ending from the start is important in order to avoid a child feeling let down or rejected. If a child is made to feel important for a time, if they share their inner feelings and emotions, their best/worst memories, if they begin to trust . . . how do they feel when they can no longer receive your time or attention?

If a child is involved in the planning they know what the rules and boundaries are. They know that for the agreed amount of sessions it is their special time, they have some involvement in the process, content and reviewing of these areas. It allows them to share the control of the work – to really feel included, involved and confirms that what they have to contribute is important. It also acknowledges that the work has a focus and time limit (which may or may not be reviewed and flexible).

**Try to make the work interesting:** Use things the child is interested in, stories, art, clay, collages, worksheets, etc.

**Who can the child tell if they want to stop coming to sessions?** This should be someone easily accessible to the child. The child needs to know they don't have to give reasons, but they do have a choice.

**Know some information about the child.** What do they like and dislike, interests, hobbies. Are they active or quiet, do they like drawing, making things, being creative? What are they good at?

**Inform the child's carer of the plan and explain the aims of the work.** The carer can then support the child if any difficulties arise, for example answering questions if the child becomes upset. Agree with the child and carer what level of information will be shared with the carer.

**Self-care:** As social workers we are trained to value each child's individuality and recognise their strengths. We are often acutely aware of the multi-faceted nature of abuse, and of the courage each child displays facing every new uncertainty, fear and confusion without the benefit of adult concepts to help understanding or measure progress. Sharing part of a child's journey, experiencing with them their feelings, thoughts, emotions – happy and sad – takes its toll on workers. It is important to acknowledge that

although we all communicate daily with children in our work, not everyone is comfortable undertaking pieces of planned, direct work with a child, particularly if the issue is around body safety. Equally, for the child's sake, issues of gender, race or culture can sometimes be the driving force behind choice.

It might in some cases be more appropriate for a co-worker to complete the jointly planned work with the key-worker acting as consultant (perhaps in return you may be able to complete a separate piece of work on your colleague's case – a kind of planned case-swap intervention – be creative).

Workers who cannot look after themselves will not be able to effectively meet a child's needs in a reliable, consistent, clear and beneficial way.

A child does not come to us with a single problem. There may be a multitude of issues to be resolved in their complex and complicated lives. It is not helpful to try to deal with them all together. This could mean jumping from one thing to another as the child brings out 'here and now' issues and may actually mirror the confusion in the child's life.

Working directly with children in a focused way can be challenging, demanding, time consuming, tiring and emotionally draining. It can also be fun and very rewarding.

Direct work takes time and commitment but is very rewarding for both child and worker. Just as workers should put a clear, thought-out framework in place for the child, we also owe ourselves the same consideration and thoughtfulness, and should commit time to putting a good support system into place for ourselves.

**Support for workers:** in the planning stages and during delivery of direct work, it helps to keep focused on whatever issues are a priority at the current time. This does not mean ignoring other things of importance to the child, but these can often be planned into further work with the child if appropriate, or reasons given to the child why these issues will not be dealt with at this time.

It also gives an opportunity to reflect on practice: to share feelings and ideas, discuss concerns, focus on the child's interactions within sessions, explore difficulties that have arisen, and also, very importantly, offers a forum to share the good experiences as well.

Support networks enable workers to keep some perspective in relation to the work. We don't have magic wands or the ability to make everything alright for a child. What we can do is help the child learn to cope and negotiate their way through situations in a more positive way. Some of the work may not impact on the child immediately; sometimes it is after the event that a child uses the skills/knowledge acquired. A child must negotiate life at their own pace. All we can do is help them acquire less destructive patterns of behaviour by encouraging awareness of alternative ways of negotiating problems/ difficulties experienced in life.

**Supervision and consultation** are two methods of support. Supervision is usually offered by line managers and should be distinctive from case management. Case management focuses on the practical tasks, supervision deals with the details of the work and feelings and issues arising from this.

Supervision can be formal and/or informal. Each worker will have their own preferred method of supervision and it is helpful to ensure that these needs are discussed with the supervisor or consultant and recorded at the outset of work.

Consultation does not necessarily have to be provided by line managers. It may be that there is a more experienced colleague who could consult to the planning, debrief and evaluation of the work. Again, think creatively and construct a support network that works for you.

## Practical ideas for some common issues

It is not the intention of this chapter to cover body safety skills in any depth, as it would warrant a workbook in its own right, and there are many available in bookshops. However, below are a few ideas that may be useful to begin with.

Children do not always understand as much as we think they do and sometimes understand things in ways we would never have expected. It is important, if a child is to feel confident again, that they have opportunity to develop a closer relationship with their safe carer (and support networks where appropriate), where they have explicit permission to take their worries, confusions, and questions, *about anyone and anything*.

There are some basic ways to let a child know that you are interested in how they feel, how they think and in what they do, and ways that support

a child to talk about feelings and to develop a feelings vocabulary.

It is not as important for a child to get answers 'right', as it is for you to understand your child's views and perceptions of their world. Working with children on these issues can give an insight into how they problem-solve and what strategies they have in place. By doing these exercises you will get to know your child better, you will start to understand how they process information and understand better and what gaps there are in their understanding.

### Identifying feelings

This can be done with younger children to start developing communication about feelings. It also demonstrates interest in how they are feeling and can be used as the child grows to expand on the ideas and discussions.

Together draw pictures of a smiley face, a sad face and a question mark. As you do them ask the child to say what they think the face picture represents. This will indicate if the child is aware of the different facial expressions. Further expressions can be added over time to extend their understanding about a range of feelings. Discussions can be widened out to include magazine pictures, storybooks, the child's school day, things at home.

### Secrets

It is important that children have an opportunity to think about secrets, as they may well have had to keep their abuse 'secret'. The child will need to hear from their safe carer that if ever anyone asks them to keep things secret in the future, they should tell them about it.

**Secrets or surprises?** Help the child to distinguish between secrets and surprises. Surprises are often associated with nice things, whereas secrets can be about bad things. However, always give the message that if the child isn't sure which it is, they should always ask you. Add cards with the words or symbols, for *secret* and *surprise* to the basic expression pictures and the question mark symbol.

Talking about secrets and surprises will help you to understand what they think secrets or surprises are, and gives an opportunity for you to give some messages about the difference.

Tell the child that the 'question mark' is for anything they are unsure of and they can point to

it at any time. Agree that when they do this, you will stop and explain whatever they are unsure about.

Place the cards face up and ask the child to use them to indicate their answers in the following games:

1. Write some scenarios out on some different cards. Place these face down and take it in turns to pick one up and answer it. You may find that the child wants to answer your question as well as their own. Some examples of scenarios might be:

– An aunty has bought one of your cousins a lovely necklace for her birthday. She asks you not to tell her.
– A child at school takes someone else's pencil case and doesn't give it back. She says not to tell anyone.
– A friend of the family wants you to sit on his knee and keeps trying to hug you when your mum isn't there. He says that it's just a game for the two of you because you are special.
– A friend of yours is making something nice for another of your friends. She asks you not to tell her.
– You are playing with friends in the park. One of them touches your private parts. They say it is just a bit of fun and not to tell anyone.

After reading each question ask:

● Is this a secret or a surprise?
● How does it make you feel?

Let the child point to the pictures. This will demonstrate their understanding. If the child doesn't get it right, try not to say they have got it wrong as children don't like to fail and it may reduce their enjoyment of the game. It may be better to say things like, 'So you think . . . I wonder what might happen if . . . do you think it would make any difference if . . . Lead them into a discussion to see if thinking through the issue helps them to come to a more appropriate stance, or to see if you can steer them to a better response.

Revisit the issue in different ways using other situations in daily life, until you feel that they have a better, or more appropriate understanding. This may need to be done over time to reinforce messages and to check them out with the child, but it shouldn't become oppressive or a 'test' that they have to get right. This is the most certain way to promote resistance and avoidance which is the very thing you are trying to avoid.

### Using work around feelings in other situations

Once the basic messages have been given, some of the scenarios could revolve around family situations, such as giving permission and strategies to the child about what to do in various situations. This helps children learn to problem solve, it can include scenarios around body safety skills or other safety situations such as being bullied, getting lost, or even moral dilemmas for older children. For example:

● Grandma comes for tea. On leaving she wants to give Joe a big kiss. Joe loves Grandma but feels he is too big to give kisses now. Is it OK to say no? What could Joe do that wouldn't upset Grandma?
● Julie was walking home from school with some friends. One of the girls' uncles saw them and said that he had a really good video game at home. He asked Julie to go to see it. What should Julie do? Is there anyone she should tell?
● Kevin saw one of the older boys at school taking some money off a younger boy. The older boy saw Kevin and said it was just a bit of fun. He offered him £1 from the money. Should Kevin take the money? What might happen if he does/doesn't? What might Kevin be worried about? Should he tell anyone?

### Families, relationships, rules, roles, boundaries

Cut out pictures from children's magazines depicting different family situations as appropriate:

- Ask the child to indicate which feeling the pictures represent. This helps to identify if children can pick up non-verbal messages from body language, facial expressions etc.
- Ask the child why they linked a particular feeling with a particular picture. Talking about feelings helps a child to develop their language skills in this area and also builds up their confidence in talking to you about these things.

### Worries/confusions

Draw a picture of a tree and pin it up somewhere the child has access to. Leave some post-it notes nearby. Tell the child that if they have any worries, confusions or anything they want to talk about to write it and put it on the tree.

This strategy could be used for any worries in or out of the home. It aims to give explicit permission to the child to talk to you about their feelings and situations that may trouble them, which they sometimes do not realise they have if they have been manipulated and told previously that you would not listen or believe them. Even if we tell children that they can talk to us, we still need to be proactive in this and demonstrate that we really mean what we say and will take the time to listen and understand what is happening for them.

# References

Bolton, F., Morris, L. and MacEachron, A. (1989) *Males at Risk: The Other Side of Sexual Abuse*. California: Sage.

Briggs, F. (1995) *Developing Personal Safety Skills in Children with Disabilities*. London: Jessica Kingsley.

Burgess, A., Groth, N., Holmstrom, L. and Sgroi, S. (1978) *Sexual Assault of Children and Adolescents*. Lexington, MA: Lexington Books.

Carroll, J. (1998) *Introduction to Therapeutic Play*. London: Blackwell.

Cupoli, J. and Sewell, P. (1988) One Thousand and Fifty Nine Children with a Chief Complaint of Sexual Abuse. *Child Abuse and Neglect*, 17.

Eckenrode, J. et al. (1988) The Nature and Substantiation of Official Sexual Abuse Reports. *Child Abuse and Neglect*, 12.

Ennew, J. (1986) *The Sexual Exploitation of Children*. Oxford: Basil Blackwell.

Fahlberg, V. (1994) *A Child's Journey Through Placement*. London: BAAF.

Finkelhor, D. (1984) *Child Sexual Abuse: New Theory and Research*. NY: The Free Press.

Finkelhor, D. (1986) *A Sourcebook on Child Sexual Abuse*. California: Sage.

Haugaard, J. and Reppucci, N. (1988) *The Sexual Abuse of Children*. Jossey-Bass.

Jewett, C. (1984) *Helping Children Cope with Separation and Loss*. London: Batsford.

Laing, B., Bogat, G. and McGrath, M. (1993) Differential Understanding of Sexual Abuse Prevention Concepts Among Pre-Schoolers. *Child Abuse and Neglect*, 17.

Nemerofsky, A., Carran, D. and Rosenburg, L. (1994) Age Variation in Performance among Pre-School Children in a Sexual Abuse Prevention Program. *Journal of Child Sexual Abuse*, 13.

Porter, F.S., Blick, L.C. and Sgroi, S.M. (1982) Treatment of the Sexually Abused Child. In Sgroi, S.M. (Ed.) *Handbook of Clinical Intervention in Child Sexual Abuse*. Lexington, MA: Lexington Books.

Regan, L. and Butterworth, J. (2005) Safe Caring. In Wheal, A. (ed.) *The RHP Companion to Foster Care*. Lyme Regis: Russell House Publishing.

Reppucci, N. and Haugaard, J. (1983) Problems with Child Sexual Abuse Programs. In Gelles, R.J. and Loseke, D.R. (Eds.) *Current Controversies on Family Violence*. Newbury Park, CA: Sage.

Rose, K. and Savage, A. (1999) Safe Caring. In Wheal, A. (Ed.) *The RHP Companion to Foster Care*. Lyme Regis: Russell House Publishing.

Saslawsky, D. and Wurtele, S. (1986) Educating Children about Sexual Abuse: Implications for Paediatric Intervention and Possible Prevention. *Journal of Paediatric Psychology*, 11.

Senn, C. (1988) *Vulnerable: Sexual Abuse and People with an Intellectual Handicap*. Downsview, Ontario: G. Allan Roeher Institute.

Webster, S. (1993) *STARS 2 for Children: A Guidebook for Teaching Positive Sexuality and Preventing Sexual Abuse for People with Developmental Disabilities*. Sexuality Education Resource Centre.

Wong, D. (1987) Preventing Child Sexual Assault among Southeast Asian Refugee Families. *Children Today*, Nov/Dec.

Wurtele, S. and Owens, J. (1997) Teaching Personal Safety Skills to Young Children: An Investigation of Age and Gender across Five Studies. *Child Abuse and Neglect*, 21: 8.

### Some useful resources: therapeutic workbooks

Blank, J. (1982) *The Playbook for Kids about Sex*. London: Sheba.

Briggs, F. (1995) *Developing Personal Safety Skills in Children with Disabilities*. London: Jessica Kingsley.

Dayee, F. (1982) *The Private Zone*. NY: Warner Books.

Elliott, M. (1991) *Feeling Happy, Keeping Safe*. Sevenoaks: Hodder and Stoughton.

Ironside, V. (1984) *The Huge Bag of Worries*. Edinburgh: Children First.

Johnson, K. (1986) *The Trouble with Secrets*. Seattle: The Parenting Press.

Johnson, T.C. (1998) *Sexuality Curriculum for Abused Children, Young Adults and Their Parents*. Self-published.

Palmer, P. (1977) *The Mouse, the Monster and Me*. California: IMPACT.

Peake, A. (1989) *My Body, My Book*. London: Children's Society.

Pithers, D. and Greene, S. (1986) *We Can Say No!* London: Arrow Books.

Rayner, C. (1978) *The Body Book*. London: Pan Books.

Rouf, K .(1989) *Secrets*. London: Children's Society.

Rouf, K. (1989) *Mousie*. London: Children's Society.

Scriptographic Publications (1988) *You're in Charge*. Alton: Scriptographic Publications.

Shore, H. (1995) *Angry Monster Workbook*. The Centre for Applied Psychology. Society Press.

Striker, S. and Kimmel, E. (1978) *The Anti-Colouring Book*. London: Scholastic Publications.

Wright, L.B. and Loiselle, M.B. (1992) *Shining Through (For Girls)*. Brandon, Vermont: Safer Society Press.

Wright, L.B. and Loiselle, N.B. (1997) *Back on Track (For Boys)*. Brandon, Vermont: Safer Society Press.

### Use of 'ordinary' books

Ordinary story books can also be used to reinforce certain messages. The following are some examples of short books with a particular theme:

**Joe Useless.** A book about a different kind of dog who seems to be useless until something happens and people recognise his worth. Written by D. Reader (1999) and available from Diamond Books in London.

**Piper.** Piper is a kind, good dog whose owner is cruel. One night he escapes and his life changes. Written by E. Clark (1995) and available from Random House Children's Books in London.

**Someone, somewhere.** A story about a young girl who never knew her mother. She escapes from an unhappy situation and finds adventure and courage. Written by H. Braanford (1995) and available from Random House Children's books in London.

**My best friend.** About valuing friendship, giving and taking in relationships. Written by P. Hutchins (1993) and available from Random House Children's Books in London.

**Nobody likes me.** A young boy tries to cope with angry feelings that burst out affecting friendship and relationships. Written by F. Weldon (1997) and available from Random House Children's Books in London.

**Grandpa Bodley and the Photographs.** The value of memories. Written by Castle and Bowman (1993) and available from Random House Children's Books in London.

# Appendix 1: A framework for identifying the focus of work with a child and the most appropriate method for undertaking this. Finkelhor's four preconditions

**1. The presence of someone with a predisposition to sexually abuse a child (completed from known information in retrospect).**
Who was the perpetrator?

Relationship to the child?

Same household?

**2. Their ability to overcome their own internal inhibitors (completed from information in retrospect).**
What is known?

How did this impact on the family?

What could the safe carer learn from this?

What might the safe carer need to know?

**3. Creating opportunity (manipulating child and safe carer – completed retrospectively).**
What were the specific circumstances, if known?

What does the safe carer know about sexual abuse, cycles of abuse, reasons why children find it difficult to tell?

What are the strengths of the child/safe carer's relationship?

What difficulties did the safe carer experience at disclosure? (How did they respond? What conflicts did they experience in believing? How did she perceive the child's disclosure?)

**4. Overcoming the child's own resistance**
What was the grooming process, if known?

Did the perpetrator use threats, bribes, tricks, coercion?

Where did the abuse take place?

Was the child protecting anyone else?

## Appendix 2: Impact Issues – Females (Porter et al., 1982)

| Damaged goods syndrome | Behaviour? | Frequency? | Whose concern? |
|---|---|---|---|
| Guilt | Behaviour? | Frequency? | Whose concern? |
| Fear | Behaviour? | Frequency? | Whose concern? |
| Depression (sadness + loss) | Behaviour? | Frequency? | Whose concern? |
| Low self-esteem and social skills | Behaviour? | Frequency? | Whose concern? |
| Hostility | Behaviour? | Frequency? | Whose concern? |
| Trust | Behaviour? | Frequency? | Whose concern? |
| Confusion | Behaviour? | Frequency? | Whose concern? |
| Pseudo-maturity | Behaviour? | Frequency? | Whose concern? |
| Self-mastery | Behaviour? | Frequency? | Whose concern? |

## Appendix 3: Impact Issues – Males (Porter et al., 1982)

| 1 Guilt | Behaviour? | Frequency? | Whose concern? |
|---|---|---|---|
| 2 Sexuality | Behaviour? | Frequency? | Whose concern? |
| 3 Anger | Behaviour? | Frequency? | Whose concern? |
| 4 Low self-esteem | Behaviour? | Frequency? | Whose concern? |
| 5 Sexual language and behaviour | Behaviour? | Frequency? | Whose concern? |
| 6 Depression | Behaviour? | Frequency? | Whose concern? |
| 7 Self harm/suicidality | Behaviour? | Frequency? | Whose concern? |
| 8 Anxiety | Behaviour? | Frequency? | Whose concern? |
| 9 Fear | Behaviour? | Frequency? | Whose concern? |
| 10 Inability to trust | Behaviour? | Frequency? | Whose concern? |
| 11 Recapitulating his victim experience | Behaviour? | Frequency? | Whose concern? |

## Appendix 4: Why All Children Need Personal Safety Skills (Briggs, 1995)

- All children are vulnerable to sexual abuse.
- All children are powerless.
- Uninformed children trust all adults.
- Young children are incapable of assessing adults' motives.
- Children are taught that goodness equates with obedience to adults.
- Children are curious about their own bodies.
- Children are deprived of information about their own sexuality.
- Uninformed children do not realise that abusive behaviour is wrong.
- Sexual abuse is often presented as evidence of affection.
- Children are even at risk in their peer groups.
- Children are confused by sexual misbehaviour.
- Children are seldom encouraged to express their anxieties and fears.

## Appendix 5: The Child's Current Eco-Map

**Who is involved with the child?**

- Main carers (known information).
- Who believes the child (known information)?
- Best friends (child's view)?
- Safe family members (child's view)?
- Who can the child talk to if they are upset/have a problem? (child's view).
- Who would help the child? (child's view).
- Who does the child go to at school if they have a problem? (child's view).
- Who is good at listening? (child's view).
- What adults/grown ups does the child go to if they need any help or need to talk about a problem or how they feel?
- Any other significant person?
- What relationships may need promoting? How/Why?
- Any other relevant information?

# CHAPTER 14

# Contact Considerations Where Sexual Abuse and Domestic Violence Feature: Adopting an Evidence-Based Approach

*Martin C. Calder and Lynda Regan*

## Introduction

The aim of this chapter is to provide a broad framework that will facilitate professionals in making an assessment that is child-centred, whilst also providing information to assist the court in its judgement. Contact is often viewed from the perspective of the rights of parents, with the inherent assumption that this will simultaneously be in the best interests of the child. The 1989 Children Act makes the assumption that contact between a parent and their child is therefore to be promoted.

The chapter recognises the dual presence of domestic violence and sexual abuse in many cases so some reference and crossover between domestic violence and sexual abuse is made. Indeed, the author has developed the domestic abuse diamond (DAD) to reflect the inter-relationship as well as co-existence of various types of harm that impact directly and indirectly on children (see Figure 14.1). The maltreatment of animals, usually pets, may occur in homes where there is domestic violence. Anecdotally, we know that animals have been abused by perpetrators to frighten their partners as a threat of potential interpersonal attacks and as a form of retaliation or punishment, and that abuse has been implicated in forced bestiality (Arkow, 1996).

## Good contact arrangements: contextual considerations

Lucey et al. (2003) have examined what contact arrangements are in the child's best interests. When approaching an assessment we have to be familiar with the context in which the dispute has arisen; it may be that there are persistent disputes between separated or divorced parents or during family proceedings after the child has been removed from their parent's care as the result of significant harm. They offer us a theoretical framework suggesting that the child must be seen as an individual growing up in the context of a family group and a wider network of significant relationships. Account must also be taken of their personal characteristics, their developmental stage, their past experiences and their current interpersonal relationships. Critical factors to consider include the part played by innate factors, the child's emotional and cognitive development, the child's vulnerability and resilience, the history of the parent-child relationship and the impact of discordant family relationships. Where separated parents do not agree and continue their disputes through arrangements about the child, contact is likely to be conflictual and traumatic; it may undermine the child's current placement and sense of stability; it exacerbates the pain and distress of separation and the child blames themselves.

Contact disputes may be appropriate and child-centred, such as concern for the child's welfare, or they may be inappropriate, such as revenge, sense of power and control over the other, or for confirmation that the other was to blame in order to protect their self-esteem; or because the struggle becomes addictive; or maybe because the child was removed by the local authority and they dispute the nature of the contact arrangements.

The purpose of contact must be explicit and clear: to provide an opportunity to impart information to the child about their family-of-origin and their life so far; to begin a process of reparation of a broken relationship; to promote experiences that facilitate their healthy emotional growth and which provide the opportunity to form and build relationships; to assess the feasibility of rehabilitation or to facilitate a clear end to the relationship. Contact must clearly be of benefit to the child. Adults need to work around the child's developmental stage, yet they should elicit and consider the child's expressed wishes. What they want, however, is not always the safest thing for them, so contact should be selected that is safe and

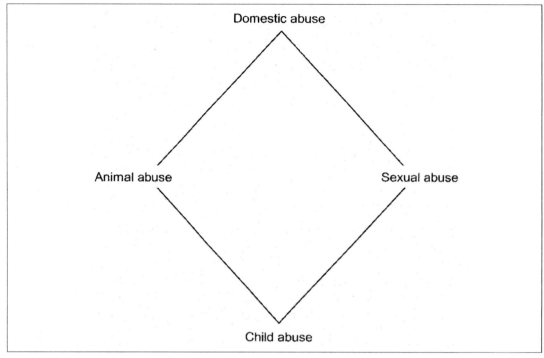

**Figure 14.1**    Domestic Abuse Diamond (DAD)

promotes their development. Contact needs to exceed being a mechanical or routine arrangement which only provides for physical proximity rather than an emotional encounter.

CAFCASS (2004) have produced an accessible overview in relation to contact. They note that views on the nature of, and the best ways to resolve contact disputes vary widely and are sometimes expressed with great emotion and conviction. Nevertheless, research and experience in Britain and other countries show high levels of consensus on a number of basic messages for families, practitioners and judges:

- There is no simple formulaic approach to contact or the apportionment of time that will meet the needs of children; each child has individual needs arising from a number of variables, personal and circumstantial, and will require an individual approach.
- The biggest and most damaging obstacle to both the quality and quantity of post-separation contact is ongoing conflict between parents or between them and the children's carers if the child is living outside the family.

- Children do not feel sufficiently informed, consulted or involved in decision-making on matters that directly concern them. When children do express clear views, they do not always feel heeded when those views fail to fit with what parents, practitioners and judges would prefer to hear.
- Though the caring of individual family members will differ in kind, quality and importance, fathers and mothers are equally important to children.

CAFCASS set out nine key principles relating to contact:

- Encourage family resolution.
- Accept each child as unique.
- Inform and listen to children.
- Children's needs take priority.
- Accept and work with diversity.
- Always address risk.
- Value all forms of contact.
- Promote fairness.
- Minimise delay and its effects.

## Contact that works should:

- Recognise that each child's needs may differ from those of brothers and sisters.
- Identify the genuine wishes of children and their parents. Where they differ, seek to encourage thought, discussion and resolution.
- Consider the quality of the child-parent relationship and the child's need for stability and continuity.
- Be realistic about the respect each parent has for the other as a carer and their ability to develop and maintain a workable, parenting relationship.
- Take account of previous childcare arrangements in the family when working with parents on how they might best continue to parent their children. Proximity, finance, transport and accommodation are likely to be more decisive factors in arranging contact than a perceived 'just' or 'ideal' plan.
- Assess the relative levels of hostility and the tendency of parents living apart to scapegoat each other. Consider the potential impact of this on the child and whether there is potential for insight and progress.
- Consider the significance of the child's extended family, whether they are sufficiently distanced from the parental dispute and can share, support and assist with arrangements.
- Consider what can be done to improve outcomes for the child by minimising negative elements and encouraging positive.
- Minimise delay in trying to repair disrupted relationships.

## Safety and risk:

- It is essential to assess and understand possible risk and then to reduce and manage that risk. The degree of the child's exposure to risk during contact needs balancing against the negative consequences of the child having no contact with those concerned.
- Use a written risk assessment to help clarify and document the risk and action you have taken. Share that with a manager when necessary.
- Take anxieties over possible abduction seriously and take whatever action is possible to reassure and/or help prevent that possibility.
- Be alert to the possible presence of undiagnosed mental health problems and substance abuse and take appropriate action.

CAFCASS concludes with recipes for good contact and contact failure.

Out of the 11 million dependent children in England and Wales, it is estimated that around 25 per cent will experience their parents' divorce before the age of 16. This equates to over 147,000 children per year who are involved in parental divorces (Bream and Buchanan, 2003). Research is also highlighting that divorce and family separation is a multi-factorial process rather than an event. Conflict is particularly damaging when it is frequent, intense, physical, unresolved, and involves the child (Grych and Fincham, 1999). It is also possible that conflict after divorce is worse for children than conflict within the marriage. Indeed, in the domestic violence sphere, children are significantly more likely to witness violence at

---

**Recipe for good contact:**
- Both parents are committed to contact
- The contact parent accepts his/her non-residential status and the resident parent proactively facilitates contact and includes the contact parent in decision-making
- Both support the children in having a relationship with the other parent and do not denigrate or threaten the other parent
- Parents adopt a realistic appraisal of each other, recognising strengths and weaknesses
- Parents recognise that there will be conflict, but learn to manage it
- Parents consult children about arrangements
- Parents find time to be alone with children without new partners always present

**Recipe for contact failure:**
- Contact poses an ongoing risk of physical or psychological harm to one or more party involved
- Not all parties are committed to contact
- At least one party seeks significant changes to the existing contact arrangements. On balance, contact is not a positive experience for all parties

**Figure 14.2** Recipes for contact (CAFCASS, 2004)

the point of contact post-separation than when the family was living together. A review of current research reveals the complexity of assessing the child's best interests after parental separation. Risk factors include erratic, hostile or depressed parenting in the custodial residence; or a resident parent with a significant psychiatric or personality disorder. Protective factors are appropriate emotional support; adequate monitoring of child's activities; appropriate discipline; age-appropriate expectations of the child (Hetherington and Stanley-Hagan, 1999).

### False allegations when parents separate

There is a widespread misperception that there is a high incidence of intentionally false allegations of child abuse made by mothers in the context of parental separation and divorce in order to gain a tactical advantage or to seek revenge from their estranged partners. Coining the term 'Parental Alienation Syndrome' (Gardner, 1999) he blames vindictive mothers for pressuring children to make false claims of sexual abuse in divorce custody disputes. While Gardner's work is largely discredited by clinical studies (Faller, 1998) and large-scale studies of custody and access disputes have found that sexual abuse allegations in the context of parental separation are relatively rare (Thoennes and Tjaden, 1990) there continue to be misperceptions about the problem of false allegations of child abuse and neglect.

Trocme and Bala (2005) differentiated unsubstantiated allegations from intentionally false ones. Most unsubstantiated allegations are the result of well-intentioned reports triggered by a suspicious injury or concerning behaviour or a misunderstood story. In contrast to unsubstantiated allegations, intentionally false allegations are intentional fabrications that are made in the hope of manipulating the legal system, or are made to seek revenge against an estranged former partner, or may be the product of the emotional disturbance of the reporter. If there is a deliberate fabrication made, it is important to distinguish between cases in which it is a parent or other adult who is taking the lead in the fabricating from those where it is the child who is fabricating the allegation without adult influence. It is also important to distinguish allegations that are clearly unsubstantiated or false, from those where abuse cannot be substantiated but remains suspected (Oates et al., 2000). In their study of 7,600 allegations they

found that more than one-third of maltreatment investigations are unsubstantiated, but only four per cent of all cases are considered to be intentionally fabricated. Within the sub-sample of cases wherein a custody or access dispute has occurred, the rate of intentionally false allegations is higher: 12 per cent. Results of this analysis show that neglect is the most common form of intentionally fabricated maltreatment, while anonymous reporters and non-custodial parents (usually fathers) most frequently make intentionally false reports. Of the intentionally false allegations of maltreatment tracked by the study, custodial parents (usually mothers) and children were least likely to fabricate reports of abuse or neglect. While the rate of intentionally false allegations is relatively low, these results raise important clinical and legal issues, which require further consideration.

### The impact of sexual abuse in the context of contact considerations

The abusive act is the culmination of a series of psychological distortions or thinking errors that the perpetrator has had to achieve. The sexual abuse of a child is not an event, but a planned process that can take a long time to progress. The perpetrator develops the capacity to deny and reframe his thoughts, feelings and actions to himself and others. Knowledge of the process of abuse for the perpetrator must be applied by the worker when assessing the child's needs in relation to contact. At the initial stage the worker can make the following assumptions:

- The development of the relationship between the perpetrator and the child is based on a distortion of thinking and action.
- Within the relationship there will be blurred role boundaries.
- There will be long-standing cognitive manipulation of the child.
- The child will lack conviction that what happened was wrong or was not their fault.
- The relationship between the child and their mother is also likely to have been distorted by the perpetrator.
- The child will believe in the domination and power of the perpetrator.
- The non-abusing carer will not have had time to unpack the overwhelming and conflicting range of emotions for themselves, let alone those of their children.

- Siblings will have experienced distortions in their relationships with other family members.

The nature of the abuse indicates that change will be an involved and gradual process. Physical separation from the perpetrator does not in itself change distorted thinking or emotional damage. The implications of all this are that in families where a child has alleged sexual abuse, contact with the perpetrator needs to be suspended. A failure to do this leaves the opportunity for the controls exerted on the child to be further exploited. The risk of any temporary damage to the adult-child relationship is far less significant than the risk of on-going damage for an abused child. If the allegation or concerns are unfounded and there are positives for the child in maintaining a non-abusive relationship, then it should be equally possible to repair any distance engendered by the separation.

Given then that sexual abuse is a process rather than an event, we should reverse the presumption of contact in cases of sexual abuse, at least in the first instance, whilst we assess clearly the potential problems of contact for the child. It is the right of the child both to embrace and reject the need for contact, which must be protected and promoted by the protective adults around them.

The role of the professional in these circumstances is two-fold; they must represent the wishes and feelings of the child and place these and other relevant views within the context of their assessment of the *welfare* of the child. This inevitably leads to some consideration of the effects or consequences of contact for the child. How a worker approaches this will depend on whether their starting point about contact is that it should promote the welfare of the child, and thereby be of positive benefit, or whether the issue is that welfare is assured as long as contact is not detrimental to the child. I will argue that for those children who have experienced sexual abuse, the approach of the worker, including their starting point, has to begin with the assumption that until there has been fundamental change, contact for the child with their perpetrator, will be detrimental.

As I have articulated in some detail in Chapter 1 there are a great many ways of trying to analyse the impact of sexual abuse on the victim so this will not be repeated here save to remind people that the sexual abuse of children follows a predictable pattern of stages or phases and

mothers will have an increased ability to understand the impact of sexual abuse when they understand the process through which sexual abuse usually progresses. It will also help them to understand why it is often so difficult for the child to tell. Most frameworks clearly highlight that sexual abuse is a betrayal of trust and a distortion of relationships and involves a degree of stimulation that is far beyond the child's capacity to encompass and assimilate. Consequently, there is interference with the accomplishment of normal developmental tasks. The progression of mastery of one's self, environment, and relationship with others is significantly disrupted by the child's permanently altered awareness and new role vis-à-vis the perpetrator.

### The child's relationship with their mother

Research highlights clearly that the perpetrator shapes and controls the relationships they have both with adults and with children in order to abuse. This clearly raises the importance of examining the distortions which may exist for the non-abusing carer. At the point of disclosure, mothers experience major cognitive and emotional dissonance. The impact reduces the likelihood that they will seek support or be able to unpack what sort of help they need. If contact is to be of positive benefit to the child it will be within the context of their relationships at home and with their main carer.

The worker must, therefore evaluate the nature of those relationships and ensure that they do not perpetuate any of the distortions established in the process of the abuse. For many, this will require some fundamental changes. It is likely that many of the practical, physical functions of parenting will have been achieved by the non-abusing carer, but the psychological functions are likely to have been undermined. For example, boundary setting, role modelling, psychological nurturance. This can result in a reversal of roles and the systems of communication between the non-abusing carer and the child can become impaired and this is perpetuated with the keeping of the 'secret' of the abuse.

As well as the direct impact on the relationship between the mother and child (these impacts most often remain hidden until a disclosure is made and sense is made of why their relationship was difficult/distant etc.), it is likely that the mother's relationships outside the family and with her partner are also distorted. Helping her to understand aspects of self and the consequent strategies used by sexual abusers includes the following:

- impaired trust
- poor self-image, including past history, difficult adult relationships including those that have been abusive, distorted body awareness, a sense of failure, limited belief in self, depression, diminished parenting skills
- denial
- distorted expectations of partner and children
- victim empathy
- poor or distorted boundary setting
- anger
- ability to communicate
- assertiveness
- impaired socialisation/social skills
- poor concrete environmental support.

In order for a non-abusing carer to understand and make changes to the distortions and then participate in planning for any future contact between the perpetrator and their children that will be safe, they need time, information and more time. The mothers need to know that they are not being judged for the actions of their partners, nor are they helpless victims in the solution. For further assessment guidance around assessment of mothers post-sexual abuse, please refer to Calder and Regan (Chapter 12) Calder, Peake and Rose (2001) and Regan (2006).

Bell (2008) identified some of the key areas that a non-abusing carer would need to demonstrate change when managing domestic violence:

- To raise their awareness of the nature and development of domestic violence and abuse and of the consequences of exposure for both themselves and their children.
- To raise their awareness about the risk posed by their partner and to help them appreciate the implications for their own and their children's safety of continued association with him (and if he is unable to evidence an ability to make changes in himself, to provide them with the emotional support needed to separate from him), and to take the steps necessary to protect themselves and their children against further violence and abuse.
- To improve their capacity to empathise with their children and to make amends for the past.

- To help them come to terms with the traumas of their childhood.
- To help them address their unmet attachment needs and to develop an improved capacity to be discerning in partner choice.
- To help them develop the capacity to recognise potential abuse in a prospective partner and to develop basic recognition and safety strategies.
- To improve their assertiveness, to differentiate between violence, aggression and expressions of anger, and to develop less destructive ways of managing intense emotions associated with vulnerability and anger.
- To help them fully understand the risk implications of their own use of aggression within intimate relationships.
- To help them to recognise and change their negative/hostile thinking patterns so as to reduce conflict in their relationships, improve co-operation with professionals, improve their social integration and promote the emotional welfare of their children.
- To help them to manage boundaries with professionals and to find ways of improving their working relationship with social services.
- To explore future contraception options and to address their apparently ambivalent attitude to pregnancy (further pregnancies would significantly increase their vulnerability, raise risk levels for any other children in their care and detract from their ability to meet their existing children's needs).
- To help them develop a pro-social support network, especially with other women, independent of their partner.
- To help them review their attitude to education and employment (unemployment, financial dependence upon men and not working outside the home are key vulnerability factors for women's further exposure to domestic violence) and to self-care (poor diet is associated with mood and aggression).

Bell also developed a useful framework for determining treatment eligibility and viability. This is shown in Figure 14.3 overleaf.

## The legal position in the UK: the bedrock of the pro-contact culture

The Children Act itself makes no mention of sexual abuse or domestic violence nor do any of the ten volumes of guidance notes accompanying it. Current research would indicate that this is a

| Factors | Unsuitable | | | Suitable | |
|---|---|---|---|---|---|
| 1. Understanding of child protection concerns | no understanding of the child protection concerns | little understanding of the child protection concerns | some understanding of the child protection concerns | understands the concerns and the purpose of treatment | fully understands the concerns and the purpose of treatment |
| 2. Attitude to child protection concerns | totally rebuts all child protection concerns | largely rebuts the child protection concerns | partially accepts the child protection concerns | accepts the child protection concerns | fully accepts the child protection concerns |
| 3. Attitude to treatment goals | refusal to address treatment goals | refusal to address some of the treatment goals | ambivalent but willing to address the treatment goals | desire to address all treatment goals | strong desire to address all treatment goals |
| 4. Willingness to work collaboratively | confrontational stance | will not collaborate (or is overly compliant) | some collaboration with the therapist | collaborates | collaborates fully |
| 5. Authenticity of presentation | previous deceit; evidence of current deceit | previous deceit; inauthentic presentation | previous deceit; evasive | previous deceit; authentic presentation | no history of deceit; authentic presentation |
| 6. Motivation to pursue change through treatment | no motivation | minimal motivation | ambivalent | some motivation | highly motivated |
| 7. Insight | no capacity or desire to self-reflect | little capacity or desire to self-reflect | some capacity and desire to self-reflect | capacity and desire to self-reflect | high capacity and desire to self-reflect |
| 8. Cognitive distortion | frequent and significant cognitive impairment | distortions of perceptions, attribution, interpretations etc. | occasional distortions | some minor distortions | no obvious distortions |
| 9. Emotional regulation | highly reactive to aversive feelings | reactive to aversive feelings | some capacity to contain aversive feelings | capacity to contain aversive feelings | high capacity to contain aversive feelings |
| 10. Attendance | less than 50 per cent attendance | irregular attendance | some unacceptable absences | no unacceptable absences | full attendance and regular punctuality |
| 11. Substance use | frequently arrives for sessions under the influence | has arrived for session under the influence | not under the influence but adverse effects from recent use | no adverse effects on treatment from recent substance use | no known substance misuse |
| 12. Assignments | unwilling or unable to complete homework | no homework completed | some homework completed | homework completed | all homework completed well |

**Figure 14.3**  Treatment viability indicators (Bell, 2008)

| Factors | Unsuitable | Context | | | Suitable |
|---|---|---|---|---|---|
| 13. Life circumstances | likely to make treatment unworkable | likely to compromise treatment | unlikely to impact on treatment | likely to support treatment | likely to enhance treatment |
| 14. Access | transport/childcare problems likely to make treatment unworkable | transport/childcare problems likely to compromise attendance | transport/childcare issues unlikely to impact on attendance | transport/childcare arrangements likely to facilitate attendance | transport/childcare arrangements likely to ensure full attendance |
| 15. The local authority's position | LA position and resourcing likely to make treatment unworkable | LA position and resourcing likely to compromise treatment | LA position and resourcing unlikely to impact on treatment | LA position and resourcing likely to support treatment | LA position and resourcing likely to enhance treatment |
| 16. Inter-agency functioning | effect of multi-agency functioning is likely to make treatment unviable | multi-agency functioning is likely to undermine treatment | multi-agency functioning is unlikely to impact on treatment | multi-agency functioning is likely to support treatment | multi-agency functioning is likely to enhance treatment |

**Figure 14.3** *Continued*

serious over-sight if the best interests of the child are to be promoted. The Act does not require courts to consider the safety of the other party or of other children in the family and seems to make the assumption that all parents behave in a reasonable and caring manner, even at the point of separation or divorce. Indeed, the Children Act 1989 fails to recognise that male violence is a significant factor in marriage breakdown and that the violence does not always end with the end of the relationship or that sexual abuse is a process that persists after the abuse incident.

Where parents do separate the act also assumes that the children will invariably benefit from having continued, frequent and substantial contact with their fathers and yet in the context of a family subject to domestic violence and sexual abuse, child contact provides a further opportunity for violence and repeat victimisation. Contact with fathers is seen as a right irrespective of the history of sexual and physical violence.

The Children Act 1989 makes the welfare of the child the paramount consideration when the court is considering an order for residence or contact. The act also provides a checklist which the court must consider. This checklist does not refer specifically to the circumstance of sexual abuse or domestic violence, although it does require the court to have regard to any harm which the child has suffered or is at risk of suffering. Such suffering could include sexual abuse or the effects of witnessing domestic violence. However, research suggests that domestic violence is not generally taken into account when arrangements for children's contact with parents post-separation are made (Hester and Radford, 1995). The outcome of negotiations, which are given preference under the 'no order' principle, may compromise the safety of the woman or the children due to a belief by all parties and the professionals that the father 'must' have direct contact. There is also a requirement for a higher standard of proof to be made available to the court where the allegations become more serious.

Three kinds of contact are possible:

- indirect contact: letters, cards and gifts and sometimes phone calls, but no face-to-face contact with the child
- direct contact: time spent with the non-resident parent, which may involve home visits
- visiting or staying contact: unsupervised visits or overnight stays, usually at the offender's home.

Further changes on family law procedures promote mediation and agreement and contribute to encouraging parental agreement with minimal delay. It also emphasises looking towards the future when past harm is an important pointer of future risk (Calder, 2003). What is clear is that mediation is not appropriate in the majority of case where there has been either sexual abuse or domestic violence: both may undermine the voluntary nature of mediation and also create an extreme imbalance of power between bargaining parties.

The courts tend to have reference to the following principles involving contact applications:

- The welfare of the child is the paramount consideration and the court is concerned with the interests of the mother and the father in so far as they bear on the welfare of the child.
- It is almost always in the interests of the child whose parents are separated that they should always have contact with the parent with whom the child is not living.
- The court has the power to enforce orders for contact which it should not hesitate to exercise where it judges that it will overall promote the welfare of the child to do so.
- Cases do unhappily arise in which a court is compelled to conclude that in existing circumstances an order for immediate direct contact should not be ordered because so to order would injure the welfare of the child.
- In cases in which, for whatever reason, direct contact cannot be ordered for the time being, it is ordinarily highly desirable that there should be indirect contact so that the child grows up knowing of the love and interest of the absent parent with whom in due course direct contact should be established (Re P contact: supervision, 1996, 2FLR314).

Throughout the 1990s domestic violence was rarely acknowledged by the courts as a cogent reason for denying contact (Humphreys and Thiara, 2002). Busch and Robertson (2000) identified some deficits by the judiciary when considering issues of residency and contact in domestic violence cases:

- Physical violence was viewed a-contextually, without any reference to the array of power and control tactics which were being utilised by perpetrators. Single acts, such as punches or kicks, were evaluated from the viewpoint of (typically) male judges as relatively trivial. Judges ignored or failed to understand the fear and intimidation which abusers could invoke by actions which, to outsiders, might seem trivial or even loving, but which were, in fact, carefully coded messages reminding women of their vulnerability to further attack.
- There was little understanding of separation violence. Judges often assumed that women would be safe from further violence once they separated from their partners. The key issue for many judges was 'why doesn't she leave?'
- Violence against a partner was typically regarded as irrelevant to custody or contact determinations. There was a view among many judges that one could be a violent spouse (even a spouse killer) but still be a good parent. Custody and contact decisions were frequently made as if a parent's violence was irrelevant to his ability to provide a physically and psychologically safe environment for children.
- Many women who gained protection orders found them to be ineffective ('just a piece of paper') as police inaction and judicial approaches commonly gave men who breached the orders no meaningful consequences. Discourses of judges and other practitioners all too often adopted the perpetrator's justifications for violence, with the violence itself characterised as relationship-based. Social, historical and cultural constructs which legitimised perpetrator violence were often unquestioned.

In the late 1990s, challenges to the presumption for contact began to be made in the context of domestic violence. In 1999, the Children Act Subcommittee of the Lord Chancellors Domestic Violence Advisory Board on Family Law issued a consultation paper on 'contact between children and violent parents: the question of parental contact in cases where there is domestic violence'. The results of this consultation led to the adoption of new guidelines to be taken into account when considering issues of child contact where domestic violence is a concern. While the guidelines fell short of recommending a change to the Children Act 1989, they do provide a challenge to the automatic assumption that contact is in the best interests of the child.

The subsequent passage of the Adoption and Children Act (2002) requires courts to take into account the impact of domestic violence on a child when making contact orders. These changes apply to applications for contact and residence and also to all proceedings where the court applies the welfare checklist under the Children Act 1989. It is hoped that the presumption in future cases would be that contact with an abusive parent is going to have an adverse effect. In effect, domestic violence formally becomes a child protection issue for the first time. Unfortunately it does not embrace all those cases in private proceedings where unsupervised contact visits may be taking place, nor does it address the issue of sexual abuse. However given the similarities of *modus operandi* and impact, then the issues around professional response and contact considerations should be similar.

As a measure of the lack of integrated thinking across government departments (Calder, 2004), the recent consultation and subsequent report *Making Contact Work* (Lord Chancellors Department, 2002) recommends stronger and legally sanctioned measures for the enforcement of contact. This appears to be advocating a presumption of contact despite the evidence-base to the contrary, which has increasingly indicated that contact does not always, or necessarily, equate with the welfare or best interests of children (Hester, 2002).

The presumption of contact is clearly a rights-based approach to legislation and policy (Bailey-Harris et al., 1999). I think it is important to clarify this issue. It is the right of the child not the right of the parent and the right of the child is a qualified one which is subject to the child's best interests. In many situations it is right and appropriate that local authorities pursue maintaining relationships where children are not living with their birth parents. However, a tension exists if the 'rights' of the parent are not assumed to be in accordance with the rights of the child. Where contact is contentious and subject to legal proceedings the reality is that children do not do the deciding, and it would be inappropriate therefore to suggest that the issue of contact is the right of the child, but more honestly, a right for the child. It is this right for the child both to embrace and reject the need for contact, which must be protected and promoted by the adults who are asked to act *in loco parentis*.

Of concern is the fact that the judicial statistics show that of 61,356 contact orders issued by the courts, only 518 cases resulted in the refusal of contact (Women's Aid, 2003). There is also evidence of contact orders being granted to

Schedule One offenders or offenders whose behaviour had caused sufficient concern for children's names to be added to the Child Protection register.

At the present time an application by the offender for a contact order is probably the easiest way to track down and harass his victims. This arises either because the court discloses the whereabouts in the paperwork; the location of the court hearing or the address of the solicitor acting for her will give the offender some idea as to the area where she lives. If the offender frames their departure as having gone missing taking the children, then the court may well instruct the police to find the child and may well order disclosure of the address to the court. Humphreys and Thiara (2002) found that 14 women in their sample (of 100) believed the child contact application of the offender was motivated by a desire to track her down. Forty-one per cent said that they had been subjected to post-separation violence as a result of child contact arrangements. They also found that handover for contact at the mother's house was the most frequent arrangement followed by handover in a public place.

Many women receive contradictory messages from different parts of the system when they should be united in supporting primary and secondary victims of domestic violence. On the one hand the child protection intervention frequently states that their partner or ex-partner represents an ongoing risk to their children and that either separation must occur or be maintained to ensure the safety of the children. On the other hand, these same men apply for, and are often granted contact with the additional problem that they continue to know where the mother lives.

Radford and Hester (2006) critically reviewed the assumption that children must have contact with their fathers and provided us with the negative consequences of contact between children and violent men. They noted that the professional approaches to domestic violence, child protection and visitation and contact are so different that they may be conceived as belonging to different planets. On the domestic violence planet the father's behaviour may be recognised by the police and other agencies as abusive in relation to the mother; his behaviour is seen as a crime and he may even be prosecuted for a criminal or public offence against him. He is thus perceived as a violent partner and the woman in need of protection. If he lands on the child protection planet he may be perceived as abusive to the mother while the parents are still together or during the process of them separating. But the focus of this planet is the protection of children not adults. It is highly unlikely that he will be prosecuted as a welfare approach prevails, although the children could be added to the Child Protection Register for emotional abuse. In order to protect the children, mothers are frequently asked to separate themselves and their children from the perpetrator if she has not already done so. On this planet the mother is seen as responsible for dealing with the consequences of the violence. In many cases the violent man disappears and the woman is left managing the intervention. If the father moves to the visitation and contact planet, there is often no apparent concrete evidence in relation to child care to question his post-separation parenting abilities. Here the emphasis is less on protection than children having two parents. Within this context the abusive father may be deemed a 'good enough' father who should at least have contact with his child post-separation if not custody or residence. The mother ends up in a difficult

situation here as she may be ordered to allow contact between her partner and the children leaving her not only bewildered and confused but again scared for the safety of her children. This three planets model shows the conceptual gap between violent men and fathers.

Jaffe and Geffner (1998) produced a useful table (see Figure 14.4 below) to differentiate between the issues raised in normal contact disputes and disputes in situations of domestic violence that is helpful for all concerned in deciding the way forward and is certainly transferable into cases where sexual abuse is a feature.

### Similarities derived from the domestic violence experiences (Calder, 2003b, 2004, 2006)

Perpetrators of domestic violence operate in a sophisticated way, designed to control their victims and disable independent thought and action. Any attempt to break out of the straightjacket heightens rather than reduces risks, thus restricting actual or perceived exit options. Professional ignorance or resource constraints can replicate the original harm by unwittingly

| Issue | Normal contact dispute | Contact dispute with allegations of abuse |
|---|---|---|
| Central issue | Promoting children's relationship with visiting parent; co-parenting | Safety for mother and children |
| Focus of court hearing | Reducing hostilities; setting schedule | Assessing lethality risk and level of violence; protection |
| Assessment issues | Children's stage of development, needs, preferences, attachments<br>Parenting abilities | Impact of violence on mother and children; developmental needs; consideration of trauma bonding<br>Father's level of acceptance of responsibility<br>Safety plan for mother and children<br>Parenting abilities |
| Planning for the future | Contact schedule that meets needs of children | Consider suspended, supervised or no contact |
| Resources required | Mediation services<br>Divorce counselling for parents and children<br>Independent assessment/evaluation | Specialised services with assessment and knowledge and training about domestic violence<br>Supervised contact centre<br>Coordination of court and community services<br>Well-informed lawyers, judges and relevant professionals |

**Figure 14.4**   Special issues in contact disputes with allegations of domestic violence

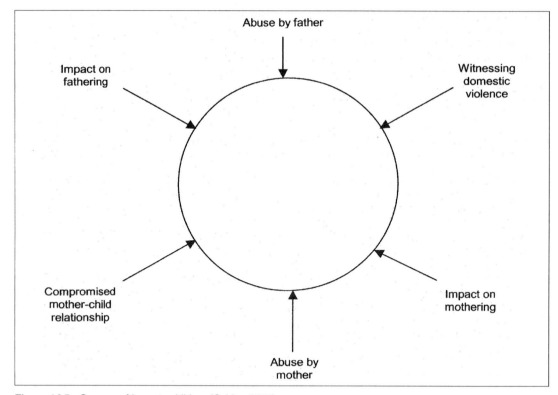

**Figure 14.5**   Sources of harm to children (Calder, 2006)

mirroring the perpetrator's controlling behaviour. Professionals can expect victims to make straightforward decisions, such as the need to separate from the perpetrator, without acknowledging the fact that the perpetrator has systematically eroded financial and emotional independence, created a context of dependency and fear, and robbed them of self-esteem and other essential components necessary for resilience-building or resilience-retention.

Perpetrators of domestic violence share many of the characteristics of sex offenders in that their primary motivating feature is the exercise of power and control. They groom the environment over a period of time to render the potential for disclosure, belief and professional action almost impossible. Children fear the cost of disclosure and their opportunities are often narrow through perpetrator threat and through the systematic undermining of their critical relationship with their mother. Children may fear the costs of disclosure in terms of disruption to their siblings, peer networks and family relationships. Women fear the costs of leaving since they are at elevated

risk, physically and emotionally, and fear potential stalking, especially if contact application to their children is achieved. Indeed, the number of children killed in court-ordered contact and the risks from domestic violence related to stalking are both high. Figure 14.5 sets out the range of impacts of domestic violence for children.

Many perpetrators restrict their behaviour to specific places or contexts, such as the home environment. Many hold down professional jobs and externally present as pillars of the community. However, they perpetuate physical, sexual and emotional abuse as well as neglect. Their control of the family is rarely restricted to the mother and there is evidence of direct harm to children other than the witnessing or awareness of domestic violence. More actively they may groom the children to perpetrate harm to their mother, or to undermine her parenting and any authority she may have had, particularly in their absence, to ensure a 24-hour, seven-days-a-week regime of control. Added to this their behaviour towards the mother may have independently drained her of the energies and confidence necessary for parenting. This familial pattern of dis-empowering the mother also conflicts with children's expectations of protection from their mothers, and further compounds the mother-child relationship difficulties as the child may apportion blame to her for not leaving the perpetrator or naming and shaming his behaviour.

Any evidence of active parenting from the mother may be witnessed by professionals as physical abuse. There is evidence that mothers may strive to regulate the behaviour of their children for fear of a severe response if witnessed by the perpetrator, and this may result in physical injuries through attempts to physically control. This is not intentional harm and in fact is driven by a need to protect their children from more severe harm from the perpetrator. The perpetrator of the domestic violence has thus successfully displaced the professional and child focus of blame to the mother, rather than the physical injury being seen as a symptom of his abusive and controlling pattern of behaviour. Mothers may also be robbed of energies and so the focus of professional concern is likely to be the mother since the concerns relate to child neglect. Professionals need to search for the origins of the presenting problem rather than dealing with the symptoms out of context. There is much in domestic violence to support the belief that men are resistant to accepting responsibility for their behaviour; they deploy effective displacement of responsibility strategies and make effective help-seeking on the part of their victims a dangerous and potentially life-threatening activity. Rather than reflecting much child protection experience that when the going gets tough, the men get going, they stay put and challenge their victims to leave if they dare.

### Professional responses

There is plenty of evidence that, unless carefully crafted, professional responses can mirror their original experiences of harm, and can escalate the seriousness, frequency and range of perpetrator behaviour. In order to try and construct a more victim-friendly intervention, it is important that we try and name those factors which contribute to a professionally dangerous response. Given that the threshold for the provision of any kind of social work service is getting tighter and retaining an incident-based focus, the issue of contact and

concerns that accumulate over a period of time will struggle to get any attention. This appears to be reflected in the demise of sexual abuse from the professional system in recent years (see Finkelhor and Jones, 2004).

What we have to do is to build a system of response that is specific to domestic violence. Like sexual abuse, domestic violence is a process. It is a pattern of behaviour rather than a series of isolated individual events. It also involves the use of power and control: the goal of the perpetrator is to ensure that he is in complete control of his partner and of the relationship. Domestic violence tends to increase in severity and frequency each time the cycle is played out unless some intervention is made.

As a consequence, we tend to respond after a serious incident in which the mother and children have been physically harmed. This is indefensible when we could have reasonably predicted that the harm would materialise and that it would be significant for the victims. One of the key professional challenges is to construct a response system that reflects the nature of domestic violence – embracing process as a predictor of likely future harm and assessing/intervening before it materialises. At the present time family experiences of social work responses tends to reinforce their negative view of social services in that when they become involved they are likely to remove the children.

A critical element of a safe professional response is for professionals to intervene to help mothers and children in a way that embraces their experiences. Expecting a mother to take immediate decisions that correspond with the professional preferences is unrealistic because:

- They are often in a state of shock.
- The risks to herself escalate significantly when she has left the home.
- The impact of sustained disempowerment and abuse on her over a period of time renders her incapable of making safe or informed choices. Figure 14.6 provides a clear structure within which the controlling aspect of the perpetrator narrows down her options.
- The mother may be resisting a move as she is frightened either of direct perpetrator retaliation on her children: or the indirect effects on the children created through moving home, such as displacement from family, peers, schooling.

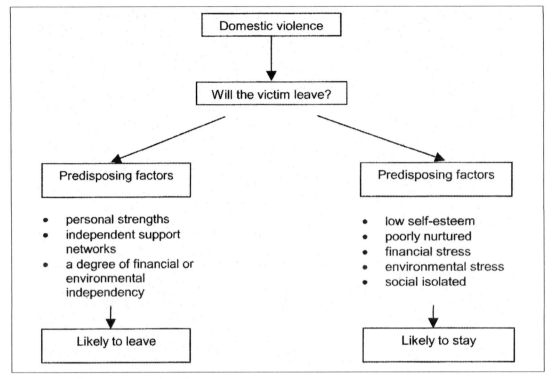

**Figure 14.6**   To leave or not to leave?

- There is genuine fear of pursuing the mother (stalking) or the children (via contact applications) and experience tells us that in many circumstances court-mandated contact has resulted in child and mother deaths.

One of the key challenges for child protection is to hold the perpetrator accountable for his behaviour and any knock-on consequences, such as displacement of the family, involvement of young people in his controlling strategy, compromised resilience or enhanced risks when he is prosecuted or in receipt of treatment. It is equally challenging for workers to approach mothers as victims lacking information and choices rather than perpetrators to avoid extending or replicating perpetrator control; to facilitate reparation of the perpetrator-initiated impairment of the mother-child relationship and the transition from victim to survivor.

Research also highlights that professional intervention heightens the risks to women and children in many circumstances. Farmer and Owen (1998) reported that mothers tend to be

under-represented in relation to offers of service and over-represented in respect of professional attempts to control them. When professionals intervene they tend to have most contact with the mothers and hold them accountable for the risks to their children rather than with the men, who tend to stay involved until they achieve their own particular outcome, such as non-prosecution, or deflection of focus on to the mother and her parenting. Mothers also report feeling unable to disclose domestic violence when professionals are making enquiries for other reasons, as they fear it will be held against them and their capacity to protect. Figure 14.7 offers a more balanced approach from professionals which is less likely to alienate mothers and more likely to hold the perpetrator culpable and responsible for the multiplicity of harm.

Workers and the courts have to be careful when considering contact decisions based on risk assessments. At the present time we have a chaotic, even polarised, system where the criminal justice field use actuarial tools to predict the likelihood of re-offending over a lifetime (not

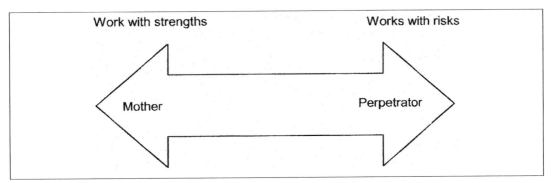

**Figure 14.7**   Risk-balancing approach in domestic violence (Calder, 2006)

when that may be, against whom, in what circumstances, or with what cost) and these could indicate a low risk of sexual re-offending but does not take account of the context or the people involved in the family situation. To uncritically import assessments and make crucial decisions around contact based on them would be indefensible (see Calder, 2008).

### Purpose of contact

The purpose of contact should be overt and abundantly clear and have the potential for benefiting the child in some way. The benefits of contact for the child include the importance of the father as one of the two parents in the child's sense of identity and value, the role model provided by a father and the male contribution to parenting of children and its relevance to the child's perception of family life as an adult.

There are many different purposes of contact including the maintenance or reparation of beneficial relationships, the sharing of information and knowledge and the testing of reality for the child. There are fewer benefits associated with indirect contact although there are some: experience of continued interest by the absent parent, knowledge and information about the absent parent, keeping open the possibility of developing the relationship and the opportunity for reparation.

### Risks and direct contact

There are a number of risks associated with direct contact. The overall risk is that of failing to meet or undermining the child's developmental needs or even causing emotional abuses and damage directly through contact or as a consequence of

contact. Specifically this includes escalating the climate of conflict around the child which will undermine the child's general stability and sense of emotional well-being. This can create a tug of loyalty and a sense of responsibility for the conflict in children, which in turn impacts and affects the relationships of the child with both parents.

There may also be direct abusive experiences, including emotional abuse by denigration of the child or the child's resident carer. There may be continuation of unhealthy relationships, such as dominant or bullying relationships, those created by fear, bribes or emotional blackmail, by undermining the child's sense of stability and continuity, by deliberately or inadvertently setting different moral standards or standards of behaviour, by little interest in the child himself or by under-stimulating or uninteresting contact. Unreliable contact allows children to be frequently let down and forcing children to attend contact against their wishes is abusive (Butler-Sloss, Thorpe and Waller, 2000). There may be a continuing sense of fear in the child; either because the child has post-traumatic anxieties or symptoms which are re-aroused by the abuser; the child may fear the violent parent and be aware of their mother's fear continuing, as well as the negative impact on the child's own attitudes to violence, to forming parenting relationships and the role of fathers. Hester and Radford (1996) found that contact after separation put children who had witnessed violence to their mothers in the difficult position of feeling that they were responsible for protecting their parents. Hester and Radford found that the children often tried to minimise the harm or keep the peace by holding back information from the father or mother, mediating between the two and covering up or toning down the violence and threats of abuse.

Bancroft and Silverman (2002) reported a number of sources of risk to children from unsupervised contact:

- risk of continued or intensified undermining of the mother's authority and of mother-child relationships
- risk of rigid, authoritarian parenting
- risk of neglectful or irresponsible parenting
- risk of exposure to new threats or acts of violence toward the mother
- risk of psychological abuse and manipulation
- risk of physical or sexual abuse of the child by the offender
- risk of inconsistency in contact attendance
- risk of the child learning attitudes supportive of domestic violence
- risk of abduction
- risk of exposure to violence in the offender's new relationships.

### Inverting legislation

The presumption of no contact until deemed to be in the child's best interests is a clear and tough position statement to adopt. It flies in the face of legislation enshrined within the Children Act and also the principle that domestic violence of itself cannot constitute a bar to contact. Some see it as just one factor in the difficult and delicate balancing exercise of discretion. In such a risk balancing exercise, in cases of proven domestic violence the seriousness has to be weighed according to the risks involved and the impact on the child against any positive factors (if any). It would need to consider the ability of the offending parent to recognise his past conduct, be aware of the need for change and make genuine efforts to do so. All these would need to be demonstrated with evidence rather than reliance on verbal assurances.

There is increasing consensus that there should be no contact unless it is proven that the contact offers something of benefit to the child and to the child's situation. Without the following it is clear that the balance of advantage and disadvantage is tipping against contact:

- some (preferably full) acknowledgement of the violence
- some acceptance (preferably full if appropriate ie the sole instigator of violence) of responsibility for that violence

- full acceptance of the inappropriateness of the violence particularly in respect of the domestic and parenting context and of the likely ill-effects on the child
- a genuine interest in the child's welfare and full commitment to the child, ie a wish for contact in which they are not making the conditions
- a wish to make reparation to the child and work towards the child recognising the inappropriateness of the violence and the attitude to and treatment of the mother and helping the child to develop appropriate values and attitudes
- an expression of regret and showing some understanding of the impact of their behaviour on their ex-partner in the past and currently
- indications that the parent seeking contact can reliably sustain contact in all senses (Butler-Sloss et al., 2000). They suggested that without the first and sixth points above they could not see how the non-resident parent could fully support the child, play a part in undoing the harm caused to the child and support the child's current situation a well as the need to move on and develop healthily.

The offending parent clearly has to demonstrate that he is a fit parent to exercise contact, that he is not going to de-stabilise the family, and that he is not going to upset the children and harm them emotionally (Sterling, 2001).

### Consequences of withholding contact

It is important to acknowledge that some consequences do arise as a result of withholding direct contact. These include the deprivation of a relationship with the biological father; loss of opportunity to know that parent first-hand; loss of opportunity to know grandparents and other relatives on the father's side of the family; loss of that parent if the child has enjoyed a positive and meaningful relationship with him; the loss of opportunity for the parent to provide positive and supportive contact; the absence of the opportunity for any repair to the relationship or to the harm done; and a lessening of the likelihood of the child being able to get in touch and form a meaningful relationship at a later stage (Butler-Sloss et al., 2000).

### Creating a context for children's healing

Bancroft and Silverman (2002) identified several elements as critical to the creation of a healing environment for children who have experienced domestic violence:

- a sense of physical and emotional safety in their current surroundings
- structure, limits and predictability
- a strong bond to the non-abusing parent
- not to feel responsible for taking care of the adults
- contact with the abusive parent
- a strong bond to their siblings.

Clearly the issue of promoting contact is a contentious one. Bancroft and Silverman argue that few children prefer to stop all contact with their abusive fathers. Rather, they generally wish to be able to continue to express their love for their father, to have him know them, and to be able to tell him about key events in their lives. They may also want reassurance that he is not in overwhelming emotional distress. However, this contact must not interfere with their other healing needs, including the strengthening of the mother-child relationship.

A child's attitude may also alter over time; once they feel safe and secure and are convinced that they will not be returning to live with the perpetrator, they may feel able to 'let go' of the trauma bond and may be able to express relief at the decisions made.

## Issues of supervised contact

The attractiveness of contact can be undermined by the hostility that children may see or sense between their parents, particularly at handover points. Workers also have to consider the potential for children to see supervised contact as something restrictive and regulating rather than safe.

There should be a second presumption that whenever there is to be any contact between children and the offending parent, it should be supervised in a safe environment and this, of necessity, precludes using relatives and friends of the offender as the supervising officer.

Sturge and Glaser (2000) identified several problems in deciding whether or not to promote supervised contact as a safe way of maintaining or forging some kind of relationship. The difficulties include:

- The quality of such experiences for a child (or parent) if this is continued over a long time. It

is an abnormal situation, it is often disliked by the child both because of its artificiality and because of the restricted opportunities for interest, fun and stimulation within it; such arrangements often make the child and parent feel tense and ill at ease and may result in the child simply holding the parent responsible for having to put up with it. This may result in further alienation and no real benefit to the child.

- There is a lack of resources: good contact centres with good facilities and good supervision are scarce and by and large not available for long-term arrangements; it is expensive.
- It is unlikely to lead to improvements in a parent's sensitivity or parenting skills or to lead to a situation where it becomes safe for the child to be alone with that parent.
- There are few situations where it might be considered if a time frame is set. It is only appropriate where the contact may be therapeutic or where change to the risk in the short-term is anticipated.

However, supervision of contact does have some purposes:

- safety from physical and emotional harm
- checks on the fitness of the parent at the start of contact and the availability of a supervisor to support the child
- to facilitate the management of contact so it is positive for the child
- support for the child to allow them to be more at ease and safe.

## What do children need in supervised contact?

Johnston and Straus (1999) examined the needs of children who have grown up in conflicted families with a history of violence. These children have often been subjected to an extraordinary range of traumatic family experiences typified by mutual distrust, fear, anger, bitterness and projection of blame. When parents separate they continue to make bad choices and conflict can escalate. For some children they find that a biological parent who has never been present or who abandoned the child for years will sometimes turn up unexpectedly to reclaim kinship and the right to visitation. The sad consequence is that these families usually provide a frightening, fragmented, contradictory and profoundly confusing experience for their children. Such children do not always view the world in expected ways. Providing children with physically safe places for contact may not be perceived as physically or psychologically safe by the child. The risks often come from different sources: 'Can I safely go between mummy and daddy?' or 'Can I safely leave mummy?' In trying to cope and survive with these profound dilemmas the child is bound to ask, 'Who can I trust? What is false and true? What is real and what is not? Who is good and who is bad?' These raise important issues for supervised contact. It cannot repair damage already done but it should aim to minimise the risk of re-traumatising the child and provide a psychologically safe environment. Maximising children's sense of predictability and control with respect to the contact experience is the first step in responding to their distrust and need for hyper-vigilance. Children are often comforted by developing rituals around contact: a familiar way of greeting, similar questions about how he or she is doing, a regular way of saying it is time to start the contact, a routine way for preparing the child for the end of the visit, and finally an agreed-upon signal for saying goodbye and leaving. Rules are also reassuring to children, such as them being the boss of touching arrangements.

### Action when contact has been suspended

Once contact is stopped the assessment will fall into the following areas:

- Individual work with the child. This work should address both the effects of the abuse for the child, validate their feelings, and counteract the distortions. They need help to understand different types of relationships between adults and to understand the things that are not acceptable. It may also be helpful to allow the child to indicate the things that were OK and not OK. Individual work with the non-abusing carer. This needs to occur at their pace and ensure they have time and opportunity to assimilate the information.
- Work with the siblings (non-abused).
- Work with the child/ren and the non-abusing carer together. This work should promote the strengthening of their relationship and systems of communication.
- Individual risk assessment and treatment of the perpetrator.

McIntosh (2002) explored the tensions for children as a result of court-ordered contact. If handled inappropriately it can mitigate against rather than promote recovery. She acknowledged that for some children, at the right time, with the right support, they can benefit from contact with the offender. The success hinges on the worker's capacity to think about the child's experiences of contact and to facilitate therapeutic contact specific to each situation in conjunction with the residential parent's and the visiting parent's ability to act on the needs of their child in contact. Through the child's eyes, success specifically hinges on the visiting parent's ability to show that they can think about, understand, and accept the child's experience.

Where there is not a clear allegation and/or the perpetrator denies any cause for concern, it is important that the assessment explores the functioning and relationships within the family as well as the original reasons for concern. At the very least, the child needs to have increased self-esteem and an understanding of where the responsibility for any abusive behaviour lies. Without the necessary changes, the physical, emotional and psychological risk to the child is unacceptable. The task, therefore in any consideration for the renewal of contact is to provide evidence that this risk is no longer significant, rather than the assumption that parent-child interaction can continue whilst an abusive 'act' does not occur.

Workers also need to consider the following of the offender:

- what is their motivation for contact: is it a desire to promote the best interests of the child or to create an opportunity to perpetuate violence, intimidation or harassment of the resident parent?
- what is their likely behaviour during contact?
- what is the likely impact of such behaviour on the children?
- their capacity to appreciate the effect of past and future violence on the other parent and the children.
- their attitude towards his past violence.
- their capacity for change and to behave appropriately.

Bancroft and Silverman (2002) identified 12 steps that are indispensable for the abuser to be able to become a responsible and safe parent and which can be used by workers to assess how far up the staircase they have come, and what they still need to achieve before safe contact can be considered:

- They must disclose fully the history of physical and psychological abuse toward their partner and children.
- They must recognise that this behaviour is unacceptable.
- They must recognise that this behaviour was chosen.
- They must recognise and show empathy for the effects of their actions on their partner and children.
- They must identify their pattern of controlling behaviours and entitled attitudes.
- They must develop respectful behaviours and attitudes.
- They must re-evaluate their distorted image of their partner.
- They must make amends both in the short and in the long term.
- They must accept the consequences of their actions for themselves.
- They must commit to not repeating their abusive behaviour.
- They must accept change as a long-term (probably lifelong) process.
- They must be willing to be accountable.

## Planning for contact: essential groundwork and ground rules

Promoting contact where it is supervised does not in itself safe-guard the child from harm nor does it promote their well-being if the areas of change have not been identified and progressed successfully. If contact is supervised, a tremendous responsibility lies with the supervisee. There are some fundamental ground rules that need to be established and agreed with the child, the perpetrator and non-abusing carer. This may fall into the following areas developed by Rose (2001):

- The purpose of contact; is this an assessment session, is it to facilitate the child therapeutically, is it taking place because of direction from the court etc?
- Venue; ensuring visibility and safety.
- Time and duration; is it sensitive to the needs of the child, including school commitments, tiredness and times of abuse etc?
- Role of the supervisor/s; there must be a shared understanding as to whether the

supervisor is there to observe and intervene if concerns are raised or has a more proactive role in facilitating the contact. It will also be important to establish for the child whether the supervisor is neutral and therefore does not have a relationship with the child, or is their ally and clearly there to empower the child.

- Child's arrival and departure from contact; who brings and takes the child, who leaves first, what greetings and goodbyes are allowed particularly in relation to physical contact?
- Agreed activities during contact; contact needs to be carefully planned and should reflect the interests of the child. It should also maximise the positive aspects of the adult's parenting skills. This should be based on the acquired knowledge of what, if anything, positively binds the child and adult together.
- Agreements about talking and touching; it is important to clarify whether kissing, hugging, sitting on knees etc. is alright or not. It is also helpful if the worker establishes with the child anything that is inappropriate or that they do not wish to talk or be asked about by the adult ie the abuse, passing messages home, providing information.
- Time alone with the child; it is crucial that everyone knows whether the child and parent are allowed to be alone together unsupervised at *any time*. This may involve making plans should the child need taking to the toilet or need a drink or snack-making etc.
- Presents; it is not unusual for estranged parents to want to bring gifts for the child. The meaning of this for the abused child must inform any decision about it.
- Intervention; the supervisor must be clear with the child and the adult how they will intervene if they are concerned during contact and what response they expect from the parent.
- Recording; if the contact is part of an ongoing assessment, agreement must be reached about what will be recorded, how it will be recorded and where the information may be shared.
- Worries and safety plans; it is important that the child identifies to whom and how they can communicate any worries they may have during contact. In my experience it can be useful to agree an 'emergency code word' that the child chooses and can use during contact if they become anxious or need the contact to stop. It is also useful if the child has access and permission to speak with an adult not involved

in supervising the contact and with whom they can express any feelings they may have.

- The non-abusing carer; it is likely that the non-abusing carer will have their own feelings about the contact and it will be important to ensure that the child understands what is to be fed back and by whom. It may also be necessary to identify what part the child wants the non-abusing carer to play after contact ie don't ask me any questions about it, I need time on my own, I need you to hug me etc.
- There should also be an agreement about immediate action the perpetrator should take to stop contact if they are aroused, and the process of debriefing within the context of any treatment they receive.

These and any other issues relevant for the individual situation must form the basis of a written agreement both with the child and the adult. The agreement with the child must reflect their age and understanding and can make use of pictures or diagrams where words are not understood. The starting point should be that the perpetrator has apologised to the child and that they alone are responsible for the abuse. The supervisor should feel confident that they are in control of the contact. The impact for the child needs to be evaluated and should take into account not only what happens during contact but what is said and how the child behaves and presents following contact.

## Conclusions

More detailed assessments are needed to explore whether contact is appropriate for individual children, starting from a premise of no contact. Where contact is considered in the child's best interests, we have to be creative in considering the best option for contact, and this may not always be face-to-face contact. Contact needs to be more carefully matched to the needs of the child and the abused parent to be safe. The greater the professionals' awareness and understanding of domestic violence, the greater the beneficial effect upon safety of child contact outcomes. This chapter has hopefully reviewed the legal position in relation to contact, considered the deficits through research and practice experience and begun to convert the evidence into a preliminary assessment framework.

## References

Arkow, P. (1996) The Relationship Between Animal Abuse and Other Forms of Family Violence. *Family Violence & Sexual Assault Bulletin*, 12: 1–2, 29–34.

Bailey-Harris, R., Barron, J. and Pearce, J. (1999) From Utility to Rights? The Presumption of Contact in Practice. *International Journal of Law, Policy and The Family*, 111.

Bancroft, L. and Silverman, J.G. (2002) *The Batterer as Parent: Addressing The Impact of Domestic Violence on Family Dynamics*. Thousand Oaks, CA: Sage.

Bell, C. (2008) Working With Mandated Domestic Violence Cases. in Calder, M.C. (Ed.) *The Carrot or The Stick? Engaging Involuntary Clients*. Lyme Regis: Russell House Publishing.

Bream, B. and Buchanan, A. (2003) Distress Among Children Whose Separated or Divorced Parents Cannot Agree Arrangements For Them. *British Journal of Social Work*, 33: 127–38.

Busch, R. and Robertson, N. (2000) Innovative Approaches to Child Custody and Domestic Violence in New Zealand: The Effects of Law Reform on The Discourses of Battering. *Journal of Aggression*, 3: 1, 269–99.

Butler-Sloss, E., Thorpe, P. and Waller, I. (2000) Re L; Re V; Re M and Re H (Contact: Domestic Violence) Court of Appeal, 19th June 2000, 2 FLR 334.

CAFCASS (2004) Contact: Principles, Practice Guidance and Procedures. (Draft 1) London: CAFCASS.

Calder, M.C. (2003) The Assessment Framework: A Critique and Reformulation. in Calder, M.C. and Hackett, S. (Eds.) *Assessment in Childcare: Using and Developing Frameworks For Practice*. Lyme Regis: Russell House Publishing.

Calder, M.C. (2003b) Child Sexual Abuse and Domestic Violence: Parallel Considerations to Inform Professional Responses. *Seen and Heard*, 12: 3, 14–24.

Calder, M.C. (2004) Child Protection: Current Context, Central Contradictions and Collective Challenges. *Representing Children*, 17: 1, 59–73.

Calder, M.C. (2006) Domestic Violence and Child Protection: Challenges For Professional Practice. *Context*, 84 April: 11–14.

Calder, M.C. (Ed.) (2008) *Contemporary Risk Assessment in Safeguarding Children*. Lyme Regis: Russell House Publishing.

Calder, M.C., Harold, G. and Howarth, E. (2004) *Children Living With Domestic Violence: Towards A Framework For Assessment and Intervention*. Lyme Regis: Russell House Publishing.

Calder, M.C., Peake, A. and Rose, K. (2001) *Mothers of Sexually Abused Children: A Framework For Assessment, Understanding and Support*. Lyme Regis: Russell House Publishing.

Faller, K. (1998) The Parental Alienation Syndrome: What Is It and What Data Support It? *Child Maltreatment*, 3: 2, 100–15.

Farmer, E. and Owen, M. (1998) Gender and The Child Protection Process. *British Journal of Social Work*, 28: 545–64.

Finkelhor, D. and Jones, L.M. (2004) Explanations For The Decline in Child Sexual Abuse Cases. *Juvenile Justice Bulletin*, January, 1–12.

Gardner, R.A. (1999) Differentiating Between Parental Alienation Syndrome and Bona Fide Abuse-Neglect. *American Journal of Family Therapy*, 27: 2, 97–107.

Grych, J.H. and Fincham, F.D. (1999) The Adjustment of Children From Divorced Families. in Galatzr-Levy, R.M. and Kraus, L. (Eds.) *The Scientific Basis of Child Custody Decisions*. NY: John Wiley.

Hester, M. (2002) One Step Forward and Three Steps Back? Children, Abuse and Parental Contact in Denmark. *Child and Family Law Quarterly*, 14: 3, 267–79.

Hester, M. and Pearson, C. (1998) *From Periphery to Centre*. Bristol: Policy Press.

Hester, M. and Radford, L. (1995) The Impact of The Children Act. in Hester, M. et al. (Eds.) *Women, Violence and Male Power*. Milton Keynes: Open University Press.

Hester, M. and Radford, L. (1996) *Domestic Violence and Child Contact Arrangements. Social Policy Research*. York: Joseph Rowntree Foundation.

Hetherington, E.M. and Stanley-Hagan, M. (1999) The Adjustment of Children With Divorced Parents; A Risk and Resiliency Perspective. *Journal of Child Psychology and Psychiatry*, 40: 1, 129–40.

Humphreys, C. and Thiara, R. (2002) *Routes to Safety: Protection Issues Facing Abused Women and Children and The Role of Outreach Services*. Bristol: Women's Aid Federation.

Jaffe, P.G. and Geffner, R. (1998) Child Custody Disputes and Domestic Violence: Critical Issues For Mental Health, Social Service and Legal Professionals. in Holden, G.W., Geffner, R.and Jouriles, E.N. (Eds.) *Children Exposed to Marital Violence: Theory, Research and Applied Issues*. Washington, DC: American Psychological Association.

Johnston, J.R. and Straus, R.B. (1999) Traumatised Children in Supervised Visitation: What Do They Need? *Family and Conciliation Courts Review*, 37: 2, 135–58.

Lucey, C. et al. (2003) What Contact Arrangements Are in A Child's Best Interests? in Reder, P., Duncan, S. and Lucey, C. (Eds.) *Studies in The Assessment of Parenting*. London: Brunner-Routledge.

Lord Chancellor's Department (2002) *Guidelines for Good Practice on Parental Contact in Cases Where There is Domestic Violence*. Prepared by the Children Act Sub-committee of the Lord Chancellor's Advisory Board on Family Law, April 2002, p. 29.

Mcintosh, J.E. (2002) Thought in The Face of Violence: A Child's Needs. *Child Abuse and Neglect*, 26: 229–41.

Oates, R.K. et al. (2000) Erroneous Concerns About Child Sexual Abuse. *Child Abuse & Neglect*, 24: 1, 149–57.

Radford, L. and Hester, M. (2006) *Mothering Through Domestic Violence*. London: Jessica Kingsley.

Radford, L., Sayer, S. and AMICA (1999) *Unreasonable Fears: Child Contact in The Context of Domestic Violence*. Bristol: Women's Aid Federation.

Regan, L. (2006) *Helping Mothers Move Forward: A Workbook to Help Provide Assessment and Support to The Safe Carers of Children Who Have Been Sexually Abused*. Lyme Regis: Russell House Publishing.

Rose, K. (2000) Contact, The Perpetrator and The Child. in Calder, M.C. (Ed.) *Complete Guide to Sexual Abuse Assessments*. Lyme Regis: Russell House Publishing.

Rose, K. (2001) Practical Exercises. In Calder, M.C. with Peake, A. and Rose, K. *Mothers of Sexually Abused Children*. Lyme Regis: Russell House Publishing.

Sterling, V. (2001) Effect of Domestic Violence on Contact. *Justice of The Peace*, 165: 599–602.

Sturge, C. and Glaser, D. (2000) Contact and Domestic Violence: The Experts' Court Report. *Family Law*, September, 615–28.

Thoennes, N., and Tjaden, P.G. (1990) The Extent, Nature, and Validity of Sexual Abuse Allegations in Custody/Visitation Disputes. *Child Abuse & Neglect*, 14: 152–63.

Trocme, N. and Bala, N. (2005) False Allegations of Abuse and Neglect When Parents Separate. *Child Abuse & Neglect*, 29: 1333–45.

Women's Aid Federation (2003) Failure to Protect? Domestic Violence and The Experiences of Abused Women and Family Courts – Executive Summary. Http://Www. Womensaid.Org.Uk Dated 24.11.03.

# CHAPTER 15

# Safe Care

*Lynda Regan and Martin C. Calder*

## Introduction

The placement of young people in substitute care is challenging for the families and the young people. Utting (1991) and Rickford (1992) emphasise the difficulties of trying to sustain appropriate placements. Practice literature suggests that placements need to be adequately prepared and supported, particularly where children have been sexually abused as this presents additional issues that need to be considered. In a study by Macaskill (1991) it was found that only 36 per cent of the foster and adoptive carers were satisfied with the background information given to them. The concerns expressed were that by omission of information, carers may well unwittingly trigger things for the child in relation to their past experiences.

Looked after children are the most vulnerable and the capacity for them to become further excluded just through the functioning of the organisation is enormous. The corporate parent has a duty to try to enter the child's world, understand their needs and provide a framework for their safe care that includes:

- support for carers to develop an understanding of the inherent vulnerabilities of the children they look after
- training for carers that helps them to consider how their thoughts, feelings and actions impact upon the children in their care
- organisational support, responsibility and accountability that enables professionals to make better and more informed decisions about the parenting vulnerable children
- a system that supports professionals and carers to have a process by which to include and involve children as much as possible (which would include monitoring and reviewing decisions made)
- for carers and professionals to have access to training that enhances their skills in communicating with young people, so that they are able to explain decisions made to the children that they are responsible for.

Children entering the care system will have a diverse range of experiences that will have shaped the ways in which they relate to other people and situations. This will include having experienced loss (of their families and everything that was familiar to them), grief, trauma and, on many occasions, abuse. These experiences and whether their needs are subsequently recognised and met, will have an impact upon how they progress.

Caring for this group of children and young people can be rewarding but also exhausting. It is not surprising that on some occasions we start to see the behaviour and lose sight of the child.

Whatever the plans are for the child, the safe carer is a crucial element. It is within the day-to-day experience of life with family and friends that the child will take their new knowledge. They can only do so if the safe adults around them make space for and encourage the changes.

Once the child is placed with a safe carer (either within the family or within the care system), there can be the expectation from the adults that the child will recognise they are safe, and as a consequence should be relieved and co-operative and grateful. McFadden (1987) in Farmer and Pollock (1998) explains that for abused children the intimacy of family life appears to involve what they interpret as a lot as sexual contact and caregivers need to help them to understand ordinary human sexuality and the role of sex in relationships. Smith (1989) suggests that for sexualised children to give up the sexual projections of the abuser means confronting the fear that they have no other value. Carers need to help young people understand how to give affection in non-sexualised ways and need to have clear frameworks in place to ensure that this is done in a sensitive and positive way.

Cavanagh Johnson (1997) provides a curriculum which can be used with young people in groups, with carers, or in parts could bring both together. She outlines the areas of importance as:

- exploring communication
- differentiating between sexual play and sexual abuse
- personal space
- sexual knowledge
- prevention of sexual misuse or abuse.

She explains that a major focus of the work is to 'increase nurturing and respectful interactions between caregivers and children. This will encourage positive attachments for the children who feel abandoned by their families and alone in out-of-home care. The residual effect of the curriculum is happier and healthier children and caregivers' (p2).

My own experience of working with young people and their carers supports this. For although the young person is the subject of a referral, the best place to start is to help the adults understand where the child's behaviours originate; to help them understand some of the dynamics and impacts of sexual abuse, so that from a more informed position they can begin to work out how to best meet their needs. There may be a need for individual work with the young person alongside this, although this is not always the case. From the start of the work, this approach also helps to locate the problem where it belongs: about what the child has experienced and not about the child themselves.

Supporting carers to be more informed helps them to identify if they have been developing a pattern of responding to behaviours presented that cause concern, rather than considering what the function of the behaviour was, and what it was telling them about the child. In order to be able to consider the practical aspects of safe caring, it is helpful if the carer or professional first reflects on their own feelings and value base in order to review their understanding of child development, behaviours and expectations of a child's behaviours. This area can often be missed, however it is important as the attachments that we all had as children influence our values and judgements about what is 'normal' and acceptable about the people around us, and as we know only too well, each person's experience is unique. This area is of particular importance if the child is in a residential home and there are different staff members providing care and support to the child as consistency can be hard to attain, and it needs clear working practice, good communication and commitment to maintain.

## Theoretical base for understanding behaviours/impacts

Child development theories tell us that adverse social relationships in childhood can affect a person's sense of well-being, self-worth, confidence and ability to form satisfying, conflict-free relationships.

The child who does not disentangle some of the distorted patterns they have learnt may carry these into adult relationships. When a child has been sexually abused by a known and trusted adult, they have received unhealthy messages about trust, adults, relationships, sex and sexuality, giving and receiving affection and attention, boundaries and self-worth. The impacts are much wider than focusing on the physical sexual experience.

Children who have experienced emotional or physical trauma may present as in control and coping well, and some resilient children may well be just that. However, some children might not be so resilient and might not 'feel' safe even if they have, or the perpetrator has, been removed. Whatever the circumstance, we know that they will (have been made to) feel some responsibility for what has happened. Porter et al. (1982) tell us that children may feel responsible on three levels:

- for what has happened to them
- for the disclosure
- for what has happened to their family following disclosure and in many cases what has happened to the perpetrator.

So despite how the child presents, there needs to be an understanding of what they may be feeling like inside. It can be likened to the analogy of the bottle of pop. It can be still and settled and then something may trigger a reaction: it could be a word, a smell, a memory, a problem they feel responsible for, and suddenly their behaviour may be too much for them to cope with and may fizz up and 'spill over'.

MacFarlane and Waterman (1986) tells us that being believed by their parent provides the best scenario for the child's recovery. What we know however, is that for some parents this may take some time as they are faced with their own emotional difficulties in coming to terms with what has happened to their child as well as the impact on their relationship, future hopes and plans.

Research by Thomas and O'Kane (1998), Plummer (2001), Daniel and Wassell (2002, 2002a,

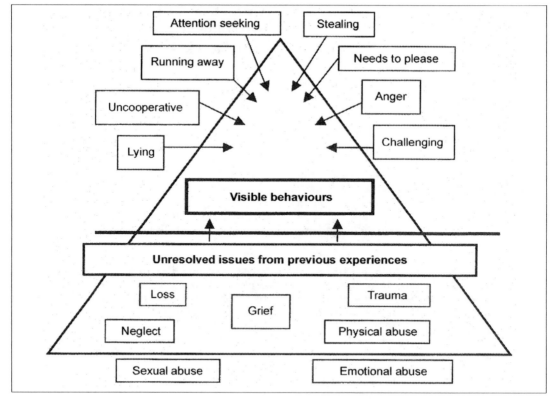

**Figure 15.1**    A child who has had negative experiences

2002b) found that children's self-confidence and sense of self-worth improves when they feel listened to and valued. It is important that children learn to see the good within themselves, know that others see it too and feel that they have something worthwhile to contribute. Combined with encouragement and positive reinforcement, these can help to reduce destructive behaviours.

### How it fits together

If the knowledge available about the child's experience and history is transferred to the triangle as shown in Appendix 1, we have a framework that allows us to understand some of the root causes of behaviours displayed and allows us a glimpse of what the child is coping with internally.

If we only see the problematic behaviours (the top of the triangle) we may respond to the child as if the behaviour identifies who and what they are. Not only does this bring us into conflict with

the child, but it also ignores the 'root' causes of the behaviour and reduces opportunities to help the child find different ways of managing their underlying issues.

As adults, when we think about the people who have meant the most to us in our lives and the qualities we valued, it is often things such as being listened to, not being judged, always being there for us, 'a shoulder to cry on'. Very few of us want someone to tell us what to do. What we often want is someone to support us through the decisions we make (whether these are perceived to be right or wrong).

Clearly, children cannot, and should not, be expected to make all the decisions, but they do have a right to be informed, included where possible and always enabled to express their opinion. Often children are wiser than we give them credit for.

Positive life experiences in childhood help us to become adults who can negotiate painful situations and have some strategies that help us

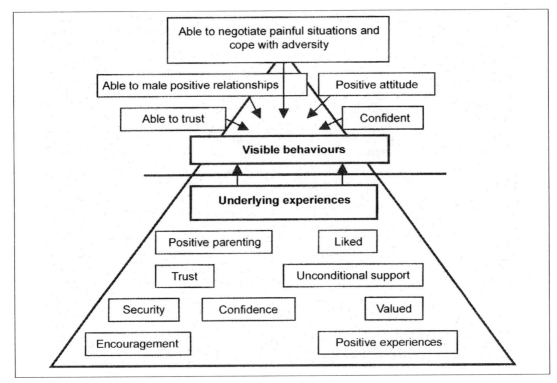

**Figure 15.2** A child who has had healthy experiences

cope with adversity. No one has a trouble-free existence, but resilience factors help us to build a secure base from which to do this.

It might be helpful for a child's carers to consider the impact of what they say and do on the child and also to think about what meaning the child will take from it. Carers are in a prime position to influence and to help children experience more positive ways of coping with difficult situations.

### Some impacts of sexual abuse

Having worked with many children who have experienced sexual abuse, their strength and courage is something that shines through. They show us that they are more than their experience and that they have the capacity to move beyond what they have been through, if only we can take the time to work at each child's own pace.

It is important that professionals and carers have an understanding of how children might have been affected by their experiences. The ten areas highlighted by Porter et al. (1982) still

continue to provide a useful way of understanding how sexual abuse may affect children. The authors note that the first five impact areas are likely to affect all children who have been sexually abused, regardless of the perpetrator's identity. The last five are much more likely from children who have been abused by someone known and trusted to them, such as a family member:

- **'Damaged goods' syndrome** – Reflects how a child may feel 'damaged' by their experience or 'different' from before. The child may also assume that others can tell just by looking at them what has happened.
- **Guilt** – Intense feelings of guilt are common once children have 'told'. Children may feel guilt on three levels:
  - responsibility for the sexual behaviour (they are often made to feel that it is their fault, they wanted it, they could have stopped it etc.)
  - responsibility for disclosure
  - responsibility for the impacts upon the rest of

the family (sometimes including the abuser who they may have very mixed feelings about. This can also be the person who provides food, shelter, clothing or other positive experiences).

- **Fear** – of consequences, reprisals and rejection are not uncommon. These can be expressed at a conscious level, or may be manifested by sleep disturbance, nightmares, anxiety etc.
- **Depression** (sadness and loss) – Children may appear sad and/or withdrawn, or they may exhibit symptoms such as excessive fatigue or repetitive 'illness'.
- **Low self-esteem** –The abusive experience on an emotional and (sometimes) physical level may reinforce the child's notion that they are bad or unworthy. It can also serve to undermine their confidence in themselves, other adults, peers and the world around them.
- **Anger and hostility** – Anger may be overt, or it may be masked by compliant behaviour.
- **Trust** – A child who has been victimised by a known and trusted person is then likely to have difficulty developing trusting relationships and may have learnt unhealthy, or unhelpful ways of relating to others.
- **Blurred role boundaries and role confusion** – The child's understanding about family life, society's boundaries and expectations and what is actually happening to them can create a puzzle that they cannot make sense of.
- **Pseudo-maturity and failure to complete developmental tasks** – A child whose healthy sexual development has been prematurely interrupted, may have confusion and conflict about sexual behaviours, boundaries, roles and expectations of their own and other people's behaviours. This may also distance them further from their peers.
- **Self-mastery and control** – The child who has been sexually abused has been taught that they have no rights, no privacy and no power. Learning that they can be appropriately assertive, have rights, choices and maintain rights over their own body, can help towards re-gaining some confidence, self-mastery and control.

As discussed earlier in this chapter, whenever we face traumatic situations, our responses and our ability to negotiate the emotions that are triggered will depend on a variety of factors from our own personalities, early childhood and life experiences. We each have our individual ways of coping and responding.

The following things can be significant in determining the extent to which a child may be impacted:

- the age of the child when the abuse began and their understanding of what happened
- the relationship of the child with the abuser (*was it someone who was known and trusted?*)
- how the child was made to comply (*tricks, force, threats, etc.*)
- what type of abuse occurred
- how long the abuse went on for
- how often the child was abused.

It is important to state that these are only 'indicators' about the severity of impacts. Each child will experience what happens in their own way, dependent upon their own set of circumstances. It is also important to remember that children go through all sorts of changes as they grow up and develop and *not every change will be linked to the abuse.*

## Caregiver engagement

Children who have been sexually abused may have sexual knowledge or perhaps ways of responding, that are considered by others as sexualised and inappropriate for their age and stage of development. In some children this will be more obvious than in others, although some children will cope in more positive ways and may not 'act out' at all. Often the adults become immobilised and feel uncertain or scared of how to respond. As a society we are still, even in this day and age, uncomfortable in talking to our children about sexual issues. If the child does act out in a sexualised way, it is important to remember that this is learnt behaviour. The child is not making a choice and is not responsible.

In these cases it is important to understand the context for the behaviour and try to establish safe 'rules' about it rather than punish the child, which would only serve to confirm that they are the problem. How a carer responds has been shown to have a direct impact on outcomes for the child. Farmer and Pollock (1998: 179) found that:

*Levels of caregiver engagement were significantly associated with the young people having been able to talk either fully or partially about their experiences of abuse and the associated difficulties which they had experienced. Over two thirds of young people in high caregiver engagement placements had been able to do so, compared with only one in eleven (one child) in low engagement placements. Just over half the children in medium engagement placements had been able to talk openly.*

*This finding suggests that children will talk about painful feelings only when they feel safe in a supportive environment and when they believe that what they say will be listened to, accepted and understood . . .*

In relation to young people also receiving therapeutic help alongside the placement it was found that:

*Those children who had **both** high caregiver engagement **and** specialist intervention were most likely to have been able to start to explore and make sense of their difficult experiences. Of the seven children who had these high levels of support and intervention, six had been able to talk either fully or partially in their care setting. On the other hand, none of the five children who had low caregiver engagement and no other intervention had been able to discuss their emotional problems.*

## Therapeutic support

Not all children who have been sexually abused need therapy and there are a range of options that need to be considered for each individual in order to provide the child with what helps them the most. Some may:

- want therapy or counselling to help them work through their experiences
- not want any help for some time
- want limited help in response to one area they are not coping well with
- not want any help at all.

## Understanding children's sexual behaviour

Individual differences between children exist across all their behaviours and abilities. Therefore, sexual behaviours will also differ and be influenced by a range of factors. These include their age, stage and level of development, family attitudes, culture, television/media, friends, family and what has happened to them previously. Not all children who have been sexually abused will present sexualised behaviours, neither has every abusing child been sexually abused themselves. Here are some general guidelines, which help towards assessing

natural and healthy sexual development in children.

Research tells us that exploration can be considered 'normal' if:

- it is occasional and limited in type and duration
- it involves children of similar ages
- it involves curiosity, not force or threats of any kind
- it is voluntary on the part of each child concerned
- the children stop when asked to do so.
  (Cavanagh Johnson, 1998: 1)

A child's experiences and transition towards adulthood can be assisted by parenting which on a developmental level encourages them to learn safely about themselves, their environment and their world and which on an emotional level acknowledges their thoughts, feelings and fears and guides them towards insight and further understanding.

Adults may feel they face a moral dilemma when considering providing a child with information on sexual health issues. In reality however, education about our bodies, how they function, feel and change, ought to be no different from learning about plants, animals and the world around us. Furthermore, any child who is not informed is at risk of abuse because, amongst other things, they may not understand what behaviour is, or is not OK, or how to actually tell someone that they need help. After all, would we decide not to teach children how to cross roads safely?

It is well documented by authors such as Briggs (1995) and Westcott and Cross (1996) that disabled children are at higher risk of sexual abuse than non-disabled children. This is because, amongst other things, they are more likely to be kept ignorant of their rights, including their right to reject unwanted touching. This is especially pertinent to individuals who are dependent upon others to meet their personal care needs, where these needs are met inconsistently and they have been denied information and support to enable them to distinguish between acceptable and unacceptable touching.

It is vital that everyone involved in the child's welfare gives consistent messages:

*I just think I was there, I was available and also my disability probably did have some bearing on the situation because of the simple reason I was already vulnerable, I already had problems and it's easiest to take the weakest one in the litter because they need more care and attention anyway and sort of . . . There's more opportunity a) for the abuse b) to cover it up.*

(Man with cerebral palsy, sexually abused by step-father in Westcott and Cross 1996: 49)

All children also need to be given opportunity to develop their vocabulary and communication skills. This is particularly important for children who have difficulties with communication, however it is an area that is often neglected or seen as unimportant. If children do not learn the vocabulary, how can they be expected to communicate their feelings and views about what is happening for them?

Briggs (1996: 27) provides us with a summary that highlights that disabled children are at a higher risk of sexual abuse than non-disabled children when they are:

- in the care of adults who have accepted the myths relating to the abuse of children with disabilities
- kept ignorant of their rights
- devalued and dehumanised by society
- not adequately protected by child care, education and justice services
- deprived of information about their sexuality, the limits of acceptable adult behaviour and their rights to reject unwanted touching
- dependant on adults for day-to-day care, becoming compliant and malleable and unlikely to know that they can take control of some aspects of their lives
- deprived of parental affection and approval
- over-protected with few opportunities for independent problem-solving
- unable to receive or communicate information about sexual matters
- lacking the confidence and assertiveness needed to complain
- unable to distinguish between acceptable and unacceptable touching due to the quantity of touching involved in their everyday care.

In addition, child victims with disabilities are the ones most likely to:

- have been abused by their caregivers
- suffer violent and prolonged abuse by multiple perpetrators
- be disbelieved or ignored when they report abuse

- be interviewed by professionals who have no specialist skills in communicating with children with special needs when abuse is reported
- to be deprived of justice and therapy, increasing their vulnerability to severe emotional disturbance, re-abuse and re-enactment of the abuse with other children.

Learning to trust and accept our feelings begins with learning to identify them. Feelings are our internal indicators for what feels OK or what does not. Talking with children about these as part of everyday life helps them to begin to build a vocabulary which, in turn, may make it easier for them to express emotions and opinions, and begin to learn some appropriate body safety and assertiveness skills. This has to include, amongst other things, 'sexual feelings' and different terminology used for 'private body parts'. Similarly, if a child uses an alternative communication system, they should have access to words, signs or symbols to help facilitate this.

It is also worth noting that there is a widespread (mistaken) assumption that knowledge will result in experimentation. International research shows however, that it is ignorance and the lack of information that leads to unsafe sex and unwanted pregnancies (Goldman and Goldman, 1988). Therefore, the major tasks as far as such issues are concerned for carers and parents of *all* children, include:

- Making sure the child has all the sex education they need, in a way they can fully understand, in order to make sense of body changes, sexual feelings and relationships.
- Giving assistance for the child to learn about keeping safe, including what is appropriate (OK) and not appropriate (not OK) sexually, acceptable places for sexual expression etc.
- Protecting the child from abuse and harm, from people who may try to coerce them into behaviours s/he does not fully understand.
- Offering the child appropriate opportunities to develop self-esteem and positive, non-abusive social and sexual relationships.

Children are taught from an early age to trust, respect and accept adult authority, often without question, especially if the adult is someone well known to them. Being obedient equates with being good. Giving children limited information about body safety in isolation from wider issues about trust, choices, assertiveness and feelings (without support and opportunity to test these out in safe relationships) places the responsibility for their safety totally with the child.

We know however, that children are incapable of understanding how abusive adults manipulate them to gain co-operation. So it follows that any framework for safe care is based upon the adults taking responsibility for the care they provide and the experiences they offer the children they look after.

Similarly, it is the adult's responsibility to make it 'safe' and to encourage children to be open and honest regarding sexual health matters. This means being proactive, not simply waiting for the child to raise the issues. Most families however, find openness about sexual behaviours, sexuality and sexual health difficult and may need support to do this.

### Problematic sexualised behaviours

From our experience, children presenting sexualised behaviours tend to make the adults around them feel uncomfortable and this can often result in a paralysis of logic whereby competent people feel suddenly lacking in confidence and ability. Having a recording framework in which to consider behaviours or incidents is often helpful in getting factual and accurate information (Appendix 1 ). This method helps to be clear about frequency and duration as sexualised behaviours can often be less frequent when recorded than carers or professionals had previously perceived them to be. This also assists the process of focusing on the child's behaviours in other settings and at other times when they aren't problematic, in order to consider the whole child and to make decisions about which intervention might be most appropriate to address the one part of the child's behaviours that is causing concern. In cases where the behaviour is frequent and concerning, the recording system provides a lot of essential information about the actual situation, before, after, who else was involved, what did or didn't work or had been tried, etc. There is no magic wand in this area of work, but there is a need to gather, collate and factual information about the child and the situation in each case.

Given that everyone has their own individual set of knowledge, attitudes and values, it is also important to recognise that in some cases there may be differences of opinion about what is or

isn't concerning behaviour. One way of identifying this and bringing it into the discussions, is for the people involved to use the pro-forma (Appendix 2). This might help to identify a common agreement on the level of concern that could indicate what happens next. This might be to identify different strategies, to include the family in a solution-focused meeting, or to refer on to children's services as a child protection issue.

## Safe care and positive communication

Each local authority will have it's own 'safe care' policy to which carers should have access. These may provide basic guidance, although, in order to be effective, they will need to be expanded and adapted to meet the needs of each individual child entering placement.

All carers have their own styles, tolerances and strengths and each family has their own routines. If a child has had a number of placements, they may have experienced a variety of different ways of doing things in relation to mealtimes, bedtimes, permission to bring friends home, jobs around the house, and so on. Additionally, if a child has been sexually abused there may need to be specific considerations.

*Sharon was terrified when her foster carers' young son came into the bathroom to use the toilet as she was getting into the bath. This family practice with their younger children had to be quickly altered as it seemed to have revived memories of Sharon's sexual abuse.*

(McFadden and Stovall, 1984)

It should never be assumed that a child will automatically know what is expected of them or that carers will understand how to provide safe boundaries. So although some careful planning needs to occur, neither should the child be greeted with a set of immovable 'rules'.

The challenge for carers and families is to make each child feel that they are valued and that they have something to contribute to the family. Only after this will the child be more likely to invest in how the family 'works'. This means being explicit about expectations, without being overly controlling. It is vital that carers don't get drawn into endless minor conflicts, as Chalke (1999: 19–20) suggests, it is better that carers save energy instead for the battles that really count.

If children understand how and why decisions are made, they are far more likely to be successful and sustained. An added bonus is that, if the foster carers own children are included in the process, then they also have opportunities to 'have their say' and express their own views and feelings.

One way of doing this would be for the carers to make up a booklet, a set of information sheets or a Family Agreement about their home. This would allow a child to understand what is expected and to express an opinion about things. If there are differences of opinion, this can be used as a way to highlight any problems and to negotiate compromises. In doing so, it is important to ask the following questions:

- How is something done?
- What is the reason for this?
- What does the child think about this and have they had other 'rules' relating to this before?

There may need to be rules around privacy. These are especially important for a child who has been sexually abused, or who has sexualised behaviours and needs clear, consistent boundaries.

Example:

---

**Privacy**

In our family we do not walk around the house without our clothes on, even if we have just had a bath.

This is so that we all have some privacy.

We each have a dressing gown that we can put on when we need to, like after having a bath or when we get out of bed in the mornings.

Does this feel OK for you?

Do you have a dressing gown of your own?

Do you need a new one?

---

Similarly, consideration needs to be given, for whatever reason, to individuals having the opportunity for 'private time'. This is particularly important where, for instance, there are no locks on the bathroom door and/or children are sharing a bedroom. Here, rules could be agreed about putting a sign on the door, letting others in the house know, and knocking when doors are closed.

There are a number of areas relating to safe care which require particular attention, for

instance bedtime routines. It is important for children to have a routine where they begin to relax and wind down energy levels before going to bed. This helps to make it feel safe and predictable for children (who may have had unpredictable things happen to them).

With younger children, bedtime stories are often a valuable part of this routine. Given the child's experiences, carers need to be mindful of their actions towards the child and try to reduce any situations where their behaviours may be misinterpreted. Some simple ways of doing this are to have some basic 'rules', such as young children don't sit on an adult's knee for a story. This can be done with the child sitting by the side of the adult, which still allows for some contact, but in a less direct way and which doesn't involve the child being as restricted.

When specific behaviours develop or boundaries need reinforcing, a useful way of addressing these with the child would be to:

- clearly identify the behaviour or situation with the child
- make explicit what isn't OK, and be positive about what is OK
- help the child understand how to achieve the change or fulfil expectations.

Children who have been sexually abused may have confusions around very ordinary behaviours and boundaries, so careful consideration needs to be given to how carers behave towards the child. Although this can raise some anxieties, mostly it is a matter of sensitivity, common sense and being aware of your own body language.

Showing consideration for these things helps to teach children that there are safe boundaries and safe adults who can respect their feelings. It teaches them that they have rights over their own bodies (which they may have been denied previously) and that it is possible for them to make choices. Involving children in this way is very empowering as it helps them feel listened to and valued.

If a child has been taught to behave sexually towards an adult, this isn't the child's fault. It does however raise concerns for foster carers, who may worry about how to respond appropriately to the child, or about the child misinterpreting their behaviour and making false allegations.

If a child does behave in ways that cause concern, it is important to address the issue without making the child feel guilty. One way of doing this is to give clear and consistent messages about the behaviour (*not the child*).

For example, using the same set of guidelines as before:

- **Identify the behaviour** – 'In our home we don't touch each other in those places, they are private'.
- **Make explicit what is and is not OK** – 'We will not touch you on your private parts, and you do not touch us on ours'.
- **Help the child achieve success** – Physically move the child to the side of you and redirect the child's attention onto something else.
- **Reinforce the message** – If this doesn't work straight away, a follow up message might be, 'In our home we show we like each other by . . . (giving hugs from the side, smiling, etc.).

Some basic messages about body safety skills, privacy and control may also be needed. If the behaviour is persistent, carers could try to reinforce messages by perhaps including a star chart or reward system for the times the behaviour is controlled. Carers should remember to reward the positives and try to ignore the times when the child slips back or forgets.

The importance of understanding the child's experiences will help to identify areas where extra sensitivity will be needed. For example, if it is known that a child has had indecent photographs taken of them (with or without their knowledge), it will be important to be clear about photographs taken while being cared for. At the very least, this would give the child a sense of what is happening and may reduce anxieties for some. For example, 'We always take photos when we go for a day out. This helps us to remember where we have been and what we did. We like to include everyone in the photos, is that OK with you?'

Similarly if photos are downloaded onto the computer, give the child a clear explanation about who will get to see them. For some children you may want to avoid downloading their pictures if that has been part of their experience.

Photographs however, are a good way to retain memories and are an important part of the child's history. Having their own album would allow some choice and control about what was kept.

We know that 'secrecy' is an issue in sexual abuse. Secrets in themselves are not bad, but some can cause anxiety. In our work, we find that using the term 'surprise' as an alternative is helpful, as it usually has positive connotations. We help children to differentiate between information that is OK not to tell, such as 'keeping a birthday surprise' and things they have been told to keep secret that they may need to tell an adult or get help with. For further information on safe care the reader is directed to a chapter by Butterworth and Regan in Wheal (2004)

## Training

*The experience of being cared for should also include the sexual education of the young person. This is absolutely vital since sexuality will be one of the most potent forces affecting any young person in the transition from childhood to adulthood.*
(Children Act Guidance and Regulations Volume 4)

All carers need adequate training on sex and relationship issues to equip them with basic knowledge, skills and awareness. They also need to be able to access targeted training to help them explore issues such as sex and sexuality and issues around children who have experienced sexual abuse, if they are to support children and young people appropriately on these issues.

There are increasing opportunities for foster carers to attend training courses in a wide range of subjects. Specifically, Standard 23.6 of The National Minimum Standards for Fostering Services (DoH, 2002: 26) states that 'Appropriate training on safe caring is provided for all members of the foster household'.

Although this area is challenging for carers, the potential benefits for the child of being helped and supported to move on from their experiences and learn more positive ways of developing healthy relationships for the future are immeasurable.

## Appendix 1

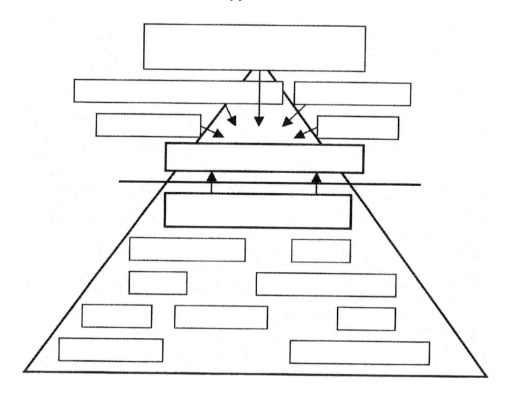

## Appendix 2: Record of Behaviour/Incident

Date/Day:                                    Time:

Name of young person:                        Who else was present:

Where did the incident take place:

---

Was anyone else involved?                    Yes/No

If yes, who?

In what capacity were they involved?

If another child was involved, was this voluntarily?

Had force/violence/coercion/threats/bribes been used?

How did the other child react?

What emotional state were they in?

Brief description of circumstances

Do you know what happened directly before the incident?

Was there anything that triggered the behaviour?
_____

If you had to intervene, what happened?

What was your response to the situation and young person?

How did the young person react?

---

What happened afterwards?

What was the young person's response?

Was the child's social worker/family placement worker informed?

If so, who?

What was their response?
_____

Anything else you feel is relevant?

---

Signed: _____    Print name: _____

Date:

Your role in relation to the young person: _____

If this record was shared/passed on to someone else:

Name: _____    Date received: _____

## Appendix 3: Behaviour Chart

> **Highly Concerning**
>
> **Worrying**
>
> **Acceptable**

Each person places the statement where they think it fits best. Consider whether there is any difference of perception, what is known about the child's age, stage of development, home situation, school, friendships, interests, what they are like in other settings, personality. It is often consideration about the context of the behaviour that helps to identify the meaning and the level of concern.

In identifying an intervention strategy, consider the following:

## The incident

**What would need to happen to move the behaviour down the concerns ladder?** For example, was there any bullying, aggression or coercing of other children? Does the child appear to think of what is happening as a joke? How does the behaviour fit with their emotional and chronological development level.

## What could other people do?

Is there any additional support that could be put in or a different strategy that could be tried? Who does the child respond to?

## What could the child do?

Try to find something positive for the child either at the point of distraction or to build self confidence in relation to 'good' behaviours. Make sure the child understands that it is the behaviour that is the problem and not them.

## An example of how this might work would be:

Think of a six year old boy who shows his penis to his class mates and they are all silly and giggly. Although he might need to learn that it isn't OK to do this, in itself it is not a highly worrying incident given his age and assumed level of development. Therefore the sticker might be placed on the border between worrying and acceptable. However if this same incident happened and the young boy tried to make another pupil touch him, do the same, or if there was any level of aggression, coercing, bullying, or separating out one particular child, then the sticker would be placed higher up the scale.

Considering all the information about the incident would help to:

- identify a level of concern that has been reached by examining all the known factors
- identify what (if anything) has already been tried
- decide upon additional strategies to manage the behaviour
- consider how to address the issue with the child, if appropriate
- indicate more serious concerns and would provide a clear basis for a referral to other agencies.

# References

Briggs, F. (1995) *Developing Personal Safety Skills in Children with Disabilities*. London: Jessica Kingsley.

Cavanagh Johnson, T. (1998) *Helping Children with Sexual Behaviour Problems: A Guidebook for Parents and Substitute Caregivers*. Dover: Smallwood Publishing.

Cavanagh Johnson, T. (1997) *Sexual, Physical and Emotional Abuse in Out of Home Care*. London: Haworth Press.

Chalke, S. (1999) *The Parentalk Guide to the Teenage Years*. London: Hodder & Stoughton.

Daniel, B. and Wassell, S. (2002) *The Early Years: Assessing and Promoting Resilience in Vulnerable Children 1*. London: Jessica Kingsley.

Daniel, B. and Wassell, S. (2002a) *The School Years: Assessing and Promoting Resilience in Vulnerable Children 2*. London: Jessica Kingsley.

Daniel, B. and Wassell, S. (2002b) *Adolescence: Assessing and Promoting Resilience in Vulnerable Children 3*. London: Jessica Kingsley.

DoH (2002) *National Minimum Standards: Fostering Services Regulations*. London: HMSO.

Farmer, E. and Pollock, S. (1998) *Sexually Abused and Abusing Children in Substitute Care*. Chichester: John Wiley & Sons.

Goldman, R. and Goldman, J. (1988) *Show Me Yours*. Melbourne: Penguin.

McFadden, E.J. and Stovall, B. (1984) *Child Sexual Abuse in Family Foster Care: Preventing Abuse in Foster Care*. Ypsilanti, MI: Eastern Michigan University.

Macaskill, C. (1991) *Adopting or Fostering a Sexually Abused Child*. London: Batsford.

MacFarlane, K. and Waterman, J. (1986) *Sexual Abuse of Young Children*. New York: Guildford Press.

Plummer, D. (2001) *Helping Children to Build Self-Esteem: A Photocopiable Activities Book*. London: Jessica Kingsley.

Porter, L., Blick, L. and Sgroi, S. (1982) Treatment of the Sexually Abused Child. In Sgroi, S. (Ed.) *Handbook of Clinical Intervention in Child Sexual Abuse*. Lexington, MA: Heath.

Rickford R (1992) *Endangered Species. Community Care*, 24: 5, 12.

Smith, G. (1989) *Personal and Professional Issues in Child Sexual Abuse, After Abuse. Papers on Caring and Planning for a Child who has been Sexually Abused*. London: BAAF.

Thomas, N. and O'Kane, C. (1998) Children and Decision Making: A Summary Report. In Phillipson, J. (1999) *Children and Decision Making: Training and Resource Guide*. International Centre for Childhood Studies, University of Wales Swansea.

Utting, Sir W. (1997) *People Like Us: The Report of the Review of the Safeguards for Children Living Away from Home*. London: Stationery Office.

Westcott, H. and Cross, M. (1996) *This Far and No Further: Towards Ending the Abuse of Disabled Children*. BASW, Venture Press.

Wheal, A. (2004) *The RHP Companion to Foster Care*. 2nd edn. Lyme Regis: Russell House Publishing.

# Russell House Publishing Ltd

We publish a wide range of professional, reference and educational books including:

**Safeguarding children and young people: A guide to integrated practice**
By Steven Walker and Christina Thurston          ISBN 978-1-903855-90-4

**Developing collaborative relationships in interagency child protection work**
By Michael Murphy          ISBN 978-1-903855-48-5

**Child exploitation and communication technologies**
By Alisdair A. Gillespie          ISBN 978-1-905541-23-2

**Children living with domestic violence: Towards a framework for assessment and intervention**
Edited by Martin C. Calder          ISBN 978-1-903855-45-4

**Secret lives: growing with substance - working with children and young people affected by familial substance misuse**
Edited by Fiona Harbin and Michael Murphy          ISBN 978-1-903855-66-9

**Preventing breakdown: A manual for childcare professionals working with high risk families**
By Mark Hamer          ISBN 978-1-903855-61-4

**Contemporary risk assessment in safeguarding children**
Edited by Martin C. Calder          ISBN 978-1-905541-20-1

**The carrot or the stick? Towards effective practice with involuntary clients in safeguarding children work**
Edited by Martin C. Calder          ISBN 978-1-905541-22-5

For more details, please visit our website: www.russellhouse.co.uk

**Parents' anger management: The PAMP programme**
By Gerry Heery                                      ISBN 978-1-905541-04-1

**The child and family in context: Developing ecological practice in disadvantaged communities**
By Owen Gill and Gordon Jack                        ISBN 978-1-905541-15-7

**Parental alienation: How to understand and address parental alienation resulting from acrimonious divorce or separation**
By L. F. Lowenstein                                 ISBN 978-1-905541-10-2

**Assessment in child care: Using and developing frameworks for practice**
Edited by Martin C. Calder and Simon Hackett        ISBN 978-1-903855-14-0

**Complete guide to sexual abuse assessments**
By Martin C. Calder et al.                          ISBN 978-1-898924-76-0

**Juveniles and children who sexually abuse: Frameworks for assessment. Second Edition**
By Martin C. Calder et al.                          ISBN 978-1-898924-95-1


For more details, please visit our website: *www.russellhouse.co.uk*


Or we can send you our catalogue if you contact us at:

**Russell House Publishing Ltd,**
4 St George's House, Uplyme Road Business Park,
Lyme Regis DT7 3LS, England,
Tel: 01297 443948
Fax: 01297 442722
Email: help@russellhouse.co.uk